Societal
Directions
and
Alternatives

Societal Directions and Alternatives

A Critical Guide to the Literature

by Michael Marien

INFORMATION FOR POLICY DESIGN
LaFayette, New York 13084

FIRST EDITION
   First Printing--June 1976
   Second Printing--June 1977
Layout and composition by Kasco Media, Inc.
Cover design by Renee Maiorana and Lyle Stander

Library of Congress Cataloging in Publication Data

Marien, Michael.   1938-
   Societal directions and alternatives.

   Bibliography: p.
   Includes indexes.
   1. Civilization, Modern--1950-   --Bibliography.
2. Policy sciences--Bibliography. 3. Forecasting--
Bibliography.   I.   Title.
Z5579.M36   [CB428]   016.909   76-9373
ISBN 0-916282-00-7

CONTENTS

PROLOGUE

The Blind Men and the Elephant: A Hindoo Fable

by John Godfrey Saxe (1816-1887) *

It was six men of Indostan
  To learning much inclined,
Who went to see the Elephant
  (Though all of them were blind),
That each by observation
  Might satisfy his mind.

The First approached the Elephant
  And happening to fall
Against his broad and sturdy side,
  At once began to bawl:
"Bless me! but the Elephant
  Is very like a wall!"

The Second, feeling of the tusk,
  Cried, "Ho! what have we here,
So very round and smooth and sharp?
  "To me 'tis mighty clear
This wonder of an Elephant
  Is very like a spear!"

The Third approached the animal,
  And happening to take
The squirming trunk within his hands,
  Thus boldly up and spake:
"I see," quoth he, "the Elephant
  Is very like a snake!"

The Fourth reached out his eager hand,
  And felt about the knee.
"What most this wondrous beast is like
  Is mightly plain," quoth he;
" 'Tis clear enough the Elephant
  Is very like a tree!"

(continued)

The Fifth who chanced to touch the ear,
Said, "E'en the blindest man
Can tell what this resembles most;
Deny the fact who can,
"This marvel of an Elephant
Is very like a fan!"

The Sixth no sooner had begun
About the beast to grope,
Then, seizing on the swinging tail
That fell within his scope,
"I see," quoth he, "the Elephant
Is very like a rope!"

And so these men of Indostan
Disputed loud and long,
Each in his own opinion
Exceeding stiff and strong,
Though each was partly in the right,
And all were in the wrong!

Moral
So, oft in theologic wars
The disputants, I ween,
Rail on in utter ignorance
Of what each other mean,
**And prate about an Elephant
Not one of them has seen!**

*The Poems of John Godfrey Saxe. Boston: Houghton, Osgood and Company, 1868; 1879, pp. 259-261.

I. INTRODUCTION

This guide to over a thousand items, primarily books, serves to identify, categorize, and comment upon much of the contemporary literature addressing four central and intertwined questions:
- Where are we?
- Where are we headed?
- What kind of society could we have?
- What are the possible strategies for achieving the desirable society?

There is no single place in which all of the literature relevant to these questions can be found. To examine the materials covered in this guide, it was necessary to visit most floors and branches of two major university libraries and a moderate-sized public library, because the literature of societal directions and alternatives is classified with anthropology, business administration, economics, history, international relations, life sciences, philosophy, political science, psychology, sociology, and urban studies. The literature also includes contributions from emerging cross-disciplinary areas such as future studies, policy sciences, general semantics, and general systems theory, as well as the decidedly non-academic realm of political tracts and polemics.

Civic wisdom would seemingly involve an extensive and continuing examination of the directions in which our society is developing, as well as the alternative visions that might inspire the design of social policy. In view of the many complex problems confronting our nation and our world, it is appropriate for our political leaders, our scholars, and our citizens to be engaged in this examination. It is particularly appropriate to do so as America's Third Century begins.

A. An Explanation of the Guide

1. Limitations

Despite the seeming breadth of this guide, there are a number of significant limitations. The scope of coverage should be clearly understood at the outset.
- **Developed Nations Only.** The literature in this guide is confined to directions and alternatives proposed for the highly developed (or over-developed) nations. The literature for developing (or poor, modernizing, Third World) nations is not unrelated to the fortunes of the relatively rich nations, but deserves a separate compendium.
- **English Language Only.** The literature under consideration is largely from and about the United States. There are also a fair number of British authors, a handful of Canadian authors, and a few translations, particularly from the French and the Russian. Ultimately, a guidebook such as this should encompass the worldwide literature on the developed nations regardless of language, in that most of the problems facing these nations are quite similar.
- **20th Century Only.** With one minor exception (no. 121), all of the literature covered here has been published in the 20th century. An expanded guide would surely include important 19th century thinkers such as de Tocqueville, Marx, Mill, and Ruskin, and range back in time to the writings of Plato. A useful introduction to thinking over the past three centuries is provided by Arblaster and Lukes, **The Good Society** (no. 797)
- **Non-Fiction Only.** With two marginal exceptions (nos. 825 and 892), fictional contributions, including the vast realm of science fiction, have been excluded. Utopian fiction, a genre that has virtually disappeared in this century (Skinner's **Walden II** is perhaps the last noteworthy example), is also excluded. Items 906 and 907 provide introductions to this realm.
- **General Literature Only.** There are some relatively narrow items covered in this guide, but there has been an attempt to restrict their number. And there is no clear dividing line between general literature and the more specialized literature devoted to matters such as population growth, the arms race, technology and society, the family, and ecology, as well as the methodology of thinking about public policy and the future. Seeking depth in any of these important areas would demand similar depth in other areas, and one could be forever at the task of identifying relevant literature. Ultimately, a series of guides to specialized policy areas such as health, transportation, housing, and justice would add greater depth to a general guide such as this one.

There are also some important qualifications to be made concerning the items that are included here.
- **Recent Items.** This guide is designed to cope with a number of loose ends, including the citation of recently-published books and books in press (e.g., items 850-890). These items are indicated as "ns" (not seen),

along with a few others that have been publicly available for some time, but somehow not personally located.

- **Annotations, Not Reviews.** Many authors provide an introduction or summation, which is quoted where appropriate. Some items have not been read thoroughly.
- **Appropriate Treatment.** Items differ in their merit. Also, some are easily summarized, and some are not. Some invite comment, or deserve it, and some are best left without comment. The annotation and commentary therefore varies in length.
- **Categorization.** There is bias in any categorization. But such packages are useful and necessary, and some attempt to categorize is considered preferable to mere alphabetization. Items are grouped together so that similarities and differences can be readily seen. This sometimes creates strange bedfellows. It should be remembered that the arrangement of items is only one of many possible arrangements. (See further comments on arrangement elsewhere in this Introduction.)
- **Obsolescence.** Certain items that are recommended, or not recommended, may very well be valued differently upon reexamination. New publications, as well as those not seen, may well deserve a higher priority than any of the items that have been seen and annotated. Such are the perils of dealing with contemporary literature. On the other hand, new is not necessarily better, and a surprising number of items in this guide have maintained their value despite the passage of time.

2. Who Might Use This Guide and How

The broad scope of materials covered here might be considered as the province of future studies or the policy sciences. It is hoped that this guide can assist both of these inchoate fields to grow in seriousness and to develop into mutually supportive undertakings that serve the public interest. But **Societal Directions and Alternatives** is not addressed merely to a small group of professionals. There are many people who obviously have considerable interest in this subject matter, and the guide has been designed for many different purposes.

Policy-makers and their staff people might use this guide to find ideas for public inquiry, legislation, and speeches, or to suggest possible consultants.

Researchers and writers in the social sciences and public affairs should benefit from the cross-disciplinary and cross-ideological access afforded here, and they may be encouraged to pursue some of the broad questions that have been raised.

Teachers at both college and high school levels should find ample material to embellish a wide variety of courses or to stimulate new courses. The rating system described below is designed to suggest appropriateness of material for various levels of sophistication.

Librarians can use this guide in reference departments and to suggest acquisitions and special displays that might stimulate reflection and discussion.

Students at both graduate and undergraduate levels should find many uses for this guide in supplementing classroom work or in directing independent study.

Citizens concerned with social reform, or with simply acquiring some understanding of our contemporary situation, should find this guide useful for browsing or for systematic study.

The variety of information offered here, however, might be overwhelming to many persons. If one does not already have an agenda for learning or research, where should one begin?

3. The Rating System

To cope with information overload, and with the problems of the beginner and the busy professional, a rating system has been devised for this guide, similar to that employed by some travel guides. There are dangers in using a rating system, for the bias of the compiler will surely be an important factor, despite attempts to be fair. But the benefits outweigh these dangers. Time is short, and should not be wasted with mediocre thinking and low priority concerns. We must begin to raise serious questions about what is most important, both in our reading agenda and in our public actions.

Criteria for recommendation are spelled out below. The ratings should be viewed as rough-gauge judgments. They are subject to change over time, as some literature grows in importance, becomes outdated, or is superseded by more important writing.

After the citation for each item, the rating appears in parentheses, e.g. (AB-3), (A-2), (C-4). If an item has not been seen, it is marked as "ns," although a brief description may still be possible by summarizing a book review or advertisement. Each rating has two parts: letters indicate level of audience, and numbers reflect judgments of quality.

Level of Audience
  A - Professional; graduate school level; technical
  B - Informed public; undergraduate level; somewhat popularized
  C - General public; high school level; highly popularized
  AB - Professional and informed public; somewhat popularized but also of importance to professionals
  BC - Informed public and general public; for use at college or high school level
  ABC - Of value to all levels; popularized, but also of importance to professionals

Quality
  1 - Highly recommended; outstanding; top priority (included in Civic Curriculum)
  2 - Recommended; important to most readers; high priority (included in Curriculum)
  3 - Good; important to some readers; generally competent; redeeming values outweigh flaws
  4 - Fair; of little or no importance; overly narrow; redeeming values do not outweigh flaws
  5 - Poor; irresponsible; simplistic; greatly flawed
  ns - Not seen; no judgment made

A total of 75 items that are rated "1" or "2" in quality are brought together in The Civic Curriculum, a listing that appears elsewhere in this Introduction.

The distinction afforded by the "Level of Audience" rating is important for a number of reasons. Many scholars will have no interest in the popular literature, and it is misleading to cite an item that would be inappropriate to their needs. Yet it is important to bridge the gulf between academic and popular literature, enabling academics to have some understanding of what is being written for popular audiences. It is also important for the users of popular materials to have some idea of what is available at the most sophisticated levels. For example, teachers at the high school level will be able to find appropriate curriculum materials placed in the context of more advanced materials. And for those persons who have an Aunt Betsy or Uncle George who can't understand what is happening in the world, this guide identifies several popular books that provide a responsible introduction (e.g., Duffus, no. 22).

The "Quality" rating is a guideline based on a mixture of three criteria: scholarly excellence, importance to public policy, and originality. Separate ratings could be made for each of these attributes, but the added complexities would outweigh any additional benefit. Scholarly excellence is defined here as the critical marshalling of a broad array of factual evidence, preferably with appropriate documentation. Works of a broad and systemic nature are generally preferred to those that focus on a narrow theme. Importance to public policy and originality are, in part, a matter of personal judgment. Strong disagreement with the opinions expressed here might lead to competitive lists of recommended reading, which would be valuable for many obvious reasons.

4. Style and Arrangement of Annotations

Wherever possible, the purpose of the book or article, as well as important ideas and conclusions, are conveyed in the author's words. This involves considerable quoting out of context, which can be a dangerous practice. It is also important to stress, again, that only some of the items have been read analytically. Comments and corrections are therefore welcomed.

Critical comments are generally placed at the end of the annotation, preceded by three asterisks (***). The intent is to segregate description and comment, but this rule has not been rigidly adhered to. Various evaluative adjectives can be found in the annotations, particularly in the initial sentences. Critical comments are necessarily concise, and should not be equated with book reviews, which allow for considerably greater depth.

Items are arranged in 16 chapters, with introductory overview comments to each chapter. The chapters are arranged so that they are either closely related to each other (Chapters 9 on Government Reform, and Chapter 10 on Economic Reform), or in sharp contrast (Chapters 11 on Redistribution of Wealth and Power, and Chapter 12 on Freedom from Government). Within each chapter, items are arranged in related clusters which are described in the introductory comments. The progression of items is generally from the most important to the least important, and then to those items not seen. Those persons who seek a broad introduction to thinking about societal directions and alternatives are advised to become acquainted with several items in each of the chapters.

There is a fundamental distinction in the classification used here. "Societal Directions" refers to literature that is largely concerned with the first two questions concerning where we are and where we are headed. "Societal Alternatives" concerns literature that focuses on the last two questions: the society we should have and how to attain it. Both description and prescription can be found in virtually every item, but most items are dominantly one or the other.

In order to avoid a distracting jumble of dots and quotation marks, some liberties have been taken with punctuation rules. The use of capital letters is generally that of the author under consideration, which explains much of the inconsistency in capitalization.

5. Influences and Acknowledgments

This guide is an experimental hybrid in style and content. It has been under development during the six years since I received my doctorate in interdisciplinary social science. My work with annotated bibliography began while serving as a Research Fellow at the Educational Policy Research Center at Syracuse. A request from the Organization for Economic Cooperation and Development (OECD) in Paris for a survey of thinking about the future of education resulted in the publication of **Alternative Futures for Learning: An Annotated Bibliography of Trends, Forecasts, and Proposals** (EPRC, May 1971. Reprinted in House Committee on Education and Labor, **Alternative Futures in American Education.** Appendix 3 to Hearings on H.R. 3606, Jan. 1972, pp. 302-446). This guide to the literature of all aspects and levels of educational policy was well-received, but did not deal with much of the general literature on our societal condition.

The most important influence in the development of **Societal Directions and Alternatives** has not been any literature guide, annotation service, or reviewing periodical. Most scholarly annotation gives equal space to each item, and arranges items in alphabetical fashion so that the reader cannot benefit from "heuristic juxtaposition." Many book reviews tend to be opportunities for the reviewer to flex intellectual muscles as the expense of the author; they also tend to be wordy and often fail to convey the author's main ideas, or one must search hard to discover these ideas. Both reviews and annotations tend to be isolated from related literature in space and time.

Rather, the major influences on this guide have come from travel guides, film reviews, and **Consumer Reports**. There are shelves upon shelves of travel guides in any bookstore, and the better ones such as Baedeker, Fodor, and Michelin rate hotels and restaurants. Why not develop a similar aid to intellectual travelers? The brief critical annotations of films in both **New York** and **The New Yorker** have served as specific influences for this guide. Many film reviewers offer lists of "Ten Best" and "Ten Worst" at the end of each year. Why not provide a continually evolving list of important work in the general area of societal directions and alternatives, and ultimately in specific policy areas dealing with matters such as health, transportation, education, justice, etc? Finally, the function of **Consumer Reports** is well-known to many: to serve as an objective intermediary between audience/consumer and performer/supplier. With a plethora of alternative futures to consider, it may well be time for "futures critics" or "idea brokers" to emerge.

All of this thinking was encouraged by the success of **The Whole Earth Catalog** in the early 1970s, which led to my consideration of a "Whole Problem Catalog," which was later discovered to be a modest version of the "World Brain" advocated by H.G. Wells in 1936 (see no. 909). In the 1972-1974 period, I received support for the preliminary stages of this guide from Julius Stulman, President of the World Institute Council. Stulman's notion of a World Institute, essentially a global think tank (no. 912), complements the World Brain idea. Several dozen of the annotations in this guide first appeared in **Fields Within Fields** (No. 13, Fall 1974), the occasional World Institute Council publication, and permission to republish them here is appreciated.

This guide could not have been prepared without the generous support and encouragement of Julius Stulman, and I am greatly indebted to him. I am also indebted to the marvelous Olin Library at Cornell University, the Bird Library at Syracuse University, the Syracuse Public Library, and Mary Fry of the LaFayette Public Library. More than a dozen periodicals deserve thanks for supplying bibliographic leads. My parents, Henry and Ida Marien, helped in a variety of essential ways. Lyle Stander and the Staff of the **Syracuse New Times** carried out the difficult task of typesetting. The inspiring spirit of a great 19th century adult educator, George Hull, encircles my workplace in the hamlet of Cardiff, New York. Finally, my wife, Mary Lou, tolerated this odyssey in fairly good humor, while supplying many valuable comments, and it is to her that I dedicate this work.

B. The Civic Curriculum: A Preliminary List of Essential Reading

The Civic Curriculum is a special listing of 75 books and articles selected from a total of over 1000 items covered in this guide. It summarizes all of those items that have been rated "1" (highly recommended) or "2" (recommended), and serves as a device for highlighting what is felt to be the most important literature. Most readers will have particular needs that go beyond the confines of this list, and will surely find many valuable items with "3" ratings, or perhaps even "4" ratings, elsewhere in this guide.

Other readers might desire some suggestions as to where to begin, and the following 15 items, all with "1" ratings, are especially recommended. Indeed, they are suggested as a general challenge to anyone's thinking about societal directions and alternatives.

- John Platt, "What We Must Do" (1969).
- Bertram M. Gross, "Planning in an Era of Social Revolution" (1971).
- Aldous Huxley, **Brave New World Revisited** (1958).
- Garrett Hardin, Exploring New Ethics for Survival (1972).
- Edward Goldsmith et al., **A Blueprint for Survival** (1972).
- Richard A. Falk, **A Study of Future Worlds** (1975).
- E.F. Schumacher, **Small is Beautiful** (1973).
- Ralph Borsodi, **This Ugly Civilization** (1929).
- James MacGregor Burns, **Uncommon Sense** (1972).
- Richard J. Barnet and Ronald E. Müller, **Global Reach** (1974).
- Herbert J. Gans, **More Equality** (1973).
- Michael Harrington, **Socialism** (1973).
- F.A. Hayek, **The Constitution of Liberty** (1960).
- President's Research Committee..., **Recent Social Trends in the U.S.** (1933).
- Alexander Solzhenitsyn et al., **From Under the Rubble** (1975).

The items listed above are also included in the following list of 75 items, about which these details should be noted: 1) No author or organization is cited more than once, so as to allow for the widest possible representation of views. 2) Each of the 75 recommended items is preceded by its item number in the full listings, where there is a complete citation and a more extensive annotation. 3) Item numbers in boldface refer to the highly recommended items listed above. 4) The number of the chapter in which an item appears is indicated in parentheses below each item number.

THE CIVIC CURRICULUM

1. Kenneth E. Boulding, **The Meaning of the Twentieth Century.** Harper
(1)   & Row, 1964. Observes that we are in the midst of a great transi-
      tion to post-civilization. Still a useful introduction to the over-
      riding problems of war, economic development, population growth,
      and chaos.   (AB-2)

3. John Platt, "What We Must Do," **Science,** November 28, 1969. An
(1)   overview of problem areas and their priorities in three future
      periods of time, serving to promote a science of survival. (A-1)

15. Luther P. Gerlach and Virginia H. Hine, **Lifeway Leap.** University
(1)   of Minnesota Press, 1973. Two anthropologists provide a sen-
      sible introduction to understanding change, systems, movements,
      and the evolutionary viewpoint.   (ABC-2)

20. Herbert J. Muller, **Uses of the Future.** Indiana University Press,
(1)   1973. A thoughtful contribution from the humanities that criti-
      cizes "futurologists" while considering the future of ignorance,
      liberalism, communication, American culture, and a possible
      universal faith.   (AB-2)

22. R.L. Duffus, **Tomorrow's News.** Norton, 1967. A responsible popular
(1)   overview of basic human dilemmas such as population, nuclear
      weapons, big government, big business, employment and jobs,
      and freedom. Still of value.   (C-2)

27. Herman Kahn and B. Bruce-Briggs, **Things to Come.** Macmillan,
(2)   1972. A somewhat popularized version of **The Year 2000,** with
      attention to both international and domestic affairs, and a great
      number of provocative ideas.   (AB-2)

29. Jean Meynaud, **Technocracy.** Payot Paris, 1964; Free Press, 1969.
(2)   A thoughtful and restrained essay on the apparent evolution from
      democracy to a scientific technocracy.   (A-2)

31. Zbigniew Brzezinski, **Between Two Ages: America's Role in the**
(2)   **Technetronic Era.** Viking, 1970. A less fearful view of "techno-
      cracy," with astute comments on the Soviet Union and global
      strategies.   (AB-2)

50. Bertram M. Gross, "Planning in an Era of Social Revolution,"
(2)   **Public Administration Review,** May/June 1971. Explores the grand
      alternatives of Techno-Urban Fascism or Humanist Reconstruc-
      tion, and the outlines of a truly civilized Post-Service Society.
      Goes further than other writers on post-industrial society. (AB-1)

74. Andrew Levison, **The Working Class Majority.** Coward, McCann &
(2)   Geoghegan, 1974. Challenges the conventional wisdom about Amer-
      ica as a white-collar society by examining the standard cate-
      gories for arraying employment data.   (ABC-2)

93. Aldous Huxley, **Brave New World Revisited.** Harper & Bros., 1958.
(3)   An essay on over-organization and propaganda prompted by the
      fear that prophecies made in Huxley's classic novel (1932) are
      coming true sooner than expected.   (AB-1)

102. George Steiner, **In Bluebeard's Castle.** Yale University Press, 1971.
(3)   A leading cultural historian describes the destruction of inner
      forms and the elimination of certain vital futures in our emerging
      "post-culture."   (A-2)

106. Andrew Hacker, **The End of the American Era**. Atheneum, 1970.
(3)   An early and challenging explanation of America's decline; the
       major reason is ungovernability.   (AB-2)

125. Aurobindo Ghose (Sri Aurobindo), **The Human Cycle**. Sri Aurobindo
(4)   Ashram, 1949. Exemplifies the non-linear alternative in viewing
       the course of human affairs.   (A-2)

131. Charles Davy, **Towards a Third Culture**. Faber and Faber, 1961.
(4)   A neglected essay on the evolution of consciousness, written in
       response to C.P. Snow's "Two Cultures" lecture (no. 891). (AB-2)

147. Alfred Korzybski, **Manhood of Humanity**. Dutton, 1921. A classic
(4)   on thinking about the future, perhaps best known for its concept
       of humans as time-binding.   (AB-2)

151. William Irwin Thompson, **At the Edge of History**. Harper & Row,
(4)   1971. Offers an elegant four-phase cyclical theory, as well as
       comments about the emerging Scientific-Planetary Civilization.
                                                                 (A-2)

170. Sir Charles Galton Darwin, **The Next Million Years**. Doubleday,
(5)   1953. Views us in the midst of the scientific revolution and fore-
       sees a fifth revolution resulting from a shortage of fuel.   (ABC-2)

171. Samuel H. Ordway, Jr., **Resources and the American Dream: Including
(5)   a Theory of the Limit of Growth**. Ronald Press, 1953. A concise
       statement of the resource problem appearing nearly two decades
       before the Club of Rome's report on **The Limits to Growth** (no.
       206)   (ABC-2)

178. Garrett Hardin, **Exploring New Ethics for Survival**. Viking, 1972.
(5)   Elaborates on various themes in the author's classic essay on
       "The Tragedy of the Commons" (no. 177), i.e., the distinction
       between price and cost.   (AB-1)

210. Willem L. Oltmans, **On Growth**. Putnam's, 1974. Interviews with 70
(5)   leading figures, generally concerning their reactions to the Club
       of Rome's report on **The Limits to Growth**. An intriguing hand-
       book of cacophony.   (AB-2)

211. Edward Goldsmith et al., **A Blueprint for Survival**. Houghton Mifflin,
(5)   1972. Reprint of the Jan. 1972 issue of **The Ecologist**; a more
       readable version of **The Limits to Growth**, with a broader and
       deeper argument.   (AB-1)

212. Dennis C. Pirages and Paul R. Ehrlich, **Ark II: Social Response to
(5)   Environmental Perspectives**. Viking, 1974; Freeman, 1974. Over-
       view of environmental problems with a broad shopping list of
       reforms, aiming for a society that nurtures human improvement.
                                                                 (BC-2)

215. Herman E. Daly (ed.), **Toward a Steady-State Economy**. Freeman,
(5)   1973. An anthology of 16 essays bringing together the most im-
       portant thinking on the problem of economic growth vs. ecological
       concerns.   (AB-2)

240. Bernard James, **The Death of Progress**. Knopf, 1973. An anthro-
(6)   pologist worries about our awesome cultural change, and argues
       for a new science and a consciously-managed world culture.   (AB-2)

248. W. Warren Wagar, **The City of Man**. Houghton-Mifflin, 1963. A his-
(6)   tory of the vision of world order or cosmopolis.   (AB-2)

252. Richard A. Falk, **A Study of Future Worlds: Designing the Global**
(6)   **Community.** World Order Models Project/Free Press, 1975. A
well-documented and comprehensive approach to imagining alternatives and attaining them--perhaps the best work yet on thinking
about alternative futures of any sort.   (A-1)

257. Louis René Beres and Harry R. Targ, **Reordering the Planet: Con-**
(6)   **structing Alternative World Futures.** Allyn and Bacon, 1974. A
college-level text that can also introduce world order concerns
to professionals.   (B-2)

298. Hazel Henderson, "The Entropy State," **Planning Review,** April-May,
(7)   1974, pp. 1-4. A succinct introduction to the decentralist argument, with a focus on the unanticipated social costs arising from
overdeveloped systems.   (AB-2)

301. Lewis Herber (Murray Bookchin), **Our Synthetic Environment.** Knopf,
(7)   1962; Harper Colophon, 1974. A prophetic argument that the modern city has reached its limits and that there are many new dangers
to human health.   (AB-2)

303. Theodore Roszak, **Where the Wasteland Ends.** Doubleday, 1972. A
(7)   sophisticated attack on reductionist science and its relationship
to urban-industrial technocracy. A far more important book than
The Making of a Counter Culture, for which Roszak is widely
known.   (A-2)

308. David Dickson, **The Politics of Alternative Technology.** Fontana/
(7)   Collins, 1974; Universe, 1975. Argues that a genuine alternative
technology can only develop within the framework of an alternative
society, and makes useful distinctions between a hard technology
and soft technology society.   (A-2)

309. Gordon Rattray Taylor, **Rethink: A Paraprimitive Solution.** Dutton,
(7)   1973. A broad synthesis serving to point us in the direction of a
need-oriented society, but one that is in no way a romantic regression.   (AB-2)

310. E.F. Schumacher, **Small is Beautiful.** Harper & Row, 1973. Widely
(7)   noted essays by a British economist that challenges the conventional wisdom of economists in particular.   (AB-1)

311. Ralph Borsodi, **This Ugly Civilization.** Simon and Schuster, 1929.
(7)   Prescribes an alternative societal future, based on organic homesteads, in far greater breadth and detail than any contemporary
work on alternatives. A prophetic classic that may be difficult
to obtain, but well worth the effort.   (ABC-1)

330. Sir Julian Huxley, **The Human Crisis.** University of Washington Press,
(8)   1963. Argues that evolutionary humanism will be the dominant
type of idea system for the next few centuries, and points to some
implications.   (AB-2)

338. Pitirim A. Sorokin, **The Reconstruction of Humanity.** Beacon Press,
(8)   1948. A far-ranging critique of plans for salvation, as a preface to
proposals for releasing the altruism and goodwill of mankind.
A sophisticated response to decadence.   (AB-2)

339. Jim Dator, "Neither There Nor Then: A Eutopian Alternative to the
(8)   Development Model of Future Society," in **Human Futures,** IPC
Science and Technology Press, 1974. A good critique of the existing literature, followed by a defense of a high-technology trans-

formational society, where each individual may become self-fulfilled. (AB-2)

365. Hadley Cantril, **The Pattern of Human Concerns**. Rutgers University
(8) Press, 1965. Analysis of interviews with nearly 20,000 people in
13 countries on universal human needs such as being hopeful,
wanting freedom, and having a sense of confidence. Important
background for futurists and planners. (A-2)

366. Karl Menninger, M.D. **Whatever Became of Sin?** Hawthorn Books,
(9) 1973. Notes that there has been an unfortunate shift in the allocation of responsibility for evil, and appeals for moral leadership. (AB-2)

375. John W. Gardner, **The Recovery of Confidence**. Norton, 1970. Wise
(9) sermonizing about many matters relevant to social renewal. Still
right on target. (ABC-2)

379. Theodore Caplow, **Toward Social Hope**. Basic Books, 1975. Describes
(9) the seven essential parts to any project of social improvement,
and assesses projects of the past two centuries that have and have
not worked. (AB-2)

380. Seymour B. Sarason. **The Creation of Settings and the Future Socie-**
(9) **ties**. Jossey-Bass, 1972. Explores a variety of considerations in
creating new organizations, or settings. Useful companion to
Caplow (no. 379). (AB-2)

381. James MacGregor Burns, **Uncommon Sense**. Harper & Row, 1972.
(9) A call to rethinking our goals and our means of attaining them,
with particular attention to the failures of thought and the ignorance of certain intellectuals. (AB-1)

382. David F. Linowes, **Strategies for Survival**. American Management
(9) Association, 1973. Proposes that successful practices of industry
should be applied to our failing non-profit organizations. Could
be some good ideas here. (AB-2)

386. Stafford Beer, **Designing Freedom**. Wiley, 1974. Explains the basic
(9) concepts of cybernetics and how they could be applied to societal
planning. (AB-2)

407. Harvey S. Perloff (ed.), **The Future of the United States Government**.
(9) Braziller, 1971. A provocative anthology from the Commission
on the Year 2000 (and the only report to be issued by any of its
working groups). (AB-2)

416. Derek Shearer, "Dreams and Schemes: A Catalogue of Proposals,"
(9) **Working Papers for a New Society**, Fall 1975, pp. 38-46. A valuable
inventory of bills, proposals, and model laws for Congress to consider, suggesting a possible and desirable society of a few years
hence. (AB-2)

431. Victor Ferkiss, **The Future of Technological Civilization**. Braziller,
(9) 1974. A well-written "exercise in utopian thinking" that criticizes
the ruling ideology of liberalism and proposes a new political
philosophy of ecological humanism. Similar to the writings of
Alvin Toffler and Charles Reich, but a marked improvement over
both. (AB-2)

434. Joseph A. Califano, Jr. **A Presidential Nation**. Norton, 1975. A thought-
(9) ful essay on the growth of presidential power, with some important

suggestions aimed toward restoring credibility and integrity. (AB-2)

451.   Edward R. Bagley, **Beyond the Conglomerates.** American Management
(10)   Association, 1975. Predicts the emergence of supercorporations
         and a possible movement to a contract state; possibilities of
         good and evil are explored.   (ABC-2)

455.   Richard J. Barnet and Ronald E. Müller, **Global Reach.** Simon and
(10)   Schuster, 1974. A thorough description of the globalization of
         oligopoly capitalism, and the new liberal vision of a world cor-
         porate society, with many sophisticated suggestions for national
         controls.   (AB-1)

486.   Robert A. Hendrikson, **The Cashless Society.** Dodd, Mead, 1972.
(10)   Argues for deliberate guidance in directing the evolution of society
         toward a desirable form of cashlessness.   (AB-2)

507.   Willis W. Harman, "Humanistic Capitalism: Another Alternative,"
(10)   **Fields Within Fields,** No. 10, Winter 1973-4, pp. 3-15. The requisite
         conditions of a humane post-industrial society concern ethics,
         various institutional changes, and changes in incentive systems.
                                                                        (A-2)

528.   Herbert J. Gans, **More Equality.** Pantheon, 1973. Deals with tough
(11)   questions that others ignore, such as social costs and equality
         vs. liberty. Advocates more equality, rather than complete equal-
         ity.   (AB-1)

531.   Jaroslav Vanek, **The Participatory Economy.** Cornell University
(11)   Press, 1971. A strong argument for a labor-managed market
         economy, with Yugoslavia seen as a prototype.   (AB-2)

539.   Irving Howe (ed.), **Essential Works of Socialism.** Holt, Rinehart
(11)   and Winston, 1970. A valuable collection of authoritative docu-
         ments.   (AB-2)

543.   Michael Harrington, **Socialism.** Saturday Review Press, 1972; Ban-
(11)   tam, 1973. The definitive work on contemporary democratic so-
         cialism.   (AB-1)

557.   Jack Newfield and Jeff Greenfield, **A Populist Manifesto.** Praeger,
(11)   1972. Offers an extensive and clearly articulated platform to
         redress the imbalance in money and power.   (ABC-2)

586.   William A Rusher, **The Making of a New Majority Party.** Sheed and
(12)   Ward, 1975. The publisher of **National Review** offers an extensive
         sketch of a possible platform for a new conservative party that
         can put together a winning coalition.   (AB-2)

588.   Robert Nisbet, **Twilight of Authority.** Oxford University Press, 1975.
(12)   Argues that the dominant element of modernity has been political
         society and that we are at the beginning of a new Reformation
         against the state.   (AB-2)

599.   F.A. Hayek, **The Constitution of Liberty.** University of Chicago
(12)   Press, 1960. An eloquent and thorough presentation of the classi-
         cal liberal political theory that favors individual freedom over
         the welfare state.   (A-1)

614.   Paul and Percival Goodman, **Communitas.** University of Chicago
(13)   Press, 1947; Vintage revision, 1960. Examines three basic com-
         munity paradigms, or model ways of life.   (ABC-2)

615. Commission on Population Growth and the American Future, **Popula-**
(13) **tion and the American Future.** USGPO and NAL Signet, 1972.
An important overview of population growth and distribution,
and many related social aspects.   (AB-2)

632. George Chaplin and Glenn D. Paige (eds.), **Hawaii 2000: Continuing**
(13) **Experiment in Anticipatory Democracy.** University Press of Hawaii,
1973. Materials associated with the Governor's Conference on the
Year 2000, summarized with valuable critical comments on why
little or no change resulted.   (AB-2)

687. Gerard K. O'Neill, "Space Colonies: The High Frontier," **The Futurist,**
(13) February 1976, pp. 25-33. The latest version of an important
proposal that might solve both energy problems and population
problems.   (ABC-2)

719. David Morris and Karl Hess, **Neighborhood Power: The New Localism.**
(13) Beacon Press, 1975. An eloquent and persuasive call for a return
to a human scale of organization as our large-scale institutions
fall apart.   (ABC-2)

723. President's Research Committee on Social Trends, **Recent Social**
(14) **Trends in the United States.** McGraw-Hill, 1933. Perhaps the most
exemplary collective effort ever undertaken to systematically
consider societal directions. Modern scholars would be well-
advised to emulate this standard.   (AB-1)

775. "2024 A.D.--A Probe Into the Future," **Saturday Review/World,**
(14) August 24, 1974. The 50th Anniversary Issue, with 17 imaginative
articles largely on world problems and outer space. A good overview of optimism.   (B-2)

779. Andrew A. Spekke (ed.), **The Next 25 Years: Crisis & Opportunity.**
(14) World Future Society, 1975. A wide variety of broad and narrow
"futurist" perspectives, with some important (and not so important) ideas.   (AB-2)

797. Anthony Arblaster and Steven Lukes (eds.) **The Good Society: A Book**
(14) **of Readings.** Harper & Row, 1971. A valuable collection of 81
writers from the 18th, 19th, and 20th centuries. A useful complement to no. 779.   (AB-2)

802. Franklin Tugwell (ed.), **Search for Alternatives: Public Policy and the**
(14) **Study of the Future.** Winthrop, 1973. Perhaps the best collection
of contemporary "futurist" writing, and a good starting point for
policy-oriented professionals.   (AB-2)

820. James Thomas Martin and Adrian R.D. Norman, **The Computerized**
(15) **Society.** Prentice-Hall, 1970. A good overview of hopes, fears,
and protective actions to be taken in light of potentially awesome
developments.   (ABC-2)

844. Alexander Solzhenitsyn et al., **From Under the Rubble.** Little Brown,
(15) 1975; Bantam, 1976. Outstanding essays of global importance by
Soviet dissidents, indicting technocracy in general as well as the
stultifying Soviet bureaucracy.   (AB-1)

913. Bertrand de Jouvenel, **The Art of Conjecture.** Basic Books, 1967.
(16) A classic work on thinking about the future, most notable in this
context for its advocacy of a surmising forum to bring together
opinions on directions and alternatives.   (A-2)

C. Some General Observations on the Literature

In the recent past, there was a consensus among many of our leading social thinkers that we lived in an affluent society, and that the inexorable direction of this society would be toward greater abundance, technology, services, bureaucracy, meritocracy, leisure, and urbanization. This Technological, Affluent, Service Society may still be our most probable, long-term future. But today it is clear that most of us are not economically secure, that the results of technology are profoundly mixed, that we cannot afford more services let alone those we presently have, that bureaucracy is insufferable, that meritocracy is far from extant, that some of us have little or no leisure while others have far more than they desire, and that the long-range trend toward urbanization has reversed.

We are at a major crossroads, both in our societal condition and in our thinking. It is a transitional era, where great changes will occur, whether or not we attempt to anticipate and direct them. Some attempt at societal management would certainly seem to be better than no attempt at all. But to undergo such an attempt there must be a recognition that we are in an Era of Paradigm Search, where our basic assumptions and models should be intelligently and systematically examined.

The broad outline of this necessary examination is suggested by the first 13 chapters in this guide. After a brief introductory chapter on general overviews of our societal condition, Chapter 2 draws together the thinking that has described and covertly promulgated the Technological, Affluent, Service Society. Such thinking often evades questions of desirability, and, as warned by René Dubos (no. 181), it assumes that trend equals destiny.

The pros and cons of the technocratic service society are shown in Chapter 3, which juxtaposes Optimists and Pessimists: the former with their generally superficial arguments that technological progress will continue to occur, and the latter with weighty arguments for cultural and social despair. Chapter 4 considers a different optimistic stance: The Cosmic Evolutionary View that describes (often with equal parts of advocacy) a vast transition leading to a humanly better condition. There is little or no interchange between writers holding this cosmic view, largely psychologists and philosophers, and those who advance the image of the service society, largely social scientists.

The items in Chapter 5, the first of nine chapters concerned with societal alternatives, raise powerful ecological arguments against the continuation of directions described by most of the writers in Chapter 2. This holistic/ environmentalist view is clearly one that can no longer be ignored. The concern for some form of World Order, the major focus in Chapter 6, will also be of increasing importance as the affairs of nations become more intertwined.

The argument for Decentralization, appearing in Chapter 7, directly challenges the feasibility and desirability of The Technological, Affluent, Service Society, as well as conventional liberal/conservative political categories. Until recently, decentralists were dismissed as escapists; today, it is more problematic as to which stance is more realistic. Chapter 8 arrays the thoughts of those who desire a society that is genuinely concerned with Human Needs, in contrast to the satisfactions and dissatisfactions resulting from our present materially oriented society.

Chapter 9 presents a variety of considerations in Government Reform through agendas, budgets, platforms, revised constitutions, and institutional change. Chapter 10, Economic Reform, focuses on large corporations as well as a variety of proposals, most notably concerning economic planning and work. Chapter 11 deals with the sensitive matter of Redistribution of Wealth and Power, particularly as advocated by socialists, populists, and Marxists. In sharp contrast, Chapter 12 is devoted to conservatives, libertarians, and classical liberals who are deeply concerned with freedom from Government. Chapter 13 on Spatial Alternatives brings together urban and megalapolitan planners, decentralists who advocate small communities, and cosmic thinkers who focus on opportunities in outer space and new styles for human habitation.

This plethora of perspectives is already unwieldy, and the cacophony may well be worsening. If this guide offers a rough approximation of what has been written, it is clear that the quantity of literature concerning societal directions and alternatives has risen steadily in this century, with a notable growth in the past few years. The rate of increase is considerably greater than the general growth rate of printed material.

Summary of Chronological Title Index (Index C)

Period	Pre-1930	1930-1939	1940-1949	1950-1959	1960-1964	1965-1969	1970-1971	1972-1973	1974-1975
No. Books and Reports	13	22	32	43	52	123	138	165	208

Such evidence of a greater "future-orientation" (only some of which is explicitly so) suggests a perturbed society, but does not necessarily indicate that the quality of thinking about societal directions and alternatives is undergoing any improvement. Publications before the 20th century have been excluded from this guide, and are therefore not contrasted with contemporary writing. But one might make such an argument simply by considering writers from early in this century such as Borsodi, the Huxleys, Korzybski, Mannheim, and Sorokin, as well as the superlative collective effort resulting in the 1933 report of the President's Committee on Social Trends (no. 723).

There has been much recent talk about futures research, futures methodology, policy sciences, systems analysis, computer modelling, and other new cross-disciplines and "intellectual technologies." But there has been little significant result. The computer model used in the first Club of Rome report created a great stir, but it should be recognized that virtually the same argument (without computer runs but with better prose) was elaborated in 1953 by Samuel Ordway as "The Theory of the Limit to Growth." (no. 171) Other than the Club of Rome studies (nos. 206 and 209) the new methodologies and techniques have made very little contribution to the broad literature of societal directions and alternatives, although they may have made important contributions to more specialized concerns.

As for future studies, there is a great confusion as to what it is, as demonstrated by the variety of titles that are freely used for different purposes by different people, e.g. futures research, futurology, futuristics, futurism, and prognostics. (Indeed, one of the current educationist fads in the elementary schools is "futuring.") The "futures field" is sometimes narrowly restricted to efforts at forecasting and to the use of certain quantitative methods such as the Delphi technique. Using a broad definition, the contents of this guide could be considered as entirely within the province of future studies.

The confusion results from the lack of a professional organization, which enables anyone to assume the title of "futurist" or proclaim any writing or activity as "futuristic." It must be kept in mind that only a few of those who write about the future choose to call themselves futurists, and only a few of those who call themselves futurists are writers and researchers. Using the "futurist" title appears to have little or no effect on the quality of thinking about the future. For example, The Civic Curriculum includes well-known avowed futurists such as Victor Ferkiss, Herman Kahn, and John Platt, but also many others who have never been considered as futurists or considered themselves as such. Conversely, there are some widely-known futurists, notably Daniel Bell and Alvin Toffler, whose contributions to the serious consideration of societal directions and alternatives are over-rated.

It is necessary to make forecasts and to consider alternative futures, as argued, for example, by de Jouvenel (no. 913). We would doubtlessly benefit from specialists in thinking about the future, perhaps occupying the Professorships of Possibility advocated by Huxley (no. 330). But thinking about the future is a very broad enterprise, and professional futurists by any definition will not necessarily make the most valuable contributions. They can easily become inward-looking "cults of cultural innovators," as warned by Mead (no. 911), or simply an isolated and impotent group of non-innovators pretending to the contrary. Whether or not one is professional, being "future-oriented" or "futuristic" is no particular virtue if one is being foolish about it. Indeed, such "future schlock" can only serve to dis-courage serious inquiry into directions and alternatives for our society as a whole and its various sectors.

The essential concerns must be kept foremost in mind: where we are, where we are headed, and what we should do. We should consider who ad-dresses them in the most intelligent and publically interested manner, regardless of professional and political labels, age and sex, scientific and academic credentials, political offices held, institutional affiliation, race and nationality, and reputation acquired at other times and in other fields.

At the same time, we must also keep in mind all of those who address the essential questions of societal directions and alternatives, regardless of their values and methodologies. This is not simply an exercise in the sociology of knowledge, but in the politics of knowledge and Realpolitik. To acquire some understanding of how we might effectively pursue the desirable human ends of peace, freedom, justice, equity, community and self-fulfillment, we must recognize that other people feel strongly that their images of society are accurate, and that their prescriptions are wise.

This guide attempts to identify what are felt to be the most intelligent responses to the essential questions, while also providing some estimate of the entire universe of response. The great variety of answers and ap-proaches to the essential questions indicates a profound and dangerous fragmentation.

One way to briefly illustrate this fragmentation is to consider the 350 societal titles summed up in Indexes D, E, and F. Index D lists 81 titles that describe our present society or era. Index E brings together 63 stage theories that seek to explain the societal transition that we may be under-going. Index F arrays 206 titles for some alternative society that we ought to have. There are undoubtedly other titles in press, and others not identi-fied here.

Some readers might delight in this pluralism, applauding the ferment and creativity that such an array suggests. We should, of course, expect and encourage a variety of positions and ideological differences: some practical and cautious views and some far-ranging and idealistic views; some short-range visions and some long-range visions; some well-conceived notions and some poorly conceived notions. We should also expect some duplication, for these images of the present and the future are in competition with each other.

But taken to an extreme, pluralism becomes cacophony, originality becomes egomania, and good intentions merely serve to waste paper and crowd library shelves. As noted by John W. Gardner (no. 373):

> The advantages of pluralism are diminished if the various elements of the society are out of touch with one another. A society that is capable of continuous renewal will have effective internal communication among its diverse elements. We do not have that today. We are drowning in a torrent of talk, but most of it only serves to raise the noise level.   **(The Recovery of Confidence, p. 58)**

This "torrent of talk" is also illustrated in the volume of interviews by Willem L. Oltmans (no. 210), who conversed with 70 major intellectual figures, largely concerning their reactions to the Club of Rome's **Limits to Growth** study (no. 206). Toward the end of the book, Oltmans made a notable observation during his interview with Richard N. Gardner (no relation to John W. Gardner, above) who edited the compendium of proposals resulting from the White House Conference on International Cooperation (**Blueprint for Peace**, no. 269). Consider this exchange by Oltmans and Gardner:

> Oltmans: What surprised me most during the research for my book was that I had always felt politicans were unable to communicate, being glued to their political ideologies, but I found to my utter dismay that the same situation prevails among scientists--or worse... And the masses are the victims. I mean the real groundswell of humanity is the victim of this immature and uncivilized behavior.
>
> R. Gardner: ...We are afflicted not only by national but by personal egoism. That is what could eventually destroy us. Many of these eminent people have such big egos that their principal preoccupation in life is to establish a piece of intellectual turf and preserve it against all comers, whatever the consequences. They're prepared to sacrifice truth--perhaps not consciously but subconsciously--to the pursuit of ideology and the pursuit of ego. This is wrong. The truly great men in history, the great scientists like Einstein, were modest men, constantly revising their ideas, listening with respect to other people with other opinions. What has happened to the tradition of Einstein? What kind of men do we have today?   **(On Growth, p. 424)**

Regrettably, this guide can offer little evidence of "modest men, constantly revising their ideas, listening with respect to other people...." The great majority of the views on societal directions and alternatives are posited with little or no reference to any other views, past or present (one indication of this being the 350 societal titles in Indexes D, E, and F.) In any established scholarly field, such hubris and lack of general scientific and scholarly standards would be intolerable. But "societal directions and alternatives" is not an established field of scholarship. It may someday be a "science" or a cross-disciplinary field, but it is certainly not deserving, at present, of even being called a new or growing field. Rather, it is a non-disciplinary No Man's Land with no standards or respect for precedent. Unlike established fields, it is neither cooperative nor competitive. There is little attempt to positively build upon the work of others, criticism goes unanswered (see Index of Selected Criticism), and there are very few attempts to promote debates or extensive exchanges of opposing views.

Individuals are responsible for this insulation, but it is not solely their fault. Our institutions serve as a mighty centrifugal force to direct attention away from serious considerations of societal directions and alternatives. Our major universities persist in training, hiring, and promotion along the lines of established disciplines. Publishing houses cater to this fragmentation, and to publishing anything that will make money, and in many instances only that which is certain to make money. Periodicals divide the task of reviewing into hundreds of separate pieces. Governments devote their research funds to specific questions, rather than sustained inquiry into fundamental matters.

By all of these processes, we lose sight of what is important and the central questions that should be addressed. Even before World War II, Mannheim lamented that "the specialized social sciences have been absorbed in details and have shut themselves off from the essential problems... (with) no one responsible for considering the problem as a whole." (no. 514) Shortly after the war, Joad (no. 116) described this condition as the "dropping of the object," warning that such behavior is the sign of a society in a decadent period. Recently, **The New Yorker** described our situation in an editorial:

> We Americans have now organized things in such a way that our control is greatest where it matters least and is least where it matters most. The route of the school bus and the price of beef we deliberate with ponderous care and hedge about with restrictions. The survival of the world we suspend from a thread.
>   (July 8, 1974, pp. 25-26)

We not only invert our priorities, but we also fail to bring our collective intelligence together in any adequate way, even as regards specific concerns. The growing difficulty in making wise action was a concern, for example, at the 1944 meeting of the Conference on Science, Philosophy and Religion (no. 726). More recently the problem was expressed by Harold Howe II, Vice President of the Ford Foundation and former U.S. Commissioner of Education:

> The worlds of science, of social science, and political decision-making are all involved in the significant decisions of the future regarding every aspect of our individual lives and of our national existence. In health, in education, in defense, in the problems of transport and communication, in the environment and the management of services in urban centers, there is inevitably a mixture of these three elements that don't understand each other well, that communicate ineptly, and that somehow combine to set the pattern of the future for all of us. It's enough to make one nervous about the future!   (Unpublished remarks, May 1974)

There is a risk in belaboring this concern about intellectual priorities and intellectual fragmentation. But there is a greater risk in denying the problem or in underestimating its magnitude. Doing so is a major cause of more problems and inadequate action.

Basically, our society lacks a comprehensive and inspiring vision, widely understood and supported, that can guide the formation of our basic policies. At present, our fortunes are directed in a piecemeal fashion that proves to be unsatisfying to many persons. Our citizenry is disinterested, or ill-equipped to participate. As noted by Harvey Perloff in the report from the Commission on the Year 2000 (no. 407), civic education is "the least understood and most neglected aspect of educational development."

Ideally, a constructive image of the future should be arrived at by democratic processes of reflection and debate by informed citizens. Less ideally, we could have a vision imposed upon us, for better or worse, by some leader. Or we could continue to drift from crisis to crisis.

Arriving at some useful image of the future that will guide the design of policy in the public interest will not be an easy task, and will require many actions on many fronts. Existing institutions should devote greater attention to promoting a useful generalist-specialist balance in their teaching and research. If widespread attention can be drawn to boxing and tennis contests, one would think that at least a modest fraction of this audience would have a similar interest in extensive debates between representatives of fundamentally opposing points of view, aired over television or recorded in the print media. Other forms of intellectual encounters might be tried, in order to get some recalcitrant scholars to consider certain views and broaden their horizons. To assist in the continuing education of political leaders, scholars, and citizens, one or more panels of qualified experts might issue a "Global Curriculum" for general concerns and various specialized concerns, on a systematic annual basis. And new institutions are needed, such as the colleges of cognitive synthesis suggested by Wagar (no. 249), the World Institute proposed by Stulman (no. 912), the surmising forum recommended by de Jouvenel (no. 913), and the World Information Synthesis and Encyclopedia advocated by Kochen (no. 915).

A new holistic science is necessary to explore the many dimensions of public policy issues. Such a science is suggested by the widespread criticism of our "normal" reductionist science in general and economics in particular (see Index of Selected Criticism), and by the corresponding advocacy of some form of systemic thinking (see Index of Selected Subjects and Ideas).

Societal Directions and Alternatives is a small step in the direction of these necessary adaptations. It is by no means a complete record of all that has been said. It does provide a broad outline of the dimensions that must be considered if we wish to seriously deal with our societal condition. If we are in a transitional Era of Paradigm Search, we should conduct the search as thoroughly and wisely as possible.

II. LISTINGS

A. Directions

Chapter 1

General Overviews of Change and the Future

The first 25 items serve as an introduction to the central questions of societal directions and alternatives. They are largely concerned with the general rate and direction of change, and they are neither markedly optimistic nor pessimistic - attributes stressed in Chapter 3.

Those persons who are unfamiliar with the subject matter of societal directions and alternatives will benefit from reading several of the items in this chapter, particularly Boulding (1), Platt (3), and Muller (19,20), which represent perspectives from the social sciences, natural sciences, and humanities respectively. More general audiences will benefit from Gerlach and Hine (15), Chase (21), and Duffus (22). Also useful are Murray (4), Michael (13), and Vickers (14).

1. BOULDING, Kenneth E. **The Meaning of the Twentieth Century: The Great Transition.** World Perspectives, Vol. 34. NY: Harper & Row, 1964; Harper Colophon Edition, 1965. 199 pp. $1.45, paper.   (AB-2)

"The twentieth century marks the middle period of a great transition in the state of the human race. It may properly be called the second great transition in the history of mankind.

"The first transition was that from precivilized to civilized society which began to take place about five (or ten) thousand years ago. This is a transition that is still going on in some parts of the world, although it can be regarded as almost complete." (p. 1)

As the first transition approaches completion, a second great transition --from civilized to post-civilized society--treads on its heels. Facets of this transition include changes in child rearing, religion and ideology, and social institutions. Postcivilization will surely be more uniform, as a result of the enormous process of cultural mixture. But we cannot know if this transition is a good change, for Orwell/Huxley anti-Utopias are possible. Indeed, this transition could be seriously delayed, or man and his planet might not make it at all. The bulk of the book is devoted to describing four traps: war, the problem of economic development, population, and entropy or chaos.

An earlier essay ("After Civilization, What?" **Bulletin of the Atomic Scientists**, Oct. 1962. Reprinted in Richard Kostelanetz, ed., **Beyond Left & Right**. NY: Morrow, 1968) contains the essential outlines of this argument.

2. FRANKEL, Charles, "The Third Great Revolution of Mankind," **The New York Times Magazine**, Feb. 9, 1958, pp. 11ff.   (AB-3)

A professor of philosophy entitles our time as the Age of Acceleration, following the agricultural revolution, which took place 25,000 years ago, and the industrial revolution, which began in the latter half of the 18th century. Both of these revolutions began as changes in ideas and tools that men had used to adjust themselves to nature. The revolution that has taken place in the last fifteen years must be put in company such as this. But the Age of Acceleration (or the Space Age or the Atomic Age) marks a change in the tempo of change, and a corresponding need to exercise more deliberate control over change.

3. PLATT, John, "What We Must Do," **Science,** 166: November 28, 1969, pp. 1115-1121. Reprinted in Franklin Tugwell (ed.), **Search for Alternatives** (Winthrop, 1973), pp. 2-17.   (A-1)

This classic essay by a biophysicist offers a concise and powerful overview of the multiple crises that confront us, with the view that "it has now become urgent for us to mobilize all our intelligence to solve these problems if we are to keep from killing ourselves in the next few years." (p. 1115)

Overview charts for the U.S. and the world are provided, indicating the priority of problem areas and the estimated time to crisis, broken down in three future periods: 1-5 years, 5-20 years, and 20-50 years. For the U.S., the problem areas in order of priority are:
-total annihilation
-great destruction or change (physical, biological, political)
-widespread, almost unbearable tension (slums, race conflict)
-large-scale distress (transportation, urban blight, crime)
-tension-producing responsive change (water supply, privacy, drugs, marine resources)
-other problems important but adequately researched (military R&D, new educational methods)
-exaggerated dangers and hopes (mind control, heart transplants)
-noncrisis problems being overstudied (man in space and most basic science)

It is concluded that "The task is clear. The task is huge. The time is horribly short. In the past, we have had science for intellectual pleasure and science for the control of nature. We have had science for war. But today, the whole human experiment may hang on the question of how fast we now press the development of science for survival." (p. 1121)

*** There has been very little change in the direction that Platt advocates. His method of arraying problems is still extremely valuable for describing societal directions. This essay is usefully contrasted with the consummately pragmatic essay by Harvey Brooks, a leading spokesman for science and a member of the much-celebrated but now-defunct Commission on the Year 2000. "Are Scientists Obsolete?" (**Science,** 186: November 8, 1974) dismisses Platt's proposals as not "in the cards politically, at least for the next decade" (p. 503). So much for courageous leadership in the scientific community.

4. MURRAY, Bruce C. **Navigating the Future.** NY: Harper & Row, Sept. 1975. 175 pp. $7.95.   (ABC-3)

A fairly well-balanced introduction to a number of concerns by the Director of the Jet Propulsion Laboratory at Cal Tech. Chapters on topics such as Science and the Mind of Man (concerning natural cataclysms, civilization, and consciousness), Runaway World (on the armaments boom, the green revolution, and H.G. Wells' scenario of "Things to Come"), on the possibility of colonizing the planets (seen as possible in the very distant future, if at all), and Dimensions of the Future (on the artificial world, genetic engineering, and homogenization).

We are seen as headed toward The Crunch: "the unprecedented period in human history when Earth becomes saturated with humans and globally unified environmentally and socially." (p. 109) Three possible outcomes are The Imperial Possibility where the world is dominated by one superpower, the Superstate Scenario featuring "an interlocking bureaucracy of the advanced nations," and a World Confederation of some sort. Several false hopes are also described: technological utopias, back to nature in communes, wisdom from some extraterrestrial intelligence, and religious utopias. Murray considers possibilities if and when we pass through The Crunch: whether a Brave New World is possible, and whether we might join a Community of the Universe (seen as probable).

Concludes that "Authoritarian America, the Superstate, or other forms of nonparticipatory authority lie in ambush for a citizenry which fails to accept the responsibility of understanding the world in which it lives." (p. 154) But Murray is optimistic that we can influence the future, and urges scientists to accept the full intellectual challenge of the modern world.

*** A useful introduction, but lacking much understanding of social institutions and missing some important documentation, i.e. there is no reference to O'Neill's proposal (No. 690) for space colonies, published half a year before this book was completed. Far more serious, Murray views a desperate need for a new world view consistent with the facts of science, but makes no reference to the classic work of Northrup (no. 271), and others such as Reiser (no. 272-274).

5. SEIDENBERG, Roderick. **Post-Historic Man: An Inquiry.** Chapel Hill: University of North Carolina Press, 1950. 246 pp.   (A-3)

A deep and eloquent essay offering insight into the future phase of man's development based on the direction and momentum of his past. "Only on the basis of the widest possible summation of the past can we hope to discern the drift into the future." (p. 177)

The central axiom is that of an increasingly organized world: an "ever-expanding trellis" along which civilization expands and develops. Such organization inevitably demands further organization, and the machine serves to accelerate this trend to the "collectivization of man."

"History thus marks a change of direction in the social structure of man, which may be subsumed as the transmutation of society as an organism into an organization of society." (p. 47) In contrast to theories of rise and fall, Seidenberg envisions a "sweeping and inescapable" determinism in the evolution of man's development, with history as a transitional stage between epochs of far longer duration. The trend toward organization "will necessarily transform society from an organic into an organizational entity." (p. 107)

The final chapter, "Values and Vistas," provides an excellent critical overview of thinkers such as Hayek, Muller, Toynbee, Jung, J. Huxley, Mumford, and L.L. Whyte.

6. SEIDENBERG, Roderick. **Anatomy of the Future.** Chapel Hill: University of North Carolina Press, 1961. 173 pp.   (A-3)

Continues the theme of **Post-Historic Man** in viewing a world moving toward total organization--a trend that came about unheralded and without the fanfare of social prophets: "the entire span of history may be regarded as a transitional era in a profound metamorphosis...our entry into a new world, different from any known in the past." (p. 41)

The striking increase in the rate of change is noted, along with dark regressions as "the obverse side of our spectacular advances." The means of life are in control, rather than the ends: "the more intangible aims and goals of man have become dissipated and obscured beneath the staggering proliferation and perfection of his mundane means." (p. 26)

The incredible increase in world population, the striking increase in organizational procedures, the expansion in the means of life, the triumphant sway of science, the continuous impact of our machine technology--"these vast and irrepressible trends, cemented by a common urgency, constitute in their massive interrelations a close-knit and sweeping determinism, a converging world movement." (p.27)

Expressing concern about what is now known by some as future shock, Seidenberg notes those who are helpless and withdrawn, psychologically alienated in the forward march of events, and wonders how man can adjust himself to this acceleration. "In giving wings to his material achievements without a corresponding enlargement of his moral vision and spiritual insight, modern man, despite his high hopes and increased powers, now finds himself more desperate and harassed than ever." (p. 43)

7. DRUCKER, Peter F. **America's Next Twenty Years.** NY: Harper, 1955. 114 pp.   (AB-3)

Examines future developments that are already under way as a result of population increases. Chapters on The Coming Labor Shortage, The Promise of Automation (technocracy under another name, where only the speed of automation is uncertain), The New Tycoons (on fiduciary managers), The Growth of Higher Education, International Economics (America viewed as a have-not nation due to lacking a supply of raw materials), and Coming Issues in American Politics (such as demands for equality and medical care for everyone).
*** Looking back twenty years later, this thoughtful essay is surprisingly accurate.

8. BAADE, Fritz. **Race to the Year 2000. Our Future: A Paradise or the Suicide of Mankind.** Trans. from the German by Ernst Pawel. NY: Doubleday, 1962. 246 pp.   (AB-4)

The Director of the Institute for Research in World Economics and a leading member of the Social Democratic Party provides a general overview of population growth, food production, the underdeveloped countries, manpower, energy, steel, education, and armaments. He points to many problems, but concludes that "this world of A.D. 2000 could indeed be a marvelous, a miraculously beautiful world." (p. 229)
*** Generally gushy hopes based on extrapolating the usual economic indicators.

9. TOYNBEE, Arnold. **The Prospects of Western Civilization.** NY: Columbia University Press, 1949. 105 pp.   (AB-4)

Four lectures delivered on the Bampton Foundation at Columbia University in April 1948: Western Prospects and Non-Western Experience, The Problem of War, The Problem of Class, and The Conflict Between Heart and Head.

One of Toynbee's concerns is the "disparity between the regular human pace of our subconscious feelings and the inhumanly accelerated pace of our technological progress." It is concluded that there are three major alternatives lying before us: catastrophe, saving ourselves at a prohibitive price (more probable), and finding some way between catastrophe and Huxley's Brave New World.

10. LAPP, Ralph E. **The Logarithmic Century.**   Englewood Cliffs, N.J.: Prentice-Hall, 1973. 264 pp. $7.95.   (AB-4)

"This book is really about a conjuction of sciences--ecology and economics, or eco-economics." (p.22) There are numerous tables to illustrate the chapters on nuclear power, the consumer avalanche, the knowledge explosion, the question of growth, and the control of technology. The potential of disaster argues for application of restraints on size.

Conscious of contributing to "a rash of author emissions," Lapp restrains himself to only one recommendation: a Global Authority on Resource Conservation to survey natural resources and make forecasts on allowable rates of depletion.

11. PIEL, Gerard. **The Acceleration of History.** NY:Knopf, 1972. 369 pp. $8.95.   (A-4)

Essays by the publisher of **Scientific American** on topics such as technology and democratic institutions, health, population, the treason of the clerks, education, the stationary state, and "the pseudoscience of futurology."

12. GABOR, Dennis. **Inventing the Future.** London: Secker and Warburg, 1963; NY: Knopf, 1964. 238 pp.   (AB-3)

Explores the three great dangers ("The Trilemma") of our civilization: nuclear war, overpopulation, and the age of leisure. Concludes that we are still the masters of our fate: "The future cannot be predicted, but futures can be invented." (p.207) "We cannot stop inventing because we are riding a tiger...we must now start thinking of social inventions to anaesthetize the tiger, so that we can get off its back." (pp. 208-209) It is hoped that consent in matters of policy can be engineered by rational persuasion.

13. MICHAEL, Donald N. **The Unprepared Society: Planning for a Precarious Future.** Foreward by Ward Madden. The John Dewey Society Lecture--Number Ten. NY: Basic Books, 1968. 132 pp. $4.95; $1.60, paper.   (AB-3)

Chapters on the following: On the Environment of the Futurist, One Way of Looking at Tomorrow (focusing on complexity, turmoil, and scarcity). Three Prepotent Technologies (cybernation, social engineering, and biological engineering), On the Changeover to Long-Range Planning, The Natural Resistances to Organizational Change, and Some Challenges to Educators.
*** Still a useful introduction to complexity and how we might cope with it.

14. VICKERS, Geoffrey. **Freedom in a Rocking Boat: Changing Values in An Unstable Society.** London: Allen Lane, The Penguin Press, 1970; Pelican paper edition, 1972. 215 pp.   (A-3)

Argues that we live in a self-exciting system, where instability is built into the culture and must get worse. Our crisis is due to explosive technology, and cultural change is required by rethinking our value structure, our blind faith in competition, the omnipotence of the firm, and the economic criterion of value.

After chapters such as The Fouled Nest, The Proliferation of Power, The Scientific Distortion, and The Need for Regulation, concludes with a chapter on "The Post-Liberal Era" (also referring interchangeably to post-liberal age and post-liberal world). The changing world situation is seen as forcing liberal democracies to face questions that the liberal age could ignore, while abandoning certain unexamined assumptions. Mankind must now conserve the planet's resources and distribute its product acceptably.

15. GERLACH, Luther P. and Virginia H. HINE. **Lifeway Leap: The Dynamics of Change in America.** Minneapolis: U. of Minnesota Press, 1973. 332 pp. $4.95 paper.   (ABC-2)

A very clear and jargon-free attempt by two anthropologists to supply four basic conceptual tools for creative participation in shaping the future: the distinction between revolutionary and developmental change, and a description of systems, movements, and the evolutionary viewpoint. Although apparently written for high school and college students, and for perplexed citizens, this volume conveys some fundamental notions that would be useful to any professional.

Revolutionary change does not necessarily use force or violence, but it does reject conventional problem-solving approaches. Developmental change is change within an established thought system or social system. Evolutionary change is seen as the interweaving of these two. Particularly useful is an explanation of change in thought systems (adapted from Kuhn's essay on **The Structure of Scientific Revolutions**), and a discussion of De Bono's distinction between lateral and vertical thinking.

The description of the variety of systems (social, ecological, political, economic, kinship, thought) and their management and control ("Practical Systematics") is also of value.

Lest one think that the pervasive change experienced in Western societies is unique to our time and our culture, the authors describe the case of the Digo in East Africa, and offer a chapter on "USA, Outside Agitator" that explores the thinking of the proponents of constructive change abroad and the changes that they have wrought.

Chapter 15 provides an excellent overview of alternatives in family structures, political systems, systems of social control, medicine, economics, religion, education, technology, and communications. The final chapter, "Fumbling Freely Into the Future," contrasts advocates of master planning such as Asimov, Forrester, Fuller, and Skinner vs. the participatory futurists who look to the bottom rather than the top for innovative solutions. But there is no choice, for, in fact, the latter is seen as really happening--a rather cheery and pluralistic view.

16. NIEBURG, H.L. **Culture Storm: Politics and the Ritual Order.** NY: St. Martins Press, 1973. 257 pp. $11.95.   (A-4)

The culture storm of the 1960's has "transformed the shape of our values and thoroughly battered all the comfortable landmarks of our civilization. In the morning of a new decade, we wake up drained of the past." (p. 1)

Culture involves "all values and resources in a web of interpersonal and intergroup transactions." It is the subjective aspect of the social system; ritual expresses and gives content to that aspect. The political order rests on a culture base. "Culture is the precurser of political and institutional change. Values change first; then everything else becomes possible." (p. 3)

Chapters on topics such as the ritual cycle, rebellions, manias and seizures, the dance of death, the arts, the media, and political thermodynamics.

*** An interesting tour of the present, but a reluctance to consider future possibilities other than the insipid statement that "The prospects for the future are for continuous evolution." (p.239)

17. MEAD, Margaret. **Culture and Commitment: A Study of the Generation Gap.** NY: Doubleday and Natural History Press, 1970. 113 pp. $5.00; $1.95, paper.   (AB-3)

A wide-ranging essay summarizing much of Mead's thinking over the past decades and adding new insights on our unique present that is "without any parallel in the past." The argument easily follows the chapter headings: The Past: Postfigurative Cultures and Well-Known Forbears (where lack of questioning and consciousness are the key conditions); The Present: Cofigurative Cultures and Familiar Peers (which is institutionalized through age grading); and The Future: Prefigurative Cultures and Unknown Children (where the child represents what is to come).

All men are seen as equally immigrants into the new era, and "Today, nowhere in the world are there elders who know what the children know, no matter how remote and simple the societies are in which the children live. In the past there were always some elders who knew more than any children in terms of their experience of having grown up within a cultural system. Today there are none." (pp. 77-78)

"Postfigurative cultures, which focused on the elders--those who had learned the most and were able to do the most with what they had learned-- were essentially closed systems that continually replicated the past. We must now move toward the creation of open systems that focus on the future--and so on children, those whose capacities are least known and whose choices must be left open." (pp. 92-93) Despite a lack of suggestions as to what is to be done with the elders, the basic argument is provocative.

18. MESTHENE, Emmanuel G. **Technological Change: Its Impact on Man and Society.** Harvard Studies in Technology and Society. Cambridge: Harvard University Press, 1970. 124 pp. $4.95; NY: NAL Mentor Books, 1970. 127 pp. $1.25.   (AB-3)

An overview of the now discontinued research of the Harvard Program on Technology and Society woven into three chapters on social change, values, and economic and political organization. The opening comments quickly dispose of "three inadequate views": the optimistic view of technology as a virtually unalloyed blessing, the pessimistic view of technology as an unmitigated curse, and the complacent historical view that technology is not worthy of special notice. Rather, technology is seen as outstripping traditional categories of thought, and established values and institutions, and necessary responses are suggested. The volume is concluded with a well-annotated bibliography of 70 items.

19. MULLER, Herbert J. **The Children of Frankenstein: A Primer on Modern Technology and Human Values.** Bloomington: Indiana University Press, 1970. 431 pp. $10.00.   (AB-3)

A balanced, "informal" volume by a well-known "nonprofessional historian" (presently a Professor of English and Government) who addresses "the general reader." The view of technology is that the consequences have been "profoundly, thoroughly mixed." After providing historical background, the impact on society and culture is explored in separate chapters on war, science, government, business, language, higher education, natural environment, urban environment, mass media, the traditional arts, religion, and people. The chapter on higher education observes the consequences of specialization and "the spell of scientific methods," with the view that "most college graduates--whatever their specialty--have too limited an understanding of our technological society for potential leaders." (p. 230) The final 3 chapters under the heading "Toward the Year 2000," examine utopian writers of the past, the individual papers from the Commission on the Year 2000, and Kahn and Wiener's **The Year 2000.** A concern for human nature and recurrent human values is expressed throughout, and it is concluded that the **Brave New World** of Huxley "looks like a real possibility, considering the nature of technological man and affluent man in America." (p. 405) As suggested by the sub-title, this volume should serve well as a primer.

20. MULLER, Herbert J. **Uses of the Future.** Bloomington: Indiana University Press, 1974.   (AB-2)

A clearly-written volume intended to raise the right questions, rather

69839

than give all the answers. Muller does not view himself as a futurist (nor is he seen as one); rather "I write as an educator in the humanities and a nonprofessional historian who has roamed all over world history..." (p.xiii)

Chapters concern The Vogue of Futurism (a good critique of futurologists, who are seen as "not very bold thinkers"), The Problem of Human Survival, Education for the Future (with a focus on the role of the humanities), The State of Ignorance, The Future of Mind, Reflections on B.F. Skinner, Possibilities of a Universal Faith, How Sick Are We? (viewing the U.S. as "A Sick Society," along the lines of a 1959 address by Adlai Stevenson on "Our Broken Main Spring"), Problems and Prospects of Liberalism Today, The Future of Communication, Perspectives from Mexico on Developing Countries and on Over-Developed America, and Speculations on the Year 2000 (mainly concerned with the state of American culture).
*** No particular focus, but nevertheless a thoughtful contribution from the humanities and a useful antidote to scientism.

21. CHASE, Stuart. **The Most Probable World.** NY: Harper & Row, 1968.
    239 pp.   (B-3)

A balanced overview of ten current trends, with chapters on technology, population, shrinking living space, megalopolis, energy, the trend toward a mixed economy, automation and computers (considering the impact on work), the arms race, nationalism, and disarmament and world order. Each of these trends are assessed as to whether they are an asset, a liability, or both.

The final chapter, "No Path But Knowledge," outlines a desirable curriculum for the education of world leaders and proposes a supranational Bureau of Standards "to evaluate and screen the consequences of large technological innovations before they go into mass production, seriously to affect the culture." (p. 209)

An Epilogue provides an optimistic scenario of the year 2001, where there is world order, environmental beauty, new towns, a world language, population growth reduced to 0.7%, fusion power, and material abundance for most persons. Such a state of affairs, however, does not appear to be the most probable world suggested in the book title.
*** Still a useful introduction to a broad range of concerns.

22. DUFFUS, R.L. **Tomorrow's News: A Primer for Prophets.** NY: Norton,
    1967. 169 pp.   (C-2)

Considers some basic human dilemmas involving population, nuclear weapons, the military, the United Nations, travel and transport, space travel, big government, big business and big labor, employment and jobs, individualism and freedom, and survival of the species.
*** A modest and responsible overview, employing simple language.

23. GORDON, Theodore J. **The Future.** NY: St. Martin's Press, 1965.
    184 pp.   (C-3)

A popular tour of largely technological matters by a space scientist who has since become a professional futurist. Topics include ways in which we may lose our liberty (behavior control, population growth, heredity control), war and how it may come about, new technologies in the home (food, diversions such as 3-D television, fuels), achievements that could affect religion (man-made life in a laboratory, discovering extraterrestrial life forms, attainment of immortality), the convergence of capitalist and communist economies, the USSR and China, and the space program.
*** The justification of the space program is one-sided, as might be expected, but the inquiry into possible impacts of other technologies is

generally well-balanced and stimulating.

24. KETTLE, John. **Footnotes on the Future.** Toronto: Metheun, 1970.
    248 pp.   (C-3)

A journalist's skimming of many matters, unfortunately with no summaries. Otherwise a balanced report of views on population, the cities, food and water, air travel, surface transportation, print, communications, the underdeveloped world, energy, medicine, education, the home, government, work, materials, money and trade, fashions, leisure, and space.

25. SHINN, Roger Lincoln. **Tangled World.** NY: Charles Scribner's Sons,
    1965. 158 pp.   (ABC-4)

Essays by a churchman based on a series of television programs appearing under the same title. "This book describes several areas of modern life in which our changing world demands decisions both of persons and of our entire society." (p. 3)
Topics include the scientific transformation of life, the affluent society, poverty in the midst of plenty, the organized society, cities, racial conflict, law, politics, and sexual ethics.
*** A competent survey of the present, but no clear summarizing image, and without any sense of societal directions and alternatives.

25a. ALFVÉN, Hannes and Kerstin. **Living on the Third Planet.** Trans. by
     Eric Johnson. San Francisco: Freeman, 1972. 187 pp. (First published in Stockholm in 1969.)   (B-3)

Discusses population, the condition of life, the cosmos, man's increasing ignorance (including ignorance of rulers), politicians, science, and the symbiosis between man and technology.

25b. LANGDON-DAVIES, John. **A Short History of the Future.** NY: Dodd,
     Mead & Co., 1936. 276 pp.   (BC-3)

Attempts to describe the most likely future by making 24 prophecies. The evolution of tools is seen as dislocating the compromise that we call democracy, creating a dictatorship of the powerful. The alternatives are fascism or communism, and it is predicted that America will enter a "ruthless" period of fascism because the age of opportunity is gone. Democracy will end by 1950--we will vote away the right to behave as such, or we will be persuaded by force.
Other prophecies include war between Germany and Japan vs. Russia, state-controlled population, work limited to three hours per day, compulsory education for all, new forms of power and new raw materials, the obsolescence of the family and home, the growth of the middle-class along with mass production and distribution, the end of crime by the year 2000, and--most interestingly--the division of mankind into 4 or 5 different sexual types.
*** Provocative and free-swinging, with interesting hits and misses.

Chapter 2

The Technological, Affluent, Service Society: Is It Viable and Desirable?

The general overviews in Chapter 1 enable a broad understanding of the massive changes that are taking place, and the major problems that we face. Terms such as Boulding's Post-Civilization (1), Frankel's Age of Acceleration (2), Vickers' Post-Liberal Era (14), and Mead's Prefigurative Culture (17) provide a general appreciation of our emerging era.

Perhaps the most widely-used label for our emerging society is that of "Post-Industrial Society" in the sense of a shift in the structure of the labor force such that more persons are engaged in the production of services than in the production of goods or foodstuffs. Daniel Bell is widely credited with first using this term in this sense. But, Bell is not the first person to use the term nor the first person to recognize the transition in the labor force. Perhaps the first person to use "Post-Industrialism" other than in passing was Arthur J. Penty, a British guild socialist who used the term in the sub-title of a 1917 book (324), and as the title of a 1922 book (325). Penty in turn credits A. K. Coomaraswamy for the term, but does not elaborate. Feeling that industrialism was doomed, Penty used "Post-Industrialism" to indicate the state of society that would follow the break-up of industrialism. Recently, this sense of the term has been employed without reference to Penty by Heilbroner (111), Wagar (249), Roszak (303), Illich (306), and Ellis (710).

The first person to write in some detail on the shift in the composition of the labor force was Roy Glenday in 1944 (43). In 1942, however, Stuart Chase recommended pursuing the goal of full employment by finding new jobs in the service trades (402), a strategy similar to that proposed by John Kenneth Galbraith in 1958 (61), and by Alvin Toffler in 1975 (47). In the United States, Stuart Chase observed the actual transition in the labor force in 1960 (62), and Victor Fuchs elaborated on the Service Economy in 1965 (44).

This history is limited of course to those items that have been identified to date. Perhaps there has been earlier usages of "Post-Industrialism" or "The Service Society" but it is not the purpose here to provide a definitive history, but only to indicate that thinking about these concerns began well before the 1960s. It is also the purpose of this chapter to point out that there are many societal labels that are worthy competitors to "Post-Industrialism," and it is important to look at all of them for various nuances in emphasis.

The items that follow are all variations on a single theme: The Technological, Affluent, Service Society. The salient characteristic of all of these items is that the author projects (or extrapolates) various social trends, and does not question the viability of such a society. A few of the authors such as Ellul (28) and Meynaud (29) question the desirability of such a society, but none of them considers the possibility of limited resources, which would challenge the likelihood of an affluent, high-consumption society (Chapter 5).

The theme of this chapter is most broadly described by the Long-Term Multifold Trend promulgated by the Hudson Institute (26,27). Post-Industrial Society, incidentally, is used in both of these books in the sense of a new economic stage of unprecedented affluence.

The next grouping of items (28-41) elaborates on the theme of Ellul's Technological Society (28). Meynaud views Technocracy (29) with alarm, but Brzezinski appears to be neutral if not favorable toward the Technetronic Society (30,31). There will be more organization (32), hopefully a Consultative Commonwealth (33) and a Managed Society (34). An understanding of this direction is enhanced by considering Cattell's prescription for Beyondism (35), Stent's view of the Golden Age (36), Russell's fears of a Scientific Society (37) and Beckwith's naive hopes for government by experts (38). Geiger assures us of a transition to a Technocratic Order, Drucker describes a Post-Modern World, an Educated Society and a Knowledge Society (40, 41), and a group of Japanese futurologists are agreed on the label of Multi-Channel Society (42).

As previously mentioned, Glenday discussed The Service State in 1944 (43), Fuchs made an "official" pronouncement in 1965 (44), which led to a book on The Service Economy (45). The Super-Industrialism promulgated by Alvin Toffler (46, 47) can best be seen as a service economy, particularly in that Toffler recommends expansion of the service sector (47). If this is to be done, the most serious questions about The Service Society as a Consumer Society have been raised by Gartner and Riessman. Gersuny and Rosengren add little to our understanding (49), but Gross raises important cautions about Techno-Urban Fascism, and offers a far look into the future in considering the outlines of a Post-Service Society (50). Lundberg recognizes the coming of "the much denounced Welfare State" (51), while Lady Williams provides acritical applause for the British Welfare State (52).

The most extensive elaboration of Post-Industrial Society is provided by Daniel Bell (53, 54, and particularly 55). The term is also used by Faunce (56), the National Industrial Conference Board (57), Touraine (58), and Emery and Trist (59). Meadows prefers Neo-Industrialism (60).

All of the above are predicated on the assumption of affluence. John Kenneth Galbraith made The Affluent Society (61) into conventional wisdom, even though his book was intended to counter conventional wisdoms. Stuart Chase looked beyond the Economy of Abundance to a new era, A Time to Live (62). Rostow's stage theory placing us in the Era of High Mass Consumption (63) was influential in shaping foreign policy, while Organski was concerned with the Politics of Abundance (64). The assumption of uninterrupted affluence in the "developed" societies was also closely related to thinking about development and modernization in the "underdeveloped" nations (65-70), a focus of many social scientists.

Affluence arising from new productivity characterizes the Revolution of the Middle Class, as seen by Bensman and Vidich (71), and the Massive Majority Middle Class Society described by Wattenberg (75). But Linder (72) questions whether we are really as affluent as we think, while Parker (73) and Levison (74) raise important doubts about the concept of the middle class.

Questions about our affluence are rather obvious by now, but even if the economic crisis proves to be temporary, and even if new energy sources are quickly developed, there are still serious doubts about the viability and desirability of the Techonological, Affluent, Service Society. Indeed, this doubt serves to characterize a large part of this guidebook to societal directions and alternatives.

26. KAHN, Herman, and Anthony J. WIENER. **The Year 2000: A Framework for Speculation on the Next Thirty-Three Years.** Introduction by Daniel Bell. NY: Macmillan, 1967. 431 pp. $9.95.   (A-3)

Considered to be a classic work by **some** futurists, this volume served as a conceptual baseline for the Commission on the Year 2000 as well as a foundation for continuing studies by the Hudson Institute. The final chapter on Policy Research and Social Change is still a valuable statement on methodology.

The text is a jumble of scenarios along with 77 tables and 33 figures, concerning economic projections, science and technology, international politics, nuclear war possibilities, and a chapter on Postindustrial Society in the Standard World. Such a society, described in a table on p. 186, has service-oriented economic activities, widespread cybernation, and high per capita income.

The Year 2000 is perhaps best known for the concept of the "Basic, Long-Term Multifold Trend," described below in its slightly updated version.

27. KAHN, Herman, and B. BRUCE-BRIGGS. **Things to Come: Thinking About the Seventies And Eighties.** NY: Macmillan, 1972. 262 pp. $6.95.   (AB-2)

A shorter, updated, and somewhat more popularized version of **The Year 2000.** Considerable attention is devoted to international affairs, with chapters on the world of the seventies and eighties, sources of stability and instability in the international system, military-technological possibilities, and the rise of Japan.

But there are also chapters on alternative U.S. futures, the countervailing forces of counterculture and counterreformation, and "The 1985 Technological Crisis" which could develop from many different technologies simultaneously breaking down or developing out of control, from bigger crises than those known in the past, or from the exponential growth of pollution and technology.

The first chapter updates the "Long-term Multifold Trend of Western Culture" described as increasingly sensate cultures, bourgeois and meritocratic elites, centralization and concentration of economic and political power, accumulation of scientific and technical knowledge, Westernization and modernization, and increasing tempo of change in all of the above. (See chart, pp. 8-9)

Chapter IX discusses the transitions from pre-agricultural to agricultural to industrial and post-industrial society. "If projections of continued economic growth in industrial societies are achieved, by the end of the century there will be another order of magnitude change in per capita income... the difficulty of speculating about a society built upon an economy of $5,000-$50,000 per capita income is suggested by our adoption of the sociologist Bell's term 'post-industrial society.'" (pp. 222-223)

The authors briefly explore "some fascinating speculatons" on identifying aspects of the new society: a post-manufacturing economy, a quarternary economy (featuring services to services), a post-economic society, a leisure society, an ennui society, a new religiosity, a learning society (favored by academics but considered unlikely), a gentlemanly society, and a "Westernistic" civilization built on Western culture.

The final chapter on The Ideology of Tomorrow makes a distinction between descriptive and normative perspectives, and claims that "we have tried to take a 'value-free' perspective." In large part this is so, but the discerning reader should note the loaded distinction between the "Humanist Left" and the "Responsible Center" (pp. 82-85) and the values that are promulgated in the "Modestly Optimistic" scenario for the U.S. (pp. 169-172). *** Despite various biases and economic misforecasting, this volume nevertheless offers a number of useful provocations.

28. ELLUL, Jacques. **The Technological Society.** Trans. by John Wilkinson. NY: Knopf, 1964; Vintage edition, 1967. 449 pp. (First published in France in 1954)   (A-3)

A sociologist's scathing "examination of the monolithic technical world that is coming to be," arguing that life cannot be happy in a civilization dominated by technique, and that it is an illusion to think that because we have broken through the taboos and rites that bound primitive man, we have become free.

Technique is defined as "the totality of methods rationally arrived at and having absolute efficiency (for a given stage of development) in every field of human activity." (p.xxv) Chapters are titled Techniques, The Characterology of Technique, Technique and Economy, Technique and the State, and Human Technique. The final chapter, A Look at the Future, notes the "incredible naivete" of scientists and warns of "a dictatorship of test tubes." (p. 434)

No solutions are proposed; the work is seen as a diagnosis and not a treatment.

29. MEYNAUD, Jean. **Technocracy**. Trans. by Paul Barnes. NY: Free
     Press, 1969. 315 pp. (First published by Payot Paris, 1964) (A-2)

The object of this thoughtful and restrained essay by a political scientist "is to analyze the spread into political life of the complex demands and workings of technological civilization..." (p.13) If political authorities do not keep a close watch on technologists, "in the end the effect would be a barely perceptible evolution towards a regime which would be democratic only on the surface." (pp. 15-16) Particular dangers are the faults inherent in bureaucratic methods: incompetence, particularism, partiality towards various social forces, and bias towards certain political ideas. Technocratic power is viewed as generally supporting the existing socio-economic order.

Chapters are devoted to Identification of Technocrats, The Field of Technocratic Intervention, The Socio-Political Significance of Technical Power, Forerunners of the Technocratic Ideology, Themes of Technocratic Ideology, and Chances of an Expansion of Technocratic Ideology.

It is concluded that "an examination of the foreseeable future reveals that there is no legitimate reason to assume that political relations will disappear: the important point is to ascertain who will be behind them and control them, and to whose advantage." (p.293)

"...the process of transfer seems to me to be under way and many signs indicate that unless some check is made...the expansion of technocracy will continue. The spirit of our day, directed towards the search for maximal productivity, is definitely favorable to technocratic ideology." (p.296) The ultimate possibility is an evolution to a scientific technocracy: " 'Scientific Society'...will perhaps replace the very fashionable but highly contestable term 'industrial society.'" (p.302)

30. BRZEZINSKI, Zbigniew, "The American Transition," **The New Republic,**
     December 23, 1967, pp. 18-21.   (A-3)

Describes America as becoming "the first technetronic society." In such a society, "Our existing post-crisis management institutions will probably be increasingly supplanted by pre-crisis management institutions, the task of which will be to identify in advance likely social crises and to develop programs to cope with them."

A profound change in the intellectual community is forecasted, with systematic elite re-training and an organizational framework redesigned to tie the educational system directly to social and political action.

31. BRZEZINSKI, Zbigniew. **Between Two Ages: America's Role in the**
     Technetronic Era. NY: Viking, 1970. 334 pp. $7.95; $2.45, paper.
                                                                     (AB-2)
A leading international relations scholar describes the transition from industrial society to technetronic society: "a society that is shaped cul-

turally, psychologically, socially and economically by the impact of technology and electronics--particularly in the area of computers and communications." (p.9) This labeling is used in preference to "post-industrial society" because "it conveys more directly the character of the principal impulses for change in our time." (p. 9)

The U.S. is seen as "both a social pioneer and a guinea pig for mankind," (p. xv) and as the "principal global disseminator of the technetronic revolution." Under these unprecedented conditions, there is an Age of Volatile Belief, leading to a worldwide condition of crumbling religions and ideologies. In a fascinating discussion of possible futures for the Soviet Union, our major adversary is seen as steeped in "dull social and political orthodoxy" and among five alternative paths for development, the most probable short-term outcome is viewed as a balance between oligarchic petrifaction and technological adaptation.

America is left to lead the way, despite problems with the New Left ("an essentially negative and obsolescent force" - p.231) and doctrinaire liberals. We are now in the midst of "The Third American Revolution" that is creating three Americas in one--technetronic, industrial, and pre-industrial--in that it "simultaneously maximizes America's potential as it unmasks its obsolescence."

Brezezinski recommends participatory pluralism, rational humanism, and a Community of the Developed Nations. The latter would be concerned with political strategy (and thus something more than OECD), but more diffused than NATO. "In the technetronic era," it is concluded, "philosophy and politics will be crucial."

*** Overly preoccupied with The New Left Reaction and The Crisis of Liberalism (each meriting a full chapter), while the problems of American obsolescence are only teasingly mentioned in passing throughout the volume. Nevertheless, this book is well written and important in the sense that Brzezinski is influential, or potentially so.

32. WALDO, Dwight (Symposium Editor), "Organizations for the Future," **Public Administration Review**, 33:4, July-August 1973, pp. 299-335.   (A-3)

Five essays from a 1971-72 lecture series at Syracuse University. Waldo observes in the introduction that nearly all of the lecturers differ from the organic-adaptive model of Alvin Toffler (in **Future Shock**) and Warren Bennis (in **Changing Organizations**), who advocate ad-hocracy and temporary systems respectively.

- Herbert Kaufman, "The Direction of Organization Evolution," argues that large-scale organization and its problems will grow worse, and criticizes the optimists who think that the future can be invented.
- William G. Scott, "The Theory of Significant People," criticizes the new elitism implicit in the writings of B. F. Skinner and José Delgado.
- Amitai Etzioni, "The Third Sector and Domestic Missions," argues that a third alternative that has grown between the public and the private sectors may be the most important alternative for the next decades. This sector includes institutions such as NASA, Amtrak, and COMSAT.
- Bertram M. Gross, "An Organized Society?" answers, probably so, either as a tighter form of Welfare State Capitalism or a less expansionist Fortress America.
- James D. Thompson, "Society's Frontiers for Organizing Activities," views formal organizations as essentially the same in the year 2000, but with greater emphasis on complex organizations of a more fluid and flexible form.

33. EULAU, Heinz, "Skill Revolution and Consultative Commonwealth," **American Political Science Review**, 67:1, March 1973, pp. 169-191.   (A-4)

The ASPA Presidential address at the 1972 Annual Meeting in Washington, D.C. The skill revolution refers to "the incredible specialization in and proliferation of occupations" and offers a complementary (not alternative) frame of reference for observing social and political situations. Proceeding on the questionable assumption that "constructs of the future are useful only to the extent that they permit us to orient ourselves meaningfully and correctly in the present" (p.171), Eulau offers the tentative construct of "the consultative commonwealth" as a more persuasive construct of the future than post-industrial society. The construct "assumes the technologization (and professionalization) of the human services but not rule by technologists" (p.169). "...the construct assumes that as a result of the prominence of old and new professions in policy making and the delivery of human services, consultative modes of interaction will be a pervasive feature of governance in the future society... Consultation will not be the dominant process but will complement, supplement, and implement other governmental processes like democratic participation, bureaucratic organization, pluralistic bargaining, or oligarchic decision-making" (p.189).
* A not-very-persuasive construct that confuses description with prescription.

34. BATES, Frederick L., "Alternative Models for the Future of Society: From the Invisible to the Visible Hand," **Social Forces,** 53:1, Sept. 1974, pp. 1-11.   (A-4)

The Presidential address delivered to the Southern Sociological Society, April 1974, confined to reviewing the work of other sociologists, particularly Bell's Post-Industrial Society and Etzioni's Active Society.
The major thesis is that there are two general forms of exchange linkages: the market form (which is supposed to prevail in a so-called free economic market characterizing relationships between organizations) and the commissary form (where social units are obligated to supply inputs or receive outputs from other social units, characterizing relationships within organizations).
In turn there are two major structural patterns through which societies perform the coordination function: the laissez-faire "invisible hand system" (the unmanaged society), and the bureaucratically organized "visible hand system" (managed society). Barring disaster, the factors operating at present (industrialization, bureaucratization, awareness of possible major crises) "will move all societies closer and closer to the managed end of the continuum." (p.6) Ultimately, "these same forces can hardly fail, in the long run, to produce a managed global society if we survive long enough for the present processes to work themselves out." (p.6) The most important issue of the future, then, is who shall manage, and how, toward what goals.
Bates argues that the greatest impact on the future of society will come from the social and behavioral sciences. "The most powerful factor leading to a managed society is the growing belief that it can be done." (p.9) To do so, advanced technologies are needed for communications, information storage, measurement, and prediction. However, "To fail in producing the desired outcomes through attempts at societal management is to fail to manage at all and simply to create the illusion of management." (p.9)
* A subtle mixture of description, promotion of social science, and recognition of possible failure at the managerial task. Possible controls over the illusion of management are not suggested.

35. CATTELL, Raymond B. **A New Morality from Science: Beyondism.** Pergamon General Psychology Series. NY: Pergamon, 1973. 482 pp. $17.00; $8.00 paper.   (A-3)

In contrast to those who seek some synthesis of science and religion, this weighty but eloquent tome, by a "noncompartmentalized scientist" who has authored some thirty books on psychology, argues for the ultimate triumph of science alone. "Religious and scientific truth must be ultimately reducible to one truth, and that is likely to be by scientific discovery. It is not, therefore, a question of bringing morality into science...but of developing morality out of science." (p. xiii)

Cattell devotes the first half of the book to stating the principles of Beyondism, and then elaborates on applications in the modern world in terms of new institutions called for in the society of the future. "Beyondism constitutes a revolution. Yet it can be achieved by steady evolutionary measures." (pp.414-415) The quintessence of Beyondist development is seen as coming from privately endowed moral research centers.

Briefly and incompletely described here, Beyondism plans for a constant revision of values by scientific research, calls for a distinct ethical value system "federated" in universalism, recognizes that any emotion (including love) can err, offers emotional support to aspiration for human advance, and is incompatible with revealed religions and Humanism. Its applications include a scientifically rational politics, eugenic control as a function of government, evolutionary values, and the respect of natural economic laws (basically free enterprise and self-adjustment).

The aim of Beyondism is clear in its application to education: "the chief challenge to education in the coming years is to teach biological and social sciences, and the arts of analyzing arguments, in such a way that a democracy may be prepared to understand the increasing role of expert research in social science in government and the growth of values." (p.380)

*** A fascinating vision of technocracy by a proponent who appears to be insulated from the descriptions and criticisms that have already been made. So much for "noncompartmentalization."

35a. NORMAN, Alfred, "Informational Society," **FUTURES: The Journal of Planning and Forecasting,** 7:4, August, 1975, pp. 321-328.   (A-4)

An economist at the University of Texas sketches a society based on technological possibilities such as total automation and a worldwide linkage of computer systems and data banks. Credit would replace money as the medium of exchange. Organizations would have no physical location, and information processing would be the principal concern of society. "As society progresses from the industrial to the informational age most routine activities will be performed by mechanical devices." (p. 323)

Individuals will be freed from having to live close to work, and a diversity of communities would offer a wide choice of lifestyles. Competition for contracts within large organizations would replace competition between them, and ownership would gradually pass to the public. Everyone would have the option of voting on every issue, since "in informational society competence implies power, the problem is how to harness the efforts of the elites to promote the public weal. For this purpose direct democracy is proposed." (p. 325)

*** An interesting scenario of a rational and technocratic society, but no comments on when it can be expected, how it will be attained, or whether it is humanly desirable. Benevolence and efficacy are major unexamined assumptions.

36. STENT, Gunther S. **The Coming of the Golden Age: A View of the End of Progress.** NY: Natural History Press, 1969. 146 pp. $4.95; $2.50 paper.   (A-4)

A molecular biologist surveys the rise and fall of molecular genetics as a paradigm of the history of creative activity in general, arguing that the internal contradictions in the progress of the arts and sciences make these processes self-limiting. The Golden Age becomes the very last stage of history, Polynesia on a global scale.

This essay is eloquent, in the manner of good scientific generalizing, and even rather interesting, as it touches on beats and hippies (as evidence of loss of Nietzschean will to power), the evolution of music, and the early writings of Dennis Gabor. But the assumptions of growing affluence and the quest for dominion over hostile nature nearing its goal, both resulting in an age of leisure, are rather shallow in the face of considerable evidence that we are not very affluent and that the attempts to control nature have been profoundly mixed in their results.

*** A neat academic exercise, but it has little to do with emerging realities.

37. RUSSELL, Bertrand. **The Scientific Outlook**. Glencoe, Ill.: The Free Press, 1931. 277 pp.   (ns)

The final section of the book (pp.203-273) discusses The Scientific Society: "an attempt to depict the world which would result if scientific technique were to rule unchecked." (p.260)

38. BECKWITH, Burnham P. **Government by Experts: The Next Stage in Political Evolution**. NY: Exposition, 1972. 166 pp. $7.50.   (B-5)

A "scientific" extrapolation that envisions the transition from democratic government to expert government, a non-hereditary, oligarchic, political meritocracy. Democratic ritual will survive, however, similar to the ritual of monarchy.

"As the social sciences advance, and as public confidence in social scientists grows, other experts and the average voter will become increasingly aware of the obvious advantages of entrusting the solution of scientists grows, other experts and the average voter will become increasingly aware of the obvious advantages of entrusting the solution of social problems to those who are most competent to solve them... As the world becomes more peaceful and prosperous, men will dispute less and less over the division of territory among nations and income among individuals." (p.153)

*** Some rather shaky premises here.

39. GEIGER, Theodore. **The Fortunes of the West: The Future of the Atlantic Nations**. Bloomington, Ind.: Indiana University Press, 1973. 304 pp.   (AB-4)

A staff member of the National Planning Association observes that "A profound transformation is now taking place with the nations of North America and Western Europe and in their relationships with one another." This transition is from the liberal Patrimonial Order of the 19th and early 20th centuries to the Technocratic Order, described in rather dull cliches on pp. 39-46.

Additional chapters are devoted to the Prospects for World Peace and War, Transatlantic Relations in the Period of the New Nationalism, and Glimpses into a Possible Twenty-First Century, examining prospects for decline and fall, and both technological and humanistic utopias (considered improbable and unlikely). Concludes with an aggressively centrist median projection depicting neither the fall nor the millenium.

40. DRUCKER, Peter F. **Landmarks of Tomorrow**. NY: Harper, 1959. 270 pp.   (AB-3)

"At some unmarked point during the last twenty years we imperceptibly moved out of the Modern Age and into a new, as yet nameless, era." (p. ix.)

The Introduction, however, is entitled "This Post-Modern World.") Drucker continues: "We thus live in an age of transition, an age of overlap... This book is a report on the new post-modern today we live in--nothing more. It does not deal with the future. It deals with the tangible present." (p.x)

The focus is on three areas: 1) the shift from the Cartesian universe of mechanical cause to the new universe of pattern, purpose, and process, and the new power to organize men of knowledge and high skill for joint effort; 2) the new frontiers, the new tasks and opportunities, and new realities such as the emergence of the Educated Society in which only the educated man is truly productive, the emergence of economic development, the increasing inability to govern and the decline of the government of the nation-state, and the collapse of non-Western culture; 3) the human situation, particularly the need to return to spiritual values. *** Essentially an early description of "Post-Industrial Society."

41. DRUCKER, Peter F. **The Age of Discontinuity: Guidelines to Our Changing Society.** NY: Harper & Row, 1969.   (AB-3)

Focuses on four major discontinuities: new technologies, the world economy (including a chapter on The Global Shopping Center), a society of large organizations (including a chapter on The New Pluralism), and the changed position and power of knowledge such that we are becoming a knowledge society--"the greatest of the discontinuities around us."

Drucker forecasts that the knowledge industries will account for one-half of the total national product in the late 1970's (p. 263), and argues that knowledge, rather than agriculture and mining, has now become the primary industry supplying the essential and central resource of production. Under these circumstances, "It is not that we cannot afford the high costs of education; we cannot afford its low productivity" (p. 334), and economic necessity will therefore force a revolution. "In a knowledge society, school and life can no longer be separate." (p. 324)

Because of our knowledge needs, "We face an unprecedented situation in which we will have to set priorities for new knowledge" (p.365) and the existing disciplines will not remain appropriate for long, if knowledge is to have a future.

42. "Perspectives on Multi-Channel Society," in Japan Society of Futurology, **Challenges from the Future. Proceedings of the International Futures Research Conference.** Vol. 1. pp. 293-390. Tokyo: Kodansha, Ltd., 1970. (English language)   (A-4)

Nine papers by Japanese scholars from a special session held at the April 1970 IFRC in Kyoto. Together, they constitute an interim report, with multichannel society seen as a world of rapid change, vast quantities of information (creating a problem of "informational pollution"), co-existence of plural value systems, structural elasticity, and peopled by "Homo Movense" (people who try to seek their raison d'etre and the supreme value of their action in mobility; people who rebel against stereotyped ideas).

43. GLENDAY, Roy. **The Future of Economic Society: A Study in Group Organisation.** London: Macmillan and Co., Ltd., 1944. 320 pp. (A-3)

A broad and far-sighted discourse viewing the problem of constructing stable economic systems as that of adjusting populations to their environments, in that no economic system can increase its content and size forever.

Chapter II, On Being a Convenient Size, describes the process of substituting man-made patterns for those of nature, the absence of checks and controls to the machine, and resulting erosion of soil. Subsequent chapters concern Control of Growth in Nature and Man-Controlled Growth.

Chapter XV, "Towards the Service State" holds that the industrial age is drawing to a close. "The immediate future of countries destined to continue to advance would seem to lie with what I have broadly termed 'services.'" (p. 242) Achievement of a real service age would require a revolution in industrial outlook, similar to the revolution in agricultural technique that accompanied the industrial revolution.

*** The argument is murky, but nevertheless points not only to the service society, but contemporary concerns with "limits to growth" and "small is beautiful."

44. FUCHS, Victor R., "The Growing Importance of the Service Industries," **The Journal of Business**, October 1965. (Reprinted as National Bureau of Economic Research, Occasional Paper 96. 30 pp.) (A-4)

Observes that the service sector now accounts for more than half of employment and Gross National Product. "This country is pioneering in a new stage of economic development. We are now a 'service economy'--that is, we are the first nation in the history of the world in which more than half of the employed population is not involved in the production of food, clothing, houses, automobiles, and other tangible goods." (p.1) The article goes on to discuss why the shift occurred and some implications for the economy.

*** Also see Victor R. Fuchs, "The First Service Economy," **The Public Interest**, No. 2, Winter 1966, pp. 7-17.

45. FUCHS, Victor R. **The Service Economy.** NY: National Bureau of Economic Research, No. 87, General Series, 1968. 280 pp. (A-4)

An elaboration of the above. The final chapter on Implications of the Growth of Services sees the personalization of work, and women increasingly able to compete on more equal terms.

*** Employs an exemplary caution, but the scope is narrow, and the notion of ever-increasing progress is strongly suggested, albeit implicitly.

46. TOFFLER, Alvin. **Future Shock.** NY: Random House, 1970. 505 pp.
(ABC-3)

Like it or not, this provocative journalistic tour of the "human side of tomorrow" (or, more correctly **some** of the human side for **some** people), is better known than any other item in this guide. The author's information in **The Eco-Spasm Report** (see below) announces that "Translated into some twenty languages, it has sold 6 million copies and been published in fifty countries." So it is important to understand what is being said, and how, and what is not being said.

Three stages of societal development are viewed: "Ten thousand years for agriculture. A century or two for industrialism. And now, opening before us-- super-industrialism."(p.16) This new stage of social development "is intended to mean a complex, fast-paced society dependent upon extremely advanced technology and a post-materialist value system." (p.434) It is also "the world's first service economy." (p. 16) Despite the shortcomings of the term, it is defended against alternative terms such as "post-industrial society," "post-civilization," "technotronic society" (sic.), and the "global village."

"What is occurring now is not a crisis of capitalism, but of industrial society itself, regardless of its political form. We are simultaneously experiencing a youth revolution, a sexual revolution, a racial revolution, a colonial revolution, an economic revolution, and the most rapid and deep-going technological revolution in history... In a word, we are in the midst of the super-industrial revolution." (p.166)

All of these revolutions bring on Future Shock, the disease of change; "the dizzying disorientation brought on by the premature arrival of the future... culture shock in one's own society..." (p.13)

More than half of the text is devoted to entertaining descriptions of the three major sources of future shock: transience, novelty, and diversity. Transience involves "the throw-away society," the new nomads (or the declining significance of place to human life), modular man (who has modular relationships with many, rather than holistic relationships with a few), the coming post-bureaucratic "ad-hocracy," and the obsolescence of information.

The novelty ratio between the familiar and the unfamiliar is seen as growing, and with the aid of science, an economy geared to the provision of psychic gratification and incorporating new family relationships is becoming increasingly dominent.

Diversity had led us to overchoice, a surfeit of subcults in the world of work and play, and a diversity of life styles enabling serial selves. This accelerating pace leads to serious physiological problems, and inappropriate psychological responses such as denial, specialism, obsessive reversion (both right-wing and left-wing), and super-simplifying.

The last four chapters of the book, concerned with Strategies for Survival, offer a massive mélange of ideas, old and new, cautious and outlandish, feasible and utterly impossible.

Chapter 17, Coping with Tomorrow, advocates a wide range of personal and social change regulators "to minimize the human damage wrought by rapid change." This would include sensory shielding, personal stability zones, situational grouping (e.g., pre- and post-natal classes) as a new social service, crisis counseling, half-way houses as "future shock absorbers," and enclaves of the past and the future.

Chapter 18, Education in the Future Tense, attacks the factory model industrial-era schools, and argues for futurizing the curriculum and helping to increase the individual's "cope-ability." Skills are particularly needed in learning, relating, and choosing. A Council of the Future is advocated for every school and community, and lifelong learning should be available on a plug-in/plug-out basis.

Chapter 19, Taming Technology, argues for conscious regulation of technological advance. "We cannot and must not turn off the switch of technological progress. Only romantic fools babble about returning to a 'state of nature.'" (p.379) Instead there should be a movement for responsible technology, creating institutions such as a "technology ombudsman" to serve as an official sounding board for complaints.

The final chapter, The Strategy of Social Futurism, flies off the deep end (or, if you will, into the stratosphere) by announcing that we are witnessing the end of technocratic planning, described as econocentric, short-range, and undemocratic. Anti-planners are attacked as "a strange coalition of right wingers and New Leftists..." (p.399) Rather, the entire society should be infused with a new, socially-aware future-consciousness, and Toffler provides a brief survey of the futures movement: "a perfectly extraordinary thrust toward more scientific appraisal of future probabilities..." (p.409) A revolution in the production of utopias is advocated: "collaborative utopianism" and the construction of "utopia factories." Utopian experiments are needed, particularly those based on super- rather than pre-industrial forms. A great international institute–a world futures data bank–should be created, for "the collection and systematic integration of predictive reports generated by scholars and imaginative thinkers in all the intellectual disciplines all over the world." (p.415) The product of such an effort would be "a constantly changing geography of the future..." And finally, there should be a revolutionary new approach to goal-setting: Anticipatory Democracy. "For under super-industrialism, democracy becomes not a political luxury, but a primal necessity." (p.420) The feedback that is facilitated is considered as essential to control. There would in effect be a continuing plebiscite on the future. To facilitate this exercise, "social future assemblies," each backed with a technical staff, are advocated for various geographic localities and social units. Each assembly might then arrive at coherent statements of priorities for tomorrow.

*** Needless to say, there are a great number of interesting ideas and well-meaning proposals offered here. But there are two major problems:

1. **Inflation of fact and expectations.** There is ringing rhetoric throughout, and a number of distortions serving to bolster the argument of accelerating change. A strong case could be made that for most people there is not much diversity, novelty, or transience. The rate of moving between homes (mobility status), for example, has remained constant for almost thirty years. As for expectations, this modest guidebook to societal directions and alternatives serves as a poignant illustration of the vast distance between reality and ideals; in this instance the ideal of a world futures data bank. Toffler's other proposals are equally unmatched by actual developments. Technocratic planning continues unscathed, while the so-called "futures movement" has resulted in virtually nothing.

2. **The book is essentially an instrument of what might be called "bourgeois populism."** The key to this interpretation is provided on pp. 36-37, where Toffler describes people of the past (70% of mankind, living as their ancestors did centuries ago), people of the present (more than 25%, molded by mechanization and mass education), and people of the future (the 2-3% of the world's population who are trend-makers without knowing it, who "live today as millions more will live tomorrow." They are richer, better educated, more mobile, and they live faster, where the action is.) It is clear that **Future Shock** has been written for and about the urbanized middle class who are acclimated to providing and consuming services. Toffler is not worried about primary needs such as food, housing, and job security, but with psychic needs of the middle class (see Chapter 17, for example). Future shock (a massive umbrella for a wide variety of behaviors) is not a problem for many people. As a Marxist might say, this book is an instrument of class struggle.

47. TOFFLER, Alvin. **The Eco-Spasm Report.** NY: Bantam Books, March 1975. 116 pp. $1.50, paper.   (ABC-4)

Based on an article in **Esquire** ("Beyond Depression," Feb. 1975), this tract is described as "an interim report" and "an experiment in what might be called 'accelerative publishing.'" (p. ix)

The result is more inflated language, this time in order to describe "super-inflation" and other economic matters. "The eco-spasm or spasmodic economy describes an economy careening on the brink of disaster, awaiting only the random convergence of certain critical events that have not occurred simultaneously--so far." (p.51)

This is not simply an economic upheaval, but something far deeper: "What is happening, no more, no less, is the breakdown of industrial civilization on the planet and the first fragmentary appearance of a wholly new and dramatically different social order: a super-industrial civilization that will be technological, but no longer industrial." (p.3) This new social order is not sketched in even rough outlines, though, nor is there any discussion as to whether it is desirable.

Toffler rumbles on to describe the energy problem and the obsolescence of economics, and to offer scenarios of super-inflation and generalized depression that might occur if action is not taken. The necessary action involves five transition strategies:

1. Restabilizing the global economy. Checking the power of the multinationals (which is in everyone's interest) with a truly transnational political movement: a World Association for Control of Transnational Systems.
2. Super-industrial stabilizers to replace or supplement those that are obsolete. This would include global, regional, and local reserve stockpiles of food and resources, and urban insurance systems "to create a new public confidence."
3. Super-Industrial employment policies. Continued conversion to a service-oriented society is advocated, in that services are labor-intensive and would serve the goals of full employment programs. "Connected up properly

with the education system, the service industry could provide dignified occupations for millions of men and women who otherwise face bleak job prospects." (p.85) There could be public service employment, but with super-industrial variety, and special incentives could be given to workers who voluntarily give up their seniority status.

4. "Super-Industrialize" national economic policy-making. Eco-spasm strengthens the case for decentralizing economic policy: "Super-industrial societies are too complex to be managed centrally in the old industrial style." (p. 92) There ought to be a devolution of power and a downward redistribution of tax revenues.

5. Accelerate the move toward anticipatory democracy. A shift from industrial-style planning to super-industrial futurism is advocated; "futurism" suggesting a broader scope of concern and a longer time horizon. Toffler describes anticipatory democracy exercises in Hawaii (see item no. 632), Iowa, and Washington, with claims that similar activities "have been held or planned in a score of states as well as various cities and regions." (p. 102) It is concluded that we must face the awesome task of designing a new civilization: "If we can look beyond the immediate, we glimpse breakthroughs to something not merely new, but in many ways juster and better." (p.105)

*** This is all very slick and superficial, and it **could** be dangerous if large numbers of people believed in it. There may indeed be a problem with industrial civilization, but a transition to "super-industrialism" does not necessarily explain it or provide an adequate base for policy. As this guide attempts to point out, there are many explanations that should be considered. The pursuit of policies based on superficial images of societal directions and alternatives could prove to be dissillusioning, if not disastrous. For example, consider Toffler's five transition strategies:

1. As pointed out by Barnet and Müller (no. 455), an ineffective attempt to control multinational corporations through some global organization could lead to further chaos; rather, national restraints may be best.

2. It will take far more than stockpiles to create a new public confidence. Moreover, Toffler never suggests where adequate funding might come from.

3. Similar to stockpiles, super-industrial employment policies may require funding that is not available. Why should services be expanded, and what is the cost in further losses of self-sufficiency? Could we return to 10% or 15% of the labor force in the agricultural sector, in contrast to less than 5% at present?

4. Decentralization is always attractive. But certain policies (e.g., concerning welfare and environmental problems) might best be dealt with on a national or even a global level.

5. Finally, anticipatory democracy. It is a very appealing idea in theory, but proponents curiously avoid the discussion of actual outcomes, which have been disappointing to date (see no. 632a). Consciously or not, Toffler may have devised a political sandbox for co-opting activists into thinking that they are participating in policy-making, while major decisions on societal directions continue to be made by the usual secluded elites. The equating of good intentions with achieved results is widespread in our society, and could very well be a hallmark of many "anticipatory democracy" exercises.

48. GARTNER, Alan and Frank RIESSMAN. **The Service Society and the Consumer Vanguard.** Introduction by Colin Greer. NY: Harper & Row, 1974. 266 pp. $8.95.   (A-3)

"We see in essence two continua: the prime course of economic development is from agriculture to industry to service with perhaps an intervening step of post-industrial or neoindustrial; the other continuum is from feudalism to capitalism to some form of socialism. The fact that socialism, historically, developed in pre-industrial societies such as the Soviet Union and China has limited what we see as the natural connection or matching stages between socialism and a service society..." (p.254-255)

The authors find it difficult "to decide whether to call the emerging society a service society or a consumer society. The future world will be both, and both will be unfulfilled unless production is organized to reflect people rather than profits, participation rather than power." (p.15)

It is predicted that the service sector (particularly human services) will continue to expand, that service growth is appropriate to meet the environmental crisis, and that credentialism will become more performance-oriented. Chapters deal with consumer power, the value explosion of the sixties, the work ethic, education, the professional-consumer dialectic, and the management of consumer-oriented practice.

*** Is expansion of the service sector inevitable and desirable? Granted this fundamental assumption, this book is valuable in raising a number of important issues. This book loses its importance to the degree that the assumption about the service society can be questioned (see chapter 7).

49. GERSUNY, Carl, and William R. ROSENGREN. **The Service Society.** Cambridge: Schenkman, 1973. 156 pp.   (A-4)

Two sociologists at the University of Rhode Island cover topics such as the rhetoric of service, the educational market place, the bureaucratization of conspicuous leisure, and the rhetoric of remedial services.

It is felt that there will be an increasing emphasis on directing consumer behavior toward the quinary sector (health care, education, recreation), because only services have a potential for unlimited growth in an environment of scarcity. "If the service society is not the wave of the future, it is undoubtedly one of the more viable alternatives for mankind." Unfortunately, the authors do not suggest what the other alternatives are, let alone examine them.

50. GROSS, Bertram M., "Planning in an Era of Social Revolution," **Public Administration Review**, 31:2, May/June 1971, pp. 259-297.   (AB-1)

(Single copies of this entire issue on "Changing Styles of Planning in Post-Industrial America" are available for $2.00 from the American Society for Public Administration, 1225 Connecticut Ave., N.W., Washington, D.C. 20036).

A lengthy essay by a leading scholar in national planning, social indicators, and systems theory. Gross discusses the acceleration of cumulative system change over the history of mankind, and various social revolutions in the past. The term Post-Industrial Society is rejected for "its modest vacuity" and Gross suggests a Service Society as a useful starting point. The major elements of such a society are outlined, with attention paid to changing technologies, changing social structures, our emerging "nation city" and world society, and the deepening crises of survival, aspirations, fragmentation, and authority.

The "grand alternatives of a new era" are seen as Techno-Urban Fascism or Humanist Reconstruction. It is cautioned that some people think that fascism has already happened in America, while others affirm that it could never happen here. "Both of these views, unfortunately, underestimate the possibility of a new-style fascism that might go far beyond anything in our past experience in developing highly organized foreign expansion and domestic repression." (p. 285) This neo-fascism, also referred to by Gross as Friendly Fascism (see item no. 103), would thrive on rationed welfare state benefits, accelerated consumerism, credentialized meritocracy, market-administration, and various technocratic evils.

In contrast, a humanist post-industrialism would feature new structures of power that provide new kinds of participation in the allocation and use of resources, shifts in values (e.g., toward cooperation instead of mastery), and "a more rational rationality" that replaces value-free or value-explicit decision-making with value-creating decision-making while developing the concept of systems synthesis and an action concept of rationality.

The possibilities of a truly civilized Post-Service Society are sketched in conclusion, where the bulk of the employed population would be involved in nonroutinized informational activities, and the boundaries between work and education obliterated as organized and unorganized learning becomes a continuing part of all human activity.

*** Raises some very important issues that the putatively "value-free" writers have ignored.

51. LUNDBERG, Ferdinand. **The Coming World Transformation.** NY: Double-
    day, 1963. 395 pp.   (AB-3)

A thoughtful but rather cheery extrapolation of social and cultural changes over the next 150 years, with chapters on topics such as social prediction, population, world economics, government, and education.

The world of the future is not labeled, but it is based on "confidently scheduled" technological developments such as automation, solar power, fusion power "making available truly unlimited energy," purification of sea water, new high-powered electric storage batteries, new chemical compounds, advanced methods of food production, weather control, and effective contraceptives.

Socially, there will be an economic trend toward equalization, centralization of the U.S. government in the national capital ("a gigantic social service institution relating to every department of modern life...the much denounced Welfare State" p.38), a radical reconstruction of cities, increasing application of scientific method, and a decline in religious fervor. Major attention is paid to learning needs and brainpower as a matter of national survival such that continuing adult education will become the largest segment of the educating system.

The concluding pages are devoted to considering "The Future of Prognostics" defined as "the systematic cultivation of social and cultural prediction" (p.351), and it is felt that the future for this enterprise would seem to be a bright one.

52. WILLIAMS, Gertrude (Professor Lady Williams). **The Coming of
    the Welfare State.** London: George Allen and Unwin, 1967. 119
    pp.   (C-5)

A slushy and acritical history, with the final chapter, Problems for the Future, trusting that the Welfare State will "modify its shape and direction as it responds to the winds of change."

Unlike the 19th century, it is asserted that most people now accept the view that the state has a responsibility for the welfare of its members, and the achievement in basic security, education, health, and housing are reviewed.

*** Problems of the state not fulfilling its responsibilities, or of negative effects of attempting to do so, are not raised.

53. BELL, Daniel. **The Reforming of General Education: The Columbia
    College Experience** in its National Setting. NY: Columbia Univer-
    sity Press, 1966; Anchor edition, 1968. 330 pp.   (A-3)

Largely about educational reform, but a brief section (pp.70-88) places this concern in the larger context of "The Tableau of Social Change." Bell discusses the rise of a welfare state, the new national society with its burgeoning intellectual class, the society becoming more "future-oriented" and planned, and the professional and technical class as the base line for future needs.

"All of this points up the fact that we are entering a 'post-industrial' society in which intellectual achievement will be the premium and in which the 'new men' will be the research scientists, mathematicians, economists, et al." (p.87)
*** All of this foreshadows later elaboration.

54. BELL, Daniel, "Notes on the Post-Industrial Society (I)," **The Public Interest**, No. 6, Winter 1967, pp. 24-35; "Notes on the Post-Industrial Society (II)," **The Public Interest**, No. 7, Spring 1967, pp. 102-118.   (A-4)

Further elaboration on aspects of The Post-Industrial Society. "...we have become for the first time a **national society** (though there has always been the idea of the nation) in which crucial decisions, affecting all parts of the society simultaneously (from foreign affairs to fiscal policy) are made by the government, rather than through the market; in addition, we have become a **communal society**, in which many more groups now seek to establish their social rights--their claims on society--through the political order; and third, with our increasing 'future orientation,' government will necessarily have to do more and more planning." (I, p.35, author's emphasis)
*** Apparently, government has yet to see the necessity for more planning, and the present revolt against bigness is very much against the notion of a national society.

55. BELL, Daniel. **The Coming of Post-Industrial Society: A Venture in Social Forecasting.** NY: Basic Books, 1973. 507 pp. $12.50. (A-4)

This widely reviewed tome is considered to be the definitive work on "Post-Industrial Society," and in certain respects it is. But it has many problems. It is a wordy assortment of essays and ideas--some fresh and challenging, some outdated, and some without empirical foundation despite the aura of thorough scholarship and Bell's reputation. There is some description, a great deal of covert prescription, and a few bare-kunckle assaults on "ecological radicals" and others such as Ivan Illich, who is seen as "a romantic Rousseauian" mouthing "cant words of modernity." Despite claims that the book was written in the past five years, the footnotes offer strong evidence of this book as a product of the 1960s.
The U.S. is used as the illustration of post-industrial society. The 1945-1950 period is seen as the birth years, while the next 30-50 years will see the full emergence of post-industrial society. The concept of such a society is a large generalization, best understood in terms of five dimensions: 1) the change from a goods-producing to a service economy; 2) the pre-eminence of the professional and technical class; 3) the centrality of theoretical knowledge as the source of innovation and of policy formation; 4) the control of technology and technology assessment; and 5) a new "intellectual technology" employed in decision-making. "The chief resource of the post-industrial society is its scientific personnel," (p. 221) and "the chief problem" in such a society is the organization of science. (p. 116)
"The central point about the last third of the twentieth century, call it the post-industrial society, the knowledgeable society, the technetronic age, or the active society, is that it will require more societal guidance, more expertise. To some extent, this is an old technocratic dream. But an earlier technocratic visionary like Saint-Simon felt that in such a technocratic society politics would disappear since all problems would be decided by the expert...It is more likely, however, that the post-industrial society will involve **more** politics than ever before, for the very reason that choice becomes conscious and the decision-centers more visible." (p. 263)
Chapter 1, From Industrial to Post-Industrial Society: Theories of Social Development, offers a broad summation of thinkers such as Dahrendorf, Lichtheim, Etzioni, Schumpeter, Weber, Lenin, Marx, Aron, Saint-Simon,

Trotsky, Burnham, Djilas, and Richta. But there is no mention of theories of rise and decline, theories of global convergence, or evolutionary theories of any kind.

Chapter 2, From Goods to Services: The Changing Shape of the Economy, offers nine tables of data to show the growth of services (transportation and utilities, trade, finance, insurance and real estate, personal and professional services, and government) relative to the growth of goods production, and the growth of white collar workers relative to blue collar workers. (For a serious challenge to this conventional wisdom, see Levison, no. 74.) Bell also discusses labor problems of the post-industrial society such as the organization of professionals and the situation of blacks and women, and constraints on change such as slow growth of productivity in services, inflation, and U.S. goods being priced out of the world market.

Chapter 3, The Dimensions of Knowledge and Technology: The New Class Structure of Post-Industrial Society, employs 30 tables of data to show the growth of science, as well as research and development spending. It is never explained why the "creative elite" of scientists are more important in the new society than wise politicians and judges, or even a good poet or novelist. There is no mention of any problem about intellectual inadequacies and the need for continuing education. Drucker (41) and Lundberg (50) are much better in this respect. Bell offers a reasonably good overview of technological forecasting (pp. 196-212), but he cites no reference later than 1968. He refers to the Delphi technique, but not to cross-impact analysis.

Chapter 4, The Subordination of the Corporation: The Tension Between the Economizing and the Sociologizing Modes, asserts that "Corporate power, clearly, is the predominant power in the society, and the problem is how to limit it." (p. 270) But then it is also asserted that "today, we in America are moving away from a society based on a private-enterprise market system toward one in which the most important economic decisions will be made at the political level..." (p. 297)

There is a useful discussion on the limitations of GNP as a measure of economic welfare, but no mention of alternatives that have been proposed, such as MEW (Tobin and Nordhaus) or NEW (Samuelson). The call for a total cost matrix that goes beyond the economizing mode to assess social costs is an important one.

Chapter 5, Social Choice and Social Planning: The Adequacy of Our Concepts and Tools, makes the important observation that we still use the language and often the assumptions of two hundred years ago. But the promise of this chapter--to question older formulations and propose "a number of new ones"--is only somewhat matched by performance. It is hardly original to conclude that "Clearly what is necessary in the next several decades is a comprehensive overhaul and modernization of governmental structure to find the appropriate size and scope of units which can handle the appropriate tasks." (p. 321) The advocacy of a System of Social Accounts, to broaden our concept of costs and benefits through better utilization of social indicators, is an important one, but has not advanced beyond Bell's contribution to the 1966 report of the U.S. Commission on Technology, Automation, and Economic Progress.

Chapter 6, Who Will Rule? Politicians and Technocrats in the Post-Industrial Society, loses itself in the mists of rhetoric with assertions such as "The technocratic mode has become established because it is the mode of efficiency--of production, of program, of 'getting things done.' (pp. 354-355) This questionable assertion is followed by an equally questionable description of the norms of professionalism and the ethos of science, and the considerable degree of equality of opportunity in the American class structure. There is no discussion of any possibility of totalitarian rule, either by technocrats or non-technocrats.

Bell concludes with a murky "Coda" entitled Agenda for the Future, which is essentially five separate essays. How Social Systems Change reiterates the notion that the autonomy of the economic order is coming to an end, while introducing the notion of a major historical change in the sundering of social function from property, and concluding with a very technical discussion of the changing relationship of status and situs. The Future of Science posits a glowing ideal on the ethos of science (seen as the emerging ethos of post-industrial society). Meritocracy and Equality offers a long discourse on Illich, Jensen, Hernnstein, Jencks, Rawls, and Young. "The post-industrial society, in its initial logic, is a meritocracy." (p. 409) But there is no discussion on the nature of present social selection (which might be described as credentialism divorced from any consideration of quality or merit), and how we might begin to attain the conditions of a meritocracy. The End of Scarcity describes the new scarcities of a post-industrial society: information, coordination, and time, and asserts that "The question before the human race is not subsistence but standard of living, not biology but sociology." (p. 465) Finally, Culture and Consciousness comments on the widening disjunction between social structure and culture, noting that "The lack of a rooted moral belief system is the cultural contradiction of the society, and the deepest challenge to its survival." (p. 480)

*** The many important ideas in Bell's book are nevertheless outweighed by the many flaws. The book's sub-title promises "A Venture in Social Forecasting" and in this respect the venture is clearly a flop, as scientific talent and universities both suffer the indignities of the economic downturn which the experts failed to anticipate. The question before much of the human race is once again one of subsistence, and there are important questions being raised about the efficacy of the technocratic mode in satisfying human needs. Even as a venture in social advocacy, Bell's society of scientific expertise may not be the most desirable alternative to strive for.

55a. BELL, Daniel. **The Cultural Contradictions of Capitalism.** NY: Basic Books, Jan. 1976. 301 pp. $12.95.   (A-4)

There is less here than one is led to expect. It must be understood that very little is said about modern capitalism (multinational corporations, for example, are discussed on pp. 207-209), although there is considerable discussion of certain aspects of high culture.

This book "stands in a dialectical relation" to **The Coming of Post-Industrial Society,** which focused on the reshaping of the techno-economic order. "In these essays, I deal with culture, especially the idea of modernity, and with the problems of managing a complex polity when the values of a society stress unrestrained appetite. The contradictions I see in contemporary capitalism derive from the unraveling of the threads which had once held the culture and the economy together, and from the influence of the hedonism which has become the prevailing value in our society." (p. xi)

Who is to blame? On the one hand Bell describes the split character of the new capitalism of abundance: demanding a Protestant ethic in production, while encouraging a fun ethic in consumption. Corporate advertising has led to a "total" seduction of the consumer. (p. 70) But then there is the "rise of the hip-drug-rock culture on the popular level...(which) undermines the social structure itself by striking at the motivational and psychic-reward system which has sustained it." (p. 54) But is this really so? Later, we are told that in the 1970s, "the cultural radicalism itself has become exhausted." (p. 144) Such are the difficulties in understanding Bell.

The major theme of the book may have major theoretical importance. Whereas, "almost all of contemporary social science thinks of society as some unified 'system'," Bell asserts that one can best analyze modern society "by thinking of it as an uneasy amalgam of three distinct realms: the social structure (principally the techno-economic order), the polity, and the culture." (p. xi) The three realms are ruled by contrary axial principles: efficiency, equality, and self-realization (or self-gratification).

The fundamental political fact of the past 25 years is seen as the extension of state-directed economies. In the next 25 years we move to state-managed societies, which emerge "because of the increase in the large-scale social demands (health, education, welfare, social services) which have become entitlements for the population." (p. 24. There is no suggestion that such societies may not be feasible or desirable.)

As concerns the cultural realm, "The adversary culture has come to dominate the cultural order..." (p. 40), subverting bourgeouis values through higher education, film, publishing, and journalism. (This is the very same argument made by Kevin Phillips, no. 585) But does it really dominate? Bell also dwells on the compartmentalization that isolates serious artists from one another, and makes specialists of critics. There is no center but only peripheries. This specialization creates "an almost unbearable strain between the culture and the social structure." (p. 95) But whereas there is impotent fragmentation in the arts, Bell remains quite neutral in describing the sciences, although he does acknowledge that the failure of liberalism has been a failure of knowledge (p. 203). Indeed, he asserts that "Ours is a society that has become 'future-oriented' in all its dimensions..." (p. 90) This is not explained in detail, but if a genuine future-orientation is a holistic reintegration of perspectives, as it ought to be, this would stand in curious contrast to the fragmentation in the arts. But Bell does not distinguish between the genuine and the specious.

As in his previous volume, this is a collection of recycled essays that does not fit together particularly well. Chapter titles are The Cultural Contradictions of Capitalism, The Disjunctions of Cultural Discourse, The Sensibility of the Sixties, Toward the Great Instauration: Religion and Culture in a Post-Industrial Age, The Public Household (see no. 396), and Unstable America: Transitory and Permanent Factors in a National Crisis. In the latter chapter, the permanent factors are a national polity, a communal society, a post-industrial world, and an urban society. The historic trend toward urbanization has reversed (nos. 709-710); one wonders whether the remaining verities are also shaky.

*** These Promising Pontifications of Mr. Post-Industrialism are difficult to digest, and may obfuscate more than they enlighten. The disjunction of realms is perhaps a useful approach, but Bell consistently uses concepts that confuse reality and idealization. There is a dazzling display of seeming erudition on cultural matters, yet there is little acknowledgement of the contemporary thinking reflected in this guide.

In the Preface, Bell says that "Any book--mine at least--is a dialogue, or sometimes a debate, with one's friend's." (p. xii) Perhaps the fundamental problem is that Bell will not go beyond his tight little circle and engage   in dialogue or debate with any of his numerous critics. Thus Bell himself may suffer from hermetic isolation, from failure to play the "game between persons" at least in the constructive way which purportedly characterizes post-industrial society.

A tiny indicator to be found in Bell's book **may** serve to explain a great deal. Throughout most of the book there is impeccable documentation, as one should expect of any serious scholar. But in the few instances where disagreement is expressed, there is also a lapse in standards. Heilbroner's recent book (no. 111) is incompletely cited on p. 27, Roszak is quoted with no citation at all on p. 143, and Gans' book (no. 528) is incorrectly cited on p. 264. The arguments of both Roszak and Gans are clearly distorted by Bell. Perhaps this is trivial or coincidental, but it might be the tip-off to a major flaw.

56. FAUNCE, William A. **Problems of an Industrial Society.** NY: McGraw-Hill, 1968. 189 pp.   (AB-4)

A sociologist at Michigan State University, largely concerned with problems of automation and alienation, notes a three-stage transition from an agricultural pre-industrial society to a mechanized industrial society, to an automated postindustrial society (without any reference to Drucker, Bell, Brezezinski, Ellul, or others with similar notions).

The final chapter, "Freedom, Control, and the Future of Industrial Society," includes a section entitled "Automation and Postindustrial So-

ciety" (pp. 162-171). The future period would possibly be an age of automation, with a labor force composed primarily of professional, technical and skilled workers (the remainder engaged in some form of independent service activity), and a shift in major goals to noneconomic concerns. The typical form of organization would be professional, rather than bureaucratic, and there is a likely decline in social structural differentiation.
** Light at the end of the tunnel.

57. MORRIS, Dubois S. (ed.) **Perspectives for the '70s and '80s: Tomorrow's Problems Confronting Today's Management.** NY: National Industrial Conference Board, 1970. 124 pp.   (A-3)

A slick wedding of a public opinion survey and a Delphi exercise, both conducted in late 1968. The Delphi survey approached 118 persons, of which 66 "distinguished experts" took part. This included 21 Presidents and Board Directors of major corporations such as Xerox, Ford, Alcoa, and U.S. Steel, and assorted professors such as Abraham Kaplan and Philip Hauser, futurists such as John Platt and John McHale, and liberals such as Barbara Ward and Gus Tyler.

Four major themes were derived from the exercise. 1) A sense of transition. "The United States is in a period of major transition. It is essentially a move from an industrial to a post-industrial society, from a pluralistic to a more centrally (or technocratically) directed nation." (p. 5) Subordinate transitions include those from rural to urban America and from a production to a service economy. 2) Obsolescence in the U.S. Infrastructure. The situation is seen as most critical in education, political institutions, legal and criminal justice systems, and food production. 3) A Shifting Power Structure in the United States, leading to greater concentration in fewer hands. 4) Confusion of Identity, Roles, Responsibilities.

Twenty specific Forecast Areas are arranged in order of National Priority Consideration, and each one contrasts the views of the panel of "experts" with those of the public. The top ten areas are divisions in U.S. society, international affairs, education, urban areas, law and order, science/technology/management of change, the economy, resources, values, and population. Energy and unemployment do not appear in any of the 20 areas.
*** Despite the biases of the panel, the approach is potentially useful. The content might not be so outdated if a broader range of expertise had been sought. Also see the IFF Delphi, no. 756.

58. TOURAINE, Alain. **The Post-Industrial Society. Tomorrow's Social History: Classes, Conflicts and Culture in the Programmed Society.** Translated by Leonard F.X. Mayhew. NY: Random House, 1971. 244 pp. $7.95.   (A-4)

A sociological exploration of old and new social classes, the student movement, the firm, and leisure activities.

59. EMERY, Frederick E. and E.L. TRIST. **Towards a Social Ecology: Contextual Appreciation of the Future in the Present.** NY: Plenum, 1973. 240 pp. $15.00; $5.95, paper.   (A-4)

A poorly organized set of essays on post-industrial society and futures methodology. Part I, "Concepts and Methods" by Emery, includes topics such as the need to find methods of complexity-reduction, early detection of emergent processes, adaptation to turbulent environments, and active adaptation. Part II, by Trist, is entitled "Aspects of the Transition to Post-Industrialism."

59a. MORLEY, James W. (ed.) **Prologue to the Future: The United States and Japan in the Postindustrial Age.** Lexington, Mass.: Lexington Books, 1974. 232 pp. $15.00.   (ns)

Includes the following essays:
- James Morley, "The Futurists' Vision"
- Robert Heilbroner, "Economic Problems of a Postindustrial Society"
- Hirofumi Uzawa, "The Transition to a Welfare Economy in Japan"
- Samuel P. Huntington, "Post-Industrial Politics: How Different Will It Be?"
- Nathan Glazer, "Information, the Postindustrial Society, and the American City"

59b. KLEINBERG, Benjamin S. **American Society in the Postindustrial Age: Technocracy, Power, and the End of Ideology.** Columbus, Ohio: Charles E. Merrill, 1973. 279 pp.   (A-3)

A welcome critique of the "end-of-ideology" ideology and how it promulgates technocratic social theory. Targets include Bertram Gross and Amitai Etzioni, with particular emphasis on Daniel Bell. Concludes that "it is quite clear that ideology has not ended, but only changed form over the past generation..." (p. 233)
*** A useful start, but there are important distinctions between Gross and Bell that are not made.

60. MEADOWS, Paul. **The Many Faces of Change: Explorations in the Theory of Social Change.** Cambridge, Mass.: Schenkman, 1971. 308 pp.   (A-4)

A rambling collection of essays by a sociologist. The initial chapter, "Industrial Society in the 1980's" states that we are "in the midst of a major shift in the culture-structure of industrial society--a shift from a mature, production-centered industrialism to a neo-industrialism (not, you will notice, a post-industrialism)." (pp. 8-9) Additional comments do not elaborate in any great detail, except to suggest that the new industrialism will be a technological society, featuring a shift from mechanization to cybernation, which in turn will involve a smaller scale of operations and an accelerated tempo of change.

61. GALBRAITH, John Kenneth. **The Affluent Society.** Boston: Houghton Mifflin, 1958. 286 pp.   (AB-4)

A best-seller in its time, serving to inbed the "Affluent Society" label into the national consciousness, although the remainder of the message appears to have been lost.
   The central argument is that, now that the nation enjoys unprecedented affluence, the old economics based on scarcity is obsolete, and we must see new problems and opportunities before us. An entire chapter is given to The Concept of the Conventional Wisdom, which is seen as protecting continuity in social thought and action.
   What we have barely noticed, Galbraith contends, is that the traditional leisure class has been replaced by another and much larger class: the New Class. The New Class is essentially the well-educated class, which derives satisfaction and enjoyment from their occupations. One of the central economic goals of our society is to eliminate toil as a required economic institution, and it is therefore recommended that the major social goal of the society should be the further and rapid expansion of the New Class. "And now to complete the case, we have a design for progress. It is education or, more broadly, investment in human as distinct from material capital." (p. 268)
*** It is a massive irony that the "Affluent Society" notion in turn became

the conventional wisdom, only recently replaced by the notion of a scarcity society. Galbraith does not use the concept of services or a service society, but this is what he is advocating by recommending the expansion of the New Class.

62. CHASE, Stuart. **Live and Let Live: A Program for Americans.** NY: Harper & Bros., 1960. 146 pp.   (AB-4)

"This book is my second attempt to appraise the problems which face our country in a time of crisis. The first was made years ago, and resulted in a book called **A New Deal,** published some months before Mr. Roosevelt announced **the New Deal.**" (p. vii. See item no. 509.)

Chase reviews major changes in the world such as the growth of population, the spread of nuclear weapons, and the decline of world resources. Major changes in America include the rise of tertiary trades ("most of us are now in the tertiary group...more than half of the gainfully employed" p. 32), automation, megalopolis, and big government.

Chapter 11 describes Four American Eras, with the U.S. seen as on the threshold of its fourth era of economic and social development. Era One, from 1620-1800 is labeled The Handicraft Society. Era Two (1800-1916) was a time of free enterprise and the making of money. Era Three (1914-1960) was characterized by The Economy of Abundance. Era Four, A Time to Live, is the unprecedented opportunity for Americans to achieve the universal goals of survival, reasonable security, and creative expression. To do so requires planning for disarmament in the world, and a National Planning Board for Domestic affairs.

63. ROSTOW, W.W. **The Stages of Economic Growth: A Non-Communist Manifesto.** NY: Cambridge University Press, 1960. 179 pp. Second Edition, 1971. 253 pp.   (AB-4)

An economist's influential and controversial description of five stages: traditional society, take-off, drive to maturity, age of high mass consumption, and beyond consumption. As of 1960, "The era of high mass consumption has by no means come to an end, even in the United States." Very little is said about the following era, except to raise questions about whether man will fall into secular spiritual stagnation, once his material needs are satisfied.

The text of the first edition is presented unchanged in the second edition (1971), with new material only in the Preface and Appendix B, "The Critics and the Evidence." The critics are confined to fellow economists, and, in sum, Rostow regards the evidence as supporting his notions.

64. ORGANSKI, A.F.K. **The Stages of Political Development.** NY: Knopf, 1965. 229 pp.   (AB-3)

Parallels Rostow, and cites him, but is more cautious in the formulation. The four stages are:
1. The politics of primitive unification, where the primary function of government is the creation of national unity.
2. The politics of industrialization, where the nation is enlarged to include the industrial elite and then the masses, who are "awakened to political interest and participation."
3. The politics of national welfare, where nations are fully industrialized and government protects capital from the people, protects people from the hardships of industrial life, keeps the economy running smoothly, provides higher living standards, and aids the disadvantaged.
4. The politics of abundance, brought on by the revolution of automation. This leads to great concentrations of economic and political power, a

new class structure headed by a small elite of planners who are set apart from the large leisured minority. The primary functions of government involve cushioning the adjustments of social reorganization.

The Trend of automation is to push the political system away from democratic responsibility to people, because industry needs guarantees of international markets and international peace. Automation may in the end bring the death of the nation-state. In the Stage 4 political system, "socialism emerges as a likely form and democratic society as a desirable form," in that the major problem of Stage 4 concerns the distribution of wealth.

65. JAGUARIBE, Helio. **Political Development: A General Theory and a Latin American Case Study.** NY: Harper & Row, 1973 603 pp. (A-4)

An extremely technical treatment of the evolution of the human species, generally seen as increasing command over the human and natural environment. Three macrostages are described: societalization (political control over society), mechanization (societal control over nature), and socioorganization (societal self-control).

66. CHODAK, Szymon. **Societal Development: Five Approaches with Conclusions from Comparative Analysis.** NY: Oxford University Press, 1973. 357 pp. $12.50. (A-4)

A political scientist at UC, Berkeley views societal development as growing systemness, while trying to discern variables of "a new framework for a multidimensional theory of societal development." Discusses evolutionary theories, development and innovation, economic and political development, and modernization, concluding that there is no alternative to development: "The only choice is between mindful and mindless development."
*** Very conventional social science with no fresh contribution.

67. HILSMAN, Roger. **The Crouching Future.** NY: Doubleday, 1975. 650 pp. $12.50. (ns)

The former Assistant Secretary of State argues that affluence brought about by technology is the dynamic, the future crouching in the present, to which we should pay most attention in searching for clues to the future shape of society.
*** "...sadly out of touch with the currents of thought and action that have the vision and moral energy capable of inaugurating constructive change." (MANAS, Sept. 17, 1975, p. 8)

68. PEACOCK, James L. and A. Thomas KIRSCH. **The Human Direction: An Evolutionary Approach to Social and Cultural Anthropology.** NY: Appleton-Century-Crofts, 1970. (BC-4)

A textbook for introductory courses organized around an evolutionary framework of five societal stages: primitive, archaic, historic, early modern, and modern. America is now experiencing the "movement beyond the early modern."

The final chapter, Sociocultural Evolution and the Future, states that the general trend of evolution is toward a faster overall rate of change, increasingly differentiated societies, and more centralization and bureaucratization.
*** A dull integration of the conventional wisdom of conventional social science.

69. WEINER, Myron (ed.) **Modernization: The Dynamics of Growth.** NY: Basic Books, 1966. 355 pp.   (A-4)

"...the most challenging problem of the twentieth century--how modernization occurs and how it can be accelerated," is explored in 25 essays by leading social scientists.
The values are perhaps typified by Robert C. Wood in "The Future of Modernization" which views the basic accomplishment of advanced societies as "technological mastery over natural resources..." (p. 41) The result is that "Healthier, more skilled, and knowledgeable people, supported by and operating a sophisticated technology that produces with increasing efficiency, enjoy circumstances of expanded personal convenience." (p. 43)

70. DAHLSTROM, Edmund, "Developmental Direction and Welfare Goals: Some Comments on Functionalistic Evolutionary Theory About Highly Developed Societies," **Acta Sociologica: Journal of the Scandanavian Sociological Association,** 17:1, 1974, pp. 3-24.   (A-5)

This review of the academic literature is pompous, naive, jargon-laden to the point of parody, and sprinkled with a number of misspellings. Concludes that there is a tendancy to project ethnocentric evaluation and beliefs into theory, and advocates a welfare approach to developmental analysis. ******* With scholarly heads in the sand such as this, no wonder we are in trouble!

71. BENSMAN, Joseph and Arthur J. VIDICH. **The New American Society: The Revolution of the Middle Class.** Chicago: Quadrangle, 1971. 306 pp. $10.00.   (AB-4)

"Since the beginning of World War II, American society has been changing continuously. This change has been in direction as well as rate. The total amount of change has been so vast and radical that it can only be recognized as a social and cultural revolution." (p. 5)
"The fundamental aspect of the New Society is an ever-increasing flood of new productivity which, when distributed, has raised the standard of living not only of the upper classes, as it has done in the past, but also of wider and wider segments of the middle classes, which have increased in numbers sufficiently to become the numerically dominant class." (p. 15)
The four major causes of this revolution are "the tremendous increase in productivity," bureaucratization, a new middle class, and large-scale government expenditures to sustain the total economy of "...this enormously productive and service-oriented society." (p. 21)
The final chapter, American Society as a Functioning System, acknowledges the problems resulting from bureaucratization, but announces that "It is impossible for American society to return to a decentralized laissez-faire state, despite the wishes of young and old reactionaries." (p. 288) ******* Insular thinking from middle-aged reactionaries.

72. LINDER, Staffan Burenstam. **The Harried Leisure Class.** NY: Columbia University Press, 1970. 182 pp. $7.00.   (A-3)

A Swedish economist focuses on the increasing scarcity of time: "We have always expected one of the beneficent results of economic affluence to be a tranquil and harmonious manner of life, a life in Arcadia. What has happened is the exact opposite. The pace is quickening, and our lives in fact are becoming steadily more hectic." (p. 1)
Chapters discuss matters such as The Disappearance of Idleness, The Decline of Service in the Service Economy, Short Cuts in Private and Public Services (further examples of the reduced quality of services, e.g.

our transition "from appetizing food to acceptable nutrition" compounded by less time to eat), The Period of Decadence (on growth mania at the individual and national level), and Economic Ultimates.

73. PARKER, Richard. **The Myth of the Middle Class: Notes on Affluence and Equality.** Foreword by G. William Domhoff. NY: Liveright, 1972. 233 pp. $7.95.   (AB-3)

A reappraisal of our images of American life, arguing that one-third of the U.S. still lives in poverty, and one-half lives below a modestly comfortable budget. Although studies of self-classification show that most Americans publically call themselves middle-class, whether blue-collar or white-collar in occupation, Parker labors at great length to show that there is a wide disparity between the upper middle class and the lower middle class.

74. LEVISON, Andrew. **The Working-Class Majority.** NY: Coward, McCann & Geoghegan, 1974. 319 pp.   (ABC-2)

This important book undermines the conventional wisdom about workers and working-class life. Moreover, "Even the venerable cliche of America as a white-collar society turns out, on examination, to be a simple deceptive misstatement of the facts. For the rest of this century, the majority of Americans will be essentially manual, rather than professional or managerial, workers." (p. 13)

Levison examines the conventional categories for arraying data on employment and finds that many working class jobs are concealed in white collar categories, e.g. postmen are better described as clerical workers. Indeed, 80% of the labor force is seen as manual or clerical. And, rather than increasing affluence, the majority of Americans live below the "shabby but respectable" standard of comfort and security.

The long-range implications are that "all the hopes progressives have for fundamental improvement must relate in one way or another to the majority of American citizens, the blue-collar workers." (p. 281) Instead, popular theories of social change have focussed on everyone but the worker as a key factor.

Full employment is seen as the most immediate and direct political goal that is possible, but there should also be a restoration of community life and promotion of job enrichment and self-management. The problem is not simply jobs, though, but employment with wages that a worker can live on.

NOTE: The rating system provides general guidelines for indicating audience level ("A" as most complex and "C" as most popular), and importance ("1" as most and "5" as least). A full explanation of the system--and its limitations--can be found on page 4.

Chapter 3

Optimists and Pessimists

The fundamental chasm between Pollyannas and Cassandras can be found throughout this guide, but this chapter contrasts the two poles in their most extreme and visible form. The overriding theme of the optimists (75-92) is that the social condition has been improving and will continue to do so. The Cosmic Evolutionary views (Chapter 4) are also largely optimistic, but are distinguished by their focus on a new developmental stage in man or society which is clearly desirable to the preceding stage. The optimists in this chapter are essentially defenders of the Technological, Affluent, Service Society. The pessimists listed in this chapter (93-121) hold the unreserved view that conditions are worsening, and little or no hope is given for reform. There are many other writers in this guidebook who hold a pessimistic view of societal directions as a necessary preface to prescribing some alternative, and their work is classified according to the nature of the prescription.

Both optimists and pessimists make extrapolative arguments that project present conditions into the future. Other than this similarity, there is an immense contrast in the quality of their intellectual foundations.

The optimists listed here are all popularizers to various degrees. Some have bellicose reactions to the "prophets of doom and gloom": Wattenberg (75), Cohn (76), Esfandiary (89-90), Farmer (91), and Tuccille (92). Wattenberg heads the list so that his "Massive Majority Middle Class" can be compared with Bensman and Vidich (71), and contrasted with Parker (73) and Levison (74). There are sincere and restrained surveys (77,78), and an exuberant portrait of The American Dream (80). Technology as the future, in a world devoid of social systems, is the unstated assumption of many of these views (e.g., 81 and 83). Beckwith carries extrapolation to the ultimate extreme (82). Roberts (84) and Osborn (85) represent the restrained but generally hopeful scientist. **U.S. News and World Report** (86-87) represents the views of a large part of the business community. Esfandiary (89-90) attempts to make a virtue out of cosmic mindlessness, while Farmer (91) and Tuccille (92) take on George Orwell's **1984**, and inadvertently support the Orwell view.

The best optimistic arguments are listed elsewhere in this guide: Maddox's attack on **The Doomsday Syndrome** (228), the report by Herman Kahn and William Brown (226), and John Fischer's **Vital Signs, USA** (628). Of those listed in this chapter, the argument by Wattenberg (75) is noteworthy.

The pessimists are virtually all academics and intellectuals, and many of those listed here are cultural historians (Huizinga, Mumford, Steiner, Lukacs, Hougan). It is of critical importance to stress that the major themes of the pessimists are quite different from those of the largely neutral social scientists who describe the Technological, Affluent, Service Society, or the optimists who defend its actual or expected material wonders. The pessimists focus on the human and cultural side which is not reflected in our social indicators.

Aldous Huxley pictures over-organization and propaganda in his revisiting of **Brave New World** (93), a classic that, along with **1984,** deserves periodic reconsideration. Goldring's view of **The Broilerhouse Society** (94) is largely in this vein. The gloom of Huizinga (95) and Ortega (96) is still useful in describing present conditions, while Mumford's dismay over technics continues largely unchanged over the decades (97-100). Steiner's views on literacy are important to consider (102), Gross (103) challenges us to think of a possible techno-urban fascism, while Lukacs (105) and Hacker (106) make strong arguments that could provide a severe test to anyone's optimism. Heilbroner, Vacca, Pawley, Hendin, (111-114) also provide strong but completely dissimilar arguments. Hougan (115) offers a new form of bleak chic in arguing for an acceptance of decadence. The final pessimist, Montgomery Throop (121), is borrowed from the 19th century as a reminder that the dismal view is nothing new.

Mankind has prevailed despite the pessimism of the past, but this is not a sufficient argument to discount the pessimism of the present. Nor is it adequate to discount gloominess as mere intellectual fashion, although intellectuals are prone to pessimism. Any full and honest view of the present condition, which is necessary to any understanding of societal directions and alternatives, must deal with the arguments of the pessimists. The few attempts to do so (122, 123) have been superficial at best.

75. WATTENBERG, Ben J. **The Real America: A Surprising Examination of the State of the Union.** Introduction by Richard J. Scammon. Garden City, NY: Doubleday, 1974. 367 pp.   (ABC-3)

"The author has on occasion been accused of being an optimist." (p. 147) This is clearly so, but the argument, embellished by great quantities of data from the Census and the Gallup poll, is impressive--at least on the surface.

"After examining the data, the conclusion here is that the human condition in America--as measured by the data--has in fact improved rapidly in recent years...improving to such a degree as to create a new human situation, a society whose massive majority is 'middle class'...a benchmark of historical importance." (p. 5) America is "the first Massive Majority Middle Class society in history." (p. 68)

Chapters cover Worker's Lib (toward cerebralization and demanualization of labor), income, education (equating success with expansion of the system), material goods, residence, black progress, the population explosion (seen as ended), and civil rights.

The three basic issues of the Massive Majority Middle Class are inflation, crime and values; in contrast, "Cause People were concerned with sexism, racism, ecology, peace and the creation of a new value system..." (p. 282)

"The dominant rhetoric of our time is the rhetoric of failure, guilt and crisis. The evidence of the data is the evidence of progress, growth and success." (p. 8)

As for the future, "The era of abundance is not ending on this earth. It is just beginning." (p. 301) We can learn humanitarian materialism: "We can--and will--learn to have both: a cleaner environment and the energy to let poor people become middle-class people." (p. 301) Americans may just respond nobly to the cause of materialism without waste: "...Americans in the decade to come will keep complaining and keep progressing." (p. 313)

*** Breezy, truculent, and tough. "Cause People" have a difficult but not impossible job in supplying counter-data, exposing distortions of the data, and showing how the official data is misleading.

75a. MOYNIHAN, Daniel P., " 'Peace'--Some Thoughts on the 1960's and 1970's," **The Public Interest,** No. 32, Summer 1973, pp. 3-12. (B-5)

A slightly revised version of the Stearns Lecture at Andover Academy which begins by noting how most social scientists were pessimistic in the early 1960's. "I don't want to be pollyannish...yet I think the situation will be different in ways that on the whole will be for the better." (p. 4)

It is asserted that most of the events that nearly tore American society apart during the 1960's "arose from conditions unique to the decade in which they occurred." This was largely a demographic matter--a youth explosion that will not occur again. As a result of this lowered birth rate, and consequent fewer numbers to educate, "The great pressures on state and local government are now receding." (p. 9)

We are entering a period of "enormous personal prosperity" and great personal opportunity. Consequently, we shall have peace, although in some respects it will be a peace of exhaustion and a peace of surfeit. "I think we have come out of our time of troubles." (p. 12)

*** This narrow-gauge optimism was perhaps politically necessary for the then-Ambassador to India, but as social science it is irresponsible. Of all the forecasts in this guide, this one, as of 1976, may well be the most off-base.

76. COHN, Victor. **1999: Our Hopeful Future.** Indianapolis: Bobbs-Merrill, 1956. 205 pp.   (C-4)

"We are living in a time of remarkable opportunity with much justification for optimism." (p. 22) This view by a science journalist is based on talks with a number of experts. Our citizens have more dignity, they have withstood the Communist world conquest, and we have remarkable scientists and tools. Chapters are devoted to homes, cities, air travel, electronics, The Era of the Robot, The Friendly Atom, solar power, food, medicine, chemicals, and space travel. Throughout the text are mini-scenarios of John and Emily Future in the year 1999 (Really!). Cohn concludes on a note of sobriety that we must choose and act between 1984 and 1999, and our fate as men or robots.

There is a strong objection to "the prophets of misery and robotism"-- the pessimists and complainers. "I am tired of hearing this sort of thing, not because it has no point--of course, much of it is well taken--but because it has been overdone and exaggerated. It confuses what may happen with what is happening, and isolates some things and ignores many others." (p. 21)

*** This critique of pessimists can also be turned on the optimists and Cohn himself. Who engages in greater exaggeration, ignoring, and confusion of what may be and what is?

77. ERNST, Morris L. **Utopia 1976.** NY: Rinehart and Co., 1955. 305 pp.   (BC-4)

A lawyer's optimistic survey of the horizon. "I am sure of my Utopia. My dream is based on the most part on nothing more than an extension of present trends." (pp. 3-4) And, as always, it simply depends on what one looks at.

Ernst discusses our new leisure and its good uses, the new era of the atomic age, population, business (democracy seen as growing in the trade unions), home and family in the push-button economy, education and the rich life, physical health, mental health (new cures seen), travel, religion, government, law, and food and farm ("I take a position on the side of the imitators of nature." p. 79)

*** Ernst is not truculent, gushy, or blatantly one-sided. He recognizes a number of problems, but hopes that they will be overcome. 1976 has arrived without the Utopia, and this book serves as well as any as a case of How To Be Sincere but Very Wrong About the Future.

78. SOULE, George. **The Shape of Tomorrow.** NY: Twentieth Century Fund, 1958. NAL Signet Key Edition, 1958. 141 pp.   (BC-3)

A restrained tour of technology that is not bubbly, but is nevertheless clearly weighted on the optimistic side. The first section, What Technology Has Done, looks at machinery and power, new materials, farming, transportation, the house, consumer goods, medical care, and uses of leisure. The second section, What Technology May Do, covers automation, new substances, nuclear energy, fresh sea-water, birth control, future income, declining hours of work, world poverty, the approaching satiety of physical goods which is seen as leading to more time for non-material satisfactions, the "rapid approach toward equality in the distribution of income," and the development of truly humane personalities in a technologically mature culture. However, cautions are expressed about possible failures to control technology for humane ends.

79. WERNETTE, John Philip. **The Future of American Prosperity.** NY: Macmillan, 1955. 272 pp.   (B-4)

A simplistic essay by a professor of business administration, "The central idea of this book is that gloom is completely unwarrented, confidence in the future prosperity of the U.S. being thoroughly justified...other countries will also experience great economic progress in the decades ahead. This bright prospect, however, could be changed--by a destructive war or moral and spiritual decay among our people." (p.vi)

79a. Editors of Fortune. **The Fabulous Future: America in 1980.** NY: Dutton, 1956. 206 pp.   (ns)

The future as viewed by 11 prominent leaders in business, labor, law, and politics.

80. BARACH, Arnold B., and the Kiplinger Washington Editors. **1975: and the Changes to Come.** NY: Harper & Bros., 1962. 195 pp.   (C-4)

A popular and starry-eyed overview of material developments, accompanied with about 100 photographs. The topics cover people and jobs, farms and businesses, laboratories and assembly lines (with more automation envisioned), houses using plastics and with streamlined kitchens, more and better education (through educational technology, of course), transportation (electronic highways and flying at Mach 3), communications (wall-sized television and push-button phones) more medical marvels such as breakthroughs in chemicals to cure cancer, and space exploration.
    "Ask the scientists, the educators, the businessmen, and the government officials what is in store. Their descriptions of what is to come may read like fantasy but are the product of informed, balanced, intelligent thought." (p. xi)
*** The American Dream incarnate, and in retrospect it is useful to look back to this innocent time and examine those promises that were realized, those that were not realized, and those that were realized for only an affluent handful.

80a. BAGRIT, Sir Leon. **The Age of Automation.** Preface by Daniel Bell. NY: New American Library, Mentor Books, 1965. 128 pp. 60¢, paper.   (AB-3)

The 1964 BBC Reith Lectures discussing automation as an extension of man, the range of applications, necessary educational changes, political considerations, and industrial and economic consequences.

"We have now reached a point where we could be moving into a golden age for the mass of human beings, with adequate food, shelter, clothing and amenities, and with the opportunity of developing their bodies and their minds to a degree that has never before been possible. The opponents of automation are basically people who are pessimists. Somehow, they do not believe that human beings can be trusted with riches and leisure." (p. 97)

Bagrit argues for a general government policy concerning automation and a Ministry of Modernization to investigate the effects of technological change, and attend to the problems of re-training and re-education.

81. STILL, Henry. **Man: The Next 30 Years.** NY: Hawthorn Books, 1968. 216 pp.   (BC-3)

An attempt "to extrapolate many of the methods and things approaching birth today into the methods of things of tomorrow. Many of these tools may lead to a better way of life, if we learn to use them." (p. 4) Chapters on population and the hopes that it will be controlled, food (adequate food for everyone is predicted), new foods (a large part of world protein may come from petroleum), water desalinization, energy and the bright prospects for nuclear fusion, transportation, communications, automation, educational technology, the possibilities of immortality, homes, experimental cities, ocean farming, space exploration, and a concluding chapter on technology forecasting.

82. BECKWITH, Burnham Putnam. **The Next 500 Years: Scientific Predictions of Major Social Trends.** Foreword by Daniel Bell. NY: Exposition Press, 1967. 341 pp.   (ABC-4)

A simplistic but imaginative extrapolation of ultimate world centralization and scientization. May offer some useful provocations for those who are not offended by the incessant scientism and optimism.

83. WARSHOFSKY, Fred. **The 21st Century: The New Age of Exploration.** NY: Viking, 1969. 173 pp.   (C-4)

A popular presentation with 142 photographs and diagrams, based on the research conducted for the CBS television series, "The 21st Century." Part I covers Tools of Tomorrow such as computers, atomic energy, and lasers, while Part II describes Targets of Tomorrow: outer space and the oceans.

84. ROBERTS, Walter Orr. **A View of Century 21.** Claremont, Calif.: Claremont Colleges, 1969. 86 pp. $3.00.   (B-3)

The Annual Lecture Series of the Claremont Colleges, delivered by the Director of the National Center for Atmospheric Research in Boulder, Colo.

Concerned with the exponential change of the present, Roberts asks whether the revolution is one or many, and argues that "the key revolution is a single, world chain-reaction of expanding knowledge and the power associated with knowledge." (p. 14) In a tone of restrained optimism, he explores the humanizing potential of computers, and hopes that the need for conservation will provide a one-world motivation even stronger than the threat of war.

Concludes with a scenario of a high technology society in the year 2000. "This hospitable planet of ours has a long and progressive future if we can turn from war and racial strife, and if we can control our avaricious tendencies to waste precious resources." (p. 19)

*** If, if, if, if.

85. OSBORN, Frederick. **The Human Condition: How Did We Get Here &
Where Are We Going.** NY: Hugh Lauter Levin Associates (1 West
39th St.), 1973. 82 pp. $4.95.   (BC-4)

Depending on one's perspective, this essay, by an anthropologist at the
American Museum of Natural History and Chairman of the Executive Committee of the Population Council, can be seen as either great and succinct
wisdom, dreary cliches, or a sophisticated form of the idea of progress via
evolution.
All men are seen as seekers for a more secure and abundant life, but
there are significant dangers today of atomic war, degradation of the environment, energy production, and the number and distribution of people.
Despite this, the outlook is positive. Selection by birth rather than death
is seen as "the greatest revolution in the processes of evolution since the
invention of sex," (p. 58) and we are "at the beginning of a revolution in
the development and training of human beings as explosive as the first
stages of the technological revolution which has so changed the physical
conditions of life." (p. 77) It is felt that there will be an increase in human
qualities such as cooperation and respect for others, and "a diminution
in qualities of self-interest and aggression which have served survival in
the past but may now be counterproductive." (p. 82) The time span for such
a needed evolution is not discussed.

86. "What Life Will Be Like 20 Years in the Future," **U.S. News & World
Report,** Jan. 14, 1974, pp. 72-75.   (C-5)

A glib composite picture, drawn from the views of unidentified "futurologists." The world of 1994 will be "a time of tremendous technical achievement," and just about everyone will be covered by national health insurance and a guaranteed minimum income. There will be smaller families,
more flexibility in life styles and career changing, and many homes heated
by solar converters.

87. "Into a New Era," **U.S. News & World Report,** March 3, 1975,
pp. 32-50.   (C-4)

A special section of seven articles, generally characterized by a restrained optimism, with modifications to the status quo.
- "How Your Life Will Change" foresees "radical shifts" but only in terms
of technology: "a new age that will operate in a framework of computer-
ization, lasers, atomic energy and satellite telecommunications now
spreading over the globe." However, there will be a rise in living standards, new respect for old values, and a continuation of U.S. primacy in
global affairs. It will be "an era of restraints after recent years of high
optimism, upward mobility and free spending." Pollution will be brought
increasingly under control, the shift toward more leisure time will continue, and most people are likely to settle in metropolitan areas. (This is
"radical"?)
- "A look at Americans in the Year 2000" extrapolates demographic data.
- "Down the Road--Better Times but a Few Bumps Too" gives estimates
from the economic unit of U.S. News, concluding that "Standards of living will improve less rapidly."
- "Big Job Ahead for U.S.--Holding on to No. 1 Spot" outlines various challenges.
- "4 Measures of World Power" provides charts on total output, financial
reserves, oil production, and grain trade.
- "Sooner Than You Think" announces new dimensions of American tech-

nology: weather forecasts more than a year ahead, a cashless society resulting from computer-controlled banking and retail systems, electric vehicles, new foods, and thoroughly computerized medicine.
"If Human Race is to Survive Into the Next Century," an interview with Loren C. Eiseley, Professor of Anthropology at the University of Pennsylvania, on science and technology in general.

88. FREEMAN, James Dillet. **The Case for Optimism.** NY: Harper and Row, 1971. $4.95.   (C-5)

A mindless and preachy embarrassment to anyone who could make a serious case for optimism. For example, "This next generation will outstrip every generation that has gone before it in scientific inventiveness, in creative power, in reasoned approach to problems, in technical ability, in the development of personality, in social skills, in artistic achievements, in the charm and refinement of its way of life." (p. 96)
*** Such mush would normally be rejected by even a vanity publisher. It even fails as a put-on.

89. ESFANDIARY, F.M. **Optimism One: The Emerging Radicalism.** NY: Norton, 1970. 249 pp. $5.95.   (C-5)

Bellicose optimism breezily touring Our Humanizing Machine Age, Breakthrough in Human Nature, The New International Economics, Mankind Converging, and other aspects of universalization.

90. ESFANDIARY, F.M. **Up-Wingers.** NY: John Day, 1973. 146 pp. $5.95. $2.95, paper.   (C-5)

"In this tract I have bypassed the plodding pace of print. Most books are too slow for our times. Up-Wingers, addressed primarily to the fluid, attempts to approximate the rhythm of electronics. Brief crisp rapid bursts of ideas intended to inform goad provoke catalyze..." (p.xi)
New dimensions are seen as emerging, going far beyond right and left, conservative and liberal, defying all the old labels. The new dimensions are up. We are at the beginning of The Planetary Movement and The Cosmic Upheaval. "Today optimism is the only relevant outlook... Ours is the First Age of Optimism." (p. 14)
The new world to be optimistic about includes a Children's Liberation Movement to do away with exclusive parenthood, replacing schools with Universal Communication, the modern commune as a vast improvement over the old exclusivist family systems, Universal Process ("a dynamic unrooted all-inclusive evolution"), mobilias (stopovers at which one should stay for no more than six months), instant communities to accommodate the new mobility, total Space Age environments to prod us to new patterns of wholesome universal life, cybernated economies, and the conquest of death; in sum, "A New World which is resigned to nothing--no pain, suffering or death."

91. FARMER, Richard N. **The Real World of 1984: A Look at the Foreseeable Future.** NY: David McKay, 1973. 210 pp. $6.95.   (C-5)

George Orwell's slogans in 1984 such as "freedom is slavery" turn the world around, but "this turning around of words can be put backward" in that one man's slavery may be another's freedom. Farmer contends that our real problem now is that we are getting freer too fast.
Chapters cover topics such as The Real World of 1884 (contrasting today's conditions to the poor conditions of the time), What is Freedom? (seen as the increasing expansion of options), The Death of the Cities

(through the rebirth of the family farm), The Minorities (less poverty and more choices seen for old people), and Public Life: The Return to Privacy (foreign affairs will fade as an issue because of a return to neo-isolation). New communications techniques are seen as giving people more flexibility and freedom, an argument is made for automotive transport as more flexible and cheaper than other forms, and in 25 years "the average family income will be about what the top five per cent is now."

"Finally, we should not overlook the tremendous progress made in management... More progress is to come, and more efficiencies will be made...lots of brilliant people are working on improvements all the time." (p. 209)

*** There may be a few worthwhile insights here, but the general argument is inept and transparent, with no attempt whatsoever at documentation.

92. TUCCILLE, Jerome. **Who's Afraid of 1984? The Case for Optimism in Looking Ahead to the 1980s.** New Rochelle, NY: Arlington House, 1975. 223 pp. $7.95.   (C-5)

Orwell's **1984** is not found in the brief listing of 46 books at the end of this curious volume. At the beginning of the volume we are told that "Even those who have not read George Orwell's famous novel, or seen the movie, know what this year signifies." (p. 3) It would appear that Tuccille is one of those who has not read the novel. As a professed optimist, though, he seeks to show that Orwell will be wrong.

He first attacks The Doomsday Brigade, composed of those who are invariably socialist or welfare-statist, with particular venom aimed at Paul Ehrlich, Michael Harrington, William and Paul Paddock, Luther Evans, Paul Kurtz, Margaret Mead, and the Club of Rome. The critique ranges from reasonable charges (problems blown out of proportion and based on a misinterpretation of facts), to snide and vicious comments.

This is followed by an acritical tour of promising technologies such as alternative automobile engines, air cushion vehicles, recycling techniques, nuclear fusion, wall-size television, and private residential Disneylands (including a self-contained one in the ocean).

The second half of the book is a scenario of the world of 1984. "What we have in reality is the mirror-image of the society portrayed in George Orwell's novel." (p. 123) Technology works on behalf of the public, multinational corporations have emerged as the principal force for peace and progress, the bulk of the planet has been converted to a more-or-less market economy, data banks have proved themselves to be "one of the most liberating influences on the human condition," the U.S. has evolved from a middle-class society to a leisure-class society with 3-day work weeks and industrial robots, Community Learning Centers have replaced public schools, food contains anti-aging additives, and there are new communities inspired by Safdie, Soleri, and Fuller. "The human condition improves because it must improve. Our technology, our spreading affluence, our creative leisure are ongoing testimonials to the genius of man." (p. 148)

Unbelievable? "We are dealing with an opposition that refuses to accept the facts of reality for what they are. If Orwell was right in one regard, it was his projection about the corruption of language into double-think. The Doomsday Brigade has honed this ability to a fine art." (pp. 157-158)

*** War is Peace, Ignorance is Strength.

93. HUXLEY, Aldous. **Brave New World Revisited.** NY: Harper & Bros., 1958. 147 pp.   (AB-1)

An essay prompted by the fear that "The prophecies made in 1931 are coming true much sooner than I thought they would." (p. 4)

The theme of Huxley's classic novel is described as "The completely organized society, the scientific caste system, the abolition of free will by methodical conditioning, the servitude made acceptable by regular doses of sleep-teaching...'' (p. 3) An interesting contrast is made with Orwell's **1984** (pp. 4-7), where the public is controlled by punishment and the fear of punishment, and Huxley concludes that the odds are more in favor of something like **Brave New World**. ''There are many roads to Brave New World; but perhaps the straightest and the broadest of them is the road we are traveling today, the road that leads through gigantic numbers and accelerating increases.'' (p. 12)

Chapters discuss over-population (which produces dictatorship), over-organization, propaganda, the arts of selling, brainwashing, chemical persuasion, subconscious persuasion, and hypnopaedia.

The chapter on Education for Freedom advocates an education in ''the facts of individual diversity and genetic uniqueness and the values of freedom, tolerance and mutual charity which are the ethical corollaries of these facts.'' (p. 129) Above all, children would be taught to distinguish truth from falsehood.

The final chapter, What Can Be Done, advocates a reduction in the birth rate and practical substitutes for our present fuels. ''To avoid the spiritual impoverishment of individuals and whole societies, leave the metropolis and revive the small country community, or alternatively humanize the metropolis by creating within its network of mechanical organization the urban equivalents of small country communities...'' (p. 142)

But it is recognized that these remedies have been offered before, and ''in spite of all this preaching and this exemplary practice, the disease grows steadily worse.'' (p. 143) It is wondered whether we really wish to act upon our knowledge, and concluded that ''Perhaps the forces that now menace freedom are too strong to be resisted for very long. It is still our duty to do whatever we can to resist them.'' (p. 147)

*** This essay deals with matters that are neglected by most writers and is still of great relevance. It is best appreciated when read with both **Brave New World** (Harper, 1932) and Orwell's **1984** (Harcourt, Brace, 1949). The former describes a well-managed society genetically stratified into Alphas, Betas, Gammas, etc. and placated by the frequent use of ''soma''--an all-purpose drug that generically suggests our present pattern of drug use. **1984** describes a considerably less benign society where material conditions are satisfactory only for the higher members of the inner party, and technology is used only for perpetual warfare. Thought control is pervasive, and ''The Principles of Newspeak'' (outlined in the Appendix) are designed to emasculate language. If ''revisited'' today would Huxley stick with **Brave New World**, or would he see a higher probability of a 1984-type of society?

94. GOLDRING, Patrick. **The Broilerhouse Society.** NY: Weybright & Talley, 1969. 226 pp. $5.95.   (ABC-3)

Although this metaphorical polemic concerns ''Broilerhouse Britain,'' the parallels to the U.S., concerning people as livestock, are obvious. The trend is toward ''a nation of processed people, scientifically conceived, produced and fed, educated by machinery, conditioned by television, housed in batteries of human nesting boxes to live out our allotted spans before being sent to the electric furnaces of the crematoria... The pressures towards such mechanized living are the same as those which produced the broilerhouse.'' (p. 9)

Industrial society is seen as becoming a huge factory farm, and individual chapters deal with living, jobs, culture, victuals, politics, morals, and travel--all described with the broilerhouse metaphor. The vital distinction is between managers (The People-Farmers) and the managed. The exceptions are The Free-Rangers (nonconformists) and the dropouts and rejects in The Broilerhouse Backyard. In general, there is a decline of standards running through the whole of life. ''If this were to be our long-term future it would mean spiritual death for our society.'' (p. 208)

It is hoped that the broilerhouse society will be replaced by a new age of aristocracy, unencumbered by serfs or a working class. In the leisure society of a "post-broilerhouse age" there would once again be a respect of craftsmanship and tradition, and a clean and uncluttered land. "I believe the human instinct toward real community and dignity will survive any processing..." (p. 216) But it is difficult to be hopeful in the wake of such a devastating critique.

*** A light but provocative polemic on some very fundamental matters. The broilerhouse theme is a bit overdone (an appendix lists 8 pages of jobs, living arrangement, culture items, victuals, etc. arranged according to "B" and "non-B" attributes), but may be valuable in stimulating classroom discussions.

95. HUIZINGA, J. In the Shadow of Tomorrow. Trans. from the Dutch by J.H. Huizinga. NY: Norton, 1936. 239 pp.   (AB-3)

The Preface warns that "It is possible that these pages will lead many to think of me as a pessimist. I have but this to answer: I am an optimist." However, the opening sentence sets the tone of this essay by declaring that "We are living in a demented world." (p. 5)

Universal education and modern publicity are seen as leading to cultural devitalization and degeneration. "The categories with which thinking has contented itself so far seem to be in dissolution." (p. 64) This has led to "a crisis of modern thought and knowledge so violent and so far-reaching as can hardly be found in any known period of the past." (p. 65) Symptoms include a lowering of standards of critical judgment, perversion of the function of science, a deterioration of moral standards.

It is a civilization at the mercy of its own intrinsic dynamism. "The gods of our time, mechanisation and organization, have brought life and death. They have wired up the whole world, established contact throughout... At the same time they have trapped the spirit, fettered it, stifled it. They have led man from individualism to collectivism." (p. 217)

Rather than sharing Spengler's fatalism, there are some grounds for hope. "It is not from intervention by social organizations that we must expect deliverance...What is required is an internal regeneration of the individual." (p. 231)

Huizinga advocates true internationalism and the new askesis--a purified culture. "There must be a possibility of conversion and reversal in the development of civilization. We are thinking here of the recognition or retrieval of eternal truths, truths that are above the stream of evolution and change. It is these values that are at stake." (p. 238)

*** A viewpoint that could be readily applied to today's condition, and quite similar to the Soviet dissidents in Solzhenitsyn et. al., **From Under the Rubble** (No. 844).

96. ORTEGA y GASSET, José. The Revolt of the Masses. NY: Norton, 1932. 190 pp. (Original Spanish edition, 1930)   (A-3)

This classic essay by a great Spanish philosopher is still well worth considering for its valuable insights into our era. One fact, for good or ill, is seen to be of utmost importance: the accession of the masses to complete social power or "the triumphs of a hyperdemocracy." (p. 17) Yet, by definition, they neither should nor can direct their own existence.

We are seen as living in a levelling period--of fortunes, culture, and the sexes. The dominant type of man today is a primitive one in the midst of a civilized world--a civilization from the 19th century summed up in two great dimensions: liberal democracy and technicism.

Chapter 12, on The Barbarism of Specialization views the man of science as "a learned ignoramus" (p. 112) who behaves in almost all spheres of life as does the unqualified mass man.

The world is seen as suffering from grave demoralization as a result of the displacement of European power. The gravest danger on the horizon is seen as state intervention.

97. MUMFORD, Lewis. **Technics and Civilization.** NY: Harcourt, Brace & World, 1934; 1962.   (A-3)

Divides the development of the machine and the machine civilization into three successive but overlapping and interpenetrating phases, with chapters III-V devoted to each one: The Eotechnic Phase (to about 1750), The Paleotechnic Phase (1750-c.1900), and The Neotechnic Phase--a true mutation that is still emerging. Concludes with a prescriptive argument for dynamic equilibrium.

98. MUMFORD, Lewis. **The Transformations of Man.** World Perspectives, Vol. 7. NY: Harper & Row, 1956. 249 pp.   (A-3)

Successive chapters devoted to six stages: Archaic Man, Civilized Man, Axial Man (in reference to the profound change in human values and goals taking place after the sixth century), Old World Man (until the 19th century), New World Man (both romantic and mechanical, seeking to leave the Old World culture behind), and Post-Historic Man. (See Seidenberg, no. 5) This final stage is a pessimistic extrapolation of capitalism, machine technics, bureaucracy and totalitarian government such that "all human purposes would be swallowed up in a mechanical process immune to any human desire that emerged from it." (p. 155)

99. MUMFORD, Lewis. **The Myth of the Machine. I. Technics and Human Development.** NY: Harcourt, Brace & World, 1967. 342 pp.   (A-4)

Aims to question both the assumptions and the predictions upon which our commitment to the present forms of science and technology, treated as if ends in themselves, have been based. Extensive space is taken to critique Karl Marx and Pierre Teilhard de Chardin.
*** Unwieldy historical analysis. Volume II (see below) is more contemporary in its focus.

100. MUMFORD, Lewis. **The Myth of the Machine. II. The Pentagon of Power.** NY: Harcourt Brace Jovanovich, 1970. 496 pp.   (A-3)

Attempts "to explore the interplay of human interests and technological pressures that conspired after the sixteenth century to dominate Western civilization. In time these forces coalesced in the unconscious as a replenished myth of the machine." (p. 164) This myth is defined more closely as "the Power Complex: a new constellation of forces, interests, and motives, which eventually resurrected the ancient megamachine, and gave it a more perfect technological structure, capable of planetary and even interplanetary extension." (p. 166) The components of the pentagon of power include power itself (manpower, nuclear power, etc.), organized political power, money power--the stimulus of profit, and publicity.
Mumford attacks visions of endless mechanial progress as "totalitarian utopias." (p. 228) He criticizes McLuhan, Fuller, Kahn, Bell, Skinner, and Seaborg, while applauding the views of Seidenberg and Huxley. "At least one thing should become clear: once the majority of any nation opts for megatechnics, or passively accepts the system without further question, no other choice will remain." (p. 332) As for those progressives who seek to destroy the past, "'Leaving the past behind' is the equivalent of leaving life behind--and with this, any desirable or durable future." (p. 391)

"For its effective salvation mankind will need to undergo something like a spontaneous religious conversion: one that will replace the mechanical world picture with an organic world picture, and give to the human personality, as the highest known manifestation of life, the precedence it now gives to its machines and computers...such changes have repeatedly occurred all through history; and under catastrophic they may occur again." (p. 413)

101. SNOW, C.P. The State of Siege. NY: Scribner's, 1969. 50 pp.   (AB-3)

The John Findley Green Foundation Lecture, delivered at Westminster College in November, 1968. This consciously pessimistic overview juxtaposes the present world-wide malaise ("We are behaving as though we were in a state of siege") with critical future problems of population growth and famine. Large-scale famines are not expected to appear before 1980, but Snow does expect a major catastrophe before the end of the century. To avoid this, population restriction and large-scale aid from the developed nations is required, but the eventuality of either is doubted. "To stint ourselves to avoid a disaster in twenty years--what body of people would ever do it? Right." (p. 38)

102. STEINER, George. In Bluebeard's Castle: Some Notes Towards the Redefinition of Culture. New Haven: Yale University Press, 1971. Paper edition, 1973. 141 pp. $1.95.   (A-2)

A notably profound and eloquent essay by a leading cultural historian. The title is based on an opera by Bartók: "We seem to stand, in regardl to a theory of culture, where Bartok's Judith stands when she asks to open the last door on the night." (p. 124) The subtitle is derived from Eliot's **Notes Towards a Definition of Culture** (1948). The contents of the book were given in lecture form in March, 1971.

The first chapter, The Great Ennui, explores the image of a lost coherence, "a great garden of civility now ravaged."

The second chapter, A Season in Hell, attempts to relate the dominant phenomenon of twentieth-century barbarism to a more general theory of culture. "The wide-scale reversion to torture and mass murder, the ubiquitous use of hunger and imprisonment as political means, mark not only a crisis of culture but, quite conceivably, an abandonment of the rational order of man." (p. 48)

Chapter three, In a Post-Culture, discusses the destruction of inner forms and the elimination of certain vital futures from the spectrum of possibility. "Technical advances, superb in themselves, are operative in the ruin of primary living systems and ecologies. Our sense of historical motion is no longer linear, but as of a spiral. We can now conceive of a technocratic, hygienic utopia functioning in a void of human possibilities." (p. 69) Further comments are made about indecent superfluities, the common formlessness or search for new forms, our filtered reality, the new leveling, and second-order psychosocial metamorphoses, concluding that "it is almost certain that the old vocabulary is exhausted, that the forms of classic culture cannot be rebuilt on any general scale." (p. 93)

The final chapter, Tomorrow, offers "conjectures as to what may be synapses worth watching...some guesses, not with a view to prophetic aptness, but in the hope that they might be erroneous in a way that will retain a documentary interest." (p. 98)

A general "retreat from the word" is seen, a debilitation of genuine literacy, of which "America is the representative and premonitory example." Replacing the traditional ideals of literate speech is a global sound-sphere, a musical esperanto, a metaculture: "Everywhere a sound-culture seems to be driving back the old authority of verbal order." (p. 118). Whereas reading is profoundly solitary, the bias of current sentiment that underlies the " 'Musicalization' of our culture" points toward gregariousness and immediate common ground. Moreover, music provides a poetry of religious emotion that is absent today in "many educated, but imperfectly coherent lives." New techniques of reproduction "no less important than was the spread of cheap mass-printing in its time, are entering our lives at numerous, shaping levels." (p. 123)

The discussion shifts to areas of science and technology that will alter basic structures of both private and social life: biomedical engineering, computers, ecological modification. "To be ignorant of these scientific and technological phenomena, to be indifferent to their effects on our mental and physical experience, is to opt out of reason. A view of post-classic civilization must, increasingly, imply a vision of the sciences, of the language-worlds of mathematical and symbolic notation." (p. 128, author's emphasis) Yet, there are certain major lines of inquiry that perhaps should not be pursued, and "It may be that the truths which lie ahead wait in ambush for man" (p. 137), and that the "old obscurantisms of religious dogma and social caste have been replaced by the even more tyrannical obscurantism of 'rational, scientific truth'." (p. 138) Nevertheless, it is expected that we shall open the last of the successive doors in Bluebeard's castle, "because opening doors is the tragic merit of our identity." (p. 140)
*** For a discussion of the various meanings of the Bartók opera, "Duke Bluebeard's Castle," see Harold C. Schonberg in **The New York Times**, Sun. May 12, 1974, p. D-15.

103. GROSS, Bertram M., "Friendly Fascism: A Model for America," **Social Policy**, 1:4, Nov./Dec., 1970, pp. 44-53.   (AB-3)

The stated purpose of this essay is to frighten people and to develop our capacity to fear, for "We need greater capacity to develop articulated fears that match the magnitude of tomorrow's dangers. We must accept the possibility that in this decade our America--despite all we may love or admire in it--may have a rendezvous with fascism." (p. 44, author's emphasis)

Gross attacks the "'Flabby' Futurism" of Bell's Commission on the Year 2000 and of **The Futurist**, as largely insipid escapism. To prepare for possible unpleasantries, Gross proposes a model of "techno-urban fascism," a new form of Lasswell's garrison state: "A managed society ruled by a faceless and widely dispersed complex of warfare-welfare-industrial-communications-police bureaucracies caught up in developing a new-style empire based on a technocratic ideology, a culture of alienation, multiple scapegoats, and competing control networks." (p. 46)

104. RIENCOURT, Amaury de. **The Coming Caesars**. NY: Coward-McCann, 1957. 384 pp.   (A-4)

An historian fears that "Our Western world, America and Europe, is threatened with Caesarism on a scale unknown since the dawn of the Roman empire." Caesarism is defined as voluntary surrender to one autocratic master. No remedy is suggested.

104a. BURNHAM, James. **Suicide of the West: An Essay on the Meaning and Destiny of Liberalism**. NY: John Day, 1964. New Rochelle, NY: Arlington House, 1975 (With a new Afterword by the author). 320 pp. $7.95.   (A-3)

Burnham feels that this book is still "the only full-scale, systematic analysis of modern liberalism (in our American sense) that has ever been made by anyone, liberal or non-liberal." (p. 313) In his Afterword, he finds nothing of importance that needs altering.

The argument is that Western civilization has been shrinking for the past two generations, both in amount of territory and proportion of population ruled. The simple underlying thesis is "that what Americans call 'liberalism' is the ideology of Western suicide." (p. 26) It is not considered as a cause of decline, but more as an expression of it.

Liberalism is seen as the prevailing public doctrine, including "a substantial majority" of those who control or influence public opinion. Among those who exemplify this view, and are criticized in the book, are W.W. Rostow, Roger Baldwin, Robert Hutchins, Norman Cousins, A.J. Muste, Arthur Schlesinger, Jr., Hubert Humphrey, Adlai Stevenson, George Kennan, and Charles Frankel.

Liberalism is seen as 19 primary ideas and beliefs, summarized in a most valuable chart (pp. 125-131), along with a vaguely conservative set of contrasting non-liberal elements. For example, liberals view human nature as changing and plastic, the obstacles to attaining the good society as ignorance and faulty social institutions, reason and science as the sole standard of truth, solutions to every social problem, the ideal government as world government, social hierarchies as evil, and social reform as equalizing conditions.

All ideological thinking is characterized by the inability to refute views by logical analysis or empirical evidence. The liberal is prevented by his ideology from distinguishing, for example, the necessary and integral role of force. Liberalism is not equipped to meet and overcome the challenges confronting Western civilization: the "jungle" spreading in our own society, population growth within the world's "backward areas," and the drive of the communist enterprise for world power.

*** A very narrow but nevertheless useful book that does indeed do a unique and excellent job in describing liberal ideology. But Burnham apparently recognizes no serious alternative view other than the conservatism that he espouses. Liberalism is criticized as being "unmistakably Left of Center" and subject to the beliefs of the radical and revolutionary Left. But there are other views such as decentralism (Chapter 7) and democratic socialism (Chapter 11) that Burnham does not acknowledge. From either of these positions, liberalism would be right of center or dead center.

105. LUKACS, John. **The Passing of the Modern Age.** NY: Harper & Row, 1970. 222 pp.   (A-3)

A sophisticated argument by an historian who sees three great ages: Antiquity, Middle Ages, and the Modern Age. The latter term no longer fits and we are seen as headed toward The New Dark Ages. Although little is said on this next stage, there is much that is offered on the devolution of the Modern Age, with chapters on the monstrosity of government, the separation of races, the purposelessness of society, the fiction of prosperity, the dissolution of learning, the meaninglessness of letters, the destruction of nature, the decay of science, and the mutation of morality. The evolution of human consciousness is not regarded as sufficient to effectively counteract this devolution.

106. HACKER, Andrew. **The End of the American Era.** NY: Atheneum, 1970. 239 pp. $6.50.   (AB-2)

A political scientist's cynical and sobering argument that America is in a time of decline because it is ungovernable, it is saddled with a second America of superfluous people, the quality of knowledge produced in the academic community is declining, Americans are no longer willing or able to be led, and there is little willingness to undergo sacrifices.

107. SCHRAG, Peter. **The End of the American Future.** NY: Simon and Schuster, 1973. 319 pp.   (AB-4)

A rambling, journalistic tour of politics and life in America. Chapter 6, "The Demise of the Mad Scientist," swings wildly at a number of futurists such as Toffler, Bell, Helmer, Fuller, and Skinner, and scores a few hits.

108. GOODWIN, Richard N. **The American Condition.** NY: Doubleday, March, 1974; Bantam Books, Oct. 1975. 436 pp. $2.95, paper.   (A-3)

A deep and murky essay by the former speechwriter and adviser to Presidents Kennedy and Johnson, concerning "the human and material circumstances responsible for the condition of life in modern America." (p. ix) The general themes of freedom and alienation (which obstructs freedom) are found throughout the book. Goodwin examines the dissolution of community and fragmentation of society, the bureaucratic institutions of the economy and the political process which sustain the dominant sources of political power, and the mechanism and techniques of institutional control over social existence. In sum, "...modern man is engaged in an unprecedented project of self-destruction." (p. 410)

Skepticism is expressed about solutions such as participation, social responsibility of corporations, environmental and consumer movements, humanizing labor, science, and self-realization efforts.

"If some find this work cheerless it is only because analysis unveils the unprecedented magnitude of the coercive power which confronts assertions of the awareness of human possibilities which, although suppressed, are fixed attributes of human existence. Cheerlessness, therefore, is not a conclusion but a preparation. To be cheerful is to accept, and one who accepts is forever without hope." (p. 421)

*** Similar to the writing of Mumford (and equally ponderous and Olympian), as well as to that of Ellul and Roszak. Difficult, but challenging.

109. CORSON, William R. **Consequences of Failure.** NY: Norton, 1974. 215 pp. $7.95.   (A-4)

A unique attempt to look at the outcome of the Vietnam War: "the pattern and inner meaning of the phenomenon of military failure and its present and future effects on the United States, its institutions, and its people." (p.9) "The unpleasantness and pain that failure causes may account for its neglect as a subject of investigation..." (p. 16) To support this view and find implications for America, Corson utilizes three case studies: the Roman Empire, the Spanish involvement in the Netherlands during the sixteenth century, and the British failure in the American revolution.

Both the direct and indirect consequences have yet to be fully felt. Some of them are: our social and institutional structures in serious disarray, a lack of confidence in our leaders, and widespread dissatisfaction. "The necessary first step to overcome failure is to at least acknowledge the fact that we have failed." (p. 150)

Three possible outcomes are viewed in their global terms. The gloomiest and most likely is one of regression, apathy, and isolationism while raiding other countries for national resources. A second possibility is one of a Fortress America, able to deal with its own domestic problems, but not willing to make sacrifices for the rest of the world. The most unlikely prospect is continuing America's world leadership, joining in a cooperative effort "to bring about a sustained balance of worldwide resource utilization, food production, and population." (p. 160)

To deal with the demoralized military, Corson recommends the use of military forces in a domestic civic action role to help solve current social problems, as well as more attention devoted to the veterans of Vietnam.

*** A thoughtful essay on an important concern, but clearly too narrow. No effort is made to consider the Vietnam failure as a symptom of a larger failure of industrial society, or to consider the widespread despair as related to anything but failure in Vietnam.

110. LORENZ, Konrad, **Civilized Man's Eight Deadly Sins.** Trans. by
     Marjorie Kerr Wilson. NY: Harcourt Brace Jovanovich, 1974.
     107 pp. (First published in Germany in 1973)   (A-3)

An ethologist's consciously pessimistic essay on overpopulation, devastation of the natural environment, the ever-increasing pace of technology,
overindulgence leading to a waning of strong feeling and emotion, genetic
decay, the break in tradition, the increased indoctrinability of mankind,
and nuclear weaponry.
No solutions are proposed, although Lorenz hopes that the dangers might
lose their terror once their causes are understood.

111. HEILBRONER, Robert L. **An Inquiry Into the Human Prospect.** NY:
     Norton, 1974. 150 pp. $5.95. (Slightly different version published
     as "The Human Prospect" in **The New York Review of Books,**
     20:21-22, Jan. 24, 1974, pp. 21-34.)   (A-3)

A bleak essay by a prominent thinker expressing little hope that social problems can be solved due to runaway population, the prospects of
obliterative war (particularly resulting from blackmail by underdeveloped
countries), and the collapse of the environment.
The central challenge is the inescapable need to limit industrial growth.
The long-term solution "requires nothing less than the abandonment of
the lethal techniques, the uncongenial lifeways, and the dangerous mentality
of industrial civilization itself." (p. 138) This involves "a 'post-industrial
society of parsimonious attitudes to production and consumption, that turns
in the direction of many pre-industrial societies toward exploration of
inner states of experience and concern for more tradition and ritual.
Unlike most writers, Heilbroner focuses on the limitations and difficulties of our capacities for response and warns of building an architecture
of hope on false beliefs, with chapters on Socio-Economic Capabilities
for Response and The Political Dimension and 'Human Nature.' Myopia
is not likely to disappear quickly, and the outlook is for "convulsive
change" forced upon us by external events.
    "...candor compels me to suggest that the passage through the gantlet
ahead may be possible only under governments capable of rallying obedience far more effectively than would be possible in a democratic setting.
If the issue for mankind is survival, such governments may be unavoidable,
even necessary." (p. 110)
*** This essay received considerable attention, particularly for the unpleasant notion cited above.

111a. HEILBRONER, Robert L. **The Future as History: The Historic Cur-
      rents of Our Time and the Direction in Which They Are Taking
      America.** NY: Harper & Bros., 1960. 217 pp.   (AB-3)

Examines our state of mind about the future, arguing that in the past we
have had the sustaining beliefs of optimism, but that this idea of progress
"has become a dangerous national delusion." (p. 178)
Optimism is inadequate because of new changes such as weapons technology, and rampant development of science and technology. It is probable
that the trend of events "will persist in directions which we find inimical
and uncongenial." (p. 178) It is concluded that we should not succumb to
false hopes or false despair: "seeing the future as part of the sweep of history, enables us to establish our place in that immense procession in which
is incorporated whatever hope humankind may have." (p. 209)

112. VACCA, Roberto. **The Coming Dark Age.** Trans. by J.S. Whale. Garden City, NY: Doubleday, 1973. 221 pp. $6.95. (First published in Italy in 1971)   (AB-3)

A very convincing argument by an Italian systems expert that our large systems will get out of control and collapse. This is most likely to happen first in the U.S. because of our great faith in technology. A Polish or Italian manager who computerizes an administrative system does not really believe that the new system will work, and he therefore preserves former antiquated systems that worked by hand. "The American manager, who tends to have greater confidence--it is sometimes limitless--in the new and indubitably advanced systems that he intends to use, is often left without reserves and may find himself in a very grave emergency, without any system at all." (p. 171)

Chapters discuss topics such as urban congestion, water and waste, a scenario of the death of New York City, social life after the Knockout, and monastic communities in the new medieval epoch. "In the imminent dark age people will endure hardship, and for the greater part of their time they will be laboring to satisfy primitive needs." (p. 212)

The few hopes that we have in making an effective stand against the breakdown of the great systems include: denouncing flagrant incompetence, more criticism of the work of scientists and professionals, and new standards or moral judgment and professional conscience.

112a. HERZOG, Arthur, "Previews of Coming Disasters: The 10 Most Likely Real Life Catastrophes," **The Village Voice,** January 20, 1975, pp. 5-8.   (ABC-3)

The author of **The Swarm** (which will soon be made into an Irwin Allen disaster movie) provides a fascinating inventory of possible disasters, each with an assessment of probability, possible magnitude, and timetable:
- Weather warfare (uncertain probability, possible elimination of mankind)
- Inadvertent Climate Modification (Cold): (quite probable, hundreds of millions dead)
- Inadvertent Climate Modification (Heat): (fair to good probability, with many dead or elimination of mankind)
- Destruction of the Ozone Shield (uncertain, but could eliminate all life)
- Peacetime Nuclear Calamity (uncertain, but could eliminate higher forms of life)
- New Killer Virus (remote probability)
- Calamitous Earthquakes (100% certain)
- Catastrophic Hurricanes (100% certain, with up to a million deaths)
- Massive Famine (virtually certain, with 50 million deaths per year)
- Steady-State Anarchy (a good probability for a return to barbarism on a universal scale)

The survey is concluded by the complaint that we don't take the future seriously: "we do not prepare for the storm because we would have to change our habits, our goals. And that is too hard and painful. We know we should change and so, we are frightened. For unlike catastrophes of the past, the new ones demand foresight and preparation." (p. 8)

*** Each of these forecasts were checked with reputable scientists; in effect this is an informal "Delphi" exercise asking some important questions that are generally neglected.

112b. "Nuclear War by 1999?" **The Washington Post Outlook,** Sunday, January 4, 1976, pp. F1 and F4.   (ABC-3)

The edited transcription of remarks by five experts at a recent Cambridge Forum panel discussion. The participants, all faculty members of the Harvard-MIT Arms Control Seminar, were Paul Doty, Richard Garwin, George Kistiakowsky, George Rathjens and Thomas Schelling.

The general consensus was that nuclear war in some form is likely before the end of this century, probably occurring as a result of the proliferation of nuclear powers and weaponry. Existing political systems have been ineffective in providing curbs to this weaponry. To survive, nations may have to surrender much of their sovereignity. But nuclear war is a more likely prospect.

As warned by Paul Doty: "We now have a period of relative public confidence that nuclear war is not imminent. This complacency can itself be a danger...we are apt to lose the vision of how absolutely catastrophic nuclear war is. But that vision is something that must not escape us." (p. F1)

112c. EPSTEIN, William. **The Last Chance.** NY: The Free Press, 1976.
260 pp. $14.95.   (ns)

The Secretary of the U.N. Disarmament Commission "examines the dangerous escalation of nuclear arms by the nuclear powers, the likely spread of such weapons to the non-nuclear powers, and their possible acquisition by criminal or terrorist groups. This book...is also a powerful plea for making use of what may be humanity's last chance to stop a nuclear disaster." (advt.)

113. PAWLEY, Martin. **The Private Future: Causes and Consequences of Community Collapse in the West.** NY: Random House, 1974. 217 pp.   (AB-3)

A British architect describes the pattern of community in the Western world as the private dwelling and the private car. Aided by a technology of socially atomizing appliances, Western society is seen to be "on the brink of collapse" as a result of this withdrawal from "the whole system of values and obligations that have historically been the basis of public, community, and family life." (p. 8)

Beyond this public withdrawal, there is a pattern of private withdrawal, very much dependent on the media, which Pawley terms "secondary reality--a kind of willful self-deception about the nature of events which is adapted as a survival strategy at all levels of society..."

It is dismally concluded that "The process of privitization is irreversible in the present circumstances of the Western world, and the allegiance of its peoples to the dreams so indiscriminately displayed within it will survive any effort at reversal short of total destruction." (p. 210)

114. HENDIN, Herbert. **The Age of Sensation.** NY: Norton, 1975. 354 pp.
$9.95.   (AB-3)

A psychoanalytic study of several hundred college students at Columbia by the Director of Psychosocial Studies at the Center for Policy Research. Both patients and non-patients were studied, in order to "get at the texture of emotional life in America through the psychodynamic study of actual lives." (p. xiv)

The final chapter is packed with dismal conclusions. "Sensation is king in a nation in which it seems the best antidote to pleasurelessness and deadness...the cultural trend is toward greater and greater stimulation of appetites...the most rapacious greed is for experience." (p. 325) Hendin also notes a preference for the meaningless and disconnected sensory episode, violent and combative competition that arouses guilt, the politicization of feeling, random and indiscriminate use of drugs, institutionalized contempt for love and tenderness, and the coincidence of social distress and private unhappiness. "Increasingly what unites people in this culture is a sense of shared misfortune and depression, a feeling of impotence in the face of forces they feel they cannot shape or control." (p. 334)

The concluding paragraph suggests that "If our physical environment is worth saving, our emotional environment is equally so, perhaps more so since the one provides us with means to sustain life and the other is our humanity: the one offers the necessities of survival, the other a life worth living...the most endangered of our vital resources is people." (p. 340)

114a. SOKOLOFF, Boris, M.D. **The Permissive Society.** New Rochelle, NY: Arlington House, 1971. 254 pp. $8.95.   (C-5)

Extreme permissiveness has engulfed a large part of America, and this is applauded and promoted by liberal intellectuals. Sokoloff describes his perspective as a biological point of view, and describes the link between the Freudian ethic and American liberalism. Chapters on crime, narcotics, sex, revolution, and liberal intellectuals.
*** A superficial right-wing polemic.

115. HOUGAN, Jim. **Decadence: Radical Nostalgia, Narcissism, and Decline in the Seventies.** NY: Morrow, 1975. 251 pp. $7.95.   (AB-3)

Free-swinging cultural analysis by a Contributing Editor of **Harper's** and "apostate freak" who argues that our situation is incurable.

"The society seems bent upon a most rapid decline, devolving toward a fascist metastate, an antiutopia of technocratic barbarism." (p. 158) Decadence is the general response to cultural decline, the interval between decline and fall. A defense of decadence is a defense of the American dream, and Madison Avenue is the machinery of our decadence.

Hougan deals with themes such as millenarian preconditions, the unraveling of America, America Flambé, emerging elitist enclaves each with its own scapegoat, Alvin Toffler ("Pimping for Progress"), problems of technology assessment (narrowness of assessors, quantitative bias, and concerned with specific innovations rather than the whole technological phenomenon--which is the greatest cause of our collective anxiety), and the **Whole Earth Catalog** ("the Last Will and Testament of the counterculture"). Considerable attention is paid to analyzing the myth of the counterculture, including an intriguing table of transitions (p. 139) through three phases: from mysticism to magic to tools.

It is asserted that this "is not a pessimistic book," (p. 8) but a relief. Indeed, it is concluded that "Reconciling oneself to the mortality of the times, moving beyond movements, is an act of private liberation that withdraws obstacles from the path of history. Letting the society strangle on its own dilemmas, rather than nagging it at attempts at its preservation in modified form, is a revolutionary path in that the society is severed from its roots, its sources or renewal." (p. 234)
*** The proportion of fresh and bold insight relative to that of repetitious and nihilistic overstatement will very much depend on one's tastes. In any event, this is the most extensive analysis to date on what has happened to the counterculture.

116. JOAD, C.E.M. **Decadence: A Philosophical Inquiry.** London: Faber and Faber, 1948. 430 pp.   (A-3)

Decadence is defined as "a sign of man's tendency to misread his position in the universe, to take a view of his status and prospects more exalted than the facts warrant and to conduct his societies and to plan his future on the basis of his mis-reading." (p. 15)

There are periods of material prosperity and technical advance known as progress, and the aftermath of such periods is decadence. In such periods the workings of the moral machinery is revealed. The seeds of decadence are sown in the periods of human success and arrogance, where man provokes the anger of the gods, as the Greeks might have put it. The book is divided into two parts. The first is devoted to General Principles, essentially an exercise in pure philosophy. The second part concerns applications, or the consideration of decadence in our time. Chapters in this part cover topics such as the culture of the many, literature, politics (with comments on socialism and planning) and specialization and decadence. Centralized states are decadent, and specialization is seen as the product of centralization. In contrast, small communities are favorable to original art and thought. To be human is, essentially, to be a non-specialized creature.

The final chapter speculates on the prospects of a decadent society, viewing the distinctive characterization of our civilization as the contrast between man's wisdom and his power. Our generation has shown a peculiar neglect of the traditional ends of human aspiration and endeavor: truth, goodness, beauty and their derivatives. These ends fill the role of the object, and "the dropping of the object" is one of the distinctive characteristics of decadent civilizations.

Joad considers the possibility of destruction, the advance of humanity towards insecthood (the ultimate expression of the dropping of the object), and movements of withdrawal. "Speculation, at all times hazardous, is particularly so at a time like the present which wears the appearance of an interim age, an age in exile between two worlds, the one dead, the other trying, yet failing to be born." (p. 421) Such interim ages are a further example of decadence.

However, "Humility and history combine, then, to teach me that what I have prophesied here will almost certainly not come to pass." (p. 421) *** Very eloquent, with considerable insight applicable to our times.

117. FRIEDENBERG, Edgar Z. **The Disposal of Liberty and Other Industrial Wastes.** Garden City, NY: Doubleday, 1975. 196 pp.   (A-4)

Gloomy and rambling essays on the mean-spiritedness of democratic life, with particular emphasis on the phenomenon of ressentiment: "a free-floating disposition to visit upon others the bitterness that accumulates from one's own subordination..." (p. xi) It is even meaner than jealousy and envy: "it envisions no satisfaction, but seeks merely to deny satisfaction to others." (p. 72)

Having despoiled the image of man, Friedenberg also has some dismal reflections on the nature of services, viewing many "clients" as conscript clienteles, who are not free to withdraw or look elsewhere for service as concerns goods, the consumer choices offered by the mass market are not real choices.

In the final chapter, the possibility is raised of a world governed by multinational corporations. "Democracy is not an alternative to fascism, but a stage in its development, an earlier form of populism." (p. 182) Men get the kind of government they can imagine: "Government cannot transcend their hopes and values, or safeguard what they do not cherish." (p. 184)

118. ROSZAK, Theodore. **Pontifex: A Revolutionary Entertainment for the Mind's Eye Theater.** Garden City, NY: Doubleday Anchor, 1974. 204 pp.   (AB-3)

A provocative, earthy, and witty play by the author of **The Making of a Counterculture** and **Where the Wasteland Ends.** Offers sardonic comments on various views of revolution as promulgated by the International Democratic Revolutionary Workers and Peasants Party of the World (IDRWPPW), the Badass Brigade, assorted feminists, and those who favor an organic commonwealth. As the society falls apart in an animalistic frenzy, efforts are made to restore law and order by Fairchild De Cream, drug dealer to the world, and his assistant, Professor Jerome Halbafter, originator of TEN PIN (Total Electroneuronic Programed Invigoration)--the ultimate freakout and source of world control. They stand behind General Thrasymachus ("Bull") Pizzle, a modern Renaissance man.

Meanwhile, the gentle protagonist, the artist, Adam, seeks out his mentor, the mystical Pontifex, who is falsely accused of instigating "the universal jail break" that engulfs them.
*** And what does this all mean? It is simply Roszak in another dimension, and quite possibly a very original slant on where we are.

119. JUNGK, Robert. **Tomorrow Is Already Here.** NY: Simon & Schuster, 1954. 241 pp.   (C-4)

A journalistic tour of weaponry, atomic energy, agriculture, skyscrapers, industrial psychology, the chemical industry and numerous other "features of a totalitarian nature" that make up "the newest world"--all that is uniform, standardized, and inhuman in its exclusive striving toward efficiency. The tendency away from freedom is seen as arising from a constant striving to open up new domains, a reaching for omnipotence. And "the shriller the happiness propaganda becomes...the more disturbing grow the doubts." (p. 11)
*** Lacks any summary comments.

120. BEX Brian L. **The Decline and Fall of the American Republic.** NY: Vantage Press, 1973. $4.95.   (ns)

"...evaluation and comparison of the U.S. and ancient Rome, showing the glories and corruption." (advt.)

121. THROOP, Montgomery. **The Future: A Political Essay.** NY: James G. Gregory, 1864, 343 pp.   (A-4)

An essay prompted by a bleak image of the nation "rushing onward toward an abyss, at the bottom of which lie national destruction and individual ruin." (p. 343)
"And I have been led at every step of my labors...to feel acutely how fearful and uncertain is the mysterious future which I have endeavored to explore, and how blindly we are all groping in the dark." (p. 343) The only advocacy that Throop offers is a trust in a Kind Providence.
*** A reminder that utter despair is nothing new.

122. BEICHMAN, Arnold. **Nine Lies About America.** NY: Library Press, 1972; Pocket Books (Revised and expanded edition, with a Foreword by Tom Wolfe), 1973. 320 pp. $1.25, paper.   (AB-3)

As described by Wolfe in the Foreword, this book explores "the modern intellectual's retrograde habits of mind." Major targets include Herbert Marcuse, Andrew Hacker, Philip Slater, Bertram Gross, Robert Heilbroner, Susan Sontag, Robert Paul Wolff, Charles Reich, and Louis Kampf. The nine lies are: America is a Fascist Country, America Means Genocide, The Bomber Left is a Moral Force, The American Worker Is a 'Honky,' American Values Are Materialistic, America is Insane, The American People Are Guilty, and America Needs a Violent Revolution.
*** Scores some points on the excesses of some writers, but also may be selecting certain topical trees from a broader forest of concern. In any event, this book is superior to Hicken (below).

123. HICKEN, Victor. **The World is Coming to an End! An Irreverent Look at Modern Doomsayers.** New Rochelle, NY: Arlington House, 1975. 223 pp. $7.95.   (A-5)

A history professor at Western Illinois University attacks campus radicals, the underground press, and the liberal establishment media. "The 1960s...was a decade of overblown rhetoric, of paranoia, of occasional doomsaying, and of maudlin sentimentality, especially on the radical left. Fortunately the great mass of the country held firm..." (p. 39)

Several pages are devoted to ecological activists, but there is no mention of the Club of Rome, and Commoner and Ehrlich are mentioned only in passing. "The truth was that by 1973 a great deal had been done to make the quality of life a little better in many places. There was actually more fresh water than ever before in history--one could see this from any low-flying plane." (p. 187)

*** Documents a great amount of inflated political rhetoric as found in newspapers, but does not deal with the more extensive world's end arguments. This book is clearly mistitled.

Chapter 4

The Cosmic Evolutionary View: High Minded Expectations

There is an alternative mode of viewing societal directions that is entirely separate from the literature of The Technological, Affluent, Service Society (Chapter 2) and its enthusiastic supporters and gloomy critics (Chapter 3).

The cosmic evolutionary view is largely held by those persons with a background in philosophy or psychology. The view is cosmic in the sense of being very broad in time and space, and "evolution" is frequently employed to describe developmental schemes of man, technology, and/or society. The view is invariably optimistic--that mankind is progressing to a more appropriate and desirable stage--and description is frequently confused with what is obviously prescription, the best-known example being Reich's assertions about evolving to Consciousness III (150).

A few of the cosmic evolutionary views are linear, such as Acland (154) and Ribeiro (155). Some suggest a profound disjunction, such as Leonard (141) and Salk (149). And others clearly employ a cyclical scheme: Aurobindo (125), Davy (131), Glasser (143), and Thompson (151). Rudhyar sees us in the midst of three cycles (140).

The chapter begins with Sri Aurobindo and Teilhard de Chardin (124-129), two major thinkers from East and West, and a modern Eastern thinker, Gopi Krishna (130). In an excellent but obscure work, Charles Davy suggests the path toward a Third Culture (131). Willis Harman and colleagues at the Stanford Research Institute proclaim The New Copernican Revolution and The Third American Frontier (135-137). Korzybski (147) and Salk (149) point toward necessary ideals for survival. Acland (154) and Ribiero (155) see socialism as the highest stage of evolution, similar to Organski (64).

New stages of technology are seen by some as necessitating new societies. Ribiero (155) views changes resulting from the thermonuclear revolution, while Polakov (156) and Nearing (157) both use the concept of the Power Age. Electronics and cybernation were popular metaphors of the 1960s, resulting in McLuhan's Electric Age (158), the Age of Cybernetics (160), the Cyber-cultural Era (161), and the Paleocybernetic Age (162).

The cosmic evolutionary view can generally be faulted for an excess of idealism and a lack of empiricism. But it is this very idealism which is lacking from the generally neutral descriptions of the Technological, Affluent, Service Society. Ultimately, in the spirit of Davy (131) and Korzybski (147), these two attributes might be productively joined.

124. GHOSE, Aurobindo (Sri Aurobindo). **The Future Evolution of Man: The Divine Life Upon Earth.** Compiled with a summary and notes by P.B. Saint-Hilaire. Pondicherry, India: Sri Aurobindo Ashram, 1963. Quest Books edition (306 W. Geneva Rd., Wheaton, Ill.), 1974. $2.25, paper. (A-3)

Views the present evolutionary crisis as a disparity between the limited faculties of man and the technical and economic means at his disposal. "Without an inner change man can no longer cope with the gigantic development of the outer life." (p.52)

The necessary transition is from mind to Supermind--a passage from Nature into Supernature--and four steps of this ascent are described.

125. GHOSE, Aurobindo (Sri Aurobindo). **The Human Cycle.** Pondicherry, India: Sri Aurobindo Ashram, 1949. 334 pp. (Originally written in the 1916-1918 period)   (A-2)

Views a transition from The Age of Individualism and Reason (Chapter II) to The Subjective Age (Chapter III). Also describes The Curve of the Rational Age (Chapter XIX) and The End of the Curve of Reason (Chapter XX), in contrast to the final chapter, The Advent and Progress of the Spiritual Age, describing a change from the mental and vital to the spiritual order of life.

*** This remarkable essay is eloquent and elevating, offering much of value in understanding our present condition and the non-linear alternative in viewing the course of human affairs.

126. TEILHARD de CHARDIN, Pierre. **Man's Place in Nature: The Human Zoological Group.** Trans. by Rene Hague. NY: Harper & Row, 1966. 124 pp. (Written in 1949 and first published in France in 1956) (A-3)

Each of the five provocative chapters represents five stages: "five phases selected to cover and picture the great spectacle of Anthropogenesis"-- A Self-Involuting World, The Development of the Biosphere, The Appearance of Man (or the "Threshold of Reflection"), The Formation of the Noosphere: A) The Expansion Phase: Civilization and Individuation, and The Formation of the Noosphere: B) The Compression Phase: Totalisation and Personalisation.

"(Man) is more than a branch, more even than a kingdom; he is nothing less than a 'sphere'--the noosphere (or thinking sphere) superimposed upon, and coextensive with (but in so many ways more close-knit and homogeneous) the biosphere." (p.80) The noosphere is "the final and supreme product in man of the forces of social ties," an irrepressible process of unification whose mechanism is governed by three well-marked periods: ethnic compression, economico-technical organization, and simultaneous increase of consciousness, science and radius of activity.

127. TEILHARD de CHARDIN, Pierre. **The Phenomenon of Man.** With an Introduction by Sir Julian Huxley. NY: Harper, 1959. 318 pp. (First published in France in 1955)   (A-3)

The four sections include Before Life Came, Life, Thought, and Survival, and chapters deal with topics such as The Expansion of Life, The Deployment of the Noosphere, The Modern Earth, and The Ultimate Earth.

*** Considered by Huxley to be the most important of Teilhard's works.

128. TEILHARD de CHARDIN, Pierre. **The Future of Man.** Harper & Row, 1964. (First published in France in 1959)   (A-3)

Chapters such as The Planetization of Mankind, The Formation of the Noosphere, On the Probable Coming of an Ultra-Humanity, and From the Pre-Human to the Ultra-Human: The Phases of a Living Planet.

129. KING, Ursala, ''Sri Aurobindo's and Teilhard's Vision of the Future of Man,'' **The Teilhard Review**, IX:1, Feb. 1974, pp. 2-5.   (A-3)

A useful contrast, which should be expanded manyfold to encompass all of the societal stage theories suggested here.

130. KRISHNA, Gopi, "Beyond the Higher States of Consciousness," **The New York Times** (Op. Ed. page), Oct. 6, 1973.   (AB-3)

The distortion of the human intellect is seen as responsible for the present unsafe condition of the world, and only a cosmic intelligence can guide human life to the destined goal. "Can even a whole galaxy of the highest intellects, in every branch of knowledge, make an accurate forecast of what would be the state of mankind after the span of only the next quarter of a century?"

Science has erred by entirely ignoring the spiritual side of man; it suffers from dogmatism, vanity, and arrogance. To bring about a harmonious development of human beings, a scientific investigation into consciousness is needed. From this, a new science will emerge, "dealing with subtle intelligent energies in the cosmos." And the right pattern of life can then be seen: a united world, harmony with nature, a life more natural and simple, and social equality.

"This may appear idealistic or even fantastic and impracticable to many people. But the conclusion is unavoidable. At its present intellectual stature, the alternatives facing the race are either self-caused annihilation with dreadful agony for myriads, or knowledge of and obedience to the laws of evolving consciousness."

131. DAVY, Charles. **Towards a Third Culture**. London: Faber and Faber, 1961. 178 pp.   (AB-2)

An eloquent essay on the evolution of consciousness, written in response to C.P. Snow's 1959 "Two Cultures" lecture. The argument is similar to that made by Theodore Roszak in **Where the Wasteland Ends**, but without the polemical style.

It is hoped that at some future time a third culture would emerge, "carrying genes from both parents but with distinctive virtues of its own." (p.90) This culture would be the successor and not the antithesis to the scientific culture. It would retain the virtues of the scientific outlook--disciplined thinking, respect for facts, testing by experiment--but it will use them differently. At the same time it will also be a religion and an artistic culture. "These three elements, essential for any fully human society, were united once; it was inevitable that they should diverge if each was to develop in freedom, but in the future it is necessary that they come together again as members of an organically differentiated whole." (p. 93)

We are presently seen as in the "onlooker age," while the next stage is called the "new imagination." The way towards this stage "will not lie through what is usually meant by psychic development, whereby a deliberate effort is made to cultivate psychic faculties, such as clairvoyance or mediumship, for their own sake." (p.115)

Davy concludes with a brief and poetic non-linear stage theory likening the history of man to the seasons. Summer comes first, when man and nature were one. Evolution proceeded to autumn, when the "skies of consciousness darkened." We are now in winter, "but the imagination of man has power to quicken the dry earth and bring in a new season." (p.173)

132. WHYTE, Lancelot Law. **The Next Development in Man**. NY: Henry Holt & Co., 1948; NAL Mentor Books, 1950.   (A-3)

The message is still of prime importance: "...if civilization is not to decline during the coming decades, it can only be through the development of a universal method of thought providing the basis for a unified humane science and for a world society." (p.vii) Unitary man, the universal type appearing in the middle of the 20th century, evolves from dissociated man and is marked by his conviction of a universal formative process.

133. ROSZAK, Theodore. Unfinished Animal: The Aquarian Frontier and the Evolution of Consciousness. NY: Harper & Row, Dec. 1975. $10.00
(ns)
"...discovers an evolutionary possibility in today's society as important as the appearance of speech or the first crafting of tools." (advt.)

134. WOLFE, Tom, "Three Merry Obsessions: Crime, Sex, Salvation," Esquire, Dec. 1973, pp. 137, 169, and 201ff.   (B-4)

Three separate essays serving as introductions to other essays. Only the final essay on "Salvation" is of concern here.
Wolfe views three Great Awakenings. The First Great Awakening came in the 1740s, helping to pave the way for the American Revolution. The Second Great Awakening came in the 1825-1850 period. Both of these movements developed during boom times that seemed materialistic, cynical, and godless.
The Third Great Awakening began at the height of the boom of the sixties, with LSD and the hippie movement, spreading to communes, encounter groups, Primal Therapy, Jesus People, Hare Krishna, Synanon, Scientology, and Maharaj Ji. "I would...predict that in the long run historians will regard the entire New Left experience with its translations of the psychedelic life (communes and all) into a political setting, as an episode in The Third Great Awakening. The Awakening began among the young but has rolled outward, giving tremendous momentum to Fundamentalists, theosophists, and other older savation seekers of all sorts." (p.310)

135. HARMAN, Willis W., "The New Copernican Revolution," Stanford Today, Winter 1969. Reprinted in **J. of Transpersonal Psychology,** 1:2 (1969).
(AB-3)
"Much evidence suggests that a group of questions relating to the commonality of and interpretation of man's subjective experience, expecially of the 'transcendental,' and hence to the bases of human values, are shifting from the realm of the 'philosophical' to the 'empirical.' If so, the consequences may be even more far-reaching than those which emerged from the Copernican, Darwinian, and Freudian revolutions."
Harman goes on to suggest some of the elements of the new science of subjective experience, which contains "significant precursors of tomorrow's image of man's potentialities." There will be a relaxing of the subjective-objective dichotomy, a renewed sensitivity to cultural bias, an accounting for the subjective experiencing of a higher self, a more unified view of human experiences and of the processes of personal change and emergence.
"It is not a question of which view is 'true' in some ultimate sense. Rather, it is a matter of which picture is more useful in guiding human affairs. Among the possible images that are reasonably in accord with accumulated human experience, since the image held is that most likely to come into being, it is prudent to choose the noblest."

136. MARKLEY, O.W. et. al., Changing Images of Man. Prepared for the Charles F. Kettering Foundation. Menlo Park, Calif.: Stanford Research Institute, Center for the Study of Social Policy, Policy Research Report 3, Oct. 1973. 347 pp.   (A-3)

A most provocative although at times innocent volume prepared by Markley and Joseph Campbell, Duane Elgin, Willis Harman, Arthur Hastings, Floyd Matson, Brendan O'Regan, and Leslie Schneider. Extra dimensions are added in appendices by Elise Boulding, Sir Geoffrey Vickers, Henry Margenau, Magoroh Maruyama, Brendan O'Regan, René Dubos, and David Cahoon. Further dimensions and criticisms are added in extensive footnotes to the text by Edgar Dunn, James Fadiman, Roland Fischer, Luther Gerlach, Charles Hampden-Turner, Stanley Krippner, Ervin Laszlo, George C. Lodge, Michael Marien, Ralph Metzner, Margaret Mead, Carl Rogers, B.F. Skinner, Robert A. Smith

III, Anthony F.C. Wallace, and John White.

Chapters are devoted to discussing images of man in a changing society, some formative images of man-in-the-universe (from antiquity to the renaissance to the industrial era), economic man, scientific influences on the image of man (including a brief review of contemporary consciousness research), the characteristics of an adequate image of humankind (entailing an ecological ethic, a self-realization ethic, multi-faceted and integrative, a holistic sense of perspective), and the processes and strategies for promoting this "evolutionary transformationalist" image in contrast to the technological extrapolationist image that we presently have.

*** The naive optimism that pervades this volume, in many instances to its detriment, is offset by its challenging integrations. The images of man promulgated here may never be widely held, but, increasingly, there is both scientific evidence and human justification for doing so. The volume is quite worthwhile as important knowledge-in-process.

137. ELGIN, Duane. "The Third American Frontier: The Evolution of Consciousness and Transformation of Society." Menlo Park, Calif.: Stanford Research Institute, Center for the Study of Social Policy, March 1975 (revised, Dec. 1975). 16 pp., mimeo.   (AB-4)

Argues that the first frontier was the open land of the West, with the challenge of settling a rich but harsh environment. The second frontier of exploiting the environment through industry and technology is now closing. The third frontier of individual and social change is now opening. "It is the frontier of the person exploring, in community with others, the next stage of the human possibility." (p.3) If we are to achieve the transition into this frontier, two closely-related ethics must emerge: a Self-Realization Ethic and an Ecological Ethic. The development of these human possibilities could lead to the reduction of physical and mental illness, improved decision-making, increased creativity, and improved education. But Elgin cautions, in conclusion, that he is "not overly optimistic that this frontier will be realized."

138. FRANCOEUR, Robert. **Evolving World, Converging Man.** NY: Holt, Rinehart and Winston, 1970. 222 pp. $5.95.   (B-4)

"This book traces the often startling and revolutionary interplay between our ever-deepening scientific image of the world and our emerging religious-philosophic image of man." (p.x) Offers some details of a new process view of man along the lines of Teilhard de Chardin's evolutionary monism.

139. HANNA, Thomas. **Bodies in Revolt: A Primer in Somatic Thinking.** NY: Holt, Rinehart and Winston, 1970. 308 pp. $6.95.   (AB-4)

A "guide for the perplexed" offered by a "happy existentialist" who is Chairman of the University of Florida Philosophy Department. The sub-title on the cover page (listed above) differs from the more lengthy one of the book jacket: "The Evolution-Revolution of 20th Century Man toward the Somatic Culture of the 21st Century."

A far greater distraction, however, is the premise on which the argument that we are in a watershed of human evolution is based: "The key to understanding this evolutionary event is that we have successfully constructed a technological society." (p. 16) Other silly assertions follow, such as the statement that men have now guaranteed their survival and thus there is no longer a need for repression--an enthusiasm that might have been accepted by some at the turn of the decade but not in the 1970's.

If this premise is set aside, the basic theme may still have some contribution to make to long-range thinking. It is argued that we are at the end of the first culture of humankind and at the beginning of a second. We are moving from cultural traditionalists and their fear-aggression drives to somatic philosophy and sensual accommodative drives. The prime question of this century is thus one of being, and the new consciousness of our bodily being. The generation gap is described as a conflict between traditional and mutant culture. Much of the book is devoted to reinterpreting major thinkers: the Somatic Philosophers (Kant, Kierkegaard, Marx, Cassirer, Camus, and Nietzsche), and the Somatic Scientists (Darwin, Freud, Lorenz, Piaget, and Wilhelm Reich).

Much like Charles Reich's attack on Consciousness II, Hanna asserts that traditional culture is dead. "Surrendering to one's own somatic being and learning the patterns of its imperatives is the educational task as of this moment. The immediate achievement of optimally adaptive human beings is the only meaningful task before men in a technological society--any other tasks are not genuine and without issue. This is what the evolution-revolution is all about, and this is where the action is, as the proto-mutants resolutely or militantly challenge the rules of our society in favor of what must come." (p.299)

140. RUDHYAR, Dane. **Occult Preparations for a New Age.** Wheaton, Ill.: Theosophical Publishing House, Quest Books edition, March 1975. 275 pp. $3.25, paper.   (A-4)

The reader is rightly cautioned that "The study of cycles is very complex and elusive," (p.115) although one might find Rudhyar making it even more so. Apparently, there are three cycles operating at this time: a great cycle for the procession of the equinoxes (100 B.C. through 2060 A.D.), a new 500-year cycle which began in 1891-1892 under the rulership of Pluto, and four 25-year seasons within each century. This, and more, is explained in chapters such as Time and the Cyclic Structure of Cosmic Processes, Human Cycles of Unfoldment, and Planetary and Social Cycles.

In a chapter on Repotentialization and the Virgin State, Rudhyar writes that "An entire society may be characterized by whether it emphasizes the mother aspect of women, rather than the Virgin of Light." The Mother represents the present stage of evolution, geared to what has been. The virginal state is oriented toward the future and "refers to a state of being in which the natural condition of productivity for exclusivistic goals implying possessiveness is transcended." (p.207) We can rise beyond compulsive living and "awaken in us the Virgin-potency..." (p.212)

141. LEONARD, George. **The Transformation: A Guide to the Inevitable Changes in Humankind.** NY: Delacorte, 1972. 258 pp.   (BC-4)

We are at civilization's end and the dawn of transformation. Our current period is unique in history: "the beginning of the most thoroughgoing change in the quality of human existence since the creation of an agricultural surplus brought about the birth of civilized states..." (p.2) The Transformation is neither utopian nor millenarian, but it does involve changes in human feeling, perceiving, and being. "Most of our current troubles from free-floating anxiety to the breakdown of craftsmanship, can be traced ultimately to the lack of a vivid unifying principle or belief system." (p.3)

Reasonably solid ground is provided by a "Concordance of Social Classifications" (p.47) which brings together the evolutionary schemes of ten thinkers, largely anthropologists.

Some questionable "signposts" are provided, though, in pointing to the direction of our inevitable journey: the sharing rather than amassing of power in politics, reduction in drug usage, the search for some paradigm beyond "man" and "woman", the erosion of the incest taboo so that all of life will become erotic, and the transformation of human beings into what amounts to a higher species.

The book becomes clearly eutopian with prescriptions such as the following: "To empty our prisons, create a new education and a new politics, end

racism, provide a decent minimum living standard for every inhabitant, open the possibilities of meaning and joy for old people, make every city a festival and the entire country a garden is, for a start, enough to engage our energy and aspiration, our enormous unused capability." (pp.206-207)
*** Regrettably, such noble aspirations cannot be necessarily equated with emerging realities.

142. FULLER, Buckminster, "Planetary Planning: The Historical Philo-sophical Background," **The American Scholar**, 40:2, Spring 1971, pp. 285-304.   (A-5)

Classically verbose and opaque Fullerese, having something to do with 12 periods of "our overall evolutionary history in which man consciously partici-pates and takes responsibility for the transformations of the environment and the consequent social behaviors of adjustment to the successively new environ-ments."
We are presently in Period Ten, where we witness ever-accelerating in-dividually intuitive withdrawals from religious groups, an emancipation of humanity from physical drudgery, a new aesthetic of intellectual integrity, etc. Period Eleven and Twelve (like the others without a name or any placement in time) defy even the semblance of annotation. Ultimately we "approach but never attain completely inclusive, infinitely incisive truth or love, or under-standing."
*** It is most relevant here to cite a general critique of Fuller's writing: "This gobbledegook of 'universe' is representative of a lot of sub-tongues spoken now by people who lead 'awesome intellectual lives.' It is speech so abstract, so far removed from anybody's experience that it is virtually out of control; anything can be said in it that the speaker has the foolish-ness or the audacity to say." (MANAS, June 25, 1975, p. 2) Liberal wor-shippers of Fuller should stop tolerating his empirical irresponsibility.

143. GLASSER, William, M.D., "The Civilized Identity Society: Mankind Enters Phase Four," **Saturday Review**, Feb. 19, 1972, pp. 26-31.   (B-4)

A neat 2 x 2 matrix offered by a California psychologist and author of **Reality Therapy** and **Schools Without Failure.** The earliest society, lasting three and a half million years, is called The Primitive Survival Society, where man's primary goal in life was survival in a rigorous environment. About 500,000 years ago, as individuals became involved in the affairs of each other, and man had time for rituals and symbols as ways in which to identify himself, The Primitive Identity Society was formed. Mankind's phase three is called The Civilized Survival Society, involving power hierarchies where individuals became subservient to the group. For the past ten thousand years, civilized survival man has struggled against a hostile environment almost entirely of his own making. But in the past twenty or so years, The Civilized Identity Society has begun to emerge, motivated by a respect for individual integrity. "The new identity society is a regeneration of intelligent cooperation and involvement, reverting back hundreds of thousands of years to humanity." (p.31)
*** The four-stage scheme is better expressed in this article than in Glasser's book, **The Identity Society** (Harper & Row, 1972. 265 pp. $5.95) which is merely a collection of informal essays on school failure, sexual behavior, reality therapy, and criminal justice. in addition to the title essay. In any event, the evidence for the Civilized Identity Society is not persuas-ive.

144. GRAVES, Clare W., "Human Nature Prepares for a Momentous Leap," **The Futurist**, VIII: 2, April 1974, pp. 72-87.   (A-3)

A complex but intriguing scheme of eight behavioral stages (six subsistence levels and two being levels) proposed by a psychology professor. Each level is designated by two letters, the first standing for the neurological system in the brain upon which the psychological system is based, the second standing for the existential problems of existence.

Subsistence Levels

1. Automatic Existence (A-N), where man seeks only immediate satisfaction of basic physiological needs.
2. Tribalistic Existence (B-O), where need is for stability.
3. Egocentric Existence (C-P), where rugged individualism dominates.
4. Saintly Existence (D-Q), arising from the view that life is not made for ultimate pleasure.
5. Materialistic Existence (E-R), where man strives to conquer the world by learning its secrets.
6. Personalistic Existence (F-S), where "man becomes centrally concerned with peace with his inner self and in the relation of his self to the inner self of others."

Being Levels

7. Cognitive Existence (G-T), where man becomes a truly cooperative individual.
8. Experientialistic Existence (H-U), where man is driven by the winds of knowledge and human faith.

"Man, at the threshold of the seventh level, where so many political and cultural dissenters stand today, is at the threshold of being human. He is truly becoming a human being." As man moves from the sixth to the seventh level, "a chasm of unbelievable depth of meaning is crossed...the gap between getting and giving, taking and contributing, destroying and constructing."(p.75)

Additional comments are offered on the G-T way of life, G-T man, human institutions at the G-T level, and the G-T way of thinking (systemic). A book that elaborates on the theory, **Up the Existential Staircase**, is in preparation.
*** Cooperation is always desirable, but there is no evidence that it is increasing. Indeed, with the unexpected reversal in our affluence, mankind may well have slipped a few notches on the ladder.

145. CALHOUN, John B., "An Evolutionary Perspective on the Environmental Crisis," **Fields Within Fields**, No. 13, Fall 1974, pp. 18-30. (Entire issue available from World Institute Council, 777 United Nations Plaza, NYC 10017, for $2.50)   (A-3)

A modified version of a longer paper appearing in **Man-Environment Systems**, (4:1, 1974) viewing seven revolutions in consciousness. "Each of the successive revolutions in consciousness reflects the attainment of humanly designed social and physical structures that serve in expanding the biological brain's capacity to acquire, transform, and utilize information." (p. 20)

We have gone through Traditional-Sapient, Living-Agricultural, Authoritarian-Religious, and Holistic-Artistic revolutions, and we are presently in the Scientific-Exploitive stage. "Projection of this evolutionary trend predicts two more such shifts: a 'communication-electronic' revolution to be clearly established by 1988, and a terminal 'compassionate-systems' revolution making its impact by 2018." (p. 20)

Further comments are made on environmental design and developing conceptual networks.

146. HEARD, Gerald. The Five Ages of Man: The Psychology of Human History. NY: Julian Press, 1964. 393 pp.   (A-4)

A murky and difficult work, presenting four 5-fold aspects of history, and generally viewing history as being psychologically driven. "I see it (the race's history) as five epochs during which, through the contraction of consciousness, man becomes first a creature of a spoken tradition; secondly, a being of protest against that stifling tradition; thirdly, a person of self-blame; fourthly, an individual of objectivity; and fifthly, an individual who is objectively aware

of his subjectivity." (p.13) A huge cycle is viewed, from the rise of the pro-
to individual to the total individual, and having completed that loop of the
spiral, "We are in the post-individual age and world." The transition is also
spoken of as that from the Humanic age to the Leptoid Age. Leptoid (derived
from "leap") suggests that this fifth stage of man requires great learning.

**146a. HEARD, Gerald. The Ascent of Humanity: An Essay on the Evolution of
Civilization from Group Consciousness Through Individuality to
Super-Consciousness.** London: J. Cape, 1929. 332 pp.   (A-4)

Views history as the story of growing consciousness, concluding with
chapters on the enlargement of individuality, both pscho-physical and psychic.

**147. KORZYBSKI, Alfred. Manhood of Humanity: The Science and Art of
Human Engineering.** NY: E.P. Dutton, 1921. 264 pp.   (AB-2)

"At present the future of mankind is dark." The conclusion of the World
War closes the period of the childhood of humanity, a period devoid of any
real understanding of values. But humanity is now "coming to its senses
and must soon enter its manhood." (p. 30) Humanity's manhood will be a
scientific period "that will witness the gradual extension of scientific
method to all the interests of mankind." (p. 46) It will be a time when patriotism will grow to embrace the world, and larger affairs will be guided
by the science and art of Human Engineering.
Engineering is "the coordinated sum-total of human knowledge gathered
through the ages, with mathematics as its chief instrument and guide." (p. 7)
Mathematics is defined as exact thought or rigorous thinking. Human engineering is built on the concept of man characterized as time-binding, in contrast to man as animal or supernatural. "This conception radically alters
our whole view of human life, human society, and the world." (p. 70) And
Korzybski (the founder of General Semantics) is profoundly aware that "definitions create conditions."
Time-binding emphasizes that we act in time as well as space. Wealth,
both material and as knowledge, is the fruit of the time-binding work of humanity. "Humans are gathering and binding the knowledge of past centuries
into sheaves for the use and development of generations yet unborn." (p. 114)
The development of higher ideals is a time-binding impulse, and survival
in time means a struggle for excellence. Viewing man as an animal leads
to "animal economics" and a brutalized industrial system; viewing man as
time-binding would lead to a humanized industrial system. Bound-up time
is of the core and substance of civilization.
The first step toward the manhood of humanity requires a new institution--
a Dynamic Department, a Department of Coordination, or a Department of
Cooperation--composed of ten sections such as Mathematical Sociology or
Humanology, Mathematical Legislation, Education, and Cooperative Banking.
It is important to note that Korzybski is a strong advocate of a holistic
science. "The primal function of a science is to enable us to anticipate the
future in the field to which it relates." (p. 39) The social sciences are not
seen as effective. "Through endless, scientific specialization scientific
branches multiply, and for want of coordination the great world-problems
suffer." (p. 38)
Many contemporary "futurists" might also heed Korzybski's wise caution
that "In relation to the past there are three wide-open ways in which one
may be a fool." (p. 169) Drifting Fools ignore the past; Static Fools falsify
the past by idealizing it; and Dynamic Fools falsify the past by disregarding
its virtues, reveling in the excitements of change. It is warned that "...the
present is the child of the past, and it is only in proportion as we thus learn
to understand the present that we can face the future with confidence and
competence. Past, Present, Future--these can not be understood singly
and separately--they are welded together indissolubly as one." (pp. 171-
172)

*** This fresh and far-sighted work is often arrogant, preachy, and repetitious, but it is well worth returning to for its many powerful ideas. Korzybski is perhaps best known for his "time-binding" concept, and it might be readily argued today that mankind is losing its time-binding capacity, rather than cultivating it, and that this has led to many of our problems.
Further articulation of "The Mechanism of Time-Binding" is in Part VII (pp. 371-564) of Korzybski's classic work, **Science and Sanity: An Introduction to Non-Aristotelian Systems and General Semantics.** Lakeville, Conn.: International Non-Aristotelian Library Publishing Co., 1933.

148. BOIS, J. Samuel. **Breeds of Men: Toward the Adulthood of Humankind.** NY: Harper & Row, 1970. 174 pp.   (AB-4)

A general semanticist and follower of Korzybski proposes a classification of men according to their semantic stage of development. This evolutionary scheme of changing human nature enables discrimination so that we may "put our future in the hands of the more advanced breeds." (p. xvii)
Breed 1 is The Primitives of all times, whose world is structured by sensory experience. TV and radio commercials are geared to this breed because "the proportion of primitives remains high."
Breed 2, The Early Classifiers, fixate the world in the categories of their native language. "It is part of our fate to manage our activities according to these definitions and to seek relief for our troubles within the framework of these predetermined categories." (p.68)
Breed 3, The Early Relators, are oriented to the notion of truth and science, thinking in terms of mechanically-interacting causes and effects. Breeds 2 and 3 "take it for granted that their knowledge gives them a real picture of a real objective world..."
Breed 4, The Postulating Breed, includes self-actualizers living in a broad space-time context, people with altruism as the dominant passion, aware of limits to discursive reason--that we live in a world that we have constructed with inherited categories and semantic structures.
Breed 5, The Participants, are those at one in a felt symbiosis with things, people, and situations, "participating with expanded awareness in the creative thrust of cosmic energy."
Our present conceptual revolution is seen as "the actual transformation of the scientific logic that has prevailed for the last three hundred years into a new perceptual, rational, and emotional semantic structure that will become the creative matrix of a new universe inhabited by a breed of men who will surpass the present generation in self-knowledge and self-mastery." (p.7)
*** An attractive ideal, but without the slightest piece of suggestive evidence that the higher breeds are increasing in number, and that the lower breeds will see fit to surrender their power to their betters. This scheme is also repeated in Bois' **Epistemics: The Science-Art of Innovating** (International Society for General Semantics, c.1972), which offers "a new science-art of utopia designing...", apparently to very few takers.

149. SALK, Jonas. **The Survival of the Wisest.** NY: Harper & Row, 1973. 124 pp. $6.95.   (A-4)

A rather murky essay intended "to draw attention to the role of value systems as control and regulatory factors which operate in an apparently 'intuitive' way, guiding man toward or away from survival." (p.48) As one might guess, "...by wisest we mean those who comprehend the survival-evolutionary process..." (p.53)
This process is described as the transition from Epoch A to Epoch B. Epoch A is anti-death and anti-disease; Epoch B is pro-life and pro-health oriented. Epoch A features self-repression and external restraint; Epoch B favors self-expression, self-restraint, and an interest in quality of individ-

uals rather than quantity.
*** Biologists and psychologists might appreciate this statement more than social scientists.

149a. LODGE, George Cabot. **The New American Ideology: How the Ideological Basis of Legitimate Authority in America is Being Radically Transformed--The Profound Implications for our Society in General and the Great Corporations in Particular.** NY: Knopf, 1975. 350 pp. $12.50.
                                                                    (AB-4)
Now a professor at the Harvard Business School, Lodge proclaims that "the United States is in the midst of a great transformation, comparable to the one that ended medievalism and shook its institutions to the ground, making way for what we now call modernity. The old ideas and assumptions that once made our institutions legitimate are being eroded." (p. 3)
Ideology is defined as "a collection of ideas that makes explicit the nature of the good community...the framework by which a community defines and applies values..." (p. 5) The traditional American ideology is composed of five great ideas: individualism, property rights, competition, the limited state, and scientific specialization.
The new American ideology concerns communitarianism augmenting and replacing individualism, rights of membership augmenting and replacing property rights, community need as an emerging criterion for the utilization of resources, the state as planner, and holism as a theory of nature. "The transition from the Old Five to the New Five has to a great extent already taken place. There can be no going back." (p. 21) The old bishops of the Lockean age such as Daniel Boone, Emerson, Carnegie, and Ford, are being replaced by the new bishops of the new ideology: Ralph Nader, Charles Reich, Philip Slater, William Irwin Thompson, and the Berrigan brothers.
The implication for managers is that they should join the side of change and survival. "The West is in the throes of another of its great adaptations. This time we can have the choice for glory, **if we will but be aware.**" (340)
*** Provocative, but superficial. The new ideology may indeed be necessary and desirable, but the crucial assessment that it has "to a great extent taken place" is unconvincing, particularly as concerns the new appreciation of synthesis in modern science. Ferkiss' argument for "Ecological Humanism" (No. 431) is far more sophisticated concerning the necessary elements for genuine ideological transformation.

150. REICH, Charles A. **The Greening of America.** NY: Random House, 1970. 399 pp. $7.95.   (AB-4)

It all seems like ancient history by now, to remember the thundering proclamation from a teacher at the Yale Law School that "There is a revolution coming. It will not be like revolutions of the past. It will originate with the individual and with culture, and it will change the political structure only as its final act." (p.4)
And, as most everyone knows by now, at the heart of everything is a change of consciousness, in that "Every stage of human civilization is accompanied by, and also influenced by, a consciousness." (p.7) Consciousness I is the traditional outlook of the American farmer and small businessman, while Consciousness II represents the values of an organization society. "They both represent the underlying form of consciousness appropriate to the age of industrial development and the market economy, bringing in the eighteenth century. Both subordinate man's nature to his role in the economic system..." (p.351)
Consciousness III is the new generation. It starts with the self and postulates the absolute worth of every human being. It rejects the manipulation of others through relationships of authority and subservience. It promotes openness to any and all experience, and is united by the energy of hope and happiness. It "sees through the Establishment verities of our society with corrosive ease." (p.229) It seeks a higher logic and a higher reason,

but it is by no means anti-technological. It "could only have come into existence given today's technology. And only Consciousness III can make possible the continued survival of man as a species in this age of technology." (p. 363) It seeks to transform work by de-institutionalization, de-alienation, and de-specialization.

Consciousness III is only a transitional stage and must by definition be always growing and changing. "So we must look forward to Consciousness IV, V, VI, and so forth; or if we say that change is inherent in the definition of III then new degrees of Consciousness III." (p.363).

*** By polarizing the good guys and the bad guys, and seeing no seamy side to the younger generation, this polemic quickly became perhaps the best-known misforecast of our time. Still, as a critique, there is a bit of baby left in the bathwater of overkill.

151. THOMPSON, William Irwin. **At the Edge of History: Speculations on the Transformation of Culture.** NY: Harper & Row, 1971; Harper Colophon Edition, 1972. 252 pp.   (A-2)

After three relatively light chapters describing the author's journeys to and through Los Angeles, Big Sur, and MIT, Thompson settles down in his "Canadian retreat" (Toronto) and describes in Chapter 4, "Values and Conflict Through History," an elegant postulation of four phases: Tribal Community, Agricultural Society, Industrial Civilization, and Scientific-Planetary Civilization, with references to Blake's fourfold vision and quadrants of ideological and functional positions. Phase III expresses maximum alienation and fragmentation. Phase IV is simply Phase I on a planetary scale: "The serpent bites its tail, and we spiral up to another plane by moving back into a correspondence with the old. A new cosmic myth succeeds the linear fragmentation of Phase III, and man once again confronts the universe with his body, mind, and soul to see that his petty industrial technology of Phase III was a very tiny thing indeed." (pp. 144-145)

*** A subsequent volume by Thompson, **Passages About Earth: An Exploration of the New Planetary Culture** (Harper & Row, 1973) rambles on about matters such as the individual as institution, the world state, and planetary mythologies, all seen as leading to Findhorn and Thompson's own community of Lindisfarne. The first book is more important; the second book (**Passages**) best seen as backup for fans of Thompson's spell-binding style.

152. JANTSCH, Erich, "Organizing the Human World: An Evolutionary Outlook," **FUTURES: The Journal of Planning and Forecasting,** 6:1, February 1974, pp. 4-15.   (A-3)

Adapted from **Design for Evolution,** Jantsch provides a complex and highly integrative view of interaction between phases or waves of organization "governed by a hierarchical relationship which also expresses policy design at different levels of human systems." (p.5) The four levels of organization are ecological, social, cultural, and psychic, and we are seen as presently in "the precarious phases of transition from predominantly social to cultural organization." (p.10)

A conscious design for world unity "is clearly outside our present organizational reach," but the fourth level of psychic organization--referring to the basic potential of man to learn how to use his psychic capabilities-- "may indeed open up new horizons and become the principal 'pulling force' for cultural design."

*** An interesting hope unaccompanied with any suggestive evidence as to even a remote likelihood of occurence.

153. RODNICK, David. **Man's Quest for Autonomy: A Background for Modernization.** Lubbock, Texas: The Caprock Press, Mar. 1974. 365 pp. $9.95.   (A-4)

On the evolution of man, with major attention devoted to Primary or Agricultural civilization, and the Secondary civilization of industry and science, but with a few comments on a Third civilization, a Tertiary one "that will not look upon production as its chief goal, but rather the solving of man's inconsiderate behavior toward his fellow men...a new civilization oriented toward solving problems--one whose roots exist at present but whose infrastructure may not come into being for another 30 to 50 years." (p.8) The concluding chapter on The World of Tomorrow offers a mixture of vaguely generalized prescription and hopeful description, e.g. "We are moving in the direction of greater human rights, a better understanding of the implications and practices of democracy, a greater political and social awareness and participation of the citizens in government in all of its phases." (p.353)

154. ACLAND, Sir Richard, "The Next Step, I," and "The Next Step, II," The Teilhard Review, VIII: 1 & 2, Feb. 1973 and June 1974. (A-4)

Two broadcasts over the BBC in 1972, arguing that "the whole process of evolution has at last, and very suddenly, put industrial technology into our hands and the egalitarian outlook into our hearts and minds...the evolutionary process requires communities in which all feel equally valued, equally involved and equally responsible. There must be a name for this; and I propose to call it Integrated Community." (I, p.7)
It is admitted that this concept is hardly new and has been "the lodestar for all the great social reformers of the last two hundred years." Such a community would be socialist, with all productive resources owned in common. It would have zero population growth, and the religious dimension of living would be rediscovered.
"We are involved in what is no less than only the sixth of the great evolutionary transformations that have raised life from one level to the next on its long journey from simplest beginnings to undisclosed destiny. We shall need to bend our whole social endeavor to the task." (I, p.8) There may be difficulties ahead, but perhaps on the further side of social failure we shall succeed.

155. RIBEIRO, Darcy. The Civilizational Process. Trans. and with a Forward by Betty J. Meggars. Washington: Smithsonian Institution Press, 1968. 201 pp. $6.50.   (AB-3)

A complex, scholarly, but still quite readable work by a Brazilian anthropologist who served as the Minister of Education and Culture (1962-1964), but with the overthrow of the Goulart regime is now exiled in Montevideo, Uruguay.
Portrays a sequence of eight technological revolutions: agricultural, urban, irrigation, metallurgical, pastoral, mercantile, industrial, and thermonuclear --as well as twelve accompanying civilizational processes. After reviewing archaic societies, regional civilizations, and world civilizations, Universal Civilization is seen as an inevitable result from the expansion of the thermonuclear revolution, arising from the industrial powers, socialistic states, and nationalistic modernizing states of the present.
Universal Civilization will not be identified with any individual race or cultural tradition. Future societies will be socialist formations of a new type, in that socialism is seen as the form most likely to provide the necessary systems of control. Differences between city and country will be eradicated, and the alienation of producer from product will be overcome. "It will also place within the reach of mankind for the first time the capacity to direct the evolutionary process itself." (p.148)

156. POLAKOV, Walter N. **The Power Age: Its Quest and Challenge.** NY: Covici-Friede, 1933. 247 pp.   (BC-4)

An engineer proclaims that "We have outgrown the technique of the Machine Age. A New production technique, power production, characterizes the new Power Age." (p.18)

Electric power available where and when it is wanted frees machines from their limitations. This leads to a different kind of economy and a different kind of social relations in a more thoroughly technologized age. A new ideal of mass production is potentially capable of providing leisure for all and eliminating insecurity. The Power Age undermines the practicality of trade barriers and questions the validity of nationalistic competition. The functions of government become broader in scope to include the planning of the national economy which would still, however, be conducted on a competitive basis. "We cannot make a 'new deal' by using the same old pack of marked cards. We must employ scientific intelligence and all available engineering means lest we perish together with the defunct Machine Age and its Faustian culture!" (p.247).

157. NEARING, Scott. **Freedom: Promise and Menace. A Critique on the Cult of Freedom.** Harborside, Maine: Social Science Institute, 1961. 202 pp.   (A-4)

We have now entered the power age, where there is a rapid extension of human understanding and the control of nature, the application of science and engineering techniques to include the direction of human society, and the unification of the planet through probes of outer space. "If the power age community is to survive and to progress, the conservation and utilization of nature, the planned direction of social forces, the development of world awareness and world loyalty, space communication and association, the prolongation and enrichment of human life and the development of human creativity must enjoy top priority in power age thinking, planning and performance." (pp.150-151)

A major theme concerns freedom and restraint, and the relation of the individual to society, which now requires more responsibility. Socialism is advocated which promotes cooperation and community. "Freedom is not enough. The power age is in desparate need not so much of free men and women as of disciplined, responsible, dedicated citizens." (p.193)

158. McLUHAN, Marshall. **Understanding Media: The Extensions of Man.** NY: McGraw-Hill, 1964. 365 pp.   (AB-4)

Argues in the Introduction that we are moving from the mechanical age to the electric age. The mechanical age allowed fragmented space and time patterns, had lineal connections and neat packages. This led to explosion, but now the Western world is imploding. "In the electric age, when our central nervous system is technologically extended to involve us in the whole of mankind and to incorporate the whole of mankind in us, we necessarily participate, in depth, in the consequences of our every action." (p.4) "The aspiration of our time for wholeness, empathy and depth of awareness is a natural adjunct of electric technology." (p.5)

After explaining the well-known and overstated slogan that "The Medium is the Message," McLuhan goes on to describe the difference between hot and cool, a leitmotif of the volume. A hot medium is high definition, filled in, extending only a single sense, exclusionary. A cool medium is more participatory and casually structured. Radio is hot and the telephone is cool, etc. Most of the book is devoted to cryptic but enticing explorations of various media such as the spoken and written word, clocks, games, the typewriter, comics, and weapons.

*** Perhaps still useful as a mind massager, but the societal stage theory is rather overstated zing-blinko, somewhat comparable to Reich's attempt to push Consciousness III.

159. ASIMOV, Issac, "The Fourth Revolution," **Saturday Review,** Oct. 24, 1970, pp. 17-20. (Part of special issue entitled "Toward the Global Village")
(B-4)
Views the evolution of human communication from speech to writing to the printing press and now to electronic communications. We are seen as having advanced as far as we can in the world of the third or print revolution, and "The race is on between the coming of the true fourth revolution and the death of civilization that will otherwise inevitably occur through growth past the limits of the third." (p.18). Once truly established, a worldwide electronic literacy would lessen differences among people, enabling the uneducated of the world to leapfrog into the culture of the fourth revolution and cities to spread out and disappear, thus alleviating overconcentration.

160. HUGHES, Harold K., "Cybernetics and the Management of Large Systems," in E.O. Attinger (ed.) **Global Systems Dynamics.** Basel: S. Karger, 1970, pp. 66-75. (A-4)

A physicist views six stages in man's development. We are presently in the Fifth Stage, the age of cybernetics (1950 to 2000), and a table is offered (p.69) contrasting the characteristics of cybernetic culture with the receding Western democracy. Cybernetic culture will feature participative democracy, localized instead of centralized decision-making, lifelong instead of limited education, cooperation instead of competition, etc. The Sixth Stage will be a new kind of steady state where we learn to abandon the inflation of population, pollution and aggression.

161. PERK, H.F. William, "The Great Transformation," **The American Scholar,** 35:2, Spring 1966, pp. 358-369. (AB-4)

A scenario written from the year 1985 and looking back to the Great Transformation of 1965-1975, which led to a worldwide cybernated productive system. This is the last of six historical periods. In the prehistoric period of Level One, man depended on himself. Level Two utilized animal power, and Level Three saw the substitution of machine power. Level Four saw the machine entering a new dimension of augmenting man's skill, and Level Five (the period just prior to the Great Transformation) saw the machine introduced for purposes of control. Level Six, the cybercultural era, "is an irreversible process that has worldwide abundance as its inevitable consequence." (p.366)

161a. SEABORG, Glenn T., "The Cybernetic Age: An Optimists View," **Saturday Review,** July 15, 1967, pp. 21-23. (B-4)

Considers the cybernetic revolution that has sprung from the scientific revolution of recent decades, and examines some of the implications such as a change in the relationship between labor and leisure, new goals for education, and a possible transition to a human-oriented society.

162. YOUNGBLOOD, Gene, **Expanded Cinema.** Introduction by R. Buckminster Fuller. NY: Dutton, 1970. 432 pp. $4.95, paper. (B-4)

From the Preface: "We're in transition from the Industrial Age to the

Cybernetic Age, characterized by many as the post-Industrial Age. But I've found the term **Paleocybernetic** valuable as a conceptual tool with which to grasp the significance of our present environment: combining the primitive potential associated with Paleolithic and the transcendental integrities of 'practical utopianism' associated with Cybernetic. So I call it the Paleocybernetic Age: an image of a hairy, buckskinned, barefooted atomic physicist with a brain full of mescaline and logarithms, working out the heuristics of computer-generated holograms or krypton laser interferometry. It's the dawn of man: for the first time in history we'll soon be free enough to discover who we are." (p.41)

163. FROMER, Manes. **Futurology and Philosophy of Technics. No. 4 The Future is Common--The End of the Capitalist-Communist Era.** Holon, Israel: Research Center of Futurology and Philosophy of Technics (46/4 Aronovitz St.), 1971. 39 pp.   (A-4)

The fourth revolution--the spiritual one--"starts in the wake of the three great technological revolutions of the middle of the century, the energotechnological, the cosmotechnical and the biotechnical revolutions..." These three technological revolutions also bring about a revolutionary transition from utilitarian technics to creative technics, with a corresponding transition from a utilitarian economy to a new creative economy.
The differences between the two are outlined on pp. 8-11, but not very convincingly. The creative economy is a rather naive scientific utopia with rule by the highly educated, and the right of creative work guaranteed to everybody.

164. LAND, George T. Lock. **Grow or Die: The Unifying Principle of Transformation.** NY: Random House, 1973; Delta edition, 1974. 265 pp. $10.00; $2.95, paper.   (A-4)

"The goal of this book and of transformation theory is to weave the new facts into an understanding of the complete human being, within the total system of being." (p.7) The book is also considered as "a general system theory; that is, it sets out to cover an extremely broad range of phenomena in many interrelated areas with a minimum number of postulates." (p.xiv)
The "total system of being" and the "many interrelated areas" are not quite as extensive as Land would have us believe. The disciplines involved here are anthropology, psychology, ethnology, ethology, physics, philosophy, and biology (p.xiii), but there is a notable lack of reference to the literature and concerns of economics, political science, sociology, and history. And thus Land's biological theory of progress exposes its arrogance and foolishness at every point where it pronounces on social phenomena.
The theory of transformation is that "psychological and cultural processes are an extension of and are isomorphic with biological, physical, and chemical processes. The single process of Nature that forms the keystone of transformation theory and that unites the behavior of all things is the process of growth." (p.8)
Three forms of biological growth behavior are identified: accretive growth, replicative growth, and mutual growth (pp.18-19). This theory is then imposed upon the evolution of Social Man (pp.42-45). The earliest cultures are seen as accretive cultures, with rigid control of information and growth by strict copying. The shift to replicative societies began with a gradual dissemination of information, and wars and missionary activity were designed to replicate culture through colonization of others. Since World War II, with the advent of more widespread mobility and information-sharing patterns, a new age of social mutualism has started to gain momentum, "and created much higher probabilities of combining new and different information, ideas, and cultures." (p.45)
"As we begin to understand more about biological systems, we can see that Man continually creates interacting systems with more mutually beneficial

potential, for example, recent developments in such things as ecology, social responsibility of corporations, extended world relationships, and crumbling social barriers." (p.69) And if this statement fails to send any social scientist through the roof, consider the following assertion about evolving mutualism: "In the development of organizations, Man has progressed from slavery, to child and indentured labor, to labor negotiations, and, today, to the modern concept of participative management." (p.160)

Making vague reference to "numerous and eminent authorities" who seek to slow down or stop industrial growth, Land counters that "There is no evidence of any successful return to a past or balanced system...Mankind's ratios of successes to failures constantly increase as he evolves himself, his thinking, and his environment." (p.73) Rather, "The idea of 'limiting growth' is anathema to Nature and to Man...Not to grow is to die." (p.74)

"The idea of technological 'dehumanization' is not withstanding once we realize that only by extending our biologic nature through the **ectosomatics** of such functions as protection, manufacturing, transportation, and communication have we been able to create the **freedom** necessary to be the agents of accelerating evolution... Technology is the self-extension that liberates Man to use his energy and information to transform our world." (p. 190, author's emphasis)

Land concludes with comments about the call to mutualism, or the pressure to create a whole organism of Mankind, and the new humanological revolution "to meet the evolving opportunities of rediscovering and improving Man and Mankind." (p.195)

*** An ambitious synthesis that attempts too much. As concerns societal directions and alternatives, the book would benefit by demonstrating some mutualism with the literature of social science and ecology. As concerns biological theory, there may be some important contributions here, but this judgment must be left to others.

NOTE: Evolutionary stage theories in this chapter and others are summarized in Index E.

II. LISTINGS

B. Alternatives

Chapter 5

Ecology and the Limits of Growth

Once again, optimism and pessimism are the central themes in the fundamentally intertwined matters of population growth, the adequacy of natural resources, the potential of certain new technologies, and pollution.

These concerns involve matters of public policy that would clearly have a significant impact on the shape of society. If one is worried about population outgrowing resources, and/or the pollution resulting from our technology, then radical changes in individual values and government policies are advocated. These pessimists (or "doomsayers") very often take a systems point of view, as exemplified by Hardin (177-178), Georgescu-Roegen (185), and the **Blueprint for Survival** (211). Their critics **(or "technological optimists")** do not generally employ a systemic approach, and their arguments serve to support the existing society, perhaps with some relatively modest modifications such as changes in the tax structure.

It is not within the scope of this guide to provide a full analysis of this argument, but only to suggest some of the vast differences that exist and to urge others to examine all sides as fairly as possible. There are many important books in this chapter that are rated "3" or higher, and it has been difficult to choose the "1" and "2" items for the Civic Curriculum. Those chosen are all pessimistic: Darwin (170), Ordway's theory of The Limit to Growth (171), Hardin (177-178), the **Blueprint for Survival** (211), **Ark II** (212), and Daly's anthology (215) that brings together the best of the "growth-mania" critics. This selection does not give equal voice to the other side. Although the optimists make strong arguments--particularly Kahn and Brown (226), Beckerman (227), Maddox (228), and Brubaker (231)--my **initial** assessment is that these arguments are addressed to elements of the whole situation, but lack the broader scope of the pessimists.

Much of the argument about ecology and the limits to **growth has been** focused on the Meadow's report to the Club of Rome (206), clearly one of the most controversial documents of recent years. But it is important to recognize that there are many other books that go further than the Club of Rome reports in prescribing what ought to be done, and that a number of "limits to growth" arguments were made more than twenty years ago--and somehow ignored. This chapter therefore begins with this neglected retrospective view.

The first item in this chapter is the 1952 report of the President's Materials Policy Commission, **Resources for Freedom** (166), a clear example of officially blindered thinking that airily dismissed population growth and paid no attention to pollution. Eight years earlier, Lewis Mumford was correctly foreseeing a transition to an age of equilibrium (167), and William Vogt (168) took a passionate ecological stance in 1948 that compares favorably with most contemporary tracts. Walter Prescott Webb announced the disappearance of The Great Frontier in 1952 (169), followed by Sir Charles Galton Darwin's forecast of the Fifth Revolution resulting from fuel shortages (170). Perhaps the most remarkable voice from the past is the Theory of the Limit of Growth proposed by Samuel H. Ordway in 1953 (171). Also in the same year, Fairfield Osborn wrote **The Limits of the Earth** (173), followed a year later by Harrison Brown's durable classic on the vulnerability of machine civilization (174).

The contemporary concern with ecology is best summarized by Hardin (177-178), Commoner (179), and Dubos (180-182). Perhaps the first economist with serious doubts was E.J. Mishan (183-184), but the most significant challenge to the conventional wisdom of economics appears to be that of Georgescu-Roegen (185). Taylor and Humpstone (189) offer an important and thoughtful critique of environmental strategy, and Rowland's summary of the Stockholm Conference is worth noting (202). Nicholson (200) proposes Ecological Humanism, but a much stronger argument for a strategy with the same title is made by Victor Ferkiss in **The Future of Technological Civilization** (431), included in Chapter 9.

The "Limits to Growth" debate began with Forrester's model (205) which led to the report by the Meadows team (206), backed up by collections of scholarly papers (207-208). The second report to the Club of Rome (209) made useful corrections to the original model, while exuding political naivete. The Club of Rome also sponsored the very stimulating interviews by Willem Oltmans (210). The considerable attention paid to **Limits to Growth** served to overshadow the British **Blueprint for Survival** (211), which is considered here to be more worthy of attention. The Ark II program proposed by Pirages and Ehrlich is a good overview of necessary reforms (212), not unlike the overview provided by Watt (213), and somewhat similar to the more radical position taken by Dumont (191). Following or paralleling themes promoted by the Club of Rome are works on the mature society (214), the steady-state society (215-216), the no-growth society (217), the scarcity society (218), and the recycle society (219-220).

The critics to the "Limits to Growth" position employ a variety of perspectives. Kahn and Brown (226) view a new societal stage of affluence (a view that Kahn has persisted with, perhaps at least partly due to his corporate support). Beckerman (227) uses conventional economics in his critique, while asserting the need to pursue conventional liberal goals. Maddox (228) scores points on those who exaggerate, while the University of Sussex group picks over the **Limits to Growth** in fine scholarly detail (229). Baxter (230) focuses only on social control devices, but Brubaker (231) offers a broad argument for a new technology course as the best of the true ultimate choices. Logan (234a), criticizes everyone for overlooking a possible cyclic decline in solar energy.

If all of this is dismal, humor (depending on one's taste) is provided by Mead (236) and **The Peter Plan** (236), the former tending more to an optimistic view and the latter tending to be more reformist.

Finally, questions are raised about both the Club of Rome and Beckerman by Emma Rothschild (237). It is a good start, but much more analysis is needed by many people as to what the various advocates are looking at, ignoring, advocating, and criticizing. This chapter will hopefully serve to suggest such an agenda.

166. U.S. President's Materials Policy Commission. **Resources for Freedom.** Five Volumes. Washington: U.S. Government Printing Office, 1952.   (A-4)

From Volume 1, Foundations for Growth and Security:

"This Report...has as its central task an examination of the adequacy of materials, chiefly industrial materials, to meet the needs of the free world in the years ahead. Even a casual assessment of these years would show many causes for concern." (p. 1)

"The greatest uncertainty that confronts us all as we attempt to pierce the fog of the next quarter century lies in the unanswerable question, will there be war?" (p. 3) As for values, the members of the Commission "share the belief of the American people in the principle of Growth," (p. 3) as well as the belief in minimum government interference in private enterprise.

In all of the five volumes, there are **no population projections whatsoever,** nor is there any mention of pollution, It is simply asserted that "This Commission does not accept the view that the world's increasing population pressures are catastrophic...Malthusian calculations have never given sufficient weight to the extraordinary ingenuity of mankind..." (p. 169)

*** And now the balance of Malthus vs. Ingenuity has shifted so that population becomes a significant variable to consider.

167. MUMFORD, Lewis. **The Condition of Man.** With a New Preface by the Author. NY: Harcourt Brace Jovanovich, Harvest Books Edition, 1944; 1973. 467 pp. $3.95, paper.   (A-3)

The case that we live in a disintegrating society, originally stated in 1944. The book explores "the tangled elements of Western man's spiritual history" with chapters such as "The Progress of Prometheus" and "Barbarism and Dissolution." Mumford's sound advice has obviously been ignored: "If we do not have time to understand the past, we will not have the insight to control the future; for the past never leaves us, and the future is already here." (p. 14)

Predating the Club of Rome by nearly three decades, Mumford argues that "an age of expansion is giving place to an age of equilibrium." (p. 398) The present period is a painful transition, leaving behind the era of expansion, associated with the rise of capitalism, militarism, scientism, and mechanization; and moving toward a period of dynamic equilibrium. "The theme for the new period will be...the resurgence of life, the displacement of the mechanical by the organic, and the re-establishment of the person as the ultimate term of all human effort. Cultivation, humanization, co-operation, symbiosis: these are the watchwords of the new world-enveloping culture." (p. 399) Mumford notes that this stabilization was suggested by John Stuart Mill in a chapter in the second volume of his Principles of Political Economy devoted to a discussion of "the stationary state."

The ideal personality for the new age is the organic person: a balanced personality "in dynamic interaction with every part of his environment and every part of his heritage;" not a specialist, but the whole man. (p. 419) To control the disintegrating forces at work in our society, it is argued that "we must resume the search for unity." (p. 14)

In the four-page Preface to the 1973 edition, Mumford announces that "Since 'The Condition of Man' appeared in 1944, the condition of man has worsened. What were once only local demoralizations or disasters now threaten to turn into planetary calamities." (p. v) In retrospect, Mumford finds very little in the work that he would care to change, either in tone or content.

168. VOGT, William. **Road to Survival.** Introduction by Bernard M. Baruch. NY: William Sloane Associates, 1948. 335 pp.   (AB-3)

A strong and passionate ecological view concerning the impact of man on his global environment, with particular emphasis on the biotic potential, or carrying capacity, of the land. The mechanization of agriculture is decried, and it is warned that the continued abuse of resources will lead to oblivion. "By excessive breeding and abuse of the land mankind has backed itself into an ecological trap." (p. 284)

In a chapter on Industrial Man--The Great Illusion, it is predicted that "As we look ahead toward a falling carrying capacity over most of the earth and toward a sharp increase in world population, we must also look for a marked decrease in our material standard of living." (p. 79) Sound familiar?

Among the "drastic measures" that are needed, we must begin to understand the dilemma and reorganize our thinking, as well as seeking to control population and restore resources.
*** Not much different from the "doomsters" of 25 years later; indeed, the emphasis on soil depletion is a point that most contemporaries have neglected!

169. WEBB, Walter Prescott. **The Great Frontier.** Boston: Houghton Mifflin, 1952. 434 pp. (University of Texas edition with introduction by Arnold J. Toynbee published in 1964)   (A-3)

The Great Frontier "has been one of the primary factors in modern history." It created a boom which lasted about 400 years (from about 1500 to 1900), as long as the geographic frontier was open. The modern age is seen as abnormal, and boom-born institutions (economic, political, and social) are seen as exceptional.
"Regardless of any techniques which may be developed to extract more from the land, there is a limit beyond which we cannot go; and if our techniques speed up the process of utilization and destruction, as they are now doing, they hasten the day when the substance on which they feed and on which a swollen population temporarily subsists will approach scarcity or exhaustion." (p. 27)
The Great Frontier has disappeared, and any new frontier cannot be compared with the old one. However, it is warned, man continues to build up the illusion that the frontier must exist somewhere. The scientific frontier is most notable, and "it is the most plausible, the most respectable, and may well be the most pernicious." (p. 288)
*** An early "limits to growth" view that places the argument in human, rather than physical terms.

170. DARWIN, Sir Charles Galton. **The Next Million Years.** Garden City, NY: Doubleday & Co., 1953. 210 pp.   (ABC-2)

Views four irreversible stages in the development of humanity: The First Revolution involved the discovery of fire; The Second Revolution concerned the invention of agriculture; The Third Revolution was the urban revolution; The Fourth Revolution is the scientific revolution where discoveries about the nature of the world have enabled man to alter his way of life. This fourth revolution has been hardly recognized, although we are in the middle of it.
Possible revolutions of the future might occur by finding some new large source of human food, or developing the ability to foresee the future with substantially greater accuracy than we now can. One view of the future is nearly a certainty: the Fifth Revolution resulting from a shortage of fuel, after we have spent the earth's stores of coal and oil. Unlike the other revolutions, this one will not lead to an increase in population, but even perhaps to the reverse.
Subsequent chapters concern topics such as population and its limitations, material conditions, the species Homo Sapiens, the importance of creeds, Man as a Wild Animal (seen as continuing to behave as such) and The Pursuit of Happiness.
Concludes that very little action can be taken about the future of the human race "for the simple reason that most human beings do not care in the least about the distant future." (p. 207)
"Attempts at improving the lot of mankind have all hitherto been directed towards improving his conditions, but not his nature, and as soon as the conditions lapse, all is lost. The only hope is to use our knowledge of biology in such a way that all would not be lost with the lapse of the conditions." (p. 208)

*** Still an excellent introductory overview (in the most ultimate sense) and notable for envisioning the energy crisis that we now face.

171. ORDWAY, Samuel H., Jr. **Resources and the American Dream: Including a Theory of the Limit of Growth.** NY: Ronald Press, 1953. 55 pp.
(ABC-2)

A cogent essay by a lawyer on the expanding industrial consumption of resources: "...it appears that we are approaching a point of declining return on scientific methods of increasing productivity from the land." (p. 19) Ordway acknowledges the one offsetting factor to this view: the hope of technological progress, and he fairly considers "The Cornucopian Faith" of the optimists.

The Theory of the Limit to Growth is based on the premise that, despite technological progress, the rising level of living consumes more resource capital than it creates. "If this cycle continues long enough, basic resources will come into such short supply that rising costs will make their use in additional production unprofitable, industrial expansion will cease, and we shall have reached the limit of growth." (p. 31)

"The price of failure to recognize the probabilities and to revise our faith, in time, could be the end of a culture." (p. 32) Our media of mass communication, for example, "would profit mankind more by sustained emphasis on the values of self-reliance, relaxation, and the nurture, not the exploitation, of natural and spiritual resources." (p. 41)

The final chapter, Toward a Balanced Civilization, advocates industrial planning and a reevaluation of the quality of the Good Life.
*** Better than anything yet issued by the Club of Rome.

172. LYONS, Barrow. **Tomorrow's Birthright: A Political and Economic Interpretation of our Natural Resources.** NY: Funk & Wagnalls, 1955. 424 pp.
(BC-3)

An early plea for "Limits of Growth" (quoting Samuel Ordway), long-range planning, and the need for understanding what lies ahead. "If we are to survive in the evolutionary chain of the ages, we must learn to preserve the means of life, instead of fouling and destroying them." (p. 405)

173. OSBORN, Fairfield. **The Limits of the Earth.** Boston: Little, Brown, 1953.
(BC-3)

"The determining question in the future of civilization is whether the supply of resources to be gained from the earth can prove adequate not only to meet the basic needs of people but to support the complex requirements of modern culture and economy." (p. 4)

The various chapters focus on particular geographic areas: Great Britain and Europe, Australia and Canada, the U.S., Africa, South America, and The Amazon, with a concluding chapter on population control.
*** A reasoned survey of limitations.

174. BROWN, Harrison. **The Challenge of Man's Future.** NY: Viking, 1954. 290 pp.
(ABC-3)

A durable classic that has gone into many printings (e.g., the 15th Printing was in 1967, and there may be subsequent ones). The obvious and simple task of the book is well-stated: "The first necessary step toward wise action in the future is to obtain an understanding of the problems that exist. This in turn necessitates an understanding of the relationships between man, his natural environment, and his technology." (pp. xi-xii)

Chapters describe the evolution of man, population, food, energy, and industrialization. The final chapter, Patterns of the Future, concerns the fragility of our machine civilization, which is seen as extremely vulnerable to disruption by war, but also vulnerable simply because of its vast interlocking networks. "Should a great catastrophe strike mankind, the agrarian cultures which exist at the time will clearly stand the greatest chance of survival and will probably inherit the earth. Indeed, the less a given society has been influenced by machine civilization, the greater will be the probability of its survival." (p. 224)

Three possible patterns of life in the distant future are seen: 1) a reversion to agrarian existence (seen as "by far the most likely"); 2) the completely controlled, collectivized industrial society; and 3) the worldwide free industrial society where human beings live in reasonable harmony with their environment (the probability of such an emergence is seen as "extremely low").

175. BROWN, Harrison, James BONNER, and John WIER. The Next Hundred Years: Man's Natural and Technological Resources. NY: Viking, 1957; Compass Books Edition, 1963. 193 pp.   (BC-3)

The result of a series of discussions between the authors (a geochemist, a biologist, and a psychologist) and the chief executives of thirty major corporations. Covers population, food, energy, and technical manpower, with a concluding discussion of the vulnerability of industrial society to disruption.

176. CHARTER, SPR. Man on Earth: A Preliminary Evaluation of the Ecology of Man. Foreword by Aldous Huxley. NY: Grove Press, 1970. 264 pp.   (AB-3)

Essays by a scientist written in the 1960-1962 period (derived from 35 broadcasts over Pacifica Foundation Radio), aiming to evolve a design-theory for the continuation of Man on Earth. Chapters such as Milk and Moral Fallout, Man the Contaminator, The Computerized Intellectuals, and The Acquiescent Society (1961).

"Man's recognition and acceptance of himself as a total human being is increasingly essential for sanity in an increasingly complex world." (p. 181) The emerging science of The Ecology of Man "holds the greatest promise for the solution of the basic questions of our time." (p. 184) The two great parent-materials of our time are seen as scientific realism and humanism; each by itself holds little promise, but their compounding may present a viable philosophic concept for our age.

*** Undoubtedly radical at the time of their writing, these essays are rather tame today, but still worth considering.

177. HARDIN, Garrett, "The Tragedy of the Commons," Science: 162, Dec. 13, 1968, pp. 1243-1248.   (AB-1)

Quite deservedly, this essay on resources, pollution, and population is considered to be one of the classic essays of our times. It is must reading for anyone who wishes to firmly grasp the fundamental principles of ecology.

"Tragedy" is used here, after Whitehead, in the sense of "the solemnity of the remorseless working of things." The "commons" refers to an obscure scenario written in 1833 by William Forster Lloyd, in the sense of the village green where various herdsmen keep their cattle. All is well as long as the numbers of livestock are kept well below the carrying capacity of the land. But as each herdsman, acting rationally, seeks to maximize his gain by adding to the herd, freedom in the commons ultimately brings ruin to all. Modern examples are briefly described, having to do with fish and whales in the oceans, cattle grazing on national forestland, and tourism in our National Parks.

The tragedy of the commons is seen as reappearing in a reverse way with pollution: rather than taking something out of the commons, it is a matter of putting something in, thus fouling our own nest. Analyzing this problem as a function of population density uncovers a neglected principle: "the morality of an act is a function of the state of a system at the time it is performed." Using the commons as a cesspool is harmless under frontier conditions; the same behavior in a metropolis is unbearable. "The laws of our society follow the pattern of ancient ethics, and therefore are poorly suited to governing a complex, crowded, changeable world."

Finally, in a crowded world, freedom to breed becomes intolerable. Appeals to conscience are seen as inadequate. Although "a dirty word to most liberals now," coercion is ultimately needed. To avoid ultimate ruin, it has to be recognized that freedom is the recognition of necessity: mutual coercion mutually agreed upon.

178. HARDIN, Garrett. **Exploring New Ethics for Survival: The Voyage of the Spaceship Beagle.** NY: Viking, 1972. 273 pp.   (AB-1)

A fresh, irreverent, witty, and authoritative volume expanding on the author's "Tragedy of the Commons" essay. In addition to including the original essay in an appendix, Hardin offers a science fictional parable about a spaceship (in four chapters introducing each of the sections of the book), and additional "non-fictional chapters" expanding on themes in the commons essay, and introducing a number of important related notions, such as the distinction between systematic Darwinian thinking vs. narrow, analytic, Newtonian thinking; the necessity of indicating "Terrae Incognitae" in our inquiries, similar to mapmakers of long ago, and the distinction between price and cost (both internal and external). The discussion of external costs, or externalities, is an important concern that is neglected by most economists.

179. COMMONER, Barry. **The Closing Circle: Nature, Man & Technology.** NY: Knopf, 1971. 326 pp. $6.95.   (ABC-3)

This well-received popularized volume by a leading ecologist is somewhat verbose and repetitious, but the central message--that the cause of the environmental crisis is technology, rather than population or affluence--should not be ignored.

The book is also a fundamental critique of our knowledge and education, as well as the resulting ignorance of fundamental concerns such as the ecosphere. The fault of technology derives from the fragmented nature of its scientific base: "The natural tendency to think of only one thing at a time is the chief reason why we have failed to understand the environment and have blundered into destroying it." (p. 26)

Commoner outlines the basic facts of the ecosphere, and devotes four chapters to describing nuclear technology, Los Angeles air, Illinois earth, and Lake Erie water. After debunking the population and affluence theories, he fingers "the technological flaw"--pointing out that new productive technologies are economic successes at the expense of ecological considerations, which do not appear in our economic accounting. Furthermore, "the country has been vastly ignorant of the extent and depth of the environmental crisis because crucial facts remained buried in inaccessible reports or shielded by official and industrial secrecy." (p. 204)

It is very difficult to estimate a point of no return because of our ignorance of hundreds of potential hazards in the environment. Nevertheless, it is estimated that major degradation will become irreparable in 20 to 50 years.

To develop an economic and social order best adapted as a partner in the alliance with nature would require many changes such as replacing synthetic materials with natural ones and synthetic pesticides with biological ones, discouraging power-consuming industries, developing transportation with maximal fuel efficiency and minimal land use, reclamation and recycling, and ecologically sound planning. "Something like one half of the postwar productive enterprises would need to be replaced by ecologically sounder ones." (p. 285) 'The replacement cost for capital equipment alone is roughly estimated at $600 billion, while the cost of efforts to restore damaged sectors of the ecosystem would be "hundreds of billion dollars." Thus, accepting a grace period of 25 years, the cost of survival (in 1958 dollars) becomes about $40 billion (far more than the annual cost of the Vietnam war at its highest point). The ecological imperative not only calls for the governance of production by a new criterion of "social thrift" rather than private gain but for global cooperation and therefore for peace among nations. "The world will survive the environmental crisis as a whole, or not at all." (p. 292)

180. DUBOS, René. **Reason Awake: Science for Man.** NY: Columbia University Press, 1970. 280 pp. $6.95.   (AB-3)

A statesmanlike appeal "concerning man's attitude toward science and the role played by scientific knowledge in human life and in the development of civilization." Social constraints on science are seen as inevitable: there is an "urgent need to correct the social absurdities and monstrosities that result from the mismanagement of scientific technology." (p. xvi)
Ecological constraints are also needed on population and technological growth, leading to a steady state. And persons are needed to work at the interface of science and society: "A Society that blindly accepts the decisions of experts is a sick society on its way to death." (p. 227)
The final chapter is devoted to "The Willed Future."

181. DUBOS, René. **A God Within.** NY: Scribners, 1972. 325 pp. $8.95; $2.95, paper.   (ABC-3)

Lofty, generalized wisdom on the past and future of mankind, with emphasis on biology, evolution, and environment. Dubos criticizes both technologic utopians and the prophets of doom, arguing that we must reverse the trend to larger agglomerations and provide a more favorable atmosphere for the development of personality.
"Civilizations commonly die from the excessive development of certain characteristics which had at first contributed to their success. Our form of industrial civilization suffers from having allowed experts to make growth and efficiency, rather than the quality of life, the main criterion of success. Among the hopeful signs of the times are the ground swell of dissatisfaction against this state of affairs and the awareness that, if things are in the saddle, it is because we have put them there. To repeat, the demonic force in our life is not technology per se, but our propensity to consider means as ends." (p. 233)
Chapters cover topics such as A Theology of the Earth, Humanized Nature, Industrial Society and Humane Civilization, and Arcadian Life Versus Faustian Civilization. Arcadian Life, symbolizing "biological adaptedness to the natural world," is the basic theme. Can we reverse the ravages of industrialization? Dubos concludes "with my own optimistic version of the humanistic faith: Trend is not destiny." (p. 291)
*** Good background reading for all levels, but perhaps overly generalized.

182. WARD, Barbara, and René DUBOS. **Only One Earth: The Care and Maintenance of a Small Planet.** NY: W.W. Norton, 1972. 304 pp.   (ABC-4)

The final section in this overview of global problems advocates A Planetary Order, offering chapters on The Shared Biosphere, Coexistence in the Technosphere, and Strategies for Survival.

We can survive only if we attain a loyalty to Planet Earth. A recognition of environmental interdependence could give us the sense of community we need to build a human world in which there would be non-violent settlement of disputes and a transfer of resources from rich to poor.

183. MISHAN, Ezra J. **The Costs of Economic Growth.** NY: Praeger, 1967. 190 pp.   (A-3)

A professor at the London School of Economics criticizes "Growthmania" and posits three choices for long-term policy: economic growth, a more equal distribution of income, and improved allocation of national resources: "the thesis is...that if men are concerned primarily with human welfare, and not primarily with productivity conceived as a good in itself, they should reject economic growth as a prior aim of policy in favor of a policy of seeking to apply more selective criteria of welfare." (p. 174; p. 163 in **Technology and Growth**) Such a policy would recognize the individual's right to amenity and promote the re-planning of cities and towns.

184. MISHAN, Ezra J. **Technology and Growth: The Price We Pay.** NY: Praeger, 1970. 193 pp.   (AB-3)

A somewhat popularized version of **The Costs of Economic Growth.** One minor difference is that "External Diseconomies" (a major concern in **Costs**) is referred to here as "Spillover Effects."

185. GEORGESCU-ROEGEN, Nicholas. **The Entropy Law and the Economic Process.** Cambridge, Mass.: Harvard University Press, 1971. 457 pp. $16.00.   (ns)

A difficult but very important work by a professor of economics at Vanderbilt University. The entropy law, or the second law of thermodynamics, asserts that the natural state of things is to pass from order to disorder; entropy is time's arrow. Entropy law rules supreme over the economic process, which is therefore seen as the irreversible transformation of low entropy into high. This view of the world is markedly different from conventional economics, which assumes a physical model of the world in which everything is reversible, e.g. the price mechanism will correct for pollution.

Georgescu-Roegen argues that economic development and mechanized agriculture are against the long-run interests of mankind. Instead, he advocates an economy based primarily on the flow of solar energy, and advocates a minimal bioeconomic program that would prohibit production of the instruments of war, lower the population level, and regard consumption for the sake of fashion as a bioeconomic crime.

*** The above is a condensation of Nicholas Wade, "Nicholas Georgescu-Roegan: Entropy the Measure of Economic Man." **Science,** 190: Oct. 31, 1975, pp. 447-450. Wade concludes that this general theory "is a powerful and ambitious synthesis that would seem to deserve more attention than has yet been its lot." (p. 450)

186. BARKLEY, Paul W. and David W. SECKLER. **Economic Growth and Environmental Decay: The Solution Becomes the Problem.** The Harbrace Series in Business and Economics. NY: Harcourt Brace Jovanovich, 1972. 193 pp., paper.   (AB-4)

"The time has come when serious choices must be made between growth and quality. This book is about those choices." (p. 2)

"In sum, in order to restore and maintain a high level of environmental quality, it is necessary to accept low rates of economic growth; and in order to ensure that everyone benefits by such a policy, it is necessary to provide a minimum income to people whether they work or not." (p. 191)

187. THEOBALD, Robert. Habit and Habitat. Englewood Cliffs, NJ: Prentice-Hall, 1972. 277 pp. $8.95.   (AB-4)

Environmental groups are seen as trying to deal with symptoms of the environmental crisis rather than with the central problem. Some groups are concerned with population growth, others with the abuse of technology. "The thesis of this book is that the causes of the environmental crisis lie far deeper. The habits we have developed during the industrial era toward our habitat are now so inappropriate that only a fundamental change in thought and action patterns will make any real difference to man's future." (p. 2)

This strange book is organized into two parts: The End of the Industrial Era and The Coming of the Communications Era. The latter is a different culture that Theobald previously called the cybernetic era. "The cybernetic era was named from the concept that nonhuman feedback mechanisms were being created: the communications era describes the overall results of this addition." (p. 145) This new era requires a transition from linear thinking to systemic thinking, where one perceives connections, interdependencies, and reciprocal relationships. It also requires a transition from the structural authority of linear organizations to the sapiential authority that is essential in dynamic conditions. In contrast to the scarcity-excess thinking of the industrial era, "Abundance can only emerge when we create systemic, sapiential authority systems." (p. 164) The final chapter describes the necessary system for distributing income in the new era, based on Basic Economic Security (BES) and Committed Spending (CS), concepts which the author has previously written about at great length.

*** Theobald also distinguishes between three styles of communication: INTER, OUTER, and SITUATIONAL. The book is described as trying to break out of the linear INTER style. Perhaps there is something profoundly fresh here, some important ideas too big to be adequately expressed. But the book might also be seen as simplistic, sloppy, and repetitious. Description and prescription are confused throughout. There are exaggerations, e.g. "As a society we are committed today to full employment." (p. 26) Chapter 5, a melange of crude charts with no analysis, purportedly constitutes a "negative scenario" that demonstrates why present trends cannot continue. A four-page "subjectively organized" bibliography succeeds in offering absolutely minimal information. And there is no index or glossary. If all of this points to the new style of communication, we may in fact be entering the non-communications era!

188. ODUM, Howard T. Environment, Power and Society. NY: Wiley-Interscience, 1971. 331 pp.   (A-3)

Employs the concepts of general systems theory and "energy language" to consider the problems of survival in our time, including questions of economics, law and religion. The concluding chapter describes three alternative futures: the future of power expanding, the future of power receding (requiring smaller cities and fewer cars), and the future of power constant. "Although there is yet excess energy, it might be better to put crash efforts into ecological engineering rather than into space." (p. 309)

*** Although "intended for the general reader," the language, as well as numerous technical diagrams, suggests that this book would best be appreciated by those with a background in the physical sciences and engineering.

189. TAYLOR, Theodore B. and Charles C. HUMPSTONE. **The Restoration of the Earth.** NY: Harper & Row, 1973. 166 pp. $7.95.   (A-3)

The teamwork of a nuclear physicist (Taylor) and a lawyer (Humpstone), who are "less concerned about pollution problems than how to go about solving them." (p.vii) The basic notion that the authors pose is the principle of containment: "a requirement that the environmental effects of human activity be confined within areas dedicated to that activity." (p. 33)

Containment aims to succeed in restoring the environment, whereas partial-release strategies seek only to maintain the status quo or reduce damage in that they are concerned with only the visible fringes of the problem. Rather than piling abatement device on abatement device, containment addresses the problem at the highest degree of abstraction. It costs less than alternative approaches, and is "the only alternative that will work and that can be put into effect during our lifetime." (p. 138) Chapters 12 and 13 explore effects of containment on daily life and on thought.

Following the containment principle, the authors propose national uniformity in emission standards, conversion of a major fraction of the world's agriculture to controlled environment greenhouses, wilderness restoration, nuclear fusion energy, closed-cycle processing plants to convert all wastes to energy and fertilizer, mass transport, covered walkways and bikeways, collecting and purifying all urban runoff and sewage water, and an international containment program featuring multilateral treaties setting uniform standards between nations.

The authors conclude: "We began by questioning two assumptions: that man is wise enough to determine how much man-made change the biosphere can support and that the way to environmental salvation lies through changing spiritual or ethical values. Discarding both, we have asserted that man has and should exercise the ability to insulate the biosphere from human activity at a cost that is not unthinkable or beyond measure but within the range or prices that we pay for other services. Containment is not a quixotic quest. It is the best of the alternative paths to the long-term preservation of the thin film of life that distinguishes our planet from its neighbors, and for all we know, from the rest of the universe." (pp. 165-166)

*** The basic notion appears well-worth considering; unfortunately, the authors do not summarize the elements of their argument or provide any footnotes or index, and their writing style is ponderous and leaden.

190. HENSHAW, Paul S. **This Side of Yesterday: Extinction or Utopia.** NY: Wiley, 1971. 186 pp. $5.95; $3.00, paper.   (AB-4)

From an evolutionary/ecological stance, it is argued that the human species "has arrived at a point in the overall cosmic scheme where continued advancement will require major shifts in attitudes and conduct with respect to reproduction, economic growth, energy development, industrialization, employment, the environment and conflict resolution--to mention only some." (p. 181) There is no clear focus, however, as to the desired end or how to attain it.

191. DUMONT, René. **Utopia or Else...** Trans. by Vivienne Menkes. NY: Universe, Sept. 1975. 180 pp. $8.50. (First published in France as **L'Utopie ou la Mort** in 1973)   (AB-3)

A steamy polemic--but a good one, with much data and many ideas--by the Director of Research at the National Institute of Agronomy in Paris. Part I attacks Herman Kahn's "semi-lunatic forecasts" and lists threats such as the danger of collapse, non-renewable resource depletion, water shortage, and the dangers of fertilizers and pesticides. Part II denounces the waste of the rich people in the rich countries, with concern addressed to advertising, private cars, excessive urban development, and the consumption of pet food. Part III argues for the inevitability of uprisings in the dominated countries.

Part IV advocates a general mobilization for Operation Survival, which would feature zero population growth, a cutback and eventual banning of arms, redistribution of wealth, a raw materials tax, cutbacks in air travel, incentives to live in the country, encouraging the sensible use of organic refuse, and the oceans becoming public property. We must put an end to waste in all of its forms "by going back to the grass roots of the peasant ethic, which is based on austerity, providence, prudence and great dignity." (p. 131) In short, Dumont advocates a socialist system geared to survival.

192. EVANS, Robert L. **The Fall and Rise of Man, If...** Minneapolis, Minn.: Lund Press, 1973. 268 pp. $6.95; $3.95, paper.   (A-4)
(Available from the author, 2500 St. Anthony Blvd., Minneapolis)

Good-hearted rambling about a variety of matters by a mathematician and past president of the Minnesota Academy of Science. The first fall of men occurred at the Tower of Babel, and the second is "still occurring through pollution and the classical four problems of war, poverty, hunger, and disease." (p. 74) Evans advocates a utopian society where there is a stress on quality rather than quantity, controlled population, and citizens supporting only those leaders who aid the whole society.

193. HELFRICH, Harold W., Jr. (ed.) **Agenda for Survival: The Environmental Crisis--2.** New Haven: Yale, 1970. 234 pp. $10.00; $2.95, paper   (ns)

194. CURRY-LINDAHL, Kai. **Conservation for Survival: An Ecological Strategy.** NY: Morrow, 1972. 335 pp. $6.95.   (ns)

An overview by a Swedish biologist of world ecological problems and the solutions that must be effected on a global scale.

195. ALLSOPP, Bruce. **The Garden Earth: The Case for** Ecological Morality. NY: Morrow, 1972. 118 pp. $5.00.   (ns)

196. KOZLOVSKY, Daniel G. (ed.) **An Ecological and Evolutionary Ethic.** Englewood Cliffs, N.J.: Prentice-Hall, 1974. 116 pp. $6.95; $4.95, paper.   (ns)

Notes by a biologist on the general themes of evolution, ecology, animism, humanism, and naturalism.

197. ROCKEFELLER, Nelson A. **Our Environment Can Be Saved.** Garden City, NY: Doubleday, 1970. 176 pp.   (C-4)

Political slush from the then-Governor of New York State, advocating "a new environmental ethic" and describing the various actions that Rockefeller had taken as Governor.

Concludes that "We are going to have to mediate the completing claims of the economy and the environment, and resolve them sensibly in the interest of the whole man, not simply economic man--not just for today, but for posterity.

"We can save our environment--and we shall save it because we must."
(p. 160)

198. EAYRS, James. **Greenpeace and Her Enemies.** Toronto, Canada: Bel-
ford Book Co., 1973 (?). $11.50.   (A-4)

A collection of essays on international affairs, held together by a vision
of a green and peaceable earth. The author is Co-Editor of **International
Journal,** published by the Canadian Institute for International Affairs.

199. CHASE, Stuart, "Green Money or Green Earth?" **The New York Times**
(Op-Ed Page), June 24, 1972.   (ABC-3)

The problems of our time are cogently summarized here in less than
500 words. "A contest is clearly gathering between the partisans of the
gross national product and of the quality of life...I believe there is an eight
major steps which sooner or later must be taken if the planet is to remain
viable." Briefly summarized, the steps are zero population growth, zero
industrial production growth, recycling and conserving material resources,
an adequate budget of the five prime essentials (food, shelter, clothing,
heath services, education) available for every human being, a decline in
the consumption of material goods in affluent societies, a sharp increase
in the social sciences "to help us deal with the severe cultural changes
that are surely coming," applied science to be carefully researched for
side effects, and some kind of organized world community.

200. NICHOLSON, Max. **The Big Change: After the Environmental Revolution.** NY: McGraw-Hill, 1973. 288 pp. $8.95.   (B-4)

The author claims experience both in public affairs and with ecological
principles, and that the book is not just another presentation of the ecological dilemma of mankind: "It starts from the point where such presentations have hitherto ended and seeks to answer the question how and where
a world which has absorbed that message can consciously undertake to redirect its social evolution so as to integrate ecological considerations."
(p. viii)
It is argued that we must face the Big Change in its entirety; yet this
event has been "swamped by countless trendy trivialities." Facets of the
Big Change include the population explosion, the changing pattern and
scale of gene flow, and the emergence of a meritocracy.
Unfortunately, the message tends to be buried in verbosity and rhetoric.
In Chapter 4, Toward Ecological Humanism, the chapter title is not defined, but there is a proposal for a Book of Man comprising several volumes
(also available in a compressed one-volume version) that is comprehensive and authoritative, expressing the continuing mission of mankind toward
higher evolution. The book would have a central role in educational curricula, with a role of unifying guidance similar to that which the Bible once
offered. Sections of the book would encompass man's environment; man's
origins and evolution; man's history, arts, science and culture; man's capabilities, faculties, weaknesses and limits; man's recent progress; and
the unsolved problems and challenges ahead. Chapter 5 suggests a world
noosphere program, and Chapter 9 proposes a College of Parenthood.

201. CALDWELL, Lynton K. **In Defense of Earth: International Protection
of the Biosphere.** Bloomington: Indiana University Press, 1972.
295 pp. $8.50.   (AB-3)

A social scientist at Indiana University devotes chapters to international

conservation efforts, problems of underestimating dangers, mobilizing international resources, inventing transnational structures, and strengthening
national capabilities. The latter offers a Ten Point Program including actions
such as making a declaration of policy, making an environmental survey,
ascertaining human resource needs, creating information systems for decision-makers, and developing public awareness.

"What is required of the peoples and nations of the Earth is that they transcend their own histories. They must learn to be more far-sighted and more
realistic then they have ever been." (p.230)

202. ROWLAND, Wade. **The Plot to Save the World: The Life and Times of
     the Stockholm Conference on the Human Environment.** Introduction
     by Maurice Strong. Toronto: Clarke, Irwin & Co., 1973. 194 pp.(AB-3)

A useful journalistic account of what happened at the 1972 Conference, as
well as the background leading to this important meeting. The appendices
are of particular interest.

Chapters are devoted to an overview of **The Limits to Growth** and **Blueprint
for Survival,** the planning of the Conference, the case of the poor nations, the
distinction between under-developed and over-developed nations, the draft
Declaration on the Human Environment, the International Conference on the
Convention on the Dumping of Wastes at Sea (held in London in Nov. 1972),
and other conferences held concurrent to the official one.

Appendix II reprints The Declaration on the Human Environment as adapted
by the Stockholm Conference, including 26 principles dealing with concerns
such as human rights to freedom and adequate conditions of life, humane
planning, abandoning projects designing for colonial and racist domination,
guarding against exhaustion of non-renewable resources, accelerating the
development of the developing countries, and the resources for improving
and preserving the environment.

Appendix 3 presents the Stockholm Conference Action Plan approved by
the 27th United Nations General Assembly. It advocates three broad types
of action--environmental assessment, environmental management, and support measures such as education and finance--and includes 109 recommendations for action at the international level.

203. STRONG, Maurice (ed.) **Who Speaks for Earth? Seven Citizens of the
     World on Major Issues of the Global Environment.** NY: Norton,
     1973. 174 pp. $6.95; $1.75, paper.   (ns)

The Distinguished Lecture Series sponsored by the International Institute
for Environmental Affairs during the U.N. Conference on the Human Environment (Stockholm, June 1972). Contributions by Barbara Ward, René Dubos,
Thor Heyerdahl, Gunnar Myrdal, Carmen Miro, Lord Zuckerman, and
Aurelio Peccei.

204. MORAES, Dom (ed.). **Voices for Life: Reflections on the Human Condition.**
     Published for the U.N. Fund on Population Activities. NY: Praeger,
     1975. 295 pp. $8.95.   (B-4)

As a capstone to the World Population Year, the following question was
asked to 25 global personalities: "What do you see as the quality of life, and
what do you think it will become in the future?" The resulting essays and
interviews do very little to answer this question: there are a number of
personal histories that fail to conclude in any general insights, and there
are many humanistic banalities.

A statement by Arnold Toynbee sets the anti-growth tone: "If mankind
is to salvage itself, it must try to return to the state of relative innocence

in which it was living before the outbreak of the eighteenth-century ethical and technological revolution in the West. In order to execute this difficult maneuver, it will have to look for inspiration, guidance, and example either in the pre-industrial West or in some non-Western region on which the pre-industrial way of life is still a going concern." (p.12) Jiddu Krishnamurti observes that we are dying because we are selfish, Heinrich Boll notes that the earth has a budget too and that we have been living on credit, Jonas Salk describes the transition from Epoch A to Epoch B (no. 149) and E.F. Schumacher expressed the hope for serious study of possibilities of a culture of poverty.

Other contributors include James Cameron, Indira Gandhi, Carlos Fuentes, Robert Kweku Atta Gardiner, Isaas Bashevis Singer, Eugene Ionesco, Lionel Tiger, Margaret Mead, Mochtar Lubis, Georges Walter, Julian Mitchell, Dipak Nandy, Barbara Ward, Arnold Wesker, Yehudi Menuhin, G. Michael Scott, Frank Hercules, Gloria Steinem, R. Buckminster Fuller, and Günter Grass.

*** So very, very little from such a putatively distinguished group. The quality of these so-called reflections is perhaps the most important message conveyed about the human condition.

205. FORRESTER, Jay W. **World Dynamics.** Cambridge, Mass.: Wright-Allen Press, 1971. 142 pp.   (A-3)

A "preliminary effort" to model world interactions, devised for a July 1970 meeting of the Club of Rome. The widely discussed Limits to Growth study (see below) followed from this work. The dynamic model described here interrelates six variables: population, capital investment, geographical space, natural resources, pollution, and food production.

This original work is perhaps best known for its argument about the counterintuitive nature of social systems in Chapter 5, Obvious Responses Will Not Suffice, where mental models are seen as deficient in contrast to computer models.

"The long-term future of the earth must be faced soon as a guide for present action. Goals of nations and societies must be altered to become compatible with that future, otherwise man will remain out of balance with his environment." (p.125) Concluding comments propose a new profession of social dynamics.

206. MEADOWS, Donella H., Dennis L. MEADOWS, Jørgen RANDERS, and William W. BEHRENS III. **The Limits to Growth: A Report for the Club of Rome's Project on the Predicament of Mankind.** A Potomac Associates Book. NY: Universe Books, 1972. 205 pp. $6.50; $2.75, paper.   (A-3)

The much-publicized, highly controversial, computer-based study of a MIT Project Team headed by Dennis L. Meadows, based on the model of Jay W. Forrester (see above), and embellished with 48 figures and 6 tables.

"Our world model was built specifically to investigate five major trends of global concern--accelerating industrialization, rapid population growth, widespread malnutrition, depletion of nonrenewable resources, and a deteriorating environment." It is readily acknowledged that this model is "imperfect, oversimplified, and unfinished" and that there is a need for more facts, particularly regarding pollution. Despite the preliminary state of this work, it was felt that the main features of the model and the findings should be summarized in a brief, nontechnical way, in order to initiate necessary debate in the wider community beyond that of scientists.

The major conclusion is that "1. If the present growth trends in world population, industrialization, pollution, food production, and resource depletion continue unchanged, the limits to growth on this planet will be reached sometime within the next one hundred years. The most probable result will be a rather sudden and uncontrollable decline in both population and industrial capacity.

"2. It is possible to alter these growth trends and to establish a condition of ecological and economic stability that is sustainable far into the future. The state of global equilibrium could be designed so that the basic material needs of each person on earth are satisfied and each person has an equal opportunity to realize his individual human potential.

"3. If the world's people decide to strive for this second outcome rather than the first, the sooner they begin working to attain it, the greater will be their chances of success." (pp. 23-24)

The first three chapters cover the nature and limits of exponential growth, and growth in the world system. Chapter 4, Technology and the Limits to Growth argues that "technological optimism is the most common and the most dangerous reaction to our findings from the world model," in that it diverts attention from the fundamental problem of growth in a finite system.

Chapter 5, The State of Global Equilibrium, describes the desirable condition where "population and capital are essentially stable, with the forces tending to increase or decrease them in a carefully controlled balance." (p.171) Such a steady state society is not anti-technological, but would welcome discoveries such as new methods of waste collection, more efficient techniques of recycling, better product design, harnessing solar energy, methods of natural pest control, and contraceptive advances. Nor would such equilibrium necessarily mean an end to progress or human development: "Equilibrium would require trading certain human freedoms, such as producing unlimited numbers of children or consuming uncontrolled amounts of resources, for other freedoms, such as relief from pollution and crowding and the threat of collapse of the world system." (pp.179-180)

Seven policies that would lead to a stabilized world model are suggested on pp. 163-164: stabilizing population by 1975 and industrial capital by 1990, reducing resource consumption per unit of industrial output to one-fourth of 1970 value, shifting economic preferences of society toward more services, reducing pollution to one-fourth of 1970 value, diverting capital to food production to produce sufficient food for all people, soil enrichment and preservation as a high priority, and increasing the durability of industrial capital.

The concluding Commentary by The Executive Committee of the Club of Rome (an informal, non-governmental association of about 70 persons of 25 nationalities), reiterates the argument that technological development and discovering new stocks of raw materials would only delay crisis, and stresses that "the conclusions of the study point to the need for fundamental changes in the values of society." (p. 188)

*** Despite the attempt to popularize the findings, the "Meadows Report" is not light reading, unless one enjoys charts showing various manipulations of the key variables. The report clearly met its aim of provoking widespread attention, but this attention appears to be not so much a reaction to what was said, but to how it was said (utilizing a computer, for better or worse), and who said it (they mysterious-sounding Club of Rome).

207. MEADOWS, Dennis L. and Donella H. MEADOWS (eds.). **Toward Global Equilibrium. Collected Papers.** Cambridge, Mass.: Wright-Allen Press, 1973. 358 pp. $18.00.   (ns)

208. MEADOWS, Dennis L. et. al. **Dynamics of Growth in a Finite World.** Cambridge, Mass.: Wright-Allen, 1974. 638 pp. $35.00.   (ns)

Presents the methodology behind The Limits to Growth and the details of a model called "World 3," a device for testing the implications of alternative assumptions.

209. MESAROVIC, Mihajlo and Eduard PESTEL. **Mankind at the Turning Point: The Second Report to the Club of Rome.** NY: E.P. Dutton/ Reader's Digest Press, 1974. 210 pp. $12.95; $4.95, paper. NAL Signet Edition, $1.95, paper.   (AB-4)

A professor of systems research at Case Western Reserve University (Mesarovic) and a professor of engineering at Hannover University in Germany, orchestrating the work of 63 collaborators and consultants, virtually all of them economists and natural scientists. Despite the pious assertion that "today's problems require knowledge from a number of, if not all, disciplines," (p. 20), the lack of any contributions by sociologists, anthropologists, historians, communications/learning experts, philosophers, and others from the "softer" areas of learning is a dramatic flaw in this report, which is technically astute but socio-politically naive.

A new and improved computer model is employed, based on multilevel hierarchical systems theory and the division of the world into ten interdependent and mutually interacting regions, analyzing alternative patterns of development over a fifty-year period. The authors explicitly criticize the "Forrester-Meadows Theses" which served as a basis for the first report, as overly homogeneous, and the prescription of equilibrium as overly simplified. To grow or not to grow is not a relevant question until growth is defined, and the authors distinguish between undifferentiated growth with its exponential increases, and organic growth, which involves a process of differentiation and dynamic equilibrium where some organs grow and others might decline.

The argument is made that the emerging world system must be viewed as an assortment of interdependencies, that delays in closing the gaps between rich and poor nations could be disastrous and delays in dealing with the population problem could be deadly, that there are limits to independence even for the biggest nations, that the only feasible solution to the world food situation requires a global approach, and that reliance on the development of nuclear energy is a "magical and dangerous solution" which is likely to be a Faustian bargain or worse.

Ignoring doomsday prophecies could make them self-fulfilling. "Our scientifically conducted analysis of the long-term world development based on all available data points out quite clearly that such a passive course leads to disaster." (p. vii in italics) In Nature, it is argued, organic growth proceeds according to a master plan, and such a plan is missing from the processes of growth and development of the world system: "...it is in this sense that mankind is at a turning point in its history: to continue along the path of cancerous undifferentiated growth or to start on the path of organic growth." (p. 9)

The gravity of this situation, unfortunately, is not matched by the trite "immediate first steps" that are recommended. On the societal level, necessary changes include long-term assessment as standard procedure in decision-making, the solution of global issues by concerted global action, the development of an international framework for cooperation, and a willingness to give top priority to the long-term global development crisis. Recommendations for individual values and attitudes include a world consciousness, a new ethic in the use of material resources compatible with the oncoming age of scarcity, an attitude toward nature based on harmony rather than conquest, and a sense of identification with future generations. All of this requires a new kind of education geared to the twenty-first century.
*** Such liberal moralizing is not new. Nor can it be expected to change the hearts and minds of a sufficient number of persons in sufficient time. Nothing is said about the role of multinational corporations or the actions that the developing countries must take themselves (e.g. **Gunnar Myrdal, The Challenge of World Poverty.** Pantheon, 1970). The so-

called systems approach, in this application, is not as holistic as it pretends to be.

210. OLTMANS, Willem L. On Growth. NY: Putnam's, 1974. 493 pp.   (AB-2)

Truly an impressive "tour d'horizon" by a Dutch journalist who has assembled 70 conversations with leading figures, generally concerning their reactions to the MIT-based, Club of Rome sponsored, **Limits to Growth** study. The questions are intelligent and learned, serving to evoke capsuled worldviews of economists such as Paul A. Samuelson, Carl Kaysen, William D. Nordhaus, Erza J. Mishan, Kenneth Boulding, Leonard M. Ross and Peter Passell; social critics such as Ivan Illich, Ernest Mandel, Noam Chomsky, Mary McCarthy, Lewis Mumford, Herbert Marcuse, and Michael Harrington; natural scientists such as Paul Ehrlich, Barry Commoner, Sir Julian Huxley, Edward Teller, Harrison Brown, and Eugene Wigner; and futurists such as Herman Kahn, Daniel Bell, Lester Brown, John Platt and Dennis Gabor.
*** A handbook of cacophony. Also see **On Growth, Two** (Putnam's, Feb. 1976. $9.95), a companion volume of conversations in the socialist nations and the Third World.

211. GOLDSMITH, Edward et al., A Blueprint for Survival. Boston: Houghton Mifflin, 1972. London: Tom Stacey, 1972. 173 pp. (First appearance as the entire Jan. 1972 issue of The Ecologist magazine)
(AB-1)
Accompanied by a statement of support by 37 leading scholars and scientists in Great Britian, **Blueprint** was published at about the same time that **The Limits to Growth** appeared, and the two were considered together at the outset. Subsequently, **The Limits to Growth** received more attention, which is unfortunate, because this is a better book.
The opening words are blunt: "The principal defect of the industrial way of life with its ethos of expansion is that it is not sustainable. Its termination within the lifetime of someone born today is inevitable--unless it continues to be sustained for a while longer by an entrenched minority at the cost of imposing great suffering on the rest of mankind." (p. 14)
The reasons for this outlook are clearly spelled out in four appendices. Ecosystems and their Disruption describes the effects of pollutants, energy consumption, thermal waste, pollution by heavy metals, and oil pollution. Social Systems and their Disruption describes cultural patterns, political institutions, and various aspects of disintegration such as crime and mental disease. Population and Food Supply covers matters such as use of pesticides and the deterioration of soil structure. The final appendix on Nonrenewable Resources briefly summarizes the outlook for fossil fuels and 16 major metals.
A systemic view is promulgated throughout, and governments are accused of seeing the world in fragments. Moreover, it is argued that governments have incentives for continued expansion of economic growth, e.g. standard of living is measured as gross national product, confidence must be maintained in the economy, and growth must be stimulated to keep unemployment at tolerable levels. The authors argue that this pattern can only be broken with a fully-integrated plan leading to the Stable Society.
"The principal conditions of a stable society...are: 1) minimum disruption of ecological processes; 2) maximum conservation of materials and energy--or an economy of stock rather than flow; 3) a population in which recruitment equals loss; and 4) a social system in which the individual can enjoy, rather than feel restricted by, the first three conditions." (p. 34)
Attaining these conditions would "probably" require seven operations: reducing environmental disruption, halting present trends, technological substitutes for dangerous components of these trends; "natural" or self-regulating substitutes where possible, the invention of energy-conserving

alternative technologies, decentralization of polity and economy at all levels and the formation of reasonably self-supporting small communities, and education for such communities.

*** This book is more readable than The Limits to Growth, and the argument is broader and deeper--dealing with necessary societal arrangements. A useful background is provided by Nicholas Wade, "Edward Goldsmith: Blueprint for a De-Industrialized Society," Science, 191: January 23, 1976, pp. 270-272.

212. PIRAGES, Dennis C., and Paul R. EHRLICH. **Ark II: Social Response to Environmental Perspectives.** NY: Viking, 1974; San Francisco: Freeman, 1974. 344 pp.   (BC-2)

"...this time the ark cannot be built out of wood and caulking. We must insure our survival by redesigning the political, economic, and social institutions of industrial society. If a new institutional ark cannot be made watertight in time, industrial society will sink, dragging under prophets of doom as well as skeptics and critics." (Prologue)

The second ark is "a society that nurtures improvement of human beings and a spirit of unity rather than one that embraces the cult of the machine." (p. 282) The initial chapters survey the worsening situation: the assault on nature, exponential growth of population, the physical limits to growth, technological momentum, increasing interdependence, and social lag.

The remainder of the book provides a broad shopping list of reforms. Many are simplistic and not very radical, but nevertheless there is a good overview of many contemporary notions. Chapter 3 covers economics, corporations, investments, consumers, and new jobs. Chapters 4 and 5 attack homogeneous legislators, centralization of power, vested interests, and irresponsibility, while supporting Rexford Tugwell's proposal for a new constitution and a Planning Branch of the federal government. Chapter 6 covers education, science, information, and mass media, suggesting reforms such as fully paid higher education as everyone's birthright, reorganizing the structure of academic disciplines, and sabbatical years for adult workers to increase university income. Chapter 7 discusses the international system and offers suggestions for a new foreign policy. Chapter 8 argues for new social priorities and a new society based on Illich's notion of a convivial society, equalizing opportunity, and a new tax policy involving a credit tax (which is related to the negative income tax and would serve to abolish welfare).

"The transformation of a society like that of the United States implies the need for a massive educational effort toward a goal unique in history--the planned evolution of a new culture." (p. 63) The authors believe that social change can take place "by working within the system and by continually pointing to the need for massive long-term structural transformations." Attaining these long-term goals requires "cultivating large numbers of well-informed, nonviolent revolutionaries. These people must use all available peaceful strategies to deflect industrial society from its suicidal course." (p. 63)

*** A comprehensive political agenda combined with a succinct overview of environmental problems.

213. WATT, Kenneth E.F. **The Titanic Effect: Planning for the Unthinkable.** Stamford, Conn.: Sinauer Associates, 1974; NY: E.P. Dutton, 1974. 268 pp.   (AB-3)

An ecologist/zoologist at the University of California at Davis seeks "to present information about important processes resulting from the interaction of economic, environmental and population phenomena in a simplified, yet valid way." (p. xi)

"The thesis of this book is that all the symptoms, good and bad, together constitute a syndrome pointing to a single acute economic ailment: excessive, unplanned, undirected and destructive growth." (p. 3) The conventional economic wisdom is defective in several respects, but can be remedied by incorporating insights from ecology and systems analysis. "The Titanic Effect" has to do with vision and planning: "The magnitude of disasters decreases to the extent that people believe they are possible, and plan to prevent them, or to minimize their effects." (p. 7)

Chapters are devoted to The Energy Crisis (dealing with questions of whether technological innovation will save us), The Rising Price of Food, Environmental Pollution, Market Saturation and Slowdown (an indicator of a malfunctioning economy), Inflation, A Coming Glut of Manpower, International Monetary Turbulence, and Overpopulation. A chapter on Scenarios of the Future posits 16 possibilities based on 4 variables: population increase, growth of GNP, resource depletion, and pollution. The four most likely scenarios are described in detail.

It is concluded that "there is only one supremely important goal for American society at present: efficiency in the use of energy and other resources. If this goal is not attained, a whole panoply of clearly disastrous consequences will follow." (p. 220) Suggested policies include minimizing the birth rate, mass transit, developing service industries, encouraging family farms and family farm cooperatives, a national energy agency to promote consistency in policy, regional land-use planning, self-regulating negative feedback systems, political accountability, citizen participation in government, and a steady-state economy (as proposed by Herman Daly). To attain such an economy, inflation must be eliminated, perhaps through a permanent wage and price freeze.

214. GABOR, Dennis. **The Mature Society.** NY: Praeger, 1972. 208 pp.
$7.50.   (AB-3)

"In this book I have tried to sketch out a Mature Society: a peaceful world on a high level of material civilization, which has given up growth in numbers and in material consumption but not growth in the quality of life, and one which is compatible with the nature of homo sapiens." (pp. 3-4)

Gabor, the recipient of the 1971 Nobel Prize in physics, does not view this society as a utopia, "though I could not avoid sketching in a few of its features." These features include stability in numbers and in material production (an ecological equilibrium with the resources of the Earth), reform of destabilizing institutions and practices, less speculation on the capital market, universal education in parenthood, unashamed elitism, and a pluralistic society of hope, play, and diversity. Such a society would be guided by two slogans: excellence instead of quantitative growth, and possession instead of consumption. Gabor also devotes chapters to discussing problems of competition, the family, freedom, stability, employment, and economics.

*** Gabor's attainable ideal is a worthwhile exercise that should be attempted by many persons.

215. DALY, Herman E. (ed.), **Toward a Steady-State Economy.** San Francisco: W.H. Freeman, 1973. 332 pp. $8.95; $3.95, paper.   (AB-2)

After a long introduction, there are 16 essays, all offering "a single, coherent point of view."

I. Biophysical Constraints on Economic Growth

-Nicholas Georgescu-Roegen, "The Entropy Law and the Economic Problem" (1971)

-Preston Cloud, "Mineral Resources in Fact and Fancy" (1971)

-Paul H. Ehrlich and John P. Holdren, "Impact of Population Growth" (1971)

-Leon R. Kass, "The New Biology: What Price Relieving Man's Estate?" (1971)
   II. The Social World and Adjustment to a Steady State
-Kenneth E. Boulding, "The Economics of the Coming Spaceship Earth" (1966)
-Garrett Hardin, "The Tragedy of the Commons" (1968)
-Herman E. Daly, "The Steady-State Economy: Toward a Political Economy of Biophysical Equilibrium and Moral Growth," (revised from 1971 lecture)
-Warren A. Johnson, "The Guaranteed Income as an Environmental Measure," (1971)
-Richard England and Barry Bluestone, "Ecology and Social Conflict" (original)
-William Ophuls, "Leviathan or Oblivion?" (original)
-E.F. Schumacher, "Buddhist Economics" (1968)
-Walter A. Weisskopf, "Economic Growth versus Existential Balance" (1965)
-Herman E. Daly, "Electric Power, Employment and Economic Growth: A Case Study in Growthmania" (1972)
   III. Values and the Steady State
-Jørgen Randers and Donella Meadows, "The Carrying Capacity of Our Global Environment: A Look at the Ethical Alternatives," (1972)
-John Cobb, "Ecology, Ethics, and Theology" (original)
-C.S. Lewis, "The Abolition of Man" (1974)
*** Steady-state economy used interchangeably by Daly with stationary-state economy and no-growth economy. Extensive definition and justification in the introduction, pp. 10-27.

216. DALY, Herman E. (ed.) **Essays Toward a Steady-State Economy.** Cuernavaca, Mexico: CIDOC, Cuaderno No. 70, 1971.   (AB-3)

   Six papers dissenting from the ruling policy of "Growthmania":
-Nicholas Georgescu-Roegen, "The Entropy Law and the Economic Problem." (1971)
-William C. Gough and Bernard J. Eastlund, "Energy, Wastes, and the Fusion Torch" (1971)
-Robert C. Heilbroner, "Ecological Armageddon" (1970)
-Barry Commoner, "The Environmental Cost of Economic Growth" (1971)
-Kenneth E. Boulding, "The Economics of the Coming Spaceship Earth" (1966)
-Herman E. Daly, "The Stationary-State Economy," 1971.
   The stationary state, seen as a necessary direction to aim for, is defined as a society in which the total population and the total stock of physical wealth are maintained at a constant level.

217. **The No-Growth Society.** Daedalus, 102:4, Fall 1973. 245 pp.   (AB-3)

   After an introduction by Mancur Olson, there are 13 essays:
-Kingsley Davis, "Zero Population Growth: The Goal and the Means"
-John P. Holdren, "Population and the American Predicament: The Case Against Complacency"
-Norman B. Ryder, "Two Cheers for ZPG"
-E.J. Mishan, "Ills, Bads, and Disamenities: The Wages of Growth"
-Kenneth E. Boulding, "The Shadow of the Stationary State"
-Richard Zeckhauser, "The Risks of Growth"
-Marc J. Roberts, "On Reforming Economic Growth"
-Harvey Brooks, "The Technology of Zero Growth"
-Lester Brown, "Rich Countries and Poor in a Finite, Interdependent World"
-Willard R. Johnson, "Should the Poor Buy No Growth?"
-William Alonso, "Urban Zero Population Growth"
-Roland N. McKean, "Growth vs. No Growth: An Evaluation"
-Mancur Olson, Hans H. Landsberg, and Joseph L. Fisher, "Epilogue"

*** Reprinted as Maneur Olson and Hans H. Landsberg (eds.) **The No-Growth Society.** NY: Norton, 1974. 259 pp. $10.00; $2.95, paper.

217a. WOLFGANG, Marvin E. (ed.) **Adjusting to Scarcity. The ANNALS of the American Academy of Political and Social Science,** Vol. 420, July 1975.   (A-3)

-Everett S. Lee, "Population and Scarcity of Food"
-James P. Grant, "Food, Fertilizer, and the New Global Politics of Resource Scarcity"
-Ian D. MacGregor, "Natural Distribution of Metals and Some Economic Effects"
-Kenji Takeuchi and Bension Varon, "Commodity Shortages and Changes in World Trade"
-Monte E. Canfield, Jr. and John R. Hadd, "Government Response to Commodity Shortages"
-Wilfrid Malenbaum, "Scarcity: Prerequisite to Abundance"
-H. Robert Sharbaugh, "Petroleum and Energy"
-Amitai Etzioni, "A Creative Adaptation to a World of Rising Shortages," advocates a Maslowian human needs perspective.
-W.W. Rostow, "The Developing World in the Fifth Kondratieff Upswing," advocates an international partnership.

218. OPHULS, William, "The Scarcity Society," **Harper's,** Vol. 248, April 1974, pp. 47-52.   (AB-3)

Generalized warnings by a Yale political scientist that the end of American abundance threatens potential dictatorship. Simpler living in harmony with nature is necessary to avoid this.

"Our awakening from the pleasant dream of infinite progress and the abolition of scarcity will be extremely painful. Institutionally, scarcity demands. that we sooner or later achieve a full-fledged 'steady-state' or 'spaceman' economy." (p. 48)

Scarcity makes muddling through as an administrative style no longer tolerable or even possible. It also threatens democracy: "The likely result of the reemergence of scarcity appears to be the resurrection in modern form of the preindustrial polity, in which the few govern the many and in which government may or may not be benevolent." (p. 52)

219. SEABORG, Glenn T., "The Recycle Society of Tomorrow," **The Futurist,** 8:3, June 1974, pp. 108-115.   (AB-3)

A University Professor of Chemistry at UC, Berkeley and former Chairman of the U.S. Atomic Energy Commission pictures the society of the 1990's as "almost 180 degrees different from what we are today, or some think we will be in the future." (p. 109)

Such a society "exercises a quiet, non-neurotic self-control, displays a highly cooperative public spirit, has an almost religious attitude toward environmental quality and resource conservation, exercises great care and ingenuity in managing its personal belongings and shows an extraordinary degree of reliability in its work. Furthermore, I see such a society as being mentally and physically healthier and enjoying a greater degree of freedom, even though it will be living in a more crowded, complex environment." (p. 109)

The recycle society will result from a number of painful shocks. It will involve a shift to the design and production of essentially non-obsolescing consumer goods, and the extensive recycle of organic material from agriculture and forest industries. Much will be required in the way of new legislation, regulation, and tax incentives. There will be a shift toward clustered, attached, and high-rise housing, and the increased use of underground space. Integrated industrial complexes will concentrate energy sources, materials, and manufacturing in single locations, and there will also be offshore nuclear-electric powerplants.

220. HUGHES, David. "Toward a Recycling Society," **New Scientist**, Jan. 10, 1974, pp. 58-60.   (B-4)

Confined to offering a few ideas on waste reclamation and the use of organic waste.

220a. U.S. Congress. House of Representatives, Committee on Merchant Marine and Fisheries. **Growth and Its Implications for the Future, Part 1.** Serial No. 93-7. Washington: U.S. Government Printing Office, May 1973. 996 pp. $4.50,paper (S/N 5270-01887).   (A-3)

A massive compendium prefaced with statements by Lester R. Brown, Robert A. Frosch, Alfred Heller, Peter S. Hunt, Dennis L. Meadows, Russell W. Peterson, and Steven Salyer.
The Appendix, beginning on p. 64, includes the entire text of **The Limits to Growth** (no. 206) and the **Blueprint for Survival** (no. 211), along with 29 other items that support or question these statements, including writers such as Carl Kaysen, Mahbub ul Haq, E.J. Mishan, Robert L. Heilbroner, Aurelio Peccei, Sir Julian Huxley, Sir Geoffrey Vickers, Henry C. Wallich, John Maddox, Herman E. Daly, and Jay Forrester.
*** By far the biggest assemblage of views on this issue.

221. GRAY, Elizabeth and David Dodson, and William F. MARTIN. **Growth and Its Implications for the Future.** Branford Conn.: The Dinosaur Press (P.O. Box 666), June 1975. 182 pp. $3.95, paper.   (BC-4)

A strange melange of charts, tables, diagrams, cartoons, questions, excerpts and choppy text, with chapters on The Parameters of Growth; Resource Availability; Environmental Pollution; Population, Food, and Land; Economic Growth--How Much and How?; Marketplace Adjustment to Scarcity; Technology as an Adjustment Mechanism; Consciousness; and The Search for Adjustment Mechanisms.
*** May be useful in the classroom.

222. CHEN, Kan and Karl F. LAGLER. **Growth Policy: Population, Environment, and Beyond.** Ann Arbor, Mich.: University of Michigan Press, 1974. 237 pp.   (A-3)

The world macroproblem is caused by the accelerating growth of population, technological development, and consumption. The authors, aided by a number of colleagues at the University of Michigan, seek to provide an overall framework and to establish criteria for coupling policy research to policy-making procedures. They propose "a comprehensive policy-making procedure, a systems approach commensurate with the dynamics and the complexity of the total ecosystem of the earth." (p. 7) This leads to a questioning of the conventional wisdom and the ability of present institutions to cope with the macroproblem, which continues to be poorly defined.

223. LECOMBER, Richard. **The Growth Objective.** Published for the International Institute of Social Economics by Emmasglen, Patrington, England, 1975. Monograph No. 3. 76 pp. $15, paper.   (ns)

224. KNOP, Ed, and Evan VLACHOS, "Examining Alternative Futures: Theoretical Considerations," **FUTURES: The Journal of Planning and Forecasting,** 7:3, June 1975, pp. 221-229.   (A-4)

An attempt to supplement Harrison Brown's classic statement, **The Challenge of Man's Future** (no. 174) with selected social science insights.
The alternatives viewed by the authors are 1) egalitarian distribution of resources; 2) a continuation of uncontrolled laissez-faire (a situation conducive to mass unrest); and 3) collective departure from growth-oriented policy, with "social differentiation, initiative, and identity/self-esteem based on the quality of our human lives and the amount of concern and self-discipline we show rather than on the quantity of our consumption of scarce resources." (p. 227) The third alternative is seen as probable, preferable, and necessary.

225. UDALL, Stewart, Charles CONCONI, and David OSTERHAUT. **The Energy Balloon.** NY: McGraw-Hill, 1974. 288 pp.   (ABC-3)

Attempts "to develop a positive program for a lean America." After reviewing the energy problem, Chapter 8 advocates "The Industrial Reformation"; a scaling down process, short-term conservation steps, a return to durable products, and getting away from being "a nation of megathinkers."
Three fallacious assumptions are assailed. 1) The Technological Transformation Fallacy that technology will beneficently transform the world; 2) The Superior Model Fallacy: the self-centered pride of Americans in the achievements of their society, which is seen as atypical in geographical blessings; and 3) The Fat Man Fallacy that the fruits of general prosperity will soon be available to poor nations; that a rising tide lifts all boats. "...a new species of special soothsayers has appeared to promulgate and expound its virtues. The most widely-known of these self-styled futurologists is Herman Kahn." (p.262)
Three basic changes are recommended for U.S. policies: rejecting "big technology" solutions to the world's problems, developing and sharing simple technologies, and promoting joint efforts in self-restraint.

226. KAHN, Herman, and William BROWN, "A World Turning Point: And a Better Prospect for the Future," **The Futurist,** 9:6, December 1975, pp. 284 ff.   (AB-3)

Argues that "The popular metaphor of explosive or exponential growth will become increasingly misleading" and that restraint of population growth is very likely to occur for a variety of reasons. Few growth curves in nature can be exponential; rather, we are entering a new phase of history with declining rates of growth, first for world population and then for Gross World Product. The present Hudson Institute analysis foresees "a world population leveling out near the end of the 21st century at about 10 to 28 billion people, with an average per capita from $10,000 to $20,000 derived from a GWP of $100 to $300 trillion. Such figures are of course rough estimates...they do not encompass the full range of possibilities." (p.285)
A very useful chart is provided (pp.335-338), contrasting the Neo-Malthusian Beliefs and Conclusions with the Post-Industrial (and Super-Industrial) Perspective. The former is characterized as viewing a fixed pie, diminishing returns from new technology, the likely failure of management, depletion of resources, cancerous growth, postponement of action as disastrous, increasing gaps in income, further deterioration of the quality of life, and a grave crisis in general. The Post-Industrial Perspective of the authors is essentially the opposite.
*** Readers are urged to contrast this article with a parallel piece by Willis W. Harman: "Notes on the Coming Transformation," in Andrew A. Spekke (ed.) **The Next 25 Years** (World Future Society, 1975. See no. 779)

Harman employs the same chart of ten categories, with the "Herman Kahn Post-Industrial Perspective" virtually identical to that portrayed above, but with a "Transformational Perspective" that differs considerably from the "Neo-Malthusian" view portrayed by Kahn and Brown. Harman's perspective advocates frugal technology, a changing social contract of business, a redefinition of growth in less economic and material terms, more emphasis on social innovation, world poverty as a continuing problem, and voluntary simplicity.

Contrasting Harman's view with the Kahn/Brown "Neo-Malthusian" view enables one to understand how Kahn paints his opponents into corners.

227. BECKERMAN, Wilfred. Two Cheers for the Affluent Society: A Spirited Defense of Economic Growth. NY: St. Martin's Press, 1975. 238 pp. $7.95.   (AB-3)

A University of London economist attacks "eco-doomsters," arguing that resources will probably not be depleted because, as demand rises, it increasingly pays to find new reserves. Concerning pollution, reductions in pollutant levels are being made in various places, and taxing polluters to cover the social cost of pollution would further this reduction. "The message of this book, therefore, is an unexciting one because it is a moderate and balanced one." (p.48)

E.J. Mishan is attacked at length, as well as The Limits to Growth report which is seen as "guilty of various kinds of flagrant errors of fact, logic and scientific method." (p.199) The anti-growth movement is seen as "basically a middle class racket" and two anti-growth camps are criticized: those who say that growth cannot continue, and those who say that growth cannot make us happier. It is yet to be demonstrated that detriment necessarily comes with economic growth.

The real issue, Beckerman asserts, is that most people still do not have conventional necessities, and that there are major continuing problems with our education, housing, and health services.

227a. SHARKANSKY, Ira. The United States: A Study of a Developing Country. NY: David McKay, 1975. 187 pp.   (B-4)

Criticizes the notion of "post-industrial society" and the prescriptions of Limits to Growth. The U.S. can be seen as a developed country, but it can also be seen as a developing country because there is considerable poverty, and great economic contrasts. Moreover, the poor states in the U.S. have characteristics in common with the politics of poor nations. Concludes that "It is neither necessary nor appropriate to ignore the demands for growth and concentrate only on conservation; or to hope for political changes that will divide a fixed economic pie into equal pieces." (p. 181)

228. MADDOX, John R. The Doomsday Syndrome. NY: McGraw-Hill, 1972. 293 pp.   (AB-3)

The editor of the prestigious British journal, Nature, attacks writers such as Paul Ehrlich, Barry Commoner, René Dubos, Rachel Carson, and William and Paul Paddock for fear-mongering and overstatement. The first report of the Club of Rome was released as the book was being completed, and it is criticized (in a Postscript) for describing the world in oversimple terms.

The common error of these prophecies is to assume that the worst will always happen. "The most serious insidious danger in the environmental movement is that it may sap the will of advanced communities to face the problems which no doubt lie ahead." (p.vi)

The first chapter, Is Catastrophe Coming?, attacks Ehrlich and Carson for overstatement. The Numbers Game argues that fertility has been declining, and that individual prosperity in the developing world will double in twenty-five years. The End of the Lode holds that there are few materials for which substitutes do not exist. The Pollution Panic scolds that "too zealous an attack on DDT and related chemicals may deprive the world of important benefits." (p.127) Ecology is a State of Mind concludes that "For the time being at least, there is no evidence that the human race has failed to profit from its relative detachment from the rest of the natural world." (p.190).

Shifting to concerns beyond ecology, Man-Made Men describes biological research and stresses that many speculations are premature; that the problems of scientific understanding are greater than legend supposes. Prosperity is Possible argues that costs of accomodating pollution can be dealt with within the system of classical economics, and that technology has improved the quality of life: "industrialization in advanced societies has brought with it more leisure, more prosperity and more freedom..." (p.236) "The speed of the white-collar revolution in the United States has been quite remarkable." (p.237) In the final chapter, What Can Be Done?, Maddox argues for using existing laws and for the benefits of science and technology in lightening labor and avoiding drudgery.

*** A challenging use of overstatement to attack overstatement.

228a. MADDOX, John. **Beyond the Energy Crisis.** NY: McGraw-Hill, 1975. 208 pp. $8.95. (ns)

228b. SAUVY, Alfred. **Zero Growth?** NY: Praeger, 1976. 224 pp. $10.00. (ns)

A French demographer argues that a sudden termination of population growth is more dangerous than overpopulation, as well as incompatible with our advances in technology. Rather than an all-encompassing policy such as zero growth, Sauvy offers solutions for specific problems "allowing us to properly channel our growth for the greater good of our environment and our economy." (advt.)

229. COLE, H.S.D., Christopher FREEMAN, et al. (eds.) **Thinking About the Future: A Critique of The Limits to Growth.** London: Chatto and Windus/Sussex University, 1973. 218 pp. (Published in U.S. under title of **Models of Doom.** NY: Universe Books, 1973, $8; $2.95, paper) (A-3)

Fourteen papers resulting from a project of the Science Policy Research Unit of the University of Sussex. In the introductory essay, Freeman argues that the Club of Rome-sponsored Limits to Growth study underestimates the possibilities of technological progress, is not sufficiently interdisciplinary, and suffers from computer fetishim.

Papers in Part I examine the sub-systems of the World Model in great detail, essentially raising objections to the assumptions. Papers in Part II examine "The Ideological Background."

230. BAXTER, William F. **People or Penguins: The Case for Optimal Pollution.** NY: Columbia University Press, 1974. 110 pp. (AB-3)

A Professor of Law at Stanford attempts to cut through the rhetorical fog and examine the complexities of attaining a "good" environment, which is just one of the set of human objectives. Baxter's criteria are oriented to people, and not penguins, and he stresses that any decision to decrease pollution will also decrease productivity.

Essentially, the essay hinges on the narrow but important problem of social control devices. Rather than tailormade government orders to reduce pollution, the technique on which we have primarily relied, Baxter argues for the class action suit for compensatory damages and the effluent tax. The final chapter is devoted to "Interregional Problems in Implementing an Effluent Tax System."

231. BRUBAKER, Sterling. **In Command of Tomorrow: Resource and Environmental Strategies for Americans.** A Resources for the Future Study. Baltimore: Johns Hopkins University Press, 1975. **177 pp.**
(A-3)

Basic recurrent themes stress the need for a long view, an interim strategy that retains options, and an awareness of diverse goals and of the potential of broader planning for minimizing goal conflict and increasing policy coherence.

Two polar cases--"the true ultimate choices"--are presented: the low technology courses of non-depleting natural technologies and a new technology course which potentially enables a higher standard of living for all.

Chapters focus on land use policy, settlement patterns (where urban growth is seen as continuing), energy alternatives, mineral policy, pollution abatement, and international responsibility.

Concludes "The United States can pioneer a future mode over the next 50-100 years based on population restraint, a restricted style of land use, a shift to inexhaustible energy sources, and greater use of common materials and renewable resources. There is no inexorable requirement for return to a primitive state or even for a no-growth society. A shift of the sort described will require conscious social decisions so as to divert the necessary resources within the required time frame." (p.170) If action must be taken now, the U.S. should proceed autonomously because of limited influence over other nations.

232. LAND, George T.L., "The Evolutionary Crisis," **The Futurist,** 9:1, February 1975, pp. 10-15. (B-4)

Charges that "the ecological alarmists have failed to reckon with three billion years of evolutionary evidence. The message of nature is clear for those with the courage to face it: **Evolution or extinction; grow or die.**" (p.10, author's emphasis) Land goes on to challenge two erroneous assumptions: the "balance of nature" idea and the concept of rapid "growth" rates. Organic growth goes through a natural sequence of stages, and psychosocial growth will soon replace physical growth; Gross National Product will yield to Gross National Process.

"In the advanced, industrialized nations of the West, growth has proceeded through infancy and childhood and is now entering adolescence... The harbingers of social maturity surround us...Never before has man enjoyed such a vision of how things ought to be. These are the marks of an organically maturing society... From an evolutionary perspective, mankind shows signs of vigorous health rather than being a terminal case, doomed by the blind tyranny of technology." (pp. 14-15)
*** The Second Report to the Club of Rome (209), not acknowledged by Land, also advocates organic growth, while taking an "alarmist" view and advocating widespread action. The metaphor of the childhood and manhood of humanity, as used by Korzybski (147), is quite different from Land's usage. Also see Land's **Grow or Die** (164).

233. PASSELL, Peter, and Leonard ROSS. **The Retreat from Riches: Affluence and Its Enemies.** NY: Viking, 1973. $6.95. (BC-4)

A breezy answer to the limits to growth pessimists, arguing that the ingenuity of science is limitless, that social costs of production can be dealt with in the market, and that only growth can aid the poor.

234. GRAYSON, Melvin J. and Thomas R. SHEPARD, Jr., The Disaster Lobby. Chicago: Follett, 1973. 294 pp. $7.95.   (C-5)

Simple-minded right-wing attack on environmentalists, conservationists, women's libbers, anti-war activists, biased journalists, left-wing academics, black radicals and others who wish to discredit America and undermine free enterprise.

234a. LOGAN, Henry L., "The Approaching Epochal Crisis," Fields Within Fields, No. 14, Winter 1975, pp. 3-6. (Entire issue available from World Institute Council, 777 United Nations Plaza, NYC 10017, for $2.50)   (AB-3)

Criticizes the Club of Rome for overlooking the capacity of the sun. "Our immediate danger is not that Man will bump into the ceiling of his resources, but that a probable cyclic decline in the Sun's energy output will cause world-wide drought." (p. 3)

Based on the evidence of tree rings, there appears to be two solar energy cycles: one of 170 years and another of 510 years. The mid-year of the next epochal crisis will be 1990. This period of low precipitation will reduce animal and human food supplies. Responding to this anticipated condition would require control of the ecologic cycle and the production of foodstuff stockpiles, which in turn requires the cooperation of global leaders.

*** This single notion of solar energy cycles could be very silly--and it could be extremely important. Has this been a neglected variable?

234b. WILCOX, Howard A. Hothouse Earth. NY: Praeger, 1975. 181 pp. $7.95.   (ABC-3)

A marine scientist and director of the U.S. Navy's Ocean Farm Project warns that the acceleration of our nuclear and fossil fuel consumption rate will lead to thermal pollution and ultimate calamity. The melting of the Greenland ice alone would raise the ocean level by about 20 feet. If the polar ice caps melt, ocean levels would be raised by 140-180 feet, major cities would be flooded, and civilization will crumble.

The alternative to present energy consumption patterns is suggested as a system of ocean farms providing food and capturing solar energy to satisfy the needs of some 20-50 billion people.

234c. GRIBBIN, John. Forecasts, Famines and Freezes: Climate and Man's Future. NY: Walker, 1976. $8.95.   (ns)

235. MEAD, Shepherd. How to Get to the Future Before It Gets To You. NY: Hawthorn Books, 1974. 228 pp. $6.95.   (C-4)

A breezy and generally optimistic tour of the technological horizon by the author of **How to Succeed in Business Without Really Trying.** Most of the text is a straight-forward popularized account of the American stream-lined dream (newly modified), interspersed with hyperbolic humor.

The first three chapters deal with the Club of Rome/Limits to Growth debate, reprinting two Jay Forrester charts from **World Dynamics.** The general position is that we are in a dangerous situation, but it is not as hopeless as one might think. Mead approvingly cites Barbara Ward and

René Dubos, and "moderates" like John Maddox, and argues that the age of creative ecology (man-made or artificial) is just beginning to dawn. As for the population problem, it is stated that the world could handle a population of 35 billion, but smaller numbers would be far more pleasant. Subsequent chapters deal with what the corporations are doing (mostly writing memos, but some are developing new energy sources and waste disposal systems), the Gross National Product and its failings as a measure (Mead suggests a Pleasure Index--or a Jolly Level or a Whee Rating-- noting that the Michelin Guide is a step in that direction), people-power (or how to sue corporations), the present problems of the communications industry, the potential "Electronic Paradise," and the possibilities of electronic education, biotechnology, and behavioral engineering.

Most parts of the book appear reasonably responsible and balanced, but every so often the values peek out from behind the humor, for example: "We have thoroughly mastered this world, almost completely whipped all contagion and disease, and every living thing is here at our pleasure." (p.213) Many people who are not "doomsters" would take strong issue with this assumption. Also, there is no attention to possible consequences of the new technologies, nor to social institutions of any kind.

*** The humor will not appeal to all, but it may be the necessary sugar-coating to get some people to consider some of the overriding problems of our time.

236. PETER, Lawrence J. The Peter Plan--A Proposal for Survival. Illus. by Walter Griba. NY: Morrow, 1976. 224 pp. $6.95.   (C-3)

The author of The Peter Principle, which explained how individuals escalate to their respective levels of incompetence, offers "A common-place approach to the survival of mankind, along with insistence on the maintenance of the best of his achievements." (p.11)

The sections and chapters (all headed by "P's") are spiced with humor, serious quotes, and numerous drawings. The Peter Proliferation describes the present destruction of the environment from a systems point of view. The Peter Planet sketches a vision of what the world could be like with solar energy, mechanical recycling, better education, peace research, and rational humanistic alternatives, as seen in Excelsior City under the leadership of Harold Foresight. The Peter Program discusses participation, performance, patrons, and protagonists who can play a role in the "transition from a destructive economy to a society based on Good and Sensible Ways." (p.249) The Peter Plan, however, is not a blueprint for a Peter Paradise.

*** The description of the Proliferation is useful; the Program leading to the Peter Planet is a variation on the standard environmentalist/ activist arguments.

237. ROTHSCHILD, Emma, "How Doomed Are We?" The New York Review of Books, June 26, 1975, pp. 31-34.   (A-3)

A review of Beckerman's Two Cheers for the Affluent Society (item no. 227) and the Mesarovic/Pestel Second Report to the Club of Rome (item no. 209), arguing that there is a great resemblance between both camps. Both optimists and alarmists advocate the same changes and the same technologies: "they will be achieved for the Club of Rome through moral regeneration and for optimists through changes in prices." (p.34)

"The Club of Rome represents the interests of the technologically and managerially sophisticated sector of industry which will prosper in a regime of growth without growth. A regime based on corporate planning, information technology, clean coal." (p.34)

Rothschild asserts that there are "very serious questions" about the modern use of technology which the Club of Rome has not addressed: e.g., the extent to which the new energy technology is sustained by military interests, and the complexity of technology that works to exclude people. The resolution favored by the Club of Rome is "an impossible hope for planning without people, without politicians, and without changes in political power." (p.34)

NOTE: The rating system provides general guide-lines for indicating audience level ("A" as most complex and "C" as most popular), and importance ("1" as most and "5" as least). A full explanation of the system--and its limitations--can be found on page 4.

Chapter 6

World Order

The growing concern about the human environment has lent additional impetus to the unmistakable trend toward human organization on a global scale, and the argument that further organization is necessary. Unlike the relatively recent attention paid to ecology and the limits to growth, visions of world order have had a long history, as ably surveyed by Wagar in **The City of Man** (248).

This chapter does not pretend to cover the literature in any comprehensive manner, particularly the scores of volumes advocating a peaceful world of some sort that appeared in the wake of World War II. Most thinking about global community has been superficial and naive. But it is important to stress that very recent work largely resulting from the World Order Models Project of the Institute for World Order (249-252, 255-256) is very sophisticated and worthy of a wide hearing. The Institute itself is attempting to promote consideration of its work by means of a school program headed by Betty Reardon and a college program headed by Michael Washburn. For further information about educational materials not listed here, write to either of these program heads c/o The Institute for World Order, 1140 Avenue of the Americas, New York, NY 10036.

This chapter begins with a modest volume by Deutsch (238), which nicely frames the questions concerning societal directions and alternatives that are dealt with in this chapter and the next one, for there are many pressures to move politics above the nation-state **and** to decentralize. Even a cautious description of trends, as supplied by Inkeles (239), indicates a profound change toward some form of world-wide society. Others (240-246) mix their description of trends with prescription that a furtherence of these trends is inevitable and necessary for survival.

A fifteenth century plan for world peace (247) serves as an introduction to Wagar's **City of Man** (248) which supplies a valuable background, as well as authority, to Wagar's attempt to revive the utopographic tradition with his own version of a desired cosmopolis (249). This early fruit from the World Order Models Project serves to introduce subsequent WOMP documents. Falk's **Study of Future Worlds** (252) is particularly important, as well as his earlier and more popularized book, **This Endangered Planet** (254), which links ecological issues to world order issues. The overview of recent thinking by Beres and Targ (257) is useful, as is Newcombe's survey of alternative approaches to world government (261).

Subsequent items propose a variety of schemes and programs: a World Homeostat System (264), Project 69 (265), a Creative Crusade (266), the Prometheus Project (267), a Blueprint for Peace (268), and a Constitution for the World (270). Both Northrup (271) and Reiser (272-274) assert that a global philosophy or ideology is needed, and their early attempts should not be ignored.

Many of the cosmic evolutionary thinkers covered in Chapter 4 (most notably Teilhard de Chardin) are prescribing some form of global harmony of integrated man and integrated society. Reiser, Kettner, and Rudhyar (272-277) infuse their visions with a mystical concern for spirit. In contrast, Fuller (278-281) advocates a form of cosmic materialism, while Hirschfeld (282) promotes what might be seen as cosmic populism. Both Fuller and Hirschfeld illustrate the dangers of well-intentioned cosmic thinking that becomes too far removed from empirical reality.

The remaining items (283-297) are largely undistinguished appeals for world harmony and the sharing of world wealth. Biéler's call for global Christian leadership (288) is heady but interesting, in contrast to an effort such as Hesburgh's (289).

Perhaps more than any other chapter in this guide, there is a clear distinction between important and unimportant reading. The new rigorous and systemic frameworks for thinking about world order and how to attain it are a clear advance over the moral pleading and grandiose schemes of the past. World order is not simply a part of international relations, but an important direction and alternative for all of today's existing societies.

238. DEUTSCH, Karl W. **Nationalism and its Alternatives.** NY: Knopf, 1969. 200 pp. $5.95.   (AB-3)

A well-known political scientist asserts that there will be no substitute for the nation-state for at least the next two or three generations.

Alternatives can be viewed in two broad categories: world government or depoliticization. The first alternative, moving politics above the nation-state, would encounter administrative difficulties, and there are no capabilities for such government now in sight. The second alternative, moving politics down to the local level, the small group, or the family, is also seen as improbable: "To ask for this sort of government is to draw a nostalgic picture of the world of a hundred years ago. It cannot be done." (p. 168)

Chapters include a discussion of nationalism in Europe and the developing countries, and the experience of regional federations.

*** A reasonable forecast of **probable** developments, circa 1969, although Deutsch might make a different assessment today. It should be noted, though, that such "neutral" forecasting evades questions of desirability and serves to create a self-fulfilling prophecy: saying that something **can't** be done is a way of inhibiting its development. The advocates of world order (Chapter 6) and of decentralization (Chapter 7) argue that alternatives to nationalism are desirable and possible.

239. INKELES, Alex, "The Emerging Social Structure of the World," **World Politics,** 27:4, July 1975, pp. 467-495.   (A-3)

The relationship of all of us, to each other and our world, is seen as undergoing a series of profound changes. "We seem to be living in one of those rare historical eras in which a progressive quantitative process becomes a qualitative transformation...we have the unmistakable sense that we are definitely set off on some new trajectory." (p.467)

"What is most distinctive about the problem before us is that it moves us beyond even the largest customary unit of social analysis, namely the nation-state, to focus on the entire human population of the globe." (p.468)

The essay proceeds to examine a number of indicators in support of this view. Autarky (being more or less completely self-contained) is seen as declining, in the face of the "exponential growth" of interconnectedness and interdependence, as illustrated by indicators of communication and travel. Integration of political units has not grown much, but there has been convergence in modes of production and patterns of resource utilization (increasingly based on inanimate power), institutional arrays (the world is increasingly cast in the bureaucratic Weberian mold), the structure and patterns of social relations such as kinship systems and class structure, systems of popular attitudes and values, and systems of political and economic control. The common feature of all states is the increasing power of the state to control the lives of its citizens.

It is cautioned that these processes are subject to countervailing trends, such as distinctive cultural traditions, which serve to mute the force of the tendency to a uniform world culture: "we can count on a very large amount of diversity throughout the world for at least another century." (p.495)
*** A bland overview that pays no attention to forces such as environmental degradation which might make world unity both necessary and desirable in the very near future. Nevertheless, this conventional survey is useful.

239a. KATZENSTEIN, Peter J., "International Independence: Some Long-Term Trends and Recent Changes," **International Organization,** 29:4, Autumn, 1975, pp. 1021-1034.   (ns)

240. JAMES, Bernard. **The Death of Progress.** NY: Alfred A. Knopf, 1973. 166 pp.   (AB-2)

A cultural anthropologist at the University of Wisconsin at Milwaukee argues that an "awesome cultural change has overtaken the present era" and worries about the likelihood that "as the world predicament of the progress culture worsens we will turn increasingly toward Great Man solutions."

James is concerned about the existence together of both the hyperrational and the antirational, viewing the counterculture as internal barbarism, but giving equal attention to the evil of good-intentioned science. Chapter IV is particularly notable for arguing "The Retreat from Consciousness" that follows the collapse of the belief in endless progress.

The final chapter, "Toward a Steady-State Ideology," outlines what is necessary to reason and work our way out of present problems as the only alternative to natural correctives. We must have a "consciously managed world culture" with a basic design similar to what biologists call an eco-climax system. Also, we "shall have to control a new science--perhaps it should be called an art--that is systemic in conception and planetary in scope." (p.145)

241. McHALE, John. **The Future of the Future.** NY: George Braziller, 1969. 322 pp. $7.95.   (AB-3)

A wide-ranging overview, aided by scores of charts and photographs, with particular emphasis on ecology, technology, and planetary resources. Chapter 1 summarizes future studies in the context of a transition toward a world-man image, and Chapter 5 continues with a survey of individual futurists and organizations studying the future, a continuing interest of McHale.

The final chapter, Toward a Planetary Society, discusses the end of economic man (presuming affluence), emerging life styles, the future city, education, and the planetary culture, concluding that "we must understand and cooperate on a truly global scale, or we perish." (p.300)

242. SOROKIN, Pitirim A. **The Basic Trends of Our Times.** New Haven, Conn.: College and University Press, 1964. 208 pp.   (A-4)

A well-known sociologist sees three basic trends: 1) a shift of the creative leadership of mankind from a monopolistic domination by Europe to the Americas, Asia, and Africa; 2) a continued decay in the sensate socio-cultural system of the West; 3) the emergence and growth of a new, integral socio-cultural order.

The U.S. and the U.S.S.R. are seen as mutually converging to a mixed sociocultural type, and world uniformity in religious and moral polarization is explored. The final chapter "sketches a new field of research--the field of the mysterious energy of creative, unselfish love which is bound to play a greatly increased role in the future of humanity if it avoids new suicidal wars."

243. JASPERS, Karl. **The Origin and Goal of History.** New Haven, Conn.: Yale University Press, 1953. 294 pp. $7.50; $1.95, paper. (A-3) (First published in Germany in 1949)

A schema of a total conception "based on an article of faith: that mankind has one single origin and one goal." A considerable part of the book (pp. 141-228) is devoted to a chapter on The Future which discusses the basic tendencies of socialism, world unity, and faith.

244. HOCKING, William Ernest. **The Coming World Civilization.** NY: Harper & Bros., 1956. 210 pp. (A-4)

A philosopher views the secularization of modern life, the impotence of the state, and the future role of Christianity.

245. McNEILL, William H. **Past and Future.** Chicago: University of Chicago Press, 1954. 216 pp. (AB-4)

An interesting view of history as the unceasing conflict between invention and custom, marked by four epochs distinguished by changes in transportation and communications. Each epoch creates a new mode of contact between alien peoples and is distinguished by an appropriate general pattern of political and cultural relationships. The Pedestrian Epoch resulted in isolated communities. The Equestrian Epoch lasted 15 centuries until the Epoch of Ocean Shipping, which gave way to The Epoch of Mechanical Transport.

Although McNeill promises to suggest the likely course of future events during the next two or three hundred years, he does not suggest any new epoch, and the bulk of the book is devoted to pleading the need for a world government. Ideally, this would be democratic, but believing "that such an ideal can never be realized" (p. 185), McNeill suggests merely what Americans in this generation could do.

246. VON LAUE, Theodore H. **The Global City: Freedom, Power, and Necessity in the Age of World Revolutions.** Philadelphia: J.B. Lippincott, 1969. 302 pp. (A-4)

An essay by an historian at Washington University in St. Louis about modernization in the global world and its problems. Chapter 2, The Age of Global Confluence, views us in an unprecedented crisis--a new and perilous beginning. "The only direction, the only hope, lies in going forward in search for a more inclusive community." (p.18)

Chapters on topics such as the crisis of mass politics, the crisis of industrialism, freedom and alienation, totalitarianism, and the burden of globalism.

246a. WELLS, H.G. **The Shape of Things to Come.** NY: Macmillan, 1933. 431 pp. (AB-4)

A short history of how the Modern World-State came about, looking back from a period 150 years in the future. The history is purportedly written by the recently deceased Dr. Philip Raven.

The old order of the 19th century, the Capitalist System, came to disaster in the second and third decades of the 20th century due to monetary instability, the disorganization of society through increasing productivity, and a great pestilence.

247. Czechoslovak Academy of Sciences. **The Universal Peace Organization of King George of Bohemia: A Fifteenth Century Plan for World Peace.** 1462/1464. Prague: Publishing House of the Czechoslovak Academy of Sciences, 1964. 122 pp.   (AB-4)

English language, with analysis by Václav Vaněček.

248. WAGAR, W. Warren. **The City of Man: Prophecies of a World Civilization in Twentieth-Century Thought.** Boston: Houghton-Mifflin, 1963, Penguin Books, 1967. 310 pp.   (AB-2)

A comprehensive, scholarly, and highly readable "biography" of the vision of world order or cosmopolis throughout history, as it has appeared in the East and the West, in Ancient Greece and Rome, in the Middle Ages, and in the present. Prophetic thinkers using various approaches are analyzed: the biological approach of Huxley and Teilhard de Chardin, the historical approach of Toynbee and Sorokin, and the "lines and spirals" approach of Hocking, Jaspers, Mumford, and Kahler. In contrast to these independent thinkers, various doctrinaire views are explored. The prospects of synthesis in philosophy, religion, knowledge, government, culture, and economics are dealth with in separate chapters, with a brief consideration in the final chapters of what might happen after a world civilization is attained. Annotated bibliography of about 100 "recent books on world order," pp. 293-302.

249. WAGAR, W. Warren. **Building the City of Man: Outlines of a World Civilization.** A World Order Book. NY: Grossman, 1971. 180 pp. $3.95, paper.   (ABC-3)

An erudite polemic attributing the "totalizing crisis" in civilization to the rate and pervasiveness of change and the lack of any totalizing response. Solutions have been piecemeal, provisional, parochial, uncoordinated, unsubstantial, and lacking prophetic moral vision.
   Assuming that reversion to primitive anarchy is unworkable, Wagar presents two options: preserving the shells of our diseased civilizations or building a new world civilization. The conventional responses are rejected: the peace movement (with its flawed utopian premises for each of the strategies of civil disobedience, diplomacy, and world federalism), salvation by science (in that many proposed solutions are "unintelligent"), and the romanticism of the New Left.
   Instead, a world revolution is proposed, with revolutionary elites developing a new ideology of world order and a new humanistic religion, building a political party, and providing doomsday insurance. But before such a party can overwhelm the nation-state system, Wagar predicts a great world war after which the species--if there are survivors--will be receptive to the arguments of a world party. (Wagar, incidentally, is a Wells scholar, and this scheme is obviously an updating of Wells' "open conspiracy.")
   A revival of the utopographic tradition is advocated, in order to set people free from their acceptance of the world-as-is. As illustration, a good portion of the book is devoted to outlining a preferred (but not necessarily ideal) world, seen as a holistic system of values and institutions.
   The chapter on Men and Women advocates the obliteration of the patriarchal society by schooling, anti-sexist evangelism, and law, while anticipating a great variety of familial structures for many different purposes. Chapter 6 on Education envisions the world citizenry devoting "at least half of its active hours to learning, both inside and outside, the formal educational

structure...at least half of those citizens employed in what we call today the 'labor force' will be educational workers." (p.122) Students will be colleagues of teachers, there will be a vast decentralization of universities so that the life of every community is enriched, and departments or colleges of cognitive synthesis will promote the necessary specialists in integration (an obviously wise and brilliant suggestion!).

"A postindustrial world civilization will also be, to a great extent, a post-economic civilization," (p.152) with government and economics receding into the background of an essentially classless society. Perhaps a century from now, there would be a government of four branches, including a World Council that supervises seven ministries. This world state would be a unitary republic of mankind, rather than a federation. The world commonwealth will be generally socialist, but authentically private, non-exploitative enterprise will be allowed. Personal income of any individual will not exceed a level of four times the universal minimum wage.

To avoid the end of all civilized life, there will necessarily be rationing of raw materials, world ecological planning, and redistribution of wealth. Incomes will necessarily drop precipitously in the Western world, and the rich will become more resourceful by winding down the advertising industry, producing more durable goods, utilizing mass transport and large communal dwellings, automating most office work, and reducing armies to a single small world peace-keeping force. "We shall be more than compensated for our losses even in a purely economic sense by the expansion and improvement of services of every kind." (p.157)

As for spatial distribution, the ascendancy of cities will not continue; indeed, cities will no longer exist as such. The center of life will become the small town, each a center of excellence, and "the world will become a single City of Man, a cosmopolis from end to end." (p.163)

*** Consciously utopographic, but why not have a number of such ideals at hand? Wagar's effort is a good model, and should stimulate other serious models, as well as classroom exercises.

250. BHAGWATI, Jagdish N. (ed.) **Economics and World Order: From the 1970s to the 1990s.** NY: Free Press, 1972. 365 pp. $3.95, paper (A-4)

The first book of academic essays to emerge from the World Order Models Project of the World Law Fund (now called the Institute for World Order). Papers arranged in 7 categories: Introduction, Global Perspectives, Socialist Prognoses, International Institutions, Latin America, Africa, and Asia.

251. MENDLOVITZ, Saul H. (ed.) **On the Creation of a Just World Order: Preferred Worlds for the 1990's.** World Order Models Project. NY: Free Press, May 1975. 302 pp. $9.95.   (A-3)

Summaries of larger works to be published in a forthcoming series.
-Ali A. Mazrui, "World Culture and the Search for Human Consensus"
-Rajni Kothari, "World Politics and World Order: The Issue of Autonomy" (see no. 255)
-Gustavo Lagos, "The Revolution of Being"
-Carl-Friedrich von Weizsäcker, "A Sceptical Contribution"
-Johan Galtung, "Non-Territorial Actors and the Problem of Peace"
-Yoshikazu Sakomoto, "Toward Global Identity"
-Paul T.K. Lin, "Development Guided by Values: Comments on China's Road and its Implications"
-Richard A. Falk, "Toward a New World Order: Modest Methods and Drastic Visions" (see no. 252)

252. FALK, Richard A. **A Study of Future Worlds: Designing the Global Community.** World Order Models Project. NY: Free Press, 1975. 506 pp. $15.00; $6.95, paper.   (A-1)

A detailed outline of the structures and functions of new world organizations necessary to ensure four overriding values: the elimination of war, poverty, social injustice, and ecological instability.

The first chapter, Points of Departure, describes the design of "relevant utopias" that include viable transition proposals. After discussing Trends and Patterns in World Society, Chapter 3, Designing a New World Order, considers the necessity of rooting reform proposals in the soil of current political, social, and economic realities, and describes nine principal types of world order systems. Designing a Preferred World Polity outlines a preference model which includes a World Assembly (the principal policy-making organ), a World Security System, a world economic system, a world system for human development, and a world system for ecological balance.

The final three chapters cover The Transition Process (stressing the mobilization of support and raising consciousness to attain a global system by the 1990s), The World Economy in a World Order Dimension, and America's Stake in Global Reform. A postscript appeals to the reader in view of the bleak prospects for adapting the WOMP/USA proposals.

*** A well-documented comprehensive approach to imagining alternatives **and** attaining them. Although Falk does not consider himself to be a "futurist," this book nevertheless appears to be, by far, the best example yet of thinking about alternative futures of any sort.

253. FALK, Richard A. **A Global Approach to National Policy.** Cambridge, Mass.: Harvard University Press. 1975. $12.50.   (ns)

"...shows how a global approach to international relations can prevent wars and solve imperative social problems." (advt.)

254. FALK, Richard A. **This Endangered Planet: Prospects and Proposals for Human Survival.** NY: Random House, 1971. 495 pp. $8.95; $2.95, paper.   (AB-3)

A cogent and well-reasoned primer on the relationship between ecological concerns and world politics, and the growing need for some form of world order (Falk is the head of the North American section of the World Order Models Project). At present, there exists "only the weakest instruments for the identification of planetary interests," and no national society can meet the challenge directed at its survival by independent action.

Falk proposes the development of "ecological politics" as a political embodiment of man-in-nature and the ideological underpinning for an adequate conception of world order. In Chapter III, the underlying causes of planetary danger are described: the state system, the paradox of aggregation (the conflict between individual and collective benefit, with credit to Hardin's "Tragedy of the Commons" argument), the efficacy of violence, the cycle of destruction due to vested interests, the hazards of velocity, and problems of alienation, manipulation, and false consciousness. The following chapter discusses the fourfold danger of the war system, population pressure, insufficient resources, and environmental overload, emphasizing their interconnected character, planetary scope, the role of archaic attitudes and archaic organization forms, the role of cumulative processes, etc.

Chapter V outlines the main features of the present system of world order and the factors contributing to world order difficulties such as emerging scarcity of vital resources, increasing extraterritoriality of critical events, the diminishing margin of decisional error, absence of knowledge about the planetary ecosystem, national constraints on international cooperation, lags in learning and behavior change, etc. In that "We are now living in the dawn of the ecological age," the need for a "genuine peace system" in place of a "spurious security system" is greater than ever.

Approaches to world order prompted by the war-prevention imperative of the nuclear age are discussed in Chapter VI (resolving inequities in wealth and power, unification, and sense of community) and Chapter VII assembles the principal elements of world-order design that will be useful in the future, concerning matters of consciousness and structure, and based on a vision of "harmony within limits." Chapter VIII suggests some first steps for world order activism: focusing on the endangered planet (through national declarations of ecological emergency, colleges of world ecology, forming a world political party), countering the war system (through national commitments against first use of nuclear weapons, strategic arms control, demilitarization), moderating population pressures, protecting the resource bases, and protecting and rehabilitating the environment (through a National Conservation Bill of Rights and Institutes of Environmental Policy). In sum, we can only rescue ourselves "by solving the whole problem of the endangered planet and by evolving the social and political forms that are compatible with a solution." (p. 413)

Chapter IX presents two images of the future: a negative sketch summarizing the endangered planet argument (the politics of despair and desperation leading to an Era of Annihilation in the 21st Century), and the positive sketch of the world order argument (decades of awareness, mobilization, and transformation, leading to an Era of World Harmony in the 21st Century).

This volume suggests the new shape of reason: shunning blind reactions by the young and "movements that have polluted their ends by adapting repugnant means," lamenting the "failure of confrontation" between optimistic and pessimistic assessments, and critical of thinking based on obsolete assumptions and narrow considerations. Although avoiding footnotes, there are numerous text references to a wide variety of fictional and non-fictional works, a modest section of chapter notes, and a good but unannotated bibliography of about 180 items.

255. KOTHARI, Rajni. **Footsteps Into the Future: Diagnosis of the Present World and a Design for an Alternative.** World Order Models Project. NY: Free Press, 1975. 173 pp. $8.95; $3.95, paper.   (AB-3)

The Founder and Director of the Centre for the Study of Developing Societies in Delhi, and the editor of **Alternatives: A Journal for World Policy,** utilizes ideas developed by Nehru and Gandhi in proposing a new structure for global politics that recognizes and affirms the autonomy of all peoples and states and the equality between them.

The most probable scenario for the future is seen as a widening North-South chasm, a gap between a tiny modernist elite and the people at large. A world state is not the answer to this crisis. Rather, there is a need to build autonomy, freedom, well-being, participation, and justice at a number of levels.

Kothari advocates a smaller number of nations (perhaps 20-25 political units) so that representation can be somewhat equalized. At the same time, there is a need to institutionalize certain processes at the regional and world levels, e.g., a world security system, and various multi-state functional authorities.

256. FALK, Richard A. et al., "State of the Globe Report 1974," **Alternatives: A Journal of World Policy** (North Holland Publishing Co., Amsterdam), Vol. 1, 1975, pp. 159-463. (Also available from Institute for World Order, 1140 Avenue of the Americas, NYC 10036)   (A-3)

The first of a series of reports by the World Order Models Project, to be published annually in **Alternatives**. In addition to Falk, this "experimental" document was prepared in collaboration with Johan Galtung, Rajni Kothari, and Saul Mendlovitz, with the assistance of Mark Blasius. It is also considered as an "action document" to serve as the basis of a forum on global developments "from the standpoint of four specific normative goals or values whose realization we consider essential for a positive world order: peace, economic well-being, individual and collective justice, and ecological balance." (p. 163)

"At the deepest level of interpretation, we believe that the existing world system is dominated by structures of exploitation and dominance consciously and actively maintained, particularly when challenged." (p. 165) The Report goes on to survey principal developments of 1974 that express these underlying characteristics: the world economy, the global food crisis, nuclear weapons, international armed conflicts, subversion and imperialism, the global context, and student political activism.

Basic trends are assessed in relation to the four world-order values, and the Report concludes with tactical recommendations in three basic areas: removing obstacles to the satisfaction of basic human needs, continuing the struggle against imperialism, and checking the state abuse of power.

An Appendix provides 32 miscellaneous documents such as the International Woman's Year Program, the world food conference declaration, and various U.N. General Assembly resolutions.

256a. COX, Robert W., "On Thinking About Future World Order," **World Politics,** 28:2, Jan. 1976, pp. 175-196.   (ns)

256b. SEWELL, James P., "Steering the New Global Forces: United States Views of an Emergent World Order," **International Journal,** 30:2, Spring 1975, pp. 326ff.   (ns)

257. BERES, Louis René and Harry R. TARG. **Reordering the Planet: Constructing Alternative World Futures.** Foreword by Richard A. Falk. Boston: Allyn and Bacon, 1974. 264 pp.   (B-2)

Clearly a college-level textbook, but a useful introduction for professionals, too. Part 1 surveys historical and contemporary models, with chapters on normative theory and academic discourse, social-critical theories of the modern state, social-critical implications of selected international relations theories, utopian and anarchist traditions, regionalist thought, world order perspectives, and human needs and the state system. Part II describes the present system of war avoidance, and offers a set of guidelines for making this concern more systematic, with chapters on Actors, Processes, Context, and Structure.

"The conception of a viable organic world community, as well as the encouragement of secondary regional and world bodies, ought to be conceived of not as an 'end state,' but as a **process of growth and humanization of the social and physical environment.** An alternative global future is both a **striving for** and an **achievement of** certain goals. The positing of alternative world futures is the first step in a process that leads man to narrow the gap between what actually exists and what potentially can be. Only when the visions are left unproposed and the commitments to **move** are left unsaid does man experience stagnation." (p. 157, authors' emphasis)

258. BERES, Louis René, and Harry R. TARG (eds.) **Planning Alternative World Futures: Values, Methods, and Models.** Praeger Special Studies in International Politics and Government. NY: Praeger, Oct. 1975. 312 pp. $20,00; $6.95, paper.   (AB-3)

Fourteen original essays assembled by two political scientists at Purdue University:
-Marvin S. Soroos, "A Methodological Overview..."
-George Kent, "Political Design"
-Louis René Beres, "...The Four Phases of World Order Design"
-Michael Washburn, "Outline for a Normative Forecasting/Planning Process"
-Davis B. Bobrow, "Transition to Preferred World Futures: Some Design Considerations"   •
-Harry R. Targ, "Constructing Models of Presents, Futures and Transitions..."
-Saul H. Mendlovitz and Thomas G. Weiss, "The Study of Peace and Justice: Toward a Framework for Global Discussion"
-Francis A. Beer, "A Methodology of World Order: Joining Humanism and Science"
-Richard A. Falk, "Reforming World Order: Zones of Consciousness and Domains of Action"
-Charles F. Doran, "Growth, Stagnation, and Alternative World Futures"
-Michael C. Stohl, "Images in the Construction and Evaluation of Alternative World Futures"
-Louis René Beres, "Behavioral Paths to a New World Order"
-Francis A. Beer, "The Structure of World Consciousness'
-W. Warren Wagar, "Imagination and Alternative World Futures"

259. LANDHEER, B., J. LOENEN, and Fred L. POLAK (eds.). **World Society: How Is an Effective and Desirable World Possible? A Symposium.** The Hague: Martinus Nijhoff, 1971. 211 pp. fl. 28.10.   (A-3)

Includes the following:
-E. Menzel, "United Nations and International Law"
-Ernst B. Haas, "Global Tasks and the UN of the Future"
-Peter Hay, "World Federalism: Regional"
-J.H.C. Creyghton, "World Order Based on the Individual and Maintained by a Political World Authority"
-J.H.M.M. Loenen, "Integrative Synthesis and Nuclear World Crisis"
-Richard A. Falk, "Bipolarity and the Future of World Society"
-E. Oberlander, "Communist Society as a World Order"
-Lin Piao, "Long Live the Victory of the People's War" (1965 text on the international significance of Mao's theory)
-T.K.N. Unnithan, "Gandhian View of a World Social Order"
-Bruno Fritsch, "The Problem of Global Social Order"
-Fred L. Polak, "Balance of Technology"
-B. Landheer, "Industrial Society as the Basis for World Society"
-Quincy Wright, "Building a Social System for Mankind"

260. ALBERTSON, Peter and Margery BARNETT (eds.). **Managing the Planet.** Englewood Cliffs, NJ: Prentice-Hall, 1972. 300 pp. $5.95.   (A-3)

An abridgement of **Environment and Society in Transition: Scientific Developments, Social Consequences, Policy Implications (Annals of the New York Academy of Science,** vol. 184, 1971. 699 pp.), containing the proceedings of the 1970 International Joint Conference on Environment and Society in Transition, held under the auspices of the American Geographical Society and the American Division of the World Academy of Art and Sciences.
Part I contains 24 essays on The Status of the Sciences, discussing the policy implications of scientific knowledge, including contributions by Jonas Salk, Hudson Hoagland, John B. Calhoun, Gardner Murphey, Jan Tinbergen, John Yehezkel Dror, and John McHale.
Part II presents brief reports from 5 multidisciplinary working groups: 1) Cultivating Resources; 2) Population, Health, and Family; 3) Scientific Knowledge, Education, and Communication; 4) Decision Processes; and 5)

Economic and Social Policy. The latter group concluded that "We are u-
nanimous in our conviction that humanity is at the danger point of its evolution." (p. 286) Critical problem areas are seen as global in scope, and solutions must therefore be sought through a global, systemic, and normative
approach. Suggested directions include the need to plan for a desirable society, the need to define a bill of rights and obligations of man in 1990,
and global population policies.

261. NEWCOMBE, Hanna, "Alternative Approaches to World Government
     II," **Peace Research Reviews,** V: 3, February 1974. 94 pp. $2.00
                                                                    (B-3)
A single copy of this worthwhile overview is available from **Peace Re-
search Reviews,** 25 Dundana Ave., Dundas, Ontario, Canada. This revised
edition of a survey appearing in Vol. I, No. 2, summarizes 183 references,
categorized into 16 approaches:
-U.N. Charter Revision
-People's Constitutional Convention
-Partial or Regional Federations
-A New or Parallel Organization Separate from the U.N.
-Gradual Expansion of International Law
-Mundialization of Cities and Government Declarations for World Government
-The World Citizens Movement
-Development Through U.N. Peace-Keeping Forces
-The Functional Approach: Expansion of International Aid and Cooperation
-Internationalism in Other Than Political Areas
-Drafting World Constitutions
-Working Through Certain Specialized Groups: Parliamentarians, Educators,
    Scientists, International Lawyers
-Initiatives by the Non-Aligned Nations, or by Becoming Non-Aligned Ourselves
-Political Parties With World Government Platforms
-A World Language, Such as Esperanto
-World Holidays

262. BROWN, Lester R. **World Without Borders.** NY: Random House, 1972.
     395 pp. $8.95.   (C-3)

Although somewhat naive, this is a good introductory overview by an expert on world food supplies. The title, incidentally, was supplied by a 19-
year-old college student in Prague.
    Part I provides an inventory of Mankind's Problems, with chapters
on the environmental crisis, the widening rich-poor gap, unemployment,
urbanization, and hunger.   Part II, Keys to our Future, has chapters
on education, population, and arms control. Part III, Creating a Global
Economy, argues that multinational corporations must be divested of national ties. "To the extent that economic integration continues to make war
a less practical instrument of foreign policy, the prospects will improve
for creating a socially and politically unified global community and for restructuring the global economy to eliminate poverty." (p. 255)
    Part IV, Creating a Global Infrastructure, argues for a global com-
munications system, English as a global language, the furtherance of a sense
of world citizenship, a global transportation system, and new supranational
institutions such as an intentional oceanic regime, a world environmental
agency to regulate the interface between global corporations and nation-
states, and supranational research institutes.
    Part V, Shaping the Future, advocates a new social ethic requiring
a new political man, and an American initiative in creating a unified global society. We either move toward a unified world, or a deteriorating one.
"The media must educate the rich in the North to what life for the poor is
like if the rich are to respond humanely to their plight." (p. 277)
*** Imaginative, but innocent.

263. BROWN, Lester R. **By Bread Alone**. NY: Praeger, 1974. 272 pp.
$3.95, paper   (ns)

Analyzes the global food crisis, "advocates population control, diet changes among the affluent minority, and improved farmland productivity in the less developed countries. He also presents a world-wide approach toward controlling runaway inflation, international competition, war and starvation-- if we are to meet the food crisis." **(The Futurist,** Aug. 1975, p. 217)

264. LASZLO, Ervin. **A Strategy for the Future: The Systems Approach to World Order**. Introduction by Richard A. Falk. NY: George Braziller, 1974. 238 pp. $3.95, paper.   (A-4)

World order "is not merely a new 'in' term for international relations theory or world politics. It is, rather, a new conceptualization in a field that embraces global ecology, geopolitics, human geography, international relations theory, anthropology, political science, and social ethics and philosophy. It is an attempt to grasp the contemporary situation on this planet in all its diversity without erecting, or conserving, artificial frontiers either between geographic or disciplinary territories." (p.xiv)
The first quarter of the book is "devoted mainly to providing the theoretical validation for purposive activism aimed at the creation of a more stable and humanistic world order." (p.61) It offers an argument for conceptual synthesis, for "unless we integrate and focus our knowledge the disorder will grow into disaster." (p.3) The Promise of General Systems Theory is described (Laszlo is perhaps the most active proponent of general systems theory today), and a systems view of future world order and sociocultural evolution is offered ("progressive hierarchization"). "We are now moving toward a global industrial and post-industrial civilization made possible through the invention of instantaneous global communication networks, worldwide trade...and increasing interdependence..." (p.39)
The bulk of the book elaborates a three-phase strategy: the era of world-system consciousness, the era of multilevel decision-making, and the era of global homeostasis. The first phase is one of mobilizing consciousness and loosening complacency. Potential disseminators include civil servants engaged with transnational issues, college faculty and students, and executives. The second phase includes the growth of various structures for multilateral decision-making. The third phase approaches the goal of Global Homeostasis by means of the World Homeostat System--a central guidance system regulating the functional states of the world system and including several dozen units (each briefly described) such as a World Revenue Service, World Economy Monitor, World Ecology Court, World Information Coordinating Board, Optimum-State Policy Review Board, and a World Population Council.
*** Pretentious and ahistorical; one does not need general systems theory to sense the path of sociocultural evolution, as indicated by many of the books mentioned in this chapter. Raising consciousness is simply a fancy term for education, particularly adult education, and the program suggested here is not convincing because it doesn't deal with existing educational and informational systems. And thus the ideal of Global Homeostasis becomes even more remote, which is perhaps just as well, for the system portrayed is a complex structure devoid of human beings.

265. PECCEI, Aurelio. **The Chasm Ahead**. NY: Macmillan, 1969. 297 pp.
(BC-3)
An Italian industrial manager assesses the macroproblems of our time, with particular emphasis on the growing cleavage across the Atlantic brought on by the technological gap: "The gap, in effect, is between the GM age and the IBM age." (p. 64) Although Americans criticize their educational system in world perspective it is seen as far ahead of other nations, a significant

gap in that "education supports the very underpinnings of the technological gap of the future." (p.50)

To facilitate "Global Dimensions to Our Thinking," a new approach called Project 69 is proposed to serve as "a multinationally sponsored feasibility study on systematic, long-term planning of world scope." (p.219)

*** Peccei is one of the founders of the Club of Rome and serves on its Executive Committee.

266. PLATT, John, "The Structure of Global Survival," **The Teilhard Review,** 6:2, Winter 1971-2, pp. 94-100. (AB-3)

The Kent State University Commencement Address of June 1971, advocating "A Creative Crusade" for global survival. "A crusade for survival will have to include forecasting and innovation, conflict resolution, global networks, new institutions to control many malfunctions, political movements to press for needed change, new human relations, and a whole new philosophy of respect and care for man and nature on our fragile planet." (p.100)

267. FEINBERG, Gerald. **The Prometheus Project: Mankind's Search for Long-Range Goals.** NY: Doubleday, 1969; Anchor Books, 1969. 264 pp. $1.45, paper. (AB-3)

A physicist discusses the unity of mankind and the need for agreement on long-range goals for humanity in the light of "impending 'world-shaking' decisions." Various forthcoming events are considered as Some Roads That Will Be Opened, i.e. biological engineering, artificial intelligence, an end to aging and death, and the possibility of interstellar communication.

Chapter 4 provides a classification and analysis of goals, distinguishing between individual goals and collective goals, intermediate goals and final goals, goals that assume an afterlife, and a possible goal of extending consciousness. Chapter 5 describes philosophical problems such as reaching agreement on goals, and the difficulties of "The Goal-Directed Society" that has adapted long-range goals.

The final chapter proposes The Prometheus Project, "a cooperative effort by humanity to choose its long-term goals." (p.222) The first step for such a project would be a world-wide publicity campaign, followed by the creation of definite opportunities for people to discuss their ideas about goals. A central organization, the Prometheus Coordinating Agency, would coordinate but not determine these discussions.

268. MAROIS, M. (ed.) **Toward a Plan of Actions for Mankind: Problems and Perspectives.** NY: Elsevier, 1974. 558 pp. $66.75 (sic.) (ns)

269. GARDNER, Richard N. (ed.) **Blueprint for Peace: Being the Proposals of Prominent Americans to the White House Conference on International Cooperation.** NY: McGraw-Hill, 1966. 404 pp. $7.95. (A-3)

President Johnson convened this Conference in Nov. 1965 and blessed it with the following message: "I am determined that the United States shall actively engage its best minds and boldest spirits in the quest for a new order of world cooperation." This volume draws together the recommendations of 30 committees involving several hundred prominent Americans, in addition to several hundred government consultants. Some 5000 people attended the conference in Washington in response to personal invitations.

Following Gardner's introduction, there are 16 chapters on the following topics (with a few of the many recommendations listed in parentheses): the arms race (non-aggression pact between NATO and Warsaw Pact countries, a versatile U.N. Peace Force, a U.N. Peace Observation Corps), peacekeeping (various proposals concerning U.N. capacities), international law (an International Law Reporter System, a court for adjudicating lower-level international disputes), human rights (U.N. Commissioner for Human Rights), cultural and intellectual exchange (64 recommendations), population (more research and education), resources (a World Institute for Resource Analysis, an International Marine Resources Agency, a Trust for the World Heritage), economic development (recommendations on technical assistance and private investment), international finance, world trade, the world's cities (a World Urban Development Research Laboratory and Institute), outer space, the use of science and technology, harnessing the peaceful atom, weather control, and Other Challenges (food and agriculture, aviation, business and industry, communications, disaster relief, education and training, health, labor, research on the development of international institutions, social welfare, transportation, women, and youth activities).

*** A useful compendium of largely unfulfilled hopes for new and expanded programs for the U.S. and the U.N.; The Great Society in its global dimensions.

270. Center for the Study of Democratic Institutions. **A Constitution for the World.** Introduction by Elizabeth Mann Borgese. Santa Barbara, Calif.: Center for the Study of Democratic Institutions, 1965. 111 pp.
(A-3)
Contains the original **Preliminary Draft of a World Constitution** (University of Chicago Press, 1948), which outlines the fundamental law for a Federal Republic of the World, as well as commentary by various staff members of the Committee to Frame a World Constitution.

271. NORTHRUP, F.S.C. **The Meeting of East and West: An Inquiry Concerning World Understanding.** NY: Macmillan, 1946. 531 pp.   (A-3)

A far-ranging volume on the resolution of ideological conflicts in the world--conflicts that must be dealt with so as to avoid misunderstanding and war. Northrup proposes "a more inclusive truly international cultural ideal which provides scientifically grounded intellectual and emotional foundations for partial world sovereignty." (p. x) Such a philosophy of culture connects the sciences and the humanities.

272. REISER, Oliver L. **A New Earth and a New Humanity.** NY: Creative Age Press, 1942. 252 pp.   (AB-3)

"Modern civilization is approaching the end of its life cycle. We are actually witnessing the collapse of a world...An old world is dying; perhaps a new one is being born." (p.91)
Creation of a new social order requires the reorganization of our ideas in many fields: a new humanism with a novel synthesis of scientific, religious, and social thought--a rediscovery of democracy through scientific humanism (a term coined by Henry Chester Tracy in 1927). Scientific humanism is simply Renaissance humanism brought up to date, fusing all thought into one great philosophical effort. Fundamental reconstructions in practice must be preceded by equally fundamental changes in theory. To facilitate such a change, Reiser advocates " a world sensorium--or world brain, to use the term proposed by H.G. Wells." (p.110) Such a sensorium would be analogous to the individual's cerebral cortex.
Three stages in human mental-social evolution are described: 1) Pre-Aristotelian or Primitive Mentality, employing a sub-verbal level of communications; 2) The Aristotelian Mentality of Classical Science and Philosophy, with its communication in verbal symbolisms; and 3) Non-Aristotelian Mentality: a super-verbal fusion of head and heart. This would address our major problem of scientific advances outgrowing our moral progress.

273. REISER, Oliver L., and Blodwen DAVIES. **Planetary Democracy: An Introduction to Scientific Humanism and Applied Semantics.** NY: Creative Age Press, 1944. 242 pp. (AB-3)

The authors aim toward pooling the genius of the race in discovery and invention, a religious concern based on scientific mysticism, a new universal theory of education, and a global democracy involving a world community, global planning, a world health service, and political security.

The two main desiderata of a new society are access to sources of raw materials and outlets for surplus commodities. A common economic-political pattern of life is needed that transcends the conflicting ideologies and ethical systems of the world. A new scientific theory is also needed; we are still operating on old Newtonian ideas, whereas we should have a theory of human relativity modeled after Einstein's theory of physical relativity.

274. REISER, Oliver. L. **Cosmic Humanism: A Theory of the Eight-Dimensional Cosmos Based on Integrative Principles From Science, Religion, and Art.** Cambridge, Mass.: Schenkman Publishing Co., 1966. 576 pp. $8.95. (A-3)

"As my interest in cosmology developed over the years, it has seemed increasingly plausible to regard the world-view of Pantheism as the most acceptable solvent of the tensions and conflicts that have emerged from the historical background of cultural evolution. As a name for this viewpoint, I have come to favor the label Cosmic Humanism. But even though I use the terms "Scientific Humanism" and "Cosmic Humanism" interchangeably, in either case this presupposes the Pantheism which is explained and supported in this work. This Hindu-Stoic-Bruno-Spinoza-Einstein cosmology is the world-view here proposed as the coming World Philosophy." (pp. xxiv-xxv)

This encyclopedia of ideas has been developed by Reiser over the past fifty years, as indicated by the author's bibliography of some 150 items (p.544-552). Among the 64 diagrams is one that reiterates the three levels of human orientation: Pre-Aristotelian, Aristotelian, and Non-Aristotelian (p.479). In the latter orientation, appropriate for a new civilization that has yet to appear, there will be multi-valued semantics, a recovery of some of primitive man's sense of the "unity of nature," coordination and synthesis of knowledge, and a new Scientific Humanism.

275. KETTNER, Frederick. **Biosophy and Spiritual Democracy: A Basis for World Peace.** NY: Vantage Press, 1954. 222 pp. (B-4)

The developer of Biosophy, "a doctrine of spiritual self-education and character improvement through intuitive interpretation," advocates a Spiritual Declaration of Independence, the synthesis of science and religion, a transition "from civilization to soulization," spiritual democracy, world citizenship, a World Academy of Democracy to spread the message throughout the world, Secretaries of Peace to encourage creative intelligence, and an Overall Board of Spiritual Strategy.

276. RUDHYAR, Dane. **Modern Man's Conflicts: The Creative Challenge of a Global Society.** NY: Philosophical Library, 1948. 228 pp. (AB-4)

Harmonization and integration are seen as needed in every sphere, with the human being as the center of the total process. To pursue the harmonizing of opposites in the lives of individuals and in our global society, chapters cover topics such as a new image of womanhood, transpersonal love, the harmonic ideal of society, the road to global harmony, and world management.

277. RUDHYAR, Dane. **The Planitarization of Consciousness.** Preface by Oliver Reiser. Wassenaar, Holland: Service Publications, 1970. NY: Harper Colophon Edition, 1972. 343 pp. $2.95.   (A-4)

Chapters organized in three parts: In the Psychological Mode, In the Metaphysical Mode, and In the Social Mode. The final chapter, The Ethics of Wholeness and the Plenary Society argues for a future planetary society that "need not be a rigidly centralized World State." Rather, it should be a multi-level society, a society with "a symbolical organic character," "holarchic" in its overall organization of activities.

278. FULLER, R. Buckminster. **Operating Manual for Spaceship Earth.** Carbondale, Ill.: Southern Illinois University Press, March 1969. 143 pp. $4.25. NY: Pocket Books, Nov. 1970. 127 pp. $1.25. (AB-4)

Fuller fumes against nations and politicians, ignorance-invented race distinctions, established ideologies that assume material scarcity, and academic specialization that may hasten our extinction.

Instead, "A new, physically uncompromised, metaphysical initiative of unbiased integrity could unify the world." (p.32) This will come about by the computer replacing man as a specialist, with man "being forced to reestablish, employ, and enjoy his innate 'comprehensivity'." (p.40) Those who are consequently unemployed will be given "a life fellowship in research and development or in just simple thinking."

Once problems are approached on a universal general systems basis, the resulting world industrialization will benefit all of humanity. "This all brings us to a realization of the enormous ..educational task which must be successfully accomplished right now in a hurry..." (p. 113)

*** Hardly an "Operating Manual," but possibly a preface to one of several that are needed to reflect several points of view.

279. FULLER, R. Buckminster. **Utopia or Oblivion: The Prospects for Humanity.** NY: Bantam Books, Matrix Editions, Dec. 1969. 363 pp. $1.25.   (BC-4)

Twelve papers based on talks or articles prepared over the past several years, providing a good overview of Fuller's thought. Especially see instructions for The World Game, the advocacy of geosocial revolutions, and the explanation of the 14 dominant concepts unique to Fuller's philosophy: universe, humanity, children, teleology, reform the environment (rather than man), general systems theory, industrialization, design science, world service industries, ephemeralization and invisible commonwealth, prime design initiative, self-disciplines, comprehensive coordination, and world community and sub-communities of world man. (pp.309-342)

The Epilogue written for this book summarizes Fuller's wildest ideas: two-mile high tower habitations, tetrahedronal floating cities, 10,000 passenger aircraft, domed-over cities, sky-floating geodesic spheres, and mobile habitats.

In summation, "The comprehensive introduction of automation everywhere around the earth will free man from being an automaton and will generate so fast a mastery and multiplication of energy wealth by humanity that we will be able to support all of humanity in ever greater physical and economic success anywhere around his little spaceship Earth. ...My intuitions foresee (man's) success despite his negative inertias. This means things are going to move fast." (p.362-363)

*** Utopia or oblivion are probably the two **least** likely prospects for humanity. Circumspect thinking, however, would probably cramp Fuller's inimitable style.

280. FULLER, R. Buckminster. **The World Game: Integrative Resource Utilization Planning Tool.** Carbondale: Southern Illinois University, World Resources Inventory, 1971. 183 pp.   (A-3)

"...The World Game is a precisely defined design science process for arriving at economic, technological and social insights pertinent to humanity's future envolvement (sic.) aboard our planet Earth." (p.2)

"...THE WHOLE STRATEGY OF WORLD GAMING IS ACCOMPLISHED BY SIMULATED EMPLOYMENT OF MY COMPREHENSIVE, ANTICIPATORY DESIGN SCIENCE WHICH ALONE HAS SHOWN ME HOW TO PROGRESSIVELY ALTER THE FUNDAMENTAL CONDITIONS UNDER WHICH HUMANITY EXISTS AND TO DO SO BY FEASIBLE AND LOGICAL MEANS." (p.6)

This strange volume is divided into four parts:
- World Game Scenario, including Fuller's 1969 testimony before the U.S. Senate Committee on Government Operations, Subcommittee on Intergovernmental Relations.
- World Game Packet, presenting some rudimentary procedures.
- Information to Begin Studying World Game, with several articles by Fuller's associates on data handling techniques.
- Readings, reprinting five articles by Fuller.

281. FULLER, R. Buckminster, "World-Around Problems: 10 Proposals," **The New York Times,** June 29, 1972, p. 37.   (AB-3)

On the occasion of turning over his life-work to a new nonprofit corporation, the Design Science Institute, Fuller has summarized the ten most crucial problems facing the world.

The highest priority of all is education: "An education revolution based on synergy...requires the reversal of our present system of compartmentation of knowledge and of going from the particular to the ever more special." It requires the elimination of all academic tenure, and "Learning is to be accomplished by use of cassette-tape video documentation with the individual child learning to find the most competent answers to the child's own questions."

Other "problems that have to be solved by bloodless design science revolution" are:
- conversion of the world accounting system
- elimination of property by making ownership onerous
- world democracy by electronic referendum
- elimination of all world sovereignties
- theoretical exploration through world game
- realization of design science competence
- recognition of humanity's unique functioning in the universe
- identification of mathematical coordinate system of universe
- philosophical realization that physical is not life
*** Fuller's silliness and wisdom in a succinct form.

282. HIRSCHFELD, Gerhard. **The People: Growth and Survival.** Published for the Council for the Study of Mankind, Inc. Foreward by Kenneth E. Boulding. Chicago: Aldine, 1973. 239 pp.   (AB-4)

A rather fresh and interesting polemic--best described as cosmic populism--by the Executive Director of CSM.

The attempt is made to explain why, throughout all of history, people have never attained lasting freedom, security, and self-determination. Politicians, businessmen, and financiers have gained, but the people have not. They have failed to benefit from expanding opportunity as a result of their lack of broad interests and political indifference. In the future, science and technology can only bring new and refined methods of exploitation.

"After more than five thousand years of societal history, the people are still the unwitting creators of new opportunity, the leadership class still the exploiters, and the middle class still the developers and refiners. If the people are to attain dignity of life, they will have to attain it through other than the traditional pattern of societal relationships." (p.151) To attain a better society, fundamental principles of the societal system must be rethought, redesigned, and reorganized. "True progress should be measured in terms of the people rather than the leadership group or the middle class." (p.160) "The conclusion seems inescapable that nothing less than a Mankind-oriented society is the solution for the problems of the people." (p.168)

The action program of Mankind Believers and a Mankind political party, described in the Appendix, is a marked degeneration of Hershfeld's argument, ending in acritical mush about the new cross-cultural art, the new economics of world trade, the new education, the new ecumenical orientation of religion, and the new international science. Few if any of these examples come anywhere near the new mankind leadership--a leadership of universality--that is advocated.

*** The analysis is provocative and the goals are noble, but the "action program" is inept--largely due to the failure to identify ineptitude in the name of Mankind which serves to inhibit any true progress toward Mankind interests.

283. WARD, Barbara. **Spaceship Earth**. NY: Columbia University Press, 1966. 152 pp.   (B-4)

"Modern science and technology have created so close a network of communication, transport, economic interdependence--that planet earth, on its journey through infinity, has acquired the intimacy, the fellowship, and the vulnerability of a spaceship." (p.vii) The four Pegram lectures go on to explore the necessity of restoring a balance of power, wealth, and ideology among the world's nations. "Then, when the grosser inequalities have been remedied, there can be more hope of building the common institutions, policies, and beliefs which the crew of Spaceship Earth must acquire if they are to have any sure hope of survival." (p.viii)

284. SHAPLEY, Harlow. **The View from a Distant Star: Man's Future in the Universe**. NY: Basic Books, 1963.   (AB-4)

An eminent astronomer writes in popular style about man's knowledge and ignorance, considering man in the frame of the universe at large: man's place in space, time and evolution, and problems of co-existing. Shapley attacks specialism in education and even wonders whether we should abandon it, feeling that "education has become largely a superficial device for concealing the ignorance within." (p.145) A "Plateau Curriculum" is advocated (pp.150-154), and comments are addressed to a "Psychozoic Kingdom" and "The Coming World State."

285. TOYNBEE, Arnold J. **Change and Habit: The Challenge of our Time**. NY: Oxford University Press, 1966. 240 pp.   (A-4)

An eminent historian argues that a World-wide World-state is necessary to avoid irretrievable catastrophe and that world authority is needed for the control of atomic energy and the production and distribution of food. "A literally world-wide world-state would be a state whose government was effective over the whole habitable and traversible surface of the planet..." (p. 115). Chapter 8 discusses various obstacles to unification, such as customary Western antipathy and race feeling.

286. HALLE, Louis J. **The Society of Man.** NY: Harper & Row, 1965 (?)
203 pp.   (AB-4)

Views a crisis in the evolution of our planet resulting from the disappearance of frontiers. Because of "upsurging" curves in population and military
and industrial power, the nation-state has been rendered unworkable. In the
final chapter, "Beyond the Nation-State," Halle suggests very little other
than the general movement "toward a permanent, worldwide organization of
man."

287. WATERLOW, Charlotte. **Superpowers and Victims: The Outlook for
World Community.** Englewood Cliffs, NJ: Prentice-Hall, 1974.
$6.95; $2.95 Spectrum paper. 181 pp.   (B-4)

Views the solution to the problems of the widening gap between rich and
poor countries in the development of world community. "The human race
seems to be evolving from premodern forms of culture into a new or modern
age; and for various historical reasons the rich countries are those who have
entered the modern age first--they are a mere two hundred years ahead."
(pp.3-4)
"The great need of Western man now is to return visionary truth to its
throne, but with rational truth as its partner, not its handmaiden." (p. 169)
The broad lines of change that are needed include conserving and exploiting
resources in the common interest, managing the environment on a global
scale, a new R & D emphasis for poor countries, disarmament, and an
overall sharing of wealth: a world welfare state. The distinctive features
of modern society are seen as a grounding in the principles of humanism
and science.
*** Clichéd liberalism.

288. BIELER, André. **The Politics of Hope.** Preface by Dom Helder Camara.
Trans. by Dennis Pardee. Grand Rapids, Mich.: Wm. B. Eerdmans
Publishing Co., 1974. (First published in Paris, 1970.) 152 pp.
$3.95, paper.   (AB-3)

A lofty call for global Christian leadership by a professor of theology
at the Universities of Lausanne and Geneva, who employs phrases such as
a solidarity city and a global homeland, responsible man and responsible
societies, global renewal, and a united worldwide society.
The church has a complicity in the arms race, and requires renewal so
that it can engage in the necessary criticism of powers. Politics and ideologies take the place of God and deceive man by giving him a reduced image
of his destiny. The Church should set these ideologies and utopias against
the knowledge of Christ: "the final and genuine goal of all of society, and
the one who can justify humanity's entire future." (p. 115) The Church has
its own model of society--Christ and his Kingdom--and must "present to
the world the goals of peace, non-violence, liberty, solidarity, disarmament, classless society, global society, etc., and to work for their political realization..." (p. 118) The Church must accept an avant-garde role
in planning and encourage a dialog open to all.
For the developing countries, Biéler suggests a more rapid rate of growth,
social justice, education related to manpower needs, and national development plans. For the developed countries, he advocates the strengthening
of international agencies, and eliminating the domination of rich countries
over poor ones.

289. HESBURGH, Theodore M., C.S.C. **The Humane Imperative: A Challenge
for the Year 2000.** The Terry Lectures. New Haven, Conn.: Yale
University Press, 1974. 115 pp.   (BC-4)

The President of the University of Notre Dame appeals to "modern Christains" to affect the course of our times by making theological and philosophical principles operative. "Rather than the scenario of global catastrophe in the days ahead, I should like to project a new world that is possible and even probable if we will dare to think new thoughts..." (p. 3)

Unfortunately, the description of the "new world" provided in this "essay in Christian humanism" is largely a cluster of pleasant banalities concerning the power of ecumenism, the growing consciousness of human dignity and human rights, population and the green revolution, global education utilizing educational television (but it will not be cultural imperialism), a triregional world of the future organized on a North-South orientation (EEC and Russia, North and South America, and the Orient), social justice as the necessary road to peace, and promoting world citizenship. Multinational corporations are not mentioned.

The greatest irritation is that Father Hesburgh speaks of completely new schemes, new and creative thoughts, and leaving the conventional wisdom behind, while failing to demonstrate anything that is new and unconventional. Such a gap between promise and performance gives "new world" thinking a bad name.

*** Hesburgh is one of the very few university presidents who has anything to say in public today. He deserves some credit, at least, for trying.

290. HOPKINS, Frank Snowden, "The Postulated Future, The Invented Future and an Ameliorated World," **The Futurist,** VII:5, Dec. 1973, pp. 254-258.   (B-4)

A former State Department planner distinguishes between the Postulated Future, the one we are most likely to drift into, and the Invented Future: "the future we might be able to achieve if we think creatively and act in a foresighted manner. It is a sort of best possible future under the circumstances of the late 20th and early 21st centuries."

As illustration, Hopkins proposes the goal of an ameliorated World: "one which is better and safer and more likely to endure than the one we have now." Two requisites for this condition are very real progress in controlling world population, and a modification of the demands of industrial man. There is little faith that government, which is seen as responding to pressures rather than planning ahead, can supply the necessary wisdom and responsibility. Rather, leadership must come from thinking individuals, from educators and communicators in general, for, to deal adequately with the future, "we must have an educated and informed public..."

291. CLARKE, Arthur C. "Satellites and the 'United States of Earth'," **The Futurist,** VI:2, April 1972, p. 61.   (AB-5)

Remarks delivered at the signing of the new INTELSAT agreements in 1971 by a noted science-fiction writer, who believes that communications satellites can unite mankind: "What the railroads and the telegraph did here a century ago, the jets and the communications satellites are doing now to all the world."

*** Although the occasion undoubtedly demanded some kindly rhetoric, it is silly and possibly dangerous to think in terms of salvation by technology, let alone a single technology.

292. DESAN, Wilfrid. **The Planetary Man.** N.Y.: Macmillan, 1972. 380 pp.   (A-4)

Incorporates Volume I, A Noetic Prelude to a United World (published in 1961) and Volume II, An Ethical Prelude to a United World. Of interest to philosophers only.

293. ULICH, Robert. **Progress or Disaster? From the Bourgeois to the World Citizen.** NY: New York University Press, 1971. 208 pp. $8.95.
                                                                              (A-5)
Considers three historical periods: the period of the bourgeois (before World War I), the years of catastrophe, and the era of mutual global inter-dependence. For each of these periods there is a discussion of the state, the economy, religion, humanism, and education, all with the aim "to inquire how the era in which we live--roughly delimited here to the nineteenth and twentieth centuries--will be judged by later generations."
* Incoherent and disorganized pedantry.

294. NEARING, Scott. **Civilization and Beyond: Learning from History. A Commentary On The Past, Present & Future of Civilization.** Harborside, Maine: Social Science Institute, August 1975. 263 pp. $3.00, paper.   (AB-5)

Surveys experiments with civilizations in the past and offers a social analysis of civilization in general: its politics, economics, sociology, and ideology. The Great Revolution of 1750-1970 is seen as making Western Civilization obsolete. The bourgeois state of monopoly capitalism is dis-integrating, but it must and can be replaced by "the universal socialist-communist state that will shepherd humanity along the difficult and dangerous path of the political life pattern beyond civilization." (p.200) The political core of this social stage will be a world government administered on the federal principle. This will be developed through the existing U.N. structure. Such a government would operate a planet-wide economy in the public interest.
* Simplistic cosmic communism.

295. NEARING, Scott. **United World: The Road to International Peace.** NY: Island Press, 1944. 265 pp.   (ns)

296. SALTER, Leonard M. **The Dynamics of World Order.** NY: Vantage Press, 1975. $4.95.   (ns)

"Stressing world peace through law...ideas on preserving our earth and population." (advt.)

297. SURSELEY, Robert J. **America's Destiny: World Union or Obliteration in Thirty Years.** NY: Exposition, Sept. 1975. $4.00.   (ns)

Chapter 7

Decentralization

It is useful to juxtapose the advocates of world order with those who face in the opposite direction toward the decentralization of all political and economic institutions. The two foci seem to be in total opposition; but, as suggested by Lakey (318), it might be possible and perhaps necessary to have both world order and decentralized community as intertwined components of "a living revolution."

A more substantial contrast is with the Technological, Affluent, Service Society. The decentralists hold an antithetical position, advocating small or "soft" technology, modest comfort for all, and a do-it-yourself philosophy. As described by E.F. Schumacher (310), it is the difference between the "people of the forward stampede" and the "homecomers" who seek to return to basic truths. Those with an intellectual or financial investment in the "forward stampede" express hope that the economy will revive or can be revived; decentralists see industrialism as a failed experiment.

The decentralist position is one that many people on both the political "left" and "right" can unite on, and the one position that clearly demonstrates why the conventional "left-right" and "liberal-conservative" political terminology is so misleading. Many advocates of decentralization view themselves as "radical" (e.g., 318-321), but there are also other varieties of radicals (Chapter 11). There is a strong kinship of decentralists to "conservatives" who detest bureaucracy and seek freedom from government (Chapter 12), but decentralists are against big government **and** big business, whereas conservatives are often blind to corporate and environmental problems.

In contrast to the previous chapter, where there are few noteworthy items, this chapter contains many outstanding works; indeed, there is a greater proportion of highly-rated items here than in any other chapter in this guide. This is a very intentional imbalance because it is felt that the decentralist argument is of fundamental importance, and that it has not been adequately considered. Ignoring an argument is not an answer, and casting decentralists aside as primitives or romantics, as many have done (e.g., Toffler, no. 46), simply indicates a failure to read the literature. Decentralists are not anti-technology, nor are they anti-scientific.

The **Blueprint for Survival** by Edward Goldsmith and colleagues (211) is an outstanding example of decentralist thinking arising out of concern for the environment. Several other decentralists with a focus on the small community, notably Arthur E. Morgan (nos. 704-705), appear in Chapter 13 on Spatial Alternatives.

The "entropy state" pictured by Hazel Henderson (298) serves as a succinct introduction to the decentralists in this chapter. Cornuelle (299) also takes a managerial point of view in his irreverent charge that official "front-office America" doesn't work. Hess (300) is another dropout from official America with a very compelling argument about rediscovering general human wisdom. Herber (now known as Murray Bookchin) was an early and eloquent critic of urbanization as dangerous to the health of the species (301), and Roszak (303) also makes the important association between urbanization and industrialization. Roszak is not against science, but he is the leading critic of the reductionist science that has characterized the industrial era. A similar critique is provided by scientists themselves: Schwartz (304) and Dubos (180). Giedion (305) provides a useful history of mechanization taking command, which serves as a background for appreciating Illich's important plea for convivial tools (306). The relationship of technology to politics and social structure is courageously explored by Dickson (308).

Taylor (309) argues for a "paraprimitive society" as necessary to promote human values, while Schumacher (310) provides a respectable case for the alternative of "Buddhist Economics." Although Schumacher is perhaps the best-known decentralist thinker at present, the most extensive thinking has been done by Ralph Borsodi, who is virtually unknown. **This Ugly Civilization** (311), first published in 1929, proposes a societal alternative that is both persuasive and highly elaborated. Any serious student of alternative futures would benefit from studying this neglected work, as well as Borsodi's encyclopedic **Seventeen Problems of Man and Society** (313), published in India in 1968.

The subsequent items, many of them steamy polemics, are not as important as the items mentioned above. Arthur J. Penty (324-325) should be noted, however, as the first writer to use "Post-Industrialism," and his distinction between the "work state" and the "leisure state" is still important.

Decentralist thinking has had a long history in both Eastern and Western thought. Doctor provides a very useful overview of "Sarvodaya" or Gandhian philosophy (327), and Huang condenses the wisdom of Lao-Tse (328). Runkle provides a history of anarchy (329) that obviously has some relevance here, although the decentralist position is more precisely defined by Borsodi as "minarchy" or minimal government. When institutions become too large, as Schumacher argues, it is reasonable for all people to consider, in a counterbalancing direction, that small is beautiful--and economical too.

298. HENDERSON, Hazel, "The Entropy State," **Planning Review: A Journal for Managerial Decision-Making,** 2:3, April-May 1974, pp. 1-4.
(AB-2)

Proposes yet another model of the unfolding shape of advanced industrial societies: "the entropy state is a society at the stage when complexity and interdependence have reached the point where the transaction costs that are generated equal or exceed the society's productive capabilities. In a manner analogous to the phenomenon that occurs in physical systems, the society slowly winds down of its own weight and complexity, with all its forces and counterforces checked and balanced in a state of equilibrium." (p. 1)

Under this condition, unanticipated social costs arise, and the costs of trying to maintain "social homeostasis" begins to grow exponentially. Traditional Keynesian remedies of pumping up the economy only serve to raise inflation rates and deplete resources.

The remedy may lie in deliberately trying to reduce interdependencies by simplifying some of the overdeveloped systems: "We might take, not the Luddite's axe, but the surgeon's scalpel..." (p. 4) The telephone system, for example, must remain large and standardized, but there could be smaller cities and corporations, a change in the mix of human and machine energy, and changes in values of life-styles such that "the entropy state might be held at bay for many generations." (p. 4) In contrast, "The Bucky Fulfilling dreams of technologically based abundance of the sixties now seem adolescent and remote." (p. 4)

*** A most concise and cogent introduction to the decentralist argument.

299. CORNUELLE, Richard. **De-Managing America: The Final Revolution.**
NY: Random House, 1975. 147 pp. $7.95.   (ABC-3)

A very popularized but insightful book by a former foundation executive
and Executive Vice-President of the National Association of Manufacturers
who quit and "rediscovered" America. Actually, two Americas: Front-
office America, the official America of social engineers and authoritarian
methods "has failed massively." And the other America, unofficial and unmanaged, which "works remarkably well."
Why is there a universal sense of failure of government programs by
their managers? Because authority isn't working the way it used to. "The
error is elemental. Social management doesn't work." Nor do the traditional
ideologies: "Conservative thought is stale and passive. Liberal thought is
hyperactive and naive. Conservatives are appealing to a faith in freedom we
never had. Liberals are appealing to a faith in government action we have
lost." (p. 19)
America is likened to the Wizard of Oz--nothing behind the glittering
front office. The social sciences are likened to alchemy in both spirit
and practice. The hollowness of licensing and credentials is adeptly exposed.
The "liberal" belief that society can be made more nearly perfect is attacked as secular religion.
A mass emancipation is beginning "and the great emancipators are the
people themselves." (p. 105) The new revolution aims for the final transformation of authority; its weapons are self-discovery and self-expression. De-management is devising methods to release the imprisoned energies, to specify results instead of specifying behavior, to define programs
in terms of outcomes instead of management intentions. A crucial element
is the awareness of institutional identity: what an institution is and what it
could be. Cornuelle attacks the limited agendas of foundations, the senility
of organizations in the "independent sector," and those corporations that
fail to exercise social responsibility. A final chapter extols the virtues
of performance contracting.
*** Not much of a conclusion, but Cornuelle nevertheless has a grasp of
certain matters of fundamental importance.

300. HESS, Karl. **Dear America.** NY: Morrow, 1975. 279 pp. $7.95.   (ABC-3)

This unusual book reflects an unusual background: a school-leaver at age
15, Hess has held a number of jobs close to the pinnacles of corporate and
governmental power, such as assistant to a corporation president, an editor at **Newsweek,** a staff member at the American Enterprise Institute for
Public Policy Research, and chief speechwriter for Barry Goldwater in
the 1964 Presidential race. This experience enables an insider's critique
of suburbia ("conquest sex" and "oblivion drinking"), corporate life
("largely mindless"; "like a pool of sharks") and bigness in general. It
has enabled a smoothly written and immensely insightful personal statement
by a drop-out from the system, now self-described as a welder and "a
writer acting on behalf of my own and my neighbor's interests." (Hess lived
in the Adams-Morgan section of Washington, D.C. and is connected with
the Institute of Policy Studies.)
Public semantics are clarified by redefining the right-left construct,
common to our political thinking. This continuum should be based on the
concentration of power, and liberals should not be seen as left wing, but as
right of center, even to the right of many conservatives. Corporate capitalism is seen as an act of theft, but state socialism is seen as the mirror
image: an act of betrayal where liberals simply seek clients for their programs. Roosevelt, for example, is not viewed as radical/liberal/collecti-
vist, but as simply taking the rough edges off of the evolving system of
concentrated power. The distinction between what Marx wrote and Marxism
as cant and political theology (pp. 156-167) is very useful.
Hess is convinced of a general human wisdom and general common sense
which rediscovers fundamental humanistic positions. This wisdom, today,

dictates a return to human scale, human purposes, and human rather than institutional values--megalopolis and the corporate state are the exact opposite of what is needed. Although Hess does not use any recurring label, the elements of the desired society are clear and sensible in the context in which they are related: industrial democracy where people participate in decisions of work as well as community, a truly free society where all have power as a result of radical decentralization, a wider diffusion of scientific and technological information, and an American language of unity and purpose centered on a view of work and workers.

Some of the ways to attain this condition, based on Hess' recent experience with his neighbors in Washington, D.C., include the use of alternative technology, growing food close to where it is eaten (thereby avoiding the waste of processing, packaging, and transport), localized health facilities replacing big competitive hospitals, and community ownership and operation or productive facilities. Hess proposes withholding tax (the very foundation of government power) subjected to continuing review, taxpayers assigning their dollars to purposes they deem useful, national defense restricted to the Polaris system and a volunteer militia, and laws requiring accountability of bureaucrats. In this way, the big-scale tragedies of farm, factory, and forum would be avoided, and we could ease our way "into a better future."

*** As a result of the crime problem, Hess has since moved to a homestead in West Virginia, although he still spends two days per week in Washington. See "The Plowboy Interview," **The Mother Earth News,** No. 37, Jan. 1976, pp. 6-14.

300a. TRACY, Phil. "If Washington is Obsolete, Can We Do It Ourselves?" **The Village Voice,** April 26, 1976, pp. 24-26.   (BC-4)

Reports that people in Washington, formerly "the temple of optimism," are now "suffering from terminal bewilderment." There has been an important change in attitudes, as citizens increasingly realize that they are asked to pay for some program, but get something entirely different in its place.

"The people who support the military-industrial complex are called conservatives. Those who champion the social service complex are called liberals. But the distinctions are meaningless. Both categories function in the same exact way." (p. 24)

A new direction is advocated to restore our instinct for self-reliance, and questions are raised about impending Washington programs such as federalized welfare, old age care, child care, nationalized health insurance (which would just make doctors and hospital administrators richer), and revenue sharing (a "shell game" allowing people in Washington to keep control of the tax money).

*** A good accounting of contemporary gut feelings, but little help is offered to get out of the bureaucratic maze.

301. ¦HERBER, Lewis (Murray BOOKCHIN). Our Synthetic Environment. Introduction by William A. Albrecht. NY: Knopf, 1962. 285 pp. Harper Colophon Edition (with new introduction). 1974. $2.95. (AB-2)

A lucid and prophetic synthesis, arguing that "The modern city has reached its limits. Megalopolitan life is breaking down--psychically, economically, and biologically." (p. 238) Agriculture has been depersonalized and overindustrialized to the point that soil needs are being overlooked: "ecological and nutrition problems created by monoculture and the land factory are likely to grow worse, and many chemical additives will be required in the mass production of our food." (p. 236) Chapters cover topics such as environment and illness, agriculture and health, urban life and health, chemicals in food, radiation, and human ecology.

It is concluded that some kind of decentralization is necessary to achieve a lasting equilibrium between society and nature, and that more localized industrial activity is likely to become more efficient. Indeed, modern technology has prepared "the material conditions for a new type of human community--one which constitutes neither a complete return to the past nor a suburban accommodation to the present...The 'urbanized farmer' or the 'agrarianized townsman' need not be a contradiction in terms." (p. 242) Life should become a more rounded experience, and this can only be done by reducing the community to a more human scale.
*** A unique integration of two isolated perspectives: health and community patterns.

302. ROSZAK, Theodore. **The Making of a Counter Culture: Reflections on the Technocratic Society and Its Youthful Opposition.** Garden City, N.Y.: Doubleday, 1969. 303 pp.   (AB-4)

The opening chapter describes technocracy and its children, arguing that "the young stand forth so prominently because they act against a background of nearly pathological passivity on the part of the adult generation." (p. 22) It is further argued that the exploration of the non-intellective powers assumes its greatest importance "when it becomes a critique of the scientific world view upon which the technocracy builds its citadel and in the shadow of which too many of the brightest splendors of our experience lie hidden." (p. 83)

Chapters III-VI explore dimensions of the counter culture: the dialectics of liberation, journey to the East...and points beyond, the use and abuse of psychedelic experience ("The Counterfeit Infinity"), and utopia, by focusing respectively on Herbert Marcuse and Norman Brown, Allen Ginsberg and Alan Watts, Timothy Leary, and Paul Goodman.

Chapter VII, The Myth of Objective Consciousness attacks conventional science with the aid of Thomas Kuhn, Abraham Maslow, Michael Polanyi, Lewis Mumford, and Jacques Ellul. An appendix of examples, "Objectivity Unlimited," supports this argument.
*** The protests of the young have waned, and this book is not of particular importance here except as a seedbed for several themes more extensively developed in Roszak's later work (see below), which has received relatively little attention.

303. ROSZAK, Theodore. **Where the Wasteland Ends: Politics and Transcendence in Postindustrial Society.** Garden City, N.Y.: Doubleday, 1972; Anchor Books edition, 1973. 451 pp. $2.95, paper.   (A-2)

"The religious renewal we see happening about us...(is) a profoundly serious sign of the times, a necessary phase of our cultural evolution, and --potentially--a life-enhancing influence of incalculable value. I believe it means we have arrived, after long journeying, at an historical vantage point from which we can at last see where the wasteland ends and where a culture of human wholeness and fulfillment begins. We can now recognize that the fate of the soul is the fate of the social order..." (p. xvii)

The basic argument is that the mindscape of our culture has been shaped over the past three centuries by modern science. We have evolved an unsatisfactory condition of urban industrialism erected upon a culture of alienation. "For the sake of the artificial environment, the soul **had** to die." (p. 419) Of particular note is the argument that humanism is bound to the single vision and reductionist intellect of urban industrial society. "Humanism, for all its ethical protest, will not and cannot shift the quality of consciousness in our society; it has not the necessary psychic leverage." (p. 417)

Chapter 1, The Artificial Environment, describes the flight from the primitive, the urban-industrial imperative, and the worldwide technological coalescence that leads to a degeneration of consciousness. Chapter 2, Citadel of Expertise, attacks the scientization of culture and is particularly important for its description of the four types of technocracy to be found in the world (pp. 38-45): suave technocracy (the ultimate expression of a mature, administered capitalism of the benign, pluralistic, swinging society), vulgar technocracy (grim, heavy-handed and monolithic as in the USSR), teratoid technocracy (push-button witch's kitchen as in Nazi Germany), and comic opera technocracy (pretentious and inept).

Part Two (Chaps. 4-7) focuses on Single Vision and Newton's Sleep: The Strange Interplay of Objectivity and Alienation, and Chapter 7, Science in Extremus: Prospect of an autopsy, along with its appendix on The Reductionist assault, is an important statement on methodology.

Part Three, The Politics of Eternity, offers chapters on topics such as Uncaging Skylarks: The Meaning of Transcendent Symbols, Rhapsodic Intellect, The Visionary Commonwealth, and Apocatastasis (or the great restoration). Essentially, the argument is that the antidote for reductionism "is a wholly new science, transformed from the psychic ground up, that will lead us to recognize with inescapable cogency what single vision will never see: that reductionism is an ugly lie and that those who extend its province degrade the truth." (p. 233)

Ecology is seen as the closest that our science has come to an integrative wisdom but little hope is held for a revolution of consciousness within the palace. "If the Reality Principle of the modern world is ever transformed, the change will happen, perversely and heretically, at the fringes of our culture and work its way in toward the center. The scientists, the guardians of single vision in urban-industrial society and the intellectual linch-pin of the technocracy, may be among the last to hear the news." (p. 378)

An outline of the elements of "The Visionary Commonwealth" is provided on p. 396; it would contain the proper mix of handicraft labor and heavy industry, non-bureaucratized social services, a rehabilitated rural life, noncompulsory education, and work as a means of spiritual growth. "The great trick is to discover what it is that holds people fast to the status quo and then to undo the knots--perhaps even on a person-to-person basis." (p. 398)

*** This extensive and sophisticated attack on reductionist science and its relationship to urban-industrial technocracy is clearly more important than The Making of a Counter Culture, for which Roszak is widely known. Wasteland is angry and passionate but it is not anti-intellectual or anti-scientific, as often charged by critics who apparently have not read the book. It argues for an alternative science and a higher reason, and a serious challenge to this argument has yet to be made.

304. SCHWARTZ, Eugene S. Overskill: The Decline of Technology in Modern Civilization. Chicago: Quadrangle Books, 1971. 338 pp. (AB-3)

"The thesis of the book is...(that) the crises that threaten human survival are inherent in science and technology and are not amenable to rectification by more science and technology...all technological solutions of problems leave a residue of unsolved problems that proliferate faster than their solutions." (p. ix)

The final chapter, Toward the Inefficient Society, argues that continuing the path to technological society "will lead either to the universal concentration camp or to biological extermination." Schwartz, a scientist, argues that the age of reason has been shown to be unreasonable. But man can rediscover himself in the philosophy of post-technological man, based on the following principles: man is within nature, there are infinite paths to the apprehension of reality, the inefficient society is a humane society (efficiency, after all, is an engineering measure), man creates himself in labor, the machine must be subservient to man, society must be free and open, and the paths to the future are varied and infinite.

*** The societal label is not a good choice, but the argument, although general, is worth a hearing.

305. GIEDION, Siegfried. **Mechanization Takes Command: A Contribution to Anonymous History.** NY: Oxford University Press, 1948. 743 pp.
(AB-3)

An exhaustive historical analysis, supported by hundreds of illustrations, of the "tools that have molded our present-day living...how this mode of life came about, and something of the process of its growth." (p. 2) The focus is on describing the humble and modest things of daily life such as changes in the baking of bread, the processing of meat, the design of furniture, implements for the bath and the household, and agriculture.

In that mechanization involves a division of labor, "the individual becomes increasingly dependent on production and on society as a whole, and relations are far more complex and interlocked than in any earlier society. This is one reason why today man is overpowered by means. No doubt mechanization can help eliminate slave labor and achieve better standards of living. Nevertheless, in the future it may have to be checked in some way so as to allow a more independent way of living." (pp. 714-715)

It is concluded that there is an illusion of progress and that the promises of a better life have not been kept. Giedion advocates a dynamic equilibrium: a new balance between the spheres of knowledge, the psychic spheres within the individual, and between individualism and collectivism.
*** Useful background reading to Illich's **Tools for Conviviality.**

306. ILLICH, Ivan. **Tools for Conviviality.** World Perspectives, Vol. 47. NY: Harper & Row, 1973. 110 pp. $5.95.   (A-3)

Illich is the author of **Deschooling Society** and the co-founder of the Center for Intercultural Documentation (CIDOC) in Cuernavaca, Mexico. This difficult but rewarding volume utilizes some of the ideas in his previous and much better-known work, and obviously reflects the perception of a world-thinker based in a less-developed country.

The first chapter describes Two Watersheds, with modern medicine employed as representative of all modern institutions. The first watershed, early in this century, was the emergence of medical science into an era of scientific verification and desirable effects. The second watershed was passed when further advances in medical science and professionalization failed to enhance human well-being. "The characteristic reaction of the sixties to the growing frustration was further technological and bureaucratic escalation. Self-defeating escalation of power became the core-ritual practiced in highly industrialized nations." (p. 8)

"The crisis can be solved only if we learn to invert the present deep structure of tools; if we give people tools that guarantee their right to work with high, independent efficiency, thus simultaneously eliminating the need for either slaves or masters and enhancing each person's range of freedom." (p. 10)

The term "tool" is used to include not only simple hardware and large machines, but also institutions such as factories and productive systems for intangible commodities such as education. "Tools foster conviviality to the extent to which they can be easily used, by anybody, as often or as seldom as desired, for the accomplishment of a purpose chosen by the user." (p. 22)

Conviviality is the opposite of industrial productivity: it is "individual freedom realized in personal interdependence and, as such, an intrinsic ethical value." (p. 11)

"As an alternative to technocratic disaster, I propose the vision of a convivial society." (p. 12) In such a society, described as post-industrial, tools would become the basis for participatory justice. Such a society would not exclude all large tools and all centralized production. "Tools for a convivial and yet efficient society could not have been designed at an earlier stage of history." (p. 33) "Our imaginations have been industrially deformed to conceive only what can be molded into an engineered system of social habits that fit the logic of large-scale production." (p. 14-15.)

Illich goes on to describe six imbalances, or ways in which people are threatened by hyper-industrialism: biological degradation, radical monopoly (dominance by one product or service), overprogramming, polarization (impelling societies to grow in population and levels of affluence), obsolescence, and frustration. Recovery of the balance of life requires the inversion of society, which requires overcoming three formidable obstacles: "the idolatry of science, the corruption of ordinary language, and loss of respect for the formal process by which social decisions are made." (p. 85)
* Rather murky in parts, but still a fresh and powerful angle of vision.

307. VALE, Brenda and Robert. **The Autonomous House: Design and ·Planning for Self-Sufficiency.** NY: Universe, 1975. 224 pp. $10.00   (AB-4)

The autonomous house is one that operates independently of any inputs except those of its immediate environment. It resembles a land-based space station.

The authors insist that this is not a regressive step. "Rather, it shows a different direction for society to take. Instead of growth, stability is the aim..." (p. 7) Once the house becomes decentralized, other systems such as self-sufficiency in food, may follow.

Costs relative to conventional housing are expected to decline appreciably in the near future, offering a standard of living that could be achievd by every person on earth. "The success or failure of the autonomous experiments that will probably be set up in the next few years may be important for the survival of mankind." (p. 11)

This stirring introduction is followed by well-illustrated semi-technical chapters on solar power, wind power, heat pumps, recycling wastes, water storage and recycling, batteries and fuel cells, heat storage, and the design for an autonomous house.
* Largely a sophisticated how-to-do-it guide, but included here particularly for the benefit of urban intellectuals to emphasize that decentralists are not necessarily romantic Luddites.

308. DICKSON, David. **The Politics of Alternative Technology.** NY: Universe, Sept. 1975. 224 pp. $7.95. (Published in England as **Alternative Technology and the Politics of Technical Change** by Fontana/Collins, 1974.)   (A-2)

A useful essay by the science correspondent of the **Times Higher Education Supplement.** Dickson tries to examine the social functions of technology and the political obstacles to the development of alternative technologies. The general thesis is that technology plays a political role in society, "intimately related to the distribution of power and the exercise of social control." (p. 10) Consequently, a genuine alternative technology can only be developed on any significant scale within the framework of an alternative society.

After chapters devoted to the case against contemporary technology, the ideology of industrialization, and the politics of technical change, Dickson devotes two chapters to describing utopian technology: technology that is satisfying to work with, controlled by producers and the community, conserving natural resources, doing negligible damage to the environment, and usable by the poorest people.

A chart on pp. 103-104 lists 35 characteristics (suggested by Robin Clarke of Biotechnic Research and Development) of a "soft" technology society in contrast to a hard technology society. Some of the traits of the "soft" technology society include craft industry, village emphasis, decentralization, few and unimportant technological accidents, diverse solutions to problems, innovation regulated by need, integration of young and old, operating modes understandable by all, and a weak or non-existant work/ leisure distinction. The power base of utopian technology would employ solar energy, wind-power, water-power, methane gas, and animal and human labor. There would be organic farming and use of locally available building materials.

Chapter 6, Intermediate Technology and the Third World, provides a particularly important critique. There are strong parallels between intermediate technology and utopian technology (such as an emphasis on labor intensive production techniques), but the difference is that intermediate technology is often seen as a complement to existing patterns of large-scale and centralized industrialization, whereas utopian technology is based on a radically new social and economic structure. Intermediate technology, already part of the conventional wisdom of development planning, "can become little more than a sophisticated extension of the ideology of industrialization..." (p. 151)

308a. BOYLE, Godfrey and Peter HARPER (eds.) **Radical Technology.** NY: Pantheon, 1976. $5.95, paper.   (ns)

Forty articles on current and alternative forms of organizing and producing food, materials, shelter, energy, and communications.

309. TAYLOR, Gordon Rattray. **Rethink: A Paraprimitive Solution.** NY: E.P. Dutton, 1973. 278 pp. $7.95.   (AB-2)

A broad, lucid, and thoughtful synthesis, skillfully utilizing history, anthropology, sociology, and psychology, with intelligent comments on economics and politics. "My object in this book is to identify the forces which are causing the 'system break' and to speed up the process of readjustment by defining the pattern we are moving towards." (p. 8) Drawing on the social sciences, Taylor attempts "to arrive at some conclusions about the kind of society we ought to be aiming at, and this will lead us into considering the complex problems of how a new kind of society could be brought about... for the first time, we are beginning to be in a position to devise, intentionally, the style of life in which we believe we should live..." (p. 11)

Taylor begins his argument by contrasting two distinct scales of contrasting value systems: patrist (hierarchical, disciplined) vs. matrist (permissive, egalitarian), and tough (hard ago) vs. tender (soft ego). As indicated by a summary chart on p. 61, the pattern of society depends on the grouping of personality elements. "In this tetralemma (and I could provide it with more horns if I used a more complex system of analysis) there is only one course that offers any hope: to use all the influence we can to crowd future generations towards the mid-position." (p. 66)

In part II (chapters 5-7), Taylor proceeds to explain why our culture is proceeding in the wrong direction. We have attempted to meet our psychological needs by the supply of goods, creating a world of substitute satisfactions: "...we need to establish a 'need-oriented society' in place of our present goods-oriented society." (p. 108) It is also noted that society continues to undermine community, and that the emerging universal culture enabled by technology destroys local variation.

A paraprimitive society is advocated, but this is in no way a romantic regression to the past (see disavowal, p. 256). Many of the elements of such a society are summarized on p. 230: a decentralization of authority and power, restoring the elements of mastery and self-determination to work and to life generally, moderating the pace of change, preventing the evasion of responsibility by corporations, and eliminating profit as the sole criterion of decision-making. A central government will still remain to conduct international affairs and handle genuinely national issues, but its main function would be that of consultant and mediator between the dispersed foci of power.

*** Very well-read and sophisticated.

310. SCHUMACHER, E.F. **Small is Beautiful: Economics as if People Mattered.** Introduction by Theodore Roszak. NY: Harper & Row, 1973; Harper Torchback Edition, 1973. 290 pp. $3.75.   (AB-1)

A British economist's lectures and published essays from the 1966-1972 period, most of the 19 items fitting together very well.

Part I on The Modern World begins with The Problem of Production, which holds that it is a fateful error to believe that this problem has been solved, and points out the failure to place a value on natural capital. Peace and Permanance argues that the foundations of peace cannot be laid by universal prosperity in the modern sense. "The cultivation and expansion of needs is the antithesis of wisdom. It is also the antithesis of freedom and peace." (p. 31) To reverse destructive trends, methods and equipment are needed which are accessible to virtually everyone, suitable for small-scale application (which is always less likely to be harmful to the environment), and compatible with man's need for creativity.

The third essay on The Role of Economics insists that "The study of economics is too narrow and too fragmentary to lead to valid insights, unless complemented and completed by a study of meta-economics." (p. 49) It is therefore the duty of economists to understand and clarify their limitations. Perhaps the most celebrated essay of this volume is Buddhist Economics, which is proposed as an alternative to the economics of modern materialism. Rather than viewing the essence of civilization as the multiplication of wants, Schumacher proposes the "systematic study of how to attain given ends with the minimum means." (p. 55)

The fifth essay, A Question of Size, states that "Today, we suffer from an almost universal idolatry of giantism. It is therefore necessary to insist on the virtues of smallness--where this applies. (If there were a prevailing idolatry of smallness, irrespective of subject or purpose, one would have to try to exercise influence in the opposite direction.)" (p. 62) The "most important" subject on the agenda of large countries today is seen as the question of regionalism, or the geographic distribution of population.

Part II, Resources, includes essays on The Greatest Resource: Education (which argues that the true problems of life are those of overcoming or reconciling opposites), The Proper Use of Land (viewing large-scale mechanization and heavy chemicalization as leading to environmental destruction), Resources for Industry (focusing on the centrality of the energy problem) and Nuclear Energy (seen as the main cause of complacency about future energy supplies). The final essay, Technology with a Human Face, introduces the notion of "intermediate technology" (or self-help technology or democratic or people's technology) that would make human hands and brains less redundant, and makes the distinction between "people of the forward stampede" who advocate more of the same, and "homecomers" who seek to return to basic truths about man and his world and place a qualitative dimension on the idea of growth.

Part III, The Third World, discusses applications of intermediate technology and the imbalance of the city and countryside as "the all-pervading disease of the modern world." Part IV, Organization and Ownership, has five somewhat more technical essays on forecasting and planning, a theory of large-scale organization, socialism, ownership, and possible patterns of ownership seen as eight different combinations arising from three basic societal choices: private vs. public ownership, a market economy vs. various forms of planning, and freedom vs. totalitarianism.

*** These essays are lucid, thoughtful, and restrained; those in the first two parts of the book are particularly important, and should serve to undermine the conventional wisdom among all but the most dogmatic of people. Also see a brief article by Schumacher, a review of his book, and an extensive interview, all in **The Futurist,** 8:6, December 1974, pp. 272-284.

310a. WINTHROP, Henry. Ventures in Social Interpretation. NY: Appleton-Century-Crofts, 1968. 551 pp.   (AB-3)

A far-ranging exploration of the impacts of science and technology, with chapters arranged in five parts: Technology and Some of Its Social Consequences; Culture, Leisure, and Education; The Burden of Social Complexity; The Pathologies of Overurbanization; and Technology, Decentralization, and the Restoration of Community.

The final part is devoted to arguing for the relevance of a philosophy of decentralization to the problems of our time, with chapters on physical decentralization, new energy sources, and technology for community. "Traditional concepts like freedom, justice, and opportunity, are in danger of being reduced to negligible proportions as a result of our increasing centralization along political, social, cultural, industrial and economic lines." (p. 413)

311. BORSODI, Ralph. This Ugly Civilization. NY: Simon and Schuster, 1929. Second Edition (Foreword by Harry Elmer Barnes), NY: Harper & Bros., 1933. 468 pp.   (ABC-1)

A truly prophetic work, with greater breadth and detail than any of the contemporary writing that seeks a viable and humane alternative to industrial/super-industrial society. Borsodi does indeed offer a "practical plan which men and women anywhere can adopt for securing food, clothing, and shelter--the essentials of life--which requires them neither to wait for a revival of business nor to wait for some revolutionary reform of the existing social system." (p.xv)

As indicated in the title, there is a passionate critique of our factory-dominated civilization of noise, smoke, smells, crowds, and urban discomfort. "It is the factory, not the machine, which has transformed man from a self-helpful into a self-helpless individual and which has changed mankind from a race of participators in life to a race of spectators of it." (p.15) The industrial states consecrate themselves to the production of wealth, rather than comfort, while perpetuating the myth that mankind's comfort is dependent upon an unending increase in production. The direction of labor into the factory and away from the home has been made to seem desirable and rational: "The real genius of our age is engaged in thinking about how to abolish labor instead of how to ennoble it." (p.341)

This critique is familar today in terms of attacks on "the corporate state," and, indirectly, as concerns the "limits to growth" debate. An additional and significant dimension of Borsodi's critique--the critique of individuals--is not fashionable today but should nevertheless be closely heeded. "Persons in the Drama" are described as herd-minded types (the average man, unconscious of his ignorance, looking for solutions exterior to self), quantity-minded types (those attracted to power and concerned with how many and how large), and quality-minded types (concerned with how fine and how unique). The cardinal principle of the good society would be to encourage those individuals best fitted to survive, not on the basis of strength but on intelligence. "In such a society the things which today are supposed to be in the interests of the masses would be subordinated to things in the interests of the superior individuals." (p.214) There would be "an aristocracy of truly superior persons," rather than one based on "false" hereditary inequality.

The key to promoting a more beautiful civilization--the superior and ennobling life--is the conquest of comfort (which in 1975 would be described as human needs). The key to promoting comfort is to establish true organic homesteads organized to function biologically, socially, and economically. Such would enable a material well-being equal to that which we now enjoy, with less unpleasant effort and greater security. The homesteads could be a natural family or a group of unrelated individuals, perhaps large enough to allow members to enjoy sabbatical leaves of absence. The home would become an "economically creative institution" and Borsodi argues at length for the superiority of home canning, baking, and preserving and against the "delusion" that factory products are desirable or economical. "Mass production of foodstuffs is essentially an outrage upon the human stomach." (p.104) Goods must be designed for use, rather than sale; to produce comfort (both mental and material) rather than wealth.

In contrast to the classic factors involved in producing wealth--land, labor, capital, and management, Borsodi employs separate chapters to describe the four factors in the production of comfort: homestead, time, machines, and wisdom. Objections are dealt with in detail, and a model constitution for a homestead is provided (pp. 330-332). Ultimately, the net gain of income would enable more books, art, travel, music--the luxuries of a cultured life. Health would be widespread, for the real cure for our ills is not in correct medication (in 1975, "quality health care"), but in correct living. Education would be drastically revised, in that schooling, according to Borsodi, is "the principal agency in keeping us ignorant."

Politically, the legislative process invariably emasculates the ideas of quality-minded men; therefore, the goal of a good society is control of an irreducible minimum of government by the quality-minded. The need for hospitals and jails would be reduced because there would no longer be the needless manufacture of idiots and criminals. Rather, all men, in due degrees, would be artists, producing beautiful things.

Many existing barriers to comfort are acknowledged, and Borsodi outlines policies which might enable us to surmount them. The barriers are economic, physiological, social, biological, religious, political, moral, psychological, educational, and individual.

In conclusion, there is little hope for improvement, for most men are seen as incurably conventional, whereas the quest for comfort requires "sensitive non-conformists" unafraid to adapt new values.
* This book may be difficult to acquire, but it surely offers a wealth of integrated insights for struggling moderns.

312. "The Plowboy Interview: Dr. Ralph Borsodi," **The Mother Earth News,**
    No. 26, March, 1974, pp. 6-13.   (C-3)

A fascinating interview with Borsodi in his Exeter, N.H. home. Borsodi still argues that distribution costs are a major neglected factor and that one-half to two-thirds "of all the things we need for a good living can be produced most economically on a small scale." (p.10)

As with other decentralists, Borsodi argues that we are living in the twilight of industrialism, and the natural materials crunch is only beginning. To remedy this situation, he would abolish special privileges for corporations, and introduce a rational system of land tenure and a rational system of money.

Living in the country, incidentally, is not seen as "the simple life." Rather, "It's much more complex than city life," because one has to master many different crafts and activities that people in the city know nothing about.

313. BORSODI, Ralph. **Seventeen Problems of Man and Society.** Anand (W.
    Rly.), INDIA: Charotar Book Stall, 1968. 595 pp.   (A-3)

This remarkably encyclopedic work had been scheduled for U.S. publication by Porter Sargent, but unfortunately was never published. The Indian edition is presently out-of-print, although a few copies may be available for $9.95 from the International Independence Institute, Box 183, Ashby, Mass. 01431.

It is described by the author as 17 separate but interrelated books, summarizing 12,000 pages of manuscript, notes and charts, and about 8,000 case studies of human action. Each of the book/chapters offers an extensive taxonomy of ideologies and philosophies from which Borsodi's views are drawn, and each is ended by an extensive bibliography, totalling, in all, about 1,200 items. Regrettably, there is no index and little in the way of overall summary.

The basic view is that "The failure of mankind to deal with both personal and social problems as they should be dealt with has its source in one great mistake: acceptance of solutions to the basic problems of man and society before all the basic problems have been adequately defined and therefore before it is possible to recognize the proper solutions of any of them." (p. 3) The most important problem in the world is that of the philosophy by which men live and by which the society is animated. i.e., the educational problem. Borsodi's book sets forth a problem-centered philosophy, in contrast to one that is "solution and subject-centered."

The focus on semantics also suggests a foundation for a genuine social science: "Until the social scientists face this problem and develop a taxonomy which is adequate to the needs of their disciplines, they will remain, I was going to say, **pseudosciences,** but I will avoid the use of that invidious term and content myself with **still-born sciences.**" (p.8, author's emphasis)

The problems are as follows:

I.   **Basic Intellectual Problems: An Introduction to Noetics**
1. Human Nature: Psyche or Soma?
2. The Universe: Chaos or Cosmos?
3. Histriography: Events and Experiences, Causes and Effects
4. Communication: Verification and Validation

II.   **Problems in Values: An Introduction to Axiology**
5. Telic Values: Convictions and Prejudices
6. Ethical Values: Good and Evil
7. Esthetic Values: Beauty and Ugliness
8. Economic Values: Wealth and Illth (advocates Adequacy Economic doctrines in contrast to affluence doctrines of capitalist and communist states)

III. **Problems of Man and Society: An Introduction to Praxiology**
9. The Psycho-Physiological Problem: Mental and Physical Health (advocates Naturalian methods and therapies)
10. The Occupational Problem: Labor and Leisure (advocates Hygienic ideologies)
11. The Possessional Problem: Trusterty and Property
12. The Organizational Problem: Enterprise and Adequacy (advocates Minimal Organization of human magnitude)
13. The Production Problem: Efficiency and Waste (advocates Qualitative Production)
14. The Distribution Problem: Acquirers, Claimants, and Apportioners (advocates a free society and a free market)
15. The Political Problem: Violence, Counterviolence, and Nonviolence (advocates Minarchy, or reducing the functions of government--but this is contrasted to Anarchy and Conservatism)
16. The Institutional Problem: Conservation and Reformation (advocates suasional methods in contrast to impositional methods)
17. The Educational Problem: Instruction and Cultivation (advocates education for excellence, rather than for competence and affluence, and Education instead of Adjustment)
*** Some publisher ought to make this extraordinary book available to Western audiences (adding an index and perhaps some summary charts). In the interim, it is important to know that this work exists. Any serious attempt to build a decentralist philosophy for the future would surely benefit from studying these pages.

314. BORSODI, Ralph, and Carter HENDERSON. **Blueprint for Monetary Survival.** 1976(?) Further information from International Independence Institute, West Road, Box 183, Ashby, Mass. 01431.   (ns)

Now "in its third draft and moving toward publication," the book "will focus on the continuing inflation and failure of the Keynesian economists to solve either the inflation or the developing recession/depression...the book will outline the entire program for policy change in banking which will be necessary for a return to any kind of economic order or stability...such changes will help to bring about a decentralized economy by providing the credit necessary for small scale enterprises and intermediate technologies (including alternative energy sources)." (From **I.I.I. Newsletter**, Jan./Feb. 1975.)

315. JENCKS, Charles, and Nathan SILVER. **Adhocism: The Case for Improvisation.** NY: Doubleday, 1972. 216 pp. $10.   (AB-4)

"Adhocism is the art of living and doing things ad hoc--tackling problems at once, using the materials at hand, rather than waiting for the perfect moment or proper approach...Adhocism has always been around but usually has been unappreciated and even scorned...Adhocism at all levels may be the solution for frustrated consumers and turned-off citizens." (book jacket)

The authors, both American architects living in England, employ 244 photos of kinky inventions which exemplify "mongrel creativity." Jencks (who wrote the first half of the book) suggests a variety of new techniques and strategies which could lead to "Consumer Democracy." To counter the present opposite movement toward extreme visual simplicity and extreme functional complexity, Jencks advocates "an Articulate Environment" which provides visual richness and diversity. He then goes on to redefine the practice of revolution beyond Vulgar Marxism to encourage the recognition and encouragement of ad hoc organization--non-violent, decentralized, and pluralist: "the desirable goal to be achieved is the federation of spontaneously forming **ad hoc** groups." (p.101)
*** Original thinking, but a bit less here than meets the eye.

316. FRIEDMAN, Yona, "Arguments for a Poor World," **Futures: The Journal of Forecasting and Planning,** 6:4, August 1974, pp. 334-339.   (A-4)

The hypothesis of a French architect "that the drift towards the poor world was triggered by the illusion of wealth and accelerated by the illusion of possibility of global communication." (p.339) The safest path for countries of the Third world would be not to oppose this process, for they would be better adapted to a poor world where there is less transportation, division of labor, and commerce. An attitude of "animal economy" would prevail, where there would be no excess accumulation or waste. Although large organizations will disintegrate, the poor world is not seen as a return to primitive life.

317. LOVE, Sam, "The Overconnected Society," **The Futurist,** 8:6, December 1974, pp. 293-295.   (C-4)

An environmentalist observes that "the historical momentum to create an ever larger and more intricate cobweb economy now is breaking down, due to serious disruptions in the energy and material flows on which the maintenance of order depends. Thus we now must look for an alternative to the overconnected society." (p.293)

Clues to a dynamic stability are provided by natural systems and their maintenance processes of decentralization, diversity, cyclical flow, and integration of components. Further comments are addressed to existing technologies such as self-sustaining houses that are necessary to construct "a small loop society."

318. LAKEY, George. **Strategy for a Living Revolution.** Published in Cooperation with the Institute for World Order. NY: Grossman, 1973. $7.95 hardcover trade edition. San Francisco: Freeman, 1973, 234 pp. $2.95 paperbound educational edition.   (BC-3)

A Quaker activist attacks the global war system, and advocates a five stage program for nonviolent transformation to an egalitarian world society. The new society would promote the full development of human beings, democratically controlled economic enterprise, simple technologies, the breakup of large cities to villages and towns, and a dissolution of the nation-state system to two levels of power: global and local. It would be a revolution on the side of life against death.

Most of the book is devoted to explaining and justifying the means to this end, with chapters devoted to each of the five stages: cultural strength through Groups for Living Revolution, propaganda of the deed, political and economic noncooperation, and intervention and parallel institutions.
*** Notable for placing decentralist concerns in a world order perspective; otherwise, an undistinguished tract.

319. BOOKCHIN, Murray (Lewis HERBER). **Post-Scarcity Anarchism.** Berkeley, Calif.: The Ramparts Press, 1971. 287 pp. $6.95; $2.95, paper.
(AB-3)
A collection of fresh and angry essays written in the 1965-1968 period, most of them published in **Anarchos** magazine, e.g. Ecology and Revolutionary Thought, Towards a Liberatory Technology, The Forms of Freedom, and Listen, Marxist!

Bookchin is critical of both capitalism and Marxism, and argues that hierarchical society has reached the culmination of its development. We are now on the threshold of a post-scarcity society, but the existing society has yet to realize the post-scarcity potential of its technology. Scarcity does not refer simply to goods: "to mean anything in human terms (it) must encompass social relations and cultural apparatus that foster insecurity in the psyche." (p. 11)

320. RASKIN, Marcus G. **Being and Doing.** NY: Random House, 1971. 449 pp.
(A-4)
A rambling polemic by a Fellow at the Institute for Policy Studies. "The collapse of the body politic forces us to think theoretically and act practically on the openings that are thus created. We are obliged to ask what is the nature of the body politic that is collapsing and to inquire into the type of body politic that it can become, within the limits of human nature and the present development of our politics and technology." Such an investigation is called a "philosophy of reconstruction."

Once the ideological and linguistic mask is lifted, the pyramidal shape of the American social, political, and economic structure can be seen. This situation is made bearable by liberal authoritarian institutions and painful by totalitarian institutions. There are four overlapping colonies:
- The Violence Colony: the most crucial and dangerous; "the central fact of human relations in American society"
- The Plantation Colony, where people work at meaningless and unreal jobs
- The Channeling Colony, which establishes standards and orders of privilege and merit for the young through schools
- The Dream Colony, particularly television, which "provides a surrogate of action and passion for the colonized"

Chapters are devoted to each of these Colonies, and to three possible reactions: immobilism, reform, and revolution.

Raskin advocates a non-hierarchic associative community that finds being through what we do. Decolonization would bring a new social contract, and "through the practice of existential pragmatism the integration of human reason and passion in the project of reconstruction." (Concluding words, p. 428.)

321. GOODMAN, Paul. **New Reformation: Notes of a Neolithic Conservative.** NY: Random House, 1970. 208 pp. $5.95.   (A-3)

A widely-known social critic, the late Paul Goodman senses in his last book that we are on the eve of a new reformation and that no institution will go unaffected. The first four chapters (pp. 3-63) examines the state of the sciences and professions. The deepest flaw of the affluent societies is "their nauseating phoniness, triviality, and wastefulness, the cultural and moral scandal that Luther found when he went to Rome in 1510." Goodman advocates prudence, ecology, and decentralization: "liberation from the Whore of Babylon and return to the pure faith." (p. 21)

322. MANICAS, Peter T. The Death of the State. NY: Putnam, 1974. 268 pp. $7.95.   (A-3)

A survey of political philosophy, with extensive footnoting. Chapters devoted to The State, Power and Authority, The Legitimate State, The Liberal State, The Democratic State, and The Liberal Moral Ideal.

The final chapter concerns The Democratic Community, where none have power over others, and all share in consciously controlling the conditions of their everyday lives. Such a community restates an old idea, presupposing radical decentralization and conditions permitting self-management--but this does not necessarily require a step backward in time.

Today's institutions are no doubt complex, but "most of the complexity is itself generated by centralization, bureaucracy and the inherent need of such structures to mystify, partialize and manipulate." (p. 251)

There are limits to the economies of scale, and modern industrial societies have long since passed these limits. Indeed, there are now many ecological, social, and aesthetic diseconomies.

323. JACOBY, Henry. The Bureaucratization of the World. Trans. by Eveline L. Kanes. Berkeley: University of California Press, 1973. 256 pp. $12.95. (First published in Berlin in 1969.)   (A-4)

A scholarly history exploring the Janus face of bureaucracy (the efficiency we need vs. the stultification it produces), utilizing perspectives from political science, economics, and sociology. "The problem that burdens everyone, even those who are unaware, is how to break the vicious circle in which the government's increasing tendency to regulate everything reduces the individual's ability to determine his own life." (p. 4)

It is argued that there could well be modes of decentralization that are contrary to the conventional wisdom of efficiency, and that democratic principles might be able to survive our "administered world."

324. PENTY, Arthur J. Old Worlds for New: A Study of the Post-Industrial State. London: G. Allen and Unwin, 1917. 186 pp.   (AB-3)

The war is seen as marking the close of an era in our civilization and "the inevitable catastrophic ending of a society which has chosen to deny the law of its own being." (p. 8) Viewing a finite world, Penty observes that "We are rapidly approaching a time when there will be no new markets left to exploit. What is going to happen when that limit is reached?" (p. 56)

The answer is prescribed in chapters such as The Evil of Large Organizations, The Strike for Quality, The Tyranny of the Middleman, The Decentralization of Industry, The Redistribution of Population, and The Destructive Consumption of Surplus Wealth.

The chapter on The Leisure and the Work State offers a clear contrast between collectivistic socialism and guild socialism. The Leisure State is "an utterly impossible dream so far as the majority are concerned" and it complements the Servile State and favors collectivism. The pursuit of pleasure leads to boredom and selfishness, and the Leisure State will eventually "fall to pieces from lack of any stability of character." In con-

trast, the Work State is associated with humanization of labor.
*** A vision that could still illuminate present concerns. The "Post-Industrial State" in the sub-title is not repeated in the text, but see the following item.

325. PENTY, Arthur J. **Post-Industrialism.** With a Preface by G.K. Chesterton. London: George Allen & Unwin, 1922. 157 pp.   (AB-4)

Post-Industrialism is defined as "the state of society that will follow the break-up of Industrialism, and might therefore be used to cover the speculations of all who recognize Industrialism is doomed." (p. 14) Penty acknowledges that he owes the term to Dr. A.K. Coomaraswamy, but does not provide further references as to where and when the term was first used.
Penty views democracy to be incompatible with industrialism, and the problem of machinery as central to the social problem. He criticizes the Socialist movement, where nationalization has become an end in itself, as well as the unfilled prophecies of Marx and Spencer about the "glorious future that would follow the unrestricted use of machinery." (p. 49)
The final chapter, "The Return to the Past," argues that when men begin to look back, "The activities of our agricultural organization societies and movements to restore the crafts and arts will appear full of significance as intelligent anticipations of the future." (p. 144)
*** Prophetic or primitive?

326. COOMARASWAMY, Ananda Kentish. **The Bugbear of Literacy.** London: Dennis Dobson, 1949. 130 pp.   (AB-4)

The author is an authority on oriental art, associated with the Boston Museum of Fine Arts from 1917-1947. He was trained as a geologist in England, where he was influenced by Ruskin and Morris, and became a champion of native cultures and handicrafts in light of their being corrupted by the invasion of Occidental industrialism.
The quantitative and material values of modern civilization are seen as suppressing the instinct of workmanship and reducing the cultures of the world to their lowest common denominator. "The bases of modern civilization are to such a degree rotten to the core that it has been forgotten even by the learned that man ever attempted to live otherwise than by bread alone." (p. 7)
Cultural bias is exposed among those who call themselves progressive and those who are called backward. Agriculture and handicraft are seen as essential foundations of any civilization; instead, we are creating "a brave new world of uniformly literate mechanics." (p. 37)
*** Eloquent and learned essays which fit in nicely with critiques by Ralph Borsodi and Ivan Illich. Also notable is the attack on Oliver Reiser's **Scientific Humanism** (nos. 272-273).

327. DOCTOR, Adi H. **Sarvodaya: A Political and Economic Study.** Bombay, India: Asia Publishing House, 1967. 229 pp.   (A-3)

A very readable scholarly survey of "Sarvodaya," the extension and application of the doctrine of Mahatma Gandhi which was formed by Gandhi's translation of Ruskin's **Unto This Last.**
Sarvodaya criticizes the present state as "the modern Frankenstein" and promulgates an alternative that stresses the completely non-violent state populated by free and equal individuals, with the village as the natural unit of collective life. It seeks the uplift or happiness of each and all, assuming that man is good at the core. Welfare is not just material, but mainly spiritual. There would be a decentralized economy in harmony with nature, stressing limited wants under the precept of "Simple living, high thinking." The Law of Return would be obeyed, returning to the soil in or-

ganic form that which is taken from it. There would be full employment; instead of man being subservient to the machine, machines would serve the interests of all. There is no objection to electricity or atomic energy if the benefits accrue evenly to all. Production of goods would be cooperative, although every man would do some farming. Barter or some sort of labor currency would serve as a substitute for the present monetary system.

The author provides a critique of the "misconceived assumptions" on which the philosophy is based, and the ideal of political and economic order. It is concluded that Sarvodaya is an unworkable utopia, but still one from which man may learn something.

*** Despite the author's lack of sympathy, the survey tries to be fair, and provides a useful bibliography (pp. 215-226) for those who wish to further explore Sarvodaya. There is much to consider, with a listing of about 160 books by or about Gandhi, about 40 books by or about Vinoba (Gandhi's disciple), and about 160 additional books on Sarvodaya and related topics.

328. HUANG, Kai-Loo, "Taoism, Economics and Ecology," **Fields Within Fields,** No. 14, Winter 1975, pp. 25-30.   (A-4)

A modern interpretation of the 2500 year old "utopia of Taoism," with its stress on the logic of relativeness, interdependence, and synthesis.

"In conclusion, I interpret **Tao Te Ching** as a reflection of Lao-Tse's methodology in dialectic, an antidote to the philosophy of Overgrowth, Rush, Contention and Exploitation of nature, men or self. The Small Country of Chapter 80 is neither a utopia for the world of nations to follow, nor a picture of the paradise for retirement. It is a kind of target for mental exercise with a view to teaching the philosophy of moderation and reservation, and in this particular case of slowing down in order to preserve one's root of life." (p. 30)

329. RUNKLE, Gerald. **Anarchism Old and New.** NY: Delacorte, 1972. 330 pp. $7.95.   (AB-4)

A philosophy professor at Southern Illinois University describes the old anarchism in 19th Century Europe and the U.S., and the new anarchists: the student left, the radical right, and existentialists. Classical anarchists are only a small remnant today. The similarities among the several varieties are that all stress freedom of the individual and elimination of existing governments. They disagree on the resulting form of society, the nature of human nature, the principles of morality and religion, and the strategy and tactics of action. The differences in the desired social order range from Individualistic Anarchy to Mutualism to Collectivistic Anarchy.

The concluding chapter, "Confessions of a Liberal," acknowledges the incompetence of government to deal with the problems of our time. "Where does the liberal stand? The liberal traditionally seeks the well-being of society. He tries to identify problems and devise rational solutions...he welcomes change as necessary for progress...he values orderly transition... The liberal, with his belief in good government, is the opposite of the anarchist." (p. 311) Liberals are urged to answer critics, cease being apologetic, and take credit for past achievements. "Liberalism is self-corrective and always looks to the future." (p. 315)

*** A useful but somewhat dated review of anarchism, with a hopelessly mushy ending. The problem with liberalism is that it **thinks** it is self-corrective, but it is not, and "looking to the future" is obviously not confined to any particular group.

Chapter 8

Human Needs

What is the nature of a good society that best serves the interests of individuals, rather than institutions? This perspective is suggested by a "eupsychic" society (347), or one that is humanized (348), sane (336), person-centered (340), non-violent (342), fraternal (344), and synergic (345).

This chapter focuses on the individual and on human relationships. Most of the items are authored by psychologists and psychiatrists, and the general view is that present societal directions are humanly disastrous. The alternatives proposed seem very desirable, but they are often vaguely general and politically blind. A frequent theme is that of self-actualization or self-fulfillment for all, and a frequent unstated assumption is that of the inherent goodness of man.

Three general items introduce this chapter in broad terms. Sir Julian Huxley (330) places the human crisis in an evolutionary perspective and makes a plausible argument for "a fulfillment society." Allsopp (331) has a similar focus on the need for quality. Martin (332) suggests the frustration that comes from aiming at "a humanly transcendent castle" but this argument is unlikely to dissuade those who seek a more humanized society.

Such a quest is not a new one, as indicated by the four subsequent items, all published before 1960. Sorokin's blueprint for **The Reconstruction of Humanity** (333) is particularly comprehensive and authoritative, and is worthy of reconsideration. Carrel (334), writing in 1935, offers an equally ambitious goal for remaking man. Fromm's "sane society" (336) is well-known, although his "revolution of hope" is somewhat more specific as to how a humanized society might be promoted (337). Insofar as a comprehensive set of programs, the report of the Joint Commission on Mental Health of Children (338) offers a portrait of the ultimate welfare state. Dator (339), a political scientist, proposes a "transformational society" with a focus on the individual, and counters possible objections to such a society. Harman (340) offers extensive justification for choosing a "person-centered society."

All of the subsequent items (341-365) are essentially apolitical, stating desirable ends with little or no sense of how they might be realized. Nevertheless, especially considered together, there is the stuff of worthy ideals: the stoa society (341), a non-violent society (342), a cooperative humane society (343), a fraternal society (344), a synergic society (345-346), Maslow's "Eupsychia" (347), humanistic society (348), and the humanistic century called for in Humanist Manifesto II (349).

Murchland (352) offers a useful survey of alienation, while Marcuse (353) takes a Marxist stance in attacking "one-dimensional society." Fill (354) views a similar condition but does not prescribe a socialist solution. Thayer (356) attacks the theories of politics and economics in order to promote his view of structured non-hierarchical social interaction.

Three books focus on the individual, but are distinctively different from other items in this chapter. Skinner's essay, **Beyond Freedom and Dignity** (360), is highly controversial but offers little substance. Delgado's view of "a psychocivilized society" is not well-developed, and Graham's plea for intelligent selection (362) appears to be equally divorced from the sociopolitical realities of the world.

The final three items, however, are very close to empirical realities. May (363) provides an important essay on powerlessness and proposes a new ethic of intention instead of the one-dimensional ethics of growth. Marris (364) offers sympathetic insights on bereavement and the management of change, while Cantril (365) suggests eleven basic uniformities of human needs which, if satisfied, could lead to an effective society.

330. HUXLEY, Sir Julian. **The Human Crisis.** Seattle: University of Washington Press, 1963. 88 pp.   (AB-2)

The John Danz Lectures, delivered by a distinguished biologist and addressed to "The Humanist Revolution" and "The World Population Problem."

In the first lecture, Huxley explains the title as "the revolution in thought and attitude now being brought about as a result of what we may call the knowledge explosion of the last hundred years. It is both a revolution and a revelation, for it is revealing a wholly new vision of man and the universe and man's place and role in the universe, in other words a new vision of human destiny." (p.3)

"...I feel quite sure that some form of what I call evolutionary humanism will become the new dominent type of idea system for the next few centuries at least." (p.21) Some of the implications include a new ethics of international aid, international world organization ("self-sufficient nationalism is no longer ethical"), and thinking in terms of diverse excellences instead of equal conformity. Instead of overconsumption and exaggerated competition for status, "our aim should be to transcend both by creating a fulfillment society." (p.28)

Embellishing Margaret Mead's suggestion for "Chairs of the Future," Huxley proposes " 'Professorships of Possibility,' on a par with law or medicine or natural science. We certainly need a new branch of study concerned with man's potentialities and their realization." (p.38)

The second lecture on the population problem argues that our aim must be for quality instead of quantity: "quality of human beings and the lives they lead. Once we have grasped this, things begin to fall into place." (p.81) And vice versa, of course.

331. ALLSOPP, Bruce. **Civilization, the Next Stage: The Importance of Individuals in the Modern World.** Newcastle upon Tyne: Oriel Press, 1969. 160 pp.   (A-4)

Concerning the "urgent predicament of mankind which is manifest in the current loss of morale, confidence, sense of direction and faith in the value of life or indeed in any values." (p. vii) Comments on people at various stages of life such as birth, education, marriage, and adult life, concluding that we need to see life whole again and to cultivate quality rather than mediocrity in people, aiming for an infinite variety of talents at many levels.
*** A thoughtful general discussion, although "the next stage" of the title is never explained.

332. MARTIN, Malachi. **The New Castle: Reaching for the Ultimate.** NY: Dutton, 1974. 209 pp. $7.95; $3.95, paper.   (A-3)

A theologian and Contributing Editor to **National Review** focuses on the castle as an old image and expression, a vision of the ideal state in which the material conditions of human living are invested by spirit and thus perfected humanly.

Chapters explore the contemporary sense of spirit in Mecca, Jerusalem, Constantinople, Rome, Pekin, Angkor Wat, and two small towns in Indiana:

"having revisited the scenes of former visions in order to catch their essences as partial analogies, we can endeavor now to trace the workings of the new vision in our modern world..." (p.187)

In all of the present dislocation there are signs of human implosion-- "a progressive clearing of ground as if for something new to be built." (p.203) "Even with our ignorance of the new castle in its full reality, we are led to the conclusion that the common thrust is toward a new liberty for the self, a liberty it has not yet known." (p.207)

It is concluded that we cannot perceive our desires but we can respond to spirit. And there is a message for would-be social engineers: "If we, men and women, were to aim at fashioning a humanly transcendent castle, it is guaranteed by that very fact not to be transcendent. And the peculiar destiny of humankind is that only by the greater than human can it be human successfully." (p.209)

333. SOROKIN, Pitirim A. **The Reconstruction of Humanity.** Boston: Beacon Press, 1948. 247 pp.   (AB-2)

Harvard's cosmic sociologist provides a passionate critique of ignorant plans for salvation along with a constructive blueprint. Part I, Quack Cures for War and Impotent Plans for Peace, castigates political cures (democracy, the U.N., world government), economic cures (capitalism, communism, fascism, and socialism), and scientific, educational, and religious cures. Democratic nations are seen as having been no less belligerent than autocratic ones; all of them neglect the decisive factor of altruism and love.

Contemporary Western culture is seen as generating egoistic forces, degrading values to the level of sensory material things. There is a misuse of science and technology, as well as religion and philosophy. Egoistic competition must be reduced, and replacing this major premise of sensate culture by the idealistic premise is "the most fundamental step toward the establishment of a creative, harmonious human order." (p.108) Changes are advocated in school, family, religious institutions, political institutions, and economic institutions. "Properly transformed, they can release forces of altruism, good will, and creative energy hitherto little exploited." (p.180)

"This ennoblement of man's conception of himself and of his cultural and social institutions inspires an attitude of reverence, respect, admiration, and love toward his fellow men, toward culture and society, toward the Infinite Manifold, and even toward the whole universe as a part of the Infinite Manifold." (p.168)

But Sorokin also keeps a foot on the ground of reality: given "the selfishness and mental aberration of our decadent society, the prospects are somewhat dubious." (p.237)

334. CARREL, Alexis. **Man the Unknown.** NY: Harper & Bros., 1935. 346 pp.   (A-3)

Argues for mental, physical, and social changes as part of "the overthrow of industrial civilization and the advent of another conception of human progress." Chapters are devoted to The Need for a Better Knowledge of Man, The Science of Man, Body and Physiological Activities, Mental Activities, Inward Time, Adaptive Functions, and The Individual.

The final chapter, The Remaking of Man, asserts that man must remake himself if there is to be any further progress. There must be a transformation of habits of thought and a return to men of the Renaissance. The separation of the qualitative from the quantitative has "led science to triumph and man to degradation."

"The making of man requires the development of institutions wherein body and mind can be formed according to natural laws." (p.286) The free practice of eugenics is advocated to lead to the development of stronger individuals, and distinctions are made between artificial health and natural health.

"Modern society should be given an intellectual focus, an immortal brain, capable of conceiving and planning its future, and of promoting and pushing forward fundamental researches..." (p.291) To this end, a thinking center is advocated, a high council where members would be free from research and teaching duties.

*** The proposed thinking center is similar to the World Brain advocated by Wells (no. 909) and the World Institute initiated by Stulman (no. 912).

335. GAUSS, Christian. **A Primer for Tomorrow: Being an Introduction to Contemporary Civilization.** NY: Charles Scribner's Sons, 1934. (A-4)

"...our faith in inevitable progress and in the future, is also weakening and dying. It is this that gives our time, in a very real sense, the aspects of a new cultural epoch. Humanity is confronted again with the necessity of making a choice." (p.282)

Nationalism, capitalism, and science are all seen as having tended to secularize life. "Our age remained unstable and restless because its center of gravity was forever ahead and outside of it and it could only maintain itself upright by continually increasing its speed." (p.283)

The first step toward a new and more satisfying culture is to relinquish our "mad race" for wealth and subject ourselves to a national discipline. Social justice--a willingness to share--must be the first step. The only new world to conquer is the inner world of man's spirit. The tragedy of our time is not that bolshevism has spread but that there is nothing of significance to oppose it.

336. FROMM, Erich. **The Sane Society.** NY: Holt, Rinehart, & Winston, 1955. 370 pp.   (AB-4)

A continuation of **Escape From Freedom** that tries to develop the basic concepts of "Humanistic psychoanalysis." Views man today as confronted with a choice between robotism and Humanistic Communitarian Socialism (in contrast to Marxist Socialism).

A sane society is one in which no man is a means toward another's ends, where acting according to one's conscience is a fundamental quality, where one is the master of his own life, where man is allowed to give expression to his inner needs. To attain it, "No change must be brought about by force, it must be a simultaneous one in the economic, political and cultural spheres." (p.361)

337. FROMM, Erich. **The Revolution of Hope: Toward a Humanized Technology.** World Perspectives, Vol. 38. NY: Harper & Row, 1968.(AB-3)

Views America in 1968 at a "crossroads": one road leading to "a completely mechanized society with man as a helpless cog in the machine," the other road leading to "a renaissance of humanism and hope." The book is based on the conviction "that we can find the necessary new solutions with the help of reason and passionate love for life."

To humanize technological society, Fromm advocates humanistic planning, activation and liberation of energies, humanistic management, humanized consumption, and psychospiritual renewal with elaboration under each of these headings.

These values are seen as finding expression only in a non-bureaucratic movement. A proposed first step is the formation of a national council which could be called the "Voice of American Conscience"--a group of 50 or so outstanding Americans who would deliberate and issue weighty statements. The Council would be tied in with Clubs of 100-300 members and smaller

Groups of 25 members. The Clubs would be autonomous, non-political, cultural centers engaged in clarifying and seriously discussing political issues. This scheme is elaborated in some detail, pp. 151-162.

338. Joint Commission on Mental Health of Children. **Crisis in Child Mental Health: Challenge for the 1970's.** Report of the Commission. NY: Harper & Row, 1970. 578 pp. $10.00   (A-3)

This is perhaps the ultimate welfare state--a comprehensive vision of a system of human services that we ought to have. It results from a 3-year study joining 13 professional associations, 500 authorities, National Institute of Mental Health funding, and ending in 136 pages of recommendations presented in the first chapter. "If vast expenditures, both human and monetary, are not made, it will in the long run be more costly in terms of mental illness, human malfunctioning, and therefore underproductivity. In this aspect of our economy, we are far behind most countries which give highest priority to the proper sheparding of their most important resource, their children." (p.xix)

The hundreds of recommendations are divided into four parts. The first part advocates a Child Advocacy System, with an Advisory Council on Children (similar to the Council of Economic Advisors) on the national level, State Child Development Agencies, and Child Development Authorities and Child Development Councils at the local levels, guaranteeing service for children and their families. The second part "strongly urges the creation of a network of comprehensive, systematic services, programs, and policies which will provide every American the opportunity to develop to his maximum potential." (p.26) This includes physical and mental health services, employment and environmental programs, social services, and education. Part three makes recommendations on research programs, and part four concerns manpower and training. In sum, "...the needs of children and youth have such low priority currently as to endanger the future quality of American life." (p.23)

*** A package of reforms so extensive and unwieldy as to defy communication to fellow professionals, let alone the general public. Unintentionally, it offers a vision of the ideal service society which, in the near future at least, is very improbable.

339. DATOR, Jim, "Neither There Nor Then: A Eutopian Alternative to the Development Model of Future Society," in **Human Futures: Needs, Societies, Technologies.** Rome World Special Conference on Futures Research 1973. Guildford, Surrey, U.K.: IPC Science and Technology Press, 1974, pp. 87-140.   (AB-2)

A provocative contribution by a futurist/political scientist at the University of Hawaii. The essay begins with a review of the American model of development as posited by Rostow, Heilbroner, and others, and the various critiques of the model by ecologists, world order supporters, decentralists, etc. including the views of Falk, Roszak, Goulet, and Lukacs.

Finding all of these positions lacking, Dator proposes his own view of the desirable future: the transformational society. The image is depicted as a series of overlapping 'S' curves of development, a set of desirable circumstances enabling "the creation of a world which maximizes our ability to live even more humanly in a situation of rapid change." (p.118)

In such a society, every person is wholly free in every way from unwanted control. The dominant unit of this future society is the individual person. The primary function of government is to provide an environment in which each individual may become self-fulfilled and self-reliant. However, a minimal set of social and environmental responsibilities is suggested.

The very rough outlines of a transformational society is one of affluence, high technology, and benign human relations. Less than 5% of the labor force would be involved in the production of goods and services. Synthesized foods would meet all nutritional and aesthetic requirements. There would be cybernetic political systems, and a reversal of the "technological impera- tive" through something like "technology assessment."

Several objections to such a society (contrary to history, contrary to human nature, too atomistic, too violent and disorderly, insufficient abun- dance) are listed, and rejoinders are made.

General actions that could hasten the Transformational Society include protecting individualizing technologies such as automobiles and bicycles and resisting deindividualizing technologies such as mass transit, en- couraging trends leading toward global consciousness coupled with local diversity and individualism, drastically reducing military expenditures, and diverting funds to "person-centered fully cybernated technological and social systems." (p. 132)

"If I have not been very specific in terms of structures, institutions, and present future-oriented policies, it was because I wanted to be as careful as I could in stating my values and goals, and because I do not want to prefigure the future with rapidly-obsolescing structures so much as infuse it with strategies and goals." (p.135)

*** A bit fuzzy, wordy, and optimistic; but also original, provocative, and well-read. This essay offers an exemplary structure: a critical re- view of the literature, a proposal that differs from existing proposals, a defense of the proposal objections, and suggestions as to how the proposal might be effected.

340. HARMAN, Willis W., "The Nature of Our Changing Society: Implica- tions for Schools," House Committee on Education and Labor, **Alternative Futures in American Education.** Appendix 3 to Hear- ings on H.R. 3606. Washington: U.S. Government Printing Office, January, 1972. pp. 6-53. (Prepared for ERIC Clearinghouse on Educational Administration, October 1969)   (A-3)

Discusses long-term societal trends, beliefs and values in transition, manifest revolutionary forces, a possible underlying conceptual revolution leading to the beginnings of a new science (see item no. 135), meta-issues of the future relevant to education policy (crises in human image, authority, economic values and pluralism), and two contrasting overall forecasts be- tween a second-phase industrial society and a person-centered society.

The second-phase industrial society (referred to in this guide as The Technological, Affluent, Service Society) is essentially an extension of present trends. Cybernation will have taken over many tasks, and there will be a bureaucratic and knowledge-based meritocratic elite. The gap between rich and poor nations will grow larger, and the arms race will continue to escalate.

The "person-centered society" marks a significant discontinuity with past trends. It would be a humanized technological society, where each individual would have sufficient resources to live in dignity, and to have a full life, including useful and rewarding work. Education would be central, and a diversity of pathways would be available. "The society will be a planned society, but planned in such a way as to deepen, not diminish, the freedom of the individual." (p.18) Priorities for technological development will be influenced by human and global needs.

"Education will center on developing self-learning habits and skills, problem-solving and decisionmaking abilities, individuality, sound valuing capabilities, capability of continuous self-renewal, and self-understanding. Education will be much more equated with life, and with the distinction between formal and informal education having become blurred, will be much more a lifetime activity." (p.19)

It is concluded that our changing society can be seen as one in the process of "choice among alternative futures, choice among alternative belief-and-

value systems, choice between ennobling versus debasing images of man,
choice of how some sense of coherent authority will be restored." (p. 49)
*** It is hardly fair to say that we **are** in such a process of choice, relative
  to what such a process could be. We certainly **ought** to be in a process of
  choice, and Harman's work is a useful starting point.

341. FOWLES, John. **The Aristos: A Self-Portrait in Ideas.** Boston: Little,
     Brown, 1964. 246 pp.   (AB-3)

A fascinating volume of wise and lucid epigrams by a well-known novelist, with chapters on The Universal Situation, Human Dissatisfaction With
the Situation, Willing and Enacting, Relativity of Recompense, The Polar
Nature of Reality, Other Philosophies (Christianity, Socialism, Fascism,
Existentialism, Lamaism, and Humanism), The Importance of Art, The Obsession with Money, and A New Education.
"The agora society must give way to the stoa society." (p. 178) The agora
society (from the Greek word for "market place") is one that is obsessed
with the getting and spending of money. The stoa society, associated with
the idea of learning and open philosophical discussion, is one that is dedicated
to healthier ends: "that is, to countering the evil effects of hazard on each
human destiny by planned social benefits, and to vastly increasing the scale,
and broadening the aims, of education." (p. 239)
The stoa society will have endless opportunities to acquire knowledge,
and all of humanity will be the leisured class. "The chief function of the
first automatized societies will be the education, improvement and enlei-
surement of the backward societies of the world. There cannot be any true
leisure until all the world possesses it equally...This is the great change
that must take place in human history." (p. 181)
"The Aristos" of the title is the new ideal man: "the best man for the
situation."
*** With the image of affluence out of fashion, the stoa society would seem
  truly utopian. The rest of the book, however, has fresh insights that
  are still relevant to the human situation.

342. KIRPAL, Prem, "Concept of a Non-Violent Social Order and Role of
     Education," **New Frontiers in Education,** IV:2, April-June 1974,
     pp. 10-16.   (AB-3)

The Director of the Indian Council of Peace Research asserts that the
concept rests on three facts and assumptions: 1) non-violence is preferable
to violence; 2) so far in history there has been no strictly non-violent social
order; and 3) a belief that such a social order is possible because of the
evolutionary principle both in society and the nature of man.
Nine conditions for realization are suggested: a social order based on
consent and participation, the recognition and acceptance of divergent forces,
maximum individual freedom, a concept and vision of Beauty, justice, a
classless decentralized society, widely-fostered cultural life, a sense of
community and belonging, and a non-violent makeup of the individual.
Current thinking about the nature of man is seen as limited and one-
sided as a result of domination by Western knowledge. A more comprehensive
and viable theory of the nature of man is needed, based on man's capacity
to live and express himself on several planes of consciousness: physical,
ethical, moral, and spiritual. Education of man must therefore be redesigned
to bring into play the potentialities of man's nature. "The choice is between
mechanistic and humanistic goals and civilizations." (p. 16)

343. SARNOFF, Irving. **Society Without Tears.** NY: The Citadel Press,
     1966. 318 pp.   (AB-3)

An anthropologist describes "our pain, despair, and inner emptiness" and how these symptoms emerge from our basic assumptions and institutions.

Chapter 9, Musings on Utopia, thoughtfully describes the desirable humane society as having a harmony between its dominant values and its major institutions. Such a society would be committed to the values of realization, while attempting to minimize the values of aggrandizement. Precedence would be given to humanitarian, equalitarian, esthetic and intellectual values. "The economy of a humane society would be entirely cooperative and devoid of any motive to profit from, exploit, degrade, manipulate, or humiliate others." (p. 222) Such a society would reject the concept of private property and would have non-hierarchical organization. Justice would be insured by devotion to humanitarian values, and crime would therefore be rare. Government would be democratic and education would be in the values of self-realization.

343a. RYAN, John Julian. **The Humanization of Man.** NY: Newman Press, 1972. 246 pp. $4.50, paper.   (A-4)

In a truly humane society, work would be a proper exercise of skill, men would work as the various kinds of artists they were meant to be, and people would be skillful in noneconomic activities as well. Ryan advocates "A Genuine World" by promoting the artistic method and the pleasures of enthusiastic creativity.

Two special offices are proposed for safeguarding citizens: that of the ombudsmen and that of the Chief Citizen of the Nation. The latter would have two functions: to represent the nation at all civic and international affairs that are purely symbolic; and to issue a non-partisan report, at least once a year, on the state of the nation. The Chief Citizen might be chosen, for example, from one of the members of the Supreme Court.

344. HAUSER, Richard and Hephzibah. **The Fraternal Society.** NY: Random House, 1963. 221 pp.   (B-4)

Signs of decay indicate the decline of the Paternal Society which has dominated human history from the beginning. It is hoped that this society will be replaced by the fraternal society where "authority and power will be delegated, not by the biggest father...but by democratic consent of the group."

Paternal society is described in terms of religious, family, politico-economic and legal structures. In contrast, the basic principles of fraternalism is that no man may live at the cost of another, and all must be allowed to develop their full potentialities. There is no need for brutality and no excuse for it. People should be treated as whole beings--a practice termed as "Wholism."

Considerable attention is given by the authors to facilitating the transition by means of the Socratic method, non-violent action research for peace, and psycho-synthesis.

345. CRAIG, James H. and Marge. **Synergic Power: Beyond Domination and Permissiveness.** Berkeley, Calif.: ProActive Press, 1974. 132 pp. $5.95; $2.50, paper.   (AB-3)

"A synergic relationship calls for openness, trust, and a commitment to work together to promote the shared and individual interests of all people in that relationship." (p. 70)

The authors synthesize a great deal of behavioral science and humanistic psychology in particular, in an uneven but intriguing attempt to push at theoretical frontiers, while writing in a popular "New Age" style. The nature of humankind and society are described as they are and as they could be. The second part of the book, Toward a Synergic Society, describes the building of synergic relationships, synergic enlightenment, and synergic conflict resolution. Synergic power "facilitates the establishment of conditions presently considered 'unnatural'--conditions under which cooperation and participation can flourish." (p. 111)

The five essential conditions for cooperative problem solving are open and honest communication, a clear picture of the problems, emphasis on human concerns, informed grass-root participation, and open-ended agreements.

*** Sounds great in theory, but, unfortunately, there is little hard evidence of successful practice.

345a. COULTER, Art. **Synergetics: An Adventure in Human Development.** Englewood Cliffs, N.J.: Prentice-Hall, April 1976. $9.95.   (ns)

346. MASLOW, Abraham H. and John J. HONIGMANN, "Synergy: Some Notes of Ruth Benedict," **American Anthropologist,** 72:2, April 1970, pp. 320-333.   (A-3)

Excerpts from lectures delivered in 1941 concerning traits of social orders characterized by high or low synergy.

347. MASLOW, Abraham, "Eupsychia: The Good Society," **Journal of Humanistic Psychology,** 1:2, Fall 1961, pp. 1-11.   (AB-3)

Based on a 1960 interview with Trevor Thomas over radio station KPFA-FM in Berkeley, Maslow sees it as "entirely valid to be imagining better societies in America at this point in our history...I think we are now ready to conceive of a 'Eupsychia'--a psychologically healthy culture--rather than just another materially-based utopia." (p. 1-2)

Either the most important or one of the most important characteristics of psychological health is seen as the ability to perceive clearly. Eupsychia would be spontaneous and democratic, with little crime and therefore not in need of armies. The main psychological block to a Eupsychia is fear (and its related traits of anxiety, inhibition, and lack of confidence).

348. GLASS, John F. and John R. STAUDE (eds.). **Humanistic Society: Today's Challenge to Sociology.** Pacific Palisades, Calif: Goodyear Publishing Co., 1972. 411 pp.   (AB-3)

A worthwhile collection of essays, generally written since 1960, arranged in four parts:
1. Humanistic Images of Man (including authors such as Carl Rogers, Erich Fromm, and Amitai Etzioni)
2. Social Science as a Humanistic Enterprise (including Willis Harman, Floyd Matson, and Kenneth Boulding)
3. Humanistic Perspectives in Sociology (including C. Wright Mills, Lewis Coser, and Peter Berger)
4. Toward Individual and Social Change (including Allen Wheelis, A.H. Maslow, Philip Slater, and Warren Bennis)

349. **Humanist Manifestos I and II.** Buffalo, NY: Prometheus Books, 1973. 31 pp. $1.50, paper.   (ABC-3)

The "Humanist Manifesto I" (pp. 7-11), reprinted from **The New Humanist,** 6:3 (1933) was committed to reason, science and democracy.

"Humanist Manifesto II" (pp. 13-24), reprinted from **The Humanist** 33:5 (1973), is more extensive and comprehensive, calling for bold and daring measures, extending the uses of the scientific method, the fulfillment of everybody's potential for human growth, situational ethics, the dignity of the individual, civil liberties, participatory democracy, transcending national sovereignty, the renunciation of poverty through economic assistance, universal education, separation of church and state, and the use of desirable technology for the good of humankind.

"The next century can be and should be the humanistic century." (p. 14)

The document was first signed by "114 individuals of prominence and distinction" and has since been signed "by countless numbers of human beings from all walks of life as a document for our time, committed to both human fulfillment and survival." (Paul Kurtz in Preface, p. 4)

*** Has yet to set the world on fire.

350. BENNIS, Warren G. and Philip E. SLATER. **The Temporary Society.** NY: Harper & Row, 1968. 147 pp.   (AB-4)

Six separate essays by one or both of the authors, aiming "to force into view certain changes affecting vital aspects of our key institutions: organizational life, family life, interpersonal relationships, and authority."

Democracy is seen as inevitable--the necessary social system of the electronic era. In the democratic family, "experiential chasms between age cohorts serve to invalidate parental authority." (p. 24) Other topics concern the new style organizations beyond bureaucracy, social consequences of temporary systems, and new patterns of leadership for adaptive organizations.

The final chapter prescribes the necessary education for the art and science of being more fully human: how to get love, to love and to lose love; how to enter groups and leave them; how to attain satisfying roles; and how to cope more readily with ambiguity. "For the most part we learn the significant things informally and badly, having to unlearn them later on in life when the consequences are grave and frightfully expensive, like a five-day-a-week analysis." (p. 127)

*** Democracy is desirable, but it is hardly inevitable in society or the family. For a skeptical response to the vision of new-style organization, see the **Public Administration Review** symposium (no. 32).

351. SLATER, Philip. **Earthwalk.** NY: Doubleday, 1974. $7.95. NY: Bantam Books, 1974. 249 pp. $1.95, paper.   (A-4)

Argues that we have developed along schizoid patterns, our minds separate from our bodies, our selves separate from community, and that we cannot construct a humane society out of the dominant trends of our present one. Many of the treasured virtues of the past such as courage and perseverence do not have survival values. They are disconnector virtues and they are ecologically unsound. In contrast, the humble virtues express humanity's embeddedness in a larger organic system.

Slater reviews the virtues of the simple community that we have left behind, but does not feel that returning to such a community is a viable goal. He does point to four general healthy directions: decentralization, deceleration, depolarization, and reconnection or recapturing primitive awareness.

Alvin Toffler, "who represents a kind of Neville Chamberlain in humanity's relation to technology" (p. 22), is attacked throughout this rambling discourse.

352. MURCHLAND, Bernard. **The Age of Alienation.** NY: Random House, 1971. 208 pp. $6.95.   (A-4)

A rather academic essay by a professor of philosophy at Ohio Wesleyan University who asserts that "Wherever the search for an understanding of the human. condition is going on today, the notions of alienation and cultural disintegration are indispensable." (p. 3) A kind of moral paralysis of the will is seen as having descended upon us.

Alienation is used broadly here to include anxiety, anomie, despair, depersonalization, rootlessness, meaninglessness, isolation, pessimism, and lack of community. "The question of how the reign of alienation may be brought to an end is the most urgent question of our time." (p. 161) Alienation is also seen as the fragmentation of experience, which raises the question of how to unify experience. But answers are not suggested.

Considerable attention is devoted to the history of the concept, with comments on Becker, Camus, Sartre, and Locke.

"Let me say, in conclusion, that some new combination of art and politics would be a most desirable form of creativity today." (p. 199, final sentence)

353. MARCUSE, Herbert. **One-Dimensional Man: Studies in the Ideology of Advanced Industrial Society.** Boston: Beacon Press, 1964; paperbound edition, 1966. 260 pp.   (A-4)

A widely-known Marxist critique, holding that "The advancing one-dimensional society alters the relation between the rational and the irrational." (p. 247)

"The goal of authentic self-determination by the individual depends on effective social control over the production and distribution of the necessities..." (p. 251)

354. FILL, J. Herbert. **The Mental Breakdown of a Nation.** NY: Franklin Watts/New Viewpoints, 1974. 136 pp. $6.95.   (BC-4)

A psychiatrist and former Commissioner of Mental Health for New York City views our accelerating mental breakdown as "the tragic result of centuries of mental conditioning to a man-estranged world view...now aided, perpetuated, and exacerbated by modern education, technology, business, and mass communications that further deform and sicken our minds." (pp. 4-5)

There is a way out and "still time to change" toward an open, trusting mutually helpful society, where the mind of man could come alive again. Such a course requires "deviewing" the "objective" world view, education to warm and deepen feelings, moving away from intellectual and depersonalized man, regaining conscious command over thought, and reintroducing will into our feelings. We must once again become conscious of basic mental health principles such as permanence, inner freedom, activity, growth, essentiality, hierarchy of being, and the feeling of belonging on one's terms.

*** Also see Hendin (no. 114) for a more restrained but no less dismal view of our mental condition, and Roszak (no. 303) for a far more extensive critique of the effects of reductionist science.

355. YABLONSKY, Lewis. **Robopaths.** Indianapolis: Bobbs-Merrill, 1972. 204 pp.   (BC-4)

The robopath is characterized by ritualism, past-orientation, conformity, image-involvement, acompassion, hostility, self-righteousness, and alienation. This behavior results from the machine domination of people in modern mass society, also described as "social machine society" and "plastic society."

The counterforces for humanistic social change include awareness, spontaneous counterculture movements, and "innovation group" vehicles. It is cautioned, though, that "Many revolutionaries and dissenters have acquired the same ahuman qualities of the robopathic leaders of the society they are attempting to destroy." (p. 135)

356. THAYER, Frederick C. **An End to Hierarchy! An End to Competition! Organizing the Politics and Economics of Survival.** NY: Franklin Watts/New Viewpoints, 1973. 232 pp. $9.95; $2.95, paper.   (AB-4)

A professor of public administration at the University of Pittsburgh attempts to outline "a formal theory of structured non-hierarchical social interaction."

"Unlike other books which address the possibilities of transforming organizations into more 'natural' or 'humanistic' communities, this one argues that instead of compromising with hierarchy, we must end it, that this is both possible and quite easy to do, and that there is a workable alternative which is not anarchy." (p. vii)

The first chapter describes The Organizational Revolution that is "now under way, one which is causing the pyramidal hierarchical walls of formal organizations to 'wither away' (in a non-Marxist sense). Because the revolution is being impeded by our outmoded theories of politics and economics, it is necessary to strip away the sham of 'democracy' (Chapter 2) and 'competition' (Chapter 3), for we cannot survive unless we find a nonhierarchical meaning for democracy and substitute cooperation and sharing for competition." (p. 6)

Favorable comments are made about the Organization Development (OD) social movement, an outgrowth of Maslow's humanistic psychology. "OD is oriented to process; it stresses interpersonal competence, collaboration, teamwork, and group dynamic skills. It seeks to instill humanistic value systems in work units..." (p. 22)

A "new social theory" is outlined in Chapter 4, based on the thinking of Arthur F. Bentley and Mary Parker Follett, and the theory is applied to U.S. policy processes in the following chapter, as concerns both the National Security Council and domestic policy.

The final chapter, A Sensuous Future or None, engages in "wider speculation about the future" by advocating a new paradigm of mutually supportive interaction where all contributions would be valued, the decline of the nation-state and of war, removing formal authority to make decisions binding upon others from all administrators everywhere, salary equalization, nonrepressive sex relationships among individuals who work together (therefore erasing all boundaries between work and love), and the reinstatement of humane competition in sports.

*** Somewhat fresh thinking that presumes the unvarying goodness of man and thoroughly confuses description and prescription--what is happening and what ought to happen. The ideals expressed here may be possible and desirable to attain, but doing so will certainly not be "easy to do." Thinking that such is the case would inhibit serious movement toward these ideals.

357. THEOBALD, Robert. **An Alternative Future for America II: Essays and Speeches.** Chicago: Swallow, Rev. and enlarged edition, May 1970. 199 pp. $6; $2, paper.   (BC-4)

A choppy melange of provocations, arguing that the most necessary changes are in the prevailing view of the nature and purpose of man. A new world is advocated which will be process-oriented rather than goal-oriented, where people will strive for self-actualization, and where education will help individuals realize their uniqueness. At a minimum, change must include income maintenance and destroying the distinction between work and labor. Although the U.N. development decade of the 1960's is acknowledged to be a failure, Theobald proposes "that we work towards an international synergetic decade of the seventies" to provide everyone with enough food, clothing, and shelter. The problem is seen as simply a question of will.

358. NATHANSON, Jerome (ed.) **Individual Excellence and Social Responsibility.** Preface by Khoran Arisian. Buffalo, NY: Prometheus Books, 1974. 87 pp. $6.95.   (AB-4)

Five revised essays originally delivered at the New York Society for Ethical Culture. "The central theme of this book is the state of the individual in America: how he is to survive, flourish, and define himself in the face of technocracy, industrialism, and governmental paternalism, all of which tend to inculcate a sense of repressive timidity in people." (p.v)
-Jerome Nathanson, "Individuality, Permissiveness, and Work"
-Ivan Shapiro, "Ethics and Civil Liberties"
-Paul Migliore, "Liberalism and the Politics of Retreat"
-Khoran Arisian, "Power: Its Use and Abuse"
-Edward L. Ericson, "Toward Economic Democracy: An American Solution," which argues against capitalist and socialist paternalism, and for the indivisibility of political and economic democracy.

359. DAVENPORT, William H. **The One Culture.** Pergamon Unified Engineering Series, Vol. 3. NY: Pergamon Press, 1970. 182 pp. (A-4)

A re-examination of the state of culture in an age of technology, and a review of C.P. Snow's two cultures argument (no. 891) ten years later, with the narrow but noble purpose of improving engineering education with more courses in the humanities and the social sciences. "Even in this age of specialization and technological stewardship it ought to be possible for scientists, humanists and laymen generally to lead fuller lives and to do it together, not apart." (p. 121) There "must be better communication among people who are intelligent, alerted, articulate, dedicated." (p. 123)
*** A high-minded statement of the goals of unity, but without any recognition, let alone analysis, of the centrifugal forces that keep people apart. This is naive in contrast to Davy's vision of "a third culture" (no. 131), which Davenport does not acknowledge.

360. SKINNER, B.F. **Beyond Freedom and Dignity.** NY: Knopf, Sept. 1971; NY: Bantam, Sept. 1972. 215 pp. $1.95, paper.   (AB-4)

A widely-known and highly controversial essay that advocates a technology of behavior to shape environment for a better society. The actual steps to be taken are not mentioned, and the defenders of freedom and dignity (presumably political conservatives) are not identified. The title is misleading, suggesting that Skinner is some sort of totalitarian manipulator, which is not the case. Rather, the position might best be seen as crypto-liberalism in its advocacy of "a planned culture."
*** Skinner's views are not developed beyond those expressed in his classic utopian novel, **Walden Two,** published in 1948. A great deal of academic energy has gone into attacking this narrow essay which offers little substance but much incitement.

360a. WHEELER, Harvey (ed.) **Beyond the Primitive Society. Operant Conditioning: Social and Political Aspects.** San Francisco: W.H. Freeman, Spring 1973.   (A-3)

Original papers dealing with the implications of Skinner's **Beyond Freedom and Dignity.** The 18 contributors include Arnold Toynbee, Arthur R.

Jensen, Max Black, John R. Platt, Dennis C. Pirages, and Lord Ritchie-Calder. The conclusion by Skinner is the only detailed published response to criticism of his book (according to an advertisement).

361. DELGADO, José M.R. **Physical Control of the Mind: Toward a Psychocivilized Society.** World Perspectives Series. NY: Harper & Row, 1969. 280 pp. $7.95; $2.25 Colophon paper edition.   (A-4)

A discussion of electronic control techniques by a widely-known Yale researcher who has pioneered in the field. Largely technical and socially naive.

362. GRAHAM, Robert Klark. **The Future of Man.** Introduction by Professor Sir Cyril Burt. North Quincy, Mass.: Christopher Publishing House, 1970. 200 pp. $7.95.   (AB-4)

An anthropologist asks that a simple principle be followed: "The more intelligent you are the more children you should have...Its wide realization could bring stability and benefit to all of mankind." (p.14) This policy results from the view that man has freed himself from the natural struggle that built high intelligence into him, and the highly competent are failing to increase in proportion to their numbers.
"Man is the heir of more than a score of civilizations, and is now in the midst of the most pervasive and powerful one which ever existed. Yet he appears to be slightly past the zenith of this civilization." (p.144)
As a successor to "cruel and enfeebled natural selection," Graham proposes intelligent selection--man's control of his own evolution. "It offers the greatest choice ever knowingly made by man." (p.153) This policy need not be imposed; rather, there are ways to encourage the multiplying of the intelligent while discouraging the unintelligent.
*** An interesting argument, but blissfully apolitical.

363. MAY, Rollo. **Power and Innocence: A Search for the Sources of Violence.** NY: Norton, 1972. 283 pp. $7.95.   (A-3)

"We live at the end of an era...The era that emphasized rationalism and individualism is suffering an inner and outer transition; and there are as yet only dim harbingers, only partly conscious, of what the new age will be." (p.47) In this present gap between ages, power is confused and "up for grabs." It becomes a new and urgent issue for everyone who is trying to get his bearings, and powerlessness becomes very painful. Language disintegrates, leading to an upsurge of violence.
In a section on The Greening and the Parching of America, May disposes of Charles Reich by asserting that "Far from Consciousness III being an answer, it would be no consciousness at all, for it lacks the dialectic movement between 'yes' and 'no', good and evil, which gives birth to consciousness of any sort...Reich has no understanding of the creeping fascism already discernable in our country." (p.54)
The concluding chapter, Toward New Community, argues that to mitigate violence, it must be recognized that violence is a symptom of powerlessness, and that ways of distributing and sharing power must be found. A new ethic of intention, assuming that each man is responsible for the effects of his actions, is seen as relevant for the emerging age, in contrast to the one-dimensional ethics of growth that never sees limits to man's potential (an error often found in the encounter-group movement).

364. MARRIS, Peter. Loss and Change. NY: Pantheon, 1974. 178 pp.   (A-3)

A thoughtful essay by a British social scientist on the relationship between conservatism, bereavement, and innovation. Conservatism is the impulse to defend the predictability of life--a fundamental and universal princicple. Arguments for social change often tend to explain conservatism as ignorance, but this impulse is "as necessary for survival as adaptability." This intolerance of relationships has far-reaching implications for the management of change. Indeed, an entire chapter is devoted to suggesting "The Conservatism in Innovation".

There are many useful insights on the management of change, i.e. "...political and scientific revolutions alike seem to evolve from the internal decay of meaningful structures. But the disintegration of social meaning encounters more anxious resistance, evokes a deeper and more intimate sense of loss, since it involves the attachments of our everyday lives; and we confront it without the supporting logic of a scientific method." (p.170)

365. CANTRIL, Hadley. The Pattern of Human Concerns. New Brunswick, N.J.: Rutgers University Press, 1965. 427 pp. $10.00.   (A-2)

The results and analysis from a massive study that involved interviews with nearly 20,000 people in 13 countries over a period of 6 years. The findings have important implications for policy design: "sound policy should be determined only on the basis of needs and attitudes of the people for whom institutions and governments are designed." (p.ix)

"The effective society is one that enables the individual to develop personal loyalties and aspirations which overlap with and are congenial to social values and loyalties..." (p.321)

Eleven basic uniformities were found: "demands human beings everywhere impose on any society or political culture"--
- survival needs
- assuring a secure beachhead to protect gains
- sufficient order and certainty for predictability
- enlarging range and enriching quality of satisfactions
- being hopeful: most people most of the time are future-oriented
- desire to make choices
- wanting freedom
- the want to experience one's own identity and integrity; the need for dignity
- a sense of worthwhileness
- a value or system of beliefs to which there can be commitment
- a sense of confidence that one's society holds out hope that aspirations will be fulfilled.

Also of interest are the five phases of individual development that parallel the genesis of economic or political stages of development: acquiescence to circumstances, awakening to potentialities, awareness of means to realize goals, assurance and self-reliance--experiencing intended consequences through action, and the final phase of satisfaction and gratification.

"A vision of a brighter future will lead only to despair or will be given up entirely unless there are some ways to start making the vision come true." (p.304)

*** A useful background to understanding our present loss of confidence and how it might be restored.

Chapter 9

Government Reform

Contemporary thinking about the reform of government can be roughly divided into three areas: enhancing administrative and democratic processes, creating new programs, and revising the structures of political thought, institutions, and the nation itself.

This chapter begins with very general concerns about the condition of the public sector. Dr. Karl Menninger's argument that we must once again consider sin (366) is intentionally placed first so that attention might be drawn to this neglected dimension. Michener (367) is also concerned about a moral collapse, while Krebs (368) and Anderson (369) express related concerns about a spiritual revival and rediscovering our "civic religion." Boulding (370) is concerned about virtue and vice, as well as cybernetic needs for the "spaceship politics" of the 21st century. Raushenbush (371) attempts to bring lessons of the past to bear on general concerns of the future. Frankel (372) offers a modern statement of the ideals of democracy and the necessary tasks for attaining "the responsible society." Gardner's discussion of the "ever-renewing society" (373) follows similar lines and is equally worthwhile. These observations are continued in **No Easy Victories** (374) and **The Recovery of Confidence** (375), the latter being particularly important for our present malaise. Boorstin (376) assures us that Americans have always been "a renovating culture."

Boorstin does not suggest that substantial changes may be needed in order to set new ideals and fulfill them. But many others do. Etzioni (377) provides a very extensive theory of "the active society" that we might choose. Caplow (379) feels that we can attain "the good society" if we undertake projects of social improvement in a more rational way. He feels that we already have most of the required knowledge, but Sarason (380) has discovered that little or no attention has been paid to the problem of creating new organizations, or settings, and offers some very valuable insights on recent failures. Burns (381) urges "uncommon sense" in our directed social change so that we might overcome the disjunction of means and ends. Linowes (382) offers a number of imaginative ideas regarding practices in industry that might be applied to the public sector under the banner of "Socio-Economic Management." Beer (386) suggests a number of cybernetic concepts to design freedom. We are also urged toward "a homeodynamic society" (388), "an experimental society" (389 and 390), online social planning (390), a participatory technology system (391), and "open systems" in general (392).

A considerably less ambitious cluster of writings should now be considered. Stern's suggestions for enhancing democracy (393) do not go as far as Frankel (372) or Gardner (373). Wilensky (394) provides a useful survey of welfare states worldwide, but does not appear to understand the necessary reforms for a genuine humanizing of the welfare state. Dahrendorf (395) proposes a few good ideas, but his agenda for "the improving society" is rather thin. Bell's advocacy of the public household and ending ideology

(396) is both narrow and obscure. Apter (397) is also fuzzy and superficial in advocating "a Socialist-Liberal solution." Rostow proposes perhaps the emptiest "American Agenda" ever (401).

In contrast, it is useful to consider some serious attempts at agendas (402-412). Chase's budget of needs and resources (402) deals with the basic issues perhaps as well as any subsequent effort. The Rockefeller Panel (403) and the President's Commission on National Goals (404) are noteworthy efforts from the early 1960's, although somewhat larded with runaway rhetoric. The "Agenda for the Nation" proposed by the Brookings Institution (406) is quite similar in format and ideology to the National Goals Commission. The report on **The Future of the United States Government** from the Commission on the Year 2000 (407) provides a broader mix of contributors and ideas. The initial step toward a system of social reporting (408) does not offer an agenda, but attempts to draw together some important base-line social indicators. The National Goals Research Staff (409) discussed general issues in the hopes of promoting a policy of "balanced growth." Meanwhile, back at Brookings, an annual analysis of the federal budget began in 1970 (410), a relatively tame effort compared to the "Freedom Budget" (411) and the "Counterbudget" (412), which both served to outline substantial across-the-board alternatives.

Less comprehensive attempts at agendas should also be noted. Stuart Udall's "Project 76" is not an "agenda for tomorrow," but an interesting scheme for involving everyone in planning one. Eldredge (414) ventures some unfashionable notions about an aristocracy of talent as the basis of "The Second American Revolution," while John D. Rockefeller uses the same title for his overview of necessary reforms (415). A third usage of this obvious title is found elsewhere in this chapter (no. 443). Shearer (416) brings together all of the bills, proposals, and model laws that are in or about the Congressional pipeline at the moment; together they form the outline of the best-of-all-possible progressive scenarios for the near future. Redburn's "Platform for the Seventies" (417) provides a number of fresh ideas that are not of any particular ideological stripe. Hamill (418) focuses his challenging agenda around the notion of abolishing welfare in New York City over a three-year period. Buckley (419) focuses on only four reforms, including a "sensible welfare system." Schlesinger (420) is concerned with only one issue, but it is a crucial one for the makeup of the U.S. budget.

Many argue, though, that substantial changes in programs cannot occur without substantial changes in our thinking, our electoral processes, and our institutions. Slomich (426), in striking contrast to Schlesinger, attacks the military megabureaucracy and advocates "The Politics of Humanism." Wheeler promulgates "The Politics of Revolution" (427) and Raskin seeks to transform American politics to a new stage (428). Beam argues for "New Politics" (429), and Lowi proposes "Juridical Democracy" as a replacement of interest-group liberalism (430). Ferkiss also proposes a new ideology (431), and goes to great lengths to argue that "Ecological Humanism" will come about through a revolution by technological man.

Califano (434) advocates a number of significant reforms such as a National Posture Statement that might close the gap between rhetoric and reality. These actions to reduce the power of "a presidential nation" could be realized, relative to improbable schemes such as thoroughly revising the constitution (435, 436, and Tugwell in Perloff, no. 407). Baldwin's interesting suggestion for 15 states (436) is somewhat similar to Sale's proposal for five separate nations (437), Hamill's proposal for a Republic of New York (439), and Toffler's speculation about an "Urban Federation" (440). Rather than secession, there might be incorporation, and the Canadians wonder about "Continental Community" (441). In contrast to this very academic inquiry, a very nonacademic utopia proposes a Republic of North America (442) as the umbrella organization to the "People's Establishment." Three other less appealing examples of "flower child politics" follow Muir's engaging fantasy.

The final item by Cornuelle (446) serves as a bridge between Chapter 9 and Chapter 10, by suggesting that rejuvenating the "third sector" of independent associations is necessary for **Reclaiming the American Dream.** It is a unique perspective that somehow gets overlooked, and complements Menninger's unique perspective (366), which introduces this chapter.

366. MENNINGER, Karl, M.D. **Whatever Became of Sin?** NY: Hawthorn Books, 1973. 242 pp. $7.95.   (AB-2)

A renowned psychiatrist observes the moral decline of our nation (even before Watergate!) and wonders what is wrong and what we can do. "We each do our part in a total process of wasting, spending, polluting, difiling, stealing, hoarding, exhausting, and destroying. We pause occasionally to gaze about in alarm and apprehensiveness; we acknowledge a general pall of depression. But no corrective peccavi or **mea culpa** escapes our lips." (p. 190-191)

Menninger makes a simple but stunningly accurate observation: "In all of the laments and reproaches made by our seers and prophets, one misses any mention of 'sin,' a word which used to be a veritable watchword of prophets. It was a word once in everyone's mind, but now rarely if ever heard." (p. 13) What happened? Certain sins such as drinking coffee have disappeared, but, more significantly, there has been a shift in the allocation of responsibility for evil. Many sins have become crimes, and policemen have replaced the priest. "Two percent of the sins of the city become 'crimes' and are thus 'appropriately' handled. But what about the other 98 percent?" (p. 18)

A skillful effort is made to supply a useful definition of sin without devolving into "a pietistic or anti-pietistic harangue." Essentially, sin is a moral failure to do as one ought toward one's fellow man. Menninger describes the modern forms of well-known sins such as pride, sensuality, gluttony, anger, sloth, greed, possession, waste, cheating, lying, and cruelty.

Acknowledging sin is the only hopeful view, and the book is concluded with an appeal for moral leadership from politicians, educators, the press, policemen, doctors, and particularly the clergy.

** An authoritative slant to an old and neglected concern.

366a. BENSON, George C.S., and Thomas S. ENGEMAN. **Amoral America.** Stanford, Calif.: Hoover Institution Press, 1975. 294 pp. $8.95.
                                                                         (A-4)

Two political scientists question the emphasis on social ethics and institutional solutions at the expense of concern for individual ethics. "Our thesis is that there is a severe and almost paralyzing ethical problem in this country." (p. 27) The authors look at existing patterns of ethical education and make suggestions for improvement in various chapters devoted to family, peers, church, school, media, intellectuals, and government.

*** A rather narrow argument in contrast to that made by Menninger (no. 366).

367. MICHENER, James A. **The Quality of Life.** Philadelphia: J.B. Lippincott, 1970; Greenwich, Conn.: Fawcett Crest Books, July 1971. 128 pp. 95¢, paper.   (BC-3)

A well-known novelist seeks "to take stock of where we are and where we are likely to go," (p. 7) impressed by the fact that America has the oldest continuing form of government on earth.

"These are our problems: finding ways to cope with a vastly increased population, keeping youth involved in our society, reconciling race differences, protecting our environment, evolving new systems for governing metropolitan areas as cohesive units rather than as fragmented parts... We are intelligent enough to restore control; we must do so because we are fighting for the continuance of a great democracy...one worth saving." (p. 128)

Particular concern is expressed about a possible moral collapse (similar to that of Germany under Hitler) and the need for new spiritual guidelines and new national goals.

*** Although a bit dated in parts, this popular overview is still worthwhile for general audiences.

368. KREBS, Hans A., "Some Facts of Life--Biology and Politics," **Perspectives in Biology and Medicine,** 15:4, Summer 1972, pp. 491-506.   (ABC-3)

A fresh and thoughtful attempt "to discuss the bearing of some general biological knowledge upon problems now facing society." Although the author is British, the comments concerning the deterioration of human conduct are applicable to all advanced societies.

The facts of life are that life must be renewed by hard effort or it will run down, a society (similar to an individual) has to earn its living, and systems must be flexible so as to adapt themselves to changing situations.

Proposals for action include more flexible and speedier machinery of government and, above all, a spiritual revival. This might be brought about by some kind of national service or community service, improving education to a higher standard of citizenship or social responsibility, and an inspiring leadership which might forego narrow party politics.

369. ANDERSON, John B. **Vision and Betrayal in America.** Waco, Texas: Word Books, 1975. 130 pp. $4.95.   (C-3)

Anderson (R.-Ill.), the third ranking Republican in the U.S. House of Representatives, describes the crises of ideals, institutions, and leadership: "the three occurring together have shaken us to our foundation." (p. 129)

A renewed commitment to the basic core values of democracy is advocated, as well as a rediscovery and rearticulation of our "civic religion": the glue of common core values that holds us together.

Institutional reforms are advocated for election procedures (matching grants are suggested), the Congressional committee system, Congressional staffing (more professionals needed), the criminal justice system, and political parties.

*** A good explanation for the grass roots voter.

370. BOULDING, Kenneth E., "Towards A Twenty-First Century Politics," **Colorado Quarterly,** 20:3, Winter 1972, pp. 309-319.   (AB-3)

Argues that the great period of change was within the lifetime of Boulding's grandfather--from 1860-1920--and that today's world is not strikingly different from 1920. Still, there is no existing political ideology that seems relevant to the 21st century. Some of the necessary characteristics of "spaceship politics" include:

1) The necessity of being cybernetic and developing an information apparatus for perceiving states of the social system.

2) Political organization must provide a satisfactory reward structure that recognizes virtue and punishes vice, and one that is able to detect one from the other.

3) A social matrix must be provided for developing satisfactory personal identities--rewards for being.

*** Perhaps overly generalized, but serves to introduce many of the remaining items in this chapter, notably Beer (386), Menninger (366), and Ferkiss (431).

371. RAUSHENBUSH, (Hilmar) Stephen. **Man's Past: Man's Future: A Humanistic History for Tomorrow.** NY: Delacorte, 1969. 308 pp. $6.95.   (AB-3)

An historian examines "lost opportunities and tragic moments in the life of past great societies" so that America might perform better. These lessons of the past are brought to bear in a wordy but most intriguing manner on four major problems that the U.S. must confront before the end of the century: depersonalization as a result of mass aggregation and technological momentum, conflict about the meaning and limits of freedom, hunger revolts and consequent revolutions, and the avoidance of destruction from our modern weaponry. Chapters are devoted to lessons from Ancient Greece, Rome, Spain, France, the American Civil War, Russia, and Germany between 1918 and 1933: "Fifteen Years of Avoidable Anarchy."

372. FRANKEL, Charles. **The Democratic Prospect.** NY: Harper & Row, 1962. 222 pp.   (AB-3)

A widely-known Professor of Philosophy at Columbia University worries that "The sense that American democracy has a prospect...is most obviously absent from the present scene...in the modern world it is motion with a meaning, change in an identifiable and desired direction, which is the basic generator of belief in a social system." (p. 179)

To restore or reaffirm belief, Frankel seeks herein to state the ideals of democracy and how they may be attained in a modern context, overcoming the politics of malaise resulting from the spector of a mass society and the disjunction of image and reality. He describes the nature of democratic consensus, the ideals of consent of the governed, an open society, and responsible government.

To recover government by consent, there is a need to reorganize voluntary associations and plan for autonomous neighborhoods within cities. An open society must face the dilemmas created by the mass media and specialized expertise. "The purpose of an open society is to produce groups of competent critics outside the inner circles, and to maintain a relevant and responsible debate on public policy not controlled by the inner circles...the debate is a public debate, and the quality of any such debate is affected by the quality of the audience." (p. 86)

Chapters also discuss The Reorganization of Work and Planning (with attention to the control of hugeness and the impact of machine production), The Welfare State ("does too much because it does too little"), and the problems of attaining The Responsible Society: professional morality, the organization of the decision-making process, visibility of decision-makers, accountability, and "effective communication between those who perform and those who judge the performance." The concluding Epilogue, Why Choose Democracy, makes a case for this ideal.

*** Important background reading, lest we forget what democracy ought to be.

373. GARDNER, John W. **Self-Renewal: The Individual and the Innovative Society.** NY: Harper & Row, 1964. 141 pp.   (AB-3)

"Apathy and lowered motivation are the most widely-noted characteristics of a civilization on the downward path." (p. xv)

In the ever-renewing society there is a framework within which continuous innovations can occur. A modern view is needed of the processes of growth, decay, and renewal: the "endless interweaving of continuity and change." Large-scale organization is not to be condemned out-of-hand; besides, "We cannot return to a simpler world...We must master the new forms of organization or they will master us." (p. 63) There are benefits to pluralism, but pluralism can work only in a society that has adequate forces of cohesion. "Extremes of pluralism can lead to utter confusion." (p. 69)

Chapters cover topics such as self-renewal (self-knowledge, love, and the courage to fail), education for versatility, innovation and creativity, obstacles to renewal, conditions of renewal (protecting dissenters and nonconformists), organizing for renewal (overcoming the filtering of experience and creating new organizational forms), commitment and meaning, and moral decay and renewal.

The chapter on Attitudes Toward the Future argues that the self-renewing society has a dominant orientation to the future ("hopelessness does not make for renewal") but must also utilize the historian. "The only sensible view of life is, and has always been, based on a clear-eyed recognition--not necessarily acceptance--of the elements of tragedy, irony and absurdity in life...anyone who does not recognize all of this is either very young or very foolish, possibly both." (pp. 111-112)

374. GARDNER, John W. No Easy Victories. NY: Harper & Row, 1968.
      177 pp.   (AB-3)

Excerpts from Gardner's speeches and writings, many of them with important insights about the future of our society and necessary directions for effective action. Particular emphasis is placed on education and learning.

375. GARDNER, John W. The Recovery of Confidence. NY: W.W. Norton,
      1970. 189 pp. $5.00.   (ABC-2)

In many respects a continuation of **Self-Renewal**, responding to concerns such as the breakdown of authority in just about every dimension, uncritical lovers and unloving critics, illegal violence on the part of authorities, and each reformer with his little bundle of desired changes.

There are things that are "gravely wrong" with our society as a problem-solving mechanism. "If we are to recover our confidence, it will have to be the confidence of maturity. And it will have to be built, as all mature confidence is built, on a willingness to face problems forthrightly and on some reasonable success in coping with them. That is hard, but adulthood is hard." (p. 19)

There is a need to repair the liberal tradition with a modern strategy of continuous social renewal. The attributes of a society capable of this renewal are pluralism, effective internal communications, the release of individual potentialities, and a restored morale that repairs the breakdown in the relationship of individual to society.

"The advantages of pluralism are diminished if the various elements of the society are out of touch with one another. A society that is capable of continuous renewal will have effective internal communication among its diverse elements. We do not have that today. We are drowning in a torrent of talk, but most of it serves only to raise the noise level." (p. 58)

*** Wise sermonizing that is still right on target. It is hoped that **Societal Directions and Alternatives** clearly demonstrates the "torrent of talk" and the lack of communication.

376. BOORSTIN, Daniel J., "Self-Liquidating Ideals," in House Committee on Science and Astronautics, The Management of Information and Knowledge: A Compilation of Papers Prepared for the Eleventh Meeting of the Panel on Science and Technology. Washington: USGPO, 1970. pp. 63-71.   (AB-4)

An eminent historian and then-Director of the Smithsonian Institution's National Museum of History and Technology argues that Americans have been led to the pursuit of self-liquidating ideals: ideals which are dissolved in the very act of fulfillment.

We are seen as a renovating culture, with recurrent needs for renewal and natural cycles of self-flagellation.

"But may not much of the peculiar greatness of our Nation consist of its uncanny and versatile powers of renewal? Again and again our nation has shown an astonishing capacity for setting itself hitherto-unimagined ideals, and then proving that these ideals can be fulfilled. And then setting still others. The burden and the challenge of being an American consist in these recurrent tests of our power of renewal. Paradoxically, this is our most distinctive and most potent tradition." (Conclusion, p. 71)

*** Let us hope that we are indeed a "renovating culture," but such unqualified cheerleading could inhibit recognition of new and unprecedented barriers to effective renovating actions.

376a. FOLLETT, Mary P. **The New State: Group Organization the Solution of Popular Government.** NY: Longmans, Green & Co., 1918. 373 pp.   (A-3)

A leading administrative theorist asserts that we have not yet tried democracy and that, under our present system, necessary social and economic changes cannot be brought about. "Our political life is stagnating, capital and labor are virtually at war, the nations of Europe are at one another's throats--because we have not yet learned how to live together. The twentieth century must find a new principle of association." (p. 3)

Follett asserts that man discovers his true nature only through the group, and advocates the revitalization of politics through non-partisan groups for begetting common ideas and a common purpose. Neighborhood organization would replace party organization by evolving a true will of the people, which would be the sovereign power of the state. "The Unified State" would bring together living groups at the local level with occupational representation. "The essence of democracy is the expression of every man in his multiple nature." (p. 295)

377. ETZIONI, Amitai. **The Active Society: A Theory of Societal and Political Processes.** NY: The Free Press, 1968. 698 pp.   (A-3)

A sociologist proposes a theory of societal self-control based on "valid social science theory" which could serve as a springboard for active participation in our "post-modern" society.

Three stages of social evolution are seen. The fused society (small, illiterate, and primitive) serves various needs with a single unit. The differentiated society (industrial societies in their laissez-faire periods) utilize a separate sub-system for each major function. The reintegrated society, an option that is open to mature societies but one that is not inevitable, develops a fused overlayer. It has the capacities of a differentiated society and the wholeness of a fused society. "It can be an active society." (p. 574)

"The active society, one that is master of itself, is an option the post-modern period opens. An exploration of the conditions under which this option might be exercised is the subject of this endeavor." (p. viii) Such a society is engaged in an "intensive and perpetual self-transformation," in response to its changing membership. It is a society that knows itself and moves toward a fuller realization of its values: "a social movement society." It would harness societal energy similar to harnessing nuclear energy. Activization must be comprehensive: appearing in all sectors and involving the participation of all major groups. To be active is to be responsive, to be in charge, and to reduce alienation.

*** The option of the active society has not been chosen, and perhaps we should start with a theory of the post-modern society that has become hyper-differentiated instead of reintegrated.

378. BREED, Warren. The Self-Guiding Society: Based on "The Active Society" by Amitai Etzioni. NY: Free Press, 1971. 242 pp. (B-4)

Etzioni asked Breed to prepare this shorter and more popularized version of his 1968 work, also published by Free Press. The attempt is textbookish, in addition to retaining the dryness and sociologese that made the previous work formidable.

An active society requires "much accurate, encompassing, and synthesized knowledge." The major flaws in post-modern society are continuing alienation and growing inauthenticity. But guided social change can be "wrought" by greater control moving downward (requiring the surrender of some power by elites) and greater consensus. "Building the good society everyone will agree presents obstacles of heroic size. And it must be the total society that is transformed; piecemeal tinkering is not enough." (p. v)

379. CAPLOW, Theodore. Toward Social Hope. NY: Basic Books, 1975. 229 pp. $11.95.   (AB-2)

Rather than viewing history as a sequence of stages culminating in the perfect society, Caplow views it as the outcome of deliberate human projects: "...although perfect social institutions are not possible or even desirable, a greatly improved society might be within our present grasp if projects of social improvement were undertaken in a more rational way... we already have most of the theoretical knowledge required for a competent social technology." (p. vii) The difficulty lies in our inability to apply existing knowledge.

There are seven essential parts to any project of social improvement: 1) a description of existing conditions; 2) a careful and honest description of the end condition to be achieved; 3) dividing the project into successive stages; 4) designing methods for getting from one stage to the next; 5) an estimate of time and resources; 6) devising procedures for measuring goal attainment; and 7) devising procedures for detecting unanticipated results.

These project elements serve as criteria for an historical assessment of change. Chapter 2, The Origins of Social Improvement, goes back 300 years to the theories of Western Europe. Nineteenth Century Trends describes modernization, the control of the physical environment, and the expansion of scientific knowledge. The Twentieth Century Viewed from the Nineteenth examines the proposals of Edward Bellamy, Karl Kautsky (the official theorist of German Marxism), and Emile Durkheim.

Chapter 5 on Twentieth Century Trends (discussing nationalism, war, and revolution) serves as a background to chapters on A Set of Successful Projects (migration of individuals and families, modernization projects, revolutionary projects, and imperialism), and A Set of Unsuccessful Projects (Marxist World Revolution, other schemes of world conquest, the League of Nations, and the United Nations). Chapter 8 examines Some Vintage American Projects (the Abolition movement, the settlement house, and prohibition), and Chapter 9 looks at The Projects of the New Deal.

Recent attempts at social change are looked at in chapters on The Coming of the Era of Protest (the Vietnam defeat, the black occupation of large cities), The War on Poverty, Social Improvement by the Courts, and Liberation Movements of racial minorities, women, and the young.

The final chapter on The Good Society offers insightful comments on social inventions and the peaks and troughs of social confidence.

*** Excellent background for anyone concerned with "inventing the future."

380. SARASON, Seymour B. The Creation of Settings and the Future Societies. San Francisco: Jossey-Bass, Oct. 1972. 295 pp. $10.50.   (AB-2)

"In the past decade or so, more new settings (leaving marriage aside) have been created than in the entire previous history of the human race."

(p. 2) But this should not contribute to the belief that real change is taking place, for there are many failures, many of which are not reported. We can set policy for new directions, but still fail despite the best of intentions. Sarason observes that, although there is an ample literature on managing established organizations, there has been little or no attention to the problem of creating new organizations, or settings: "a general problem the understanding of which may be extremely important, if not crucial, to what is and will be happening in our society." (p. 19)

The aim of the book is to arouse interest in the problem and suggest what some of the basic concepts might be. Sarason draws heavily on his experience as Director of the Yale Psycho-Educational Clinic, and sprinkles the text with examples of marriages, the Russian and Cuban revolutions, communes, mental health clinics, schools, and theatrical productions--all various instances of setting creation. There is considerable wisdom here, although it is somewhat frustrating to the reader (but perhaps cautious on the part of the author) that there are no conclusions or recommendations for further inquiry.

Among other introductory comments, Chapter 1 discusses the extraordinary difficulty of accepting the concept of the universe of alternatives: "it is usually only after failure and catastrophe have occurred that respect is given to the concept and then in the form of a postmortum on a dead setting." (p. 18) Chapter 2 stresses "Before the Beginning"--that new settings always arise in some relation to existing settings. Subsequent chapters discuss choosing the leader, formation of the core group, the myth of unlimited resources (a major pitfall), resources and values (tendency to think of solutions exclusively in terms of professionalism and specialization), symptoms of decline (boredom, or the departure of the leader), building as distraction (frequently disrupting goal attainment), the social ization of the leader (distinguishing between men of action and men of theory), the feelings of the leader, problems of control (with an excellent section on the value of the external critic--pp. 250-251), and the new setting as a work of art. The next-to-last chapter is devoted to a critique of B.F. Skinner, arguing not that his position about ideal societies is wrong, but that "it is incredibly incomplete."

381. BURNS, James MacGregor. **Uncommon Sense.** NY: Harper & Row, 1972. 196 pp. $6.95.   (AB-1)

An eloquent and authoritative critique by a distinguished political scientist and historian at Williams College. "This book is a call to undertake that most demanding and revolutionary of all activities--rethinking our goals and our means of attaining them. It proposes that we neither patch up our system nor overthrow it, but that we transform it by keeping what is essential to our supreme ends and abandoning anything else that stands in the way." (p. x)

The major concern has to do with directed change: change harnessed to broadly held ends. We have failed to deal with interlocked national problems because of sporadic and piecemeal action. "Underlying these political and institutional failures, however, and stunting our capacity to criticize and reform the political system, are crucial failures of thought." (p. 8) The central problem in American thought is not the supremacy of means over ends, but the disjunction of means and ends.

Chapters are devoted to The Failure of the American System, The Illusion of Practical Progress, Foreign Policy: Piety and Practice, Overturning the System (attacks the long and slow gradualism of the "raising-of-consciousness" approach, and "revolution" as another "sponge word"), The Mobilization of Change (requiring the analysis of factors that block social change and the definition of ends), Beliefs as Guides to Action, The Transformation of Government, A Party Fit to Govern, and The Crisis of Leadership.

The best government would seem to be local government, but it is inadequate to deal with national problems. Suggestions include regional federal agencies to mobilize money and talent, the localization of federal power, a strengthening of the presidency, presidential leadership in building a wide variety of supranational institutions, public planning, and a national movement involving a coalition of the concerned.

Some harsh comments are directed to the intellectuals, who are "always" the spokesmen of uncommon sense: "Not only have some intellectuals exhibited in self-imposed exile, at home or abroad, a large measure of purism, sectarianism, and downright snobbery; they have shown a perverse hostility and ignorance toward the political system within which men of affairs have to act. They have dwelt on Utopian goals without any consideration of the means required to reach them...Few have been the intellectuals in America who understood the need not for rejection of the world of power but for a combination of confrontation of it and involvement with it." (p. 164)

382. LINOWES, David F. **Strategies for Survival: Using Business Know-How to Make Our Social System Work.** NY: AMACOM (A Division of the American Management Association), 1973. 231 pp.   (AB-2)

Suggests that the successful practices of industry should be applied to non-profit organizations, which are seen as failing. Socio-Economic Management (SEM) is a "logical extension of socio-economic accounting," and would pinpoint "profitable" programs and reject impractical endeavors, undoing the "government=appropriations lie" that spending money is synonymous with doing the job.

The rules are proposed for SEM, including matching standards and goals to human needs, applying funding for results, the use of discretionary funding as an incentive, multi-disciplinary planning, social profitability audits, and establishing public visibility. Two of the more intriguing chapters discuss the socio-economic audit as a mechanism for asking the right kinds of performance questions, and socio-economic councils or "survival squadrons" as watchdog groups at every level of government and society. *** Appears to offer a number of fresh and important ideas.

383. GROSS, Bertram M. **The Managing of Organizations: The Administrative Struggle.** NY: The Free Press, 1964. 971 pp. (2 Vols.)
(AB-3)
A massive and far-ranging work on administrative theory that devotes chapters to The Rise of the Administered Society and resulting Threats to Mankind, seen as dehumanization, the sickness of society, and the possibility of self-destruction.

"The administrative revolution is here to stay. Modern man has no escape from the complexities of organizations and their management. In fact, we shall probably have much more of these phenomena. This is the central probability that must govern any realistic ideas concerning the future of society." (p. 808)

Chapter 30, The Challenge of the Administered Society, explores various strategies to cope with this condition such as countervailing organization, the potentials of organizational democracy, an attack on spiritual poverty, more mature conceptions of national planning, and a realistic stance between cynicism and idealism.

383a. VICKERS, Sir Geoffrey. **Making Institutions Work.** NY: Wiley, 1973. 187 pp.   (A-3)

Eleven essays, most of them previously published, including The Demands of a Mixed Economy, Who Gets What, Towards a More Stable State, The End of the Individualist, and The Management of Conflict.
*** Wise and thoughtful, but without any particular focus.

383b. CORNFORD, James (ed.) **The Failure of the State: On the Distribution of Political and Economic Power in Europe.** Totawa, NJ:
Rowman and Littlefield, 1975. 198 pp. $17.50.   (A-3)

Six papers by members of the Department of Politics, University of
Edinburgh, concerning France, Italy, Great Britain, Germany, Eastern
Europe and the EEC, and how present dilemmas have been perceived and
debated.
The failure of the state is characterized by the loss of responsiveness
which their assumption of wider responsibilities has raised, and there
has been a sacrifice of political values as a result of the steps necessary
to fulfill these obligations. Considerable attention is devoted to the issue
of centralization vs. decentralization.
*** Deals with some universal problems in modern governance.

383c. GUTTMAN, Daniel and Barry WILLNER. **The Shadow Government:
The Government's Multi-billion-dollar Giveaway of its Decision-
making Powers to Private Management Consultants, "Experts" &
Think Tanks.** With an introduction by Ralph Nader. NY: Pantheon,
1976. 354 pp. $10.00.   (ns)

A report from Nader's Center for the Study of Responsive Law, arguing
that the federal bureaucracy has not grown, but that there has been a growth
in the volume of Federal contracts, last year totalling $110 billion, of which
a significant amount goes to consultants and experts. But this industry is
shrouded in secrecy and unchecked by public accountability. There is nothing
in the record of these consultant firms to justify the money spent. Rather
than solving problems, these consultants are more likely to provide the
illusion of action. (From **New York Times** review, 4-26-76).

383d. RICHARDSON, Elliot. **The Creative Balance: A Post-Watergate Look
at the American People and Politics.** NY: Holt, Rinehart & Winston,
June, 1976. $12.95.   (ns)

383e. DOUGLAS, Paul H. and J. Enoch POWELL. **How Big Should Government Be?** Washington: American Enterprise Institute for Public
Policy Research, 1968. 212 pp. $4.50.   (ns)

384. CROZIER, Michel. **The Stalled Society.** NY: Viking, 1973. 177 pp. $6.95.
                                                                (A-3)
An essay by a leading French sociologist, originally published in Paris as
La Société Bloquée (Editions du Seuil, 1970). Although thinking is directed
primarily to French society, blockages such as centralized administration,
caste systems, and rigid education and thinking are seen as "an essential
characteristic of modern advanced societies."
"Ultimately we shall find that the best opportunity for renewal lies at the
level of intellectual methods..." (p.149) Three principal approaches are suggested: developing a capacity for serious analysis, understanding the process
of change and appropriate behaviors for controlling it, and directing greater
concern to the development of institutions.

385. PLATT, John, "Social Traps," **American Psychologist,** 28:8, Aug. 1973,
pp. 641-651.   (A-3)

Social traps, like fish traps, are situations in society "where men or
organizations or whole societies get themselves started in some direction
or some set of relationships that later prove to be unpleasant or lethal and

that they see no easy way to back out of or avoid." An example is Hardin's "Tragedy of the Commons," where individual advantage leads to collective damage for the group as a whole. Platt goes on to suggest some types of traps and ways out, such as changing reinforcement relations. The study of social traps could become "a whole new discipline" in that such traps "represent all of our most intractable and large-scale urban, national, and international problems today" (p.651).

386. BEER, Stafford. **Designing Freedom.** London: John Wiley & Sons, 1974.
       100 pp. $8.95.   (AB-2)

The text of the 1973 Massey Lectures (six radio broadcasts sponsored by the Canadian Broadcasting Corporation), devoted to explaining the basic concepts of cybernetics and how they could be applied to societal planning.

It is argued that we live in "a dinosaur society" where institutions are unable to respond in time. There has been an insistence on variety reducing methods which worked in a bygone epoch, but are now working to seal our doom. Our existing liberty is largely illusory, and our institutions of education and publishing serve to dangerously constrain variety. Our science has been sold in the wrong way and for the wrong reasons. "Our institutions are failing because they are disobeying laws of effective organization which their administrators do not know about..." (p.19) "Civilization is being dragged down by its own inefficiency." (p.89)

But efficiency does not entail tyranny if we get the system right, and science could be used for liberation. Based on his recent experience in Chile, Beer argues that it is possible to redesign institutions of government according to cybernetic principles, and that it had been done within two years. Institutions can be designed with liberty as an output.

The barriers to redesign are bureaucracy, which must be dismantled, and the availability of money. The costs associated with major projects are seen as unreal, and many new projects could be financed by eliminating bureaucracy.

So that we may realize The Free Man in A Cybernetic World (the title of the final lecture), "The continuous process of liberating our minds from the programs implanted in our brains is a prerequisite of personal evolution." (p.87) Corrective action requires new channels of communication, including new educational and publishing systems. Better and more dynamic models of the components of the economy are needed, but these models must be created by the workers themselves. And computer power should be freed so that people could engage in their personal evolution.

*** Some very fresh and sophisticated ideas are presented in Beer's unique informal style, which includes child-like drawings by the author. Readers with a background in the physical sciences should be quite excited by this populist cybernetician; those with a background in the humanities will feel that Beer should collaborate with a good editor.

387. BEER, Stafford. **Platform for Change: A Message from Stafford Beer.**
       NY: Wiley, 1975. 457 pp.   (AB-3)

Beer has served as the President of the Operational Research Society and of the Society for General Systems Research. This strange but engaging book offers conventional prose on white pages (reprinted addresses and articles largely circa 1970-71), and unconventional "word groupings" (not poetry, Beer insists), on yellow, orange, and blue pages, in order to break our habits, for

"Man is a prisoner of his own way of thinking
and of his own stereotypes of himself
His machine for thinking
the brain
has been programmed to deal with a vanished world." (p.15)

The most recent and interesting address is "Fanfare for Effective Freedom:

Cybernetic Praxis in Government" (1973), which describes Beer's assistance to Salvador Allende's Chile before "the assassination/of a poor country/by the rich world." (p.453)
*** Fresh and well-meaning, but overly disjointed (e.g., no index or table of contents); brain food for advanced hippies.

388. BLAKELY, R.J. **Toward a Homeodynamic Society.** Boston: Center for the Study of Liberal Education for Adults, 1965. 54 pp. $1.50. (Notes and Essays on Education for Adults, no. 49)   (AB-4)

"This essay is an attempt to answer two big questions: 'What are the important social trends? What are their implications for education?'...The major trend of the present age is to increase knowledge and power. The major problem is the widening gap between knowledge and power and our ability to control them. The major implication is that our learning to control knowledge and power must overtake our learning to increase knowledge and power." (p. iii) In going on to advocate the homeodynamic, inventive society, Blakely distinguishes between three types of learning (hereditary-cultural, adaptive cultural, and inventive-cultural), and the necessary learning for the adult as parent, citizen, and worker.

389. JUNGK, Robert, "Toward an Experimental Society," **The Humanist,** 33:6, Nov/Dec 1973, pp. 39-41. (Special issue on "Images of the Future: The Twenty-First Century and Beyond," edited by Robert Bundy)   (AB-4)

An optimistic image of the future "based on the hope and the possibilities for human development." Advocates tapping the creativity buried in "Every-man," taming technology and making it responsive, the enhancement of human senses, real democracy with a new kind of town hall in every community, creative social planning, a medium for communicating and evaluating social experiments, and a yearbook of social experiments. Jungk recognizes that the experts will say that it cannot be done, but concludes that "In the difficult times ahead, we need imagination more than ever before."
*** Is imagination needed even to protect vested interests?

390. SACKMAN, Harold. **Mass Information Utilities and Social Excellence.** Princeton, NJ: Auerbach, 1971. 284 pp.   (A-4)

After a general discussion of computers and the public interest, and the status of man-computer experimentation, Chapter 11 outlines "Online Social Planning" in the hope that mass information utilities may revolutionize social planning as we understand it today by greatly increasing participation. This leads to "The Experimental Society" where mass information utilities, linked to real-time information bases in the public domain, enable the public to "scan the social scene, identify problems, contribute to social control and provide continuing corrective feedback on the interplay of pluralistic social experimentation." (p.257) This experimental ethos would of course require continuing lifelong information and education.
*** The assumptions that the public can learn and will learn are extremely optimistic. Still, the argument is interesting, and there is no harm in small-scale experimenting with "the experimenting society."

391. LEONARD, Eugene et al., "MINERVA: A Participatory Technology System," **Bulletin of the Atomic Scientists,** XXVII:9, Nov. 1971, pp. 4-12.   (A-4)

Outlines the components of a system ("Multiple Input Network for Evaluating Reactions, Votes, and Attitudes") that would enable large groups of dispersed citizens to regularly interact among themselves and with their leaders. Several access options are discussed, such as grafting MINERVA on to local networks financed by CATV operations. The authors, all on the staff of the Center for Policy Research, conclude that "There seems little doubt that MINERVA, or its experience-modified descendant, will be an integral part of the social-communication structure of those future societies which prove viable in the coming age of mass participation."

392. KARIEL, Henry S. **Open Systems: Arenas for Political Action.** Itasca,
     Ill.: F.E. Peacock, Loyola University Series in Political Analysis,
     1969. 148 pp.   (A-3)

A political scientist's essay on how we might "pry open" our personality systems, our social system, and our system for gaining scientific understanding. "Development is promoted by settings sufficiently open and challenging to encourage the individual to become equivocal and multidimensional--to become a person." (p.77)

393. STERN, Frederick Martin. **Life and Liberty: A Return to First Prin-**
     ciples. Foreward by Seymour Martin Lipset. NY: Thomas Y.
     Crowell, 1975. 212 pp. $7.95.   (A-4)

A polite call for more democracy sustained by enlightened citizens. The initial chapter, First Principles of an Organic Society, borrows biological principles to support the unarguable assertion that "To follow the pattern of life, a society ought to give the greatest possible freedom to internal pressures--the thoughts, wishes, and criticisms of its individual members. Spontaneity, diversity, and cooperation, the birthright of all living matter, are equally essential to the survival and prosperity of a nation." (p.9)
     Subsequent chapters discuss topics such as Two Theories on Ending Class (supplied by Tocqueville and Marx), Equality and Liberty Inseparable, Conflict and Authority, Pluralism and Productivity, and Depersonalization.
     Concludes with proposals for widening employment opportunities by reducing unjustifiable educational standards, increasing paraprofessional jobs, expanding cooperatives, reforming corporation laws (approving many of Ralph Nader's proposals), and an all-embracing system of administrative courts (beyond those advocated by the Hoover Commission in 1955 and similar to those operating in France and Germany).
     *** Reasonable as far as it goes, but the scope of necessary reform does
         not seem to be adequately appreciated. Gardner and Frankel go much
         further.

394. WILENSKY, Harold L. **The Welfare State and Equality: Structural and**
     Ideological Roots of Public Expenditures. Berkeley: University of
     California Press, 1975. 151 pp.   (A-3)

A sociologist's "first report" of a long-range comparative study of welfare states. "My main aim is to discover the structural and cultural determinants of the welfare state and to explain why rich countries, having adapted similar health and welfare programs, diverge sharply in their levels of spending, organization and administration of services and benefits, and styles of administration." (p.xi)
     "On the basis of a cross-sectional analysis of sixty-four countries I conclude that economic growth and its demographic and bureaucratic outcomes are the root cause of the general emergence of the welfare state..." (p. xiii)
     The final chapter, The Impact of the Welfare State on Real Welfare. examines both economic and noneconomic effects, as well as the conservative and radical criticisms of the welfare state. "Whatever their political persuasion,

critics of the welfare state share a tendency to select particular segments and programs, impute utopian goals to them (too often based on the agency's own exaggerated claims) and then conclude that the action falls short." (p.110)

Wilensky concludes that "the problem is to humanize the welfare state and make it more effective at a time when costs are climbing, and simultaneously to transform it into a welfare society that can cope with universal issues of civilized survival." (p.118)

*** Presumes affluence and its continuation, but otherwise a valuable survey.

395. DAHRENDORF, Ralf. **The New Liberty: Survival and Justice in a Changing World.** Stanford, Calif.: Stanford University Press, June 1975. 102 pp. $5.95. (A-4)

The 1974 BBC Reith Lectures delivered by a widely-known sociologist who is the Director of the London School of Economics. "The new liberty which we can hope and work for, is a liberal response to a world which is in a process of radical transformation." (p.4) In the advanced societies of the world, the dominant theme of progress and linear development appears to be spent. The new theme is still uncertain in its contours, but it is not a negation of growth; rather, it is improvement or qualitative development. "We are living in a period in which our potential for realizing human life-chances has outgrown the ways in which these life-chances are organized in our societies." (p.23) Human life-chances are what is considered here as liberty, and as mattering most in the world.

Dahrendorf objects to the two Club of Rome reports for being overly gloomy and exaggerating survival issues "to the point of obliterating the overwhelming significance of justice, and of liberty." (p.10) And for those who think that small is both beautiful and feasible ("a misplaced romanticism"), it is asserted that "large administrative facilities have become indispensable." (p.40)

The Improving Society is advocated, where walls are broken down between education, work, and leisure: the unnecessary cubicles of an inherited division of labor, and where public control and individual rights are recovered from bureaucracies. Steps in the right direction include a renovation of the international system (e.g., transforming the FAO into an effective instrument to insure global production and distribution of food), a new concept of public service that would provide for public services at all times via a public service contract, and sabbaticals for everybody.

*** Relatively little is suggested here, and "the new liberty" seems more to be a weak apology for the welfare state.

396. BELL, Daniel, "The Public Household--on 'Fiscal Sociology' and the Liberal Society," **The Public Interest,** No. 37, Fall 1974, pp. 29-68. (A-4)

A murky essay on political philosophy. In contrast to the domestic household and the market economy, there is now a third sector--more important than the two familiar ones: "which has come to the fore in the last 25 years, and which in the next 25 will play an even more crucial role, the public household." (p.29) This term, with connotations of family problems and common living, is preferred to the more neutral but more widely known terms of public sector or public finance (as expressed in government budgets).

"What is clear is that the revolution of rising expectations, which has been one of the chief features of Western society in the past 25 years, is being transformed into a **revolution of rising entitlements** in the next 25." (p.39, Bell's emphasis. Such a statement is not at all "clear," either as description or prescription.)

"The centrality of the public household in a modern interdependent society is inescapable." (p.48) Accordingly, Bell explores four issues that must be resolved in forming the political philosophy of the public household: the relevant units and the balances of rights among them, the tensions between liberty and equality, the balance between equity and efficiency, and the dimensions of the public and private spheres.

Concludes that "manifest destiny is shattered, the Americanism has worn thin, and only the hedonism remains. It is a poor recipe for national unity and purpose.

"Yet in trial and defeat--and there has been defeat--a virtue emerges: the possibility of a self-conscious maturity that dispenses with charismatic leaders, ideological doctines, and manifest destinies, and which seeks to re-define one's self and one's liberal society on the only basis on which it can survive. This basis must be created by conjoining three actions: re-affirmation of one's past...recognition of the limits of resources and the priority of needs...and agreement upon a conception of equity which gives all persons a sense of fairness and inclusion in the society...This would be a kind of social compact, but a social compact that, though renegotiated in the renewable present, does not, cannot, ignore the past." (p.68)

*** The End of Ideology (a sort of liberal utopia) rides again. This essay, somewhat expanded, appears as the final chapter in Bell's latest book, **The Cultural Contradictions of Capitalism** (see item no. 55a).

397. APTER, David E. **Choice and the Politics of Allocation: A Developmental Theory.** New Haven: Yale University Press, 1971. 212 pp. $7.95 (A-4)

On the relationship between development and order: "To identify systems of order that do not penalize development and patterns of development that do not jeopardize order is the object of this inquiry...Our immediate concern is with finding a suitable political framework for maximizing both these variables." (p.6)

Development (seen as expanding choice) is divided into two growth stages: industrialization and modernization (the dissemination of knowledge and the roles appropriate to it).

The final chapter, Toward a Socialist-Liberal Solution, views the future as a reconciliation system "in which decentralized planning rather than entrepreneurship will be characteristic." (p.201) It will be a "socialism of high participation by means of a rationalized bureaucracy combined with instrumental values," arising not from dramatic or revolutionary change, but from "the continuous transformation of the simple into the complex..." (p.203)

As for any alternative to this direction, "The suggestion to return to a simpler environment can be discounted as sentimental, similar to the attempt to found simple communes and New Harmonies in the face of an industrial way of life." (p.201)

*** A superficial characterization of the decentralist argument, and a confusion of description and prescription.

398. MOYNIHAN, Daniel P. **Coping: Essays on the Practice of Government.** NY: Random House, 1973. 430 pp. $10.00   (A-4)

A collection of 22 previously published papers, including "Bosses" and "Reformers": A Profile of the New York Democrats, The Case for a Family Policy, Traffic Safety and the Body Politic, The Crises in Welfare, The Education of the Urban Poor, The Politics of Stability, Liberalism and Knowledge, and Policy vs. Program in the 1970s.

These essays are prefaced by a notable piece of gobbledegook: "Long-range forecasting steadily becomes more rigorous and valuable. And yet the here-and-now and the close-at-hand are the dominant facts of public life, and the proper study of those who would take part in it. That the people must have vision I do not doubt; but what leaders need is foresight. That at least is the sum of my experience. Those I have respected most and most tried to emulate have not tried to think immensely far ahead, but only a little way ahead: their art is not that of prophesying, but of coping." (p.4)

*** There is no evidence that forecasting (which is **not** prophesying) has yet to become "more rigorous and valuable" and perhaps our leaders have been too much in the "here-and-now" which is why they are not adequately coping. One would hope for more bolder thought from Moynihan.

399. RAWLS, John. A Theory of Justice. Cambridge, Mass.: Belknap Press of Harvard University Press, 1971. 607 pp.   (A-3)

Very well-received by the academic community, this tome on political philosophy attempts "to generalize and carry to a higher order of abstraction the traditional theory of the social contract as represented by Locke, Rousseau, and Kent." (p.viii)
"The Concept of a Well-Ordered Society" (pp. 453-462) defines such a society as "one designed to advance the good of its members and effectively regulated by a public conception of justice." (p.453)
*** Academic chic in other contexts, this highly theoretical work is not of immediate relevance to considering societal directions and alternatives.

400. PFAFF, William. Condemned to Freedom. NY: Random House, 1971. 210 pp. $6.95.   (A-4)

Arising out of his work at the Hudson Institute, Pfaff describes in this murky essay not only a crisis of government and policy, but a refutation of certain fundamental assumptions about liberal politics. The New Populism and The New Left are seen as reflecting "The Burst Structures of Liberal Society."
"What is required, and constitutes the immense and honorable responsibility of political men, is radically intellligent and courageous reform of liberal politics...a radical liberalism, or a rational radicalism--or an existential radicalism." (p.193) The first need is to clear away obvious social and economic problems; then there has to be a reconsideration of the right structure of liberal government. "The crisis of liberalism comes out of the fact that we are condemned to freedom." (p.181)

401. ROSTOW, W.W. The Diffusion of Power: An Essay in Recent History. NY: Macmillan, 1972. 739 pp.   (AB-4)

A lengthy essay on continuity and change in the 1957-1972 period by the former Chairman of the Policy Planning Council at the Department of State and special assistant to President Johnson for national security affairs, now on the faculty of the University of Texas. The book is largely concerned with international affairs--particularly the diffusion of power away from Moscow and Washington--but there are also some observations on domestic affairs that should be noted.
"The central question on the international scene remains this: can the intimately interconnected world community of nations organize the diffusion of power in ways that lead to relatively stable peace; or will the diffusion of power lead to increasing violence and chaos?" Rostow employs a simplistic projection of per capita GNP to the year 2000 for the developed and less developed world, warning that "Advances through the stages of growth will not be smooth and uneventful for either the presently developed or less developed nations." (p.583) There is a recognition of the limits to growth argument with the forecast that "A new agenda of balance will gradually supersede the old agenda of uninhibited growth..." (p.583)
The last part of the book is entitled "The Present and the Future," with the final chapter devoted to The American Agenda. It is conducted that "Clearly, the most basic task of American society is to find its way to regular growth without inflation." (p.590) Rostow expresses confidence "that

the American political process is, in the widest sense, committed to act" (p. 591), and he advocates "a maturing of the American style." (p. 602) It is also necessary to strengthen the ability to find compromise between diverse groups and interests. "In domestic life the elaborate and subtle partnerships that already suffuse the working of American society require refinement--if possible, refinement where power and authority can be diffused to state and local institutions capable of bearing increased responsibility." (p.604)

An appendix definition of "The National Interest" states that "It is the American interest to maintain a world environment within which American society can continue to develop with the humanistic principles that are its foundation." (p.605)

*** The great depth of this essay is more than cancelled by the notable lack of breadth, e.g. the failure to pay any attention to multinational corporations. Rostow is one of "The Best and the Brightest" who mired our nation in the Vietnam war. His statement about the "humanistic principles" of our society indicates his continuing unwillingness or inability to distinguish principles from performance and intentions from reality. As for "The American Agenda," seldom has so little been said by one whose experience would seemingly prepare him to say something of importance.

402. CHASE, Stuart. **Goals for America: A Budget of Our Needs and Resources.** NY: Twentieth Century Fund, 1942. 134 pp.   (AB-3)

Part of a series (entitled "When the War Ends") of exploratory reports on postwar problems. The "Budget" is not a financial statement, but one of physical resources and requirements.

"Unemployment is the cancer of high-energy societies," (p. 11) and it is recommended that the Goal of Full Employment be pursued by finding new jobs "in the service trades." (p.109) In a statement that is still highly relevant today, Chase declares that "The democracies have got to find a permanent way to full employment, and a way to give their citizens a sense of function, of belonging to the community." (p. 12)

To satisfy the Goal of Survival, there must be adequate military protection, complete and final abolition of chronic unemployment, holding our natural resources at par, and minimum standards for the well-being of the entire population, expressed in a National Minimum Budget. Well-being is described in terms of The Big Five: food, shelter, clothing, health service, and education, and a chapter is devoted to each of these concerns.

*** Fresh and cogent thinking about problems that are still with us.

403. The Rockefeller Panel. **Prospect for America: The Rockefeller Panel Reports.** Garden City, NY: Doubleday, 1961. 486 pp.   (AB-4)

Six reports from the Special Studies Project of the Rockefeller Brothers Fund, organized in 1956 to define problems and opportunities in the next 10-15 years, to clarify national purposes and objectives, and to develop a framework of concepts and principles on which national policies and decisions could be based.

The reports of each panel were published separately in the 1958-1960 period, concerning foreign policy, military aspects of international security, foreign economic policy, and, domestically, economic and social aspects (including policies to promote growth and human welfare programs), the pursuit of excellence (on the educational system and uses of talent), and The Power of the Democratic Idea (on the ideals of democracy, consensus, civil liberties, pluralism, and the private sector).

The sanguine expectations of the time are well-reflected in the following: "With our growing population, our extraordinary record of rising productivity, the inherent dynamic in our free enterprise economy, there is every reason to face the future with full confidence that we shall measure up to the challenges that lie ahead." (p.333)

404. President's Commission on National Goals. **Goals for America: Programs for Action in the Sixties.** Administered by The American Assembly. Englewood Cliffs, NJ: Prentice-Hall, Spectrum Books, 1960. 372 pp.   (AB-3)

Comprises the Report of the Commission (pp. 1-31), and 16 chapters by individual authors, both "designed to encourage informed discussion."

The Report is divided between "Goals at Home" and "Goals Abroad." The former category concerns The Individual, Equality, The Democratic Process, Education, The Arts and Sciences, The Democratic Economy, Economic Growth, Technological Change, Agriculture, Living Conditions, and Health and Welfare. "Goals Abroad" concern Helping to Build an Open and Peaceful World, The Defense of the Free World, Disarmament, and The United Nations.

The chapters are as follows:
- Henry M. Wriston, "The Individual"
- Clinton Rossiter, "The Democratic Process"
- John W. Gardner, "National Goals in Education"
- Warren Weaver, "A Great Age in Science"
- August Heckscher, "The Quality of American Culture"
- Clark Kerr, "An Effective and Democratic Organization of the Economy"
- Herbert Stein and Edward F. Denison, "High Employment and Growth in the American Economy"
- Thomas J. Watson, Jr., "Technological Change"
- Lauren K. Soth, "Farm Policy for the Sixties"
- Catherine Bauer Wurster, "Framework for an Urban Society"
- Dr. James P. Dixon, Jr., "Meeting Human Needs"
- Mortin Grodzins, "The Federal System"
- Wallace S. Sayre, "The Public Service"
- William L. Langer, "The United States Role in the World"
- John J. McCloy, "Foreign Economic Policy and Objectives"
- William P. Bundy, "A Look Further Ahead"

405. LECHT, Leonard A. **Goals, Priorities, and Dollars: The Next Decade.** NY: The Free Press, 1966.   (A-3)

An initial effort by the National Planning Association Center for Priority Analysis to reconcile aspirations, suggested by the President's Commission on National Goals, with financial resources.

406. GORDON, Kermit (ed.) **Agenda for the Nation.** Washington: Brookings Institution, 1968. 620 pp.   (A-3)

An effort supported by a grant from the Ford Foundation and resulting in 18 essays on domestic and foreign affairs, "addressed to all who play a role in the formulation of public policy."

The essays on domestic concerns are as follows:
- Charles L. Schultze, "Budget Alternatives After Vietnam"
- James L. Sundquist, "Jobs, Training and Welfare for the Underclass"
- James Tobin, "Raising the Incomes of the Poor"
- Kenneth B. Clark, "The Negro and the Urban Crisis"
- Anthony Downs, "Moving Toward Realistic Housing Goals"
- James Q. Wilson, "Crime and Law Enforcement"
- Ralph W. Tyler, "Investing in Better Schools"
- Clark Kerr, "New Challenges to the College and University"
- Herbert Stein, "Unemployment, Inflation, and Economic Stability"
- Stephen K. Bailey, "Managing the Federal Government"

407. PERLOFF, Harvey S. (ed.) **The Future of the United States Government: Toward the Year 2000.** Prefaced by Daniel Bell. NY: George Braziller, May 1971. 388 pp. $7.50.   (AB-2)

A report from the Commission on the Year 2000 of the American Academy of Arts and Sciences, with 19 essays plus panel discussions, grouped in six categories.

In the Foreword, Daniel Bell discusses three structural changes in the U.S.: the creation of a national society, a communal society (with the growth of nonmarket public decision-making and the definition of social rights in group rather than individual terms), and a post-industrial society.

In the Introduction, Perloff outlines four groups of societal problems of primary concern to the government in the next decades: pressures on the individual, threats to internal cohesion of society, deterioration of the environment, and strains of world responsibility. "If American government is to cope effectively with future problems, it must reevaluate the philosophical bases for governmental policy and action, and reformulate organizational and operational principles." (p. 6) Moreover, there is the problem of "building a sufficiently strong base of general public understandng and participation to support the growing jurisdiction and power of government... Civic education should be greatly improved, but today it is the least understood and most neglected aspect of educational development." (p. 22)

I. **Rights and Values**
- Kenneth L. Karst, "Individual Rights and Duties in the Year 2000," advocates diversity, flexibility, and options.

II. **Promoting Civic Order and Political Cohesion**
- Harold Orlans, "The Fragmentation and Cohesion of Society," compares scenarios of fragmentation, amorality, and armed anarchy vs. a society of cohesion and civility.
- Matthew Holden, Jr., "The Future of Black-White Relations," argues that an American Apartheid is less improbable than a color-blind political community, but that a plural society of some sort is most probable.
- John G. Wofford, "Retaining Alienated Minorities in the Political Mainstream," focuses on blacks, upper middle-class youth, lower middle-class whites, and the anti-communist right, with a belief that the two-party system will survive into the 21st century.
- James L. Sundquist, "Politics in the Year 2000," projects an activist-conservative axis for the two parties unless disrupted by problems of race or foreign policy, as described in two "surprise" scenarios. Also comments on party attachment and alienation.
- John Voss, "Comment on 'Politics in the Year 2000'," views a decline of traditional ideologies and a weakening of party structures.

III. **United States World Responsibilities**
- Lester R. Brown, "The Nation-State, The Multinational Corporation, and the Changing World Order," approves of growing economic interdependence leading to closer political relationships.
- Herman Kahn, "The Military," sees military force as generally less central, and views it in four alternative contexts: an integrated and peaceful world, an inward-looking neo-isolationist world, a disarray world, and an uncontrolled arms race world.

IV. **Social Change and Adaptability of Governmental Institutions**
- Donald A. Schon, "Maintaining an Adaptive National Government," offers thoughts on managing the process by which new ideas come into good currency, and on the policy keyboard where problems cut across multiple policy areas.
- Robert R. Nathan, "Relations of the Public and Private Sectors," views the increase in total production and the rise in living standards as bringing about a modest degree of cooperation between government, business, and labor.
- James David Barber, "Some Consequences of Pluralization in Government," offers an excellent list of 17 impacts of pluralization

(or adding new units), all of which might lead to a government largely irrelevant to social concerns.

V. The Future of National Governmental Institutions

- Rexford G. Tugwell, "The Shaping of the Constitution for 2000," indicates the need for constitutional revision in either a deteriorating crisis-ridden society or in a progressive society. Proposals include new groupings of former states and a central government of six branches: political, planning, legislative, internal affairs, judicial, and the presidency.
- William M. Capron, "The Executive Branch in the Year 2000," offers ideas for intergovernmental relations and executive branch reorganization.
- Rep. John Brademas, "Congress in the Year 2000," discusses democratic participation, the policy-making and monitoring functions, and various reforms in management and the use of technology.

VI. The Future of Urbanism and of United States Federalism

- Martin and Margy Meyerson, "...The Quality of the Urban Environment," see a greater possibility for metropolitan government and other urban reforms if the total package of national, state and large-enterprise activity were to be reformulated.
- Rep. Henry S. Reuss, "State and Local Government," proposes a modernization act that would lead to fewer local governments, metropolitan government, the short ballot, decentralized democracy, and ombudsmen.
- Richard P. Nathan, "Intergovernmental Relations," provides a rich prescriptive scenario of decentralization (excepting nationalized welfare), with features such as functional flexibility grants, non-highway overhead aid, and Metro-Center aid.

407a. WOLFF, Robert Paul (ed.) **1984 Revisited: Prospects for American Politics.** NY: Knopf, 1973. 201 pp. $2.95, paper.   (ns)

"The six original essays demonstrate how an understanding of political and social realities reveals the probable shape of the future." (advt.)
- Todd Gitlin, "...How Young Activists Will Get to 1984"
- Gene L. Mason, "The Future of Repression"
- Robert T. Nakamura, "Congress Confronts the Presidency"
- Michael P. Lerner, "The Future of the Two-Party System in America"
- Ira Katznelson, "Urban Counterrevolution"
- Frances Fox Piven, "The Urban Crisis: Who Got What and Why"

408. U.S. Department of Health, Education, and Welfare. **Toward a Social Report.** Washington: U.S. Government Printing Office, 1969. 101 pp. $0.55.   (AB-3)

An attempt to systematically measure the social well-being of the United States, and an important preliminary step toward a regular system of social reporting. Seven areas were selected for initial study with the aid of existing data: health and illness, social mobility, physical environment, income and poverty, public order and safety, participation and alienation, and learning, science, and art.

Concluding comments on the development of policy accounts are particularly important because of potential contributions to "truly rational" decision-making. "Ultimately, we must integrate our social indicators into policy accounts which would allow us to estimate the changes in a social indicator that could be expected to result from alternative levels of expenditure on relevant public programs." (p. 101)

409. National Goals Research Staff. **Toward Balanced Growth: Quantity with Quality.** Washington: U.S. Government Printing Office, July 1970. 222 pp. $1.50.   (AB-3)

Outlines options open to policy-makers and the advantages and disadvantages of various actions in areas of population growth and distribution, environment, education, consumerism, technology assessment, basic natural science, and economic choices.

This report does not attempt to duplicate the efforts in **Toward a Social Report,** but seeks to be "a springboard for discussion and an aid to decision."

The central theme of "balanced growth" arises from the new awareness that growth in population, wealth, military strength, and scientific capability is not enough. "Yet our need is not to stop growth, but to redirect it...we need to refine and elaborate a concept of 'balanced growth,' and to develop the guidance mechanisms through which it can be achieved on a sustainable basis." (p. 23)

*** Perhaps overly generalized and vague, but an interesting and important beginning. Unfortunately, the National Goals Research Staff was disbanded shortly after publication of this report.

410. SCHULTZE, Charles L., with Edward K. HAMILTON, and Allen SCHICK. **Setting National Priorities: The 1971 Budget.** Washington: The Brookings Institution, 1970. $6.50; $2.95, paper.   (AB-3)

The first in a series of annual books by Brookings staff members that analyzes the major issues in the President's budget, outlines the alternative choices in each sector, and discusses costs and benefits of each alternative.

411. A **"Freedom Budget" for All Americans: Budgeting Our Resources, 1966-1975 To Achieve "Freedom From Want."** NY: A Philip Randolph Institute (217 West 125th. St.), revised edition, October, 1966. 84 pp. $1.00.   (AB-3)

A "fundamental approach to the elimination of poverty" generally endorsed by more than 200 signatories, including Daniel Bell, Richard A. Falk, John Kenneth Galbraith, Bertram M. Gross, Michael Harrington, Martin Luther King, Jr., Gunnar Myrdal, David Riesman, and Albert Shanker.

Poverty can "and therefore must" be abolished within ten years. The focus is on the Federal Budget because it is "the most powerful single instrument of national economic and social policy." (p. 8)

"The 'Freedom Budget' differs from previous worthy efforts to set forth similar goals because it fuses general aspirations with quantitative content, and imposes time schedules. It deals not only with where we must go, but also with how fast and in what proportions. It measures costs against resources, and thus determines feasible priorities. It is not only a call to action, but also a schedule for action." (Introduction)

The seven basic objectives are to restore full employment and maintain it, to assure adequate incomes for those employed, to guarantee a minimum income to all who cannot or should not be employed, to wipe out ghettos and provide a decent home for every family, to provide modern medical care and educational opportunity for all, to overcome other manifestations of neglect in the public sector (pollution, transportation, resource development), and to unite full employment with full production and high economic growth.

*** A useful device for articulating societal alternatives.

412. BENSON, Robert S. and Harold WOLMAN (eds.). **Counterbudget: A Blueprint for Changing National Priorities, 1971-1976.** Foreword by Sol M. Linowitz. Published for the National Urban Coalition. NY: Praeger, 1971. 348 pp. $8.95; $2.95, paper.   (AB-3)

The American malaise is seen as the distance between the national ideal and the national reality. To close this gap, the U.S. should pursue six major goals in the 1971-1976 period: 1) full employment; 2) equal opportunity to participate in American society; 3) providing basic necessities to all; 4) rectifying the imbalance in revenues between federal, state, and local governments; 5) assuring adequate national security; and 6) meeting obligations to assist in the economic development of the world's less developed nations.

To move toward these goals, there must be a reordering of budget priorities, an increase of revenues through more equitable taxation, and a reshaping of government to assure a more responsive and effective delivery of programs and services.

413. UDALL, Stewart L. **1976: Agenda for Tomorrow.** NY: Harcourt, Brace & World, 1968. 173 pp.   (BC-3)

The Secretary of the Interior in the Johnson administration proposes Project 76 as a commemoration of our bicentennial: "a vast project to make all our cities fair, and all our human relations amicable." (p. 83)

Project 76 would be formulated by a massive White House conference involving a wide variety of "eminently talented citizens." The entire political leadership would participate, and every community would be involved "in the drafting of a master plan to achieve the redesign and renovation of its entire environment no later than the year 2000." (p. 84)

In addition to the defense and elaboration of Project 76 in Chapter 5, there are other chapters describing "New Dimensions of Conservation" (such as a National Scenic Rivers System and a Council of Environmental Advisors), "Population, Parenthood, and the Quality of Life," and "The Renewal of Politics" (enabled in part through an annual national assessment).

In conclusion, Udall states that "I am convinced that the American experiment will falter unless our agenda for tomorrow embraces and includes goals and purposes as spacious and ennobling as those of the Founding Fathers." (p. 157)

*** An intriguing plan for action of Great Society dimensions.

414. ELDREDGE, H. Wentworth. **The Second American Revolution.** NY: Wm. Morrow, 1964; rev. ed., Washington Square Press, 1966. 402 pp.   (AB-3)

A sociologist explores the question of elite power and society, with chapters on traditional democracy in a revolutionary world, classical thoughts on rulers, man as seen by the behavioral sciences, social stratification, the upper class and the elite, Communism, fascism, the underdeveloped countries, and new sources of power (science, technology, the managerial revolution, and thought control). Concludes by promulgating Jefferson's concept of an aristocracy of talent. The Second American Revolution would be planful, with a powerful executive branch of government staffed by the best. "It is the contention here that a thorough rethinking of democratic ideology and structure based on sophisticated human and social models can lead to economic and political devices which can manage our world for humanistic goals..." (p. 336)

415. ROCKEFELLER, John D., 3rd. **The Second American Revolution: Some Personal Observations.** NY: Harper & Row, 1973. 189 pp. $6.50.   (BC-3)

A popular synthesis of contemporary liberal/humanist thinking by the Chairman of the U.S. Commission on Population Growth and the American Future and brother of Nelson Rockefeller. The basic view is that old patterns are breaking down and that change is necessary. Chapters discuss blacks, youth, the new values, etc., with an advocacy of organizational self-renewal, a humanistic capitalism, corporate responsibility, a giving society, a learning society, and a planning society. The final chapter lists five fundamental elements to a life of quality: human dignity, belonging, caring, each person attaining his full potential, and beauty.

416. SHEARER, Derek, "Dreams and Schemes: A Catalogue of Propsoals," **Working Papers For a New Society,** 3:3, Fall 1975, pp. 38-46.
                                                                (AB-2)
A very useful survey of bills, proposals and model laws for Congress to consider. "Taken as a whole, the list is a practical surrogate for the real platform the Democratic party will never write. It indicates what it may be possible to hope for from the elections of 1976." (pp. 38-39)
- Tax Reform: The Tax Justice Act of 1975 to close various loopholes.
- Full Employment: The Equal Opportunity and Full Employment Act of 1975 (the Hawkins-Humphrey Bill) to transform the U.S. Employment Service into the Job Guarantee Service.
- Controlling Corporations: a federal chartering bill is being drafted by Mark Green of the Nader Corporate Accountability Group; major provisions include corporate democracy, strict antitrust standards, corporate disclosure, and the rights of employees. Another complementary approach is to set up countervailing public economic power in the form of competitive public enterprise.
- Economic Planning: the Balanced Growth and Economic Planning Act of 1975 is considered by the author to be mild and relatively ineffective.
- Alternative Economic Development: a bill has been drafted by Ralph Nader and the Cooperative League of the U.S.A. to establish the National Cooperative Development Bank. Another major proposal is the Kennedy-Javits bill to create a National Community Development Banking system which would stimulate noncorporate economic development.
- Energy: a bill by Sen. Stevenson for a Federal Oil and Gas Corporation (FOGCO) to develop resources on federal lands. Also a Public Utilities Commission Act, being drafted by Sen. Metcalf, to mandate certain policies and structures.
- Food and Agriculture. The Farmer-Consumer Direct Marketing Act of 1975, introduced by Congressman Vigorito, would stimulate direct marketing of food. The Family Farm Act, sponsored by Sen. Abourezk, would prohibit large nonfarm corporations from engaging in agriculture. The Reclamation Lands Authority Act would redistribute federal land to small farmers and co-ops.
- Transportation. The Ground Transport Act, introduced by Sen. Kennedy, would change the dominant position of General Motors in public transportation. A model Railroad Nationalization Bill is being drafted by writer Michael Harrington.
- Banking and Credit: a model Consumer Credit Act has been drafted by the National Consumer Law Center.
- Community Control. The Neighborhood Government Act of 1975, sponsored by Sen. Hatfield, would give tax credits for individuals who allocate their federal tax payments to a neighborhood government corporation.
- Workplace Democracy: The Worker Alienation Research and Technical

Assistance Act, introduced by Sen. Kennedy in 1972, would take some
steps toward opening a national debate on humanizing jobs.
- Health Care: the National Health Rights and Community Service Act,
drafted by Congressman Dellums, is considered by the author as
the most far-reaching of the many national health insurance bills
now under consideration.
*** A valuable inventory suggesting a possible society of a few years hence.
This approach might be even more valuable if somehow joined with a
general inventory of long-term societal problems (e.g., Platt, no. 3).

417. REDBURN, Thomas, "A Platform for the Seventies," **The Washington
Monthly**, 6:8, October 1974, pp. 8-18.   (ABC-3)

Popularly written, cogent, and breezy, this lead article in a section
entitled "What Do We Do Next?" advocates the following:
- A negative income tax providing an income cushion for everyone.
- Abolishing social security in favor of a guaranteed income.
- Student loans to finance post-secondary education, via an Educational
Opportunity Bank.
- A new system of health care financing.
- Changes in the tax system (e.g. taxing all income equally) to encourage
competition.
- Abandoning the idea of prisons as rehabilitation centers and viewing them
simply as places for the punishment of infractions.
- Legalizing victimless crimes to free the courts and the police.
- Reducing the number of tenured positions in the civil service.
- A National Defense Railroad Act to create a genuinely effective rail
system.
- Dismantling aircraft carriers, cutting back the ratio of support to com-
bat troops, and abolishing the Reserves and the National Guard--
but maintaining an efficient fleet of Polaris submarines with nuclear
missiles, and modernizing the B-52.
- Developing a variety of small-scale energy sources, rather than placing
our fate "in the single salvation of nuclear power."
- Thinking seriously about world government and bypassing the United
Nations.
- Using food as a bargaining weapon in international relations.
- Abolishing the operations division of the CIA.
- Abolishing the USIA while expanding and internationalizing the Peace
Corps to work on small-scale agricultural and educational projects
and help settle tribal disputes.
*** Good ideas for any political platform or civic discussion group.

417a. AULETTA, Ken, "An Agenda to Save Our City: 44 Proposals That
Could Help Turn This Town Around," A Special Report, **New York**,
9:12, March 22, 1976, pp. 39-54.   (ABC-3)

There are three interrelated agendas here: for the city itself, the state
of New York, and the U.S. Government.
The Agenda for the City makes 22 proposals, including scrapping the
three-year fiscal plan, balancing the budget, reconstituting management
(by reforming civil service, abandoning seniority, etc.), drafting a plan
for economic development, selective tax reductions to make the city competitive with other locations, changing rent control laws, expanding tourism,
legalizing sports and casino gambling, and reducing the disparity between
the 7.4% of federal tax income that the city gives and the 5.5% of the aid
that is returned to state and local government.
The Agenda for the State advances 12 proposals, including a state bank,
a state small business administration, regional taxes, a state energy policy,
and changes in the state aid formula for education.

The Agenda for Washington includes compelling states to cooperate regionally, a new federal welfare policy, national health care, improving mass transportation, funding more public works and jobs, a federal urban bank to make low-interest loans for economic development projects, a national energy policy, and a tax break for tenants.

It is concluded that the city's crisis teaches the limitations of what government can do, as the Depression taught the lessons of unfettered free enterprise. "My own candidates for the most dangerous people in New York today are those who ignore the facts of this city's predicament. That includes city or state officials who would still dare to drape their revenue projections around false assumptions--creating still new deficits--or who only complain about what the federal government can do while neglecting what they must do." (p. 54)

418. HAMILL, Pete, "Welfare Must Be Abolished," **The Village Voice,** September 29, 1975, pp. 7-8.   (ABC-3)

A fresh polemic based on seeing the cost of welfare as the true cause of New York City's fiscal crisis. More than a million people are on welfare, costing almost a billion dollars in direct handouts and close to $5 billion in services such as police, fire, schools, and hospitals.

"At the very least, the federal government must do the following:" 1) assume the real cost of welfare in the city for a three-year period; 2) establish day-care centers to free a large number of welfare mothers for employment; 3) create a massive jobs program for the city with emphasis on goods-producing industries set up on the principle of worker control; and 4) setting a deadline for abolishing welfare. The goods to be produced would be geared to the needs of the city: automobiles designed for city use (possible steam-powered), three new subway systems, 20-30 story greenhouses for truck farm crops, and a fair share of modern smokeless industry.

Funding for this program could be raised by cutting off all aid to dictatorships, an excess profits tax on oil and gas companies, chopping $40 billion out of the $106 billion Department of Defense budget, reducing the CIA budget, and tying highway funds into the development of mass transport systems.

Hamill concludes by noting that New York sends the federal government $16 billion a year in tax revenue and gets back only $3 billion. If the federal government does not act, then Mayor Beame should declare the Republic of New York. "Given our own money--that $16 billion a year--we could do all of the above ourselves." (p. 8)

419. BUCKLEY, William F., Jr. **Four Reforms--A Guide for the Seventies.** NY: G.P. Putnam's Sons, 1974. 128 pp. $4.95.   (A-4)

America's best-known conservative writer argues for the following: 1) A Sensible Welfare System, with social welfare benefits redistributed among states. 2) A Simplified Tax, including a complete overhaul of the Federal tax system, imposing a uniform tax of 15% on all income, and eliminating all progressive features. 3) Noncoerced Education, amending the constitution to allow public aid to nonpublic schools. 4) Speedier Justice, through repealing the Fifth Amendment against self-incrimination in order to reduce crime.
*** This skimpy list is not integrated into any overall vision, and can hardly serve as "A Guide for the Seventies" for any political interest. It should be noted, though, that the reforms are proposed in a piecemeal form that is relevant to the realities of the legislative process. It also helps to have a brother in the U.S. Senate!

420. SCHLESINGER, James R., "A Testing Time for America," **Fortune,** 93:2, February 1976, pp. 75 ff.   (AB-3)

The former U.S. Secretary of Defense, dismissed in November 1975, describes the growing specter of Soviet hegemony, arguing that "at no point since the 1930's has the Western world faced so formidable a threat to its survival." (p. 75)

Americans take security for granted, but the U.S. is seen as the only potential counterweight to the military and political power of the Soviet Union. Trade is no panacea. The Soviets now outspend the U.S. in virtually all major categories of defense activity, and these estimates are probably understated. The USSR has been increasing its military expenditures in real terms at 3% or more per year, while U.S. expenditures have been shrinking at about the same rate.

"Undoubtedly, in the existing political climate, many people really do not want to know the facts. Acceptance that the balance is indeed tipping implies difficult decisions." (p. 149) As the military balance continues to tip, there will be a rising level of risk, and a growing reliance on early recourse to nuclear weapons--a poor man's strategy because of its low cost.

"The deterioration of the military balance both draws upon and contributes to the loss of will. In that loss of will--with all that it reflects regarding the decline of confidence and moral stamina--lies the not-so-hidden crisis of Western civilization...Without enduring American strength, Western civilization will not survive." (p. 153)

*** A narrow argument that does not consider world order possibilities, but an important and disturbing view that will not go away and has major implications for societal directions and alternatives as expressed in the federal budget.

421. McCARTHY, Eugene J. **The Hard Years: A Look at Contemporary America and American Institutions.** Introduction by Tom Wicker. NY: Viking/A Richard Seaver Book, Oct. 1975. $8.95. 229 pp.
                                                                          (C-4)

Rambling and disconnected thoughts by the former U.S. Senator from Minnesota, occasional Presidential candidate, and poet (three poems are included here).

The analysis of contemporary America is not very deep or original, nor are the proposals. McCarthy advocates depersonalizing the Presidency ("We do not need Presidents who are bigger than the country, but rather ones who will speak for it and support it."), more concern in the selection of the Vice-President, more responsible political parties, universities being apart from society, abandoning the cult of the expert, and one system of justice for all Americans. Elements of needed corporate reform include greater freedom for corporate employees, making corporations operate within the law, imposing certain social responsibilities, and re-examining the political power of corporations.

To improve the economy, there should be limited wage/price controls, selective credit controls, selective excise taxes, selective use of investment credit and accelerated depreciation, a partial subjection of the Federal Reserve Board to Treasury policy, elimination of unnecessary military expenditures, and elimination of waste in the nongovernmental economy.

Comments are also made on matters such as the military, the CIA, lobbyists, language and politics, poetry and war, intellectuals and politics, and censorship.

422. RIBICOFF, Sen. Abraham. **America Can Make It!** NY: Atheneum, 1972. 242 pp.   (C-4)

Chapters on America's Present Condition (frustration and loss of confi-

dence), school integration, housing, the working class, welfare and poverty, the individual in society, and the economy (advocating joint long-range planning by government and industry, and new mechanisms to promote technological progress). Touching all bases, Ribicoff states that we must maintain a credible defense posture while reordering domestic priorities, concluding that "Our challenge today is to bring together idealism and workable solutions to our problems. I believe we can do it. If so, America can make it." (p. 242)
*** Rather doubtful with both the idealism and the solutions offered here. Less cheerleading and more homework is needed.

423. ROGOW, Arnold A. **The Dying of the Light: A Searching Look at America Today.** NY: G.P. Putnam's Sons, 1975. 384 pp. $10.00.   (AB-4)

A rambling and verbose tour of American culture by a CUNY political scientist, with chapters such as The Decline of the Superego, Political Economy and Other Cruelities, Phallic Culture, City Blues, The Uses of Crime and Violence, The Pursuit of Suburbia, and The Abdication of One-Eyed Kings. Of all the developments mentioned, "I view the decline of the superego and the conflict between hedonism and scarcity as the most threatening to the future of Western civilization." (p. 13)
"But while I regard the light that once blazed so brightly, that once was hailed as a beacon to the world, as a dying light, I do not think of it as dead. Not yet." (p. 16) The future of American democracy is seen as depending on our willingness to settle for less, and a standard liberal litany follows about what could be done to make a more egalitarian world and just society. We could divert wealth to the poor by reducing military expenditures and diverting capital and labor to rebuilding cities and creating low-cost public housing. Money incentives could promote integration. The only other option is a garrison state.
"The vital questions for the future are not whether there are to be restrictions, but by what methods these restrictions are to be decided upon and to whom and in what manner they will be applied." (p. 323)

424. RIESELBACH, Leroy (ed.) **People vs. Government: The Unresponsiveness of American Institutions.** Bloomington: Indiana University Press, 1975. 384 pp. $15.   (ns)

Essays on the Presidency, Congress, the Supreme Court, the federal bureaucracy, state and local government, the military, and the police. The lead essay by Rieselbach is entitled "An Unresponsive America."

425. CANTY, Donald. **A Single Society: Alternatives to Urban Apartheid.** NY: Praeger, 1969. 181 pp.   (C-4)

Focuses on the slums and ghettos of the cities, arguing that there is a "lack of national will to change the trend toward further division and discord." The goal of a single society requires a national policy of building choice and helping the disadvantaged to catch up.

426. SLOMICH, Sidney J. **The American Nightmare.** NY: Macmillan, 1971. 285 pp.   (AB-3)

A deep and eloquent critique by a political scientist who has worked for the CIA and in Army think tanks. Concerns include the flight from responsibility (which has led to "a massive assault on the future"), the fragmentation of work and living patterns, the politics of death, space exploration, final solutions, the military megabureaucracy, suburbia as a gadget, the mechanization of political science and scientism in general, and "the dybbuk of technological obsession."

The Politics of Humanism is proposed: a cluster of policies essential for our survival, including a weapons moratorium, arms control and disarmament, a supranational legal and political order, an intensive long-term national dialogue in open forums, and public education in foreign affairs. Domestically, necessary programs include mass transit, land banks and open spaces, diverse communities, people living near work wherever possible, strict regulations on vehicles, rigid pollution programs, reforming education to include a politics of humanism, humanizing bureaucracy, metropolitan government, interstate compacts, restoration of historical perspectives, and a President who seeks to arouse the best in America.

"A universal social order, if it comes about, will be reached through the politics of power, which is the politics of balance of power, and through the recognition of common human purpose among men. It is this that the technological obsession obscures in our vision of others and destroys in our vision of ourselves." (p. 238)

"The hope of this nation, that of any nation, is its people. You are that hope. The entire system of expertise and secrecy designed to prevent the people of this country from determining their own destinies is basically a fake." (p. 284)

"A democratic politics of humanism...will value community and interrelationships among men, subject technique and power to quality and purpose, promote regionalism, conduct a politics of dialogue, restrict bureaucratic nihilism and corporate secrecy, and eliminate industries and economic and bureaucratic institutions and practices antithetical to the country's ecologic health and democratic purposes." (p. 239)

*** Notably comprehensive in diagnosis of domestic and global difficulties, and in the prescriptions offered.

427. WHEELER, Harvey, **The Politics of Revolution.** Berkeley: The Glendessary Press, 1971. 305 pp. $6.95.   (AB-3)

A Senior Fellow at the Center for the Study of Democratic Institutions takes a broad view of politics "similar to that of the ancients, for whom politics was the architectonic science." The book concerns the American Revolution of the 1970's, with revolution defined as "the dialectic of two competing cultural systems warring against each other in the same society" (p. 9) and as a condition of systemic rather than incremental change. "Revolutionary crisis has the function of revealing the inadequacy of mere reform and demonstrating the necessity for overall structural, or revolutionary, transformation." (p. viii)

Chapters and sections of chapters are devoted to the limits of confrontation politics, the rise and fall of Marxist ideology, the rise and fall of American liberal democracy, the obsolescence of the American party system, and the nature of the "Intentional Society" that is advocated (with particular emphasis on its necessarily revised constitution).

The era of the "Learning Society" is technologically possible today. But it is not only media alone, but the proper content: "a new science of politics combining ecology, information theory and dynamic programming, all brought together in an organic or biology-oriented framework, rather than in a mechanistic one. Beyond this we shall have to devise an applied political science capable of transmitting this ecological wisdom to the average citizen for rational and deliberate application at the polls." (p. 36)

Dangers are noted, however, and the book concludes with a discussion of "The Manipulative Spector," as contrasted with the prospects for "A New Age of Wisdom."

428. RASKIN, Marcus G. **Notes on the Old System: To Transform American Politics.** NY: David McKay, Fall 1974. 180 pp. $6.95.   (A-4)

An "attempt to describe some of the workings of the American System" by the co-director of the Institute for Policy Studies. The governing principles of American life, serving as a "handbook for tyranny," are that everything is for sale, people are innately selfish and individualistic, and that the state has a mandate to act as "moral legislator" for all of its citizens. "In the modern-day United States, neither a democracy nor a republic exists in operation. The state helps the powerful." (p. 4)

After several chapters on the presidency and Nixon in particular, the evolution to the present state of affairs is described in terms of three stages: 1) class law protecting growth of American capitalism; 2) para-law and the national security state, enabling high levels of military spending; and 3) the Leader-Commander State where law is made by whim and command, as in the Nixon administration.

A new stage is advocated where authority, responsibility, and the law are located in the people, and where there is open debate of presently-hidden questions. Raskin proposes the use of grand juries (several to be located in each congressional district) as forums of investigation and debate to stimulate the consciousness of the people.

*** A somewhat thin vision of means and ends.

428a. ROELOFS, H. Mark. **Ideology and Myth in American Politics.** Boston: Little, Brown, March 1976. c.220 pp.   (ns)

Views congenital problems of American government and concludes that there will be no revolution or fundamental reform.

429. BEAM, George D. **Usual Politics: A Critique and Some Suggestions for an Alternative.** NY: Holt, Rinehart and Winston, 1970. 196 pp.   (AB-4)

A political scientist at the University of Illinois at Chicago Circle feels that if any country has the possibility for developing the good and free life, it is the United States.

"Why has this promise not been realized? It is my contention that part of the answer is linked to a concept of politics that mitigates against the sort of thinking and action necessary to achieve the good and free society. This concept of politics I call 'usual politics.' It is ably captured in Madison's **Federalist** No. 10, which defines the good society by its procedures rather than by its attainment of certain goals and values. These procedures are group conflicts that result in balance and in compromise, and certain institutional arrangements, such as separation of powers and federalism. The assumption is made that these procedures are the good and free life and that they operate in a neutral manner to assure the best possible society." (p. v) But the usual politics of groups in balance is not a neutral process, and usual politics centers too much attention on social pluralism and voting as the means for dealing with power and preference.

The final third of the book sketches the proposed alternative of "New Politics." Such an alternative depends on "the modification or destruction of the deterministic world view," which is presently seen as permeating the whole range of political discussion. "What is needed is an explication which, while recognizing the limits of all human action, calls attention to the reality of options and the means for bringing them to fruition." (p. 147) An alternative set of concepts is needed that gives to questions of value and reform techniques "the same status and legitimacy as the questions relating to empirical data and system maintenance." (p. 149)

In the final chapter, Beam rejects liberalism, the right, and traditional radicals (including the New Left). New Politics is committed to the goals of the good life and "begins with the values of freedom and individual development as bases for evaluating the existing procedures." (p. 186) It is "action in gear with reality," with different strategies for insiders and outsiders. It is "a contemporary revolution of the whole--an administrative, mili-

tary, and economic revolution" (p. 188), but it is not necessarily mass-based politics.
*** A rather academic exercise, quoting only political scientists, and directed more to a fairly useful critique of political science than of politics. No comments are made on how New Politics is to be brought about, and politics and political science continue as usual.

430. LOWI, Theodore J. **The End of Liberalism: Ideology, Policy, and the Crisis of Public Authority.** NY: Norton, 1969. 322 pp.   (A-3)

A self-confessed "polemic" by a political science professor at the University of Chicago: "its principal target is the modern liberal state itself, its outmoded ideology, and its delf-defeating policies."
"The corruption of modern democratic government began with the emergence of interest-group liberalism as the public philosophy." (p. 287) Interest-group liberalism cannot plan, cannot achieve justice, weakens democratic forms and power, and produces an apologetic political science. Lowi advocates a "radical platform" leading to Juridicial Democracy. This would involve restoring the rule of law, rule of law by administrative formality, the fostering of a "truly independent and integrated administrative class"--a Senior Civil Service, restoring regional government, expanding fiscal policy as an instrument of control, and a tenure-of-statutes act.

431. FERKISS, Victor. **The Future of Technological Civilization.** NY: George Braziller, 1974. 369 pp. $12.50.   (AB-2)

An important and well-written "exercise in utopian thinking" by a Professor of Government at Georgetown University. The four sections of the books are devoted to a criticism of the ruling ideology of liberalism, the development of a new political philosophy of ecological humanism, sketching some of the elements of a planetary society governed by ecological humanism, and describing how we will get there from here.
In Part I, Liberalism and Beyond, Ferkiss distinguishes between pre-modern, modern, and post-modern stages, and it is argued that the modern era is drawing to a close. The on-coming society will be a technological society, but to be viable, it must regard economic and technological growth as merely instrumental values. There will be no escape from "the all-pervading influence of technology" and to meet the needs of growing population, "an increasingly complex system of management and communications will be required." (p. 17) The major problem is that we face many physical and social threats, but we are still subjected to the power of outmoded but entrenched ideas--the philosophy of liberalism which holds that the principle purpose of human society is to increase individual self-aggrandizement. "The only hope lies in a revolution in political philosophy." (p. 6)
There is an extensive description of the philosophical foundations of liberalism, with particular emphasis on Locke, as well as the triumph and decay of American liberalism. "One of our difficulties as a people in coming to grips with our current problems is that, having no adequate, accepted, popularized name for our current system, we continue to mouth the ideals and ideas of the past; though knowing in our hearts they are meaningless, we are unable or fear to give the new reality a new name. Perhaps the best term for it is neoliberalism...It differs from traditional liberalism...in that the competitors for power and profit are now no longer individuals but organized groups..." (p. 44) This is described by some as pluralism, but Ferkiss deftly points out the biases in such a view, arguing that, new or old, liberalism has failed because it is historically outmoded.
Chapter 6 criticizes alternative philosophies as "Roads to Nowhere." Radical liberalism (or reform liberalism) places more emphasis on equality and less on materialism, but fails to recognize the extent of the necessary changes in consciousness, while lacking a vision of the good society because

of the focus on means rather than ends. Today's conservatism, embracing the liberal capitalist tradition, is "a futile and tawdry political movement" largely composed of "liberals in flimsy disguise." Conservatism "in the name of patriotism and loyalty is committing treason against the American earth and the American community." (p. 67) Socialism is also inadequate, and Ferkiss criticizes Marx and Engels and their modern American heir, Michael Harrington, who is seen as holding inadequate views on controlling technology and unreal visions of the coalition between labor and the new working class. The New Left has had only limited theoretical success and has been a practical political failure. Anarchists, including ecoanarchists such as Murray Bookchin, offer a responsible critique of technology but hold romantic notions of laissez-faire. Additional comments are aimed at Lewis Mumford, Charles Reich, Jean-Francois Revel, Theodore Roszak, Jacques Ellul, Reinhold Niebuhr, and Walter Lippmann.

Part II proposes ecological humanism as the necessary political philossophy for technological man after an extensive discussion of political philosophy, and its tasks of dealing with definitions of man, the universe as it affects man, and the relationship between man's values and the way in which the universe works. To be meaningful for our time, a philosophy must be universally relevant and capable of being incarnated. Among many matters discussed here are human needs in social perspective and the common good, and a broader definition of freedom which recognizes that whatever affects our future qualifies our freedom.

Part III describes the politics, economics, and culture of the humane society governed by ecological humanism, although consciously avoiding great detail. Such a society is above all an active learning society, constantly creating new patterns of equilibrium. Political intelligence is adequate to cope with the problem of information overload, and there is adequate political will to act. The economy will be planned, with equalized economic well-being and control of technology, all governed by a new and more realistic economic theory. There would be cultural pluralism, freedom of speech, rational majority rule, planetary patriotism, and human self-actualization. The role of today's multinational corporations in such a society of the future is not described.

Part IV describes--very unconvincingly--how ecological humanism will come about. A revolution is seen as necessary, the "The revolution will come into being when a sufficient number of people recognize that the future cannot be a simple projection of the past but requires a conscious choice between liberation and destruction." The revolution must be led by technological man, who will be "inspired by a philosophy based on naturalism, holism and immanentism--the philosophy of ecological humanism." (p. 264. This is described in Ferkiss' previous book on **Technological Man**. Braziller, 1969.) Most technological men and women will necessarily come from the ranks of the middle class.

The revolution will be a non-violent, open conspiracy, a piecemeal process of creeping convergent revolution, a process of social learning and self-conscious evolution. It will not be centrally directed, and, rather than dropping out, ecological humanists will work for change within the system. This strategy will require both dedication and sophistication. "The advantage of those committed to ecological humanism will be their superior perception of the significance of what is happening and their superior awareness of how what they and others are doing is shaping the future..." (p. 272) A cultural war will be waged against nationalism, militarism, addiction to consumer goods, philosophical dualism, and psychological rigidity. Ecological humanists "will aim at results rather than emotional catharsis." (p. 273, author's emphasis.) Above all, they will be futurists, in the best sense of the word. This revolution must also create a global political system and a steady-state world, which would be the basis for new adventures in human development.

*** Ferkiss is one of the very few widely-read authors. His unannotated bibliography of 700 books and 500 articles is impressive, as is his critique of many of the authors that he cites. Although more sophisticated, Ferkiss is much like Alvin Toffler in the breadth of his integrative prowess and his faith in the middle class. There is also a bit of Charles Reich reflected in Ferkiss' faith in "The Immanent Revolution"--indeed, Ferkiss makes two references to Reich's greening of America as "prematurely heralded" (pp. 20 and 268).

But Ferkiss is subject to many of the flaws that he finds in others. Perhaps his most fatal flaw is his faith that technological man, with his sophistication, superior perception, and steady aim at results in shaping the future, has arrived or will arrive in sufficient numbers in sufficient time. Unfortunately, many ecological humanists (conventionally known as liberals) are politically inept, and have no sense whatsoever about results. Until this fact can be dealt with, the revolution of technological man is just another romantic notion. The book nevertheless warrants consideration as a successor and improvement on Toffler and Reich.

432. BAHM, Archie, "Demo-speci-ocracy," **Policy Sciences,** 3:1, March 1972. pp. 97-106.   (A-3)

"Demospeciocracy is a new system of government designed to combine the advantages of both democracy and specialization. It aims not only to sustain but to revive and promote the now-sagging virtues of democracy by providing more people with greater incentive to vote, and vote intelligently. It seeks to restore power to legislate directly into the hands of the voter, in contrast to the current indirect system delegating such power to representatives. But it also proposes to adapt the methods of science and technology to settling questions of public policy." (p. 97)

After discussing six assumed principles, nine basic and necessary agencies are proposed for the system, involving initiators, steerers, researchers, informers, examiners, voting supervisors, planners, judges, and administrators.

It is hoped that demospeciocracy might get started by some political unit willing to try it out on an experimental basis, perhaps with foundation support.

433. SNEED, Joseph D. and Steven A. WALDHORN (eds.) **Restructuring the Federal System: Approaches to Accountability in Postcategorical Programs.** NY: Crane, Russak, 1975. 261 pp. $16.00.   (ns)

434. CALIFANO, Joseph A., Jr. **A Presidential Nation.** NY: W.W. Norton, Sept. 1975. 338 pp. $9.95.   (AB-2)

A thoughtful essay by the former Special Assistant for Domestic Affairs to President Johnson on the growth of presidential power: "As a result, we approach the final decades of the twentieth century more as a presidential nation than as a republic of deliberately fragmented power." (p. 5) If we fail to take any action, the forces now at play in our society will give more power to the president.

Chapters examine the executive branch, Congress as the "separate but unequal branch," relationships with governors and mayors ("Caesar among Centurions"), the media, special interests, the courts, and presidential personality.

The final chapter offers a number of important proposals for reform. A Presidential Powers Impact Statement Act, similar to environmental impact statements, would "require the Congress and the executive branch to analyze the impact of each significant new legislative program or administrative action on the powers of the presidency." (p. 283) Legislation is also proposed to require that certain specific reports accompany the president's State of the Union messages, which are seen as "optimistic sermons."

Presidents should also be required to present an annual National Posture Statement "with reports that provide a specific measure of his branch's performance against legislative programs enacted by the Congress and promises the president has made about these programs." (p. 286) The reports would project the five-year costs of all domestic program decisions, set forth the basis for selecting one alternative over another, and estimate the financial and social costs of failure to pursue a particular program.

Other suggestions include the indication of costs in all presidential messages to Congress, candidates estimating the costs of fulfilling their campaign promises, public financing of elections, a six-year term for the president with possibilities for re-election (in that it takes this period of time to set programs into motion), four-year terms for Congressmen, higher pay for Congressmen so as to reduce the potential for corruption, and a vast executive reorganization into functionally oriented departments.

These suggestions are aimed toward restoring credibility and integrity. "The president and the Congress have repeatedly refused to act in accordance with their own rhetorical and legislative commitments." (p. 289) These exaggerated promises have been debilitating to the fabric of American society.

*** Some modest but very important suggestions.

434a. DIMOCK, Marshall E. **The New American Political Economy: A Synthesis of Politics and Economics.** NY: Harper and Bros., 1962. 306 pp. (A-3)

"Political economy is the pursuit of the better life through a wise admixture of institutions and voluntarism. It involves a vivid awareness of the concept of the public interest, which it makes the ultimate regulator of public policy." (p. viii)

After discussing a number of policy decisions relevant to the domestic economy, competitive balance, foreign policy, and husbanding natural and human resources, Part III argues for fundamental government reforms such as a decentralization of federal functions, the eventual establishment of regional governments, and an 8-man inner executive group to make the Presidency effective.

435. HARDIN, Charles M. **Presidential Power & Accountability: Toward a New Constitution.** Chicago: The University of Chicago Press, 1974. 257 pp. $7.95. (ns)

"A proposal for effective realignment in the balance of power between the President and Congress and between the federal government and the people. A book to raise public consciousness of the need for profound constitutional change. An affirmation of belief that American democracy can not only survive such change but can be strengthened by it." (advt.)

436. BALDWIN, Leland D. **Reframing the Constitution: An Imperative for Modern America.** Santa Barbara, Calif.: American Bibliographical Center-Clio Press, 1972. 145 pp. (A-3)

In order to encourage more effective and flexible government, an historian draws on the best of the American and British systems, proposing "changes relevant enough to promise a solution to our problems, but not radical enough to destroy our traditional democratic ideals." (p. x) The changes are grouped in four categories:

1. Larger and more viable States. Fifteen states are proposed, each with a reasonable degree of topographical, historical, cultural, and economic affinity: Alleghenia (Pennsylvania through Northern Virginia, with Washington D.C. no longer a Federal district), Appalachia, California (essentially Southern California), Chicago, Deseret, Erie, Hawaii, Mississippi, Missouri, New England (including upstate New York), New York

(including parts of Connecticut and New Jersey), Oregon (possibly including Alaska), Savanna (essentially the deep South), Sierra (northern California), and Texas.
2. Less separated powers. Congress would become a unicameral body of 200 members elected to five-year terms. The Senate would be reconstructed as a separate court of last resort and board of censors and ombudsmen presided over by a Chief Justice who would also serve as titular Chief of State, thus relieving the President of part of his great burden.
3. The party system. Parties would be made more responsible and responsive. The party electing a plurality of Congressmen would also win the Presidency. The office of Vice-President would be abolished.
4. Overcoming the problems of majority rule.
The book is concluded with a Revised Constitution of the United States comprised of nine Articles
*** Several interesting notions worthy of consideration.

437. SALE, Kirkpatrick, "One Nation, Divisible," **Newsweek**, November 17, 1975, p. 15.   (C-4)

Observes that our country is "too elephantine" and that it might be divided into five new nations, each with 40 million people.

438. SMART, Ian, "The Advanced Societies: Revolution or Devolution?" **International Journal**, 27:3, Summer 1973, pp. 403-417.   (A-4)

Discusses secession **in situ,** which is a form of devolution rather than revolution. The post-industrial stage of societal development is seen as enhancing prospects of devolutionary secession as governments are found incompetent. "Something might conceivably be done to recreate and legitimize an option of controlled secession through mobility within the government's overall jurisdiction, by allowing people to choose freely between alternative sub-jurisdictions: a type of regionalization to accommodate political, rather than ethnic, groups." (p. 417)

439. HAMILL, Pete, "Don't Tread on Us: New York Should Secede From the Union," **The Village Voice**, June 23, 1975, pp. 13-15.   (ABC-3)

Like all colonies, New York has a severe balance of payments deficit. The time is now ripe to revolt and declare the Republic of New York. A governmental structure would be created similar to that of Switzerland, and the city would be a free port similar to Hong Kong. Everyone would donate one day of work each week to rebuilding the city, in the pursuit of a single goal of a humane state. The most rational system of operation would be one of democratic socialism.

440. TOFFLER, Alvin, "Secession Shock: It's Later Than You Think," **The Village Voice**, August 14, 1975, pp. 20 ff.   (C-4)

A hearty affirmation of Hamill's "splendidly imaginative" article, a "brilliant polemic...(that) should stir enormous controversy."
This impulse for secession is placed in the context of Toffler's vision of the emergence of super-industrial civilization. "Now, for the first time, there exists the opportunity to create an Urban Federation--a kind of quasination made up of largely noncontiguous cities banded together to challenge the centralized power of the federal government and its voracious tax collectors." (p. 23)

441. AXLINE, Andrew W. et. al. (eds.) **Continental Community? Independence and Integration in North America.** Toronto: McClelland and Stewart, 1974. 302 pp.   (A-4)

Twelve essays written primarily by political scientists. Very academic and narrow.

442. MUIR, John. **The Velvet Monkey Wrench.** Santa Fe, New Mexico: John Muir Publications (P.O. Box 613), 1973. 246 pp. $3.00, paper. (BC-3)

The author of a popular Volkswagen repair manual ascends to grander matters: "a blueprint for a consentual (sic.) society." The language is mangled throughout by use of the informal hippie argot, with expressions such as "dig," "OK," "a gas," "groovy," "like," and "you gotta." But the advocated "People's Establishment" or "the new Establishment" is highly detailed in many respects, and the R. Crumb-like cartoon illustrations by Peter Aschwanden, although not particularly relevant to the text, are uniquely charming. Muir, incidentally, is not to be confused with the fabled naturalist of the same name.

The principles underlying the proposed vision are multi-valued lives, living without contention, maximum unemployment (there is plenty of work to be done, but automation will allow more living time), and total concern for ecology. The basic cells of social organization are to be neighborhoods of 500-1500 people, with neighborhood representatives forming into a Council of Two Hundred, and 1700 Councils in turn forming the Republic of North America (RNA). Land is not owned, but leased, with fees depending on the use or misuse of land and cancellation upon any evidence of pollution. Credit becomes the new name for money, and everyone is allotted a fair share of the economy. A single card with a person's identification numbers and thumbprint replaces money, which becomes electrical impulses stored in computers. This numbering system, however, will secure individual privacy.

Until age 12, the young will be cared for in Neighborhoods, and from ages 12-19 they become the responsibility of Councils and live in Council Houses or miniature Neighborhoods. In education, a heavy emphasis is placed on audiovisual methods, with the philosophy that children must be allowed to learn everything they can as freely and openly as possible.

There is also an attempt to elaborate on necessary steps to attain this vision. Baby Steps include selling the book, registering and voting, buying land and growing healthy food, eating well, and working to "Lay on everybody the communication of love between People." Giant steps follow the point when sales of **VMW** pass one million (presuming that buyers read the book and are strongly convinced), and a corporation (VMW, Inc., of course) is set up to facilitate communications. The first political step is to eliminate hand guns; the second is to run for office, for "We have to be part of the establishment in order to change it." The philosophy is more or less summarized on pp. 162-163 with a list of 19 things for Children to know. Meanwhile, the folks at **VMW**, Inc. are organized into 26 design sections devoted to concerns such as Human Engineering, Media, Boundary Patrol, Computer, Power, Transportation, Council Centers, and Protection Organizations. The book is concluded with 33 steps for "Getting it on," or facilitating Change Day, once adequate political power is obtained.

*** Could very well be seen as THE counter-culture utopia; imaginative ideas and charming cartoons outweigh the gross abuses to the English language, and an utterly unreal plan of action.

443. GARCIA, John David. **The Moral Society: A Rational Alternative to Death.** NY: Julian Press, 1971. 353 pp. $8.95.   (B-4)

A simplistic joining of the cosmic evolutionary viewpoint to a political strategy. Man is seen as evolving to ever-greater mind: ever-greater awareness through increasing complexity. "An extrapolation of evolutionary trends in general, and human evolution in particular, indicates that mankind is about to undergo another evolutionary joining in which the whole becomes more aware than the sum of the parts...the human joining will be a psychosocial process in which men, machines, and collective knowledge become a single super-organism in which each person remains free and individualized." (p.xxi) This new organism is the Moral Society. Teilhard de Chardin is acknowledged as the first person to discuss this concept under the "more limited" notion of "the Noosphere."

It is first necessary to create the Ethical State: "a nation which is structured to increase total awareness." This will be done by the organization of Protagonists (deliberate players of the Game of Life, which is the basis of all evolution), who will withdraw support from bureaucracies, establish feedback with the nations of the world by educational means, form a political force for electing ethical men to office, and implement an ethical constitution.

The outlines of an Ethical State are provided in Chapter 6. Among its many features are an educational system that produces generalists, essentially capitalist industry in order to maximize feedback, and democratic government with male-female pairs holding all offices. Once the Ethical State includes all mankind, the Moral Society will be created, but "The Earth is merely the first stage, or better still the launching pad, for the Moral Society. Only in the infinity of outer space can man have an infinite future." (p.83) And thus the Moral Society evolves "toward the infinite Cosmic Moral Society of all joined Moral Societies... " (p.86)

*** Didactic, repititious, and arrogant: e.g., the book jacket proclaims that this is "possibly the most important synthesis in history..." A very remote possibility.

444. FLATTO, Elie. **The Second American Revolution: Decline and Fall of the Presidency.** NY: The Arica Press (Box 4405, Grand Central Station), 1974. 93 pp. $1.85, paper.   (C-5)

Asserts that America is facing a crisis of authority which would have occurred no matter who occupied the White House, for "The Presidency is obsolete and irrelevant!" (p.x)

As the divine right of kings was once toppled, "Today again the concept of authority is being challenged as man goes from an industry-corporation technology to a post-industrial, electronic one...In a world that is electronically unified, where territory simply ceases to matter, authority in general may become obsolete and anachronistic." (pp.2-3)

The Second American Revolution is seen as a prologue to a World Revolution, leading from passive deputization to active involvement and participation, from punitive and authoritarian authority to that authority which tribalizes people to larger communal wholes. Much of this essay serves to vilify Nixon (the personification of the system) and to glorify McGovern (The Tribal Leader).

*** Trendy black and white nonsense; McLuhanism at its worst.

445. STEVENS, L. Clark. **est: The Steersman Handbook. Charts of the Coming Decade of Conflict.** NY: Bantam Books, October 1971. 154 pp. $1.50, paper.   (C-5)

Cosmic cant about "est" (Electronic Social Transformation) based on the erroneous but then-fashionable demographic assumption that "...by and large, the vast majority of those under 30 support the Movement while the vast majority of those over 40 support the Establishment." (p.8)

Beyond even revolution, "what is now unfolding is no less than the transformation of all things" (p. 1), a transformation of constant, inexorable change; a pervasive shift in the fundamental Nature of Being, based on the great awakening words of today: Peace, Love, Freedom.

There is a basic polarization between the print-conditioned linear forces of the Establishment, and the non-linear lifestyle of the Movement, which cannot be led because "It has no authoritarian leaders and no submissive followers. What it does have is brothers and sisters, peoples of the world who relate with love, in peace and freedom, to their household earth." (p.36)

Est will replace politics and go beyond guerilla warfare by the application of peacefare. "The Est people with their comprehensive capability have the advantage of simulsensory awareness over members of the Establishment who are limited by separate-sense, compartmented habits of thought... the pattern of Est action involves the entire, together, historical accumulation of mankind's capabilities." (p.113)

The political strategy for the movement is to concentrate forces on one state, and the governorship of California is suggested. "The Capture of California" would provide an important base of influence for the critical presidential election of 1976, "which will determine the ultimate fate of the biosphere. The last chance to change Executive direction. The point of no return." (p.154)

Once in power, the Movement would limit corporate power (especially the size of enterprises) to permit the U.S. Constitution to function. There would be organic neighborhoods, each individual would find self-expression, and nations would be vestigual structures.

*** A plastic Flower Child stew combining pieces of Marshall McLuhan, Buckminster Fuller, Lewis Mumford, J. Krishnamurti, Che Guevara, and Bobby Seale. Little wonder that "the Movement" died from intellectual malnutrition.

446. CORNUELLE, Richard C. **Reclaiming the American Dream.** NY: Random House, 1965; Vintage edition, 1968. 171pp.   (ABC-3)

Argues that the liberals cannot succeed by continuing to promote big government, and that the conservatives cannot succeed because they are without a program for a better society. Beyond the concepts of the public sector and the private or commercial sector, there is a third sector: the independent sector of associations such as churches, foundations, fraternal and service organizations, labor unions, and private hospitals and schools-- "a Kaleidoscope of human action."

If fully mobilized, this independent sector could put everyone to work, wipe out poverty, stop juvenile crime, renew our towns and cities, stop pollution, etc. Competition with government is not only legitimate but necessary. But many organizations in the third sector are seen as still operating in the 19th century. There is a need for research, development, mobilization, and information, and each of these strategic elements are described.

There is a "compelling drive" among many to serve, whether it stems from self-denial or egomania; "the service motive is at least as powerful as the desire for profit or power." (p.61)

This interesting and original appeal concludes with a notion from Saul Alinsky that "if a three-sector society becomes a two-sector society, it will soon become a one-sector society." (p.167)

*** A valuable and woefully neglected angle of vision. Interestingly, Cornuelle's recent book, **De-Managing America** (no. 299) takes a somewhat different position by attacking the first two sectors and proposing decentralization, rather than action by the third sector.

Chapter 10

Economic Reform

Intertwining of the "public" and "private" sectors of society continues to grow; hence considerations of reforming the government are logically followed by considerations of reforming the economy. Indeed, economic reforms can readily be seen as a special category of governmental reforms, for most proposals concern how much and what kind of governmental intervention in economic affairs.

Before listing the items that focus on economic reforms, it is important to consider recent trends in corporate evolution--a fundamental reality that is neglected by a surprising number of writers who dwell on societal directions and alternatives. It may be unpleasant to deal with the new world of conglomerates and multinationals, but, along with nations. they are the central social institutions of our global society.

Galbraith's "New Industrial State" (447) that is characterized by these large corporations serves to introduce this chapter, and the extensive research by Blair (448) emphasizes the increasing concentration of wealth and power. Bannock worries about "The Juggernauts" (349), while Barber surveys "the Goliaths" (450). Bagley (451) speculates about the formation of supercorporations and the possibility of "the contract state." Such a view is not unlike Webb's speculative scenario, written in 1937, about turning government over to the corporations and revising the constitution to reflect this reality (452).

Such indelicate matters were not discussed by the 1972 White House Conference on the Industrial World Ahead (453), an otherwise extensive anthology. The participants at the White House Conference, as well as other writers on corporations, have also neglected the cultural aspects viewed by Haden-Guest (454): "The Paradise Program" of emerging world empires such as Muzak, Hilton, and Coca-Cola, who are "landscaping the future" in prosaic but significant ways.

The most extensive treatment of the multinational aspects of corporations is provided by Barnet and Müller (455), who focus on the world managers and their impact. A somewhat similar view is taken by Stephenson (457), who suggests the changes in governments and trade unions that will develop out of the "coming clash." But there are those--notably the corporate defenders--who argue that the portrait of unleashed corporate power is exaggerated or out-dated, and that governments worldwide are holding the "Multinationals at Bay" (458). Who holds the upper hand, and what should be the balance of corporate and governmental power? The answers to these questions are of fundamental importance.

The radical answer to this question is that this is an Age of Imperialism (459), and an Age of Multinationals (460), and that the food and energy crisis are a result of greedy multinational corporations (463). Alternative views of world economic crisis focus on the world monetary order (464) and long-range cycles identified by Kondratieff (465).

Prescriptions for the global economy include a new world economic order (473), a World Industry Redistribution Plan (474), a mankind-oriented approach for global corporations (475), a world without war (476), and an exuberant extrapolation of a benign capitalism coexisting with world order (477).

This well-intended innocence is also reflected in many of the proposals for domestic reform advanced by business leaders. The "New Industrial Revolution" of decentralization and industrial democracy, proposed by Filene in 1925 (478), eloquently expresses many of the hopes of subsequent leaders, such as the "Second Industrial Revolution" of "Creative Capitalism" proposed by Kosmetsky (479). Haggerty urges "A Productive Society" (480) through a National Development Act, and Foy proposes a very narrow "progressive program" (481) to overcome lags in capital investment. Lundborg envisions more social responsibility as leading to a "Future Without Shock" (482), and Ramo considers "electronic free enterprise" as a humanizing option (483).

A wide variety of other schemes follow (nos. 486-506), in no particular logical sequence. Hendrikson's proposal for "A Cashless Society" (486) seems to be particularly of worth. Melman's argument that industrial inefficiency in "The Permanent War Economy" is aggravated by the subsidy of state capitalism (487) is unique and important. Barnet (488) makes a somewhat similar point in advocating a National Conversion Commission to steer us away from "The Economy of Death." Reagan (489) is notably prophetic in advocating various reforms for a "Managed Economy," and Ulmer's "Plan for Stability" appears to contain some worthy suggestions. The Kelso proposal for Universal Capitalism (497) is a fresh approach. A unique slant on distribution is provided by Borsodi's 1927 book (505), and by Stulman's recent proposal for a "Third Industrial Revolution"(506).

Harman's challenging essay on "Humanistic Capitalism" (507) serves to introduce the subject of planning by its emphasis on somehow aligning the private sector with overall societal goals. The concern with planning is hardly new, and it is important to consider some of the literature from several decades ago so that old arguments are not needlessly repeated. In 1932, Chase proposed a National Planning Board (509), Soule advocated "A Planned Society" (510), and Beard brought together views on "A Planned Economy" (511). During the World War II years, a fundamental debate developed. Mannheim (514, 515) made an extensive case for democratic planning that is still important to consider. Drucker (516) wrote against centralized planning, but Hayek went further in his classic essay on **The Road to Serfdom** (517), which was seen by Finer as **The Road to Reaction** (518).

In response to recent economic troubles, the Initiative Committee for National Economic Planning was formed (519), and it should be noted that its membership and endorsement can hardly be considered as "radical." The most significant planning-related legislation that might be passed in the near future is the Hawkins-Humphrey Equal Opportunity and Full Employment Act, described in the ANNALS volume edited by Moses (522). Also of note in this volume is the essay by Moses on 16 different ways to estimate unemployment levels. The focus on full employment serves to introduce five additional items that focus on work; the HEW Special Task Force Report (523) is particularly important. Reforming the economy through the reform of work is continued in Chapter 11 on Redistribution.

---

447. GALBRAITH, John Kenneth. **The New Industrial State.** Boston: Houghton Mifflin, 1967. 427 pp.   (A-3)

The Industrial System--that part of the economy characterized by large corporations--is seen as the dominant feature of The New Industrial State.

This New Industrial State is guided by the "technostructure" (all of those who bring specialized knowledge to bear on decision-making), in contrast to the entrepreneurial leadership of the past.

Whether capitalist or communist in origin, industrial systems are seen as convergent in their development, and planning is replacing the market.

But rather than consumers instructing business firms on what to produce, "the revised sequence" suggests how large firms arrange consumer behavior to satisfy the needs of the firms.

448. BLAIR, John M. **Economic Concentration: Structure, Behavior, and Public Policy.** Foreword by Gardiner C. Means. NY: Harcourt Brace Jovanovich, 1972. 742 pp.   (A-3)

An extensive tome on "the continuing rise in economic concentration as a result of inadequate reinforcement of antitrust laws. Between 1947 and 1968, the 200 largest manufacturing corporations increased their share of manufacturing assets from 47.1% to 60.4%. Between 1947 and 1967, their share of value added by manufacturing increased from 30% to 41%. Blair argues that an understanding of this structure and behavior cannot be gained from any of the existing theoretical models.

Sections of the book are concerned with The Dimensions of Concentration, Centrifugal Forces, Centripetal Forces, Concentration and Economic Behavior, and Concentration and Public Policy. The final chapter explores the option of state ownership, concluding that "In the communist countries, as in the capitalist world, oligopoly stands as the principal barrier to the achievement of better economic performance." (p. 706)

449. BANNOCK, Graham. **The Juggernauts: The Age of the Big Corporations.** Indianapolis: Bobbs-Merrill, 1971. 363 pp.   (AB-3)

Argues persuasively that "the mature corporation is rapidly becoming the dominant form of industrial organization in the second half of the twentieth century." This change has resulted from the dispersion of ownership and its separation from control, and a scale of operations so large that no individual can comprehend it and imprint his personality on it. The system no longer works "primarily in the interests of the consumer but in the interests of a minority of managers. Yet, thanks to a highly developed ideology it receives society's support." (p. 307)

However, "I do not believe that the substitution of state for private industry will do anything to remedy the shortcomings of the new order described in this book." (p. 323) Rather, Bannock advocates moving away from concentration and centralization, restoring greater economic competition.

450. BARBER, Richard J. **The American Corporation: Its Power, Its Money, Its Politics.** NY: E.P. Dutton, 1970. 309 pp. $7.95.   (AB-3)

A former counsel for the U.S. Senate Anti-Trust Subcommittee describes a "silent revolution" that most people have failed to appreciate. But, "To be ignorant of these forces of change in business is to acquiesce in the kind of society that they will resolutely mold..." The change is such that the old demarcation between public and private no longer has meaning.

Chapters describe The Corporate Goliaths, The Postindustrial State, Business and Higher Education, science and business, social problem solving, the world economy, internationalization, and The Political Dimensions of Corporate Supranationalism. An era of superaffluence and greater urbanization is projected, but this apparent misforecast does not necessarily invalidate the rest of the analysis.

It is concluded that "The failure of government to meet the challenge of business power is, in the final analysis, a risk to democracy itself." (p. 300) If government wants a larger role, there must be a reform of Congress. Government must also become aware of industrial plans; otherwise, "big corporations are going to pretty much shape the future of the world." (p. 299)

450a. MARRIS, Robin (ed.) **The Corporate Society.** London: Macmillan, 1974. 403 pp. (Dist. in U.S. by Wiley/Halstead.)   (A-3)

The second volume of a project sponsored by the now-defunct Harvard Program on Technology and Society. The first volume, **The Corporate Economy,** was published by Harvard University Press in 1971.

The 9 essays are by Emmanuel Mesthene, Thomas Schelling, Irene Taviss, Tom Burns, Joseph Bower, Kenneth Arrow, Richard Musgrave, Mancur Olson, and E.J. Mishan, with extensive commentary on each by Marris.

451. BAGLEY, Edward R. **Beyond the Conglomerates: The Impact of the Supercorporation on the Future of Life and Business.** NY: American Management Associations/AMACOM, 1975. 213 pp. $11.95.
                                                                        (ABC-2)

The President of a Wilmington, Del. consulting firm offers two heavyweight ideas in a lightweight prose style: the probable emergence of supercorporations and the possible coming of the contract state.

Two new kinds of huge corporations are predicted for the period between the later 1970s and 1990: one-two dozen supercorporations, and scores of semisupercorporations. Supercorporations have four hallmarks: they are greater than $1 billion in sales or assets, they grow at an average rate of 10% annually (about twice the average rate), there is extensive diversification into at least three disparate industries, and there is "a rare degree of resourcefulness, flexibility, aggressiveness, and creativity." The supers will usually but not necessarily be multinational in scope. They will arise out of the form of the conventional corporation and the "swinging conglomerates" of the sixties. Their emergence "is likely to hit us harder than any other business happening in this century--for better or worse." (p. vii)

After briefly surveying the Limits to Growth debate, Bagley concludes "that economic growth will remain as high a priority as environmental improvement." (p. 18) It is also assumed that "Our postindustrial society will be even more wealthy, prone to change, and socially restive than the one that laid to rest our happier days. Within this new society, we can expect the supercorporation to be a prime mover." (p. 151)

Chapter 14 argues that supercorporations will support the movement to a contract state, where there would be a multi-billion dollar increase in state contracting. Advantages and disadvantages are explored, but it is recognized that the situation is too new to be fully considered at this point. The final two chapters explore the possibilities of how the supercorporations may aid some of the poor nations and sponsor new cities.

*** The serious reader should not dismiss these notions because of their decidedly non-academic presentation. Despite the informality, there are some important considerations here, and Bagley tries to be neutral about these developments, stressing possibilities of good and evil.

452. WEBB, Walter Prescott. **Divided We Stand: The Crisis of a Frontierless Democracy.** NY: Farrar & Rinehart, 1937.   (AB-3)

Fresh but uneven thinking, with some rambling and an over-reliance on a sectionalist theme of the North vs. the South and West.

It is still useful to consider Webb's concept of a new feudalism based on finance capitalism and distribution. On the right of the President "lies a strange form of corporate fascism and business feudalism." (p. 217) The new fief is not a plot of ground but a segment of business. The chapter on chain operations is quite prophetic.

"The closing frontier and the growing corporations--both synonymous with decreasing common opportunity--are offered as mated keys to the recent crisis of the modern world's first great democracy." (p. vi)

As a "purely intellectual exercise," Webb suggests a plan to fit the existing forces of society, in contrast to pursuing the romantic notion of democracy: that is, to turn the government over to corporations and let them run it. A new constitution would be devised that recognizes and acts upon facts. The executive would be headed by the most powerful firm. The upper house of the legislature (the Council of Corporations) would be composed of representatives from the 200 largest corporations, while the lower house would have delegates from various interest groups. The War Department, of course, would be in the hands of the munitions makers.

*** In modern parlance, we would call this exercise a "scenario," and it is a most intriguing one.

453. White House Conference on the Industrial World Ahead. **A Look at Business in 1990.** Washington: U.S. Government Printing Office, Nov. 1972. 369 pp. $5.25.   (A-3)

A massive conference held in Washington in February 1972, attended by some 1500 decision-makers, and resulting in 53 contributions arranged in seven sections:

1. A Conference Overview, includes remarks by President Nixon, Secretary of Labor Hodgson, Secretary of the Treasury Connally, the usual exuberant forecast by Herman Kahn, a more restrained forecast by The Conference Board, and a description of revolutionary change and basic choices by Willis Harman (see no. 508).
2. The Social Responsibility of Business includes contributions by Roy Amara, Arjay Miller, Hazel Henderson, Paul N. Ylvisaker.
3. Technology and Resources for Business includes contributions by Michael Michaelis, Joseph L. Fisher, Simon Ramo, Nathaniel A. Owings, George Kosmetsky, and Athelstan Spilhaus.
4. The Human Side of Enterprise includes articles on manpower, labor-management relations, minority groups, and planning.
5. Structure of the Private Enterprise System includes articles on the financial system, consumer demand, and a world of capital scarcity.
6. World Business and the Economy of 1990 focuses on the economy of the world, the developing countries, and trade with the Communist countries.
7. A Conference Summary by Maurice Stans focuses on the "outstanding potentials" for a better America and the need for better public understanding on how productive the economic system is.

454. HADEN-GUEST, Anthony. **The Paradise Program: Travels through Muzak, Hilton, Coca-Cola, Texaco, Walt Disney and other World Empires.** NY: Morrow, 1973. 310 pp. $6.95 (Published in Great Britain in 1972 as **Down the Programmed Rabbit Hole.**)   (ABC-3)

"I am interested in the myths, the global imagery which has inevitably been created by the business empires. It has as much to do with landscaping the future as the political wheeling-and-dealing or the wielding of economic strength." This is not a critique or a celebration, but poking around the myth factories and talking to the responsible people. "They turn out to be high-minded, mostly, and gifted with terrible innocence...On the other hand, they tend to be sublimely incurious as to effect. There is nothing that cannot be controlled and merchandised." (p. viii) In addition to the travels indicated in the sub-title, the author visits with Edgar Rice Burroughs, Inc., **Reader's Digest,** McDonalds hamburgers, and **Penthouse** magazine.

*** A light and humorous tour, by a writer who has been called "the English Tom Wolfe," uncovering an important dimension of the future that has been neglected by most writers. Indeed, the societal directions suggested here may be among the most significant of any to be found in this guide.

455. BARNET, Richard J. and Ronald E. MÜLLER. **Global Reach: The Power of the Multinational Corporations.** NY: Simon and Schuster, 1974, 508 pp. $11.95. (Shortened version in **The New Yorker,** Dec. 2 & 9, 1974.)   (AB-1)

A fresh and authoritative analysis of a critical concern by a founder and co-director of the Institute for Policy Studies and an economics professor at American University.

"The global corporation is the most powerful human organization yet devised for colonizing the future." (p.363) Its managers "are the first in history with the organization, technology, money, and ideology to make a credible try at managing the world as an integrated unit." (p.13) "The global corporation is the first institution in human history dedicated to centralized planning on a world scale." (p.14) In turn, this has produced "an organizational revolution as profound in its implications for modern man as the Industrial Revolution and the rise of the nation-state itself." (p.15)

The managers of the global corporation now see the nation-state as the chief obstacle to planetary development--a view the authors consider as far more radical than anything ever proposed by the World Federalists. Only the threat of nationalization keeps the managers from transforming the world political economy through their increasing control of three fundamental resources: the technology of production, finance capital, and marketing. The global shopping center is increasingly sparked by the cult of bigness and the science of centralization, leading to "the supreme political issue of our time: i.e., whether it is really 'rational' to attempt to organize the planet through centralizing technologies into ever-larger pyramidal structures." (p.44)

The authors present a strong case that it is not rational. The principal elements of the global transformation are the globalization of oligopoly capitalism, an overriding interest in global profit maximization, a shift of new production to the poor nations (changing the employment patterns and living standards in the U.S.), and a new concentration of political power in private hands. The result is increasing affluence for a small transnational middle class and "escalating misery for the great bulk of the human family." (p.184) The diet of the bottom 40-60% of the world's population is getting worse, compounded by the increasing concentration of income and elimination of jobs, the increasing corporate control of arable land, and the control of ideology through advertising leading to a change of diet for the worse. Even in the U.S., there is a growing gap between the rich and the poor. Global corporations aggravate this social balance, as well as the ecological balance (by requiring a throwaway society) and the psychological balance (by destroying possibilities of real community).

However, the old "Public Be Damned" style has disappeared. "In its place is a liberal vision of a world corporate society promising peace and abundance." (p.120) The global managers have an invincible faith in their power to do good, a form of self-protective ignorance. The mortal enemies of the global managers are three recent ideological movements: the advocates of a no-growth economy, the anticonsumption movement, and the antihierarchy movement. What should these movements do to develop countervailing power?

The authors recommend "fundamental reforms in the process by which information crucial for society is produced, used, and diffused." (p.369) In short, there must be adequate disclosure by requiring corporate records to become public documents and requiring corporations to disclose the extent and nature of their reserves.

An international agency might prove to be the best way for corporations to escape regulation, because "present international agencies or any new agency in the forseeable future are too weak to regulate the corporate giants. To pretend otherwise is to settle for the patina of regulation instead of the substance." (p.373) Rather, there should be a restoration of powers to national governments and local communities.

The productive system must be regulated to support national development objectives. There must be clearly articulated national priorities through a national development plan that sets out a vision of the society we hope to achieve. The three essential aspects of this plan are investment in the U.S. to meet needs of people, more equitable distribution of income and wealth through a decentralized economy, and reasonable self-sufficiency in raw materials and goods. The authors also advocate debate on new forms of public ownership and control of strategic industries, a tax law that does not encourage foreign investment, major investment in the development of job-creating alternative technologies, new standards for quality and a new holistic definition of efficiency. To give greater bargaining power to communities, corporations should file a plan with authorities to cover their local operations. Public directors should be added to boards, and members of regulatory commissions should be elected. In sum, the values needed for survival "turn out to be the familiar democratic values preached by prophets and sages since the beginning of history--respect for human dignity, justice, frugality, honesty, moderation, and equality." (p.386)

*** There is no better book to enable an understanding of the realities of global corporations and the implications for public policy. Absolutely essential for anyone concerned with societal directions and alternatives.

456. BLAKE, David H. (ed.) **The Multinational Corporation. The ANNALS of the American Academy of Political and Social Science**, Vol. 403, Sept. 1972.   (A-3)

Thirteen articles on implications for executives and trade unions, consequences for international economics and politics, and impacts on Europe, developing countries, and the U.S.

The final contribution by Howard U. Perlmutter, The Multinational Firm and the Future," outlines three developmental stages in our "primary reality," The Emerging Global Industrial System (Fig. 1, p.142):

1) The Era of National Global Systems (1970-1980)
2) The Era of Bi-and Tri-National and Regional Global Systems (1980-1990)
3) The Era of Geocentric and Geocentroid Global Systems (1990-??)

457. STEPHENSON, Hugh. **The Coming Clash: The Impact of Multinational Corporations on National States.** NY: Saturday Review Press, 1973. 186 pp. $7.95.   (AB-3)

The editor of the London **Times Business News** focuses on the 300-400 multinational companies that are profoundly contradicting our 16th century ideas about sovereign nation states. The capacity of international industry to physically move its location has resulted in a fundamental change in the balance of power between industry and government.

Some of the effects include a new mobility of workers and jobs, a new protectionism dictated by corporate managements rather than governments, undermining the entire basis of traditional trade theory, finance departments of international corporations effectively becoming their own international bankers, and destruction of the Bretton Woods international monetary system.

"It seems for the moment as if industrial management is the only organism which has found the capacity to emerge from the restrictive and increasingly irrelevant chrysalis of the nation state. In due course the pressure will become irresistable for a basic change in the attitudes of governments and trade unions alike. But that moment has not yet come: the slow process of development will occupy the whole of the 1970s." (Conclusion, p. 175.)

458. "Multinationals at Bay" (Special Section), **Saturday Review**, January 24, 1976, pp. 12-30.   (B-3)

Four articles comprising the Annual International Business Review, introduced by the comment that "Multinational corporations are today on the

defensive: increasingly, they are being pilloried by consumer groups, unions, the media, Congress, and various international organizations...Are these attacks warranted? Or are multinationals, on balance, a force for good?" (p. 12)
- Gurney Breckenfeld, "Coping With the Nation-State," outlines the pros and cons of five major questions: 1) Are multinationals exporting U.S. jobs? 2) Do they create "export platforms" abroad to ship cheaply-made goods back to the U.S.? 3) Are multinationals the villains of the currency crisis? 4) Do they exploit the economies of the under-developed countries? 5) Do they evade taxes abroad by rigging prices?
- Rawleigh Warner, Jr. (Chairman of Mobil Oil), defends the multinationals.
- Richard C. Longworth, "Writing the Rule Book," discusses the formulation of laws that could effectively control but not strangle the big corporations.
- Donald Kirk describes actions being taken by the United Nations.
- *** A fairly useful introduction, although leaning toward the corporate point-of-view. Why not stage a genuine debate between the most articulate critics and defenders?

459. MAGDOFF, Harry. **The Age of Imperialism: The Economics of U.S. Foreign Policy.** NY: Monthly Review Press, 1969. 207 pp.   (AB-3)

"Imperialism is not a matter of choice for a capitalist society; it is the way of life of such a society." (p. 26) The distinctive features of the new imperialism are: 1) England no longer the undisputed industrial power, and, 2) within industrial nations, power shifting to a relatively small number of firms. The newer features of imperialism involve a shifting of emphasis from rivalry to a struggle against contraction, the new role of the U.S. as the leader of the system, and the rise of international technology.
*** A cogent Marxist perspective providing analysis but no prescription.

460. SCHEER, Robert. **America After Nixon: The Age of the Multinationals.** NY: McGraw-Hill, 1974. 326 pp. $7.95.   (BC-4)

A spirited Marxist argument by a former editor of **Ramparts** and one of the early critics of the Vietnam war. The title is based on "the notion that Nixon's troubles are symptomatic of a more general crumbling of the American political system. This age of the multinationals represents a time when effective control over what is important has passed to the new breed of transnational corporations." (p. xi)
Chapters attack Nixon, Kissinger, Rockefeller, the corporate growth mania, corporations and the energy crisis, foreign aid, and South Korea as an example of American foreign political and economic policy. The myths that problems of the poor countries were being solved "enabled citizens of the economies of waste to acquiesce to the ripoffs of the multinational corporations." (p. 163)
Concludes with a poorly-supported hope that there is a new populist political majority, in that more than 80% of Americans see corporate control over the political process as dangerous. (The depth of this opinion, and its priority over other concerns, is not considered.) No suggestions are made for dealing with the multinationals once the broad-based "left force" gains political power.

461. WILLIAMS, William Appleman. **The Great Evasion: An Essay on the Contemporary Relevance of Karl Marx and on the Wisdom of Admitting the Heretic into the Dialogue about America's Future.** Chicago: Quadrangle, 1964. 189 pp.   (AB-3)

Americans have made Marx into Lenin, Stalin, and the Soviet Union, but "We have never confronted his central thesis about the assumptions, the costs, and the nature of capitalist society." Galbraith's "Affluent Society" is seen as "a complacent, inaccurate, misleading and dangerously stultifying exercise in self-congratulation." (p. 231)

Chapters are devoted to The Expansion of the Marketplace and Capitalist Foreign Relations, Increasing Misery and Increasing Proletarianization, and Capitalism and the Creation of an Ethical and Equitable Community.

462. ROSEN, Sumner M. (ed.) **Economic Power Failure: The Current American Crisis.** NY: McGraw-Hill, 1975. 297 pp. $8.95; $3.95, paper. (AB-3)

Forty selections arranged in ten sections: The End of the Keynesian Era?, Oil, The Changing World Economy, The End of Imperialism?, Corporate Dominance, Multinationals, The Military Economy, Unequal Shares and Unfair Taxes, Losers (the unemployed, farm workers, the aged), and Our Long-Run Fate: What Choices? Who Chooses? The selections include essays such as E.F. Schumacher, "Buddhist Economics," and Gar Alperovitz, "Toward a New Society."

*** A good selection of critical essays to serve as a contrast to corporate apologetics.

462a. The Staff of The Washington Post. **Bad Times and Beyond.** NY: Dell/ Laurel Original, 1974. 239 pp. $1.75, paper. (BC-4)

There is no introduction or index to this jumbled collection of essays, accompanied with excerpts from selected position papers and transcripts of the White House "Economic Summit" Conferences of September 1974. Among the 14 articles are:
- Haynes Johnson and Noel Epstein, "Deferring the American Dream"
- Bernard D. Nossiter, "The International Connection"
- J.W. Anderson, "Fueling the Energy Crisis"
- Amitai Etzioni, "The Psychology of Inflation"
- Herbert Rowan, "Prescription for Recovery"

463. ARONOWITZ, Stanley. **Food, Shelter and the American Dream.** NY: The Seabury Press, 1975. 188 pp. $3.95. (AB-4)

Focuses on the food and energy crises, and the recent transformation of American capitalism involving "quantum leaps of accumulated international wealth, control, and power." Some features of our present condition include the penetration of government agencies by corporations, the growing rigidity of cultural institutions, and repressive measures such as lying and surveillance to sustain adherence to corporate practices. Aronowitz warns of "the distinct probability of the emergence of new forms of authoritarian rule at home." (p. 163)

Stemming inflation is seen as depending entirely on finding ways to expand production of real goods--an option that is foreclosed by the international commitments of U.S. corporations.

463a. BARRACLOUGH, Geoffrey, "The Coming Depression," **The New York Review of Books,** June 27, 1974. (ns)

The first of three articles in **NYRB**; the other two are "The World Crash" (January 23, 1975), and "The World Economic Struggle" (August 7, 1975).

Argues that we are in the death throes of capitalism and that reactions by the men of power are all disastrously wrong.

464. CAIRNCROSS, Frances and Hamish McRAE. **The Second Great Crash.**
Englewood Cliffs, NJ: Prentice-Hall, 1975. 120 pp. $5.95.   (B-3)

An explanation of the breakdown of the world economic system by two
British economists associated with **The Guardian.** The Second Great Crash
has already happened in the sense that "most major stock markets had already fallen by more than they did in the original Great Crash of 1929."
(p. 5)
After a general discussion of the causes of accelerated inflation and the
instability of the world monetary order, the authors focus on the recent
quadrupling of the price of oil as a watershed. "Without it, the fragile economic situation would have been worrying but not frightening." (p. 39) The
bulk of the book is devoted to the consequences of the inability of the oil
producers to spend their money.
Little is offered in the way of forecast and prescription. However, the
authors warn of the grave danger of major countries losing control of their
currencies if they expand their economies to deal with unemployment.
And in an appendix considering the plight of the developing countries, it
is argued that the politics of food will surely dominate the end of this decade as the politics of oil has dominated the mid-1970's.
***Useful as background.

465. SHUMAN, James B. and David ROSENAU. **The Kondratieff Wave.** NY:
World, 1972. 198 pp.   (BC-4)

Based on the theory of economic waves proposed shortly after World
War I by the Russian economist Nikolai D. Kondratieff. Shows how the long
economic wave, lasting approximately 52 years, has operated in American
history, and predicts euphoria and contentment in the 1970's followed by
a crash in the 1980's. The authors urge that we plan for this event.
*** An imaginative approach, but rather vague about when we can expect
the pre-crash "euphoria and contentment."

466. GILPIN, Robert. **U.S. Power and the Multinational Corporation.** NY:
Basic Books, 1975. $10.95.   (ns)

466a. GILPIN, Robert. **The Multinational Corporation and the National Interest.**
Prepared for the U.S. Senate Committee on Labor and Public
Welfare. Washington: U.S. Government Printing Office, 1973. 85 pp.
(ns)

467. GILPIN, Robert, "Three Models of the Future," **International Organization,** 29:1, Winter 1975, pp. 37-60.   (A-3)

The triangular relationship of the U.S., Western Europe, and Japan is
seen in disarray. Three models of the future, drawn from current writings
in international relations, are evaluated as answers to the question of whether
the interdependent world economy can survive the political environment
of the future. Faults in each model are discussed:
- The Sovereignty-at-bay Model, views a relatively benevolent system of
national economies enmeshed in a web of economic interdependence,
with the nation-state as an anachronism.
- The Dependencia Model, the Marxist view of ultraimperialism: a hierarchical and exploitative world order.
- The Mercantilist Model, views the nation-state and national interests
as the primary determinants of the future role of the world economy,
with manipulating economic arrangements to maximize their own interests.
Gilpin concludes that few new international institutions will be created

but it is likely that existing institutions will be "profoundly altered." The world economy may be fragmenting into regional trading and monetary blocs. This could be prevented if the U.S. were to reassert its waning hegemony, but is this the wisest policy? In the long run, it is seen as perhaps more costly.

468. BALL, George W. (ed.) **Global Companies: The Political Economy of World Business.** Englewood Cliffs, NJ: Prentice-Hall, 1975. 179 pp. $7.95; $2.95, paper.   (ns)

469. KAHN, Herman (ed.) **The Future of the Corporation.** NY: Mason & Lipscomb, 1974. $8.95.   (ns)

470. SAUVANT, Karl P. and Bernard MENNIS. **Emerging Forms of Transnational Community.** Lexington, Mass.: Lexington Books, Jan. 1976.
                                                                    (ns)

471. SAUVANT, Karl P. and Farid G. LAVIPOUR (eds.) **Controlling Multinational Enterprises: Problems, Strategies, Counterstrategies.** West View Press, March 1976. $25.00.   (ns)

472. HUFBAUER, G. C., et al. **U.S. Taxation of American Business Abroad.** Washington: American Enterprise Institute for Public Policy Research, 1975. 101 pp. $3.00, paper.   (ns)

"Five tax experts discuss the inequities and problems caused by the current tax laws--and each has his own idea of how to change those laws." (advt.)

472a. BUNDY, William P. (ed.) **The World Economic Crisis.** A **Foreign Affairs** Book. NY: W.W. Norton, 1975. 252 pp. $8.95.   (AB-3)

Eleven essays on topics such as the oil crisis, energy interdependence, world food supply, U.S. trade policy, and non-fuel minerals.

473. de MONTBRIAL, Thierry, "For a New World Economic Order," **Foreign Affairs,** 54:1, October 1975, pp. 61-78.   (A-4)

An exploration of possibilities in a few essential areas, rather than a detailed plan. Our problems are seen as stemming from monetary disorders, and thus "monetary stability is a prerequisite for economic stability." It is also argued that the number of actors in the economic "game" must grow, and that mechanisms must be developed to ensure mutual rights and equality. "A new world economic order would retain the fundamental principles of economic liberalism while introducing certain nuances." (p. 78) The changes, for example, would include an international monetary system based on fixed parities, and free trade within zones seeking integration. *** Even if successful, would this liberal tinkering deserve to be called a "new" economic order?

473a. McHALE, John and Magda. **Human Requirements, Supply Levels and Outer Bounds: A Framework for Thinking About the Planetary Bargain.** NY: Aspen Institute for Humanistic Studies (717 Fifth Avenue), 1975. 92 pp.   (ns)

The "planetary bargain" is a new international economic order that is both just and workable, and the McHales offer a framework for answering the question about meeting basic requirements without transgressing the carrying capacity of the biosphere.

474. KAYA, Yoichi, and Yutaka SUZUKI, "Global Constraints and a New Vision for Development--II," **Technological Forecasting and Social Change,** 6:4 (1974), pp. 371-388.   (A-4)

Two members of the Japan Work Team of the Club of Rome, employing the simplistic Rostow model of economic take-off (see no. 63), view the development of manufacturing industry as indispensable. But the greatest obstacle to the economic growth of the developing nations is their inability to secure markets for their products.
"The most effective solution would be for the advanced nations to modify their own industrial structure so as to create markets throughout the world for the products of the developing nations... In the advanced nations, knowledge-intensive and agricultural industries could be further developed to make up for the industries given up. This type of policy would certainly help the developing nations effectively." (p. 374) Such a "World Industry Redistribution Plan" is seen as "a kind of international division of labor."
*** There is no suggestive evidence of any new-found altruism among the advanced nations, or how such a policy would "certainly help" the developing nations.

475. JANTSCH, Erich. **Technological Planning and Social Futures.** NY: Wiley/Halstead, 1972. 256 pp.   (A-3)

Sixteen previously published articles such as Forecasting, Planning, and Policy Formation (1970), Toward a Methodology for Systemic Forecasting (1970), Adaptive Institutions for Shaping the Future (1969), Growth and World Dynamics (1971), and Toward the Inter-and Trans-disciplinary University (1970), which recommends a new and active role for the university in society--an active institution in the process of planning. Roles for the World Corporation (1971) notes two approaches to world integration: imposing Western patterns on the rest of the world, or coordinated development efforts geared to different cultural patterns so as to regulate the world as a "trans-cultural system." The primary role of the world corporation should be a "total-mankind-oriented approach to shaping the systems of human living." (p. 200) Corporate policies "ought to be conceived and planned as integral parts of a policy for mankind..." (p. 6)
In sum, "the entire process of rational creative action is spotlighted from forecasting and planning...to institutional and instrumental change..." (p. 6)
*** Well-intentioned technicism serving to highlight the disparity between the rational idealism which it espouses and the sordid realities which it ignores. What world corporation will voluntarily seek the betterment of mankind? What university will become truly trans-disciplinary?

476. BERNAL, J.D. **World Without War.** London: Routledge & Kegan Paul, 1958. 308 pp.   (A-3)

A scientist views most of the world's troubles as having been brought about by the instabilities of the capitalist form of production, and proposes "a complete transformation of the material basis of human society all over the world."

Bernal advocates the constructive use of science for peace, a restoration of purpose to life, a society in which everybody can be effective throughout their lifetime, and a new age that rediscovers the spirit and practice of beauty.

477. POSNACK, Emanuel R. **The 21st Century Looks Back.** NY: The William-Frederick Press, 1946. 241 pp.   (BC-4)

A wildly optimistic extrapolation onto a global scale, with extensive arguments as to the superiority of the condition of "dynamic equilibrium" over Socialism and Communism. In the 21st Century, there would be equitable distribution of earnings and business opportunities, a free flow of men and information in a world of free enterprise, and the abolition of monopolies (except for justifiable government monopolies). There would be World Government with a Global Constitution, a Global Statistical Service providing immediate supply and demand data, a Global Transportation Authority, and Global Stabilization to assure fixed relationships among world currencies.
*** Clearly an overdone utopia, but with some interesting ideas not unlike the more sophisticated proposals for "Global Homeostasis" recently made by Laszlo (no. 264).

478. FILENE, Edward A. **The Way Out: A Forecast of Coming Changes in American Business and Industry.** NY: Doubleday, Page & Co., 1925. 306 pp.   (ABC-3)

An eloquent essay by the founder of the great Boston department store, insisting that forecasting is a "necessary prelude to any intelligent business planning," (p. 50) and that the long view is "the only business-like view." (p. 53) Filene's long view is a well-intended prescription with many notions advocated by today's corporate leaders.

"I believe that the modern business system, despised and derided by innumerable reformers, will be both the inspiration and the instrument of the social progress of the future." (p. 29) The great paradox around which the book is written is that "We can repeat the causes and reverse the results of the old Industrial Revolution." (p. 184)

A New Industrial Revolution is advocated that would decentralize industry away from cities, regularize production and distribution, solve the problem of unemployment, and deal with the effects upon workmen of repetitive labor. "This is a pretty large order, but it can be filled." (p. 66) Super-competition is seen as leading to mass production and mass distribution, and industrial democracy--where employees have a stake and some control in the conditions of work--is seen as inevitable. The obstacle to this development is the ignorance of employees and employers.

Chapter 10 advocates mass production and distribution by "Fordizing America." Contemporaries can chuckle at the forecast come true: "it is only a question of time until we shall be living in a Fordized America." (p. 176)

479. KOZMETSKY, George. "Education as an Information System," in House Committee on Science and Astronautics, **The Management of Information and Knowledge: A Compilation of Papers Prepared for the Eleventh Meeting of the Panel on Science and Technology.** Washington: U.S. Government Printing Office, 1970. pp. 89-106.   (AB-4)

The Dean of the Graduate School of Business at the University of Texas views our society in a transition from the First Industrial Revolution to the Second Industrial or Socio-Economic-Cultural Revolution. We are also in a period where the successes and deficiencies of national capitalism have created the need for "creative capitalism."

"Creative capitalism must advance our society beyond the need for imperialism or exploitation of people. Creative capitalism's success depends on its creation of wealth in a manner that truly establishes the community of humanity as the goal of our society. Wealth produced under creative capitalism must be distributed in a manner that makes it possible to increase the standard of living of all the people in the world. The new institutions or complexes upon which creative capitalism is based will make it possible to solve in a timely basis our social problems simultaneously while creating wealth and providing for meaningful leisure for all people in the world." (p. 98)

480. HAGGERTY, Patrick E. **The Productive Society.** 1973 Benjamin F. Fairless Memorial Lectures. Pittsburgh: Carnegie Press, 1974. 174 pp. $8.95. (Distributed by Columbia University Press)   (AB-3)

The Chairman of the Board and Chief Corporate Officer of Texas Instruments, Inc. begins his lecture by acknowledging critics such as Lewis Mumford, Charles Reich, B.F. Skinner, and Philip Berrigan. Nevertheless, there has been progress and conventional indicators are employed (with the aid of 57 charts) to demonstrate increases in GNP per capita, education, and life expectancy.

"Is growth obsolete? We think not. Although GNP and other national income aggregates are imperfect measures of welfare, the broad picture of secular progress which they convey remains after correction of their most obvious deficiencies." (p. 53) There is no reason to arrest growth to conserve natural resources, although there is good reason to provide proper economic incentives to conserve them.

Haggerty argues that there is a strong correlation between a high-productivity society and the real quality of life. To further this condition, he suggests that we should write laws and organize institutions to achieve the maximum possible alignment between interests of the individual, the employer, and the state, and that there should be a general emphasis on individual initiative and responsibility.

A National Development Act of 1976 is proposed as a natural evolution from the Employment Act of 1946. Under such an act, it would be the policy and responsibility of the Federal Government to seek an ever-improving standard for every citizen, to encourage free and competitive enterprise, to minimize the inclination to inflation, and to foster the growth of knowledge in all fields. Similar to the Council of Economic Advisors established in the 1946 legislation, the new act would provide for a Council of National Development Advisors.

*** A useful primer in corporate reasoning.

481. FOY, Lewis W., "A Progressive Program For 'A Backward Nation'," 1975. 4 pp. Available from Office of the Vice President for Public Affairs, Bethlehem Steel Corporation, Bethlehem, Pa. 18016.   (C-4)

Address by the Chairman of Bethlehem Steel Corporation to the Downtown Rotary Club, Washington, D.C., July 23, 1975. The U.S. is seen as a backward nation as a result of lags in capital investment, economic growth, plant modernization, and productivity.

To get our nation moving forward again requires "an enlightened and coherent Federal income tax program." Five measures are suggested as "rock-bottom requirements": an effective capital recovery system (revising depreciation rates for plant and equipment), immediate write-offs for pollution control outlays, a boost of the investment tax credit to 12%, doing something about double taxation of corporate profits, and maintaining the existing depletion allowance rates.

482. LUNDBORG, Louis B. **Future Without Shock.** NY: W.W. Norton, 1974.
155 pp. $6.95.   (C-5)

Liberal banalities from the Chairman of the Bank of America, who attempts
to identify the choices that our society faces. The book was apparently
stimulated by the rude shock of a 1970 bank burning in Isla Vista, California.
Lundborg advocates and foresees trends such as more social responsibility for business, profit optimization rather than maximization, and a flat-
tened (more egalitarian) organization chart.
"In short, over the next decade or so I see the business system of A-
merica evolving into more socially oriented, humane, and responsive insti-
tutions--and in the final analysis, more beneficial institutions--more beneficial to the society, to the employee, and to the shareowner." (p. 100)
*** The gross mistitling is matched by the gross confusion between description and prescription.

483. RAMO, Simon. **Century of Mismatch (How Logical Man Can Reshape
His Illogical Technological Society).** NY: McKay, 1970. 204 pp.   (C-5)

Loosely used language and hortatory notes by the Vice Chairman of the
Board of TRW, Inc. The good society is more or less suggested in Chapter
6, The Electric Supermarket, which advocates On-Line Democracy, Electronic Free Enterprise, and an automated society based on the free choice
of the individual and technology for the benefit of citizens and consumers.
It is contended that reasoning such as the computer's can make man smarter,
which in turn leads to rapid social advance (p. 127). This condition is contrasted to Chapter 5, The Robot Society where automated information is seen
as keeping track of everything and directing all activity in accordance with
rigid rules. Part III, clearly mislabled "The History of the Future," includes chapters such as The Systems Approach, and The Technique of An-
ticipation."

484. RYAN, Paul. **Birth and Death and Cybernation: Cybernetics of the Sacred.**
NY: Gordon and Breach, Social Change Series, 1973. 176 pp. $9.95.
Doubleday Anchor, July 1974.   (BC-5)

New age fragments, poems, and photographs, mostly reprinted from the
Gordon and Breach periodical, **Radical Software.** Advocates cybernetic guer-
rilla warfare and an Information Economy.
"Our capitalist economy renders life unidimensional--more and more the
same; uniformity via homogeneous quantification. By contrast an information
economy thrives on variety and diversity, quality not quantity, differences
that make differences." (p. 93)
*** Peurile.

485. STERN, Frederick Martin. **Capitalism in America: A Classless Society.**
NY: Rinehart & Co., 1951. 119 pp.   (AB-4)

A collection of anti-communist letters to a friend in a European nation,
arguing that there is a trend toward a classless society in the U.S. and that
the advancement of dignity and prosperity for all cannot be realized without
capitalism. "Our workers have their full share of political power. Consequently, there is no class hatred or class struggle." (p. 9)
*** Thoughtful, but exaggerated and one-sided.

486. HENDRICKSON, Robert A. **The Cashless Society.** NY: Dodd, Mead & Co., 1972. 254 pp. $8.95.   (AB-2)

Further proliferation of a cash and carry society throughout the world is seen as contributing to the forces of resource depletion that the Club of Rome has identified. A structure and method of governing the economic system is needed to exercise global control over money as cash. Cashlessness would probably be its most significant characteristic. But "utopians and futurists" are attacked for thinking that this trend will be automatic and painless. The intent of the book is to "consider the consequences of failure to bring the deliberate guidance of human foresight to bear in directing the evolution of society toward a cashlessness that is fundamental and not superficial." (p. 11)

The desirable form of a cashless society would link all local banks and credit rating institutions to each other. Individuals would be issued a single national credit card bearing signature, photograph, fingerprints, and voice recognition computer print. In this way, the proliferation of the aggregate totals of money and the demands it makes on scarce resources of the earth would be placed under rational control, opening the way "toward a more rational general society." This would not repudiate monetary capital created in the past, but would instead accept it as a stable face value. The central bank control of individual credit would be the most effective way to regulate economic activity. In sum, the cashless society would eventually remove the economic shackles which largely prevent self-actualization. It can also serve in many ways to reduce crime.

*** The possibility of totalitarian control is a great and obvious danger, although it is considered somewhat by the author. Otherwise, this book deserves consideration: it is well-written and provocative, and appears to be sophisticated in dealing with social alternatives. The sophistication of the economic ideas, however, is a matter that cannot be judged here.

487. MELMAN, Seymour. **The Permanent War Economy: American Capitalism in Decline.** NY: Simon and Schuster, 1974. 384 pp. $9.95.   (AB-3)

No punches are pulled in this trenchant thesis by a Professor of Industrial Engineering at Columbia, who opens his book with the assertion that "The decline of the United States as an economic and industrial system is now well under way. This is a consequence of the normal operation of a thirty-year military economy fashioned under government control at the side of civilian capitalism. The new state-controlled economy, whose unique features include maximization of costs and of government subsidies, has been made into the dominant economic form in American capitalism." (p. 11) This process is not unique to the U.S., though, but is "shared by all states that try to sustain permanent war economies." (p. 12)

Melman attempts to demystify the conventional wisdom that war and preparing for war brings prosperity. He assails the ideological consensus of the economists and attacks economics textbooks. Considerable data are assembled to show that industrial inefficiency is commonplace, and is aggravated by the subsidy pattern of "state capitalism" which has made firms failure-proof, and has had highly destructive effects on the rest of the economy and society.

The remedy proposed in Chapter 8 is "Economic Reconstruction Without Centralism" and suggestions are made for reducing the military budget to the benefit of non-military activities.

*** On brief scanning, the central argument would seem to be a unique one and well-worth considering. But Melman's efforts to make his point, which is (perhaps necessarily) an over-simplified view of our societal problems, are quite transparent. Moreover, the remedy for the situation is rather bland. Despite this, Melman's basic view deserves attention.

488. BARNET, Richard J. **The Economy of Death.** NY: Atheneum, 1969.
201 pp.   (ABC-3)

A "taxpayer's guide to national security" arguing that our defense policy
is "dangerously irrational" and explaining the role of the military-industrial complex in setting national priorities.

The initial chapter discusses how many nuclear weapons are needed and
what is necessary for effective deterrence. The third chapter proposes "a
strategy for shifting from an Economy of Death to an Economy of Life."
This would involve a downgrading of the role of military power in foreign
policy, increasing national security through arms control, and improving
the machinery for setting national priorities. A National Conversion Commission is proposed to assist in manpower retraining and relocation, and
to prepare a national conversion plan. "To invest in the reconstruction of
American society means redistribution of wealth and power, while military socialism for the most part means subsidizing the rich." (p. 160)

Enacting these policies would require a movement of Americans who see
militarization as the primary national security problem.
*** Still relevant and important.

489. REAGAN, Michael D. **The Managed Economy.** NY: Oxford University
Press, 1963. 288 pp.   (AB-3)

Advocates more effective public control over the economy, based on the
view that "the American economy no longer functions in accord with Adam
Smith's concept of the invisible hand but is increasingly administered by
corporate executives and government officials." Three possible lines of
development are seen for the modern corporation in terms of power and social accountability: a "fascistic" rule by an industrial elite, a diminution
of corporate power, and a continuation of present trends, but with increased
public controls.

Numerous proposals are made, all considered to be consistent with the
technological and political imperatives of the age: corporate regulations,
by federal charter, restricting non-economic activities of corporations,
public members of corporate boards, a government-industry investment council to relate government responsibilities under the employment act, variable
tax arrangements to even out the investment cycle, State of the Union messages looking five or more years ahead, the reorientation of the system in
the direction of Presidential planning, and a general strengthening of the
federal government's capacity for policy planning: "the intelligent antici-
pation and analysis of problems." Such planning is seen as an essential
countervailing device, as well as an independent need.
*** Many proposals here that are only now being considered seriously.

490. COLEMAN, James S. **Power and the Structure of Society.** Fels Lectures on Public Policy Analysis. NY: W.W. Norton, 1974. 112 pp.
$6.95; $1.95, paper.   (A-4)

Four lectures promising a sketch, "with broad strokes," of the emergent structure of modern western society. The broad strokes are hardly
visible, though, in this difficult and rather narrow study of the growth of
corporations and corporate actors, with emphasis on the transition to a
new stage in the 20th century where actors have come to be largely autonomous.

Pathways to control of corporate actors include 1) new options of choice
to bring control back to individuals (e.g., the voucher system in education);
2) creating countervailing actors such as trade unions; and 3) state control (e.g. nationalization of industry).

491. STONE, Christopher. **Where the Law Ends: The Social Control of Corporate Behavior.** NY: Harper & Row, 1975. $12.95.   (ns)

A professor of law at the U. of Southern California explores how the law can be used to reform corporate practices while preserving managerial independence.

492. ULMER, Melville J. **The Welfare State: U.S.A. An Exploration In and Beyond the New Economics.** Boston: Houghton Mifflin, 1969. 203 pp.   (AB-3)

A University of Maryland economist argues that we have been living in a welfare state for more than a generation and that it is not something that can be turned on or off at will. After discussing the new economics in theory and practice, inflation, unemployment, and quantity and quality in economic life, Ulmer concludes with a three-point Plan for Stability:
1) A National Services Administration (NASAD) to coordinate all activities bearing on unemployment, welfare, and poverty, with the purpose of aiming toward full employment without inflation.
2) A new technique for flexible fiscal controls involving refundable taxes.
3) A vehicle for improving relations between capital and labor: a National Incomes Board to reflect the public's interest in price stability. The Board would not be a controller, but a negotiator, persuader, and arbitrator.

493. OKUN, Arthur M. **Equality and Efficiency: The Big Tradeoff.** Washington: Brookings Institution, 1975. 124 pp. $6.95; $2.95, paper.   (A-4)
The 1974 Godkin Lectures at Harvard on a recurrent two-part theme: "the market needs a place, and the market needs to be kept in its place." (p. 119)
"The fulfillment of the right to survival and the eradication of poverty are within the grasp of this affluent nation. And within our vision is the target of half of average income as the basic minimum for all who choose to participate in the community's economic life." (p. 117)
Concludes that "A democratic capitalist society will keep searching for better ways of drawing the boundary lines between the domain of rights and the domain of dollars." (p. 120)
*** And perhaps such a society will not "keep searching," particularly if it is no longer affluent. A clear example of narrow-gauged liberalism.

494. BOWIE, Norman E. **Toward a New Theory of Distributive Justice.** Amherst, Mass.: University of Massachusetts Press, 1971. 148 pp. $9.00.   (A-4)

A very academic exercise in moral philosophy, demonstrating the inadequacy of the three traditional formulas of distributive justice: utilitarian, egalitarian, and socialist. Bowie argues that adherents do not understand the nature of the problem (choosing among legitimate values and ordering them as the situation warrants), traditional formulas are not sufficiently inclusive, and the formulas cannot be applied in every situation.
The proposed alternative is a middle course which employs flexible principles applicable to four conditions: extreme scarcity, subsistence, comfort, and affluence.

495. THEOBALD, Robert (ed.) **Social Policies for America in the Seventies: Nine Divergent Views.** Garden City, NY: Doubleday, 1968. 216 pp.   (AB-3)

"This book is concerned with the possible alterations in our economic and social values and systems as we enter a world that is being fundamentally altered by the impact of science and technology." (p. ix)
- Leon Keyserling argues for further economic growth and technological development.
- Garth Magnum offers a proposal for providing everyone with jobs, utilizing the government as employer of last resort.
- F. Helmut Weymar advocates bonuses for those who earn their way out of poverty.
- Arthur Pearl proposes new careers for the poor.
- Lawrence Suhm suggests cumulative earned leave as a new tool for economic planning.
- Louis Kelso and Patricia Hetter argue for capital rights for all, rather than jobs for all.
- Robert Theobald warns that the present policy goals on which existing policies are founded may not remain valid.
- John Holt advocates the schooling of inner-directed individuals who can make intelligent and free decisions.
- John McHale offers a global view of resource distribution in order to advance "a more equitable world society."

495a. LEKACHMAN, Robert. **Economists at Bay: Why the Experts Will Never Solve Your Problems.** NY: McGraw-Hill, 1976. $8.95.   (ns)

Essays on the politics of unemployment and poverty, and on the folkways of economists, who are seen as preferring conventional and accepted theory, even thought it leads them to dangerous errors.

495b. LEIBENSTEIN, Harvey. **Beyond Economic Man: A new Approach to Microeconomic Theory.** Cambridge: Harvard University Press, Jan. 1976.   (ns)

496. GALBRAITH, John K. **The Good Economy.** Boston: Gambit, Jan. 1976. $12.95.   (ns)

497. KELSO, Lewis, and Patricia HETTER. **How to Turn Eighty Million Workers into Capitalists on Borrowed Money.** NY: Random House, 1967. 198 pp.   (AB-3)

Criticizes Galbraith's image of the "affluent society" as a mirage, and encourages the nonaffluent to set about to make the small but decisive changes to create a truly affluent economy and affluent world.
   Universal Capitalism is proposed, "an economic system in which all citizens (either as members of families or as individuals) own or have effective opportunity to own viable holdings of productive capital..." The main premise is that capital, rather than labor, is the source of affluence. Mass production must be balanced by commensurate power of mass consumption. It is assumed that everyone wants to produce their own wealth and hates to receive charity, and that the most important value of the good society is freedom and the diffusion of economic power. It is also assumed that leisure is essential to a civilized definition of affluence.
   Proposed strategies include a Second Income Plan to build the industrial power of the people and the power of the masses to consume it, relevant

changes in tax policies, and capital ownership for corporate employees.
*** A fresh and challenging proposal. Also see earlier books by Kelso, a San Francisco attorney: Louis Kelso and Mortimer J. Adler, **The Capitalist Manifesto** (Random House, 1958) and Louis Kelso, **The New Capitalists** (Random House, 1961). For a recent report on one of Kelso's proposals, employee stock-ownership plans or ESOP's (essentially a profit-sharing trust), see **U.S. News and World Report,** June 9, 1975, pp. 68-69.

498. ROBERTSON, James. **Profit or People? The New Social Role of Money.** London: Calder and Boyars, 1975. 95 pp.   (ns)

Advocates a replacement for the market system in a post-capitalist, post-socialist society.

498a. ROBERTSON, James, "Can We Have a Non-Profit Society?" **The Sunday Times** (London), May 19, 1974, p. 62.   (AB-3)

A British economist argues that "whether we like it or not, the traditional profit mechanism is already on the way out." Profits have been falling over the past quarter of a century, and there is a complex of moves (such as consumer protection laws and employment laws) designed to make companies socially responsible. Further changes toward "a non-profit economy" are seen as inevitable, leading to a downgrading of the status of shareholders.

These long-term trends "signal the end of an era in which the traditional profit mechanism could be regarded as the mainspring of the economy. A more open system will now allocate resources and distribute purchasing power, the idea of fairness will take precedence over the idea of utility, and financial planning will become concerned with balancing cash flows. "We have the makings of a coherent, evolutionary programme of institutional reform for a post-capitalist and post-socialist society."

There are three possible paths of development: a socially responsible free enterprise system without profits, a centralized state society, and centralized corporate-statism. The British financial establishment is urged to grasp the opportunity to pursue the desirable first alternative.

499. DYE, Rex. **Capitalism in a Changing World.** Economics Research, 23587 Novi Road, Northville, Mich. 48167. 1975(?) 229 pp. $9.50.
                                                                              (ns)
"...analyzes causes of the impending breakdown of capitalistic economic structure and action needed for its survival...Depression is inevitable unless we conform to basic laws under which capitalistic organization must function." (advt.)

500. ALBUS, James S. **Peoples' Capitalism: The Economics of the Robot Revolution.** Lanham, Maryland: Peoples' Capitalism (8667 Brae Brook Drive), 1975. $7.50; $2.95, paper.   (ns)

A plan to "revitalize the free enterprise system, and realize the ideals of Jeffersonian Democracy in post-industrial America" by creating three new institutions: 1) a semi-private investment corporation called the National Mutual Fund which would make stock purchases from private industry and pay profits to the general public; 2) a Demand Regulation Policy to provide sufficient savings to offset NMF investment spending; 3) a cabinet-level Department of Science and Technology to finance and direct long-term research into major productivity producing technologies.

Such a plan will solve recession and inflation simultaneously, resolve the conflict between economic growth and environmental preservation, promise an unprecedented degree of individual freedom, cure poverty and old age insecurity without taxing the rich, achieve economic equity without destroying incentives, and open up a new road to economic development for emerging nations.

501. RAYMOND, Fred I. **The Limitist.** NY: Norton, 1947. 166 pp.   (A-4)

A rather limited argument that capitalism does not distribute benefits satisfactorily, but socialism is not the answer. Rather, a "new method of government" is proposed that limits the control of the individual and the control of the government. This condition would be the opposite of socialism, making capitalism work in accordance with classical theory through the use of limitist laws as methods of control instead of taxation and regulation. Model limitist laws for Commerce and for Agriculture are proposed in two separate chapters.

In conclusion, under limitism, "We would have saved the private ownership system and freed it from the excesses which have wrecked it periodically throughout history and threaten to wreck it now." (p. 166)

502. VAN PETTEN, A.A. **The Prosperity Plan.** The Build-A-Better World Series. Utopian Publishers, 1972. 235 pp. (Available from The Prosperity Plan, Box 419, Woomera, South Australia, or 9052 Pioneer Drive, Huntington Beach, Calif. 92646)   (C-4)

An American businessman advocates "a continual voluntary redistribution of real wealth from inefficient users to efficient users...best accomplished by private lending at low rates of interest."

The Prosperity Plan includes five points:
- Eliminating taxes on transactions.
- Establishing a prosperity fund to ensure a minimum standard of survival.
- Deriving all necessary government revenue from an inefficiency tax proportionate to the inefficiency in the use of real wealth.
- Allowing an exemption of $20,000 per person in the inefficiency tax so as to protect the poor, the middle class, and the aged.
- Assessing all real wealth at the highest current offer.

Van Petten discusses his proposals in the form of dialogues with other economists such as Adam Smith, Malthus, Keynes, Keyserling, and Galbraith showing how their thinking is fallacious or how it supports the Prosperity Plan.

503. "A Strategy for Prosperity" (SR Special Report), **Saturday Review,** July 12, 1975, pp. 10-41.   (B-4)

The Report is introduced as follows: "...Can bold public-policy strokes speed our recovery? Or should we sit tight and count on the natural play of market forces to turn the tide and start us uphill again?

"For the answers, SR's editors went to Secretary of the Treasury William E. Simon, five senior professors at the Harvard Business School, Gurney Breckenfeld of **Fortune**'s board of editors, and six future corporate leaders. Their judgment provides no less than a set of blueprints for recovery and renewed national prosperity." (p. 10)

In the lead article, "Getting Government Out of the Marketplace," Secretary Simon objects to three "solutions" in particular: greater federal spending, wage and price controls, and rationing. The workable approach that the Ford administration is trying to follow includes fiscal and monetary discipline, expanding unemployment compensation, reform of federal regulatory practices, tax reform to create an environment more conducive to economic growth, energy self-sufficiency, and strengthening the free-enterprise system: "recent history shows that the government, despite its splendid intentions, is incapable of matching the vitality, the wisdom, and the ingenuity of free men." (p. 20)

The Harvard professors hold forth on "Recovery and Beyond," Breckenfeld warns of "The Perilous Prospect of a Low-Growth Economy," and the future leaders from the Advanced Management Program of the Harvard Business School engage in "Challenging the Doomsayers."

*** A one-sided forum that presents the corporate point-of-view, but hardly "a set of blueprints."

504. BUCKLEY, Senator James L. and Senator James A. McCLURE. **An Alternative Economic Plan: A Proposal for Growth Without Inflation.** American Conservative Union, Education and Research Institute, 422 First St., S.E., Washington, D.C. 20003. June 1975. 20 pp. $1.00.   (A-4)

Two conservative Republican senators disagree with the Senate Budget Committee and recommend an alternative budget with a maximum ceiling of $340 billion (in contrast to outlays of $365 billion). It is not a stingy budget--it does not deny us a reasonable national security budget as some would do--but it is not a reckless budget. Too much new money would guarantee inflation and cause even higher interest rates than in 1974.

505. BORSODI, Ralph. **The Distribution Age: A Study of the Economy of Modern Distribution.** NY: D. Appleton & Co., 1927. 321 pp.   (AB-3)

Fresh, forerunner, pro-consumer thinking, pointing out that what we are saving through lower costs of production is being lost through higher costs of distribution. "This study makes it plain that only about one-third of the consumer's dollar spent at retail is paid for production while two-thirds is paid for distribution." (p. vi)

Marketing methods are seen as increasingly a manufacturer's necessity, rather than reflecting the needs of society. Borsodi proposes more genuine competition, more cutting of costs, more consumer buying power, and more patronage of the arts in order to make life more worthwhile. "The world--to be a tolerable place for a really civilized people--should consist of only two classes: artists and patrons of artists...To produce great artists, we need great audiences--sensitive, critical, educated audiences." (p. 320)

506. STULMAN, Julius, "The Third Industrial Revolution," **Fields Within Fields,** No. 10, Winter 1973-4, pp. 83-94. (Entire issue available from World Institute Council, 777 United Nations Plaza, NYC 10017, for $2.50.)   (A-3)

An intriguing attempt "to sketch the barest outlines of how we might deal with man's economic concerns, in their broadest sense..." Essentially, it would involve intensive development of existing technology in the form of containerization and computers, influenced by brainpower applied through World Institute methodology. (See J. Stulman, "The Methodology of Pattern," **Fields Within Fields,** 5:1, 1972; also J. Stulman, "The World Institute: Key to Mankind's Emergence," **Fields Within Fields,** No. 11, 1974.) Added together, this would lead to "a whole new system for producing and distributing the world's goods which, in turn, will literally mean a Third Industrial Revolution..." (p. 83)

Stulman, who first conceived of containerization, feels that present applications are still quite primitive, and suggests a number of advances that might make redesign of distribution systems possible. Moreover, "intermodular containers of goods can be seriously considered as a realistic, flexible new monetary supplement that will aid international trade and, by greatly increasing the value of raw and semi-processed materials, be of particular importance to developing nations." (p. 84)

Such a systc n will give everyone more and take nothing from anyone. It will utilize unused production capacity, manpower, and buying power, while eliminating waste. By yielding end-products for a growing do-it-yourself market, it might create greater opportunities for individual self-development and freedom.

*** An imaginative essay that may well contain the seeds of important developments.

507. HARMAN, Willis W., "Humanistic Capitalism: Another Alternative," **Fields Within Fields,** No. 10, Winter 1973-4, pp. 3-15 (Entire issue available from World Institute Council, 777 United Nations Plaza, NYC 10017 for $2.50).   (A-2)

A modified version of a paper appearing in the **Journal of Humanistic Psychology** (Winter 1974). The "high-technology free-enterprise industrial state" is seen as unable to resolve the problems of employment, distribution, and making organizational microdecisions serve the public interest. Enlarging the public sector or returning to self-sufficient small communities are not viable solutions.

The requisite conditions of a humane post-industrial society concern ethics, institutions, and incentive systems. The basic failures of our society can only be resolved if the dominance of the growth-and-consumption ethic is replaced by an ecological ethic and a self-realization ethic.

Necessary institutional changes include 1) aligning goals of private sector organizations with overall societal goals; 2) assuring opportunity of all persons to be full and valued participants in society; 3) restructuring all organizations so that they enhance, not diminish, man; 4) a more effective mechanism by which individual microdecisions aggregate to more satisfactory macrodecisions; 5) encouraging widespread citizen participation in designing the future; and 6) promoting adult and career education needs.

Changes in incentive structures might include measures such as a "forgiven tax" on corporations (a tax that would be forgiven provided the money is used for specified humanizing purposes), a selective graduated wage subsidy (to lower corporate costs to the point where desired activities become economically feasible for private enterprise), and new institutional forms such as general benefit corporations. Such changes in incentive structures are necessary so that corporations will not suffer economic disadvantage from taking actions to enhance humane employment.

Under humanistic capitalism, unemployment would be ended by a combination of measures involving action by the private and voluntary sectors, "enhancement income maintenance" programs (available to those who wish to carry out some project of manifest social value), government public works, subsistence income maintenance, and a universal unemployment insurance program. There would be integrated planning involving "a well-coordinated network of planning units at local, regional, national, and planetary levels." And there would be a redistribution of wealth and power through "progressive tax structures for income and various expanded ownership schemes for capital."

"In the end, good business policy must become one with good social policy." (p. 14)

*** A concise array of valuable ideas.

508. HARMAN, Willis W., "Key Choices of the Next Two Decades (An Exploration of the Future)," **Fields Within Fields,** 5:1, 1972, pp. 82-92. (Slightly different version appears in the volume resulting from the White House Conference on the Industrial World Ahead--item no. 453.)   (A-3)

An earlier argument in favor of "humanistic capitalism," concluding that "we can choose either to understand and move with the tides of history, whatever they may be--or to attempt to resist them. Upon that choice may rest in great measure the state of business in 1990--and beyond." (p. 92)

509. CHASE, Stuart. **A New Deal.** NY: Macmillan, 1932. 275 pp.   (B-3)

"We have left the economy of scarcity behind and entered the economy of abundance--though very few of us realize this, and most of our thinking is still in terms of scarcity economics, a cultural lag which we shall presently discuss." (p. 1) The problem of distribution, however, has not been solved, and a drastic change in the economic system is advocated. This change is going in the direction of the left road--of more collectivism--and there are three main routes: a violent revolution, a commercial dictatorship, and change within the outline of the law and American tradition.

This last route is greatly preferred, and "The Third Road" is described in detail (pp. 173-193). Its goal is "to give the economy of abundance a chance to function, which means bringing distribution to a par with production; to banish economic insecurity and give mankind at last an opportunity to breathe deeply and to live." (p. 189)

"The Third Road attempts to dissolve capitalism with a minimum of governmental interference. It shifts new purchasing power into consumer's hands, and shifts new investment from socially destructive fields to socially useful ones, particularly public works." (p. 241)

Among many suggestions, Chase proposes a National Planning Board to find facts on a gigantic scale, and endorses Sen. LaFollette's pending bill for a National Economic Council. To deal with unemployment, spreading out work is advocated: increasing the size of payrolls and decreasing the hours of work. The final chapter, "On Changing a System" advocates local shock troop units of the intelligent minority (after H.G. Wells' open conspiracy), planning from the bottom up as well as the top down, and regional industrial audits.

*** Many ideas packaged into a popular style; Chase might well be seen as the Alvin Toffler of his time!

Is this the source of "The New Deal"? In response to a personal inquiry, Chase explained that some chapters from this book were published in **The New Republic** before July 1932, when Franklin D. Roosevelt first used the "New Deal" slogan. It is not known whether Roosevelt or Raymond Moley (credited with supplying the term, according to the **Encyclopedia Brittanica**) were inspired by Chase's use of the term. Chase modestly suggests that "the whole matter may just be a coincidence." (Letter to Marien, January 5, 1976.)

510. SOULE, George Henry. **A Planned Society.** NY: Macmillan, 1932. 295 pp.   (AB-3)

Criticizes our "Unmanaged Civilization" and exposes the dilemma of liberalism whereby dissatisfaction prevails with a society based on liberal principles. Liberals fail to understand that the true fulfillment of the individual requires intelligent integration of the society. "Of all idle Utopian dreams, unlimited capitalistic competition is the most fanciful." (p. 183)

The main objective of planning is to increase the standard of living, particularly that of the poor. The chief cultural value of planning is that "we shall be at work, through society, mastering our life and creating it as a whole." (p. 283)

Prophetically, Soule recognized that "The fight for a planned economy is likely to be a long and arduous one." (p. 281)

511. BEARD, Charles A. (ed.) **America Faces the Future.** Boston: Houghton Mifflin, 1932. 416 pp.   (AB-3)

A valuable anthology edited by the sometime President of the American Political Science Association. Part I, The New Intellectual and Moral Climate, includes 9 articles. Part II, Blue-Prints for a Planned Economy, contains the following among its 13 articles:

- Charles A. Beard, "A 'Five-Year Plan' for America" which proposes a National Economic Council to coordinate the divisions of the economy and a Board of Strategy and Planning to survey resources and forecast production levels.
- Nicholas Murray Butler, "Unemployment"
- Gerard Swope, "Stabilization of Industry"
*** The U.S. Council of Economic Advisors, formed in 1946, performs many of the functions proposed by Beard's Board of Strategy and Planning.

512. EZEKIAL, Mordecai. **Jobs For All: Through Industrial Expansion.** NY: Knopf, 1939. 229 pp.   (AB-3)

The unofficial views of a U.S. Department of Agriculture economist who feels that if we can plan in time of war, we can plan democratically in times of peace, creating a positive program to make real work for all: "There should be a stirring call to press forward now for a full-bodied War on Poverty." (p.7)

To counter unstable employment and the failure to produce enough to meet needs, Ezekial proposes a program of Industrial Expansion. "The essential idea of Industrial Expansion is to have each of the key basic industries prepare tentative programs for expanding its operations and pay roll in the year ahead..." (p.17) Government contracts would provide for public purchase of any unsold portion of programmed production.

Subsequent chapters describe this proposal in great detail, and Chapter 6 examines alternative proposals. The final chapter deals with political aspects, arguing that Industrial Expansion will protect and intensify democracy, while preserving and utilizing the most valuable elements of capitalism.

513. BURKE, Chester H. **Meritism: The Middle Road.** Los Angeles: Parker & Baird Co., 1939, 343 pp.   (C-4)

A former banker proposes a "scientific economic system" with 16 major precepts. These include complete employment, democracy, economic policies divorced from politics, no competition between government and business, the merit principle (proper rewards for talent, skill, and effort), the profit motive, sound money (currency based on gold), balanced budgets, reasonable taxes, and world peace (arising from assurance of right to work). Meritism is also described as "intelligent planning made feasible without autocratic domination."

To popularize the subject, the book is awkwardly written in the form of a fictitious conversation. To further accomplish his ends, Burke organized the American Institute of Meritism, which is described in the final chapter.

514. MANNHEIM, Karl. **Man and Society In an Age of Reconstruction: Studies in Modern Social Structure.** London: Kegan Paul, Trench, Trubner & Co., 1940. 469 pp. (Expanded English edition of 1935 German original)
(A-3)

Written "from the point of view of a man for whom freedom and personal responsibility were the highest of all values...(but) A realistic description and a theoretical analysis of what was happening in the crisis of liberal democracy seemed to him more important than a mere ideological assertion of the merits of freedom and self-determination." (p.5)

The main cause of maladjustment is seen as the clash of principles between laissez-faire and planless regulation. Planning is seen as inevitable, but it is hoped that it will take a different form from that conceived by dictatorships. "If we are to direct the social forces effectively we must not remain absorbed in the continued pursuit of short-run interests. The new form of policy can only succeed at a much higher level of consciousness, a consciousness with a taste for experiment." (p.7)

Mannheim's critique of the applicability of the sciences to public policy is prophetic of the many comments that are made today: "The specialized social sciences have been absorbed in details and have shut themselves off from the essential problems..." (p.31) "As long as scientific knowledge is scattered among the different specialists no one is responsible for considering the problem as a whole, and it passes into the hands of those who have a speculative axe to grind." (p.32)

*** Still an important work on democratic planning. The bibliography of about 1700 items (pp.383-455) is particularly noteworthy.

515. MANNHEIM, Karl. **Diagnosis of our Time.** NY: Oxford University Press, 1944. 195 pp.   (A-3)

The profound argument of an eminent sociologist for democratic planning--planning for freedom--and a militant democracy. Such a democracy would develop a new attitude toward values differing from the relativist laissez-faire of the previous age.

The "main problems of our time" are expressed in questions such as: Can there be planning based on coordination yet leaving scope for freedom? Is there a form of planning which moves in the direction of social justice?

In an argument that is still applicable to the 1970's, Mannheim insists "there must be something, a third way, between totalitarian regimentation on the one hand and the complete disintegration of the value system at the stage of laissez-faire on the other." (p. 29)

516. DRUCKER, Peter F. **The Future of Industrial Man: A Conservative Approach.** NY: John Day, 1942. 298 pp.   (A-3)

World War II is seen as being fought for the structure of industrial society, and as the first war to be fought as an industrial war--where industry is the main fighting force itself.

"It is extremely probable that America will extend her sphere of influence, expand her political and military radius, and take the lead in economic or social developments abroad..." (p.270) Drucker also feels that only the U.S. can find a nontotalitarian way to a free industrial society, and this cannot be through centralized planning.

"The planning philosophy of today is not a program of preparedness but of unpreparedness. It asks us to give up all possibilities of choice, of experimentation, and of pragmatic testing in favor of an untried miracle. It demands that we trust in the ability of the twentieth century 'expert' to foretell the future." (p.288)

Rather, it is argued that we should plan for a great number of varied alternatives and build genuine local and decentralized self-government, avoiding both totalitarian planning and 19th century laissez-faire. The present moment is seen as a fortuitous time to start, when all are united in the purpose of winning the war.

517. HAYEK, Friedrich A. **The Road to Serfdom.** With Foreward by John Chamberlain. Chicago: University of Chicago Press, 1944. 248 pp.
(AB-3)

An eloquent anti-planning classic by an Austrian economist who views the rise of fascism not as a reaction against socialist trends, but a necessary outcome. Socialism is seen as the most important species of collectivism. It seeks to abolish private enterprise, although economic planning, "the prime instrument of socialist reform, can be used for many other purposes." (p.33)

"It is of the utmost importance to the argument of this book for the reader to keep in mind that the planning against which all our criticism is directed is solely the planning against competition--the planning which is to be substituted for competition." (p. 42) It is also acknowledged that an effective competitive system requires an intelligently designed legal framework.

Mannheim's **Man and Society in an Age of Reconstruction** is seen as an "extreme position." Democracy is an essentially individualist institution in irreconcilable conflict with socialism. "When it becomes dominated by a collectivist creed, democracy will inevitably destroy itself." (p. 70) Stuart Chase is attacked for thinking that political democracy can remain if planning is confined only to economic matters. Sir Richard Acland's "Common-Wealth" movement is seen as the "most totalitarian form of English socialism." (p.212)

In sum, "Though we neither can wish nor possess the power to go back to the reality of the nineteenth century, we have the opportunity to realize its ideals--and they were not mean...The guiding principle that a policy of freedom for the individual is the only truly progressive policy remains as true today as it was in the nineteenth century." (p.240)

517a. FINER, Herman. **The Road to Reaction.** Boston: Little, Brown, 1946. 228 pp. (AB-3)

Hayek's **Road to Serfdom,** described as "The Reactionary Manifesto," is seen as "the most sinister offensive against democracy to emerge from a democratic country for many decades." (p. ix) The competitive system is attacked for its insecurity and egoism, and socially responsible power is advocated as the better path to abundance.
*** A steamy rebuttal that scores some good points.

518. GROSS, Bertram M. (ed.) **Action Under Planning: The Guidance of Economic Development.** NY: McGraw-Hill, 1967. 314 pp. $12.00.
(A-3)

Eleven essays as follows:
- Bertram M. Gross, "Planning the Improbable"
- John Friedmann, "The Institutional Context"
- Fred G. Burke, "The Cultural Context"
- Lynton K. Caldwell, "The Biophysical Environment"
- Zygmunt Bauman, "The Limitations of 'Perfect Planning'"
- Peter J.D. Wiles, "Economic Activation, Planning, and the Social Order"
- Bertram M. Gross, "Activating National Plans"
- INTERPLAN Executive Committee, "Developing National Planning Personnel"
- Robert J. Shafer et al., "What is National Planning?"
- Peter J.D. Wiles et al., "Some Fundamental Questions on National Planning"
- Michel Crozier et al., "Attitudes and Beliefs on National Planning"

519. Initiative Committee for National Economic Planning, "For a National Economic Planning System," **Social Policy,** 5:6, March/April 1975, pp. 17-19.   (AB-3)

The Committee was formed in October 1974 to promote discussion on the need for economic and social planning, "not only to enable us to avert hardship and disaster, but to guide the economy in a direction consistent with our national values and goals." (p. 17) Among the members of the Committee are Wassily Leontief and Leonard Woodcock (co-chairmen), Anne Carter, John Kenneth Galbraith, Robert Heilbroner, and Robert Lekachman. Among the endorsers are Kenneth Clark, Gerard Piel, Arthur Schlesinger, Jr., Melville J. Ulmer and Willard Wirtz.

The key recommendation is an Office of National Economic Planning which would work out alternative long-term economic programs (15-25 years) and alternative plans of intermediate length (5-6 years). It would develop programs in specific areas where there are discernable national needs, e.g., energy, transportation, and housing. The Council of Economic Advisors would become a part of the Office and continue to concentrate on short-run problems.

"Above all, planning is a way of looking at economic problems as a whole, providing the information needed to set explicit priorities in the use of resources, and guiding all sectors of the economy toward the attainment of our chosen goals." (p. 18) This influence would be exerted with economic techniques such as tax incentives and disincentives, selective credit controls, guidance of basic capital flows, and mandatory resource allocation.

520. MILLER, S.M., "Planning: Can It Make a Difference in Capitalist America?" **Social Policy,** 6:2, Sept.-Oct. 1975, pp. 12-22.   (AB-3)

General comments on the Initiative Committee for National Economic Planning and the various aims of planning: crisis stabilization, establishing social priorities, planning as policy, physical controls, planning for capital supply, anti-antitrust, and promoting incomes policy. Various benefits and dangers are also explored, concluding that "planning is not necessarily a progressive measure, even though it may contain progressive elements." (p. 22)
*** A useful and cautious overview.

520a. ROOS, J.P., "Theoretical Problems of Democratic Planning," **Acta Sociologica,** 17:3, 1974, pp. 217-235.   (ns)

520b. STEIN, Herbert. **Economic Planning and the Improvement of Economic Policy.** Washington: American Enterprise Institute for Public Policy Research, 1975. 33 pp. $2.00.   (ns)

The former chairman of the Council of Economic Advisors analyzes the proposed Balanced Growth and Economic Planning Act of 1975, discussing its possible implications, and whether it can be democratic and consistent with freedom. (From AEI catalog)

520c. NUTTER, G. Warren. **Central Economic Planning: The Visible Hand.** Washington: American Enterprise Institute for Public Policy Research, 1976. 23 pp. $1.50.   (ns)

521. GRAHAM, Otis L., Jr. **Toward a Planned Society: From Roosevelt to Nixon.** NY: Oxford University Press, Jan. 1976. $11.95.   (ns)

522. MOSES, Stanley (ed.) **Planning for Full Employment. The ANNALS of the American Academy of Political and Social Science,** Vol. 418, March 1975.   (A-3)

Moses, an Assistant Professor of Urban Affairs at Hunter College (CUNY), states in the Preface that "This volume concerns itself with questions that are at the center of man's personal existence and also constitute the basic fabric of social business." (p. ix)

"The current apprehension and fear about the nation's future is more than a crisis of economic recession or possible depression. It relates to a general perception of a lack of vision and purpose in the direction of national affairs...At a time such as this, questions of unemployment and full employment become perceived as central social issues affecting the entire society, and not simply the interests of the groups directly impacted...This volume should not be thought of as a blueprint for full employment, but rather as a guide and stimulus to reconsidering some of the basic principles and tenets of American democracy, which have been debased increasingly during the past decades." (p. xii) The 15 articles are as follows:

- Bertram M. Gross and Jeffrey D. Straussman, " 'Full' Employment Growthmanship and the Expansion of Labor Supply." Argues that restrictive definitions of full employment have obscured the growing supply of labor willing and able to work for pay.
- Augustus F. Hawkins, "Planning for Personal Choice: The Equal Opportunity and Full Employment Act." This proposed legislation by Congressman Hawkins (co-sponsored by Senator Humphrey) is one of the most significant pieces of social legislation now pending in Congress.
- Hubert H. Humphrey, "Guaranteed Jobs for Human Rights." Describes the evolution and expansion of the right to meaningful employment.
- Stanley Moses, "Labor Supply Concepts: The Political Economy of Conceptual Change." Most notable for a remarkable table on p. 38 depicting 16 different ways to estimate unemployment, resulting in percent of labor force unemployed ranging from 2.7% to 61.2%.
- Frank F. Furstenberg, Jr. and Charles A. Thrall, "Counting the Jobless: The Impact of Job Rationing on the Measurement of Unemployment." Attacks the narrow official definition of unemployment.
- K. William Kapp, "Socio-Economic Effects of Low and High Employment."
- James O'Toole, "Planning for Total Employment." O'Toole was chairman of the HEW task force producing **Work in America** (see below).
- Robert Lekachman, "Managing Inflation in a Full Employment Society."
- Elizabeth Wickenden, "A Guaranteed Income: Supplement to Full Employment Guarantees."
- David Livingston, "Labor Unions and Full Employment."
- Bernard E. Anderson, "Full Employment and Economic Equality."
- Irma Diamond, "The Liberation of Women in a Full Employment Society."
- Eleanor Gilpatrick, "Education for Work: A Full Employment Strategy."
- David C. Warner, "Fiscal Barriers to Full Employment." Shows how changes in taxes, subsidies, and methods of government purchase and regulation may lead to more productive use of the nation's human and nonhuman resources.

*** Contrary to the wishful thinking of Moses that employment is presently perceived as a central social issue, the literature surveyed in **Societal Directions and Alternatives** suggests quite the opposite: most writers who propose societal alternatives pay little or no attention to employment. Certainly there should be more attention paid to this focus, and to the proposed Hawkins-Humphrey bill.

On the other hand, it is notable that this volume is, in turn, isolated from the literature of societal directions and alternatives. None of the articles have a broad, future-oriented focus. Although "A Full Employment Society" is used in the title of two essays, there is no attempt to elaborate on the concept.

The use of the term "Employment" instead of a broader concept such as "Occupation" prejudices the discussion toward jobs in the employ of others and against a basic policy that would promote both welfare-state jobs **and** self-sufficient occupations as advocated by decentralists (Chapter 7). We obviously cannot return to a society where practically everyone is self-sufficient, but it is dangerous to accelerate the trend to a society where everyone is dependent.

522a. GARTNER, Alan, William LYNCH, Jr., and Frank RIESSMAN (eds.) **A Full Employment Program for the 1970s.** NY: Praeger, May 1976. c.250 pp. $17.50; $5.95, paper.   (ns)

Shows how full employment can be developed without inflationary consequences, how it would be paid for, how it would affect a wide variety of social diseases such as crime and drug addiction, and how a fully employed society can be established.

522b. O'TOOLE, James (ed.) **Work and the Quality of Life: Resource Papers for Work in America.** Cambridge, Mass.: MIT Press, 1975(?). $15.00; $5.95, paper.   (ns)

523. Special Task Force to the Secretary of Health, Education, and Welfare. **Work in America.** Report of the Task Force. Prepared under the Auspices of the W.E. Upjohn Institute for Employment Research. Cambridge: MIT Press, 1973. 262 pp. $2.95, paper.   (AB-3)

A unique report supervised by James O'Toole, Chairman of the Task Force. Rather than the usual list of recommendations, the report attempts "to draw attention to some of the policy implications of the issues of work and its dissatisfactions, to provide a framework for viewing the interrelationships between work and other basic institutions, and to lay the groundwork for changes in policy, both private and public." (p. xix)
The institution of work is considered to be "a point where considerable leverage could be exerted to improve the quality of life...And significant numbers of American workers are dissatisfied with the quality of their working lives. Dull, repetitive, seemingly meaningless tasks, offering little challenge or automony, are causing discontent among workers at all occupational levels. This is not so much because work itself has greatly changed; indeed, one of the main problems is that work has not changed fast enough to keep up with the rapid and widescale changes in worker attitudes, aspirations, and values." (pp. xv-xvi)
After exploring the effects of work problems on various segments of society, and the physical and mental health costs of jobs as they are now designed, the report takes up the redesign of work, which is the "keystone" concern. This includes participation in work decisions and profits, self-renewal programs, career education, and Federal manpower policies.
*** Lacks the broad futures perspective of Harman's "Humanistic Capitalism" (no. 507), and the broad economic perspective of Vanek's "Participatory Economy" (no. 531), but is still important, particularly if considered with Harman and Vanek.

524. LAMOTT, Kenneth, "Proposed: That Every American Should Get One Year Off in Every Seven," **Esquire,** Feb. 1974, pp. 63ff.   (B-4)

Suggests a Universal Sabbatical System (U.S.S.) similar to the academic sabbatical, with a stipend amounting to two-thirds of an employed person's average salary during the preceding six years. Housewives will also, somehow, receive a stipend. The U.S.S. is seen as reducing welfare rolls, and stimulating the growth of educational and travel industries, while attacking the roots of alienation of the worker from his work.

525. BEST, Fred (ed.) **The Future of Work.** Human Futures Series. Englewood Cliffs, NJ: Prentice-Hall, Spectrum Books, 1973. 179 pp. $2.45, paper.   (AB-3)

The following are among the 17 selections:
- C. Wright Mills, "The Meanings of Work Throughout History"
- Abraham Maslow, "A Theory of Human Motivation: The Goals of Work"
- Robert Heilbroner, "Work and Technological Priorities..."
- Peter Drucker, "Evolution of the Knowledge Worker"
- Marshall McLuhan, "Learning a Living"
- Robert Theobald, "Guaranteed Income Tomorrow: Toward Post-Economic Motivation"
- Herman Kahn and Anthony Wiener, "The Future Meanings of Work..."
- Jacques Ellul, "...Humanity as a Cog in the Machine"
- Carolyn Symonds, "Technology and Utopia"

525a. PARKER, Stanley. **The Future of Work and Leisure.** NY: Praeger, 1971. 160 pp. $6.50.   (A-3)

Work and leisure is seen as part of the same problem, and, to facilitate rewarding work, the conclusion distinguishes between segmentalist policies and holist policies. The former aim at limited goals and practical reforms, whereas "...a holist theory of society will insist that more far-reaching policies aimed at changes in the social and economic structure as a whole are necessary." (p. 142)

525b. FAIRFIELD, Roy P. (ed.) **Humanizing the Workplace.** Buffalo, NY: Prometheus Books, 1974. 265 pp. $11.95.   (ns)

526. DICKSON, Paul. **The Future of the Workplace: The Coming Revolution in Jobs.** NY: Weybright and Talley, Jan. 1976. $15.00.   (ns)

527. EHRENREICH, John and Barbara. **The Politics of Work.** NY: Random House, 1976.   (ns)

NOTE: The items in this guide considered to be most deserving of attention--all with "1" or "2" ratings--are summarized as "The Civic Curriculum," pp. 7-13. Also see the explanation of the rating system on page 4.

Chapter 11

Redistribution of Wealth and Power

Redistribution is an important aspect of both reforming the economy and reforming the government. But it is a very sensitive question that is often ignored, which in turn can give tacit concurrence to present patterns of allocating who gets what.

This chapter could easily borrow the title of **More Equality** from Gans (528), for it concerns those visions of societal alternatives where a--if not the--major focus is a change in the shares of material wealth and political power. Gans does not advocate complete equality, unlike many others in this chapter, but merely seeks to reduce inequality to acceptable levels. The distinction is a central one.

Another major distinction is in the means to facilitate redistribution. There is an immense difference between democratic socialists, who seek to work peacefully within the legal framework, and "revolutionaries" of various shades and stripes who advocate an overthrow of existing structures as a necessity to end the evils of capitalism. Both of these positions are often lumped together as "the extreme Left" or "the radical Left."

A final distinction concerns the issue of collectivism vs. freedom as envisioned by advocates of redistribution, and their opponents. The advocates view freedom of the individual arising from participation in political and workplace decisions, and from the economic security provided by the government. This economic security may or may not involve nationalization of industry. Opponents of redistribution fear chaos in leadership, and government intervention as diminishing individual freedom (see Chapter 12). The difference in these two views is largely a matter of which individual freedoms are under consideration.

Gans' essays (528) begin this chapter as a demonstration that one can discuss redistribution as a pragmatic matter of costs and benefits, and that it is not necessarily a "radical" concern, as suggested in the subtitle of the Benello/Roussopoulos anthology on "Participatory Democracy" (530). Vanek also takes a pragmatic stance in arguing for the efficacy of "The Participatory Economy" (531). This slant on the redistribution of power is also known as self-management (532), organizational democracy (533), and worker's participation (534). In contrast, Nader argues that worker control is not necessarily good for the consumer or for the environment, and suggests the outlines of a "consumer-owned economy" (535). A somewhat similar perspective is developed by Hampden-Turner's strategy of social marketing which would focus on Community Development Corporations (536). Perhaps these perspectives will be brought together in the **Encyclopedia for Social Reconstruction** that is under way at the Institute for Policy Studies (537).

Socialism in its broadest sense is introduced by the Campen bibliography (538). Many of the preceding items in this guide explicitly use the "socialist" title, or are close to much if not all of what socialists have advocated for some time. But "socialism" is a widely-used and abused term, much like "democracy" and "freedom." In the U.S., many people view it as a close kin to communism, and in certain respects it is, as indicated by the essential works selected by Howe (539). But there is also a non-Marxist socialism represented in the Howe anthology, and in the U.S. this tradition has been exemplified by Norman Thomas (554, 555) and Michael Harrington (540-545), who is clearly the leading contemporary spokesman. His definitive work on **Socialism** (543) offers a reasonable and well-developed vision of a societal alternative, and his advocacy of a Presidential Report on the Future (542) in 1968 goes beyond anything yet to be advocated by any "futurist." Interestingly, Harrington has never been viewed as a "futurist" nor has he ever viewed himself as such. John Kenneth Galbraith, a widely-known writer on societal directions and alternatives, is similarly not considered as a "futurist." Yet, his prescriptions for "a new socialism" that enhances the power of the market system (546), and the need to improve the efficiency of public management (547), are potentially important elements in virtually any desirable future.

Other socialist thinking has not been effective. The 1964 "Triple Revolution" memorandum from the Center for the Study of Democratic Institutions did not mention "socialism" but advocated redistribution and increased investment in the public sector. This document received much attention, at least, whereas other hopes for a new revolution (550) or a healthy society (551) are ignored. This is hardly new. In 1907, for example, Upton Sinclair wrote "in all seriousness" that a revolution was on the horizon, leading to the "Industrial Republic" (553). Norman Thomas was more restrained in advocating the "Cooperative Commonwealth" (554) and the socialism necessary to succeed the New Deal (555). It is important to all who are concerned with societal directions and alternatives to consider the reasons for the failure of this "Alternative Vision" in the 1930s. Warren's analysis points to the need for a vision that is placed within the American millenial tradition (556), similar to the warning by Gans that an American model of equality must be individualistic (528).

"Populism" is another way to consider redistribution, although in many respects it is difficult to distinguish from democratic socialism. The Newfield/Greenfield "Manifesto" (557) offers an extensive platform and is perhaps most representative of this position. The three books by Fred Harris (558-560), a contender for the Democratic Presidential nomination in 1976, offer a popular introduction, as does the "People's Platform" proposed by Senator Mike Gravel of Alaska (561).

Finally, there is revolution in its many forms, introduced by the reflections of Arendt (567) and Ellul (568). Ellul's attack on "Vulgarized Revolution" is usefully contrasted with Revel's exuberant hopes for "The New American Revolution" (569) which were often equated with Reich's expectations for Consciousness III (150). Other French writers have recently proposed "The Radical Alternative" (570) and "Christian Marxism" (571).

Ellul's concern with a "necessary revolution" based on modern realities serves as a critique of what might be called the "Old Left," which wallows in a rut of rage against capitalism (572-583), as it tries to formulate a new cultural revolution (579) or an evolutionary transition (580). Even Marcuse recognizes a great deal of "false consciousness" (581), but offers little to promote emancipation. Gerassi (582) offers a rather shallow justification for acting first and thinking later. In a concluding contrast, Crozier's concern with repressing revolution and subversion of the state (584) provides a mirror image--the reaction to those who would commit violent revolution.

---

528. GANS, Herbert J. **More Equality.** NY: Pantheon Books, 1973. 261 pp. $7.95.   (AB-1)

Essays by a Columbia University sociologist "about equality of results, or rather, about **more** equality. It assumes that perfect or complete equality is not a realistic goal, albeit a proper topic for utopian thought. Instead, the book deals with the possibilities and problems of achieving greater equality, considering particularly the economic, social, political, and other consequences, including undesirable ones, that would follow in the wake of reducing inequality (pp. xi-xii). And the book delivers exactly what it promises! (Note that Gans is **not** advocating equality of results.)

Chapter 1 on The Equality Revolution notes a continuing rise in expectations and suggests the basic requirements for "A More Egalitarian Society." Methods or models for achieving equality have historically been collectivist, whereas an American model must be individualistic. It should allow liberty to continue and should not nationalize industry. Free choice must be maximized wherever possible. The American Malaise is slightly revised from the **New York Times Magazine** article (see below).

Some Problems of Equality discusses incentives, individual striving, and scarce resources. "The major defect of complete equality is the defect of all single-value conceptions: if equality is the all-encompassing goal, then all other goals, regardless of their desirability or necessity, become lower in priority, and no society can function by pursuing one goal above all others... The real issue, at least from the point of view of pragmatic social policy, is more equality, that is, how much present levels of inequality of income and power should be reduced." (p.67) Chapter 4 plays devil's advocate and reviews 15 positive functions (social, economic, and political) of poverty and inequality, e.g. the dirty work gets done, and the poor absorb the costs of change in society. Chapter 5 discusses Political Inequality and Majority Rule. The Possibilities of Income Redistribution explores tax reform, particularly the Credit Income Tax and its economic and social effects.

Some Proposals for Research on Equality suggest studies to analyze egalitarian relationships and to explore some of the observations that were made in the preceding essays. The final chapter, Some Utopian Scenarios, discusses considerations under conditions of economic equality, political equality, racial equality, sexual and familial equality, educational equality (among teachers and students), and cultural equality of taste levels.

In a concluding Epilogue, Gans finds little evidence that the country is moving toward more equality, "and even some indication that it is now moving in the opposite direction." (p.235) Still, in the long run, as a result of the pressure of expectations, the prospects are seen as more encouraging than the current situation would suggest.

*** Grapples with the tough questions, such as social costs and equality vs. liberty, that others have yet to recognize, or choose to ignore.

529. GANS, Herbert J., "The American Malaise," **The New York Times Magazine,** Feb. 6, 1972, pp. 16ff.   (AB-3)

Countering President Nixon's assertion that the American malaise is associated with too much affluence and a loss of will to improve, Gans argues that the problem has developed in part from "the closing of the gap between people's aspirations and expectations, and a recent widening of the gap between these expectations and their achievement." (p.16) Moreover, "matters previously decided by fiat, consensus, or by the application of traditional values now have to be negotiated, and in many ways, America has become a negotiating society." (p.24) "The final and perhaps most important reason for the malaise is that the new expectations are developing in an old economic and political system which cannot really deal with them." (p.26)

Gans concludes that these rising expectations are not necessarily a sign of decline: an adaptive redistribution of income would justify optimism about the future, but if the poor are further squeezed and if they fight back, "America will one day fall apart from internal strife."

529a. SHOSTAK, Arthur B., Jon VAN TIL, and Sally Bould VAN TIL. **Privilege in America: An End to Inequality?** Englewood Cliffs, NJ: Prentice-Hall, 1973. 150 pp. $6.95.   (ns)

"An argument from social scientists that inequality is inevitable if A-merican goals continue to be set by political leaders and academics whose programs assume that it is an unavoidable and even socially useful fact of life. In the course of challenging this notion, the authors evaluate several plans for income redistribution." (World Future Society Book Service)

529b. LEVINE, Donald J. and Mary Jo BANE (eds.) **The "Inequality" Con-troversy.** NY: Basic Books, 1975. 338 pp. $17.50; $6.95, paper.
                                                                                        (ns)

529c. BROWNING, Edgar K. **Redistribution and the Welfare System.** Wash-ington: American Enterprise Institute for Public Policy Research, 1975. 131 pp. $3.00.   (ns)

529d. BROWNING, Edgar K., "How Much More Equality Can We Afford?" **The Public Interest,** No. 43, Spring 1976, pp. 90-110.   (A-4)

"Although some government statistics misleadingly indicate otherwise, it is clear that the distribution of income has become dramatically more equal in recent years as a result of egalitarian policies. Moreover, the massive redistribution currently taking place each year makes it very costly to attempt to move still further toward equality. I will show why by exam-ining the economic and ethical implications of additional redistribution." (p. 90)
*** The key to this challenging but very one-sided argument is that the income level of those officially classified as poor does not include the value of "in-kind" transfers from the government. But if the income of the poor is to be redefined by some allowance for government goods and services, one must also attempt to make a similar calculation for the income of the non-poor, a task that Browning does not even acknowl-edge. There are many government services such as education, trans-portation, police protection, and dispensing information where the non-poor receive both greater quantity and quality. All things considered (and one should also measure differences in wealth as well as income), there **may** be a general trend toward greater inequality.
     This essay is an excellent example of what can be considered as either overly narrow or reductionist calculation, and/or crypto-conser-vatism.

530. BENELLO, C. George and Dimitrios ROUSSOPOULOS (eds.) **The Case for Participatory Democracy: Some Prospects for a Radical Society.** NY: Viking, 1971; Compass edition, 1972. 386 pp. $2.95, paper. (A-3)

"Participatory democracy assumes that in a good society people participate fully, and that a society cannot be good unless that happens. Participation and control must be **one.**" (p.6) The thrust of the 21 essays is to seek struc-tural changes in a depersonalized system that is closing out true democracy. Among the contributions are:
- Don Calhoun, "The Human Material" (concerning the nature of man)
- Stewart E. Perry, "...the Genesis of the Community Development Copora-tion"
- James Gillespie, "Toward Freedom in Work"
- Murray Bookchin, "Toward a Liberatory Technology"
- Gerry Hunnius, "The Yugoslav System of Decentralization and Self-Management"

- John D. McEwan, "The Cybernetics of Self-Organizing Systems"
- Arthur W. Chickering, "How Many Make Too Many?" (on the relationship between personal development and size)
- Murray Bookchin, "The Forms of Freedom"
- Christian Bay, "'Freedom' as a Tool of Oppression"
- Colin Ward, "The Anarchist Contribution"

531. VANEK, Jaroslav. **The Participatory Economy: An Evolutionary Hypothesis and a Strategy for Development.** Ithaca, NY: Cornell University Press, 1971. 181 pp. $6.50. 1974 edition; $2.45, paper. (AB-2)

Also known as the labor-managed market economy, the participatory economy is seen as a new major economic system, differing from both western capitalism and the Soviet-type command economy. This volume offers fresh and cogent general thoughts for a general audience, summarizing the essentials of Vanek's earlier study addressed to fellow economists (**The General Theory of Labor-Managed Market Economies.** Cornell, 1970).

The five defining characteristics of a participatory economy are: firms controlled and managed by those working in them, equitable income sharing, the working community not having full ownership (thus being unable to destroy real assets or sell them), a market economy with fully decentralized decision-making, and freedom of employment.

Galbraith's "New Industrial State" is seen as an evolutionary substage of a more general trend. Arriving at this desirable condition is described in terms of transition from the left (from a Soviet-type command economy), and transition from the right. Chapter 3 asks "How Well Can the Participatory Economy be Expected to Operate?" and argues that it would do as well as any existing economy. Chapter 4 describes the economy of Yugoslavia as a prototype, and Chapter 5 places the economic theory in the context of a theory of social evolution.

Vanek concludes by hoping that the less-developed countries can skip developmental stages and move directly to a state of socioeconomic equilibrium.

532. ADIZES, Ichak and Elisabeth Mann BORGESE (eds.). **Self-Management: New Dimensions to Democracy.** Studies in Comparative Politics, No. 7. Santa Barbara, Calif.: ABC-Clio, Aug. 1975. 192 pp. $12.75; $4.75 paper. (ns)

Documents a 1971 conference held at the Center for the Study of Democratic Institutions, bringing together scholars and diplomats to discuss experiments in self-management underway in Yugoslavia, Israel, and Norway.

533. "Organizational Democracy: Participation and Self-Management" **Administration & Society,** 7:1, May 1975. (ns)

Seven articles as follows:
- Carole Pateman, "A Contribution to the Political Theory of Organizational Democracy"
- David Ellerman, "The 'Ownership of the Firm' is a Myth"
- A. Covarrubias and J. Vanek, "Self-Management in the Peruvian Law of Social Property"
- Michael Brower, "Experience With Self-Management and Participation in United States Industry"
- Cornell Self-Management Working Group, "Toward a Fully Self-Managed Industrial Sector in the United States"
- G. David Garson and Michael P. Smith, "On Public Policy for Self-Management: Toward a Bill of Rights for Working People"

534. POOLE, Michael. **Worker's Participation in Industry.** Boston, Mass.: Routledge & Kegan Paul, 1975. 198 pp. $15.00.   (ns)

Views participation as part of the exercise of power in society, and reviews various participation programs in various industrial societies.

535. COCKBURN, Alexander, and James RIDGEWAY, "Ralph Nader Forecasts Big Change Coming in the 1980s," **The Village Voice,** Sept. 29, 1975, pp. 16ff.   (AB-3)

An interview with Ralph Nader in an attempt to pin down his long-term strategy and long-term vision. Nader feels that the situation is not yet bad enough for any fundamental change, but by the 1980s people will start losing faith in the economic system.

Nader advocates a consumer-owned economy which would not require any change of habits, but only changing ownership of stores and other institutions. "Once you get a consumer-owned retail economy you get a massive increase in collective bargaining power... Once you start with food, which is always easiest, you can go into cooperative credit unions, cooperative housing, cooperative entertainment, cooperative adult education, cooperative banks, and so on." (p.19)

Nader's solution is contrasted with worker control of industry, which is good for worker conditions, but "not necessarily good for the consumer and not necessarily good at all for the environment." (p.16) The main obstacle to facilitating consumer co-op development is seen as the lack of credit. *** Brief, but illuminating; an elaboration would be useful.

535a. 1976 Public Citizen Platform (Brochure). Public Citizen, P.O. Box 19404, Washington, D.C. 20036. Single copies free with stamped self-addressed envelope; greater quantities are $.10 each.   (AB-3)

Headed by Ralph Nader, Public Citizen "advocates structural reforms in tax policy, antitrust enforcement, corporate accountability, freedom of information, health care delivery, occupational health, safe energy production, consumer choice in the marketplace and citizen participation in government decision-making."

The Platform "proposes avenues to secure citizen control over the quality of life and the quality of justice," with 27 general proposals such as reimbursement for the costs of citizen participation, expanding the use of ballot box instruments such as referendum and recall, consumer cooperatives, a patient's bill of rights, complete product information, decentralization of energy sources, closing tax loopholes, and reforming the IRS.

536. HAMPDEN-TURNER, Charles. **From Poverty to Dignity: A Strategy for Poor Americans.** NY: Anchor Press/Doubleday, 1974. 300 pp. $8.95; $3.50, paper.   (A-3)

The exposure to communications and advertising is seen as leading to passivity, self-indulgence, and submission. "The theme of this book is that what is frustrating our attempts to turn rhetoric into reality is the lack of an adequate theoretical framework with which to fuse competing perspectives towards human development." (p.xi)

The fusion of competing perspectives is demonstrated by the advocacy of Community Development Corporations (a synthesis between business corporations and community change agencies), and a strategy of social marketing (a synthesis between advertising and Movement politics). Such a strategy would offer goods for sale on the basis of the humanity and social purposes behind the products. This would lead to self-recognition of one's individuality and competence, as well as synergistic relations with others.

Another proposal is a non-manipulative sociology that would give attention to the creation of social matrices in which innovation, self-reliance, and resourcefulness could occur. The book is concluded with a chapter entitled "1983: Scenes from a Liberated Culture."
*** Very original and complex thinking that suffers from a disjointed presentation. The style is similar to the author's previous work, **Radical Man: The Process of Psycho-Social Development** (Anchor, 1971).

537. **Draft Prospectus for the Encyclopedia of Social Reconstruction: Plans & Practices for a New Society.** Washington: Institute for Policy Studies (1520 New Hampshire Ave., N.W.), 1973. 227 pp.   (A-3)

An ambitious and potentially important project that aims to be a tool for people to develop knowledge to build a new society that seeks "survival, human-ness, equality and an end to colonizing thought and action." (p.29) The project seeks to clarify the spirit of the time. "We will show how to rebuild what is to be rebuilt, who are the allies and who are the opponents." (p.15)

The General Editors are Marcus Raskin and Richard Barnet, and among the 24 other editors are Gar Alperovitz, Hannah Arendt, Murray Bookchin, Karl Hess, Christopher Jencks, James Ridgeway, Arthur Waskow, and Garry Wills. The quarterly journal, **Working Papers for a New Society,** is connected with the project.

There will be 17 major categories of the Encyclopedia: Bringing Up Children, Culture and the Arts, Health and Medicine, The Law and the State, Liberation of the Spirit, Living With the Process of Nature (with an Agriculture subsection), The Neighborhood, Natural Resources and Energy, Political Economy, Psychostructure and Character, Regional Development, Relations of Peoples and States, Reconstructive Knowledges, Cities and New Towns, Third World Cultures and Politics in the U.S., Tools and Technology, and Women and Men. The bulk of the Prospectus is devoted to describing questions to be considered under each of these categories.

538. CAMPEN, Jim (comp.) **Materials Relevant to Constructive Thinking about Socialist Alternatives for America: A Bibliography.** Resource Materials in Radical Political Economics, Vol. 1. Ann Arbor, Michigan: Union for Radical Political Economics (c/o Michigan Union), Spring 1974. 122 pp.   (AB-3)

An annotated bibliography of 577 items "potentially useful to people interested in exploring the possibilities for a humane, democratic socialism in this country." (p. 3) Includes a selective listing of 54 items (of which 25 are most highly recommended), not unlike "The Civic Curriculum" in this guide. Index to author only.

The five sections are as follows:
1) Socialist Thought: histories and surveys of socialist thought, Marxist, anarchist, utopian, and fictionalized speculation.
2) Socialist Experience: socialist countries, other countries, the American experience, and "So-called Primitive Societies."
3) Aspects of the Socialist Alternative for America: economics, self-management, participatory democracy, ecology, design and planning, sex roles, education, human nature, etc.
4) Alternatives to Socialism for America: establishment and humanist futurology, counter-cultural alternatives, reformed capitalism.
5) Complements to Thinking About the Socialist Alternative: critical analysis of the capitalist system, strategic thinking, and radical periodicals.
*** A complementary guide to **Societal Directions and Alternatives** that is broader in certain respects and narrower in others. Campen's URPE guide offers access to more foreign materials, more materials by American radicals, and more items of a specialized nature (Sections

1-3). This guide offers a far broader range of alternatives and complements to the socialist alternative (Sections 4 and 5 in the URPE guide).
The Campen guide is more generous in its praise of many items.
Both guides appear to be animated by similar views of the desirable
society; the major difference between the guides is in the perceived
viability of various strategies for attaining the goal.

539. HOWE, Irving (ed.) **Essential Works of Socialism.** NY: Holt, Rinehart and Winston, 1970. 406 pp.   (AB-2)

Authoritative documents for purposes of political reflection and historical
evidence, with a conscious effort to omit esoteric and "internal" kinds of
radical polemics. Items are grouped in five sections:
1. The Founding Fathers: Marx and Engels, including "The Communist
   Manifesto."
2. The Social Democratic Tradition: Kautsky, Plekhanov, Luxembourg, and
   Edward Berstein on "Evolutionary Socialism."
3. The Bolshevik Tradition: Lenin, Trotsky, Bukharin, etc.
4. Non-Marxian Socialism: Mill, Wilde, Orwell, Morris, Shaw and Russell.
5. Recent Socialist Thought: Djilas, Strachey, Harrington, Bell, Buber,
   Lange, Lichtheim, Cole, Walzer, etc.
*** A valuable collection that lives up to its title.

540. HOWE, Irving and Michael HARRINGTON (eds.) **The Seventies: Problems and Proposals.** NY: Harper & Row, 1972. 519 pp. $12.50.
                                                                   (AB-3)
A useful but somewhat outdated introduction to democratic socialism, by
way of 28 essays originally appearing in **Dissent.** The common theme is one
of a major social and political crisis that requires radical changes such as
a major extension of reforms designated as the welfare state, a significant
redistribution of income, wealth, and power, the eradication of racism and
poverty, and the major components of the economy collectively owned and
democratically controlled. The articles focus on immediate and middle-
range domestic problems, for example:
- Michael Harrington, "American Society: Burdens, Problems, Solutions,"
    advocates socialized investment on a national scale within the frame-
    work of planning, and an Office of the Future in the White House.
- Irving Howe, "What's the Trouble? Social Crisis, Crisis of Civilization,
    or Both?"
- Robert Lekachman, "Between Apostles and Technicians: Mind-Blowing
    and Problem Solving"
- Leon Shull and Stina Santiestevan, "What Do We Want Right Now? Legis-
    lative Proposals for Reform," recommends public service employment,
    a guaranteed income, raising the minimum wage, and national health
    insurance
- Arnold S. Kaufman, "A Political Strategy for Radical Liberals," argues
    for a new coalition strategy in the Democratic Party.

541. HARRINGTON, Michael. **The Accidental Century.** NY: Macmillan, 1966;
Baltimore: Penguin Books, 1967. 322 pp.   (A-3)

Concerns the contemporary decadence, with a focus on what is dying in
order to understand what is being born. The accidental revolution is the technological and cybernetic transformation that is being carried out in a casual
way. It has introduced doubt and contradiction into every Western creed.
"In order to choose the new society rather than being chosen by it, the
West must make this accidental century conscious and truly democratic.
And this goal I would call socialism." (p. 277) Laying the ground for his subsequent book, Harrington proclaims that "only the emergence of a democratic

Left holds out the possibility of the United States measuring up to its challenge." (p. 302)

The heart of the socialist hope is that the people democratically control the technology of production; however, "the nationalization of industry is a technique of socialism, not its definition. It is one extremely important way of abolishing the political and social power that results from concentrated private ownership... But there are other ways to forward the democratization of economic and social power. Fiscal and monetary policy, a cooperative sector, and taxes are among them." (p. 279)

542. HARRINGTON, Michael. **Toward a Democratic Left: A Radical Program for a New Majority.** NY: Macmillan, 1968; Batimore: Penguin Books, 1969. 314 pp.   (A-3)

Observes the contrast of American pretense and practice, and attacks the rhetoric of President Johnson as "windy futurism." The problem with the War on Poverty is that not enough visionaries preceded the practical men. "For the next time the nation decides to start moving again, there must be a democratic Left with some idea of where it is going." (p. 12) The horizon of this book is therefore set 20 years in the future, offering a program that is located between immediate feasibility and ultimate utopia: a program that goes beyond the New Deal, which has now become the status quo.

The "Social-Industrial Complex" is attacked for its sinister potential, and the ideology of anti-ideology is assailed. It is argued that a new poverty and a new racism is being created.

The response to this condition requires an unconditional war on poverty to destroy every slum within ten years and to have actual full employment. Agencies are needed for democratic planning that allocates more resources according to criteria of social need. Chapter 5, Tentative Proposals for a New Civilization, advocates a revolution in knowledge so that society is provided with intelligible information about the choices before it. Of particular interest is the proposal for a periodic Report on the Future by the President, projecting basic choices before the country and the estimated costs of alternative programs. This would be presented to a Joint Congressional Committee on the Future, which would hold public hearings. "The House and Senate will then debate, and vote on, the general economic and social orientation of the American Government during the next period." (p. 115)
*** Outdated in its discussion of politics, but the proposals are still important.

543. HARRINGTON, Michael. **Socialism.** NY: Saturday Review Press, 1972; Bantam, 1973. 436 pp.   (AB-1)

The opening sentence offers an important challenge: "Socialism has known increments of success, basic failure and massive betrayal. Yet it is more relevant to the human construction of the twenty-first century than any other idea." (p. 3) There will be collectivism in the 21st century; the major question is whether its form will be totalitarian, bureaucratic, or democratic: "...the socialism defined here does not pretend to be the wave of the future. It is simply our only hope." (p. 10)

The first 11 chapters are historical. Chapter 12, Beyond the Welfare State, asserts that there will be planning in the future, and that the only question is what kind and for whom. The three main areas of programs to democratize economic power are the socialization of investment, progressive socialization of the functions of corporate property, and tax policy as an instrument for social justice.

Chapter 13, Beyond the World Market, argues that capitalism perpetuates ancient wrongs and economic backwardness. Communism is perhaps relevant, but totalitarian. World and regional economic planning is needed, as well as a transformation of trade and aid policy.

Chapter 14 elaborates on the contemporary vision of socialism: a society in which compulsory work and money would both tend to disappear: "all men will work like artists, out of an inner need and satisfaction, and not because they are forced to earn their daily bread." (p. 368)

The most basic premise of socialism is that "man's battle with nature has been completely won and there is therefore more than enough of material goods for everyone." (p. 344) As a result of this change, cooperation rather than competition becomes natural. Harrington is not convinced by the ecological pessimism of those such as Boulding and Heilbroner, for socialism could speed up three important trends: technological innovation, population control, and a change in consumption attitudes. Under a socialist system, waste and pseudo-needs would be eliminated--an important consideration in calculating the limits to world resources. If abundance is not possible, neither is socialism in the full sense of emancipating personality; however, in "a spaceship society," socialism could promote fairness in rationing.

Criticisms are made of both Daniel Bell and Theodore Roszak, with the conclusion that "It will never come to pass in its ideal form, yet it is important to detail the dream in order to better design each approximation of it." (p. 344)

*** Clearly the definitive work, for the moment at least, on contemporary socialism.

544. HARRINGTON, Michael. **The Twilight of Capitalism.** NY: Simon & Schuster, May 1976. $9.95.   (ns)

545. Democratic Socialist Organizing Committee, "Toward a Socialist Presence in America," **Social Policy,** 4:4, Jan.-Feb. 1974, pp. 5-10. (AB-3)

A statement by Michael Harrington and the Committee, outlining the principles of the organization, which identifies with the tradition of Debs and Thomas. Democracy is the essential point. "Planning, nationalization, and the other traditional socialist proposals are not socialist when they are not accompanied by democracy." (p. 6)

As for government programs, "the failures of the sixties show that underfinanced programs which rely on the social conscience of the private sector will not accomplish their proclaimed goals..." (p. 7) It is necessary to go beyond the conventional liberal wisdom: "the problems before America today cannot be solved on an ad hoc basis. They require democratic planning, the posing of alternatives, basic changes. Our technology and world are revolutionary and our choices are going to be radical, whether we know it or not." (p. 10) It is hoped that the Democratic party can be turned into a new kind of mass political party with a democratic left program. The ultimate aim is "to create the conditions of freedom for all mankind and an end to every form of domination." (p. 10)

546. GALBRAITH, John Kenneth. **Economics and the Public Purpose.** Boston: Houghton Mifflin Co., 1973. 334 pp. $10.   (A-3)

Continues the thinking in **The Affluent Society** and **The New Industrial State** with a focus on the theme of unequal development and the associated inequality of income. A key concept is that of the planning system: the giant firms that do not conform to the neoclassical model, and are not passive in response to the market or the state. Galbraith advocates "The New Socialism" which retrieves the state for the public purpose by radically enhancing the power and competence of the market system in relation to that of the planning system.

The most formidable task of reform is The Emancipation of Belief (Chap. 22), specifically the belief that the purposes of the planning system are those of the individual. Such an emancipation would lead to the emancipation of the state; in turn, "seven lines of public action become possible--and necessary." These include measures to equalize power and competence in the economic system, enhance inter-industry coordination, and ensure that public expenditures serve public purposes.

547. GALBRAITH, John Kenneth, "Tasks for the Democratic Left," **The New Republic,** August 16 & 23, 1975, pp. 18-20.   (A-3)

The failures of the democratic left in all countries have been in controlling inflation while avoiding unemployment, and the dilemma of public ownership of failed corporations. The prime political task of the democratic left is not to deepen the faith, but to improve the capacity for performance: "extension of the area of public ownership is only possible politically and economically as the reputation for efficient public management is affirmed. That is now the absolute essential." (Concluding words, p. 20)

548. FROMM, Erich (ed.) **Socialist Humanism: An International Symposium.** Garden City, NY: D˜ubleday, 1965; Anchor edition, 1966. 461 pp.
(A-3)
Socialist Humanism is seen as one branch of contemporary Humanism, which is defined as "the belief in the unity of the human race and man's potential to perfect himself by his own efforts." Fromm brings together 36 essays, of which 31 were written specifically for this volume. The final item is "The Triple Revolution" memorandum from the Center for the Study of Democratic Institutions (no. 549).

549. Ad Hoc Committee on the Triple Revolution. **The Triple Revolution.** Santa Barbara, Calif.: Center for the Study of Democratic Institutions, 1964. (Reprinted in Fromm, no. 548)   (B-4)

A memorandum sent to the President in March 1964, with 24 signatories, including W.H. Ferry, Todd Gitlin, Michael Harrington, Tom Hayden, Gunnar Myrdal, Gerard Piel, Michael D. Reagan, Ben B. Seligman, Robert Theobald, Alice Mary Hilton, David T. Bazelon, and Linus Pauling.
The statement "demands a fundamental re-examination of existing values and institutions" in the light of three separate and mutually reinforcing revolutions involving cybernation, weaponry, and human rights. The first has led to a new era of production distinct from the industrial era; the new weaponry has eliminated war as a method for resolving international conflicts; and the worldwide demand for full human rights is now "clearly evident."
Among the proposals for action are a "massive" program to build up the educational system, "massive" public works, a "massive" program of low-cost housing, rapid transit systems, low-cost public power systems, rehabilitation of obsolete military bases, a major revision of the tax structure aimed at redistributing income, new planning institutions at every level of government, and increased investment in the public sector. "With the emergence of the era of abundance we have the economic base for a true democracy of participation..."
*** A widely-recognized document in the 1960's which in retrospect exemplifies the massive rhetoric of that time. In the 1970's, we face a triple failure: less abundance, a greater threat of war, and a probable decline in human rights (particularly in a global sense). Today, the only effective argument for massive change may probably be one that spells out desirable actions in terms of social costs and benefits.

550. LERNER, Michael P. **The New Socialist Revolution: An Introduction to its Theory and Strategy.** NY: Delacorte, 1973. 332 pp.   (BC-3)

"This book is an attempt to explain why the only changes that will make sense in America are those that will move the society to socialism, a socialism that will be a far cry both from the 'welfare statism' of Sweden and the bureaucratic regimes of Eastern Europe...(it) can be realized in this country only through revolutionary struggle." (p.xi)

Part 1 provides Analysis, with chapters on powerlessness, imperialism, racism, and sexism. Part 2, The Revolutionary Strategy to Change America, argues that the current crisis is economic and political, and attacks the liberal position which serves to strengthen the foundation of rule by elites. Radicals take liberal ideals seriously. Chapters concern those who will make the revolution, strategy and tactics, and violence (self-defensive violence seen as necessary).

Part 3 describes The New Society where it is technologically possible to eliminate scarcity, and where democracy will be extended to every area of our collective lives. After the revolution there will be electronic participation, a decentralized economy, regional and national planning, experimentation in communities, rotation of job assignments, rebuilding and decentralizing cities so that they are aesthetically pleasing, free essential services, free cultural activities, trial by peers, abundance for all, full development of each person, and permanent liberation of women.

*** Everything for everyone, if we can only get it together. The New Society is obviously idealized, but its description is quite extensive.

551.TANZER, Michael. **The Sick Society: An Economic Examination.** Chicago: Holt, Rinehart & Winston, 1971. 260 pp. $5.95.   (AB-3)

Concerning "the deleterious effects on human life of a society dominated by socially irresponsible corporations" which more or less control the federal executive government.

The illnesses of the sick society includes overseas involvement (Vietnam is not seen as an accident), black poverty, alienation, the international money crisis, and the growth of credit capitalism leading to the domestic economic crisis. These illnesses cannot be remedied within the framework of the present corporate-dominated society.

Two "cures" are examined. State capitalism would involve widespread intervention, but still leave ownership in the hands of corporate stockholders. Socialism, or collective public ownership, could take many possible forms. Some of the general principles underlying the basic institutions of "a healthy American society" (which is also a healthy socialist society) would be an economy serving real needs rather than trivial desires, a more egalitarian distribution of income, and widespread planning and coordination.

552. BENNETT, Roy, "The Coming Renaissance of Socialism," **Social Policy,** 4:4, Jan.-Feb. 1974, pp. 11-18.   (AB-3)

Examines new trends on the European left--particularly in France, Italy, and Great Britain, and their relevance to the potential for a socialist movement in the U.S.

553. SINCLAIR, Upton. **The Industrial Republic: A Study of the America of Ten Years Hence.** NY: Doubleday, Page & Co. 1907. 284 pp. (B-4)

A widely-known social reformer views the evolutionary process in two waves: political and industrial. The political phase took place in the late 18th century, and rapidly developing forces are now ushering in the Industrial Revolution: "an organization for the production and distribution of wealth, whose members are established on the basis of equality; who elect representatives to govern the organisation; and who receive the full value of what their labor produces." (p.x) Such a socialist society will have abolished exploitation and the competitive wage system. Competition has made men selfish and deceitful; "cooperation will make them beautiful and sincere." (p.274) The final chapter describes The Cooperative Home, or colony--presently known as communes.

"...I write in all seriousness that the revolution will take place in America within one year after the Presidential election of 1912; and, in saying this, I claim to speak, not as a dreamer nor as a child, but as a scientist and a prophet." (p.xiv)

*** Sinclair himself provides a most appropriate comment on p.257 in recounting that H.G. Wells sent a copy of **A Modern Utopia** to him, with the following inscription: "To the most hopeful of Socialists, from the next most hopeful!"

554. THOMAS, Norman. The Choice Before Us: Mankind at the Crossroads.
        NY: AMS Press, 1934; 1970.   (AB-3)

The basic views of America's foremost Socialist during the thirties. The Cooperative Commonwealth is advocated, with features such as nationalization of industry with compensation rather than confiscation, social insurance, civil liberty, a single-chambered Congress, and a redistribution of national income that would give workers collectively the fruits of their labor. "Today the best service that America can render the world is to fulfill her most glorious traditions and to rescue herself from the death grip of a disintegrating capitalism." (p.234)

555. THOMAS, Norman. After the New Deal, What? NY: Macmillan, 1936.
        245 pp.   (ABC-3)

The most probable answer to the question posed in the book title is "Fascism," and the only escape is a well-organized effort to build the co-operative commonwealth. Socialism is the only reasonable way of life, but it is certainly not inevitable.

Chapter VII provides a clear definition of the socialist position. "Social ownership of the great means of production and distribution is necessary for planning. It is the only bais on which we can end the dominion of profit." (p. 158) In this day and generation, it is seen as the condition of true democracy. Three principles are advanced: "1) No income for any able-bodied adult without work; no long search for work in vain; 2) a minimum standard of decent living for all; 3) above the minimum an approximation to reward according to deed..." (p.161)

Among the many proposals are a minimum income for each worker of $2000-$2500 per year, housing all people in comfort and beauty, a shorter working week and enriched leisure, and self-governed industries. A better basis for liberty will be provided by this wider security.

Chapter IX spells out the differences between Socialists and Communists, a critical distinction that many on the political right prefer not to make.

556. WARREN, Frank A. An Alternative Vision: The Socialist Party in the
        1930's. Bloomington: Indiana University Press, 1974. 273 pp. (A-3)

In examining the reasons for the failure of socialism in the 1930s, this scholarly work by an historian at Queens College also provides some very fundamental insights about all proposals for societal alternatives, and essentially, the politics of ideas.

Particular emphasis is given to the "realist" critique of socialism that argues for a politics of limited objectives and compromise. Warren attacks

Daniel Bell's books on radicalism, Arthur Schlesinger's pragmatic liberal politics, and Bernard Johnpoll's recent book on Norman Thomas. The "realistic" stance tells more about the values of its spokesmen than of the failures of the Socialist Party.

It is argued that socialism was rejected not because it was millenial, but because its millenialism ran counter to the American tradition of millenialism, seen as individualistic, moralistic, and open-ended. An extensive section is devoted to recounting ideas of Leon Samson during the 1930s, who argued that every concept in socialism had its counter-concept in Americanism.

The problems that bother many in society today "are connected with a restricted concept of politics that has developed the present environment and rationalized it." (p.177) The Socialist ideal of liberating human personalities was and is "a deep statement about the goals of any meaningful politics." (p.177)

557. NEWFIELD, Jack and Jeff GREENFIELD. **A Populist Manifesto: The Making of a New Majority.** NY: Praeger, 1972. 221 pp. $5.95. (ABC-2)

In the interests of "a new populism," the authors propose a platform for a movement that does not yet exist. Admitting that their fundamental argument is "wholly unoriginal," the first priority of politics is seen as the redress of the imbalance in money and power. Present policy is based on fear; therefore, the only antidote to fear is self-interest, rather than moralistic or humanitarian appeals.

Three beliefs govern the manifesto: that wealth and power are unequally and unfairly distributed in America today; that the key to any new political majority is a coalition between blacks and moderate-income whites; and that the new populism differs from the New Frontier and New Left in its synthesis of many radical and some conservative ideas, i.e. being decentralist, participatory, and anti-imperialist.

Separate chapters are devoted to banking, utilities, taxes, crime, the media, health care, unions and work, regulatory agencies, foreign policy, and opening up the political process, with proposed populist policies clearly outlined for each problem area.

*** Particularly noteworthy for the clear outline of a comprehensive program.

558. HARRIS, Fred R. **The New Populism.** NY: Saturday Review Press, 1973. 209 pp. (C-3)

A very popularized blast at the evil of concentrated power by the former Democratic senator from Oklahoma.

559. HARRIS, Fred R. **Now is the Time: A New Populist Call to Action.** NY: McGraw-Hill, 1971. 238 pp. $6.95. (C-4)

Chapters such as Let the People Rule, The Right to Health and Life, People and National Priorities, Income for the People, and People and Foreign Policy.

560. HARRIS, Fred R. **Alarms and Hopes: A Personal Journey, A Personal View.** NY: Harper & Row, 1968. (C-3)

Final chapter on "The Future of America" advocates an end to racism, renewing a feeling of community, getting our national priorities straight, more jobs, business enterprises in poor areas, calling America to greatness, and a system of national social accounting to measure the quality of American life.

561. GRAVEL, Senator Mike. **Citizen Power: A People's Platform.** NY: Holt, Rinehart and Winston, 1972. 284 pp.   (BC-3)

"Every idea (or plank) I outline here, however radical it at first seems in the context of today's politics, is basic to our spirit and consistent with our history." (p. xi) Sen. Gravel (Dem.-Alaska) argues that liberals have not made good on their promises, but have instead served to abet the increas3 and centralization of wealth and power. A people's platform would seek to change this condition, in pursuit of its basic goal of encouraging citizens in autonomous nonregulated activity.

Chapters cover "Who Stole the American Dream?," revitalizing the governmental process through public financing of elections, a New Internationalism promoting cooperation and assistance as well as foreswearing unilateral resort to force, limiting "The Warfare State," work and the workplace, reducing poverty by allowing people to control their own lives, an economy of and by the people based on realistic tax reform, health policy, equal opportunity in education, energy policy, crime and punishment, and "An End to Secrecy." Appendix C reprints the Populist Party Platform adapted at an 1892 People's Party Convention in Omaha--a statement that is still relevant today.

562. LAZARUS, Simon. **The Genteel Populists.** NY: Holt, Rinehart & Winston, 1974. 303 pp. $8.95.   (AB-3)

A Washington lawyer argues that "the new populism of the early 1970s has vented a philosophical crisis of American liberalism" (p. xv), in that the great liberal reform programs often did not work at all and sometimes caused harm.

Chapters cover the new populist revival, the similarities to old Progressives and differences from old New Dealers, the notions of Jack Newfield and Jeff Greenfield, the captivity of government, the powerlessness of people, the pageant of reform, the elite ideocracy, the genteel populists, the reformer's dilemma of populism or paternalism, antipopulist liberalism and public-interest law.

Concludes that public interest law is no harbinger of revolution, but may nevertheless be a hopeful omen as concerns reformers such as Ralph Nader and John W. Gardner. "Rather than dreaming of taking power, they are working on mechanisms to check power." (p. 271) It is recommended that reformers should focus less on promise-making and more with improving promise-keeping.
*** Narrow, but with useful observations.

563. DELLINGER, Dave. **More Power Than We Know: The People's Movement Toward Democracy.** NY: Doubleday, 1975. 326 pp. $10.   (ns)

564. The Peoples Bicentennial Commission. **Common Sense II: The Case Against Corporate Tyranny.** NY: Bantam Books, April 1975. 108 pp. $1.25, paper.   (C-5)

A steamy tirade against corporate domination of the individual, authored by Jeremy Rifkin in an attempt to be a modern Tom Paine.

The amount of space spent in the indictment outshadows the miniscule description of the advocated transition from a Corporate Economy to a Democratic Economy. Essentially, all that is said is that new politicians are needed who will pass and implement new laws.

The concluding chapter offers "A Platform to Unite America," described as "A Declaration of Economic Independence," most of which again is devoted to indictment. The direction to aim for is described in one page: "the abolition of these giant institutions of tyranny and the establishment of new economic enterprises with new laws and safeguards to provide for the equal and democratic participation of all American Citizens in the economic decisions that affect the well-being of our families, our communities, and our Nation.'' (p. 101) The enterprises will be decentralized, with control being shared jointly by workers in the plants and by the local communities in which they operate, with similar patterns of shared control exercised on a regional and national level.

565. GEORGE, Robley E. **Common Sense II: On the Further Design of Government in General.** Jericho, NY: Exposition, 1972. 273 pp.
(C-5)

Centered around the single proposal of a democratically set limit to wealth, combined with guaranteed income and good social system design. Extensive efforts are made to answer the possible arguments against this floor and ceiling approach.
* Title promises far more than it delivers, the book is wordy and pretentious, and the style employs a hip-like and very unfunny humor directed to the sub-literate. Perhaps the best example around on how not to make an impressive argument.

566. STANBURY, James. **The California 2000 Campaign: The Populist Movement With A Meaning for All America.** Jericho, NY: Exposition 1974. 160 pp.
(C-4)

Populism, or New Politics, is seen as blending the best of socialism and libertarianism. The Campaign is dedicated to ten goals, to be achieved by the year 2000 through state budgetary policy: tax justice, equal rights, jobs for all, conservation of natural resources, control of corporations, participatory democracy, an end to crime, free schools, total health care, and a peace state.
A California 2000 Petition Drive is attempting to place a sweeping tax reform proposition on the ballot. Essentially, there would be a single tax paid into Social Security-Plus, and a phasing out of regressive levies and loopholes.
Part III explains the history of populism in America, why Stanbury intends to run for State Treasurer in 1978, and the politics of love: "The job is to make community safe for diversity. Love is the answer; and Populism is love, in the only form it can find political expression." (p. 160)

567. ARENDT. Hannah. **On Revolution.** NY: Viking, 1965. 344 pp.   (A-3)

Wars and revolutions have determined the physiognomy of the 20th century, and still constitute its two central political issues. "Historically, wars are among the oldest phenomena of the recorded past while revolutions, properly speaking, did not exist prior to the modern age; they are among the most recent of all major political data. In contrast to revolution, the aim of war was only in rare cases bound up with the notion of freedom..." (p. 2)
This may no longer be a century of wars, but "it seems more than likely that revolution, in distinction to war, will stay with us into the foreseeable future." (p. 8)

568. ELLUL, Jacques. **Autopsy of Revolution.** Trans. by Patricia Wolf. NY: Knopf, 1971. 300 pp. (First published in France in 1969)
(A-3)

Largely historical, in order to comprehend the current situation, the relationship between revolt and revolution, and the intellectual thrust of revolution. Chapter 4 on Vulgarized Revolution attacks the flagrant misuse of the term to designate practically anything.

The necessary revolution is that which must be made in order to effectively change the destiny of modern man. Our society is basically technological and statist, and a necessary revolution will have to be founded upon these realities. Any other revolution is inadequate and inconsequential. Things that are perceived as motives for revolt, such as imperialism and hunger, have no bearing on necessary revolution.

The most hopeful solution "lies in the revival of citizenship, a reawakening to the virtues of individuality, and the cultivation of democratic human beings." (p. 282)

569. REVEL, Jean-François. **Without Marx or Jesus: The New American Revolution Has Begun.** With an Afterword by Mary McCarthy. Trans. by J.F. Bernard. Garden City, NY: Doubleday, 1971. 269 pp. $6.95.   (A-4)

"The revolution of the twentieth century will take place in the United States. It is only there that it can happen. And it has already begun." (p. 1) The first world revolution--the political transformations of the second half of the 18th century--substituted institutions for the despotism of rulers. The second world revolution must replace the despotism of institutions in the area of international relations. The revolution that mankind needs will abolish national sovereignty, eliminate the possibility of internal dictatorship, offer world-wide economic and educational equality, and allow complete ideological, cultural, and moral freedom. "Obviously this is a utopic program, and it has nothing in its favor, except that it is absolutely necessary if mankind is to survive." (p. 182)

The U.S. is seen as the country most eligible for the role of prototypenation in that it has five prerequisite conditions for revolution: a critique of economic and social injustice, a critique of management, a critique of political power, a critique of culture, and a vindication of individual freedom. Arguments are made as to why the revolution cannot take place in the communist countries, Western Europe, or the Third World.
*** Silly then, sillier now.

570. SERVAN-SCHREIBER, Jean-Jacques and Michel ALBERT. **The Radical Alternative.** NY: Delta Books, 1972. $2.45, paper. (Published as **Ciel et Terre** in Paris by Editions Denoel, 1970.)   (BC-3)

The advocated reforms are grouped under four main themes:
1. Separation of political power from economic power by eliminating state aid to business firms and applying the rigor of the laws of competition and profitability. An Economic Security Fund would be established for the benefit of all social groups which are victims of development.
2. Access to social equality, with primary education beginning at the age of two and subsequent education aiming for the full development of individual personality. Permanent education (lifelong learning) would replace the adolescence-prolonging higher education of the present, and a civic service would replace compulsory military service.
3. The end of hereditary private power by giving wage-earners the possibility of choosing directors.
4. Redistribution of public power through eliminating national sovereignty, in that the traditional structure of political power, confined with national frontiers, no longer allows effective control over the economy.

571. GARAUDY, Roger. **The Alternative Future: A Vision of Christian Marxism.** Trans. by Leonard Mayhew. NY: Simon & Schuster, 1974. 192 pp. (Published in Paris as **L'Alternative--Changer le**

Monde et la Vie. Robert Laffont, Collection "Liberties 2000", 1972.)
(BC-4)
Elaborates the main lines of the radical critique by French youth against
the content and value of what they are taught. Education destroys personality
instead of developing it, while side-stepping problems that deal with ends.
Garaudy is against both capitalism and Stalinist technobureaucracy, while
advocating a changed consciousness, cultural revolution, global prediction
and global planning. The ultimate objective is a socialism of self-management. This cannot be achieved piecemeal, but only through a majoritarian
revolution enabled by an electoral coalition of all the groups with grievances
against capitalist monopolies.
*** Clearly written, but nothing new.

572. U.S. Labor Party. **Presidential Platform '76: A New Kind of World
Leadership for the U.S.A.** Campaigner Publications, 231 W. 29th
St., New York, NY 10001, May 1975. 54 pp. $1.00.   (AB-5)

Robust rhetoric by Lyndon H. LaRouche, Jr., the Labor Party candidate
for President. "At this moment we have entered into the collapse phase of
the worst depression in all recorded history...at least several times worse
than that of the 1930s." (p. 6) But if the proposals of the Labor Party are
enacted, "the depression collapse-spiral can be halted (for North America,
Western Europe, Japan) within approximately any thirty days..."
"Contrary to the myths of "limits to growth,' a fraud created and circu-
lated by the Rockefeller brothers and their lackeys, there are no objective
'ecological' or other outer boundaries preventing an immediate and sustained
rapid expansion of industrialized development of the globe." (p. 6)
The three basic points of the global policy are 1) a commitment to developing fusion power or Controlled Thermonuclear Reactions (CTR); 2)
accelerating development of industrially advanced foci, and 3) raising the
level of agricultural output and productivity in all areas. The three basic
points for domestic recovery for the U.S. are 1) a general debt moratorium;
2) an emergency nationalization mechanism for insuring the integrity of
functioning of the banking system; and 3) "government-credit-supported
production-development programs amounting to an estimated $200-250 bil-
lions per year to mobilize full-scale production around a focus on priority
needs of global and national economic development."
After a long and rather academic discourse on science policy and economics, nine pieces of legislation are proposed (e.g. Emergency Agricultural Production Act, Mideast Peace and Reconstruction Act, Emergency
Housing Act), as well as proposed "Articles of Impeachment of Nelson
A. Rockefeller."
*** Rockefeller will not lose any sleep over this challenge.

573. SHEPPARD, Barry, et. al. **A Revolutionary Strategy for the 70s:
Documents of the Socialist Workers Party.** NY: Pathfinder Press,
March 1972. 96 pp.   (C-5)

Three documents presented at the 1971 SWP convention, all amply laced
with suffocating rhetoric, while viewing recent failures of capitalism, successes of the noble worldwide Trotskyist forces, and the bright prospects
for attaining "the final victory of the world revolution."

574. KOLKO, Joyce. **America and the Crisis of World Capitalism.** Boston:
Beacon Press, 1974. 202 pp. $7.95.   (A-5)

Aims to "raise some important questions of the world economy and to
ascertain new pressures toward crisis or consolidation." (pp. xiv)
Concludes that "Capitalism in the sytemic, compulsive sense is the

origin of the current malaise around the globe, and it allows for no reform.
It is less the acts of perverse men than the operation of the system which
has not changed in fundamentals and which inexorably will continue to reach
into the lives of the people in all corners of the world and destroy through
war, repression, and exploitation until the system itself is destroyed. Yet
the operations of the capitalist system can and will engineer its own demise...
The social movement of resistance that can potentially transform that collapse
into a new and better society must come from the political struggle of the
working class..." (p.180)

No way is seen to work within the system to reform or modify it. As for
the future, "One cannot predict the outcome; one can only comprehend the
forces of crisis." (p.183)

575. COOPER, David (ed.) **To Free a Generation.** NY: Collier Books, 1969.
207 pp. paper. (A-4)

Presents some of the addresses delivered at the Congress on the Dialectics
of Liberation, held in London in 1967, which was "concerned with new ways in
which intellectuals might act to change the world." Consciously blends
"theorists" such as Gregory Bateson, Herbert Marcuse, R.D. Laing, Jules
Henry, and Paul Goodman, with "activists" such as Stokeley Carmichael.
*** Inbred and impotent.

576. MOORE, Barrington, Jr. **Reflections on the Causes of Human Misery
and upon Certain Proposals to Eliminate Them.** Boston: Beacon
Press, 1972. 201 pp. (A-3)

An eloquent Marxist view, learning on the writings of Marcuse, Kolko, and
Magdoff, with chapters on the unity of misery, war and cruelty, hunger and
injustice, and intellectual freedom and scholarship.

The U.S. is seen as "Predatory Democracy" and the final chapter views
the decay of legitimacy and of traditional authority, as well as "a large
reservoir of active opposition." The prospects for reform and revolution are
reviewed, concluding that "some form of democratic and humane socialism
may well be the most desirable set of social arrangements. But the obstacles
are staggering." (p.192)

577. DOWD, Douglas F. **The Twisted Dream: Capitalist Development in the
United States Since 1776.** Cambridge: Winthrop, 1974. 315 pp. (AB-4)

"The United States is in the midst of a developing social crisis, at once
economic, political, and moral, simultaneously domestic and international.
The Twisted Dream seeks to identify and explain the nature of and the reasons
for this crisis." (p.xi)

The basic theme of the book is that the U.S. is a capitalist society, and
capitalism is a system requiring expansion and exploitation. It is concluded
that, if social crises become more pronounced, "it seems highly likely that
American-style fascism would be attempted." (p.297) Hope is held, however,
for an American revolutionary socialist movement.

578. RUBENSTEIN, Richard E. **Left Turn: Origins of the Next American
Revolution.** Boston: Little, Brown, 1973. 286 pp. $8.50. (AB-4)

Aims to demonstrate "that there is both a necessity and a potential for
revolution in America," with revolution defined as "a rapid, drastic altera-
tion of the political system which will destroy the economic basis for big
business' domination of American social and political life and which will
bring the working class majority to power." (p.xi)

Part I describes the exhaustion of the liberal reform tradition, Part II describes the relationship between coalition government and class conflict, and Part III analyzes contemporary changes in class structure and political forms. The basic argument is that "the American system of coalition government has lost the capacity to absorb and redirect social change...our options are narrowing down. Americans will soon be compelled to decide whether to move decisively Right or Left--whether to support an American-style fascism or a new type of socialism." (pp.xi-xii) As concluded in the final sentance: "Business oligarchy or worker's democracy: it must be one or the other." (p.250)
*** Superficial and unconvincing.

579. BROWN, Bruce. **Marx, Freud and the Critique of Everyday Life: Toward a Permanent Cultural Revolution.** NY: Monthly Review Press, 1973. 202 pp. $7.50.   (A-5)

Tired, inbred, and inflated rhetoric piled into unwieldy sentences. Weighty analysis with considerable reference to Marx, Freud, Habermas, Marcuse, Reich, and Fromm.
"The movement is presently in crisis. As the contradictions of advanced capitalism grow ever more intense, the profound inhumanity and moral bankruptcy of the system is revealed to ever greater numbers of people, but the New Left has no theory and strategy of cultural revolution capable of giving direction to this constantly enlarging fund of disaffection and revulsion." (p.30)
Chapter 6 explains a transition "From Crisis Capitalism to a Bureaucratic Society of Manipulated Consumerism," while Chapter 7, "Toward a Method for the Revolutionary Reconstruction of Everyday Life," advocates localized centers of cultural contestation and self-management as a principal goal of reconstruction.
"What today is called cultural revolution is none other than the totalization and reinvogoration of all the liberatory endeavors launched by past generations of revolutionaries." (p.196)

580. BOGGS, James and Grace. **Revolution and Evolution in the Twentieth Century.** NY: Monthly Review Press, 1974. 266 pp. $10.00. (BC-4)

Two activists in the labor and radical movements in Detroit suggest ethical psychodynamics (a new concept of human identity to extend the dialectical development of humanity), rather than property relations, as the key to enduring social revolution. The authors have written previously on this "fundamental and dangerous contradiction in our society between economic overdevelopment and political or human underdevelopment." (p.8)
In order to make an evolutionary transition from a bourgeois outlook to a socialist outlook, every person should begin to live on a socialist basis in relation to other individuals, races, and nations. A cadre organization is recommended for educating the masses. However, there is no Promised Land: "humankind will always be engaged in struggle, because struggle is in fact the highest expression of human creativity." (p.266)

581. MARCUSE, Herbert. **Counterrevolution and Revolt.** Boston: Beacon Press, 1972. 138 pp. $7.50.   (A-4)

America's leading Marxist theorist describes the paradox of low revolutionary potential (counterrevolution) at the height of capitalist development as deceptive, for "a new pattern of disintegration and revolution emerges, corresponding to, and engendered by, the new phase of capitalism: monopoly-state capitalism. And understanding this, in turn, calls not for the reversion but for the restoration of Marxian theory: its emancipation from its own fetishism and ritualization, from the petrified rhetoric which arrests its dialectical development. The false consciousness is rampant on the New as well as Old Left." (p.29)

Marcuse announces that "The emancipation of consciousness (is) still the primary task," but does not suggest how this might come about. Unsurprisingly, he proclaims that "Strategies must be developed which are adapted to combat the counterrevolution," but does not suggest what they might be.

*** Heavy and obscure. Perhaps there are important nuances here, but it is more likely that the robust language is largely stale, even as it attempts to describe the new.

582. GERASSI, John (ed.) **The Coming of the New International: A Revolutionary Anthology.** NY: World, 1971. 610 pp. $15.00.   (AB-4)

The writers in this massive anthology "are all comrades" and it is explained that many do not write well because they were or are men of action. The selections come from 22 countries, including China, India, Vietnam, Palestine, South Africa, Cuba, Venezuela, and the U.S., and there is an extensive introduction to the writings of each country.

There is also an extensive 81 pp. introductory overview, The Future is Revolution, in which it is contended that human progress has always come about through confrontation and revolution. "In the decades to come, familiar concepts will be discarded, systems will be smashed, empires will be destroyed. Once again, the future is Revolution." (p. 1)

Liberals "ask 'What after the Revolution?' because they don't want a revolution." (p. 80) The world that is wanted will have no masters or slaves, it will be administratively decentralized and will recognize no "supernatural" talents, and necessities will be free. But this is seen as a dream that is far away, and it is necessary to first "excise the cancer." (p. 81)

583. FRANKLIN, Bruce (ed.) **From the Movement Toward Revolution.** NY: Van Nostrand Reinhold, 1971. 169 pp. $3.95, paper.   (BC-4)

An anthology of materials from the U.S. on civil rights, Vietnam, black power, Chicano liberation, and women's liberation, representing groups such as SDS, the Weathermen, SNCC, and the Black Panthers.

"1960-1970 was the decade of the birth and growth of a pre-revolutionary movement. The odds are that 1970-1980 will be the first decade of revolutionary practice." (p. 160) Depends on who makes the odds.

584. CROZIER, Brian. **A Theory of Conflict.** NY: Scribner's, 1974. 245 pp. $12.50.   (A-4)

A conservative work of political and moral philosophy that is concerned with revolutionary conflict. The state is necessary, but rebellion against it is inevitable. "I conclude that in our time the alternatives to pluralism are the authoritarian way and the totalist (which I suggest as a less umbrous substitute for totalitarian)..." (p. viii. Note the assumption of "pluralism" rather than, say, the Marxist assumption of imperialism.)

It is also noteworthy that Crozier states the "Axioms" on the nature of the human animal: 1) man is innately envious and aggressive (after Ardrey and Lorenz); 2) his nature is not subject to change (no social theory predicated on the perfectability of man has been validated by events); 3) his behavior is susceptible to change for better or worse; 4) he has an overwhelming need of order; and 5) human progress is dependent upon free inquiry. (One can at least agree with the last axiom!)

Chapters concern topics such as Prevention of Conflict, Repression of Conflict, and The Problem of Subversion. It is possible to contain subver-

sion, but the real danger lies "in the reluctance or inability to see sub-version as a problem until it is too late." (p. 205) Moral courage is required to overcome the inevitable accusations of being illiberal or fascist.
*** Subversion is viewed here in the narrow and conventional sense, rather than in the broader sense that could consider, say, subversion of the biosphere in the same light as subversion of the state.

Chapter 12

Freedom from Government

The desire for more equality is often opposed by the search for more liberty. At the farthest extremes of these positions, the hatred of "capitalist imperialism" is matched by that of the "socialist state." But not all of the literature in this chapter, nor in the previous one, should be dismissed as steamy polemics.

There is a remarkably small quantity of literature concerned with conservatism, libertarianism, classical liberalism, and purist capitalism. The number of items in this chapter is less than half of the number of items in the previous chapter alone. But conservatives also consider themselves to be directly opposed to the "leftist" liberal position, which represents a large portion of the literature covered in this guide. This liberalism is viewed as the "Suicide of the West," according to James Burnham (no. 104a). In contrast, Victor Ferkiss argues that it is classical laissez-faire liberalism that has brought us to our present difficulties (no. 431).

Conservative thought tends to dwell on a standard theme: that government unduly restricts individual effort, and that public sector activity is inept in contrast to the efficacy of the private sector. The major blind spot in this argument is also standard: there is seldom any acknowledgement of the role of large corporations and how they impinge on certain individual freedoms and restrain free competition. Unless the realities of large conglomerates and multinational corporations are seriously considered, liberals and radicals are quite justified in arguing that the conservative stance favors the goliaths of the "private" sector. Advocacy of a "free society" can thus be readily seen as a strategy to promote license for corporations.

Nevertheless, the argument for freedom has considerable merit from an economic and a humanistic point of view. In addition, it should be heeded simply because the conservative position is politically potent in the U.S. Although not well-represented in academia, as consistently reiterated in the **National Review**, there is considerable conservative sentiment in state governments, in the U.S. Congress, and in the Office of the President during recent years.

This point about political clout is made very clear by the demographic analysis of Phillips (585), who criticizes the minority of "new mandarins" who shape and market ideas and information, and makes some astute comments on "The Dynamics of Liberal Failure." Rusher (586) makes a similar argument against the "guardian state" and proposes an extensive platform for a new majority party whose policies would be considerably different than the prescriptions of many social scientists and liberal intellectuals.

The general critique against the state is perhaps best argued by Nisbet (588), who advocates the recovery of pluralism and a new laissez-faire, in contrast to "the vast clerisy" of political power. Roche (589) offers a similar view in explaining why we are a "bewildered society." Lane (591) and Twight (592) hold extremely polarized positions.

Rather than focus on the ills of the state, others seek to provide a positive philosophy. The libertarian view is close to the conservative and classical liberal views. The anthology assembled by Machan (593) serves as a worthy introduction. For the academic with a taste for elegant political philosophy, Nozick (594) is clearly the contemporary theoretician. On a more popular plane, Friedman (595) gives a provocative introduction to "anarcho-capitalism," and Rothbard (596) surveys "the new libertarianism."

The older thinking about classical liberalism is introduced by Lippmann's 1937 inquiry into the principles of "the good society" (598). Perhaps the most extensive and eloquent defense of this position is Hayek's ideal of **The Constitution of Liberty** (599). Roepke's defense of the free market (600) is also noteworthy. The other items have not been seen or are not as valuable. Mention should be made of Ayn Rand's essays on capitalism (607), for her novels are widely known, and her protégé is the current Chairman of the Council of Economic Advisors. (In contrast, could one ever imagine a protégé of Herbert Marcuse attaining a position of great influence in the U.S. government?) One might also note a curious collection of Morman essays (611), including a contribution from a former U.S. Secretary of Agriculture. To conclude on an amusing note, there is indeed a "Foresight Through Hindsight" Series (612), not to be confused with any present-day "futurist" thinking. It is noteworthy that "futurist" thinking by virtually any definition is quite foreign to any of the writing in this chapter.

585. PHILLIPS, Kevin P. Mediacracy: American Parties and Politics in the Communications Age. NY: Doubleday, 1975. 246 pp. $8.95.   (A-3)

Now a nationally syndicated columnist, Phillips received considerable attention from **The Emerging Republican Majority** (Arlington House, 1969), an exhaustive demographic analysis in the cause of right-wing politics. The demographics are back again (17 maps and 25 charts) along with considerable historical analysis, and a fresh view of American society that borrows from and improves upon the writings of Daniel Bell and Herman Kahn.

Phillips describes "a fundamentally changed era" of new alignments based on new socioeconomic criteria, and therefore a watershed in American politics. Instead of an aristocracy or a democracy, the dominant influence of the media has resulted in a mediacracy. America's "new mandarins" are people who shape and market ideas and information. Liberalism is the ideology of this privileged sector of the population because of economic interest in social and research spending. The knowledge sector has a vested interest in change, which is essential in keeping demand for their products.

The major political cleavage now developing is between the New Politics/ knowledge sector (about 10-20% of the population), and the 60%-70% square majority. "Nothing is more central to the controversiality of the new class than its 1963-72 attempt to sidestep existing outlooks and institutions and reprogram American society. Conceiving themselves unfettered by the past, the new elite thought that society could be unfettered--and old restraints cast aside." (p. 34) "The Great Society's helter-skelter approach--a mixture of When-I-was-a-boy-on-the-Pedernales New Deal optimism, poor planning, recklessly distributed cash, and knowledge-sector avarice--produced the inevitable mediocre results." (p.45) Comments such as these, concerning the "Dynamics of Liberal Failure" and other aspects of post-industrial society (Chap. 2, pp. 13-80) serve as an important and well-documented critique of recent years. The rest of the book, however, gets lost in demographic analysis and suggestions (but no descriptions nor even a speculative scenario) of portentious political changes.

*** Smoothly written, with many good ideas, but, as with all conservative presentations, the one-eyed analysis is obvious. Too much power and influence is ascribed to the liberal mediacrats, while not a word is said about the corporate tycoons, whose excesses are still a major political issue. For a stunning contrast, compare Phillips to Herbert I. Schiller, **The Mind Managers**. (Boston: Beacon Press, 1973. 214 pp. ($9.95.) With an equal amount of documentation, Schiller makes the com-

pletely opposite argument: that the media promote consumerist ideology in the service of a corporate economy, and that communication
has become an instrument of repression. Nevertheless, Schiller concludes that "a gradually heightened consciousness, despite a more
tightly controlled communications system, may develop its own means
to force the social changes so desperately needed in this country today."
(p.191)

586. RUSHER, William A. **The Making of the New Majority Party.** NY:
Sheed and Ward, 1975. 222 pp. $6.95. (Also see condensation: "A
New Party: Eventually, Why Not Now?" **National Review,** May 23,
1975, pp. 550-555.)   (AB-2)

The publisher of **National Review,** America's leading journal of conservative opinion, argues that "America is now paying the long-deferred
price of economic policies pursued, in a spirit of irresponsibility compounded by ignorance, by every administration of both parties for over
forty years." (p.204) An endlessly proliferating series of rights is issuing
forth from the "Guardian State." However, it is noted that among those
who indicated a choice between liberal and conservative in a May 1974
Gallup Poll, 59% chose a conservative orientation.

The time is now ripe for a political readjustment and a new major party
(for present purposes named the Independence party) that would replace the
Republican party as the GOP once did to the Whigs. This new majority party
must behave as such and put together a winning coalition ("The Great Coalition") of economic and social conservatives. Economic conservatives are
essentially middle class, while social conservatives are predominantly
lower middle class people who work with their hands. Circumstances now
bring these two groups together in shared social values of "unapologetic
patriotism, anti-communism, a strong defense, respect for law, distrust
of big government, and allegiance to the traditional mores..." all of which
are under attack by the "liberal verbalist elite" which is supported by its
constituency geared to the welfare ethic. "That assault defines the truly
key issue of our time." (p.208)

A rough sketch of a possible platform is offered in Chapter 6. The "golden
formula" in domestic affairs is to honor and reward work. This would be
done by reducing welfare payments (although no one in the nation would be
without basic support), profit-sharing, tax simplification and reform, and
having mail delivered by the private sector. There would be a ban to school
busing and an unqualified school voucher system to promote freedom of
choice. Rusher advocates far stricter anti-wiretapping and bugging laws,
and enforcing the fairness doctrine among the liberal-dominated television
networks. The whole administration of justice should be overhauled to make
punishment more certain, more prompt and in some cases more severe.
There should be sound measures to protect the environment, but a recognition
of the "demagogic" attacks on business and jobs. Conservatives, we are
told, do not believe in governmental efforts to achieve Zero Population Growth
or in "cataclysmic fantasies of the Club de Rome type" (p.100). In foreign
affairs, a strong defense is advocated to support the best interests of the
U.S. in its struggle against communism.

In sum, "only the political coalition I have described has, in America
today, both the numbers to win and the moral resources necessary to guide
this country through its present crisis and...rededicate it to its original
principles." (p.217)

*** A persuasive argument for the political attainment of a societal alternative. Liberals, progressives and reformers obviously do not share
these values and perceptions, but would benefit from reading this book
which is consummately concerned with a **winning** coalition. The chances
of an Independence party are not great, but political events could,
suddenly, make this book into an extremely important and prophetic one.

587. BUCKLEY, Sen. James L. If Men Were Angels...A View from the Senate.
NY: Putnam's, 1975. $8.95.   (ns)

Demonstrates the failure of centralized federal programs, arguing that
government cannot do what it pretends to do (or does so at great cost) and
that various grants and programs have created a vast client empire where
behavior is determined by the dictates of grantsmanship. Buckley proposes
that government be turned back to the states and counties and that various
programs be eliminated. (From review in **The New Republic**, Oct. 25, 1975)

588. NISBET, Robert. Twilight of Authority. NY: Oxford University Press,
1975. 287 pp. $10.95.   (AB-2)

Nisbet is a well-known scholar in the history and philosophy of social
and political thought, as clearly reflected in this curious and provocative
essay. He is not well-versed in contemporary thinking, but this book--or
at least the first two chapters--is well worth considering.
In Chapter 1, The Political Community at Bay, it is argued that the dominant element of modernity in the West has not been technology nor industrialism, but political society. A vast clerisy of power exists, but there is
also a gathering revolt against it. "Clearly we are at the beginning of a new
Reformation, this time, however, one that has the political state rather than
the church as the central object of its force..." (p. 6) Nisbet goes on to describe the declining trust in leaders, government as deception, the decay of
political parties, the growth of democratic royalism, the obsolescence
of ideology (the conservatives were wounded by Watergate while the New
Left has retreated from objectivity), bureaucracy ("the transfer of government from the people"), and the erosion of patriotism.
Chapter 2, The Crumbling Walls of Politics, describes the loss of social
roots (through decline of community, dislocation of kinship, and erosion of
the sacred), the pains of affluence, inflation (seen as more devastating
than depression), the loss of both heroes and villains, the escape from culture (the trivialization and hubris of science, the hollowness of the social
sciences, and the general loss of confidence in knowledge because of fragmentation into tiny coteries and elites), the corruption of both spoken
and written language, the loss of the authority of the university, and the
triumph of the subjective through increasing preoccupation with self.
The next two chapters are most interesting, but not clearly convincing.
The Lure of Military Society argues that "The recipe for militarism in
a society is basically twilight of authority in the civil sphere" (p. 146),
and attempts to link intellectuals with a fondness for military pursuits.
The New Science of Despotism attacks the new equality of condition and
result as leading to uniformity and centralization, and a second managerial
revolution of government regulators.
The final chapter on The Restoration of Authority outlines the elements
of a genuine social regeneration: the recovery of pluralism (consisting of
the maximum possible freedom for each sphere of society, decentralization of social initiative, government power, hierarchy, and tradition), the
restoration of social initiative, a revival of the prestige of the private as
contrasted with the public, a renascence of kinship, a revival of localism
and voluntary association, and a new laissez faire to create a setting in which
social inventions would flourish: "...the greatest need in our age is that of
somehow redressing the balance between political-military power on the one
hand and the structure of authority that lies in human groups such as neighborhood, family, labor union, profession, and voluntary association." (p. 276)
*** An excellent political and cultural analysis combined with the standard
neglect of any attention to multinational corporations, international relations, and the environment. The unexamined assumption of affluence
should also be noted.

589. ROCHE, George Charles, III. **The Bewildered Society.** New Rochelle, NY: Arlington House, 1972. 346 pp.   (AB-3)

The President of Hillsdale College observes that increasing material prosperity is an incomplete answer to fulfilling lives. Security for the individual is at the expense of conformity. "If men are to live as men, they must do so on a human scale. Rather than big business and big government, both liberals and conservatives should complain of big society." (p. 13)

Part I offers chapters on bureaucracy, technology, urbanization, and mass culture, concluding that we have been robbed of our most precious possession: traditional American self-reliance and self-determination. Part II, The Politics of Bewilderment, argues that government has been deeply involved in the enmassment of society.

It is concluded that people can look only to themselves for salvation, with an emphasis on freedom, rather than adjustment. There is a need to combine libertarian and conservative attitudes to offer a vision of "elbow room" for our civilization--room for the individual to discover and pursue his own goals.

To this end, Roche advocates decentralized politics, keeping government out of the marketplace, stemming environmental decay through protecting private property rights, product users paying the full costs of production, restoring the dignity of work, cultural diversity, and a new elite of disciplined self-actualizing individuals. This would provide "A Reason for Living."

590. WOOLDRIDGE, William C. **Uncle Sam The Monopoly Man.** New Rochelle, NY: Arlington House, 1971.   (ns)

Demonstrates why private competition would result in much better service for mail delivery, coinage, courts, roads, police and fire protection, and schools, as opposed to the assumption of a government monopoly for certain public services.

591. LANE, Thomas A. **The Breakdown of the Old Politics.** New Rochelle, NY: Arlington House, 1974. 308 pp. $8.95.   (B-4)

A free-swinging conservative polemic viewing the source of our problems as the drift to socialism. Socialist elites, "hidden in and controlling the political parties, are the chief enemy of America today. Their purposes and methods are deeply hostile to our system of representative government." (p. 55) Socialism leads to either dictatorship or an inefficient and insufferable bureaucracy--the fundamental disability in either case is hierarchical structure. Full employment policy is seen as a major step toward socialism, and the cause of national decline and demoralization. The moral climate is characterized by socialism atheism, the licensing of pornography, limiting population growth (Lane contends that food supplies are more adequate than ever before in history), and the legalization of abortion. This corruption is seen as a failure of politics.

Even Richard Nixon is attacked for his liberalism, and Lane stresses the rule of the late Ludwig von Mises: political interference produces results contrary to its purposes.

"The country approaches its 200th birthday in a remarkable state of distress. It is returnung to the paternalism and authoritarianism which the Founding Fathers rejected...Because both political parties are committed to the socialist course, the people have no voice representing their traditional political ethic." (p.265)

The advocated new directions include purifying the electoral process which is presently subverted by the power of money, maintaining a climate of individual responsibility in freedom, restoring the decentralized constitutional order, reduction of all government spending, and recognizing the reality of Communist power and purpose in the world.

*** Pretty much the standard conservative critique that ignores large corporations, environmental degradation, and promiscuous military spending. Nevertheless, this book is useful to juxtapose against the simpler liberal/humanist critiques in order to see the mirror image of the unbalanced argument.

592. TWIGHT, Charlotte. **America's Emerging Fascist Economy.** New Rochelle, NY: Arlington House, 1975. 315 pp. $12.95.   (A-5)

"The term 'fascist' is an emotionally charged, vituperative label more often mindlessly affixed to one's opposition than dispassionately analyzed. This book has two primary aims: first, to describe objectively the salient economic policies of a fascist state...and second, to outline the highly developed structure of United States statutes and judicial decisions adopting similar premises...it is objectively accurate to label the prevailing American economic structure fascist..." (Opening sentences, p. 13)

"There are only two philosophic models for political and economic systems, collectivism and individualism." (p.14) The essence of fascism is collectivism. Fascism is the antithesis of limited government and seeks to obliterate individual right. It gives lip service to capitalism, but a fascist economy is run from the top by political authorities. A subtle consequence is to make people psychologically dependent on the government for their economic well-being. A recent refinement is "participatory fascism" or the ostensible inclusion of all dissident parties within the economic decision-making process.

With this conceptual framework, a massive amount of documentation follows on interstate commerce, money and banking, regulation, product quality control, government dominion over labor, agriculture, and international economic policies, concluding that "A marked acceleration of America's fascist economic policies commenced during 1973 and 1974." (p.260)
*** A strong candidate for All-Time One-Sided Argument.

593. MACHAN, Tibor R. (ed.) **The Libertarian Alternative: Essays in Social and Political Philosophy.** Chicago: Nelson-Hall Company, 1974. 553 pp. $12.50.   (AB-3)

A useful anthology by an Assistant Professor of Philosophy at SUNY Fredonia and a senior editor of **Reason,** with the intent "to reclaim or reinstate America's unique political tradition." (p.495)

There are 37 articles by writers such as Murray N. Rothbard, Milton Friedman, Thomas S. Szasz, John Hospers, and Yale Brozen, arranged in seven sections: Justice, Liberty and the Individual; State and Societies; Contemporary Statism; Free Societies and Foreign Affairs; Economics and the Free Market; The Free Society; and Prospects and Obstacles to Freedom.

594. NOZICK, Robert. **Anarchy, State, and Utopia.** NY: Basic Books, 1974. 367 pp. $12.95.   (A-3)

An important work of libertarian political philosophy by a Harvard professor. "Our main conclusions about the state are that a minimal state, limited to the narrow functions of protection against force, theft, fraud, enforcement of contracts and so on, is justified; that any more extensive state will violate persons' rights not to be forced to do certain things, and is unjustified; and that the minimal state is inspiring as well as right." (p.ix)

Part I justifies the minimal state, while Part II develops a theory of justice and criticizes other theories, especially that of John Rawls. Part III discusses a framework for utopia.
*** Widely and favorably reviewed by the academic community, but not of immediate relevance to societal directions and alternatives.

595. FRIEDMAN, David. **The Machinery of Freedom: Guide to a Radical Capitalism.** NY: Harper & Row, 1973; Harper Colophon edition, 1973. 239 pp. $2.25, paper.   (ABC-3)

A challenging and very clearly-written book advocating libertarianism and an "anarcho-capitalist society." The author describes himself as "an Adam Smith liberal" and "a Goldwater conservative," and also happens to be the son of the renowned conservative economist, Milton Friedman.

"The central idea of libertarianism is that people should be permitted to run their own lives as they wish." (p.xiii) A libertarian society would have no welfare or Social Security, nor any laws against drugs, gambling, and pornography.

After an extensive defense of the notion of private property, a "Libertarian Grab Bag" of ideas is offered to sell off the state in small pieces. This includes a voucher system for schools, a free-market university ("Adam Smith U.") which would replace the present corporate structure with a number of separate organizations and encourage free-lance teachers, private postal companies, private protection agencies, and subcity governments. The removal of immigration barriers would produce more wealth for all by bringing cheap and unskilled labor into the country. The transfer of streets and highways to private ownership could lead to variable tolls which would reduce traffic congestion. The American Arbitration Association could replace the courts in the function of enforcing contracts. Drug companies would be free to sell anything, subject to liability for damages. Pollution would be reduced by converting unowned resources into property and encouraging the owners to sue polluters.

The major premise is that "Wherever there is a government monopoly, there is inefficiency, bad service, and an opportunity for profits." (p.109) In response to the socialist claim for the benefits of cooperation over competition, Friedman responds that the institution of private property allows for cooperation within competition. We have followed the socialist vision, and it has led us to where we now are. (Socialists, of course, claim that the vision has never been genuinely tried.)

To get from here to there, Friedman advocates education, demonstrations through alternative institutions, and the creation and support of libertarian proposals.

*** Friedman does not mention large corporations and how to respond to oligopolistic situations. Other than this standard blind spot, this is a lively and imaginative work that might be particularly good for provoking classroom discussion.

596. ROTHBARD, Murray N. **For a New Liberty.** NY: Macmillan, 1973. 327 pp. $7.95.   (B-4)

The new libertarianism, "rightest" on some issues (free enterprise, private property, and the horror of the welfare system) and "leftist" on others (the Vietnam war, the draft, civil liberties) is described as developing from a 1969 schism in Young Americans for Freedom (YAF), and emerging as an important force in the early 70's. Within the movement, there is a spectrum ranging from old-fashioned laissez-faire economics people, followers of Ayn Rand, anarcho-capitalists, believers in absolute pacifism or "autarchism," and radical libertarians.

Crucial problem areas in the society such as welfare, education, taxes, pollution, and services are all blamed on government, and libertarian applications are proposed. In truly partisan fashion it is explained that "the libertarian doctrine is not utopian but eminently realistic, because it is the only theory that is really consistent with the nature of man and the world." (p.308)

*** It is problematic as to whether such a wide collection of beliefs adds up to "a movement."

597. TUCCILLE, Jerome. **Radical Libertarianism: A Right Wing Alternative.** Indianapolis: Bobbs-Merrill, 1970. 109 pp. $5.00.   (C-5)

Covers the thinking of Karl Hess (in his pre-decentralist period) and Murray Rothbard, reviews topics such as the rift between libertarians and conservatives and the rediscovery of anarchy, and proposes radical community decentralization--an anarchist alternative expressed by Paul Goodman and Norman Mailer.

A blueprint for liberty is offered to achieve a laissez-faire society that abolishes the military draft and federal licensing. As for foreign policy, "the legal monopoly on the use of force and weapons of defense should be taken away from the state" (p.72) and the free market should be left to provide for its own defense.
*** Steamy and shallow.

598. LIPPMANN, Walter. **An Inquiry into the Principles of The Good Society.** Boston: Little, Brown, 1937. 402 pp.   (AB-3)

The first half of the book is concerned with The Providential State and The Collectivist Movement, with chapters on "The Dominant Dogma of the Age," totalitarian regimes, planning vs. democracy, and democratic collectivism. "Throughout the world, in the name of progress, men who call themselves communists, socialists, fascists, nationalists, progressives, and even liberals, are unanimous in holding that government with its instruments of coercion must, by commanding the people how they shall live, direct the course of civilization and fix the shape of things to come." (p.4)

The second half of the book is devoted to advocating The Reconstruction of Liberalism and The Testament of Liberty, with chapters such as the political principles of liberalism and the government of a liberal state. The basic argument is that a social philosophy is needed that obeys the laws of the industrial revolution. The first principle of our economy "is the increase of wealth by a mode of production which destroys the self-sufficiency of nations, localities, and individuals, making them deeply and intricately interdependent." (p.165) The division of labor is the prime factor in the modern economy, and "the new mode of production is incomparably more efficient..." (p. 168) The free market is the only way in which specialized labor can be synthesized into useful work. Historic liberalism is the philosophy of the industrial revolution, rather than a reaction against it, as is the case with collectivism, which seeks to abolish the regulative principles of the market.
*** Very clear thinking based on a limited number of premises.

599. HAYEK, F.A. **The Constitution of Liberty.** Chicago: University of Chicago Press, 1960. 569 pp.   (A-1)

An eloquent, thorough, and restrained presentation of the classical liberal point of view. "My aim is to picture an ideal, to show how it can be achieved, and to explain what its realization would mean in practice." (p.vii)

The basic principles on which this civilization was built are seen as falling into increasing disregard and oblivion. If "the necessary condition for a free evolution--the spirit of individual initiative--is lacking, then surely without that spirit no viable civilization can grow anywhere." (p.5)

Hayek seeks "not to provide a detailed program of policy but rather to state the criteria by which particular measures must be judged if they are to fit into a regime of freedom." (p.5) The parts of the book concern The Value of Freedom (with chapters on responsibility, equality and merit, and majority rule), Freedom and the Law (with chapters on topics such as coercion and the state, economic policy, and constitutionalism), and Freedom in the Welfare State (with chapters on labor unions, social security, taxation, the monetary framework, housing and town planning, agriculture and natural resources, and education and research).

As concerns the Welfare State, "Though **some** of the aims of the welfare state can be achieved **only** by methods inimical to liberty, **all** its aims may be pursued by such methods." (p. 260, author's emphasis) It is noted that the outlook of the great majority of the electorate is increasingly determined by people in employed positions, leading in turn to policies that make employed positions more attractive. But, it is rightly asked, should society be turned into "one great hierarchy of employment?" (p. 119) As for world order, until the protection of freedom is more firmly secured than it is now, "the creation of a world state probably would be a greater danger to the future of civilization than even war." (p. 263)

The final chapter, Why I Am Not a Conservative, argues that conservatism cannot offer an alternative to the direction in which we are moving, but simply slows down undesirable developments. In contrast, classical liberalism is not averse to evolution and change.

*** Present measures to support full employment might accommodate this position by also considering measures to encourage self-employment.

599a. A Discussion With Friedrich A. von Hayek. Washington: American Enterprise Institute for Public Policy Research, 1975. 20 pp. $1.50.
(ns)

The leading figure in the Austrian school of economics and 1974 Nobel Prize recipient addressed a group of economists at AEI in April 1975. This pamphlet contains his address on the errors of Keynesian economics, and his interchange with the audience. (From AEI catalog)

600. ROEPKE, Wilhelm. A Humane Economy: The Social Framework of the Free Market. Chicago: Henry Regnery Co., 1960. 312 pp. (First published in Germany in 1958.)   (AB-3)

In our age of highly developed industrial economy, an economic order ruled by free prices and free markets "is the only economic order compatible with human freedom..." (p.5)

The author is firmly against collectivism, concentration, management, and administrative machinery. "In all fields, mass and concentration are the mark of modern society; they smother the area of individual responsibility, life, and thought and give the strongest impulse to collective thought and feeling." (p.7)

The public sector is at fault: "the most immediate and tangible threat is the state itself...The bloated collossus of the state, with its crushing taxation and boundless expenditure, is also chiefly to blame for the smoldering inflation that is a chronic evil of our times." (p.33)

601. FRIEDMAN, Milton. Capitalism and Freedom. Chicago: University of Chicago Press, 1962. 202 pp.   (ns)

602. EVANS, M. Stanton. Conservatism and Freedom. New Rochelle, NY: Arlington House, Nov. 1975. $8.95.   (ns)

603. GRIFFIN, Clare Elmer. The Free Society. Washington: American Enterprise Institute for Public Policy Research, 1965. 138 pp.   (AB-3)

Intended "to present a long-standing philosophy variously suggested, though not adequately defined, as free enterprise, free society or 'liberalism' in the old classic sense." (p.v)

"A good society will be one in which as many people as possible will be as free as possible to seek as successfully as possible the ends that to them seem good." (p.13) The basic elements of classic liberalism include individualism, belief in the decency of people (tempered by the idea that man is neither angel nor beast), and rationality.

It is felt that there has been a departure from the fundamental tenets of traditional liberalism, an expansion of the functions of the state, and a shift to a social welfare emphasis. People have become careless of the blessings that they have merely inherited.

Griffin concludes by outlining the features of a positive program of liberalism: vigilance to preserve elements of freedom, holding in check the power of coercion, and preserving competition.
*** Scholarly, restrained, and cogent.

604. CLARK, William R. **Toward a Free Society.** Philadelphia: Dorrance & Co., 1969. 144 pp.   (AB-4)

Acknowledging the ideas of the conservative economist, Milton Friedman, Clark sees the policies of the U.S. government as introducing a form of collectivism and undermining the foundations of American greatness. Large organizations are the true enemy of liberty, and the state is the most powerful of all. Many changes are advocated, all in the direction of increasing human dignity and emphasizing man's importance as an individual. The strategy for attaining a free society (which essentially is the opposite of the liberal's Great Society), is that of winning minds in the universities.

605. AYRES, C.E. **Toward A Reasonable Society: The Values of Industrial Civilization.** Austin: University of Texas Press, 1961. 301 pp. (A-4)

A rambling defense of "the industrial way of life."

606. BROWN, Susan Love, et al. **The Incredible Bread Machine.** San Diego, Cal.: World Research, Inc. (11722 Sorrento Valley Road), 1974. 192 pp. $1.95, paper.   (C-4)

The "bread machine" is capitalism, and government intervention is a "no-dough" policy. The six young authors argue for private property, laissez-faire capitalism, and a free society, and against the anti-individualistic principles of socialism, communism, and fascism.
*** Enthusiastically reviewed in **National Review** (Oct. 10, 1975) and **The Wall Street Journal** (Jan. 31, 1975). So grand to see those young 'uns thinking right.

607. RAND, Ayn. **Capitalism: The Unknown Ideal.** NY: New American Library, 1966. 309 pp.   (AB-3)

This collection of 22 essays from **The Objectivist Newsletter** is described by Rand as "a nonfiction footnote to **Atlas Shrugged,**" her major novel that promotes the values of selfishness over those of altruism. In addition to 16 essays by Rand, there is one by Robert Hessen, two by Co-Editor Nathaniel Branden, and three by Alan Greenspan, who is presently Chairman of the U.S. Council of Economic Advisors.

Capitalism is defined as "a social system based on the recognition of individual rights, including property rights, in which all property is privately owned." (p.11) The only function of government in such a society is the task of protecting man's rights. All human relationships are voluntary. The cardinal difference between capitalism and collectivism is private property, which protects the right to disagree.

"The moral justification of capitalism lies in the fact that it is the only system consonant with man's rational nature...its ruling principle is: justice." (p.12)

608. VON MISES, Ludwig. **Omnipotent Government: The Rise of the Total State and Total War.** New Haven: Yale University Press, 1944; New Rochelle, NY: Arlington House, 1969.   (A-4)

A discussion of international problems and how government interference raises the domestic costs of production. "Durable peace is only possible under perfect capitalism, hitherto never and nowhere completely tried or achieved." (p.284)

The final section of the book, The Future of Western Civilization, criticizes the delusions of world planning and various peace schemes. No compromise is seen as possible between planning and free enterprise.

609. VON MISES, Ludwig. **Theory and History: An Interpretation of Social and Economic Evolution.** New Haven: Yale University Press, 1957; New Rochelle, NY: Arlington House, 1969. 384 pp. $10.00.   (A-4)

Criticizes the program of collectivism, scientism, planning and the suppression of economic freedom, the ideology of equality in wealth and income, and the idea of equal distribution of land. The final chapter, Present-Day Trends and the Future, asserts that the hopes of the philosophers of the Enlightenment have been discredited. "Instead the trend is toward totalitarianism, toward socialism." (p.350)

610. WILKIE, Leighton A. and Richard S. RIMANOCZY. **The Principles of American Prosperity.** Old Greenwich, Conn. 06970 (143 Sound Beach Ave.), Devin-Adair, 1975. 237 pp. $3.95.   (ns)

"Examines man's economic progress from toolmaking in the Stone Age to today's system of free enterprise capitalism." (advt.)

611. VETTERLI, Richard (comp.) **The Challenge & the Choice.** Salt Lake City, Utah: Bookcraft, Inc., 1969. 286 pp.   (B-5)

Essays by leading Mormons such as David O. McKay (President of the denomination), Ezra Taft Benson (Elder and former U.S. Secretary of Agriculture), and various professors at Brigham Young University. Topics cover Socialism, Communism, The Welfare State, Good Government, The American Heritage of Freedom, The Way of the Intellectuals, War and Peace, and The Great Gift of Freedom.

In sum, the writers attack "political and intellectual sycophants who rise to pinnacles of power," defying God, morals, reason, history, experience, and the welfare of their people. Polarization is seen between the well-financed forces of false propaganda and the forces of freedom. The correct choice for mankind is that of God and time-proven principles of eternal value leading to hope, freedom, peace and prosperity.

612. LONG, Hamilton Abert. **Your American Yardstick: Twelve Basic American Principles underlying the traditional American philosophy of Man-over-Government.** "Foresight Through Hindsight" Series, No. 2. Philadelphia: Your Heritage Books, Inc., 1963. 397 pp.   (AB-4)

The present generation is seen as confused, having betrayed and abandoned traditional American principles proclaimed in the 1776 Declaration of Independence. "This philosophy is an indivisable whole and must be accepted or rejected as such." (p.xxv) Long proposes the term of American Traditionalist for adherents.

The twelve principles are: The Spiritual is Supreme, Fear of Government-

Over-Man, Unalienable Rights--From God, Man Organizes Governments to be his Tools, Limited Government, Decentralized Government, Equality, Life and the Pursuit of Happiness, Liberty, Private Property, Limited Taxes, and Limited Powers of the Majority.
*** This "study-guide" includes a great number of varied materials which provide a useful background. The basic idea is interesting, particularly for the American Bicentennial. However, the nature of our present confusion is not explained, nor is any strategy for restoration of principles offered.

613. COSER, Lewis A. and Irving HOWE (eds.) **The New Conservatives: A Critique from the Left.** NY: Quadrangle, 1974. 343 pp. $9.95. (ns)

Chapter 13

Spatial Alternatives

This final chapter in the "Societal Alternatives" section concerns space: the probable and desirable distribution of human population. The consideration of how and where people will live together is often a neglected dimension. Yet, such matters can serve as an overview of the human condition, and in many respects this chapter is a reprise of the preceding 12 chapters.

A general overview of change, as in Chapter 1, is provided by the Commission on Population Growth and the American Future (615). The Technological, Affluent, Service Society of Chapter 2 is a highly urbanized society--a view reflected by many items in this chapter, notably the Advisory Commission on Intergovernmental Relations (617) which concluded that urbanization is "inevitable and a natural concomitant of an increasing technological age." The cosmic evolutionary view in Chapter 4 is in great evidence here, exemplified by Buckminster Fuller (682), and Gerard O'Neill (687-689), who outdoes Fuller in audacity and practicality! The decentralization theme of Chapter 7 is a major concern of both communards (695-703), and those who seek small rural communities and neighborhood power (704-720). Redistribution is a major concern of the land reform movement (713-714), and freedom from inept government is the theme of Banfield's assault on liberal programs that fail to solve the ills of "the unheavenly city" (638-639).

The organization of this chapter generally follows this progression. Essentially, there are three broad groups: the liberal-urbanist literature, the cosmic views (which are generally extrapolations of urbanism), and the decentralist writing (which is the direct opposite of the cosmic view). The only writers to juxtapose these basic ways of life are the Goodman brothers (614), and their classic essay on **Communitas** begins the chapter.

The Commission on Population Growth and the American Future (615) considers urban-rural distribution, but does not deal with certain fundamental questions, as pointed out by Sen. Cranston. The Commission's finding that 64% of the population would **prefer** living in open country or small towns is a significant one, and could have been used to predict the historic reversal in demographic trends, whereby rural areas are now growing faster than urban areas (709-710). Perhaps this shift is only a temporary aberration, but it also may signal a profound change in thinking about spatial and societal alternatives.

We do not yet have a national growth policy, as the Congressional Research Service concludes (616), but there is an implicit body of policy that favors urbanization and other actions that aggravate our social problems. A national policy was advocated by the Advisory Commission on Intergovernmental Relations (617) in 1968. Focusing on urban policy and urban problems at the exclusion of rural problems (618-620), however, overlooks what may be the major source of urban problems: pressures to deplete the rural population, which forces migration to the cities.

This long-term trend was viewed in the early 1960s as leading to the formation of megalopolis (622), and the spreading of cities (623) has been recently noted as leading to the urbanization of the suburbs (625) and "a suburban nation" (626). Willbern noted this trend in 1964 as "The Withering Away of the City" (627).

These trends (621-627) serve as a background for several items that describe attempts to promote changes at the local and state levels. Fischer (628) offers an optimistic view of development districts, metropolitan planning, and regional councils. The California Tomorrow Plan (629) proposes a comprehensive planning process. The Alternatives for Washington process of involving a great number of citizens in thinking about the future (630) appears promising. Goals for Dallas (631) also involved a great number of people, but it is not clear as to how things have been made better. The Hawaii 2000 experience (632) appears to have been equally long on enthusiasm and short on results, but offers some valuable lessons for those who are serious about "Anticipatory Democracy,"

This participatory process might be improved if information on alternative ideals and strategies were to be made available. Pure ideals are suggested by Marks (633) and Haworth (634), while Schneider (635) reviews the history of idealized cities. Jensen (636) encourages us to aspire to "cities of vision." On the other hand, Banfield (638, 639) asks us to accept the "unheavenly city" and to recognize that government cannot solve problems and that liberal programs make the problems worse. It is doubtful that any liberal has been convinced.

Most schemes to save the city are put forth not as ideals, but as practical proposals. In the style of the spend-more sixties, Faltermayer recommends more spending (640). Linowitz (641) makes a weak and narrow argument for saving the cities through means such as Metropolitan Development Corporations. Bent (642) advocates intersystem linkage, similar to Higbee's call for better network coordination (643), and Meier's prescription for a carefully-designed and globally interconnected metropolis (644). Arango (645) proposes a Pan-Urban Land System, while Dantzig and Saaty (646) sketch a general plan for "Compact City." Wolf's overview of new directions (647) is perhaps the best survey of new planning ideas. (But where will we get the money?) Blair (649) views all of these problems on a global scale.

New towns are a distinct class of proposals (664-668) that have evoked considerable interest and enthusiasm, although Clapp (664) wonders whether it is an idea whose time has passed. In contrast, MacCallum (669) views an evolution to the proprietary and contractual community. This cosmic view serves to introduce many others with far-ranging and unconventional notions (670-694).

The late C.A. Doxiadis was a widely-respected cosmic thinker who founded the science of "Ekistics" (670) and developed the notion of "Ecumenopolis" (674) over a period of 15 years. Safdie's Habitat (677) is relatively tame in contrast to the "Arcologies" of Soleri (678). Compared to this "ecological architecture" that is built upwards, Mason (679) proposed underground as the ecologically correct direction. And then there are the tetrahedral and domed-over cities of Fuller (682). But this is hardly the last word in far-out thinking, for all of the items noted to this point have confined the human population to the planet earth.

Migration to outer space has been a science fiction staple for many years, and a few recent non-fiction writers (683-686) have pointed to the potentials of the space age. But migration has heretofore been confined to considering settlement of planets. This "hangup" was overcome by the Princeton physicist, Gerard O'Neill, who made a serious proposal for space colonies in 1974. By 1975 they were being touted as satellite solar power stations and the answer to our energy problems (687-688), although they were first proposed as the answer to the world population problem (689-690). A similar proposal for "flying cities" has been made by Berry (691). It is important to recognize that there is a pre-existing lobby to support the space colonies idea: namely, NASA and the aeronautical industry. For better or worse, this idea will surely be debated in Congress and perhaps acted upon so that NASA may once again have a mission. In contrast, Soleri (678) is slowly building his prototype arcology in Arizona without any public support, and it is highly doubtful whether any of Fuller's gigantic designs will ever gain financial backing.

At this point, the perspective shifts down from the heavens to the opposite extreme: the small community. To many persons, this means religious and countercultural communes, and there has been a fair amount of attention paid to such experimentation (695-703). But this enterprise should be placed in perspective, for even under the most generous possible estimate, the number of persons involved in forming a possible "alternative society" (703) is not, at this time, more than 1% of the U.S. population, and no doubt closer to 0.1%. In contrast, more than 30% of the population still lives in nonmetropolitan areas, and in the 1970-1973 period this proportion was growing (709), contrary to all of the expert forecasts.

Much attention is paid to urban problems, but what of the small community? The late Arthur E. Morgan has contended for some time that the primary community is the only way to live well (704, 705). Sarason has recently examined the neglect of the sense of community by psychologists (706). In the Sarvodaya tradition (327), Hoffman argues for an organic garden culture (707), while Bookchin takes a radical stance that megalopolis must be destroyed (708). Ellis views "the new ruralism" (710) as an essential component of the post-industrial age.

A technocratic version of "the new rural society" is proposed by Goldmark (711), who sees new communication networks as decentralizing business and government. Another option is returning people to the agricultural sector by promoting land reform (713-714). The Community Land Trust could become a significant tool to promote rural new towns (715), while Community Development Corporations (717) could promote a new era of rural development.

The focus on the small community is not confined to rural areas, however. Kotler proposes neighborhood corporations (718), while Morris and Hess (719) describe a comprehensive process to promote "the new localism." The neighborhood development associations proposed by Falk (720) are similar to the rural CDC's. These developments could be very important for the future of our society. Interestingly, they were not generated by any urban experts or public commissions.

In the recent past, those who placed their hopes for the good society in communes have been considered as romantics. But this is unfair. In reviewing the literature of urban planning, new towns, great architectural designs and voyages into space, one can find an equal amount of faith that these solutions would each lead to the good society. And in reviewing the results of these notions, one can probably find a ratio of success to failure similar to that experienced by communes. Perhaps the best society might be one where there is a high proportion of successes for all of the spatial alternatives that are attempted.

614. GOODMAN, Paul and Percival. **Communitas: Means of Livelihood and Ways of Life.** Chicago: University of Chicago Press, 1947; revised second edition, Vintage, 1960. 248 pp.   (ABC-2)

A cultural criticism of physical plant and regional plans--"not an indictment of the American way of life, but rather an attempt to clarify it and find what its possibilities are." (p. 6)

After a critical history of planning, the authors offer 3 community paradigms (or model ways of life): 1) Efficient Consumption (based on the premises of official economics); 2) Elimination of the Difference Between Production and Consumption (the Borsodi ideal of small units with relative self-sufficiency); and 3) Planned Security with Minimum Regulation (whereby minimum subsistence is available to all).

*** The only book yet located which attempts to examine fundamental spatial alternatives, rather than assuming the inevitability or desirability of one or another.

615. Commission on Population Growth and the American Future. **Population and the American Future.** Report of the Commission. Washington: U.S. Government Printing Office, 1972. 186 pp. $1.75, paper (S/N 5258-0002). NY: NAL Signet, March 1972. 362 pp. $1.50, paper.   (AB-2)

An overview of population growth and distribution, the economy, resources and the environment, government, education, and various social aspects of population growth. The text and appendices of the two editions appear to be identical, with the exception of a summary Compilation of Recommendations in the Government edition (pp. 141-147) that is absent in the Signet edition.

Between 1900 and 1970, the rural population declined from 60% to 26%. By the year 2000, 85% of the population will live in metropolitan areas (a projection that may be erroneous in light of recent demographic changes). Yet, in a national opinion survey conducted for the Commission in 1971, only 12% of the population lives in the open country, but 34% would prefer to live there. In contrast, 33% live in small towns or cities (30% preferring to live there), 28% live in medium-sized cities or suburbs (22% preference), and 27% live in larger cities or suburbs (14% preference). The Commission concludes that "Americans are urban and becoming more so, but many people evidently dislike the trend." (p. 34; p. 36 in NAL edition. Also see Sundquist, no. 712.)

No convincing economic argument was found for continuing national population growth, and slowing down the rate of growth would ease the problems facing government. However, "Under the most optimistic assumptions, at least 50 million more people will be added to our population before the end of the century." (p. 60; p. 89)

Most of the recommendations of the Commission concern policies for limiting numbers by birth control, education, and restricting immigration. But there is also a question of urban-rural distribution, dealt with in Chapter 14, National Distribution and Migration Policies.

It is recognized that "social and environmental problems are often aggravated by the continued growth of large population concentrations," and that these factors must be given more importance in policy decisions. But despite this concern, and the data that people **prefer** living in open country or small towns, the recommendations are surprisingly bland and evasive, and no statement is made as to the **preferable** urban-rural balance. The Commission recommended guiding urban expansion (through comprehensive land-use and public facility planning, more extensive human capital programs, and more low and moderate income housing in the suburbs), aiding depressed rural areas (through programs emphasizing human resource development, worker relocation counseling, and creating new jobs nearer to or within declining rural areas), and various institutional responses at the federal state, and local levels.

The missing dimension to this concern is provided in a separate statement on depressed rural areas by Sen. Alan Cranston (D.-Cal.) (pp. 152-153; pp. 272-273), who observes that farms are increasingly large-scale and mechanized and that agriculture is increasingly dominated by conglomerates seeking vertical integration. These huge corporations have little stake in rural communities, and are a major factor in the reduction of farms and the farm population, often with the encouragement of federal policies. Cranston argues that the temptation should be resisted to assume that only new industry can revitalize rural America, and suggests further investigation of these issues so as to truly maximize the individual's freedom of choice about where to live and work.

*** In addition to a neglect of agricultural policy, one might also wonder why the Commission did not consider the influence of welfare policies on migration patterns.

616. U.S. Library of Congress, Congressional Research Service. **Toward a National Growth Policy; Federal and State Developments in 1974.** A Report Prepared for the Use of the Joint Economic Committee, Congress of the United States. Washington: U.S. Government Printing Office, Sept. 1975. 350 pp. $3.20, paper. (Bibliography, pp. 200-350) (A-3)

"The basic purpose of this report is to relate Federal and State actions that took place in 1974 to the national urban and rural development objectives set forth by Congress." (p. 1) Three similar reports have been released in the past three years.

The eight parts of national growth policy identified in the Housing and Urban Development Act of 1970 include general statements such as continued economic strength of all parts of the U.S., and treating problems of poverty and employment comprehensively. In this report, these components are consolidated into six chapters: Effective Areawide Planning and Delivery of Services, Rural Development and Economic Growth, Renewing Old Communities, Toward a Decent Home, Improving the Environment, and Improving Government Capability.

Within each chapter, there is a report on laws enacted, significant legislation receiving attention and likely to be passed in 1975, major actions taken by the Executive Branch, and major Congressional and Executive reports and hearings. Laws enacted by States are also reported on.

It is concluded that "There is not now any common ground of agreement on a specific national growth policy or even whether such an approach would be useful...Policies have been reactive rather than anticipatory. In recent years, the record of Federal activities in trying to encourage metropolitan regional governance, improve the economic opportunity in rural and central city depressed areas, stabilize rural development or provide housing for low and moderate income families has not been conspicuously successful." (pp. 150-151)

However, the sum of this activity is recognized as an implicit body of policy. Among the 16 unintentional directions are the promotion of industrialization in American agriculture, the favoring of new housing construction on undeveloped suburban tracts over rehabilitation of existing community structures, promoting the use of surface and air transport, and minimal public attempts to influence the flows of manpower.

The appendices provide descriptions of about 375 federal research projects in progress, and an annotated bibliography of about 1800 items.

*** A very useful ongoing report on our national growth policy, such as it is, as well as a valuable reference tool.

617. Advisory Commission on Intergovernmental Relations. **Urban and Rural America: Policies for Future Growth.** A Commission Report. Washington: U.S. Government Printing Office, April 1968. 186 pp. (A-3)

Chapters on The Pattern of Urbanization, Economic Growth: The Regional, State, and Local Experience, The Impact of Recent Urbanization Trends, New Communities in America and Their Objectives, and Guidance and Controls for Large-Scale Urban Development and New Communities.

After a discussion of arguments pro and con, "the Commission concludes on balance that a national policy to deal with urban growth would be desirable.

"While agreeing that urbanization in varying degrees is, of course, inevitable and a natural concomitant of an increasing technological age, the Commission also believes that a combination of public and private actions can mitigate certain adverse effects of present urbanization trends. Specifically, we note the diseconomies of scale involved in continued urban concentration, the locational mismatch of jobs and people, the connection between urban and rural poverty problems, and urban sprawl." (p. 129)

*** Urbanization, of course, is perhaps no longer seen as inevitable--a shift in the perception of societal directions that could help mitigate the adverse effects that the Commission noted.

618. MOYNIHAN, Daniel P. (ed.) **Toward a National Urban Policy.** NY: Basic Books, 1970. 348 pp. $7.95.   (AB-3)

A Forum series of the Voice of America, resulting in 25 essays, including Philip Hauser on population, Robert Wood on intergovernmental relations, Nathan Glazer on housing, John Meyer on urban transportation, Marion Folsom on community health planning, Glenn Hilst on pollution, James Wilson on crime, Lee Rainwater on poverty, and Scott Greer on urban renewal.

The initial essay by Moynihan outlines "Fundamental of Urban Policy" such as attacking poverty and the social isolation of minority groups, creating an urban balance by being sensitive to the disruption of social services and housing by programs such as highway construction, offering incentives for the reorganization of local government in order to overcome fragmentation and obsolescence, a restoration of the fiscal vitality of urban government through federal urban policy, equalization in the provision of public services, and better information and more research.

618a. MUCHNICK, David M., "Death Warrant for the Cities? The National Urban Policy," **Dissent,** 23:1, Winter 1976, pp. 21-32.   (ns)

619. U.S. National Commission on Urban Problems. **Building the American City.** NY: Praeger, 1969. 500 pp.   (A-3)

Chaired by Paul H. Douglas, the Commission recommended orderly urban growth, a new generation of housing codes embracing higher standards, a new system of building codes, more labor efficiency coupled with job security, a real political commitment to solve our problems, revenue sharing, federal income tax revision, more authority for local government, full-value assessment, reduction of housing costs, and a decent home for every family.

620. HARRIS, Sen. Fred R. and Mayor John V. LINDSAY. **The State of the Cities.** Foreword by Sol M. Linowitz. NY: Praeger, 1972. 114 pp. $4.95; $1.95, paper.   (ns)

The Report of the Commission on the Cities in the '70's, arguing that conditions since the mid-60's have worsened, and pointing to reforms that can be achieved only by concerned national leaders.

621. ELDREDGE, H. Wentworth, "Alternative Possible Urban Futures," **FUTURES: The Journal of Planning and Forecasting,** 6:1, Feb. 1974, pp. 26-41.   (ABC-3)

A valuable survey of existing and emerging types of cities, grouped in two basic categories:
- Type A: Almost Certain to Continue. Includes megalopolis, metropolitan central city, smaller central city, small central city or town, satellite cities, inner suburbs, outer suburbs, exurbia, new towns (with 5 sub-groupings) and rural/agricultural settings.
- Type B. Far-Out Potential Environments. Includes mega-structures or mini-cities, the water city, underwater and underground habitations, communes and other societal innovations, and the wired city.

It is glumly concluded that "quite probably, 'more of the same' will be the lot of Western urbanism for the rest of this century and probably well on into the next." (p. 38)

*** Some major catastrophe such as that suggested by Herzog (no. 112a) could change this probability derived through extrapolation into a mere possibility. The survey omits communities in outer space but is otherwise instructive

622. GOTTMAN, Jean. **Megalopolis.** NY: Twentieth Century Fund, 1961. 810 pp.   (A-3)

A pioneering study of the developing pattern of the urbanized northeastern seaboard.

623. CLAWSON, Marion, "The Spread City," **Resources,** No. 44, Sept. 1973.
                                                                                (A-4)
The head of Resources for the Future, Inc. proclaims that "Barring some wholly new development not now foreseen, or perhaps foreseeable, the population of the United States will continue to concentrate in Metropolitan areas. The nonmetropolitan areas...are essentially stagnant." (p. 5) Clawson forecasts an expansion of the city into the suburbs and rebuilding older city centers.
*** It was indeed not foreseen that by 1975 the cities would be broke and that population would grow in the nonmetropolitan areas, relative to the now-stagnant metropolitan areas. Still another instance of being blinded by the conventional wisdom.

624. CLAWSON, Marion, "The Future of Nonmetropolitan America," **The American Scholar,** 42:1, Winter 1972-73, pp. 102-109.   (AB-4)

Argues that the nonmetropolitan society and economy, presently seen in decay, "would be more viable if the population were substantially regrouped into a degree of agglomeration." This could be preceded by functional restructuring, e.g., several small counties and small towns adapting a single government and working toward a single set of integrated services. Population regrouping to larger centers of perhaps 25,000 could be aided by federal and state technical assistance and direct subsidy.
*** The values of efficiency vs. the unrecognized values of community.

625. MASOTTI, Louis H. and Jeffrey K. HADDEN (eds.). **The Urbanization of the Suburbs.** Vol. 7, Urban Affairs Annual Reviews. Beverly Hills, Calif.: Sage Publications, 1973. 600 pp. $20.00.   (A-3)

Nineteen original contributions organized in six parts: historical perspectives on suburbanization, social structure and social process, government and politics, suburban issues in the seventies (zoning, police, problem-solving), the economics of suburbia, and looking ahead. In the concluding epilogue, Masotti suggests four alternative urban futures (continued sprawl, intensification, planned suburban growth, and resettlement of the central city), and discusses factors in the future shape of suburbia such as personal attitudes, land-use controls, fiscal inequities, and the changing roles of governments. The volume is concluded with an alphabetized bibliography of about 900 items (pp. 545-592).

626. MASOTTI, Louis H. (ed.) **The Suburban Seventies. The ANNALS of the American Academy of Political and Social Science,** Vol 422, Nov. 1975.   (A-4)

The preface announces that "America has become a suburban nation during the last 15 years while almost no one was looking," (p. vii) and 13 articles explore various facets of this transition. Of particular interest are "Suburbia and the Metropolitan Turf" by Robert L. Lineberry, "Beyond Suburbia" by Sylvia F. Fava, and "From Suburb to Urban Place," by David L. Birch.

627. WILLBERN, York. **The Withering Away of the City.** University of Alabama Press, 1964. 139 pp.   (AB-3)

Argues that two revolutions are taking place: the rise of the urban way of life and the outward explosion of our urban centers. "The more urban we become, the more shaky become both the concept and the reality of the city." (p. 33)

628. FISCHER, John. **Vital Signs, U.S.A.** NY: Harper & Row (A Cass Canfield Book), 1975. 197 pp. $8.95.   (ABC-3)

A long-time editor of **Harper's** Magazine feels that the Good Society may be too much to hope for, but if enough people keep trying, "we might--just possibly--come within reach of something that could be called the Almost Good Society." (p. 1)
The outlines of such a society are suggested by the recent social inventions described in this book--new institutions which, "rather than Charles Reich's dreams of the counterculture--might be the real greening of America...Now and then I got the feeling that all of these inconspicuous changes could add up to the biggest transformation America has experienced since the Civil War." (p. 7)
Although there is no master planning in the U.S., there is piecemeal planning, and some of these plans get carried out. Examples described include development districts (a new form of local government beginning in 1960 in Georgia; by 1973 there were 600 such districts in 49 states), the Twin Cities Metropolitan Council (which is not a consolidated government, but a structure to handle those functions that must be handled on an area-wide basis), new towns in town (with the example of Gloria M. Segal's development on the edge of Minneapolis), the strong county-wide government that reclaimed Jacksonville, Fla., various unofficial **ad hoc** metropolitan planning efforts in the Seattle area, new towns, the New York State Urban Development Corporation, the Appalachian Regional Commission, and the ten federal Regional Councils (established in 1969) which could become true provincial governments. The final chapter is a paean to the small town of Guilford, Conn., where Fischer lives, and the possibilities for rejuvenating small towns in an attempt to disperse population.
*** All well and good, but the pessimist can easily answer that it might be too little, too late. Nevertheless, if the reader needs a happy book that is still responsible, this is one of the best.

629. HELLER, Alfred. (ed.) **The California Tomorrow Plan.** Los Altos, Calif.: William Kaufmann, Inc., 1972. 120 pp. $2.50, paper.   (AB-3)

A book developed by California Tomorrow, a nonprofit organization formed in 1961 which publishes the quarterly journal **Cry California.** This revised edition of "A First Sketch" published in tabloid newspaper format in 1971, suggests two alternative futures: California One (the continuation of the present way of solving problems) and California Two (a coordinated approach to comprehensive state and regional planning). The key policies would be to provide adequate political strength, adequate economic strength, a guide to the distribution of population, and a guide to resource use.

629a. ALEXANDER, Christopher, et. al. **The Oregon Experiment.** NY: Oxford University Press, 1975. $12.50.   (ns)

Reports on the execution of the ideas of a user-created master plan for the expansion of the U. of Oregon--"a complete working alternative to our present ideas about architecture, building and planning." Alexander and associates have developed six dynamic principles: organic growth (creating harmony and user satisfaction), participation (effective communication between users and designers), piecemeal growth, patterns, diagnosis, and coordination. (Library of Urban Affairs, advt.)

630. EVANS, Daniel J., "Rediscovering the Future," **National Civic Review.** 65:1, Jan. 1976, pp. 6-11. (AB-3)

An address by the Governor of Washington at the November 1975 National Conference of the National Municipal League, relating the successes of Alternatives for Washington: "a process for citizen participation and de-cision-making for the future."

In brief, 150 citizens, representing a wide variety of backgrounds, de-voted four 3-day weekends to looking ahead and identifying discrete alter-natives. They developed 11 alternatives, which were then discussed by more than 2000 participants in a series of regional meetings. The alterna-tives were then described in a TV program, followed by a questionnaire sent to a cross-section of viewers, resulting in more than 65,000 responses. Enthusiasm has been high, and many local communities have initiated their own programs.

The most popular future for Washington was the spreading out of industry so people could grow up and live in the smaller communities where they were born.

Gov. Evans wisely concludes on a note of restraint: "Now we have finished phase one. Phase two will be the more difficult process of taking those somewhat utopian dreams, applying some costs to them and identifying the laws and the policies necessary to get from here to there." (p. 10)

631. Goals for Dallas: Achieving the Goals. Dallas, Texas: Goals for Dallas (One Main Place), August 1970. 313 pp. (AB-3)

Stimulated by **Goals for Americans** (no. 404), this forth volume from Goals for Dallas represents the culmination of nearly five years of effort, with the participation of over 100,000 citizens of Dallas and neighboring towns. The aim of the exercise, as stated by Erik Jonsson, Mayor and Chairman, was "to leave this city better and more beautiful than it was left to us." (p. xiv)

Twelve Task Forces were assembled on government, design of the city, health, welfare, transportation and communications, public safety, elemen-tary and secondary education, higher education, continuing education, cultural activities, recreation and entertainment, and the economy of Dallas. Each group identified the steps to achieve the goals, the public and private or-ganizations to be involved, and the costs.

*** The general thrust of the recommendations is that of expanding existing institutions, with no questioning of performance or of projects such as the Dallas-Fort Worth Regional Airport. Nevertheless, even as an exercise in maintaining the status quo, this well-intended document would seem to offer some important lessons for community-wide planning.

632. CHAPLIN, George and Glenn D. PAIGE (eds.) **Hawaii 2000: Contin-uing Experiment in Anticipatory Democracy.** Honolulu: University Press of Hawaii, 1973. 491 pp. $9.95. (AB-2)

Materials associated with the Governor's Conference on the Year 2000, stimulated by the Commission on the Year 2000, and held in August 1970. A Hawaii State Commission on the Year 2000 was formed in 1971.

This anthology includes pre-Conference presentations by James A. Dator and Robert Theobald, and Conference addresses by Alvin Toffler, Arthur C. Clarke, Robert Jungk, Yehezkel Dror, Alfred Pasatiempo, Sr., and Bob

Krauss. There are Task-Force reports in ten areas: people and life styles, quality of personal life, natural environment, housing and transportation, political decision-making and the law, the economy, science and technology, education, the arts, and Hawaii and the Pacific Community. And there are responses from Conference observer-consultants: John McHale, Hidetoshi Kato, Raymond G. Studer, and Hahn-Been Lee.

The final summation by the editors is by far the most important section. Sketches of "Alternative Hawaiis" include Hawaii as an ideal American state, a battlefield for protracted struggle, a restoration to the true kingdom of Aloha, a Pacific coconut republic and playground of the world, an ecological commonwealth (either a back-to-nature version or a technology-nature symbiosis), and as world headquarters of the United Nations.

But the editors also provide a valuable critique. The task force approach produced a fragmented picture, and there was a failure to obtain an integrated overview. Few of the participants were well-trained for the task of writing scenarios and developing action programs: "Our experience shows that most of us need training in the creation of alternative futures." (p. 460) There was also a failure to bridge the gap between the "creative futurists" and the "critical presentists." And there was insufficient time to develop any legislative proposals.

*** This unique volume brings together a great deal of exuberance and rhetoric, along with many ideas. The futurists got their suntans and the participants undoubtedly had a good time. The big question is whether conditions in Hawaii are any different (or may possibly be different) as a result of this Conference. The critique by the editors suggests why little or nothing has happened, and should be read by anyone who is seriously interested in change, as contrasted to sandbox democracy.

632a. BAKER, David, "State Goal Groups: Performance and Potential," **World Future Society Bulletin,** X:2, March-April 1976, pp. 5-14.
(AB-3)

A sober survey of the 14 state level efforts at futures planning and goal setting that have been organized since 1970. In general, "these efforts have still not fully succeeded in turning around the states or in gaining wide support," as a result of five problems: inadequate funding, dealing with the comprehensiveness and time dimensions of "futures" and "goals," politics, state bureaucracies, and the commission structure itself.

"The groups have experienced their greatest successes in educating participants about current state problems, projecting alternatives in various sectors of state activity, and devising general goals for state action." (p. 10)

633. MARKS, Peter, "Vision of Environment," **American Scholar,** 40:3, Summer 1971. pp. 421-431. (AB-3)

A Cornell ecologist sketches the broad outlines of a utopian environment that blends urban and rural life. The major components are "enlightened cities, unblemished country, and a cheap, clean, quiet and fast means of getting from one to the other and back." The suburb is an unhappy compromise; it offers nothing that is not better in either the country or the city.

634. HAWORTH, Lawrence. **The Good City.** Bloomington: Indiana University Press, 1963. 160 pp. (A-4)

A philosopher's attempt to develop a systematic theory of urban life, connecting it with ethical principles and city planning. The leading ethical ideas are power, freedom, and community.

"The idea of a Good City is the idea of the form the urbanized nation should take. Power, freedom, and community define a national ideal fully as much as they define an ideal for city, metropolis, or megalopolis." (p. 198)

635. SCHNEIDER, Wolf, Babylon Is Everywhere: The City as Man's Fate.
NY: McGraw-Hill, 1963. 400 pp.   (AB-4)

A history of cities. Part 7, The City of the Future, covers the history
of idealized cities and the possibility of a beautiful city.

636. JENSEN, Rolf. Cities of Vision. NY: Wiley/Halstead, 1974. 382 pp.
                                                              (A-3)
"Sooner or later...it is certain that much of the argument put forward
in this work must form the basis of rational urban planning and design
policies if cities are to be retrieved from their...drive to destruction."
(p. vii)
"More and more people are moving into cities and this process will inevitably continue." We need determination, allocation of funds as a top
priority, and trained and imaginative planners. Construction of new towns
and cities should be halted until the priority task of dealing with existing
cities has been carried through. Flight from the city or policies of dispersal cannot solve the problem.
Rather than mechanistic urbanism, new techniques of planning are urgently
needed: "The cities of vision, to which we should aspire, would thus become
the creative masterpieces of enlightened individuals, endowed with foresight; as well as a reversion to urban areas with a highly-developed visual
emphasis as the essential prerequisite for the habitat of urban Man." (p. 5)
*** Good arguments accompanied by 200 illustrations.

**637. LONG, Norton. The Unwalled City: Reconstituting the Urban Com-
munity.** NY: Basic Books, 1972. 208 pp. $8.45.   (AB-4)

Major problems are not seen as stemming from inadequate resources,
but from the failure to utilize them. We should apply the lessons of foreign
aid to the city. The final chapter, A Possible Future: The City as a Humane
Cooperative, sees the tragedy of the city as a loss of purpose and self-
direction. The city is run neither by nor for its inhabitants.

**638. BANFIED, Edward C. The Unheavenly City: The Nature and Future
of Our Urban Crisis.** Boston: Little, Brown, 1970. 308 pp. $6.95.
                                                              (AB-3)
A genuinely controversial book by a Professor of Urban Government at
Harvard and head of President Nixon's task force on model cities, who
attempts "to think about the problems of the cities in the light of scholarly
findings." (p. vii) Banfield assures his readers that he is well-meaning,
although he fears that "This book will probably strike many readers as the
work of an ill-tempered or mean-spirited fellow." (Opening sentence,
p. vii)
After chapters on metropolitan growth, social class, race, unemployment, poverty, schooling vs. education, crime, rioting, and the future of the
lower class, "It is impossible to avoid the conclusion that the serious problems of the cities will continue to exist in something like their present form
for another twenty years at least," (p. 255) and they will not be "solved"
by programs of the sort now being undertaken. Rather, the tendency of these
programs is to prolong the problems and possibly make them worse.
One of the barriers to dealing effectively with problems is the virtues of
the American political system whereby power is widely distributed so that
organized interests can veto measures that would benefit large numbers
of people. The "democratic" formulation of problems (e.g. viewing poverty
as a lack of income rather than an inability to work) is another barrier,
as well as the faith in the perfectability of man.
Government cannot solve the problems of the cities, but some problems

might disappear as a result of economic growth, demographic change, and continuing "middle- and upper-class -ification."

"To the pessimist, the prospect is that a new conventional wisdom about the problems of the city, the product of many millions of dollars' expenditure on research, cast in the language of systems analysis and the computer, will only compound the existing confusion. The optimist, however, will see reason to believe that facts, rational analysis, and deliberation about the nature of the public interest will play a somewhat larger part than hitherto in the formation of both opinion and policy." (Concluding sentences, pp. 262-263.)

*** Guaranteed to raise the hackles of anyone not predisposed to Banfield's views. But if one believes in dialectic to sharpen one's thinking, this is one of the few books on urban affairs to do it with. This stance is somewhat like that of Kahn and Bruce-Briggs (no. 27) and Wattenberg (no. 75).

639. BANFIELD, Edward C. **The Unheavenly City Revisited.** Boston: Little, Brown, 1974. 358 pp.   (ns)

A major revision and expansion of the above work, continuing to challenge the "crisis" view that today's cities are in decline.

640. FALTERMAYER, Edmund K. **Redoing America: A Nationwide Report on How to Make Our Cities and Suburbs Livable.** NY: Harper & Row, 1968. 242 pp.   (BC-4)

Concludes that "It is well within our capabilities to arrest the chaos that is enveloping us, and to create a vastly more livable country. If we can resist quick and inexpensive compromises, and hold out for ambitious plans that 'stir men's blood...'" (p. 205) Recommends about $20 billion in additional annual expenditures for the cities, an environmental lobby to press for public arrangements over private needs, and more environmental concern on the part of everyone.

*** Classic spend-more liberalism of the sixties.

641. LINOWITZ, Sol M. **This Troubled Urban World.** Claremont, Calif.: Claremont College, 1974. 69 pp. $4.00.   (AB-5)

The former Ambassador to the Organization of American States and present Co-Chairman of the Urban Coalition views the transition to the "first urban age" when the majority of mankind will live in cities or metropolitan areas. It is felt that "our cities can and will survive as the bastions of our civilization," (p. 5) and that Americans can adapt their heritage to new realities.

To counter "the myth that Americans do not like living in cities," (p. 14) Linowitz cites data on population growth in metropolitan areas (but he does not consider data on preferences: where people would like to live).

To save the cities, Linowitz advocates Metropolitan Development Corporations financed by bonds and grants, urban homesteading, and new kinds of education connecting students with jobs.

*** A weak argument from someone who should know better.

642. BENT, Alan E. **Escape from Anarchy: A Strategy for Urban Survival.** Memphis, Tenn.: Memphis State University Press, 1972. 200 pp. $6.95.   (A-4)

"...applies the theoretical framework of systems models and cybernetics analysis in building an intersystem linkage between the urban system and the political system." (p. 6) National controls based on a Keynesian view of the economy are seen as necessary to overcome inertia and chaos, as well as a full utilization of a hierarchy of planning levels.

643. HIGBEE, Edward. **A Question of Priorities: New Strategies for Our Urbanized World.** With an Introduction by R. Buckminster Fuller. NY: Morrow, 1970. 214 pp. $6.00.   (B-4)

The whole of humanity is seen as switching from an agrarian to an urban resource base, thereby becoming increasingly interdependent on the manmade synthetic environment of integrated resource-supply systems. The sickness of cities is seen as the result of the failure to change institutionally. Governments should develop the same degree of network coordination that characterizes modern business and industry.

Chapter 5, A Society of Responsibility, defines such a society as one which facilitates the full social maturation of all its citizens through its institutional networks. To do this, a "mammoth transfer" of wealth from war to peace is required as a first step toward the ecological welfare of total world humanity.

644. MEIER, Richard L. **Planning for an Urban World: The Design of Resource-Conserving Cities.** Cambridge, Mass.: MIT Press, 1974. 515 pp.   (A-4)

The fundamental problem for most people is seen as survival, and rambling, but far-ranging, commentary is devoted to famine, possible challenges, ecumenopolis, the Green Revolution, energy and water supply, the uses of space and time, and communications. There are also 12 scenarios on topics such as Bombay's future, improving Singapore, a New Ice Age, and poor cities subjected to an energy squeeze.

"Cities are destined to become the normal habitat for man. When human populations are numbered in the multiple billions, the metropolis must become home for all but a minor fraction. Only in the highly organized, carefully designed, and globally interconnected metropolis does any hope exist for coping successfully with prospective resource scarcities." (p. 9)

*** An urban version of a non-affluent technological society, but does not consider alternative formulations such as the **Blueprint for Survival** (no. 211) before placing its hope "only" in the highly organized metropolis.

645. ARANGO, Jorge. **The Urbanization of the Earth.** Boston: Beacon Press, 1970. 175 pp.   (A-4)

Views the traumatic process of adaptation to the scientific and industrial era as irreversible. The Pan-Urban Land Use System (PLUS) is advocated to replace promiscuous and amorphous growth with a system of Urban Units (sectors of approximately 2 square miles) integrated with open land. When the city needs to grow, it would create a new Urban Unit, like a plant producing a new leaf.

PLUS is not a plan, but an organic process: "a way in which urban areas should be organized so that they can be planned." It is a sizable investment, but continuing to patch up that which does not work ("shells of the agricultural era") is a useless waste.

646. DANTZIG, George B. and Thomas L. SAATY. **Compact City: A Plan for a Livable Urban Environment.** San Francisco: Freeman, 1973. 244 pp.   (AB-3)

Compact City is a possible new city that would be inexpensive to build and maintain, yet spacious. Services would be fully available at all times. There would be no suburban sprawl, traffic jams, smog, and urban blight.

This ideal serves as a yardstick of what might result by replacing the patchwork approach of the present with the "total-system interactive approach" for redesigning cities. The objective is to make cities into convenient, simple, exciting places to live, and to make them more flexible. Chapter 3 offers a general plan for a Compact City of 250,000 population in a 2.2 square mile area, and Chapter 4 sketches the ideal transportation plan.

Even if this ideal is out of sight, the overview of past solutions appears worthwhile: Ebenezer Howard's garden cities, Greenbelt communities, Frank Lloyd Wright's decentralized cities (see no. 681), satellite cities, Le Corbusier's "Glorious City," Jane Jacobs' conditions for reconstruction of cities, and Soleri's Arcologies (see no. 678).

647. WOLF, Peter. **The Future of the City: New Directions in Urban Planning.** NY: Watson-Guptill, Whitney Library of Design, 1974. 207 pp. $20.50.   (ABC-3)

A slick survey of contemporary liberal hopes, embellished with 146 illustrations of past and present proposals and attainments. At the end of each chapter there is a summary of New Directions viewed as probable and desirable.

Chapters cover Downtown, The Street, The Urban Highway (must be integrated with total community development objectives), Public Transportation (must be expanded to serve outlying areas), Housing, The Urban Environment (stressing redevelopment of river and lake edges), Historic Preservation (a new emphasis on districts rather than single buildings), Land Use Regulation (more support for New Town development), and New Directions in Planning (such as growing concern with process and flexibility).

A sanguine conclusion assails the belief that cities are in decline: "In focusing on where change is beginning to appear, where new trends are beginning to be in evidence, and the quality of new planning concepts only recently evolved, it becomes evident that the future of the city is indeed promising." Most cities have grown too far and too fast, "But American cities of the later 1970's and beyond may well be more contained, more humane, and far more desirable." (p. 194)

*** The city planner's version of "Light-at-the-End-of-the-Tunnel," and a noteworthy example of prescription posing in the language of description.

648. DAHINDEN, Justus. **Urban Structures for the Future.** NY: Praeger, 1972. $25.00.   (ns)

More than 400 photographs and plans reveal the exciting potential of new building and city structures: cellular construction, clip-on, plug-in cities; marine structures; and bridge structures to span existing cities." (Book club advt.)

649. BLAIR, Thomas L. **The International Urban Crisis.** NY: Hill and Wang, 1974. 176 pp.   (B-4)

An overview of the similarity of urban patterns and problems worldwide, with chapters on The Urban Explosion, Slums and Suburbs, Movement and Congestion, Pollution and the Environment, and Alienation, Conflict, and

Violence. The final chapter provides a bland survey of the usual solutions for transport, new towns, metropolitan-regional planning, reforming government structures, and planning urban futures. This is concluded with a liberal exhortation for responsible technology and improved coordination: "Competition must be phased out and replaced by socially responsible economies, political forms, and social values." (p.165)
*** Useful as an introductory survey of urban problems.

650. ELDREDGE, H. Wentworth (ed.) **World Capitals: Toward Guided Urbanization.** Garden City, NY: Anchor Press/Doubleday, 1975. 642 pp. $19.95.   (AB-3)

The justification for this lavish anthology is that the ruling ideology of the 20th century is nationalism, and that capital cities bear an important symbolic torch. Capital cities can be seen as the best that man can do: if he fails in this respect, can he build a glorious city anywhere else?

Eleven case studies are dealt with in four sections: Western Old World (Stockholm, Paris, London), Western New World (Washington, Toronto, Caracas), Non-Western (Moscow, Tokyo), and Developing Nations (Chandigarh, Dakar, Brasilia). Toronto and Chandigarh are provincial capitals of especial note.

The final section on Managing Urbanism offers three chapters by Eldredge. The Urban Malaise summarizes the lessons learned from the above cases. Alternative Possible Futures (see no. 621) provides a taxonomy of types of settlement. A National Urban Plan and Delivery System describes the promise of futurism, the policy sciences, social indicators, and behavioral technologies, and advocates a national urbanization policy as an act of will. It is warned that no plan will lead to great trouble, and that two disastrous poles must be avoided: anarchy and "planned centralized macroincompetence."

651. ELDREDGE, H. Wentworth. (ed.) **Taming Megalopolis: An Introduction to Urban Planning and Urbanism.** 2 vols. NY: Praeger, 1967. 1200 pp. Doubleday Anchor edition, 1967.   (ns)

A reader for graduate and advanced undergraduate students in courses on city planning, urban sociology, local government, urban design, urban geography, etc.

652. LEVIN, Melvin R. (ed.) **Exploring Urban Problems.** Boston: Urban Press, 1971. 667 pp. $12.50.   (B-4)

A reader dividing 19 selections into five sections: The Urban Planners' Trinity (population, land use, and economic base), The Physical Structure of Urban Areas (housing, transportation, environment), Social Problems and Programs (education, poverty, race, crime), Approaches to Urban Government, and Overview of Problems.

653. CHINOY, Ely (ed.) **The Urban Future.** NY: Lieber-Atherton, 1973. 179 pp.   (B-4)

An anthology of possibly-outdated materials by York Willbern (1964), Catharine Bauer Wurster (1963), John Friedmann and John Miller (1965), Jean Gottman (1966), Paul Ylvisaker (1961), Nathan Glazer (1959), Mortin Grodzins (1957), the National Commission on the Causes and Prevention of Violence (1969), and Russell Baker (1965).

654. GALE, Stephen and Eric G. MOORE (eds.) **The Manipulated City: Perspectives on Spatial Structure and Social Issues in Urban America.** Chicago: Maaroufa Press, 1975. 366 pp. $5.95, paper.   (ns)

655. BOURNE, L.S. **Urban Systems: Strategies for Regulation.** NY: Oxford University Press, 1975.   (ns)

"This book is the first to compare and evaluate different national urbanization policies. It provides a survey of the theory of urbanization and describes the strategy behind government policy in Britain, Sweden, Australia, and Canada." (advt.)

656. GRIFFIN, Charles W., Jr. **Taming the Last Frontier. A Prescription for the Urban Crisis.** NY: Pitman, 1974. 260 pp. $8.95.   (ns)

657. MEAD, Margaret. **World Enough: Rethinking the Future.** Photographs by Ken Heyman. Boston: Little, Brown, March 1976. $17.00. (ns)

Explores the impact that post-World War II technology, planning, and political strategy has had upon people across the globe, pointing out that experience has proved to be more complex than any planner could have possibly foreseen. Argues for a rethinking of the premises from which planners have worked in the past, in order to instill "human scale" into architecture. (Library of Urban Affairs, advt.)

658. ALLSOPP, Bruce. **Towards a Humane Architecture.** London: F. Muller, 1974. 111 pp.   (ns)

659. BERRY, Brian J.L. **The Human Consequences of Urbanization.** NY: St. Martin's Press, 1973. 205 pp.   (ns)

660. HAWLEY, Amos H. and Vincent P. ROCK (eds.) **Metropolitan America in Contemporary Perspective.** NY: Wiley/Halstead Press, July 1975. $25.00.   (ns)

An analysis of approaches for dealing with urban areas, sponsored by the National Academy of Sciences.

661. CHUDACOFF, Howard P. **The Evolution of American Urban Society.** Englewood Cliffs, NJ: Prentice-Hall, 1975. 280 pp. $12.50.   (ns)

662. WILSHER, Peter and Rosemary RIGHTER. **The Exploding Cities.** NY: Quadrangle, 1975. 238 pp. $8.95.   (ns)

663. RASKIN, Eugene, A.I.A. **Sequel to Cities: What Happens When Cities Are Extinct.** NYC (10010): Block Publishing Co., 915 Broadway, 1975. $1.95, paper.   (ns)

663a. LOTTMAN, Herbert R. **How Cities Are Saved.** NY: Universe Books, April 1976. $10.95.   (ns)

663b. CAPUTO, David A. **Urban America: The Policy Alternatives.** San Francisco: W.H. Freeman, April 1976.   (ns)

663c. WILHELM, Paul and Robert TORRONE. **Urban Growth.** Rochelle Park, NJ: Hayden Book Co., 1975. 160 pp. $3.25, paper.   (ns)

663d. LINEBERRY, Robert L. and Louis H. MASOTTI (eds.) **Perspectives on Urban Policy.** Lexington, Mass.: Heath/Lexington Books, Policy Studies Organization Series, 1975(?). 240 pp. $16.00.   (ns)

663e. GREENBERG, Martin and Ralph CLEM. **City: Two Thousand A.D.** NY: Fawcett World/Crest Original, July 1976. $1.95, paper.

664. CLAPP, James A. **New Towns and Urban Policy: Planning Metropolitan Growth.** NY: Dunellen, 1971. 342 pp. $12.50.   (A-3)

"This study is basically concerned with an investigation of the relevance and feasibility of new towns policy in the light of the increase of private new town development and a diverse literature on metropolitanism." (p. xii) Chapters discuss the new town concept, an historic overview, the case for new towns, characteristics of American new town developers and developments, operational considerations for new towns policy, and the feasibility of the new town concept.

It is concluded that "most American new towns show, aside from the process of development, little if any significant distinction from the characteristics of development in other suburban areas." (p. 282)

"Generally, it appears that many proponents of new towns have placed unwarranted faith in physical determinism and the ability of the new town concept to effect desired changes in the social and economic structure of the metropolis." (p. 284)

The major obstacle to a new towns policy is the fact that the U.S. has no concerted public policy. The new town idea is also frustrated by the fragmented governmental structure of the metropolis. Public programs established to date appear inadequate. The goals of the new town concept do not mesh with the structure of the modern metropolis, "and in this respect the new town concept may well be an idea whose time has passed." (p. 287)

665. GALANTAY, Ervin Y. **New Towns: Antiquity to the Present.** NY: George Braziller, 1975. $15.00; $5.95, paper.   (ns)

Explores every facet of new town development and predicts that several hundred new towns, designed to contain 20-30 million people, will be founded in the next 25 years. (Library of Urban Affairs, advt., April 1975)

666. OSBORN, Frederic J. and Arnold WHITTICK. **The New Towns: The Answer to Megalopolis.** Introduction by Lewis Mumford. Cambridge, Mass.: MIT Press, revised edition, 1969. 456 pp. (First published in Great Britain in 1963.)   (AB-4)

A broad account of the new towns in Great Britain, with two-thirds of the book devoted to a description of 23 individual new towns.

667. SMITH, Fred. **Man and His Urban Environment: A Manual of Specific Considerations for the Seventies and Beyond.** With an Introduction by Laurence S. Rockefeller. NY: Man and His Urban Environment Project (30 Rockefeller Plaza, Room 5600), Nov. 1972. 57 pp. $2.00.   (AB-3)

A well-written pamphlet attempting a "fresh perspective" on major problems. "As a result of basic ignorance, we are so inundated with urban confusion that we do not really know what our problems are, though we are saturated with their consequences...What is really needed is insight and a determination to isolate those points at which the city fails us..." (p. 4)

The first part of this "manual" starts with a listing of fundamental **needs** (as distinguished from **wants**, which are embellishments and limitless): livable shelter, effective services, reasonable security, hope for personal and community improvement, a source of income and sense of belonging, a minimum of waste, adequate transportation, and a minimum of pollution. To find viable answers, New Towns as pilot plants are advocated, following the precedent set by the British.

"It becomes increasingly evident that what we need--and what we lack-- is a comprehensive, integrated Urban System that combines the physical design of the city with the pattern of its direction and Management." (p. 16) To this end, the second part discusses New Town development through public corporations, and through federal and state assistance. Part III sketches a prototype New Town project for a population of 150,000.

Nine fundamental man-environmental relationships are suggested for investigation: ethnic and cultural patterns, employment, consumption, recreation, justice, health, education, cultural institutions and activities, and corporations. The final part offers a chart suggesting how an interested group can carry the intent of this study forward.

668. BRECKENFELD, Gurney. **Columbia and the New Cities.** NY: Ives
   Washburn, 1971. 332 pp. $8.95.   (C-4)

A history of the new town experience in Europe and the U.S., with about half of the book devoted to an exuberant account of Columbia, Maryland, and its chief planner, James Rouse.

"I believe that new towns are an essential part of the needed restructuring of our urban apparatus...such a renovation must occur if private enterprise, political liberty, and a healthy American civilization are to survive." (p. 1)

668a. LANGORD, Letitia C. and Gwen BELL, "Federally Sponsored New
   Towns of the Seventies," **Growth and Change,** 6:4, Oct. 1975, pp.
   24-31.   (ns)

668b. GOLANY, Gideon and Daniel WALDEN (eds.) **The Contemporary New
   Communities Movement in the United States.** Urbana: University
   of Illinois Press, 1974. 154 pp. $12.50.   (ns)

Ten essays on topics such as enabling legislation at the federal level, national growth policies, new town governance, social issues, and new town case histories.

668c. GOLANY, Gideon (ed.) **Strategy for New Community Development
   in the United States.** NY: Wiley/Halstead, 1975. 293 pp. $28.00. (ns)

An outgrowth of a seminar at Pennsylvania State University, with 11 essays on topics such as regional and national growth policy, economic considerations, communication needs, population redistribution, and sociological issues. (From **World Future Society Bulletin,** March-April, 1976).

669. MacCALLUM, Spencer H. **The Art of Community.** Menlo Park, Calif.: Institute for Humane Studies, Inc., 1970. 118 pp.   (AB-3)

An interesting combination of perspectives from real estate and anthropology. The hotel is discussed as a model of the modern city, in that the key principle of organization is not kinship, interest, or sovereignty, but contract. Other forms of proprietary community such as trailer parks and industrial parks are then explored.

"A main theme of this (essay) has been that the period of sovereignty is but the unstable transition between two levels of human social organization--the kinship level and the contractual." (p. 103) An extension of proprietary community is advocated, leading to a society of individual contracts.

670. DOXIADIS, Constantinos A. **Ekistics: An Introduction to the Science of Human Settlements.** NY: Oxford University Press, 1968. 257 pp.(AB-3)

The major work of a major urban planner, clearly outlining the author's holistic approach. Chapter 4, Ekistic Evolution, describes the transition from megalopolis to ecumenopolis, the universal human settlement. The impact of predicted population growth appears to inexorably lead from connected cities to metropolises to megalopolises. "Thus, it is quite probable that all settlements will become interconnected to form a continuous system covering the inhabitable earth...the Ecumenopolis is already beginning to take shape and if we do not intervene actively, it may take shape as a city bearing in its very roots the elements of death." (pp. 217, 218) Ecumenopolis is thus born as a dying city due to the slow death of its many centers.

The shortening time span in each of the five phases of human settlements is also noted: primitive non-organized (unknown time period), primitive organized (10,000-12,000 years), static cities (5000-6000 years), dynamic cities (200-400 years), and the single static settlement.

671. DOXIADIS, Constantinos A., "The Coming Era of Ecumenopolis," **Saturday Review,** March 18, 1967, pp. 11-14.   (B-3)

Population growth will create "a universal city, Ecumenopolis, which will cover the earth with a continuous network of minor and major urban concentrations of different forms...the pressure of population on resources will be such that important measures will have to be taken so that a balance can be retained between the five elements of the anthropocosmos in a universal scale." (p.13) The anthropocosmos (the real world of man) contains nature, man himself, society, shells (or structures), and networks.

672. DOXIADIS, C.A. **Dynapolis, the City of the Future.** Athens, Greece: Doxiadis Associates, 1960. 77 pp.   (ns)

673. DOXIADIS, C.A. **Anthropopolis: City for Human Development.** Athens, Greece: Athens Center of Ekistics, 1974.   (ns)

The first book in a series of four, describing a City for Human Development, or the city we need as humans.

674. DOXIADIS, C.A. and J.G. PAPAIOANNOU. **Ecumenopolis: the Inevitable City of the Future.** Athens, Greece: Athens Center of Ekistics, 1974. 469 pp. (U.S. edition published by W.W. Norton in 1975. $14.95; $5.95, paper.)   (A-3)

The second of four volumes "which try to help the understanding of what is going to happen to our human settlements and what we can do to save them. It deals with the inevitable changes in their scale from the small polis (town or city of the past) to the present-day megalopolis and to the City of the Future or Ecumenopolis." (p.xii) The third book, **Building Entopia,** will describe the city that combines our hopes and goals with reality. The fourth book is called **Action for Human Settlements.**

The first statement of the ecumenopolis concept was made in 1961, and this book is the fruit of a 15-year study, bringing together 153 figures and 34 tables, with the claim that the general concept of Ecumenopolis, without any doubt, is a valid image of the future of urbanization on this planet. "The main trends of present technological and economic progress cannot, and should not be reversed. This means that a universal system of life will be formed, with a population which will stabilize at between 15 and 25 billion..." (p.37)

We are in the middle of an explosion of many forces, but there is no reason for pessimism; we are simply suffering from growing pains. The reason for this growth is the change in the capacity of the globe as a container to support Anthropos. "It should be entirely possible with the advanced technologies and high incomes anticipated for the period of Ecumenopolis to produce adequate supplies of....resources to sustain a larger global population..." (p.268)

"The present systems are going to go on changing for two main reasons: people will continue to flow into the cities because of the greater advantages they can obtain there, combined with the decreased need for agricultural labor..." (p.279) This great migration is "sure to continue."
*** A great deal of work based on the increasingly questionable premises of The Technological, Affluent, Service Society.

675. TOYNBEE, Arnold. **Cities on the Move.** NY: Oxford University Press, 1970. 257 pp.   (AB-4)

The final chapter concerns "The Coming World City," with due credit to the Doxiadis concept of ecumenopolis. The world city is seen as "a certainty," with "all but a fraction of mankind...living within the confines of a World-City that will occupy only a fraction of the planet's land surface." (p.200) It is also proclaimed that "food-producers will become a dwindling minority."

Consequently, there is an extensive argument for the use of trains rather than autos, and a brief argument for the necessity of a world government to manage the World-City. Concludes that "Since our ancestors rose to the occasion, we, their descendants, are presumably capable of emulating them if we display the courage, vision, and inventiveness that were our ancestor's salvation." (p.247)
*** For a discussion of cities that may be literally "on the move," see Adrian Berry's views on flying cities (no. 691).

676. SAFDIE, Moshe. **For Everyone a Garden.** Cambridge, Mass.: MIT Press, 1974. $25.00.   (ns)

The Israeli architect known for Habitat '67 offers solutions to the problems of mass transit, low-income housing, pollution, and human design, with models of his current and future projects.

677. SAFDIE, Moshe. **Beyond Habitat.** Edited by John Kettle. Cambridge, Mass.: MIT Press, 1970. 244 pp.   (ABC-3)

Comments on city design in general and on the building of Habitat in particular (including 55 photos of Habitat designs).
The number one political issue of our time is that we must have planning,

but we must also "liberate the individual from the bureaucratic oppression that commonly results from central planning." (p.232) The concept of private ownership of land in the urban context is obsolete; indeed, air rights may be more significant than surface rights.

Safdie advocates an Environmental Bill of Rights outlining the basic housing and community requirements of every citizen. This would include a national transportation master plan, a five-year program to end all pollution, and a master plan for urban dispersal.

678. SOLERI, Paolo. **Arcology: The City in the Image of Man.** Cambridge, Mass.: MIT Press, 1969. 122 pp.   (AB-3)

An outsize 24"x14" to counterbalance the striking assertion on the first page that "This book is about miniaturization."

To counter ecumenopoly ("The Map of Despair"), Soleri proposes miniaturization in order to minimize the prime handicap of the physical world: the time-space straight jacket. Arcology (derived from "ecological architecture") refers to a one-structure system which is central to the organization of the city as the wholeness of a biological organism. It is "coherent, meaningful life totally tri-dimensional--human scale within megastructure--ecological relevance--conditioned open city--fruition in implosion."

The book is not considered to be a blueprint for a city-civilization, but only a guideline for a new option. It is composed of "a critical part and a constructive part." Part I includes 55 cosmic schematics--crude sketches to illustrate concepts such as The World of Man and Society, Wholeness and Flux, and Aesthetogenesis.

Part 2 is composed of very detailed and elaborate designs for 30 arcologies to accommodate various topographic conditions, i.e. sea cliff (Arcoforte), coastal flat region (Babelnoah), farm land (Arcvillage I), desert land (Arkibuz), cold region (Arcollective), dam site (Babeldiga), and mesa topography (Arcosanti). The latter is the design that Soleri is engaged in building near Phoenix, Arizona.

*** A nice place to visit, but would someone want to live there? There is not harm in an experiment, and Soleri is building a prototype arcology for 3000 inhabitants. Work on "Arcosanti Community" has been going on for 5 years, but is still less than 2% completed. **(The New York Times,** Thursday, Nov. 20, 1975, p. 39) Also see Donald Wall, **Visionary Cities: The Arcology of Paolo Soleri** (Praeger, 1971), which is largely photographs of models with a few visionary statements by Soleri. The 1969 MIT Press Book is far better.

679. MASON, Roy, "Underground Architecture: What Lies Ahead May Be Beneath Us," **The Futurist,** X:1, February 1976, pp. 16-20. (B-3)

A survey of various experiments, concluding that "The increasing need to improve the quality of the environment and conserve energy suggests that we should review our tendency to build upward, and instead consider going down into the ground, thus re-establishing our oneness with it. Some day soon, underground homes, offices, and factories may become our natural habitat, and we can let the surface of the earth go back to natural wilderness." (p.20)

This article is followed by Malcolm Wells, "Why I Went Underground" (pp. 21-24), in which an architect describes the virtues of his office.

*** Certainly an interesting option, although, as a forecast, the notion that most of us will "soon" be underground is obviously rhetorical excess.

680. ENTWISTLE, Clive, "Holopolis: Some Ecological Effects of Our Urban Environment and a Program for Its Systematic Regeneration," in BROOKS (ed.), **The Changing World and Man** (1970), pp. 42-63 (see No. 758).   (A-4)

Holopolis is an urban environment that is whole in all the senses, designed to favor the emergence of healthy people. We can regenerate existing obsolescent cities with the Holopolitan system, which is seen as entirely within our economic reach today. The presentation includes 8 figures.

681. WRIGHT, Frank Lloyd. **The Industrial Revolution Runs Away.** NY: Horizon Press, 1969. 187 pp.   (B-4)

A revision of Wright's **The Disappearing City** (1932). The new text is accompanied with a facsimile of the original text, revised in Wright's hand, on facing pages. The volume was issued in a limited edition of 1250 copies.
The city of the future is called Broadacre City because it is based on the spacing of a minimum of an acre to a family. It would stress individuality and "organic architecture" which is seen as the only architecture of democracy. Similarly, Broadacre City is "the only possible city looking toward the future." (p. 73)
*** Lofty, overgeneralized, and repetitious.

682. FULLER, R. Buckminster. "City of the Future," **Playboy,** Jan. 1968. pp. 166 ff.   (B-3)

Offers a drawing of a tetrahedral city and an explanation of this "entirely feasible and practical new way for men to live together economically." The pictured city, consisting of 3 triangular walls of 5000 living units each, can be placed on land or it can float. Such a floating city could house a million people.
There is also an argument for domed-over cities which "would reduce energy losses--either in winter heating or summer cooling--to 1/85 of the present level. It would obviate snow removal. The savings in ten years would pay for the dome." (p. 230)
Environmental conditions have frustrated the realization of man's potentials, but "The comprehensive introduction of automation everywhere around the earth will free man from being an automaton..." The new life pattern might become that of "frequency-modulated occupancy of rented space in mobile hotels or in dwelling machines..." (p. 230)
*** Freedom is slavery???

682a. BORGESE, Elisabeth Mann. **The Drama of the Oceans.** NY: Harry N. Abrams, 1976. 258 pp. $25.00.   (ns)

The chairman of the Planning Council of the International Ocean Institute views oceans as the last frontier. Includes a chapter on ocean architecture, describing plans for island cities of various sizes. Such architecture is seen as the next stage in a great two-stage migration of human population: from the country to the city, and from the city to the coastlines.

683. RITNER, Peter. **The Society of Space.** NY: Macmillan, 1961. 144 pp.   (A-4)
Rambling essays on The Rejuvenation of Idealism, Other Forms of Life, Youth and Work, Love, Art, and The Empire. Three kinds of space are considered: inside the human head, the dimensions of choice opened up by the technological revolution, and the extraterrestrial environment.

684. HUBBARD, Earl. **The Search Is On: A View of Man's Future from the Perspective of Space.** Los Angeles: Pace Publications, 1969. $1.25, paper.   (ns)

Discusses indulgent society vs. transcendent society, the age of awareness, and a synthesis of mankind. A limited future is seen for man on earth, and it is now time for man to be "born into the universe."

685. WOODWARD, Herbert N. **The Human Dilemma.** NY: The Brookdale Press, 1971. 198 pp. $5.95.   (ABC-3)

A well-read businessman expresses his concern about the growth of machine technology and population, and the need for new frontiers. "...I believe the earth and even the solar system will ultimately prove too finite for man so that he must plan to move up and out for the long-term benefit of the species." (p. ix)
We are seen as presently in the atomic age. Although the potential of atomic power has been scarcely tapped, the implications of the approaching space age are even greater. "Man is now opening the door to the most expansive and exciting period in his history." (p. 117)
*** Modest and well-written.

686. "Unibutz, 'Out of This World'," **Fields Within Fields,** 4:1, 1971. 71 pp. (Available from World Institute Council, 777 United Nations Plaza, NYC 10017, for $2.50.)   (A-4)

Six essays centered on the notion of Unibutz (Universal-Kibbutz), proposed by Robert A. Smith III as "a global goal which honors the work of three outstanding behavioral pioneers who departed from us within the last decade--Douglas McGregor, Gordon Allport, and Abraham Maslow." (p. 14) This seeding operation would launch three spaceships, each carrying 100 or more passengers (symbolic of the voyage of Columbus) for the purpose of erecting a settlement on a distant planet. (Smith is a Behavior Analyst with NASA.) Contributors include Smith, A. Reza Arasteh, Oliver L. Reiser, Thomas Broussard Turner, S.B. Sells and E.K. Eric Gunderson, and James L. Daniels, Jr.

687. O'NEILL, Gerard K., "Space Colonies: The High Frontier," **The Futurist,** X:1, February 1976, pp. 25-33.   (ABC-2)

A popularization of the author's ideas based on his presentation to the World Future Society's Second General Assembly (June 1975), and on testimony before Congress (July, 1975). An elaboration of the space colony concept appears in **Physics Today** (no. 689), and an elaboration of the satellite solar power station notion appears in **Science** (no. 688).
In the **Physics Today** article, the colonies were justified as a means of relieving population pressures on earth. In the **Futurist** article, it is argued that Island One (the first colony) could pay back all of the total investment (plus 10% interest) in 24 years by manufacturing satellite solar power stations which would convert solar energy to electricity and beam it by microwaves to earth, where it would be reconverted to ordinary electricity. This investment approach is particularly useful to O'Neill's argument in that the present estimated cost for the first colony is now $100 billion (with a possible variation of $50 billion in either direction), in contrast to the original "spartan" estimate of $30.7 billion in the **Physics Today** article.
The widespread interest in the space colonies idea, suggested by information accompanying this article, has also accelerated expectations: "The human race stands now on the threshold of a new frontier whose richness

is a thousand times greater than that of the new western world of 500 years ago...That frontier can be exploited for all humanity..." (p. 26)
*** Clearly an important alternative that, like it or not, will be receiving considerable attention. The major counterargument is that of time: how can we manage our affairs on earth for the several decades until the energy benefits of space colonies may be available, and until they are a living option for a substantial number of people? Will the immediate psychic benefits of a major and possibly multinational effort outweigh the costs at a time of vast cutbacks in the public sector?

688. O'NEILL, Gerard K., "Space Colonies and Energy Supply to the Earth," **Science,** Vol. 190, Dec. 5, 1975, pp. 943-947.   (A-3)

"The feasibility of establishing manufacturing facilities in a high orbit is under discussion. They could be used for the construction of satellite solar power stations from lunar materials. Estimates indicate that this may be considerably more economical than constructing power stations on the earth and lifting them into orbit." (Summary, p. 947)

689. O'NEILL, Gerard K., "The Colonization of Space," **Physics Today,** Sept. 1974, pp. 32-40.   (A-3)

Any migration into outer space has heretofore been confined to considering the settlement of planets. Breaking through this "mental 'hangup'" a Princeton physicist argues that the region beyond earth is not a void but should be seen as a culture medium, where abundant energy can be obtained from the sun, materials can be acquired from the moon and the asteroid belt, and rotational acceleration can substitute for Earth's gravity.
O'Neill then launches into a detailed plan for building space colonies inside coupled pairs of rotating hollow aluminum cylinders (in seasonal counterpoint), landscaped to resemble earth-like environments by dividing the circumference into alternating strips of land area (valleys) and window area (solars). Climate would be to one's liking, dependent simply upon the opening and closing of solar mirrors.
An initial model could be in operation by 1988, housing 10,000 people. About 1000 yards long--the size of a supertanker--the colony would be located between the Earth and the moon, and 98% of the colony's mass would be obtained from the moon's surface. The cost for this model, estimated in some detail, would be $30.7 billion, about equal to the $33 billion spent on the Apollo program. "Model 2" would be ten times as large in area and population, but would cost no more than the first colony because "Model 1" would be a factory-city producing nearly all the necessary components for "Model 2."
After these two initial colonies, construction costs would taper off as space-based industry becomes stronger and asteroid materials are used. "Model 3," requiring virtually no assistance from Earth, could be ready by the year 2002. "Model 4" would reach optimal size: 16 miles long, 4 miles in diameter, 100 square miles of land mass, and supporting several million people. These colonies would duplicate themselves in geometric progression, each doubling requiring about 6 years. By the middle of the 21st century, there might be some 500 colonies.
Emigration could then reverse the rise in the Earth's population, in that the new habitats would be "far more comfortable, productive and attractive than is most of Earth." Moreover, nearly all industrial activity and heavy power usage could be moved away from Earth's fragile biosphere. The colonies would provide self-sufficiency and independence, as well as havens for endangered animal species. Indeed, with this new mode of ex-

pansion, "the ultimate size limit for the human race on the newly available frontier is at least 20,000 times its present value."

All of this is predicated on existing technology, assuming only structural materials that already exist. "Within a development that may span 100 years, this assumption is unrealistically conservative."

690. ASIMOV, Isaac, "Colonizing the Heavens," **Saturday Review,** June 28, 1975, pp. 12-17.   (ABC-3)

A popularization of the above. Also see another popular summary in **The Sciences** (New York Academy of Sciences), July/August 1974, pp. 15-20, accounts in **The New York Times** (May 13, 1974, p. 1) and **Time** (June 3, 1974, p. 51) and O'Neill's own popular account in **The Los Angeles Times** (July 30, 1974). O'Neill issues an irregular "Newsletter on Space Colonization" from his office (Jadwin Hall, P.O. Box 708, Princeton, N.J. 08540).

691. BERRY, Adrian. **The Next Ten Thousand Years: A Vision of Man's Future in the Universe.** NY: Saturday Review Press/E.P. Dutton, 1974. 250 pp. $8.95.   (AB-3)

An optimistic view of possibilities in outer space, with harsh words for the Club of Rome. Chapter 2, No Limits to Growth, argues that the complete destruction of the human race and the world as a habitat for life would be an almost impossible task. As for resources, "Even if the Earth's resources prove ultimately to be finite, those of the solar system and the great galaxy beyond are, for all practical purposes, infinite." (p. 53)

Citing the Russian astronomer, N.S. Kardashev, Berry describes three phases of a planetary civilization: Phase 1 civilizations draw upon energy resources of a single planet; Phase 2 civilizations utilize the entire parent solar system with the dismantling of some planets for raw materials; and Phase 3 civilizations exploit whole sections of a galaxy.

The possibilities of colonizing the moon and Venus are discussed, and Chapter 12 on Flying Cities argues that we should not build more big cities on earth; instead, there could be a series of cities shaped like gigantic wheels, each twenty or so miles in diameter, where inhabitants could reproduce any earthly conditions they desire, including great agricultural fields or hydroponic farms beneath transparent domes.

It is concluded that the Rousseau-like dreams of a return to nature assume that man is free to shape his future, but man can only choose within narrow limits: "there is only one forward path, the path to unending technological expansion." (p. 194) Sooner or later, "we shall go forward to ever more magnificent achievements." (p.196)

*** The Idea of Progress elevated into the heavens. Arrogant, but provocative.

692. MARUYAMA, Magoroh, and Arthur HARKINS (eds.) **Cultures Beyond the Earth: The Role of Anthropology in Outer Space.** NY: Vintage, 1975. 206 pp. $2.95, paper.   (ns)

"A group of anthropologists, scientists, writers, and an Apollo flight technician use the tools and lessons of anthropology to speculate on how we should approach the coming age of space exploration and settlement. Subjects discussed include the physical design of space colonies; political, educational, and social systems; and first contact with non-human cultures." (**The Futurist,** Feb. 1976, p. 48.)

693. GILFALLAN, Edward S., Jr. **Migration to the Stars: Never Again Enough People.** Washington, D.C.: Robert B. Luce Co. (dist. by David McKay), 1975. 226 pp. $8.95.   (ns)

694. STINE, G. Harry. **The Third Industrial Revolution.** Introduction by Barry Goldwater. NY: G. P. Putnam's Sons, 1975. 192 pp. $7.95.
                                                                          (C-3)
An aeronautic engineer and rocket specialist advocates a "Third Industrial Revolution" via the exploitation of the solar system. It is argued that outer space is the best place to locate industrial operations, thereby freeing earth to be a garden planet. An extensive description of orbiting space factories is provided.
*** Quite popularized, but interesting.

695. KANTER, Rosabeth Moss. **Commitment and Community: Communes and Utopias in Sociological Perspective.** Cambridge, Mass.: Harvard University Press, 1972. 303 pp. $2.95, paper.   (A-3)

A critical and well-balanced comparison of contemporary communes with the utopian communities of the past. A major distinction is between retreat communes, which are generally anarchic, and service communes, which are generally well-ordered.
"The utopian vision of the harmonious, integrated, loving community --the communal enclave of warm, close, supportive relationships--does not always occur according to scenario. Reality modifies the dream." (p. 213)
However, "Utopian communities are important not only as social ventures in and of themselves, but also as challenges to the assumptions on which current institutions are organized." (p. 236)
*** Also includes an unannotated bibliography (pp. 270-286) of about 360 items.

696. BOUVARD, Marguerite. **The Intentional Community Movement: Building a New Moral World.** Port Washington, NY: Kennikat Press, 1975. 207 pp. $12.00.   (AB-3)

A good overview, with chapters on history, religious communities, anarchism and decentralism (including a section on Ralph Borsodi, pp. 90-94), the Twin Oaks community (modeled after Skinner's **Walden Two**), and the communitarian subculture.

697. JEROME, Judson. **Families of Eden: Communes and the New Anarchism.** NY: The Seabury Press, 1974. 271 pp.   (AB-4)

A good, but rambling, survey, most notable for its estimate that there might be as many as 30,000 communes, in that many are unnamed and unpublicized. As of 1973, there were at least 5,000 prominent ones. In all, there may be more than three-quarters of a million people living in communes (p. 18).

698. REXROTH, Kenneth. **Communalism: From Its Origins to the Twentieth Century.** NY: The Seabury Press, 1974. 316 pp. $12.95.
                                                                          (ns)
Argues that the birth of a new society--the way out of the contemporary crisis--is indicated by interest in communalism.

699. VEYSEY, Laurence. **The Communal Experience: Anarchist and Mystical Counter-Cultures in America.** NY: Harper & Row, 1973. 495 pp. $15.00.   (A-4)

An historian at the U. of California at Santa Cruz concentrates on several 20th century American communities which have been influenced by anarchism or religious mysticism, and places them in the context of the history of American radicalism.

700. ZABLOCKI, Benjamin. **The Joyful Community: An Account of the Bruder-hof, a Communal Movement Now in Its Third Generation.** Baltimore, Md.: Penguin, 1971. 362 pp. $1.95, paper.   (AB-4)

A sociological case study of a community which began in Germany in the 1920s, migrated to the U.S. in 1954, and is presently a federation of three colonies located in New York, Pennsylvania, and Connecticut, totalling 750 persons. The Bruderhof community is held together by a common religion: "a radical, fundamental Anababtist Christianity." Most of the membership has joined in the past ten years, and survival through three generations is seen by Zablocki as a major accomplishment.
It is felt that the intentional community exemplified by the Bruderhof could never be a widespread model, but it contains important lessons about how people can reestablish contact with the feeling life.

701. FAIRFIELD, Richard. **Communes USA: A Personal Tour.** Baltimore, Md.: Penguin, 1972. 400 pp. $3.50, paper.   (C-4)

After a brief historical survey, the publisher of **The Modern Utopian** offers informal descriptions of Marxist/Anarchist communes, scientific ideological groups such as Walden Two, modern religions, hip communes, group marriage, service communities, and youth communes.

702. HEDGEPATH, William and Dennis STOCK, **The Alternative: Communal Life in New America.** NY: Macmillan, 1970. 191 pp. $7.95.   (C-4)

A paean to communal living, with dozens of lovely photographs supported by glowing rhetoric...a **National Geographic** by and for the counterculture. The commentary proclaims that the new consciousness is happening, must happen.

703. CONOVER, Patrick W., "The Potential for an Alternate Society," **The Futurist,** VII:3, June 1973, pp. 111-116.   (B-3)

A sociologist quotes Richard Fairfield, editor of **The Modern Utopian,** as estimating that there are now about 2000 communes in the U.S., and adds his own suspicion that this is only a small fraction of the total. Conover also estimates at least 200 underground newspapers (supported by at least three underground news services), about 500 Free Schools and over 250 Free Clinics.
The question is whether "the various alternate institutions can become sufficiently integrated so that an enduring alternate society will emerge"--essentially a sub-society within the large one. To do so, the various groups must be coordinated, and factors that encourage and discourage cooperation are discussed. "All considered, there appears to be a very realistic potential for the establishment of an alternate sub-society..." In turn, such a society "might check a movement toward an anti-utopia and even become a center for the American experience as a whole." (p.116)
The article includes a good list of 28 selected readings and a typology of 16 types of communes suggested by Herbert Otto.

704. MORGAN, Arthur E. **The Small Community: Foundation of Democratic Life. What It Is and How to Achieve It.** NY: Harper & Bros., 1942. 312 pp.   (AB-3)

A study of the small, primary community where, more than anywhere else, it is felt that men can find the way to live well. "Today, as in the ancient past, the small community is the home, the refuge, the seed bed, of some of the finest qualities of civilization." (p.10)
Chapters cover topics such as community leadership, the community

council, community social services, community economics, and the relationship to larger social units (each level of society should exercise minimal necessary control over subordinate units).

Present-day community is seen as being dissolved, diluted, and submerged by modern technology, commercialism, mass production, propaganda, and centralized government. But the community need not disappear: "The very changes which are destroying it have put into our hands the means for recreating it in a finer pattern." (p.13)

705. MORGAN, Arthur E. **The Community of the Future: and the Future of Community.** Yellow Springs, Ohio: Community Service, Inc., 1957. 166 pp.   (AB-3)

Notes by the former president of Antioch College and chairman of TVA, contending that the small face-to-face community is a fundamental and necessary unit of society. Most of the book is devoted to describing the characteristics of a good community, with chapters on common functions, outside relationships, the physical setting, local government, economic life, education, religion, recreation, and present-day intentional communities. In sum, it is argued that the community of old may be integrated with the values of modern technology and urban culture, creating a social unit with the advantages of the old and the new, and the serious disadvantages of neither.

706. SARASON, Seymour B. **The Psychological Sense of Community: Prospects for a Community Psychology.** San Francisco: Jossey-Bass, Feb. 1974. $12.95.   (ns)

"All people need a sense of common responsibility and purpose--to feel part of a group they can depend on and contribute to--but few actually do. The lack of...the psychological sense of community is widely felt today in every part of our society, but the need for creating and maintaining it has been either ignored or misunderstood." (advt.)

Chapters concern topics such as the neglect by American psychologists, over-emphasis on the individual at the expense of considering cultural factors, and social action as a vehicle for learning.
*** Appears to be addressed primarily to behavioral scientists, but may offer some valuable insights for all social scientists concerned with spatial alternatives.

707. HOFFMAN, Daniel P. **The Coming Culture.** Forward by Oliver L. Reiser. Thanjavur, India: Sarvodaya Prachuralayam, 1964. 129 pp.
                                                                                (C-4)

A jumbled argument by an American for decentralized, self-reliant and self-governing communities of 1000-5000 people, based on an organic "garden culture" where everyone would have the opportunity to work the land without buying it. Cities as we know them today and violence would disappear, with creativity as "the link that unifies man and nature."

708. BOOKCHIN, Murray. **The Limits of the City.** NY: Harper Colophon, 1974. 147 pp. $2.75, paper.   (AB-3)

A "radically critical" view of the degraded standards of contemporary urbanism, arguing that the roots of the urban crisis lie in the social system that has created it.

It is concluded that to restore urbanity, "the megalopolis must be ruthlessly destroyed and replaced by new decentralized ecocommunities" that possess the best features of the polis and the medieval commune. "The alternative to this development can only be the horrifying disintegration of urban life into a condition of chronic social war, personal violence, and bureaucratic mobilization." (p.139)

709. BEALE, Calvin L., "Renewed Growth in Rural Communities," **The Futurist**, IX:4, August 1975, pp. 196-202.   (AB-3)

"The remarkable recent reversal of long-term population trends is demonstrated by growth in nonmetro counties of 4.2% between April 1970 and July 1973, compared with 2.9% in metro counties." (pp. 197-198) Decentralization in manufacturing has been a major factor, as well as retirees moving to rural areas, the development of state colleges in rural areas, and a change in attitudes.
"The trend in the United States since 1970 was not foreseen in the literature of scientific and public discussion of even 3 or 4 years ago...Much new thought is needed on the probable course of future population distribution in the United States, uncolored either by value-laden residential fundamentalism or by outmoded analytical premises." (p.202)

710. ELLIS, William N., "The New Ruralism: The Post-Industrial Age Is Upon Us," **The Futurist**, IX:4, August 1975, pp. 202-204.   (B-3)

"The U.S. Bureau of Census population projections for 1970-1973...show that people are leaving the urban centers in droves and moving to the remote, rural and least developed parts of our country..." (p.203) With the exceptions of Delaware and Florida, the 20 most rapidly growing states today are rural. "The abrupt reversal of trends which have held for over 100 years puts in serious doubt many national policies and future projections." (p.204)
This important observation is coupled with the expectation that this "new ruralism" is becoming the tool of the post-industrial age, which will emphasize the meeting of man's psychic needs.
*** The return of the Penty usage of "post-industrialism" (nos. 324 and 325) in a modern form. Also see Roszak (no. 303).

710a. STERNLIEB, George and James W. HUGHES (eds.) **Post-Industrial America: Metropolitan Decline and Inter-Regional Job Shifts.** 1976. $12.95.   (ns)

Essays examining the new economic and demographic trendlines away from older metropolitan regions, the causes underlying these trends, and policy implications.
*** Library of Urban Affairs Alternate Selection for June 1976. Publisher information not available.

711. GOLDMARK, Peter C., "Tomorrow We Will Communicate to Our Jobs," **The Futurist**, VI:2, April 1972, pp. 55-58.   (B-4)

The inventor of the long-playing phonograph record and Electronic Video Recording focuses on new communication networks that could promote the decentralization of business and government, and create "the new rural society." There is no intention to deurbanize America, but to halt migration and accommodate the new Americans to be added to the population by the year 2000. "We would like to give all Americans an opportunity to work and live in small but attractive rural communities. The persons who choose to settle in these communities will become the new rural society." (p.56)
For an elaboration of this article, see **The 1972/1973 New Rural Society Project.** Report to the U.S. Dept. of Housing and Urban Development under

Contract No. H-1694. (National Technical Information Service, Springfield, Va. May 1973. 116 pp. $6.25, paper. #PB-231 826.) The project was conducted by Fairfield University (Fairfield, Conn.), in cooperation with Goldmark Communications Corporation.

712. SUNDQUIST, James L. **Dispersing Population: What Americans Can Learn from Europe.** Washington: Brookings Institution, 1975. 290 pp. $9.95.   (AB-3)

Examines programs in Great Britain, France, Italy, Netherlands, and Sweden of incentives and disincentives offered by governments to plan for and regulate where new jobs are offered workers. The first and last chapters discuss the American experience and why little has been accomplished relative to European nations. Concludes that dispersal is an attainable goal that is not unduly costly.
*** A thorough study, particularly noteworthy for the summation of data on preferred and actual place of residence, pp. 24-30.

713. BARNES, Peter, "Land Reform," **The New Republic,** June 5, 12, and 19, 1971.   (ns)

Three articles on The Great American Land Grab, The Vanishing Small Farmer, and The Case for Redistribution.
*** A 64 page booklet by Barnes, **The Sharing of Land and Resources in America,** is available from **The New Republic** for $2.00.

714. BARNES, Peter (ed.) **The People's Land: A Reader on Land Reform in the United States.** Edited for the National Coalition for Land Reform. Emmaus, Pa.: Rodale Press, Book Division, Feb. 1975. 260 pp. $6.95, paper.   (ABC-3)

The goal of the land reform movement is a society based on democratic, egalitarian, and ecological principles. This handsome and provocative volume brings together 42 brief selections under 7 categories: Historical Perspectives; Regional Perspectives; Food, Farms and Technology; Water and Energy; Taxes; Small Towns and Rural Poverty; and Co-Ops, Land Trusts and Land Reform.

715. SWANN, Robert S., Shimon GOTTSCHALK, Erick S. HANSCH, and Edward WEBSTER. **The Community Land Trust: A Guide to a New Model for Land Tenure in America.** Prepared by the International Independence Institute. Cambridge, Mass.: Center for Community Economic Development (1878 Massachusetts Ave.), 1972. 118 pp. $3.50, paper.   (A-3)

A "preliminary" introduction to a concept that is described as more or less theoretical at this time, but one that could become an important tool for low-income communities in urban and rural areas to gain control of the developmental process in their own neighborhoods.
"Today's poverty, unemployment, and urban misery are in no small part due to the thoughtless malappropriation of rural land which has taken place at an ever-increasing pace over the last century and a half." (p. xv)
To counter this trend, the community land trust is proposed. It is a quasi-public legal entity chartered to hold land in stewardship. It is not concerned with common ownership, but with ownership for the common good. The trust holds land in perpetuity, with long-term leases to users who are expected to preserve or enhance the value of the land. Absentee control and sub-leasing are proscribed. Improvements such as homes and industrial

enterprises may be owned individually or cooperatively. (The word "trust" is derived from Ralph Borsodi's idea of "trusterty," or natural resources, as contrasted with "property," or man-made resources. See no 313.)

One of the major applications of the trust idea is in the promotion of rural new towns, in that the trust would be a mechanism for attracting investment money or government support. There might eventually be regional land trusts formed from existing communities.

Perhaps the foremost example of a community land trust is New Communities, Inc. of Lee County, Georgia, which is described in Chapter 3. (pp. 16-25) The remainder of this book is devoted to describing how land trusts can be brought about, with chapters on organizational structure, land acquisition, financing, social planning, land policies, taxation, and zoning.

716. GOTTSCHALK, Shimon S. **Communities and Alternatives: An Exploration of the Limits of Planning.** Cambridge, Mass.: Schenkman, 1975. 170 pp. $9.95; $5.95, paper. (Also distributed by Halsted/ Wiley)   (ns)

717. DEATON, Brady J., "CDCs: A Development Alternative for Rural America," **Growth and Change: A Journal of Regional Development,** 6:1, Jan. 1975, pp. 31-37.   (A-3)

The Community Development Corporation is a broad class of general nonprofit service corporations to develop revenue-generating businesses controlled through community ownership. Deaton provides an overview of various CDC ventures, noting that, in the past, public efforts to stimulate small business enterprise have often been stopgap in nature and incomplete in comprehension.

But we are now seen as entering a new era of rural development efforts. "In response to community pressure, public policies are being modified in line with the idea of self-determination--and this is far more pervasive than is reflected in the simple notion of revenue sharing." (p. 31)

*** Also see **Growth and Change,** 7:1, Jan. 1976, pp. 48-50, for an exchange between Deaton and D. Jeanne Patterson, who feels that CDCs are an unlikely means of encouraging rural America.

718. KOTLER, Milton. **Neighborhood Government: The Local Foundations of Political Life.** Indianapolis, Ind.: Bobbs-Merrill, 1969. 111 pp. $4.95.   (ABC-3)

Asserts that there is presently a movement for local control of cities and that the neighborhood is the source of revolutionary power, with "local liberty as its modest cause." The impoverishment of political life is seen as resulting from the growth of central administration.

Localism, but not separatism, is advocated. This would be enabled by neighborhood corporations, and the revision of city constitutions to distribute power among neighborhoods and to federate that power in a common city government.

719. MORRIS, David, and Karl HESS. **Neighborhood Power: The New Localism.** An Institute for Policy Studies Book. Boston: Beacon Press, June 1975. 180 pp. $3.45, paper.   (ABC-2)

The neighborhood is the way people naturally live together, and the fundamental unit of democracy. "Neighborhood life is the life that brings or tries to bring as much of human life together as possible. It is one special argument of this book, in fact, that in a new birth and building of neighborhood life, all human activity could be brought back together so that work, play, love, life, politics, science, and art could be a shared experience by people sharing a space...in a humane setting." (p. 13)

The authors disagree with the critics of small-scale organization who claim that there are vast economies of scale in the centralization of services such as police, fire protection, and trash collection. Rather, the large-scale institutions are seen as falling apart, and it is felt that the rise of great city problems is related to the rise in great city political power.

The book calls for a return to a human scale of organization and to a sense of community. It describes a comprehensive process: "ways to control local wealth, mechanisms for stabilizing land values, ways to establish community financial institutions, the potentials and limitations of neighborhood manufacturing...(and) the goal of local self-reliance and resident participation in decision-making." (p. 14)

Chapters cover topics such as developing neighborhood awareness, the local economy, housing, government, production, and intercommunalism, concluding with an intriguing and coherent scenario of "A Neighborhood of the Future" which contrasts the newly-attained good life with the old life of the neighborhood as a small underdeveloped nation.

*** An eloquent statement of the decentralist position and a challenging contrast to liberal urban planners. Also see David Morris and Karl Hess, "Neighborhood Technology," **Working Papers for a New Society**, 3:1, Spring 1975, pp. 62-67, and **Dear America** by Hess (no. 300).

720. FALK, Joe (ed.). **Cooperative Community Development (A Blueprint for Our Future)**. Shawnee Mission, Kansas: The Future Associates (P.O. Box 12), 1975. 268 pp. $2.95, paper.   (C-3)

An ingenuous volume based on Falk's experience in Kansas City. Falk is really the author of the entire book, but refers to himself as "editor," perhaps to stress the value of cooperation, which is a dominant theme.

Cooperative Community Development is a way of organizing that "will enable us to decentralize, democratize and humanize the planning, decision making and actions of all of our existing bureaucratic systems." (p. xvi) It involves the formation of neighborhood development associations to enable people to go into business together, and regional development associations to assist the neighborhood groups. In turn, this leads to a new form of society: Cooperative Capitalism.

The book is largely a do-it-yourself guide, with a focus on possibilities for real estate development, financial services, cooperative production, marketing and buying, and education.

*** The innocence and exuberance is not unlike that of **Synergic Power** (345) and **The Velvet Monkey Wrench** (442), but there seems to be many good ideas here that have been carried out to some degree. (It would be useful to have a disinterested observer report on what has actually happened.) Despite vast differences in style, Falk's aims are similar to those of Morris and Hess (see above). The difference is that Falk envisions cooperation with existing institutions, whereas Morris and Hess feel that replacement is necessary.

II. LISTINGS

C. Miscellaneous

Chapter 14

Anthologies and Symposia

This chapter brings together collective efforts that consider societal directions and alternatives not classified elsewhere in this guide. In most instances, the effort is too broad to fit any of the 13 previous category/ chapters.

Time and space limitations have made it necessary, in many cases, to provide only a partial listing of contents or simply to suggest the basic categories of the various collections. In instances where there are widely-known contributors, names are listed so as to suggest the ideological cast of each work. It is noteworthy that certain specialists in generalities keep reappearing through the years: for example, Kenneth E. Boulding, Bertrand de Jouvenel, Margaret Mead, Hans J. Morgenthau, Lewis Mumford, and Arnold J. Toynbee. Mumford appears in collections published in 1928 and in 1974 (nos. 721 and 774). Mead appears in collections published in 1943 and 1976 (nos. 725 and 785), and in many interim collections.

Original collections (721-785) and the collections of reprinted essays or readers (786-807), are each listed chronologically. Of the original anthologies and symposia cited here, the number published appears to have peaked in the 1968-1972 period. Of the 23 readers cited here, 19 were published in the 1970-1973 period. Economics is undoubtedly one of the factors responsible for the quantitative decline in recent years.

Insofar as trends in quality, it might well be argued that collective efforts have gone downhill since 1933, when the President's Research Committee on Social Trends published its massive report on **Recent Social Trends in the United States** (723). This report made an exemplary effort to view the situation as a whole and to interrelate the various elements, each of which was carefully and extensively considered. Most subsequent efforts have simply brought together a collection of undistinguished essays with little or no attempt at synthesis by the editor. There is occasional discussion among participants. There is no instance here of prolonged debate between sharply contrasting viewpoints, in part because most collections are ideologically consistent.

In addition to **Recent Social Trends** (723), another notable early effort was the Conference on Science, Philosophy and Religion in Their Relation to the Democratic Way of Life (726), held in 1944. The distinguished contributors and their deliberations were not unlike those of the Rockefeller Panel (403), the President's Commission on National Goals (404), and the "Agenda for the Nation" proposed by a volume from The Brookings Institution (406). All of these efforts are similar to the over-rated collection of working papers issued in 1967 by the Commission on the Year 2000 (741). Of comparable quality are the three volumes sponsored by the American Institute of Planners (743-745), and the Great Society Seminar at Syracuse University (746).

Volumes that were explicitly "futurist" began to emerge in 1969 with the publication of **Values and the Future** (752), and the proceedings of the First

International Futures Research Conference (753), held in Oslo in 1967. Proceedings of the Second IFRC, held in Kyoto, appeared in 1970 (754). The next lengthy compilation of futurist essays does not appear until the 1975 collection published by the World Future Society (779).

The 1968 Princeton seminar sponsored by The International Association for Cultural Freedom (755) deserves note, as does the experimental Delphi exercise conducted by the Institute for the Future (756). For better or worse, the Delphi can be seen as a symposium of anonymous participants. The set of 17 prospective studies published as part of Plan Europe 2000 (768) is similar to the standard pattern of specialized experts established by **Recent Social Trends** and its inferior successors.

Periodicals have published a number of collections (particularly, it seems, in recent years), most notably the two hopefests in **Saturday Review/ World** (775-776) and the low-horizon Bicentennial issue of **The Public Interest** (781).

Among the readers, Kostelanetz was the first to publish an anthology of futurist writings, and all four of his anthologies (787, 791, 792, 805) are still worthwhile. The Arblaster and Lukes compilation of 81 selections from the 18th, 19th, and 20th centuries (797) offers valuable historical depth for beginning students. Possibly the best collection for beginning students at the high school level is **Futures Conditional** (798). At an upper division or professional level, the best introductory collection of futurist writing is provided by Tugwell (802). Clarke's new anthology of decentralist and ecologically-oriented readings (807) contrasts sharply with all of the other items in this chapter--an important reminder that a thorough consideration of the entire array of alternative futures has seldom, if ever, taken place.

---

721. BEARD, Charles A. (ed.) **Whither Mankind: A Panorama of Modern Civilization.** NY: Longmans, Green and Co., 1928. 408 pp.   (AB-3)

The 16 essays generally concerned with machine civilization and science include Bertrand Russell on science, Julius Klein on business, Sidney and Beatrice Webb on labor, Emil Ludwig on war and peace, Havelock Ellis on the family, Lewis Mumford on the arts, John Dewey on philosophy, Stuart Chase on play, and Carl Van Doren on literature.
*** Also see Beard, ed., **America Faces the Future** (1932), no. 511.

---

722. BROWNELL, Baker (ed.) **Society Tomorrow.** Man and His World, Vol. Six. Northwestern University Essays in Contemporary Thought. NY: D. Van Nostrand, 1929. 185 pp.   (AB-4)

Includes 5 essays:
- George Soule, "Toward Economic Liberty"
- Earl Dean Howard, "Economic Problems of Tomorrow"
- Ralph E. Heilman, "Modern Industry and Social Control"
- A.R. Hatton, "The Future of Urban Politics and Government"
- W.L. Bailey, "Cities Today and Tomorrow"

---

723. President's Research Committee on Social Trends. **Recent Social Trends in the United States.** With a Foreward by Herbert Hoover. NY: McGraw-Hill, 1933. 1568 pp. (2 Vols.)   (AB-1)

This massive and truly exemplary effort was initiated by the President in September 1929 to report on social trends so as to "supply a basis for the formulation of large national policies looking to the next phase in the nation's development." (p. xi) Wesley C. Mitchell served as Chairman of the Committee, William F. Ogburn was Director of Research, and Howard W. Odum was Assistant Director of Research.

The 29 chapters by individual authors form an important and comprehensive anthology--yet these chapters are a mere summary of 13 additional volumes of special studies and supporting data.

The 95 page introduction is outstanding and should be read by anyone interested in social science, future studies, or policy studies. "It may indeed be said that the primary value of this report is to be found in the effort to interrelate the disjointed factors and elements in the social life of America, in the attempt to view the situation as a whole rather than as a cluster of parts." (p. xiii) This is in fact achieved in the "Review of Findings" (pp. xi-lxxv), under three broad categories:
- Problems of Physical Heritage (discusses land, minerals and power).
- Problems of Biological Heritage (discusses immigration policy and the quantity and inherited quality of the population).
- Problems of Social Heritage (discusses material culture, distributing the costs of progress, the need for economic planning, social organizations, consumers, minority groups, children, women, housing, schools, the arts, public welfare, medicine, crime, the costs of government, laws, democracy, and international relations).

The fundamental principles underlying the report are "that social problems are products of change, and that social changes are interrelated." (p. lxx) The conclusion advocates an integration of social intelligence and of social effort, rather than a policy of drift. The type of planning needed is not economic planning alone, but a "new synthesis" including scientific and educational aspects.

The emphasis of the report is on a method to approach social problems: "the Committee is not unmindful of the fact that there are important elements in human life not easily stated in terms of efficiency, mechanization, institutions, rates of change or adaptations to change...The clarification of human values and their reformulation in order to give expression to them in terms of today's life and opportunities is a major task of social thinking." (p. lxxv) Unfortunately, these concerns are largely omitted by today's social scientists.

*** Quite possibly the most outstanding collective effort ever to systematically consider societal directions and alternatives (although emphasis is largely on directions). Subsequent efforts reflected in various anthologies and symposia (and in **Toward a Social Report**, no. 408), are weak and disorganized in comparison. It is regrettable that **Recent Social Trends** has been forgotten, rather than serving as a standard to be surpassed.

724. COLE, G.D.H. et al.   **What Is Ahead of Us?** NY: Macmillan, 1937.
192 pp.   (A-4)

Six Fabian Lectures revised for publication:
- G.D.H. Cole, "Can Capitalism Survive?" expresses socialist confidence that it cannot survive indefinitely.
- Sir Arthur Satter, "Economic Nationalism: Can It Continue?"
- Wickham Steed, "Dictatorships: What Next?"
- Sidney Webb, "The Future of Soviet Communism"
- P.M.S. Blackett, "The Next War: Can It Be Avoided?"
- Lancelot Hogben, "Planning for Human Survival"

725. ANSHEN, Ruth Nanda (ed.) **Beyond Victory.** NY: Harcourt, Brace, 1943. 291 pp.   (AB-4)

The 21 essays include:
- Arnold J. Toynbee, "Has Christianity a Future?"
- Margaret Mead, "The Family in the Future"
- Alexander Meiklejohn, "Education and the Future"
- James Bryant Conant, "Science and Society in the Post-War World"
- Carl J. Hambro, "World Organization"

The other essays cover topics such as peace, economic organization, Russia, the former colonial peoples, and social security.

726. BRYSON, Lyman, Louis FINKELSTEIN, and Robert M. MACIVER (eds.)
      Approaches to National Unity. NY: Harper & Bros., 1945. 1037
      pp.   (A-3)

The fifth meeting of the Conference on Science, Philosophy and Religion in Their Relation to the Democratic Way of Life, held at Columbia University, September 1944.

The accelerating increase of knowledge "has created an unbalance which is apparently making wise action more difficult for us, than for many who knew far less. At any rate our age which requires, beyond all those before, a mastery of various fields of knowledge for the solution of its complex and intricate problems, seems singularly unable to focus its energies and wisdom on them." (p. v) The introduction also comments on intellectual insulation and inadequate thinking based on a narrow range of learning and experience.

The papers are organized in two sections: The Problem of Group Tensions, and The Problem of Communication of Knowledge and Experience. Among the contributors are Pitirim Sorokin, Karl W. Deutsch, Robert J. Havighurst, Clyde Kluckhohn, Hans J. Morgenthau, Norman Cousins, Elton Mayo, and other luminaries.

Perhaps the broadest contribution is Roy Wood Sellars, "A New Age of Enlightenment," where it is argued that we are on the verge of the birth of an era of worldwide enlightenment reflecting a philosophy of "reformed, evolutionary materialism."

*** The introduction nicely states the problem of bringing knowledge to bear on human problems; unfortunately, the contributors proceed in the usual fragmented style. Nevertheless, it is an interesting symposium, not unlike the later deliberations of the Commission of the Year 2000 (no. 741).

727. **The Prospect Before Us: Some Thoughts on the Future.** London: Sampson Low, Marston & Co., Ltd., 1948. 266 pp.   (A-4)

After the Foreword by Lord Elton, there are nine essays on the future of religion, science, literature, drama, education, music, art, medicine, and politics.

728. BLIVEN, Bruce (ed.) **Twentieth Century Unlimited: From the Vantage Point of the First Fifty Years.** Philadelphia: Lippincott, 1950. 315 pp.   (AB-3)

Most of these essays first appeared in **The New Republic.** Topics cover world government, the atom in peace and war, science, medicine, food, population, politics, business, trade unionism, education, art, music, writing, amusement, manners and morals, and the cities.

729. BRYSON, Lyman (ed.) **Facing the Future's Risks: Studies Toward Predicting the Unforseen.** NY: Harper & Bros., 1953. 318 pp.   (AB-3)

The report of a conference held in New York City in 1952, marking the 200th anniversary of the successful establishment of mutual insurance in America. The 13 essays cover topics such as probability and statistics, physical science and the future, psychology, biology, population trends, women and values, crime, political change, and America's economic greatness.

730. The Future of Man. A Symposium Sponsored by Joseph E. Seagram & Sons, Inc. NY: 1959. 58 pp.   (AB-3)

Talks by and discussion among Robert Frost, Julian Huxley, Devereux Josephs, Ashley Montagu, Hermann Muller, and Bertrand Russell, in commemoration of the new Seagram building.

731. HOAGLAND, Hudson, and Ralph W. BURHOE (eds.) Evolution and Man's Progress. NY: Columbia University Press, 1962. 181 pp. (First published in **Daedalus,** Summer 1961)   (AB-3)

Essays by James F. Crow, Herman J. Muller, Julian H. Steward, B.F. Skinner, and Henry A. Murray, as well as a symposium on "Cultural Evolution as Viewed by Psychologists," bringing together H.A. Murray. B.F. Skinner, A.H. Maslow, Carl Rogers, L.K. Frank, and others.

732. ARON, Raymond (ed.) World Technology and Human Destiny. Ann Arbor: University of Michigan Press, 1963. 246 pp.   (A-3)

The Basel-Rheinfelden conference, with three papers by Aron, Eric Voegelin, and Charles Morage. About three-quarters of the volume is devoted to an extensive discussion of industrial society in the USSR, the Third World, and the West by 21 participants, including Bertrand de Jouvenel, George Kennan, Charles Lindblom, Michael Polanyi, Robert Oppenheimer, and Eugene V. Rostow.

733. de JOUVENEL, Bertrand (ed.) Futuribles: Studies in Conjecture I. Geneva: Librarie Droz, 1963. 321 pp. (English language)   (A-3)

Seven essays on the future of Britain, Burina, Black Africa, Pakistan, the forms of government, and Western man.

734. de JOUVENEL, Bertrand (ed.) Futuribles: Studies in Conjecture II. Geneva: Librarie Droz, 1965. 375 pp. (English language)   (A-3)

Five lengthy essays concerning forecasting in international relations and the possibilities of a federative Europe.

735. Syracuse University Research Corporation. The United States and the World in the 1985 Era, and **Appendixes One and Two to the Previous Volume.** Syracuse: SURC, 1964. 145 pp. and 155 pp. respectively.   (A-4)

A series of projections prepared for the U.S. Marine Corps. by S.U. physical and social science faculty with the assistance of outside consultants. These two volumes are followed by two additional volumes entitled **Science and Technology in the 1985 Era** (47 pp. and a 405 pp. Appendix).

736. "Symposium on the Future," The New York Times Magazine, April 19, 1964.   (ns)

Contributions by Henry Steele Commager, H.L. Dryden, J.B.S. Haldane, Margaret Mead, Clarence Randall, and Arnold Toynbee.

737. "The Prospects of American Civilization: An Inventory of Human Hopes," **Saturday Review,** August 29, 1964.   (AB-4)

The 40th Anniversary Issue, featuring 24 articles such as:
- Arnold Toynbee, "Conditions of Survival"
- R. Buckminster Fuller, "The Prospect for Humanity"
- Allen Nevins, "The Outlook for Greatness"
- John Lear, "The Future of God"
- Roscoe Drummond, "Is the Government Ready for the Future?"
- Barbara Ward, "The Uses of Prosperity"

738. CALDER, Nigel (ed.) **The World in 1984.** (2 Vols.) Baltimore, Md.: Penguin Books, 1965. 215 pp. and 205 pp. 95¢ each.   (AB-3)

The complete **New Scientist** series, first published in Great Britain in 1964, with about 100 contributors from many countries offering short essays on the next 20 years as seen through their specialities.
Volume 1 concerns science and technology, with topics such as space exploration, natural resources, oceans, chemicals, computers, and biology.
Volume 2 concerns institutions and nations, with articles in the following categories: Human Mind, Health, Domestic Life, Government, Education, Cities, Leisure and the Arts, Trade, International Relations, Britain, North America, Latin America, Africa, Asia, and The World in 1984.

739. ROTSTEIN, Abraham (ed.) **The Prospect of Change: Proposals for Canada's Future.** University League for Social Reform. Toronto: McGraw-Hill, 1965. 361 pp. $6.00.   (ns)

Anthology of 16 articles designed to stimulate public debate on policy issues such as the economy, regional development, labor, foreign investment and trade, education, social welfare, and the arts. (Hugh Stevenson, U. of Western Ontario)

740. HILTON, Alice Mary (ed.) **The Evolving Society: First Annual Conference on the Cybercultural Revolution--Cybernetics and Automation.** NY: Institute for Cybercultural Research, 1966. 410 pp.
(A-4)
Contributors include Paul Armer, Ben B. Seligman, Donald N. Michael, Hannah Arendt, and Ruth Nanda Anshen. The editor's contribution, "The Bases of Cyberculture..." exuberantly announces that "The magnificent promise of the dawning age of cyberculture is the complete emancipation of human beings from drudgery and scarcity that is achievable with cybernation. A humane and civilized society...will be feasible for the first time..." (p. 8) *** Such were the enthusiasms of the 1960s.

740a. MORPHET, Edgar L. and Charles O. RYAN (eds.) **Prospective Changes in Society by 1980.** Designing Education for the Future: An Eight-State Project, Vol. 1. NY: Citation Press, 1967. 268 pp.
(ns)
Original essays by non-educators serving to launch several additional volumes by educators, e.g. Vol 2. **Implications for Education of Prospective Changes in Society** (Citation, 1967).

741. BELL, Daniel (ed.) **Toward the Year 2000: Work in Progress. Daedalus,** 96:3, Summer 1967. 363 pp. (Republished by Beacon Press, 1969. 400 pp. $3.95, paper)   (A-3)

This first report from the Commission on the Year 2000 received wide-spread attention at the time of its issue. But it hardly begins to approach "the real need in American society," as articulated by Chairman Daniel Bell, "for some systematic efforts to anticipate social problems, to design new institutions, and to propose alternative programs for choice." (p. 648)

Essentially this is an anthology of 22 papers on specific social problems, sandwiched between two sections of dialogue resulting from Working Session I held in October 1965 (27 participants), and Working Session II held in February 1966 (33 participants).

The papers, on brief examination, appear no better nor worse than any of numerous other anthologies that bring together leading experts in special-ized areas. Herein are Herman Kahn and Anthony J. Wiener on the next 33 years, Fred Charles Ikle on social predictions, Donald A. Schon on forecast-ing, Martin Shubik on information, Leonard J. Duhl on planning, Harvey S. Perloff on urban development, Daniel P. Moynihan on federal-local relation-ships, Lawrence K. Frank on the need for a new political theory, Stephen R. Graubard on university cities, Harold Orlans on educational and scientific institutions, Ernst Mayr on biological man, Gardner C. Quarton on behavioral control, Krister Stendahl on religion, Erik H. Erikson on youth, Margaret Mead on the life cycle, Harry Kalven, Jr. on privacy, George A. Miller on psychology, David Riesman on meritocracy, John R. Pierce on communi-cation, Eugene V. Rostow on international society, Samuel P. Huntington on political development, and Ithiel de Sola Pool on the international system.

The volume ends with a note on the eight working parties: Values and Rights, The Life Cycle of the Individual, The International System, Intellectual Institutions, Science and Society, The Social Impact of the Computer, Biomed-ical Sciences and Technology, and The Structure of Government. Only the last group, headed by Harvey Perloff, has issued a report (see no. 407). The other groups have not been heard from, and the Commission has since disbanded.

*** In retrospect, this anthology is perhaps most notable for the disparity between its promises and the subsequent performance of the Commission.

742. American Academy of Arts and Sciences. **America's Changing Envi-ronment. Daedalus,** 96:4, Fall 1967.

This anthology grew out of a study initiated by the Academy entitled "1976: Planning the American Future." Rather than mere shopping lists of desirable reforms, study groups were asked to concentrate on fundamental kinds of change that need to be considered, and substantial changes that might take place. This publication stems from a group led by Roger Revelle with a focus on "Resources, Conservation, and Recreation," but the 15 pa-pers are devoted to broad concerns. Among them are:
- F. Fraser Darling, "A Wider Environment of Ecology and Conservation"
- Hans H. Lansberg, "The U.S. Resource Outlook: Quantity and Quality"
- Nathaniel Wollman, "The New Economics of Resources"
- Athelstan Spilhaus, "The Experimental City"
- Harold Gilliam, "The Fallacy of Single-Purpose Planning"
- George J. Maslach, "The Reorganization of Educational Resources"

743. EWALD, William R., Jr. (ed.) **Environment for Man: The Next Fifty Years.** Bloomington: Indiana University Press, 1967. 308 pp.   (A-3)

The first of three volumes resulting from a two-year consultation spon-sored by the American Institute of Planners. The 12 papers in this volume were presented at an August 1966 meeting in Portland, Oregon, devoted to the theme of "Optimum Environment with Man as the Measure." The pa-pers are concerned with the physiological, psychological, and sociological impact of the physical environment, and include the following:
- René Dubos, "Man Adapting: His Limitations and Potentialities"

- Bertram M. Gross, "The City of Man: A Social Systems Reckoning"
- Stephen Carr, "The City of the Mind"
- Stanley J. Hallett, "Planning, Politics, and Ethics"
- Moshe Safdie, "Habitat '67"
- John T. Howard, "Some Thoughts on the Future"

744. EWALD, William R., Jr. (ed.) **Environment and Change: The Next Fifty Years.** Bloomington: Indiana University Press, 1968. 397 pp.   (A-3)

Papers commissioned for the 1967 Washington Conference, the second part of the two-year AIP consultation. The general concern was to articulate the necessary philosophy for a creative development of our environment. Among the 24 contributions are:
- Pierre Bertaux, "The Future of Man"
- Bertrand de Jouvenel, "On Attending to the Future"
- Herman Kahn and Anthony J. Wiener, "Faustian Powers and Human Choices..."
- Claude Brown, "The Effective Society"
- Robert Theobald, "Planning with People"
- Gunnar Myrdal, "The Necessity and Difficulty of Planning the Future Society"

745. EWALD, William R., Jr. (ed.) **Environment and Policy: The Next Fifty Years.** Bloomington: Indiana University Press, 1968. 459 pp.   (A-3)

These papers were also commissioned for the AIP Washington Conference, but are more specific and action-oriented. Each author was asked to specify steps to be taken and implications at all levels of government. Critiques follow each paper.

This volume is in the tradition of bringing together leading experts on various specialized functions: Bayard Rustin on minority groups, Robert Hutchins on education, Odin Anderson on health services, William Stewart on health, Sebastian de Grazia on leisure, Kevin Lynch on "The Possible City," Max Feldman on transportation, Charles Abrams on housing, Jack Meltzer on manpower, Lyle Fitch on national development, Joseph Fisher on natural resources, Herbert Simon on research, Daniel Mandelker on new incentives and controls, and Alan Altshuler on new institutions.

746. GROSS, Bertram M. (ed.) **A Great Society?** Foreward by Stephen K. Bailey. NY: Basic Books, 1968. 362 pp. $8.50.   (AB-3)

A unique and lively anthology of 13 articles, 11 of them presented at the Great Society Seminar held in honor of Arthur F. Bentley at Syracuse University during 1965-1966. The volume is described in the Foreward as a "White House-Academia Dialogue," in that President Lyndon B. Johnson provided five specific questions for consideration, in response to seeing an outline of the seminar plan. Unfortunately, there was no response to the academic response, although such a dialogue might ideally be conducted on a continuing basis.

The essays are not at all oriented to short-term concerns, but contain many ideas that are still valuable in considering the creation of any great or good society. The opening summary, "The President's Questions--And Some Answers," is loaded with interesting notions such as State of the Metropolis Reports, seven civilian RAND corporations, more and better use of pilot projects, more awards for efforts that fulfill national purposes, and referring to "A", rather than "The" Great Society. Also of interest:
- Herbert Marcuse, "The Individual in the Great Society"
- Norton E. Long, "Local and Private Initiative in the Great Society"
- Hans J. Morgenthau, "The International Aspects of the Great Society"

- Daniel Bell, "The Adequacy of Our Concepts" (essentially Chapter 5 in *The Coming of Post-Industrial Society*, no. 55)
- Peter F. Drucker, "New Political Alignments in the Great Society"
- Frank E. Manuel, "Reflections on Great Societies"
- Kenneth E. Boulding, "The Great Society in a Small World--Dampening Reflections from the Dismal Science," in which the notion of "the spaceship economy" is introduced, perhaps for the first time
- Alvin Toffler, "The Politics of the Impossible--Art and Society"
- Bertram M. Gross, "Some Questions for Presidents," which offers some important considerations about the President as truth teller, peacemaker, champion of justice, humanist, and learner.

747. Toward the Year 2018. Edited by the Foreign Policy Association. NY: Cowles Education Corporation, 1968. 177 pp.   (B-4)

The introduction by Emmanuel Mesthene boasts that "The chapters in this volume aim to set the technological context of social and international policy over the next fifty years." (p. vii) But the 13 papers merely follow the standard pattern of liberal experts cautiously peering somewhat forward: D.G. Brennan on weaponry, Gordon MacDonald on space, Najeeb Halaby on transportation, J.R. Pierce on communication, Thomas Malone on weather, D. Gale Johnson on food, Anthony Oettinger on educational technology, Ithiel de Sola Pool on behavioral technology, Charles R. DeCarlo on computer technology, Philip Hauser on population, Herman Kahn and Anthony Wiener on economics, and Roger Revelle on oceanography. The shallow optimism that pervades the volume is reflected in Charles A. Scarlott's paper on energy, where it is stated that the U.S. "should continue to have ample amounts of energy at acceptable cost to meet a greatly augmented demand." (pp. 122-123)

748. ROTHBLATT, Ben (ed.) Changing Perspectives on Man. Chicago: University of Chicago Press, 1968. 298 pp.   (AB-4)

Thirteen selected Monday Lectures delivered in the 1966-1967 period, including:
- John R. Platt, "The Two Faces of Perception"
- Theodosius Dobzhansky, "Darwin vs. Copernicus"
- Kenneth E. Boulding, "Revolution and Development"
- William H. McNeill, "The Peasant Revolt of Our Times"
- Robert Gomer, "The Tyranny of Progress"

749. GUNN, James E. (ed.) Man and the Future. Lawrence, Kansas: The University Press of Kansas, 1968. 305 pp.   (A-4)

The proceedings of the Inter-Century Seminar celebrating the centennial of the University of Kansas. Nine contributions by eminent leaders covering time and prophecy, law, the scientific revolution, prospects for humanity, the world community, the theater, penology, space exploration, and the changing university.

750. The Editors of News Front. The Image of the Future. NY: Year, Inc., 1968. 255 pp.   (C-3)

The 10th Anniversary issue of **News Front,** a management magazine, bringing together 53 brief articles on topics such as tomorrow's society, the economy, management, science, international relations, probing the future (an abbreviated version of the 1964 Helmer and Gordon Delphi study at RAND), space travel, the computer, mass transit, drugs, and medicine.

751. WARNER, Aaron W., Dean MORSE, and Thomas E. COONEY (eds.). **The Environment of Change.** NY: Columbia University Press, 1969. 186 pp.   (AB-3)

Proceedings of two conferences held in 1966 and 1967 under the sponsorship of *Time* magazine. The general focus was the impact of science and technology on society. Each of the seven essays is followed by discussion.
- Sir Isaiah Berlin, "The Hazards of Social Revolution"
- I.I. Rabi, "The Revolution in Science"
- Jacob Bronowski, "The Impact of New Science"
- David Sidorsky, "Scientific Revolution and Cultural Continuity"
- Eli Ginzberg, "Technology, Work, and Values"
- Everett M. Kassalow, "Change and the Less-Developed Countries"
- Loren C. Eiseley, "Alternatives to Technology"

752. BAIER, Kurt, and Nicholas RESCHER (eds.) **Values and the Future: The Impact of Technological Change on American Values.** NY: Free Press, 1969. 527 pp.   (A-3)

The 17 original essays are aimed "toward the discovery of ways of guiding social change in directions which are at the least not incompatible with the realization of our deepest values, and perhaps even helpful to it." (p.v) Some groundwork is laid for a new profession of "value impact forecasters," especially through methodological pieces by Rescher, Gordon, and Helmer. The other essays are largely focused on economics, and the editors readily confess the weakness of excluding views of anthropologists, sociologists, and psychologists. Among the essays are:
- Kurt Baier, "What is Value?"
- Olaf Helmer, "Simulating the Values of the Future"
- Theodore J. Gordon, "The Feedback Between Technology and Values"
- Bertrand de Jouvenel, "Technology as a Means"
- Kenneth E. Boulding, "The Emerging Superculture"
- David Lewis, "New Urban Structures"
- John Kenneth Galbraith, "Technology, Planning, and Organization"
The volume is concluded with two bibliographies (pp. 472-512): the first lists 300 uncategorized items on technological progress and future-oriented studies; the second offers about 500 categorized items on theory of value.

753. JUNGK, Robert, and Johan GALTUNG (eds.) **Mankind 2000.** Oslo: Universitetsforlaget, 1969; London: Allen & Unwin, 1971. 367 pp. (A-3)

Contributions to the First International Futures Research Conference, held in Oslo in 1967. Largely grouped in four sections:
- International Futures: Jan Tinbergen, Seymour Melman, Charles E. Osgood, Peter Menke-Gluckert, Arthur I. Waskow, etc.
- Material and Technological Development: Richard L. Meier, Hazan Osbekhan, Fritz Baade, Dennis Gabor, etc.
- Goals and Human Implications: Richard E. Farson, John G. Papaioannou, etc.
- The Role of Future Research: Edward S. Cornish, Nigel Calder, John McHale, Ossip Flectheim, Yehezkel Dror, David E. Miller, I. Bestushev-Lada, Fred L. Polak, etc.
*** The final section is important for professional futurists.

754. Japan Society of Futurology. **Challenges from the Future.** Proceedings of the International Futures Research Conference, Vol. III. Tokyo: Kodansha, Ltd., 1970. (English language) 431 pp.   (A-4)

Divided into three sections:
- Section 6, New Values: New Man, offers 14 papers on topics such as post-

industrial civilization, social philosophy, images of man, human potential, values, and language.
- Section 7, Social Systems and Social Innovation, carries 11 papers on topics such as bureaucratic systems, technology assessment, and social planning.
- Section 8, World Futures, has 14 papers on topics such as space exploration, peace research, structural pluralism, the developing countries, France 2000, technological development, Latin America, arms control, and urban development.
*** A total of four volumes resulted from the second IFRC meeting (held in Kyoto in April 1970); the other three volumes are devoted to more specialized concerns.

755. DUCHÊNE, François (ed.) **The Endless Crisis: America in the Seventies.** NY: Simon & Schuster, 1970. 310 pp. $7.50; $2.75, paper.   (A-3)

A December 1968 seminar at Princeton held under the auspices of The International Association for Cultural Freedom, and co-chaired by Jean-Jacques Servan-Schreiber and Carl Kaysen. The title page pretentiously describes the meeting as "A Confrontation of the World's Leading Social Scientists on the Problems, Impact and Global Rule of the United States in the Next Decade." It is somewhat less than this, but still an interesting assemblage.
The papers and proceedings are divided into four sections:
- The Crisis of Liberalism: with contributions by some three dozen persons, including John Kenneth Galbraith, Sam Brown, Stanley Hoffman, Roy Innis, and Edward Shils.
- Post-Industrial Society: Daniel Bell, Robert Lifton, Michel Crozier, Zbigniew Brzezinski, etc.
- Global Power or Self-Restraint: Martin Peretz, George F. Kennan, George Ball, etc.
- Postscript: Intellectuals and Power: Arthur M. Schlesinger, Jr., Henry Kissinger, etc.

756. DE BRIGARD, Raul, and Olaf HELMER. **Some Potential Societal Developments, 1970-2000.** Middletown, Conn.: Institute for the Future, IFF Report R-7, April 1970. 134 pp. (IFF now located at 2740 Sand Hill Rd., Menlo Park, Calif. 94025)   (A-3)

An experimental attempt to employ the Delphi method in forecasting societal developments with a panel of 34 members. Potential developments are assessed in major categories of urbanization, the family, leisure and the economy, education, food and population, international relations, conflict in society and law enforcement, national political structures, values, and the impact of technology on government and society. At the end of each section there is a brief but valuable discussion of "some policy issues raised by the preceding expectations."
In the final section of the report, the panelists estimated to the year 2000 the course of 46 statistical indicators such as GNP, divorce rate, education expenditures, life expectancy, income levels, and overseas travel.
*** The coordinators of this exercise provide substantial qualification to their effort. Given the multitude of topics explored, the panel was hardly large enough to provide a broad array of expert opinion for each concern. Nevertheless, this exercise suggests the outlines of what could be attempted on a much broader scale. Also see the Delphi exercise performed under the auspices of the National Industrial Conference Board, no. 57.

757. WALLIA, C.S. (ed.) **Toward Century 21: Technology, Society, and Human Values.** NY: Basic Books, 1970. 318 pp. $8.95.   (A-4)

A 1968 Stanford University lecture series resulted in these 24 articles grouped in five general categories: biopsychological perspectives, science and creativity, technology and economic development, the political system, and humanistic perspectives.

758. BROOKS, Chandler McC. (ed.) **The Changing World and Man: The Cultural and Social Environment of Man. Its Significance for His Biological Performance.** Brooklyn, NY: Downstate Medical Center, Dept. of Physiology, 1970. 123 pp.   (AB-4)

Among the eight papers resulting from a visiting scholars program are:
- Carleton S. Coon, "Human Evolution and the Avalanche of Culture"
- Elting S. Morison, "Man in Modern Times"
- Clive Entwistle, "Holopolis..." (see no. 680)
- Arnold J. Toynbee, "History's Challenge to Human Nature"
- Rev. John M. Culkin, S.J., "Life in a Postliterate World"

758a. LINDEN, Allen M. (ed.) **Living in the Seventies.** Toronto: Peter Martin Associates, 1970. 250 pp. $3.95, paper.   (ns)

"A thoughtful, stimulating collection of 25 articles prepared...for policy makers in the federal Liberal party. Topics...include articles on technology, satellite communications, various urban problems, law reform, civil and human liberties, crime and justice, privacy, poverty, guaranteed annual income, economic policy, agriculture, environment, labour, media policy..." (Hugh Stevenson, U. of Western Ontario)

759. CLARKSON, Stephen (ed.) **Visions 2020: Fifty Canadians in Search of a Future.** Edmonton, Alberta: M.G. Hurtig, Ltd., 1970. 290 pp. $2.95, paper.   (BC-3)

A project to celebrate the 50th anniversary of **Canadian Forum,** resulting in 50 short articles, stories, or poems grouped under four themes:
- Obsession: world obliteration, or Canada dragged under by U.S. disintegration or expansion.
- Realities: the future of death, sex, trade unions.
- Hopes: Canada as the true and free North, and man as liberated.
- Contexts: the new technology; relating to the past.

760. Editors of The National Observer. **The Seventies: A Look Ahead at the New Decade.** A Dow Jones Book. NY: The National Observer, 1970. 165 pp. $1.95.   (ns)

After an overview on "Whither the '70s?" articles are devoted to space, the economy, medicine, foreign policy, Vietnam, the arts, oceanography, politics, education, travel, manners and mores, and America seen from abroad.

761. BELL, Wendell, and James A. MAU (eds.) **The Sociology of the Future: Theory, Cases, and Annotated Bibliography.** NY: Russell Sage Foundation, 1971. 464 pp. $12.50.   (A-3)

Contains 12 essays on topics such as images of the future, utopia construction, images of future leisure, Canada's future, the urban future, and organizational change. An excellent bibliography compiled by Bettina J. Huber (pp. 339-454) annotates 257 items, about half of which are concerned with methodology.

762. HANCOCK, M. Donald, and Gideon SJOBERG (eds.) **Politics in the Post-Welfare State: Responses to the New Individualism.** NY: Columbia University Press, 1972. 335 pp.   (A-4)

Sociologists and political scientists provide 14 original essays on socio-political change in the U.S., Great Britain, and Sweden. The major theme is that, through modern technology, man can lapse into a totalitarian condition, or fashion new alternatives enhancing political fulfillment. The volume is intentionally balanced between pessimists who view collapse or repression, and optimists who foresee modifying change or radical change.

763. MARUYAMA, Magoroh, and James A. DATOR (eds.) **Human Futuristics.** Honolulu, Hawaii: University of Hawaii, Social Science Research Institute, 1972. $7.00.   (ns)

Based on the cultural futurology symposium held at the 1970 meeting of the American Anthropological Association. Among the 12 essays are:
- Elise Boulding, "Futuristics and the Imagining Capacity of the West"
- Albert and Donna Wilson, "Future-Orientation..."
- Thornton Page, "Man in Space"
- Margaret Mead, "A Note on Contributions of Anthropology to the Science of the Future"
- Sue-Ellen Jacobs, "Towards Polyocular Anthropology"

764. FINKELSTEIN, Louis (ed.) **Social Responsibility in an Age of Revolution.** NY: Jewish Theological Seminary of America, 1971. 283 pp. (A-4)

"The present volume is a modest effort to analyze some of the normal dilemmas of our time, and to indicate elements of hope for the future." The 10 essays include:
- Philip Sporn, "Ethics and Business"
- Charles Merrill, "Reflections on Over-Population"
- Walter Kaufmann, "Doubts About Justice"
- Reinhold Niebuhr, "Religion in a Pluralistic Culture"
- Earl Warren, "Toward a New Cultural Federalism"

765. RADEST, Howard B. (ed.) **To Seek a Humane World.** Buffalo, NY: Prometheus Books, 1972. $5.95.   (ns)

Essays presented at the International Humanist and Ethical Union Congress held at M.I.T., including contributions from Barry Commoner, Noam Chomsky, Sen. Walter Mondale, Jerome D. Frank, Jo Grimmond, Lord Ritchie-Calder, Paul Kurtz, and Edward L. Ericson.

765a. ROSLANSKY, John D. (ed.) **Shaping the Future: A Discussion at the Nobel Conference.** Amsterdam: North Holland, 1972. 102 pp. $7.50. (Dist. in U.S. by Fleet Academic.)   (B-4)

Five addresses delivered primarily for students at Gustavus Adolphus College, St. Peter, Minn. in 1971:
- John McHale, "Shaping the Future: Problems, Priorities, and Imperatives"
- Norman E. Borlaug, "The World Food Problem: Present and Future"
- Anthony J. Wiener, "Faust's Progress: Methodology for Shaping the Future"
- Joseph Sutter, "The Perils of Futurist Thinking: A Common Sense Reflection"
- Glenn T. Seaborg, "Shaping the Future--through Science and Technology"

766. URBAN, G.R. (ed.), in collaboration with Michael GLENNY. **Can We Survive Our Future? A Symposium.** London: The Bodley Head, 1971. 400 pp.   (AB-3)

Edited versions of interviews by Urban and Glenny in 1970-1971, which were broadcasted over Radio Free Europe. Arranged in three sections:
- The Impact of Science on the Moral Options of Man (Arnold J. Toynbee, Jacques Ellul, Erich Jantsch, etc.)
- Growth, Controls, and Responsibility (Edward Shils, Michael Shanks, Andrew Shonfield, Dennis Gabor, Herman Kahn)
- Choosing the Future (Maurice Duverger, Ossip K. Flechtheim, Brian Aldiss, etc.)

767. EBLING, F.J., and G.W. HEATH (eds.) **The Future of Man.** Published for the Institute of Biology. London and NY: Academic Press, 1972. 211 pp.   (A-4)

Proceedings of a symposium held at the Royal Geographical Society in London during April 1971. The 12 papers cover topics such as the distribution of homo sapiens in Great Britain, conservation, the future of the family, reproduction, aging, drugs, war, and scientific responsibility.

768. **The Future Is Tomorrow: 17 Prospective Studies.** Plan Europe 2000. Published Under the Auspices of the European Cultural Foundation. The Hague: Martinus Nijhoff, 1972. 583 pp. (2 vols.) 65 fl.   (A-3)

The 18 essays are in five major sections: Cultural and Political Aspects, Environment, Economics, Work and Leisure, and Information. Includes contributions by writers such as Michael Young, Jean Gottman, Jan Tinbergan, Bertrand de Jouvenel, and Pierre Piganiol.

769. MEYERS, William (ed.) and M. Vincent HAYES (asst. ed.). **Conversion from War to Peace: Social, Economic and Political Problems.** NY: Gordon & Breach, 1972. 121 pp. $5.95; $2.50, paper.   (AB-4)

Abstracts from two 1969-1970 conferences conceived by the Fund for New Priorities in America, unfortunately with no introductory or summary comments. The 35 contributions are arranged in eight categories as follows: Introduction to Conversion, Conversion and Radical Change, Conversion for Whom?, Conversion and a Military Society, Role of Corporations, Role of Education, Manpower Problems, and Other Problems. The list of contributors is notable for its variety of professors (such as Seymour Melman and John Steinhart), activists, journalists, and labor leaders, along with a steelworker and a Politician (Sen. Thomas Eagleton).
*** Possibly a few worthwhile bits and pieces to be mined here.

770. WOLFGANG, Marvin E. (ed.) **The Future Society: Aspects of America in the Year 2000.** The ANNALS of the American Academy of Political and Social Science, Vol. 408, July 1973.   (A-4)

Revised presentations at the 77th Annual Meeting. Wolfgang states in the Preface that "Futuristic studies are all around us and are growing enormously each year" (a somewhat overstated exuberance). The eight essays are as follows:
- Suzanne Keller, "The Future Role of Women"
- Leslie T. Wilkins, "Crime and Criminal Justice..."
- Wilfred Molenbaum, "World Resources for the Year 2000"
- Anthony J. Wiener, "The Future of Economic Activity," argues that the

Neo-Malthusian position is unpersuasive.
- Bertram S. Brown, "Mental Health in the Future"
- George E. Ehrlich, "Health Challenges of the Future"
- John A. Morsell, "Ethnic Relations of the Future"
- Sen. Philip A. Hart, "The Future of the Government Process"

771. BUNDY, Robert (Guest Editor), "Images of the Future: The Twenty-First Century and Beyond," **The Humanist,** 33:6, Nov.-Dec. 1973, pp. 12-55.   (AB-3)

A special issue of futurist essays, although the essays are not so futuristic as to live up to the inflated sub-title of "The Twenty-First Century and Beyond."
- Fred L. Polak, "Responsibility for the Future"
- Lester R. Brown, "Issues for an Image"
- Jacques Ellul, "Search for an Image"
- Geoffrey Squires, "Poetry, Reduction, and the Future"
- Manfred Stanley, "Three Post Political Futures"
- Robert T. Francoeur, "Human Nature and Human Relations"
- Elise Boulding, "Religion, Futurism, and Models of Social Change"
- Robert Jungk, "Toward an Experimental Society" (see no. 389)
- Paul Kurtz Interview with Herman Kahn: "On Humanism, Economic Growth, Energy, and The Meaning of Life"
- A.J. Christiansen, S.J., "Blind Prophets and Quick-Witted Kings: A Survey of Eight Books"
- Robert Bundy, "Epilogue: Over the Edge of History"
- ******* A clothbound edition with the same title and somewhat expanded contents is available from Prometheus Books, 923 Kensington Ave., Buffalo, NY 14215 for $12.95.

772. KANTOR, Rosabeth Moss and Louis A. ZURCHER, Jr. (eds.) **Alternative Institutions.** (Special Issue) **Journal of Applied Behavioral Science,** 9:2/3, 1973. Single copy, $4.50.   (A-4)

Articles on 19th century utopian thinkers, an alternative to public welfare, community economic control, free schools, counterculture marriages, and the changing character of urban middle-class life styles.

773. STULMAN, Julius, and Ervin LASZLO (eds.) **Emergent Man: His Chances, Problems and Potentials.** A World Institute Creative Finding. NY: Gordon and Breach, 1973. 185 pp. $8.95.   (AB-3)

Eleven essays first appearing in **Fields Within Fields:** Abraham Maslow on humanistic biology, Gardner Murphy on creativity, D.L. Stacy on art, Sidney J. Parnes on creative potential, Ervin Laszlo on "Reverence for Natural Systems," Noel McInnis on gestalt ecology, Willis W. Harman on alternative futures, Robert A. Smith III on synergistic organization, Oliver L. Reiser on cyclic-creative cosmology, Robert A. Smith III on "Unibutz," and Julius Stulman on the World Institute.

774. Rome World Special Conference on Futures Research, 1973. **Human Futures: Needs, Societies, Technologies.** Guildford, Surrey, ENGLAND: IPC Science and Technology Press, 1974. c.180 pp. $14.00 (ns)

Includes papers by Bertrand de Jouvenel, John McHale, Maurice Guernier, Lewis Mumford, Sam Cole and Craig Sinclair, Jim Dator (see no. 339), William Simon, Harold A. Linstone, and Yehezkel Dror.

774a. CLARKE, Ronald O. and Peter C. LIST (eds.) **Environmental Spectrum: Social And Economic Views on the Quality of Life.** NY: D. Van Nostrand Co., 1974. 161 pp. $2.95, paper.   (ns)

Papers presented at an Oregon State University symposium, held in May 1973, exploring the relationship of economic growth to the quality of life.

775. "2024 A.D.--A Probe Into the Future," **Saturday Review/World,** August 24, 1974.   (B-2)

The 50th Anniversary Issue, featuring 17 articles as follows:
- Norman Cousins, "Prophecy and Pessimism," notes the significant absence of doomsday prophecies in this issue, and criticizes the vulnerability of projections based only on facts of the present.
- René Dubos, "Recycling Social Man," offers a picture of what human beings can achieve, based on a policy of regionalism.
- Andrei D. Sakharov, "Tomorrow: The View From Red Square," sees a a world of flying cities and arctic farming.
- McGeorge Bundy, "After the Deluge, the Covenant," envisions global law arising out of a period of famine and nuclear warfare.
- Milovan Djilas, Emmet John Hughes, Lord Trevelyan, and Kei Wakaizumi, "A World Atlas for 2024," provide four different predictions of changes in national borders.
- Moshe Safdie, "Beyond the City Limits," describes the architecture in the welfare world of 2024.
- Clare Booth Luce, "The 21st-Century Woman--Free at Last?"
- Kurt Waldheim, "Toward Global Interdependence," projects the role of the U.N.
- Neil A. Armstrong, "Out of This World," describes underground lunar colonies and other bases on the planets.
- Wernher von Braun, "Space Riders in the Sky," shows how satellites will solve our problems on earth.
- Jacques Cousteau, "The Perils and Potentials of a Watery Planet"
- Michael E. DeBakey, M.D., "The Medical Prognosis: Favorable, Treatable, Curable"
- Harold Howe, II, "Report to the President...on Education"
- Fred M. Hechinger, "The Case for Educare and the Open University," a scenario of the Educare Act of 2008.
- Isaac Asimov, "Clippings from Tomorrow's Newspapers"
- Rev. Theodore M. Hesburgh, "Will There Still Be a God?"
- Norman Podhoretz, "The Literary Light as Eternal Flame"
*** A good survey of contemporary optimism.

776. "An Inventory of Hope: A Special Double Year-end Issue Devoted in its Entirety to the Restoration of Confidence," **Saturday Review/World,** December 14, 1974.   (B-3)

The 17 gloom-chasing contributions are as follows:
- Norman Cousins, "Hope and Practical Realities," hopes that we can release human energies and live up to our moral capacity.
- Maurice Strong, "The Case for Optimism," describes ten steps for a better world.
- Orville Freeman, "I Have a Plan," proposes a scheme for averting famine.
- Robert McNamera, "Greening the Landscape"
- David Rockefeller, "Living in a Wizardless World"
- William Ruckelshaus, "Yes--The Environment Can Be Saved"
- Glenn Seaborg, "Finding a New Approach to Energetics--Fast!"
- Albert Rosenfeld, "Medicine's Mighty Molecules"
- Theodore Taylor, "Strategies for the Future," describes the Committee

for the Future, controlled environment greenhouses, and space colonies.
- "Toward a Restoration of Confidence" offers a portfolio of statements by various leaders.
- René Dubos, "The Humanization of Humans"
- Yehudi Menuhin, "Art as Hope for Humanity"
- Lewis Foy, "An Optimist's Checklist" (Foy is Chairman of Bethlehem Steel)
- Charles Yost, "How to Save the United Nations"
- Susan Schiefelbein, "Future Promise," an intriguing compilation of portraits of 32 young leaders (ages 24-43)--essentially the contributors to **Saturday Review** hopefests of several decades hence!
- Susan Heath, "In Support of Humankind: A Sampler of New Books," provides excerpts from 12 books on ecology and world order.
- "The Young Hopefuls," offers portraits on 17 young writers of fiction and non-fiction.

777. "This Fractured Democracy: A Special 60th Anniversary Supplement," **The New Republic,** November 9, 1974, pp. 13-35.   (AB-3)

Six essays as follows:
- Hans J. Morgenthau, "Decline of Democratic Government," on powerlessness and the political vacuum.
- C. Vann Woodward, "What Became of the 1960s?" on the end of activism and the vision of the "postindustrial, technetronic utopia."
- Irving Howe, "Historical Memory, Political Vision," on the fleeting New Left.
- Marcus G. Raskin, "Ersatz Democracy and the Real Thing"
- James Chace, "The Kissinger Years," on foreign policy.
- Abe Fortas, "Strengthening Government to Cope with the Future"

778. "What Are America's Prospects," **Skeptic: The Forum for Contemporary History,** No. 6, March/April, 1975, pp. 45-57.   (BC-4)

Interviews on this question with Clare Booth Luce, Leon H. Keyserling, Jonas Salk, Theodore M. Hesburgh, and David Dellinger. Diversity without depth.

779. SPEKKE, Andrew A. (ed.) **The Next 25 Years: Crisis & Opportunity.** Foreward by Nelson A. Rockefeller. Washington, D.C.: World Future Society, June 1975. 376 pp. $8.00, paper.   (AB-2)

Most of the 43 contributions were presented in some form at the World Future Society's Second General Assembly, held in Washington during June 1975, and this volume was produced in conjunction with the Assembly. There is an interesting mixture here of broad concerns and more specialized papers on topics such as future studies, women, sex, graphic design, the criminal justice system, and methodology. Among the general contributions are:
- Roy Amara, "The Next 25 Years: Crises and Challenges"
- John Platt, "The Future of Social Crises"
- Willis W. Harman, "Notes on the Coming Transformation"
- Herman Kahn and William Brown, "A World Turning Point--And a Better Prospect for the Future" (see no. 226)
- Magoroh Maruyama, "The Post-Industrial Logic," views the emergence of a new scientific paradigm based on heterogenistic principles.
- Ervin Laszlo, "The Emerging World Polyarchy"
- Stuart Conger, "Social Inventions"
- Jay W. Forrester, "Understanding Social and Economic Change in the United States."

*** A wide variety of perspectives ranging from silly to very profound. Selective use of this volume could be profitable. The blessing of slightly more than 100 words by the Vice President of the United States may set some record for brevity!

780. America's Continuing Revolution: An Act of Conservation. Washington: American Enterprise Institute for Public Policy Research, 1975. 398 pp. $12.00.   (A-4)

A handsome volume of lectures sponsored by the American Enterprise Institute in celebration of the U.S. Bicentennial, delivered during the 1973-1974 period at historic sites across the nation.

The introduction by Stephen J. Tonsor states four basic questions that should be the spirit of bicentennial inquiry: "Where are we? By what route have we come? What are the unfinished tasks? To what ought we aspire?" (p.xi) On brief examination, the lectures appear to concentrate largely on the second question of historical routes. This is not surprising, for there is a clear conservative or conservative-liberal cast to the contributors: Irving Kristol, Martin Diamond, Paul G. Kauper, Robert A. Nisbet, Gordon S. Wood, Caroline Robbins, Peter L. Berger, Daniel J. Boorstin, G. Warren Nutter, Vermont Royster, Edward C. Banfield, Leo Marx, Ronald S. Berman, Kenneth B. Clark, Forrest Carlisle Pogue, Seymour Martin Lipset, Charles Burton Marshall, and Dean Rusk.

781. "The American Commonwealth--1976," **The Public Interest,** No. 41, Fall 1975.   (AB-3)

The Bicentennial issue of **The Public Interest** which also serves to mark the 10th anniversary of publication. The 10 essays are as follows:
- Daniel P. Moynihan, "The American Experiment"
- Samuel P. Huntington, "The Democratic Distemper"
- Martin Diamond, "The Declaration and the Constitution..."
- Aaron Wildavsky, "The Past and Future Presidency"
- James Q. Wilson, "The Rise of the Bureaucratic State"
- Nathan Glazer, "Towards an Imperial Judiciary?"
- Irving Kristol, "Corporate Capitalism in America"
- Seymour Martin Lipset, "The Paradox of American Politics"
- Robert Nisbet, "Public Opinion versus Popular Opinion"
- Daniel Bell, "The End of American Exceptionalism"

782. "The American System" (Special Bicentennial Issue), **Fortune,** April 1975.   (AB-3)

"This special issue--FORTUNE's contribution to the nation's Bicentennial celebration--assesses the American system, that enduring but constantly evolving pattern of political, economic, cultural, and ethical arrangements." (p.2)
- "How President Ford Views the System" (excerpts from an interview)
- Max Ways, "A Proposition That Freed a Torrent of Individual Energies," on liberty and its limits.
- Thomas Griffith, "Reshaping the American Dream"
- Edmund Faltermayer, "Ever Increasing Affluence is Less of a Sure Thing"
- Daniel Bell, "The Revolution of Rising Entitlements"
- Charles G. Burck, "The Intricate 'Politics' of the Corporation," on the need to reconcile a diversity of interests.
- A. James Reichley, "A Foreign Policy for the Era of Interdependence"
- Juan Cameron, "Black America: Still Waiting for Full Membership"
- S. Frederick Starr, "Color the New Generation Very Light Green," argues that the work ethic is alive and well among the young.

783. "What Kind of Future for America?" **U.S. News & World Report,** July 7, 1975, pp. 44-50.   (C-4)

Interviews with "leading scholars whose views represent a wide range of opinions" concerning our "heritage and prospects for the future."
- Richard B. Morris, President-Elect of the American Historical Association, hopes that national pride will return.
- Benjamin R. Barber, a political scientist at Rutgers, hopes that America will make the next century a truly global century.
- Gloria Steinem, editor of **Ms.**, advocates revolutionary feminism.
- Charles A. Berry, head of the U. of Texas Health Science Center, foresees increased life spans.
- Robert Penn Warren, novelist and poet, comments on culture and politics.
- David Packard, Chairman of Hewlett-Packard, is "very optimistic" about the future of business.
- Andrew F. Brimmer, former member of the Federal Reserve's Board of Governors, foresees somewhat more coordination between public and private sectors.
*** A scattered and superficial mélange of non-radical opinions.

784. "Is Democracy Dying? Verdict of 8 Leading World Scholars," **U.S. News & World Report,** March 8, 1976, pp. 50-67.   (BC-3)

Interesting interviews with the following:
- Samuel P. Huntington, who views a move into a phase of deep cynicism.
- Max Beloff, who views the U.S. in a healthier condition than his own Britain.
- Robert L. Heilbroner, who views a crisis of political faith.
- Charles Frankel, who views a return of practicality and idealism in combination.
- William H. McNeill, who views the deepening pessimism as new in its intensity and depth.
- René Dubos, who views an evolutionary step toward participatory democracy.
- Friedrich A. Hayek, who views democracy as suffering from a mistaken construction of institutions, leading to unlimited government.
- Michel J. Crozier, who views a decline of democracy as a result of bureaucratic complexities.
*** All but the first two of these scholars have books that are annotated in this guide.

785. MARUYAMA, Magoroh and Arthur HARKINS (eds.) **Cultures of the Future.** NY: Free Press, 1976. (Two vols.)   (ns)

Contributions organized in eight parts:
- The Future as a New Dimension of Anthropology (Margaret Mead, Elise Boulding, etc.)
- Anthropological Insights for Social Policy: Western Views
- Anthropological Insights for Social Policy: Third World Views
- Conceptualization of the Future in Various Cultures
- Anthropological Perspectives of Social Movements and Cultural Trends
- Perception, Action, Research Paradigm and Policy Design
- Education Toward the Future
- Future Cultural Alternatives: Imaginative Use of Anthropology

786. BURKE, John G. (ed.) **The New Technology and Human Values.** Belmont, Calif.: Wadsworth Publishing Co., 1966. 408 pp.   (ns)

An introductory reader focusing on problems such as education, leisure, automation, population, privacy, and government.

787. KOSTELANETZ, Richard (ed.) **Beyond Left and Right: Radical Thought for Our Times.** NY: Morrow, 1968. 436 pp. $2.95, paper.   (B-3)

A good selection of futurist thinking that is radical in the non-political sense: "...neither their prose nor their thought is as simplistic or as obvious as partisan polemic or political platforms." (p. xiii) Among the 36 selections there are 5 by Buckminster Fuller, 3 by Herman Kahn, and 2 each by Kenneth Boulding and Simon Ramo. Others included here such as Daniel Bell, Karl Deutsch, Paul Goodman, Zbigniew Brzezinski, Hans Morgenthau, Robert Theobald, Marshall McLuhan, and Oliver Reiser.

788. DUNSTAN, Maryjane and Patricia W. GARLAN. **Worlds in the Making: Probes for Students of the Future.** Englewood Cliffs, NJ: Prentice-Hall, 1970. 370 pp. $8.95; $6.50, paper.   (C-4)

A trendy textbook joining liberal rhetoric with a focus on megatechnology. The seven sections of excerpts and essays are as follows:
- Grokking the Problem: Robert Heinlein, Alvin Toffler, Buckminster Fuller, etc.
- Coping With Change: Ken Kesey, Ralph Ellison, Joseph Heller, Eldredge Cleaver.
- Exploring Spaceship Earth: Arthur C. Clarke, C.A. Doxiadis, and B. Fuller.
- The Machine--Enemy or Ally? Theodore J. Gordon, Robert Heilbroner, D.S. Halacy, and Glenn T. Seaborg.
- Evolution or Revolution: Robert Theobald, Lewis Mumford, Hal Hellman, George B. Leonard, and Albert Rosenfeld.
- Discovering Human Nature: Carl Rogers, Alan Watts, Eric Berne.
- Inventing the Future: Richard E. Farson, Lillian Smith.

789. MICHAEL, Donald N. (ed.) **The Future Society.** New Brunswick, NJ: Transaction Books, No. 17, 1970. 131 pp. $2.95, paper. (Dist. by E.P. Dutton)   (AB-4)

Seven reprinted essays from **Transaction/Society**, which the editor sees as stressing the conditions of transition:
- Melvin M. Webber, "The Politics of Information" (1965)
- Robert A. Skedgell, "How Computers Pick an Election Winner" (1966)
- Warren G. Bennis, "Post Bureaucratic Leadership" (1966)
- Fred Davis, "Why All of Us May Be Hippies Some Day" (1967)
- Kenneth Keniston, "How Community Mental Health Stamped Out the Riots (1968-1978)" (1968)
- Commentaries on Reports from Iron Mountain (1968)
- Helen P. Goudner, "Children of the Laboratory" (1967)
*** "Some Elements of The Future Society" would be a considerably more accurate title.

789a. DOUGLAS, Jack D. (ed.) **Freedom and Tyranny: Social Problems in a Technological Society.** NY: Knopf, 1970. 289 pp.   (ns)

790. OFSHE, Richard (ed.) **The Sociology of the Possible.** Englewood Cliffs, NJ: Prentice-Hall, 1970. 398 pp. $8.50; $4.95, paper. (ns)

Readings dealing with social possibilities in the areas of population, race relations, social organization, interpersonal relations, etc.

791. KOSTELANETZ, Richard (ed.) **Social Speculations: Visions for Our Time.** NY: Morrow, Jan. 1971. 306 pp. $7.50; $2.95, paper. (B-3)

In his introduction, The Politics of Speculation, the editor states that "a social thought truly relevant to our times must turn from negative carping, no matter how perceptive, into offering visions of what can, and ought, to be done. The ineffectuality of what is known today as 'radical thought' points up the need for a revolution in how we think about fundamental social change..." (p.19)

The 35 selections favor what might be called cosmic technocratic thinking that advances a bold but benign technological transformation. They are organized in four sections:
- History: Buckminster Fuller, Nigel Calder, Oliver Reiser, Karl W. Deutsch, Herman Kahn, Dane Rudhyar, Burnham Putnam Beckwith, etc.
- Technologies: Theodore J. Gordon, Hasan Ozbekhan, J.C.R. Licklider, Isaac Asimov, etc.
- Environments: Anthony J. Wiener, Fritz Baade, Don Benson, Dandridge M. Cole on "The Ultimate Human Society," etc.
- Cities: Martin and Margy Meyerson, Kenneth B. Clark, Athelstan Spilhaus, Geoffrey A. Jellicoe on "Sea City," selections on Buckminster Fuller's floating and domed cities, etc.
*** An interesting array of big technology solutions, but with a notable absence of attention to issues such as freedom vs. equality, centralization vs. decentralization, large corporations, and real life politics. The volume is thus somewhat mistitled.

792. KOSTELANETZ, Richard (ed.) **Human Alternatives: Visions for Us Now.** NY: Morrow, 1971. 297 pp. $7.95; $2.95, paper.   (B-3)

In contrast to **Social Speculations,** published earlier in 1971, this anthology "is more specific, more personal and perhaps more practical." (p. vii) Kostelanetz courageously states his presuppositions in the Preface: that change is the metaphysic of our age, that our existence is now more amenable than ever before in history, and that optimism is a more persuasive intellectual posture than pessimism. The editor's own position is described as "techno-anarchist," but very few of the 34 selections could ever be considered as anarchist or decentralist. There is even a conscious attempt to describe the omissions in this volume (seen as international relations and New Left writings). But there are also omissions that are not recognized--essentially the same as in the previous volume, despite attempts to be "more practical." The six sections are as follows:
- Knowledge: Edmund Carpenter, Buckminster Fuller, Herbert Simon.
- Organisms: Allen Ginsberg, John Platt, Gerald Feinberg, etc.
- Economics: Robert Theobald, Buckminster Fuller, David T. Bazelon.
- Politics: Herman Kahn, Seymour Melman, John Diebold, Grenville Clark, etc.
- Education: Don Fabun, Paul Goodman, Caleb Gattegno, Anthony Oettinger, etc.
- Planning: L. Moholy-Nagy, Charles DeCarlo, John Cage, James Bright, the O.E.C.D. Bellagio declaration, etc.
*** Another stimulating compilation; economics and politics are considered here, but very lightly.

793. PIRAGES, Dennis C. (ed.) **Seeing Beyond: Personal, Social, and Political Alternatives.** Reading, Mass.: Addison Wesley, 1971. 342 pp. $3.95, paper.   (B-3)

The 28 selections are arranged in six sections:
- One Dimensional Society: The Need to See Beyond
- Galloping Technology: Contemporary Human Problems
- The Individual: Toward a Multidimensional Mind
- Interpersonal Relations: A Return to the Extended Family
- Metropolis and Community
- Social Engineering: Politics and Behavioral Science

794. KAPLAN, Max, and Philip BOSSERMAN (eds.) **Technology, Human Values, and Leisure.** Nashville, Tenn.: Abingdon Press, 1971. 256 pp. $6.50; $3.50, paper.   (ns)

Contents include the following:
- Robert Theobald, "Thinking About the Future"
- Emmanuel G. Mesthene, "Technology and Humanistic Values"
- Harrison Brown, "Technology and Where We Are"
- Joffre Dumazedier, "Leisure and Post-Industrial Societies"

795. LAUDA, Donald P. and Robert D. RYAN (eds.) **Advancing Technology: Its Impact on Society.** Dubuque, Iowa: William C. Brown Co., 1971. 536 pp. $6.95, paper.   (B-4)

A massive volume of 59 selections, including:
- Ben B. Seligman, "The Social Cost of Cybernation"
- Sebastian de Grazia, "Leisure's Future"
- Athelstan Spilhaus, "The Next Industrial Revolution"
- Philip M. Hauser, "The Chaotic Society..." (see no. 813)
- Jacques Ellul, "Technique in Civilization"

796. DOUGLAS, Jack D. (ed.) **The Technological Threat.** Englewood Cliffs, NJ: Prentice-Hall, 1971. 185 pp. $5.95; $2.95, paper.   (AB-3)

A reader with selections grouped under five headings:
- American Society as a Technological Society: Daniel Bell, Irene Taviss.
- The Impact of Technology on American Values: Robert Nisbet, Karl Mannheim.
- The Impact of the Electronics Revolution: David Riesman, Norbert Wiener.
- The Threats of Alienation and Social Technology: Daniel Bell, Carl Rogers, B.F. Skinner.
- The Impact of Technology on Political Values: C. Wright Mills, Lawrence K. Frank, Edward T. Chase.

797. ARBLASTER, Anthony, and Steven LUKES, (eds). **The Good Society: A Book of Readings.** NY: Harper & Row, 1971; Harper Torchback, 1972. 436 pp. $3.95, paper.   (AB-2)

A very valuable collection of 81 authors from the 18th, 19th, and 20th centuries, including names such as Adam Smith, Immanuel Kant, Thomas Paine, William Blake, Robert Owen, Thomas Carlyle, Alexis de Tocqueville, Karl Marx, William Morris, Oscar Wilde, Emile Durkheim, Georg Simmel, Max Weber, Bertrand Russell, Karl Mannheim, Walter Lippman, Mao Tse-Tung, A.A. Berle, Jr., George Orwell, David Riesman, S.M. Lipset, and Che Guevara.

In the thoughtful 21-page introduction, the authors "hope that our anthology contains enough evidence to demonstrate that poets, novelists and essayists, as well as politicians and revolutionaries, make their own uniquely valuable contributions to the discussion of the issues which specialists in political and social theory are sometimes apt to regard as their private preserve." (p. 1)   The authors also hope to demonstrate the "crucial importance" of values and ideals.
*** The breadth and historical depth of this collection serves as a welcome antidote to various innocents who assume that thinking about the future began in the past decade.

798. THEOBALD, Robert (ed.) **Futures Conditional.** Indianapolis: Bobbs-Merrill, 1972. 357 pp.   (C-3)

A broad selection of essays, poems, and cartoons on topics such as the nature of time, choosing your view of the future, revising the constitution, life-styles, education and pollution. Included are authors such as Robert A. Heinlein, Mark Rudd, Joseph Wood Krutch, John W. Gardner, Willis Harman, Neil Postman, Arthur Waskow, and A.H. Maslow.

799. JAMES, Dorothy Buckton (ed.). **Outside, Looking In: Critiques of American Policies and Institutions, Left and Right.** NY: Harper & Row, 1972. 437 pp. $4.25.   (ns)

800. RASMUSSEN, John P. (ed.) **The New American Revolution: The Dawning of the Technetronic Era.** NY: Wiley, 1972. 250 pp. $11.00; $5.95, paper.   (ns)

Articles grouped in seven categories:
- The Idea of Post-Industrial Society: Arthur M. Schlesinger, Jr., Zbigniew Brzezinski, Herman Kahn and Anthony Wiener, etc.
- The Reign of Automation: Marshall McLuhan, Lewis Mumford.
- Megalopolis: The Present and Future of the Super-City: Studs Terkel, Paul Goodman, Norman Mailer.
- Technology's Children: Kenneth Keniston, Buckminster Fuller, etc.
- Technology and the Global Environment: Pennfield Jensen, Lord Ritchie-Calder.
- A Question of Control: Michael Harrington, Jacques Ellul.
- As the Future Unfolds: Walter Goldstein on "The Technology Gap."

801. TOFFLER, Alvin (ed.) **The Futurists.** NY: Random House, 1972. 321 pp. $3.95, paper.   (AB-5)

"The purpose of this collection is to make accessible a few of the works of the best-known and, at the moment, most influential futurists." (p.5)
Who or what is a futurist? "The word now denotes a growing school of social critics, scientists, philosophers, planners, and others who concern themselves with the alternatives facing man as the human race collides with an onrushing future." (p.3) We are also informed that today's futurists are wary about dogmatic statements and focus instead on the array of alternatives open to decision-makers, and that this book reflects "what constitutes the emerging 'establishment' within the futurist movement." (p.9) The 22 selections are divided into three categories:
- Social Critics: Paul Ehrlich, Margaret Mead, John McHale, Marshall McLuhan, Robert Jungk, Arthur I. Waskow, and Alvin Toffler.
- Scientists: Arthur C. Clarke, Olaf Helmer, Herman Kahn and Anthony J. Wiener, Theodore J. Gordon, M.S. Iyengar, I. Bestushev-Lada, and Erich Jantsch.
- Philosophers and Planners: Kenneth E. Boulding, Yujiro Hayashi, Daniel Bell, Ossip Flechtheim, Bertrand de Jouvenel, Fred R. Polak, John Wren-Lewis, and R. Buckminster Fuller.
*** A fair introduction to some of the leading future-oriented thinkers, although the categories are poorly drawn. More important, the writers do not constitute a "school"; they have little in common except for some future-orientation, and the rhetoric about "the futurist movement (having) spread rapidly around the globe" should be laid to rest or severely modified in light of actual developments. These essays are no doubt stimulating, but very few of them examine an "array of alternatives," which is supposedly the distinguishing mark of the futurist. One of the great barriers to serious thinking about the future is the inflated statements and outright myths about the extent and impacts of "futurism," as promulgated by bubbly supporters such as Toffler.
Some of the writers here are certainly "establishment," and parti-

cular note should be made of Igor Bestushev-Lada, described by Toffler as the "Top Soviet futurist." More correctly, Bestushev-Lada (whose article here fulminates about "Bourgeois 'Futurology' and the Future of Mankind") is essentially the "official" Soviet futurist, who monitors Western futurists and counters with stale Marxist rhetoric. Bestushev-Lada might be profitably compared with the leading "unofficial futurist," Alexander Solzhenitsyn (nos. 843-844), who has the freedom to express some profound thoughts about the future, but has yet to be considered as a futurist. The important lesson here is that those who call themselves futurists do not necessarily have more significant or influential views of the future than those who do not call themselves futurists.

802. TUGWELL, Franklin (ed.) **Search for Alternatives: Public Policy and the Study of the Future.** Cambridge, Mass.: Winthrop Publishers, March 1973. 335 pp.   (AB-2)

A worthy collection of some of the best futurist writings in recent years, introduced by John Platt's classic essay on "What We Must Do" (see no. 3).
Part One, On Knowing the Future: Approaches and Interpretations, has 11 essays on prediction (Bertrand de Jouvenel, O.D. Duncan, Olaf Helmer, and Nicholas Rescher), imagination and values (Elise Boulding, Irene Taviss), the alternative futures approach (Herman Kahn), the Delphi technique and cross-impact matrix (Selwyn Enzer, Robert H. Ament), participatory future studies (Arthur I. Waskow), speculative scenarios (Paul Ehrlich), and models and cybernetic anticipations (Jay W. Forrester).
Part Two, On the Shape of the Future: Institutions and Policy Systems, has 5 essays on the international system (Johan Galtung), the post-industrial society (Daniel Bell), political futures (Bertram Gross on friendly fascism, see no. 103), alternative planning systems (Donald N. Michael) and beyond bureaucracy (Alvin Toffler).
*** A good starting point for policy-oriented professionals.

803. SCHEIBER, Jane L. (ed.) **America and the Future of Man: A Reader for the First Course by Newspaper.** San Diego: University of California, University Extension, 1973. 322 pp. (Published by CRM Books) (B-3)

This reader of 50 selections reproduces the 13 brief essays which ran in some 200 participating newspapers, and adds additional materials for those students pursuing the subject in somewhat greater depth and for credit at some 200 cooperating colleges.
Authors of original contributions and reprinted pieces include Daniel Bell, C.A. Doxiadis, E.J. Mishan, Barry Commoner, Richard J. Herrnstein, Kenneth E. Boulding, Garrett Hardin, Philip Morrison, Bentley Glass, Leon R. Kass, and Paul Ramsey.

804. THEOBALD, Robert, and Stephanie MILLS (eds.) **The Failure of Success: Ecological Values vs. Economic Myths.** Indianapolis: Bobbs-Merrill, 1973. 277 pp.   (C-4)

A reader of articles, cartoons, and quotations, organized in four sections: Economists vs. Ecologists, What Do We Mean by Development, The Search for a New Ethic, and Changing Personal Success Criteria.

805. KOSTELANETZ, Richard (ed.) **The Edge of Adaptation: Man and the Emerging Society.** Englewood Cliffs, NJ: Prentice-Hall, 1973. $6.95; $2.45, paper.   (ns)

Has 15 essays in four parts: impact and potential of new technologies, changes in the common environment, changes in social mores and behavior, and strategies for coping with the emerging society.

805a. SHOSTAK, Arthur B. **Modern Social Reforms: Solving Today's Social Problems.** NY: Macmillan, 1974. 411 pp. $4.95, paper.   (BC-3)

A textbook/reader with lengthy introductions to 15 articles on reforms in education, labor, justice, communities, health, and environment. Approaches to various issues are seen in terms of conservative, liberal, radical, and visionary viewpoints (with the implication that visionary is superior).

In the introduction, it is forecasted that the reform agenda of the 1970s will differ substantially from recent reforms. It will be more eclectic, but fewer reforms will be adapted, in that proposals will have to meet a new test of social accounting evaluation.

*** Breezy, but interesting. The sub-titling is a bit promiscuous, for we seldom "solve" social problems.

806. NORMAN, Maxwell H. (ed.) **Dimensions of the Future: Alternatives for Tomorrow.** NY: Holt, Rinehart and Winston, 1974. 306 pp. $4.95, paper.   (ns)

Fiction and essays divided into 13 chapters.

807. CLARKE, Robin (ed.) **Notes for the Future: An Alternative History of the Past Decade.** NY: Universe Books, Feb. 1976. 240 pp. $10.00; $4.95, paper.   (ns)

An anthology of visions on man's endangered future and how civilization can survive. Contributors include W.H. Auden, Murray Bookchin, Georg Borgstrom, Harrison Brown, Derek Bryan, Barry Commoner, Paul Ehrlich, Robert Graves, Garrett Hardin, Judson Jerome, Jerome Lettvin, Malachi Martin, Donella Meadows, Theodore Roszak, E.F. Schumacher, John and Sally Seymour, Henryk Skolimowski, John Todd, Peter Van Dresser, and Lynn White, Jr. (publisher's information)

> NOTE: The items in this guide considered to be most deserving of attention--all with "1" or "2" ratings--are summarized as "The Civic Curriculum," pp. 7-13. Also see the explanation of the rating system on page 4.

Chapter 15

Unclassified

Publications that have not been seen and cannot be classified on the basis of their title alone, and views of societal directions and alternatives that do not fit into the previous 14 chapters, are found here. New categories are obviously suggested, but the number of items identified is not large enough to warrant separate grouping.

There are general views on the condition of America (808-814), and general approaches to alternatives via the systems view (815) and innovations (816). There are surprisingly few instances where an array of alternative futures is examined. Ewald (817) offers a credible if somewhat simplified effort, the Stanford Research Institute (818) provides an array of interesting but inconsistent visions, and Agel (819) presents a collage of ideas that could be seen as "alternative futures" in the loosest sense.

There are specific views of a certain technology or trait characterizing the society. "The Computerized Society" (820) is a particularly persuasive view of a probable future, while "The Immortalist State" (822) is a remote possibility that could be thrust upon us by bio-medical researchers. Such a development would give considerable impetus to the cause of the new feminism, and the "cybernetic socialism" advocated by one of the movement's more radical thinkers (823). The definitive work on meritocracy was published in 1958 by Michael Young (825), and it also remains as the definitive futures history, or scenario. In contrast, Hutchins advocates an egalitarian "Learning Society," a secular ideal no less remote than the Kingdom of God that is promised by Christian fundamentalists (827-830).

The vision of a new society resulting from the second coming of Christ is widely held, and the Billy Graham explanation (827) is perhaps as good as any to be found. The books of Hal Lindsey (828) are particularly popular with campus audiences. The extensive cultural analysis by Sorokin (832) suggests an interesting parallel in his assertion that an idealistic culture will arise from the "fiery ordeal of catastrophe" that will result from our sensate culture.

There are doubtlessly many books devoted to societal directions and alternatives for other developed nations. The few mentioned here are only meant to suggest what might be included in a more extensive guide. Of particular interest is the recent **samizdat** (or self-published) literature from the Soviet Union. Amalrik (842) was sent to a labor camp for suggesting a pessimistic societal direction. Solzhenitsyn proposed a societal alternative (843) and was deported. The dissent from the Soviet Union is not a mere internal matter, but is a critique of The Technological Society in its communist form, as clearly indicated by the extraordinary collection of critical essays collected by Solzhenitsyn (844). This view might be seen as "spiritual decentralist"; in contrast, Sakharov (845) and Medvedev (846) advocate democratic reforms, but a far less radical change in societal directions.

Items 850-890 have not been seen, and are listed alphabetically. Many of them are listings from the most recent edition of **Forthcoming Books,** and it should be cautioned that the titles and publication dates are subject to change.

808. FAIRLIE, Henry. **Spoiled Child of the Western World: The Miscarriage of the American Idea in Our Time.** Garden City, NY: Doubleday, Jan. 1976. 350 pp. $8.95.   (A-3)

"This book has not been a work of prescriptions; America has enough of prescriptions with too little sense of a common endeavor. If anything, the argument has been the initial response of an outsider to the humanism of the American tradition and experience..." (p. 325)
Fairlie is a native Londoner now living in Colorado. Chapters in this rambling tour include The Americanization of the World, The Do-It-Yourself God Kit, The Exhaustion of the Self, The Boundaries of Affluence, and The Revolt Against the Democratic Idea in America. Along the way he attacks conservatives, liberals, the failure of the sociological imagination, Daniel Bell and other "intellectual technologists," Konrad Lorenz, and the withdrawal of the citizen from politics.

809. HOFFER, Eric, "What We Have Lost," **The New York Times Magazine,** October 20, 1974, pp. 110-117.   (B-4)

America's only philosopher-longshoreman observes that "We are living in an epoch of great disillusionment," and that the essential attributes of a vigorous country are courage and a passion for excellence.
The reversion of social decline is possible and "America can become hopeful only by placing itself in the van of mankind; by mobilizing all its energies and know-how to solve the problems which now plague the world--and solve them speedily and dramatically." (p. 117) Rather than relying on a great leader, the solution of these problems "must become a vast communal undertaking."

810. TUCHMAN, Barbara W., "History as Mirror," **The Atlantic Monthly,** 232:3, Sept. 1973, pp. 39-46.   (B-3)

Describes calamities of the 14th Century because "I think a backward look at that disordered, violent, bewildered, disintegrating age can be consoling and possibly instructive in a time of similar disarray...In human affairs as in nature, decay is compost for new growth." (p. 39) Modern doomsayers are criticized for their extrapolation. Tuchman concludes that "like our ancestors, we, too, will muddle through." (p. 46)
*** A most instructive argument; however, unique aspects of our age, such as nuclear weaponry, are not considered.

811. de GRAZIA, Alfred. **Eight Bads--Eight Goods: The American Contradictions.** Garden City, NY: Doubleday Anchor, 1975. 268 pp. $2.95, paper.   (B-3)

"These are lectures to the Chinese. They are built around two favorite Chinese ideas: the idea of contradictions...and the idea of numbered slogans of things to be sought after or avoided...I wonder whether the Chinese will ever hear the lectures. It doesn't matter. They were really written for Americans." (Foreword)
The eight bads are living in the past, practicing deception, exalting idols, becoming dependent, dividing the soul against itself, setting one above another, setting one against another, and being proud. The greatest bad is considered to be the bureaucratization of America. A chart (pp. 120-121) contrasts the U.S. with 13 other nations, as concerns the eight bads.

The eight goods are being honest, joining together, solving problems, producing goods, caring for everyone, dispensing justice, making friends, and ruling well. The greatest good is considered to be the openness of America. A chart (pp. 242-243) contrasts the U.S. with 13 other nations, as concerns the eight goods.

In concluding part one, America is seen as "A Culture of Force."

In concluding part two, America is seen as "A Culture of Freedom."

* Very interesting.

812. WESCOTT, Roger W. **The Divine Animal: An Exploration of Human Potentiality.** NY: Funk & Wagnalls, 1969. 340 pp.   (BC-4)

A light and rambling discussion by an anthropologist concerning instincts, communications, the evolution of language, states of consciousness, America as an underdeveloped country, impending globalization, etc. "The United States is simultaneously radical in technology, liberal in politics, conservative in economics, and reactionary in religion." (p. 282)

813. HAUSER, Philip M., "The Chaotic Society: Product of the Social Morphological Revolution," **American Sociological Review,** 34:1, Feb. 1969, pp. 1-19.   (A-3)

Based on the Presidential Address to the 1968 annual meeting of the American Sociological Association. Contemporary society "is realistically characterized as 'the chaotic society.'" (p. 1) The cause of this chaos is the social morphological revolution which consists of increased size, density, heterogeneity, and tempo of change.

814. TURNER, Jonathan H. **American Society: Problems of Structure.** NY: Harper & Row, 1972. 299 pp. $4.95, paper.   (B-3)

A textbook that "attempts to develop a new approach to the study of social problems in America. Primary emphasis is placed on the fact that social problems are structural in origin and persistence." (p.xv) The four generic types of structures dealt with are residential communities, social strata, social institutions, and ecological communities. Chapters deal with cities, segregation, inequality, poverty, minorities, criminal justice, government, education, pollution, and population growth.

* Nothing remarkable and little in the way of summary, but otherwise a good overview.

815. ACKOFF, Russell L. **Redesigning the Future: A Systems Approach to Societal Problems.** NY: Wiley-Interscience, 1974. 260 pp. $10.95.   (B-4)

Views a transition from The Machine Age to The Systems Age. The former is characterized by analytical thinking based on doctrines of reductionism and mechanics. But this is now being supplemented and partially replaced by the doctrines of expansionism and teleology, and a new synthetic mode of thought. This "postindustrial revolution" is based on automation, and its key idea is interaction.

Chapters are devoted to each of the three organizing problems of the systems age: The Self-Control Problem (concerning systems that can cope with increasing complexity), The Humanization Problem, and The Environmentalization Problem.

Chapters are then focused on eight particular problems: education, the generation gap, race, crime, health, solid waste and litter, transportation and the city, and underdeveloped countries.

* A brief examination suggests that this well-meaning but immodest volume is not as systemic as it pretends, and may be dangerously simplistic. We undoubtedly could benefit from "a new synthetic mode of thought," but unqualified claims that a systems view is being taken when important elements (system components or critical linkages of system to environment) are being ignored, can only serve to aggravate our problems and erode the potential of synthetic thinking.

816. GABOR, Dennis. **Innovations: Scientific, Technological, and Social.** NY: Oxford University Press, 1970. 113 pp. $4.95; $1.95, paper.   (AB-4)

A brief survey of 137 inventions and innovations that we might anticipate: 73 of them "hardware," 27 biological, and 37 social. The discussion of developments in the hard sciences is generally intelligent, although there is a failure to explore the possibility of negative consequences.

The discussion of social innovations is superficial and naive. For example, the section on crime and corruption fails to acknowledge any need for reforming prisons and courts. Student violence is seen as resulting from the large number of students combined with institutional permissiveness. Futuristic studies are advocated, but narrowly defined to include only a handful of technocratic elites.

*** An admirable attempt to be comprehensive, but the social naiveté of the natural scientist is in great evidence here. It is regrettable that Gabor, a Nobel Prize winner (for his invention of holography), cannot express some humility in the face of social complexities.

817. McCUE, Gerald M., William R. EWALD, Jr., and the Midwest Research Institute. **Creating the Human Environment: A Report of the American Institute of Architects.** Urbana: University of Illinois Press, 1970. 339 pp. $4.95, paper.   (AB-3)

Essentially three separate documents: the first 151 pages by Ewald is a valuable and wide-ranging "Reconnaissance of the Future." The Midwest Research Institute is responsible for the section on the building industry (pp. 155-251), and McCue addresses the Future of the Profession (pp. 255-339) and makes numerous recommendations.

The Ewald section sees four paths to the future: Revolution (leading to a people's democracy and a spontaneous society), Reason (leading to a planning democracy and scientific humanism), Response (continuing traditional and corporate democracy), and Reaction (leading to a paternalistic society and an elite society). There are also projections of innumerable indicators, and comments on organizing knowledge to create a humane future environment.

818. ELGIN, Duane S., David C. MacMICHAEL, and Peter SCHWARTZ. **Alternative Futures for Environmental Policy Planning: 1975-2000.** Washington, D.C.: Environmental Protection Agency, Office of Pesticide Programs (EPA-540/9-75-027), Oct. 1975. 286 pp. (Copies may also be available from the Center for the Study of Social Policy, Stanford Research Institute, Menlo Park, Calif. 94025)   (A-4)

One-half of this report is devoted to elaborating ten "alternative future scenarios" which are grouped around three main themes: industrial success achieved through existing political, economic, and social forms; industrial failure without alternative values or reformed institutions; and industrial transformation to a new paradigm of "frugal" values that incorporates the principle of Buddhist economics.

*** On the surface this appears to be an exemplary use of futures research. On closer examination, the scenarios tend to be cliché-ridden and remarkably evasive on basic matters such as the composition of the labor force, the spatial distribution of the population, and--most surprisingly--

the system of agriculture employed. The authors seem to be oblivious to the possibility of a largely (if not totally) pesticide-free organic system, which, of course, would seem to be of central importance to policy planning for the Office of Pesticide Programs!

819. AGEL, Jerome. **Is Today Tomorrow? A Synergistic Collage of Alternative Futures.** NY: Ballantine Books, Nov. 1972. 191 pp. $1.95, paper.   (C-3)

The same zing-blinko style that Agel pioneered in previous paperbacks on Marshall McLuhan (**The Medium is the Massage** and **War and Peace in the Global Village**), Buckminster Fuller (**I Seem To Be a Verb**), and Herman Kahn (**Herman Kahnsciousness**). This mélange of notes, quotes, and photos does not concern any individual, but everyone and everything.

There are two interesting sections here. On pp. 33-57 there is a listing of some 700 words and phrases suggesting various possibilities such as aging delayed, daily brownouts, telekinetics, retirement at 22, one currency for the world, modification of the solar system, and no advertising. No doubt useful for stimulating classroom essays and discussion.

And on pp. 129-169 there are the unedited responses from about 90 experts (including many well-known futurists) to the question "Do you believe that young people can handle curricula on the future?" Obviously, most respondents answered positively.

820. MARTIN, James Thomas and Adrian R.D. NORMAN. **The Computerized Society: An Appraisal of the Impact of Computers on Society Over the Next 15 Years.** Englewood Cliffs, NJ: Prentice-Hall, 1970. 560 pp. $10.95.   (ABC-2)

The authors assert that "a critical point is at hand. In the years immediately ahead, there will be a sudden massive spread of computer usage that will affect the lives of almost everyone." (p. v) This spread will be due to mass production with a very sharp drop in cost, standardization allowing cheap reproduction of programs, new storage and retrieval capacity, and linkages to the telephone network allowing linkages with other computers. "The impact of the computer and new tele-communications facilities is going to be more sweeping than the impact of the automobile." (p. vi)

Chapters are divided into three sections: Euphoria, Alarm, and Protective Action. The first section discusses positive prospects such as uses in finance, law enforcement, teaching, medicine, transportation, and government. The section on Alarm offers a balancing set of chapters on threats to privacy, machine error, crime and sabotage, bewilderment, power, and changes in employment patterns. The final section on Protective Action covers handling change (advocating long-range planning), changes needed in education at all levels, needed laws, security devices, control over accuracy, an Ombudsman, and responsibilities of systems scientists.

*** Simply-written and well-balanced, although the impact may not be as soon or as sweeping as anticipated.

821. LANDERS, Richard R. **Man's Place in the Dybosphere.** Englewood Cliffs, NJ: Prentice-Hall, 1966. 266 pp.   (B-4)

Concerning the transition from the biosphere to the dybosphere: "the realm of artificially created things which behave in a life-like manner." (p. 4) Man is seen as increasingly mechanistic, while machines are becoming more humanoid, thus resulting in a convergence of a biogenic machine and a dybogenic man.

*** Such thinking, quite characteristic of the automation-conscious sixties, would be quickly challenged today.

822. HARRINGTON, Alan. **The Immortalist: An Approach to the Engineering of Man's Divinity.** NY: Random House, 1969; Avon Discus edition, 1970. 287 pp. $1.25, paper.   (AB-3)

Contends that a society of immortal men will come about (provided that the species refrains from destroying itself) and that such a society ought to be pursued as a conscious goal. "Our new faith must accept as gospel that salvation belongs to medical engineering and nothing else...Does such a project seem quixotic now? Perhaps so, but it will not tomorrow." (p. 27) The final chapter offers comments on what the Immortalist State might be like.
*** An interesting long shot which could lead to many dramatic changes.

823. FIRESTONE, Shulamith. **The Dialectic of Sex: The Case for Feminist Revolution.** NY: Morrow, 1970; NY: Bantam, 1971. 242 pp. $1.25, paper.   (B-4)

The new feminism aims to overthrow the class system based on sex. A "cybernetic socialism" is advocated, whereby "the establishment of the household as the alternative to the family for reproduction of children, combined with every imaginable life style for those who choose to live singly or in nonreproductive units, would resolve all the basic dilemmas that now arise from the family to obstruct human happiness." (p. 238)
The four minimal demands for any alternative system are 1) the freeing of women from the tyranny of their biology by any means available, 2) economic independence and self-determination of all, 3) the total integration of women and children into the larger society, and 4) sexual freedom.

824. GORNICK, Vivian, and Barbara MORAN (eds.) **Woman in Sexist Society.** NY: Basic Books, 1971. 515 pp. $12.50.   (ns)

824a. "U.S. National Women's Agenda," **Social Policy,** 6:5, March/April 1976, pp. 24-25.   (AB-3)

A listing of 93 national women's organizations, and the priorities and goals that they advocate, arranged in 11 categories: fair representation and participation in the political process, equal education and training, meaningful work and adequate compensation, equal access to economic power, quality child care for all children, quality health care and services, adequate housing, just and humane treatment in the criminal justice system, fair treatment by and equal access to media and the arts, physical safety, and respect for the individual. Further information can be obtained from the Women's Action Alliance, 370 Lexington Ave., Room 601, New York City 10017.

825. YOUNG, Michael. **The Rise of the Meritocracy, 1870-2033: An Essay on Education and Equality.** London: Thames & Hudson, 1958; Baltimore, Md.: Penguin Books, 1961. 190 pp.   (A-3)

A brilliant and witty scenario by a sociologist who writes as a sociologist in the year 2033, defending the existing order and providing historical background for government leaders. The history describes how brainpower planning became more effective as the measurement of merit (intelligence and effort) became more effective, so that, in 2033, "The world beholds for the first time the spectacle of a brilliant class, the five percent of a nation who know what five percent means." (p. 103) The most intelligent children received the best education, and, consequently, the gap

between social classes became wider, with social inferiors being inferiors in other ways as well.
*** An exemplary model of a "future history" informed by social science. No subsequent attempt at scenario writing has ever come close to this standard. Indeed, the topic of social selection itself is an important matter that is seldom discussed. Our society is obviously not a "meritocracy;" how should it be characterized in terms of social selection, and what could it be? (See Michael Marien, "Beyond Credentialism: The Future of Social Selection," **Social Policy,** 2:3, Sept.-Oct., 1971, pp. 14-21.)

826. HUTCHINS, Robert M. **The Learning Society.** NY: Praeger, 1968; New American Library, Mentor Books, 1968. 173 pp. $1.25, paper.
(AB-4)
Discusses educational issues that may emerge before the end of this century. "The essay concentrates on the most important of the emerging issues. In general, they are those brought about or at least accompanied by affluence and technological change, by the evolution of a world community and a world order, and the dissolution of the class structure of all societies." (p. vii)
Concludes by foreseeing and advocating a learning society. "This would be one that, in addition to offering part-time adult education to every man and woman at every stage of grown-up life, had succeeded in transforming its values in such a way that learning, fulfillment, becoming human, had become its aims and all its institutions were directed to this end." (p. 165)
In that machines can do for modern man what slaves once did for a few, such a vision can be realized. "A world community learning to be civilized, learning to be human, is at last a possibility. Education may come into its own." (p. 166)
*** Such starry-eyed slush from Hutchins is quite disappointing, particularly so because many educators are using the "learning society" banner without any sense as to whether more learning is taking place relative to the past, and relative to our needs. It may be more profitable to see our society as an "ignorant society" where learning needs have been outdistancing attainments. (See Michael Marien, "The Discovery and Decline of the Ignorant Society, 1965-1985," in Thomas Green, ed., **Educational Planning in Perspective.** Guildford, Surrey, England: FUTURES-IPC Science and Technology Press, Fall 1971, pp. 80-89.) A society deserves the title of "learning society" only when there is evidence that it is closing the gap between learning needs and attainments.

827. GRAHAM, Billy. **World Aflame.** Garden City, NY: Doubleday, 1965. NY: Pocket Books, 1967. Old Tappen, NJ: Spire Books, 1967. 224 pp.
(BC-4)

The world's best-known evangelist asserts that "Ultimately, the Bible looks into the future to foresee a new world in which peace and righteousness prevail. There is to be world peace. There is to be a new social order. There is to be a new age. There is to be a completely new man in whom will be no false pride, hate, lust, greed, or prejudice. This will be the climax of human history. This age will be unlike anything the world has ever known. The Kingdom of God will triumph...Until the coming of the new social order in God's direct intervention, the world will continue to plunge from crisis to crisis. In the midst of these trials and tribulations, we must determine which way God is moving in history--and then get in step with God!" (pp. xv-svi)
Evidence abounds that we are in the midst of Satan's World. Chapter 1, Flames Out of Control, describes the population explosion, lawlessness, racial tensions, Communism, and uncontrolled science. Chapter 20, Signs

of the End, adds distressed and bewildered nations, abundance together with millions starving, the world on a moral binge, and a falling away from the faith.

"The salvation of society will come about by the powers and forces released by the apocalyptic return of Jesus Christ... The second coming of Christ will be so revolutionary that it will change every aspect of life on this planet." (p. 174)

*** A persisting vision, still believed in by millions--in marked contrast to the secular views of societal directions and alternatives, each of which is held by very few persons, albeit, in some instances, elite persons. The vision of a coming Kingdom encourages religiosity (getting in step with God) and, conversely, political passivity.

828. LINDSEY, Hal, with C.C. CARLSON. **The Late Great Planet Earth.** Grand Rapids, Mich.: Zondervan Publishing House, 1970. 192 pp. (C-4)

The same message as above, delivered in a still more popular form by a traveling speaker for Campus Crusade for Christ. "God's kingdom will be characterized by peace and equity, and by universal spirituality and knowledge of the Lord... The Great Society which human rulers throughout the centuries have promised, but never produced, will at last be realized under Christ's rule." (p. 177)

*** Similar to the Graham book (above), the front cover of this book proclaims over 500,000 copies in print. Lindsey has also published subsequent volumes on the same theme.

829. WILLIS, Hugh Evander. **The Good Society: The Goal of Law and the Religion of Jesus, the Unconscious Goal of Creative Evolution, and the Coming Purposeful Goal of Life.** NY: Vantage Press, 1958. 642 pp. (B-4)

A Professor of Law Emeritus at Indiana University seeks "not to put forth another dream utopia, but to build on the foundation of all past human experience by restating the fundamental principles of Jesus' plan for a good society..." (Preface)

The good society is seen as democracy: self-government towards the ends of equality, liberty, and the common good. "The good society has not developed in the United States primarily due to the failure of the family, the schools, and the churches to give training in moral standards and spiritual ideals, and of government to apply them..." (p. 44)

*** Preachy.

830. OTIS, George. **The Solution to CRISIS-AMERICA.** With a Foreword by Pat Boone. Revised and Enlarged Edition. Old Tappan, NJ: Spire Books, 1972. 120 pp. 95¢, paper. (C-5)

Tub-thumping evangelism promulgating RESURRECTION-AMERICA. "What America needs is a focus on her spiritual and moral ecology. We have polluted our souls worse than our streams!" (p. 116)

831. ANDERSON, John B. **Between Two Worlds: A Congressman's Choice.** Grand Rapids, Mich.: Zondervan Publishing House, 1970. 163 pp. (C-4)

A personal perspective on institutions and issues, and on the world of God and the world as it is, by an Illinois Congressman who is the third-ranking Republican in the U.S. House of Representatives.

The first five chapters are devoted to personal chitchat. Chapter 6, What Kind of Society Do We Want? says nothing in a pleasant manner, i.e. "To build a decent, just, humane society in America will require the commitment of vast resources under the direction of our most talented leaders." (p. 50) The first priority for our society "is a recognition of the absolute importance of spiritual as opposed to purely material values." (p. 50)

Chapter 7 provides A Republican Credo that advocates the extension of freedom, decentralization of power, fiscal restraint, and participation. Subsequent chapters discuss Vietnam, the arms race, equality, poverty, crime, and the environment.

Chapter 17, Toward a New Christian Social Ethic, argues for an ethic that looks to both the spiritual and physical elements in life--"an integrated ethical system that reunites personal responsibility with social responsibility." Anderson argues for a more positive outlook toward government and more participation by Christians. As for the good society, "I believe that the perfect society will always pass us by... Perfection in personal and social relations is something reserved for the Kingdom of God." (p. 147) *** Good-hearted, rambling rhetoric.

832. SOROKIN, Pitirim A. **Social and Cultural Dynamics.** NY: American Book Co., (Four Volumes), 1937-1941.   (A-3)

The four volumes in this massive effort have the following titles:
1. **Fluctuation of Forms of Art** (ns)
2. **Fluctuation of Systems of Truth, Ethics, and Law,** 1937. 727 pp.
3. **Fluctuation of Social Relationships, War and Revolution,** 1937. 636 pp.
4. **Basic Problems, Principles, and Methods.** 1941. 804 pp.
The final volume offers an extensive analysis of cultural change, with a concluding chapter on The Twilight of our Sensate Culture and Beyond, which views a dismal future of continued atomization of values, disintegration of the family, waning of creativeness, and social anarchy.

However, this sensate culture will be succeeded by an idealistic culture: "purified by the fiery ordeal of catastrophe" (p. 778), a new constructive period will occur--a noble society built upon integralistic principle.

833. MELKO, Matthew. **52 Peaceful Societies.** Oakville, Ontario: Canadian Peace Research Institute Press, 1973. 223 pp.   (ns)

"Comparative analysis of 52 societies that have achieved and maintained internal peace for more than a century." The four sections of the book are The Discovery of Peace, Conditions Favouring Peace, The Termination of Peace, and Some Generalizations Concerning Peace. (Annotation from Hugh Stevenson, U. of Western Ontario.)

834. ECONOMIC COUNCIL OF CANADA. **Annual Review Series.** Ottawa: Information Canada, Annual Since 1964. Various Prices.   (ns)

"The best single source of socio-economic future projections produced in Canada and probably the most influential in terms of setting government industrial and general economic policy priorities. Over the years, their projections and policy advice have also directly influenced educational and major social policy considerations at federal, provincial, and local levels. Until recently, the Economic Council of Canada has performed as something of a national think tank, assuming the major responsibility for societal forecasts in the absence of other agencies deliberately designed to fulfill the need for comprehensive policy insights."
Sample reviews include:
- Eleventh Annual Review: **Economic Targets and Social Indicators.** 1974. 264 pp. $4.00.
- Tenth Annual Review: **Shaping the Expansion.** 1973. 211 pp. $3.50.
- Ninth Annual Review: **The Years to 1980.** 1972. 117 pp. $2.50.
(Hugh Stevenson, U. of Western Ontario.)

835. BERTIN, Leonard. **Target 2067: Canada's Second Century.** Toronto: Macmillan of Canada, 1968. 297 pp. $8.95.   (ns)

A survey of more than a hundred leading Canadians in business, government, science, the arts and education, along with the author's own analysis. Generally optimistic. (Hugh Stevenson, U. of Western Ontario.)

836. SOUTHERN, Michael (ed.) **Australia in the Seventies.** London: Penguin, 1974. 40p, paper.   (ns)

837. FABUN, Don. **Australia 2000.** NY: Free Press, 1975. 188 pp. $13.95.   (ns)

838. STILLMAN, Edmund, "Le Boom," **New York Times** (Op-Ed), July 23, 1973.   (B-4)

The director of the European division of the Hudson Institute argues that, after Japan, France is the most dynamic economy in the world. It has the fastest growing rate of productivity increase, and the boom should continue, at least in the short-term future. "Thus France is likely to emerge before the end of the present decade with the world's third or fourth highest standard of living--behind the United States and Sweden but very possibly ahead of Canada."
*** Typical Hudson Institute hyper-optimism, based on a narrow set of measures that may be (and certainly ought to be) outmoded in the next decade.

839. KAHN, Herman. **The Emerging Japanese Superstate: Challenge and Response.** Englewood Cliffs, N.J.: Prentice-Hall, 1970. 274 pp. $7.95.   (ns)

Predicts that by 1990 Japan will probably pass the U.S. in per capita income, and that, by 2000, Japanese GNP will equal that of the U.S.
*** One of the leading candidates for All-Time Poor Forecast?

840. KEENE, Donald, "Letter From Tokyo: The Short, Happy Life of Japan as Superpower," **The New York Times Magazine,** March 3, 1974, pp. 19ff.   (B-3)

Argues that the "recent period of Japanese glory, from 1969 to 1973, ...has ended with dramatic suddenness." The gains achieved after years of immense effort have been canceled out by international developments over which the Japanese have no control. Housing is a particular problem, and prophecies of disaster abound.

841. MATSUHITA, Konosuke. **Japan at the Brink.** Tokyo: Kodansha, April 1976. $6.95.

842. AMALRIK, Andrei. **Will the Soviet Union Survive Until 1984?** NY: Harper & Row, 1970. 93 pp. $4.95.   (ns)

A Soviet historian and playwright sees the entire Soviet state crumbling as a result of a stagnant bureaucracy.
*** As a result of disseminating such "falsehoods derogatory to the Soviet

state and social system," Amalrik was sentenced to a Soviet labor camp. This book was part of the evidence against him at his 1970 trial. (**The New York Times**, May 23, 1973, p.8)

843. SOLZHENITSYN, Alexander. **Letter to Soviet Leaders.** Trans. by Hilary Sternberg. London: Collins/Harvill, 1974. 64 pp.   (AB-3)

A modified version of an unanswered letter, now made public after Solzhenitsyn's enforced deportation.

The chief dangers facing the country in the next 10-30 years are "war with China, and our destruction, together with Western civilization, in the crush and stench of a fouled earth." (p. 8) There is a summarization of **The Limits to Growth** (no. 206), and a conclusion that a civilization greedy for perpetual progress has now choked and is on its last legs.

A zero-growth economy is recommended, in addition to renouncing the gigantic scale of modern technology. There should be internal growth, rather than an external expansion of power, and an opening up of the vast Russian Northeast is urged, in order to escape the "utterly unnatural urban life." There should also be a renunciation of psychiatric violence and a free art and literature.

Ideology is seen as inhibiting the building of a healthy Russia. It is charged that Marxism failed to predict a single event in terms of figures, quantities, time-scales or locations.

844. SOLZHENITSYN, Alexander, et al. **From Under the Rubble.** Trans. under the direction of Michael Scammell. Boston: Little Brown, 1975. NY: Bantam, April 1976. 308 pp. $8.95; $1.95, paper.   (AB-1)

Eleven extraordinary essays by Solzhenitsyn and six dissidents still living in the USSR. Although primarily an attack on the Soviet regime, these fresh and profound essays are of importance to the future of all developed nations, and are united by their advocacy of a moral revolution and a new life of repentance and self-restraint.

- "As Breathing and Consciousness Returns" by Solzhenitsyn notes that "For decades, while we were silent, our thoughts straggled in all possible and impossible directions, lost touch with each other, never learned to know each other, ceased to check and correct each other...Powerful and daring minds are now beginning to struggle upright, to fight their way out from under heaps of antiquated rubbish." (p. 4) The essay goes on to review the thinking of Andrei Sakharov, and to soundly criticize it: "Incomplete liberation from modish dogmas imposed by others is always punished by intermittent failures of vision and overhasty formulations." (p. 13)
- "Socialism in Our Past and Future," by Igor Shafarovich (a mathematician and algebraist), argues that our era is a turning point. He ranges far back into history to examine socialism as "one of those basic and universal forces that have been in operation over the entire span of human history." (p. 45), concluding that universal socialism would lead to "the withering away of all mankind, and its death." (p. 61)
- "Contemporary Socioeconomic Systems and Their Future Prospects," by Mikhail Agursky (a cyberneticist), argues that there are more resemblances than differences between capitalism and communism. Both stimulate consumption and planned obsolescence, although the process is less efficient in the Soviet Union. Both systems are rapacious plunderers of natural resources, and the selfish interests of corporations is similar to the worldwide expansion of communism. The defects of totalitarian societies are discussed, as well as those of contemporary democratic societies, where certain freedoms, such as acquiring arms, are "being turned inside out." The socioeconomic system of the future will resemble that of neither East or West. "A just and rational system can be built only on a foundation

of spiritual and moral values." (p. 81) The economy should break manufacturing down into smaller units with an advanced science and technology base and all employees participatng in management. The abolition of the gulf between physical and intellectual labor will be an essential feature, and there will be a decline of urban population. The political structure will require a high degree of self-discipline, and a mass media freed from commercial and propagandist characteristics. Media censors acting as judges should be freely elected.

- "Separation or Reconciliation? The Nationalities Question in the USSR," by Shafarovitch, is conscious that Soviet problems are local manifestations of natural laws common to all mankind. Attempting to rethink "decolonization" it is argued that the formation of "pocket-handkerchief states" brings no relief from familiar troubles.
- "Repentance and Self-Limitation in the Life of Nations," by Solzhenitsyn, attacks "the arrogant insensitivity of the modern trend in the social sciences" (p. 106), prophesying that true repentence and self-limitation will soon reappear and that a hollow place in modern man is ready to receive them. Repentance is necessary for survival, and the only starting point for spiritual growth; we must stop blaming everyone else, always claiming that we alone are in the right.
- "The Direction of Change," by A.B. (a pseudonym), views Russia as in "a lamentable state" and in need of new spiritual energies--a Christian consciousness.
- "Russian Destinies" by F. Korsakov (a pseudonym) concerns the cleaning of the soul and the return to the Church.
- "The Schism Between the Church and the World," by Evgeny Barabanov (an art historian), reviews the historical failures and sins of the Church, concluding that "Today, as never before, a Christian initiative is needed to counter the godless humanism which is destroying mankind..." (p.192)
- "Personality and National Awareness," by Vadim Borisov (a young historian), laments that "the degeneration of national awareness started in earnest with the spread of atheism, rationalism, positivism and materialism." (p. 213) The convergence of socialism and technocracy is not fortuitous; the "new society" envisages the disappearance of the personality and to destroy historical memory. Universal mechanical unity does not raise the standard of existence, but brings disintegration and destruction.
- "The Smatterers" by Solzhenitsyn attacks the Russian intelligentsia which today means merely the educated stratum; in fact, they are "the semieducated estate," the smatterers. He advocates "an honest society" by urging his countrymen not to lie, to take part in the lie, or to support the lie.
- "Does Russia Have a Future" by Shafarovitch sees mankind as having entered a blind alley, and urges fighting one's way out of antiscience, antiliterature, and the superorganized traits of modern society: "...nothing matters more at the present time than joining forces to debate the vital issues of our country's future--for no ideas can develop in isolation, undebated." (p. 291)
*** In addition to the eloquence and forcefulness of these essays, one should note that unlike Western anthologies, thinkers with backgrounds in both the sciences and the humanities are not only brought together in this volume, but their styles are virtually indistinguishable from each other. In contrast, the West suffers deeply from the "smatterer" and the "two cultures" problems.

845. SAKHAROV, Andrei D. **My Country and the World.** NY: Knopf, 1975. 109 pp. $5.95; $1.95, paper.   (ns)

The distinguished Russian physicist and Nobel Peace Prize laureate advocates fundamental reforms in his country to make it open and democratic. He depicts a moral decline under the party's rule since 1917, a sea of human misery, and the spread of drunkenness and crime. In global terms, the nuclear arsenal of the Soviet Union is a danger to all mankind.

His ideas for reform include a multiparty system, amnesty for political prisoners, limited restoration of private enterprise, an end to censorship, and allowing republics such as Latvia and Armenia to secede from the Soviet Union if they wish. (From review in **New York Times,** Nov. 14, 1975)

846. MEDVEDEV. Roy A. **On Socialist Democracy.** Trans. from the Russian and Edited by Ellen de Kadt. NY: Knopf, 1975. 405 pp.   (AB-3)

Medvedev is a free-lance historian and sociologist, and one of the dissident intelligentsia in Russia whose writing is now being made available to Western audiences. The author remains a Marxist, while condemning Stalinism and the ways in which it still survives. He feels that there can be no genuine socialism when democracy is absent and that the present bureaucratic structure has become an impediment to progress in almost every area of life. He advocates a gradual and evolutionary process of introducing and strengthening democratic freedoms. Change will have to come through the communist party and the eventual conversion of its leadership.

In a special six-page introduction to the English language edition, written in May 1974, Medvedev reiterates his argument, insisting that "The demands of development conflict with the behavior of the bureaucratic oligarchic caste governing the country. This is what has created an objective need for reform, an objective need for the democratization of social life." (pp. xix-xx)

847. STOJANOVIC, Svetozar. **Between Ideals and Reality: A Critique of Socialism and Its Future.** Trans. by Gerson S. Sher. NY: Oxford University Press, 1973. 240 pp. $7.00; $2.95, paper. (First published in Yugoslavia in 1969)   (A-3)

A Yugoslav Marxist examines the Marxist governments in Europe, seeing the statist myth of socialism as the greatest myth of the twentieth century. The concluding chapter, Toward a Mature Communism, argues that "Mature communism is distinguished by its realistic and multilateral evaluation of the possibilities of human nature...immature communism absolutizes the principle of social equality, negating the principle of individuality in the process." (p. 209)

848. MODRZHINSKAYA, Y.D., et. al. **Future of Society: Marxist and Non-Marxist Forecasts of Scientific and Social Developments.** NY: Beekman Publishers Sept. 1975. $12.50.   (ns)

849. SAIFULIN, Murad (ed.) **The Future of Society.** Moscow, USSR: Progress Publishers, 1973. 375 pp.   (ns)

"The book is avowedly ideological in content and purpose. However, the critical evaluations of 'bourgeous' scholars are insightful and useful. Discussions of the contributions of scientific socialism and Marxism-Leninism to scientific forecasting are very disappointing--grandiose claims and predictable cliches with no critical analysis. Nevertheless, the book does provide a good introduction to the 'world view' underlying the policy process in the USSR." (Gary C. Shaw in **Policy Studies Journal,** Summer 1975)

850. BECKER, Theodore L. **Your Country Tis of Thee: Making a Constitutional Revolution.** Boston: Allyn and Bacon, Jan. 1976. $9.50. (ns)

851. BELLAK, Leopold. **Overload: The New Human Condition.** NY: Human Sciences Press, 1975. 224 pp. $9.95.   (ns)

851a. CALDWELL, Lynton K., "Managing the Transition to Post-Modern Society," **Public Administration Review,** 35:6, Nov.-Dec. 1975, pp. 567-571.   (ns)

852. CALLENBACH, Ernest. **Ecotopia: The Notebooks and Reports of William Weston.** Berkeley, Calif.: Banyon Tree Books (1517 Francisco St.), 1975. 167 pp. $2.75, paper.   (ns)

853. COMMONER, Barry. **The Poverty of Power.** NY: Knopf, May 1976. $8.95 (Excerpts published in **The New Yorker,** Feb. 2, 9, and 16, 1976)   (ns)

854. COOPER, John Charles. **The Recovery of Ameria.** Philadelphia, Pa.: The Westminster Press, 1973. (Out of Print)   (ns)

855. COUSINS, Norman. **The Celebration of Life: A Dialogue on Immortality and Infinity.** NY: Harper & Row, 1974. $4.95.   (ns)

856. CROZIER, Michel, Samuel P. HUNTINGTON, and Jaji WATANUKI. **The Crisis of Democracy.** Report on the Governability of Democracies to the Trilateral Commission. NY: New York University Press, 1975.   (ns)

857. ELLISON, Jerome. **A Serious Call to an American (R)Evolution.** NY: Bulldog Books, 1967; Berkley Medallion Books, 1971. 160 pp. $1.25, paper.   (ns)

858. ETZIONI, Amitai. **Demonstration Democracy.** NY: Gordon & Breach, 1970. 108 pp. $7.95; $2.50, paper.   (ns)

858a. ETZIONI, Amitai, "The Crisis of Modernity: Deviation or Demise?" **International Journal of Comparative Sociology,** 16:1-2, March-June, 1975, pp. 1-18.   (ns)

859. EXTON, William, Jr. **The Age of Systems: The Human Dilemma.** NY: American Management Association, 1972. 261 pp. $13.75   (ns)

860. GARLAN, Patricia W. and Maryjane DUNSTAN. **Star Sight: Visions of the Future.** Englewood Cliffs, NJ: Prentice-Hall, Feb. 1976. $6.95, paper.   (ns)

861. GAVIN, James M., "A Strategy for National Survival," **California Management Review,** 17:4, Summer 1975, pp. 5-10.   (ns)

862. GOLDWATER, Barry. **The Coming Breakpoint.** NY: Macmillan, March 1976. $8.95.   (ns)

863. GREENWOOD, D.J. **Unrewarding Wealth.** NY: Cambridge University Press, April 1976.   (ns)

864. HALL, Edward T. **Beyond Culture.** Garden City, NY: Doubleday Anchor, Jan. 1976. $7.95.   (ns)

865. HEILBRONER, Robert L. **Business Civilization in Decline.** NY: W.W. Norton, Feb. 1976. $6.95; $2.50, paper.   (ns)

866. HUMMER, Ralph P. and Robert ISAAK. **Politics for Human Beings.** North Scituate, Mass.: Duxbury Press, 1975. $7.50.   (ns)

867. JANTSCH, Erich. **Design for Evolution: Self-Organization and Planning in the Life of Human Systems.** NY: George Braziller, 1975. 322 pp. $5.95, paper.   (ns)

868. JOHNSON, Gerald W. **The Imperial Republic: Speculations on the Future, If Any, of the Third U.S.A.** NY: Liveright, 1972. $5.95.   (ns)

869. KAHN, Herman et. al. **The Next Two Hundred Years.** NY: Morrow, May 1976. $8.95; $2.95, paper.   (ns)

870. LASSWELL, Harold D. **Future Systems of Identity.** NY: Grossman, 1976.   (ns)

870a. LEVITAN, Sar A. and Robert TAGGART. **The Promise of Greatness.** Cambridge: Harvard University Press, May 1976. $15.00.   (ns)

871. LEVY, Marion J., Jr. **Modernization: Latecomers and Survivors.** NY: Basic Books, 1972. 160 pp. $5.95.   (ns)

871a. LOEBL, Eugen. **Humanomics: How We Can Make the Economy Serve Us--Not Destroy Us.** NY: Random House, 1976. $6.95.   (ns)

872. MAYER, Martin. **Today and Tomorrow in America.** NY: Harper & Row, Feb. 1976. $8.95.   (ns)

873. MOORE, Truman E. **Nouveaumania: The American Passion for Novelty and How It Led Us Astray.** NY: Random House, October 1975. $7.95.   (ns)

874. MOSBY, Robert. **Decline in the Anglo-Saxon World Leadership and the Historical Future of Humanity.** American Classical College Press, Jan. 1976. $25.00.   (ns)

875. NICHOLLS, David. **The Pluralist State.** NY: St. Martins, 1975. 179 pp. $18.95.   (ns)

876. PACKARD, Vance. **A Nation of Strangers.** NY: McCay, 1972. 368 pp. $7.95.   (ns)

876a. PERELMAN, Lewis J. **Global Mind: Beyond the Limits to Growth.** NY: Mason Charter, June 1976. $15.00.   (ns)

877. PHILLIPS, Bernard S. **Worlds of the Future: Exercises in the Sociological Imagination.** Columbus, Ohio: Charles E. Merrill, 1972. 337 pp. $4.95.   (ns)

878. RICHARDSON, Norman W. and Thomas H. STUBBS. **Evolution, Human Ecology, and Society.** NY: Macmillan, Feb. 1976. $5.95, paper.   (ns)

879. ROSS-MACDONALD, Malcolm, et. al. **Life in the Future: Prospects for Man and Nature.** Garden City, NY: Doubleday, July 1976. $14.95.   (ns)

880. ROSTOW, W.W. **Politics and the Stages of Growth.** NY: Cambridge University Press, 1971. 410 pp. $9.50.   (ns)

881. SCHLESINGER, Stephen. **The New Reformers: Forces for Change in American Politics.** Boston: Houghton Mifflin, 1975. $7.95.   (ns)

882. SCITOVSKY, Tibor. **The Joyless Economy: An Inquiry Into Human Satisfaction and Consumer Dissatisfaction.** NY: Oxford University Press, March 1976. $11.95.   (ns)

883. SERVICE, Elman R. **Origins of the State and Civilization: The Process of Cultural Evolution.** NY: Norton, 1975. 362 pp. $12.50; $4.95, paper.   (ns)

884. SHAPIRO, H.R. **The Bureaucratic State: Party Bureaucracy and the Decline of Democracy in America.** Samizdat Press, 1975. 32 Court St., Suite 506, Brooklyn, NY 11201. $11.95; $4.95, paper.   (ns)

885. SMITH, Lewis G. **Towards A Pro-Life Society.** Boston: Branden, Nov. 1975. 142 pp. $6.95, paper.   (ns)

885a. SOLOMON, Ezra. **The Anxious Economy.** NY: Simon & Schuster, April 1976. $7.95; $3.93 paper.   (ns)

886. STAVRIANOS, Leften S. **The Promise of the Coming Dark Age.** San Francisco: W.H. Freeman, May 1976. $7.95; $3.95, paper.   (ns)

886a. STRETTON, H. **Capitalism, Socialism and the Environment.** NY: Cambridge University Press, May 1976.   (ns)

887. THEOBALD, Robert. **Beyond Despair: Directions for America's Third Century.** Washington, D.C.: New Republic Book Co., Feb. 1976.   (ns)

888. THOMPSON, William Irwin. **Evil and World Order and Other Essays.** World Perspectives, Vol. 50. NY: Harper & Row, April, 1976. $7.95.   (ns)

888a. TYLER, Gus. **Scarcity: A Critique of the American Economy.** NY: Quadrangle, April 1976. $7.95.   (ns)

889. WOLFF, Robert Paul. **The Poverty of Liberalism.** Boston: Beacon Press, 1968. 200 pp. $5.95.   (ns)

889a. YARTZ, Frank et al. **Progress and the Crisis of Man.** Chicago: Nelson-Hall, May 1976. Text ed. $9.95.   (ns)

890. ZIJDERVELD, Anton C. **The Abstract Society: A Cultural Analysis of Our Time.** Garden City, NY: Doubleday, 1970. $5.95.   (ns)

Chapter 16

Background Information

Various "literary friends and relatives" that have inspired this guide, or serve as a supplement to it, deserve some recognition.

One of the major problems to which this guide is addressed is that of intellectual fragmentation. C.P. Snow described the situation in his classic "Two Cultures" essay (891), and Arthur Koestler has recently underscored the problem in his acerbic novel, **The Call Girls** (892).

This guide is also about images of the future, both descriptive and prescriptive. A deeper understanding of the importance of the image of the future is supplied by Polak's extensive and authoritative reflections (893), and by Boulding's briefer essay (894). The consideration of ideals is a related concern, and Stebbing's justification for doing so (895) is an important antidote to the scientism that has suppressed serious consideration of human values and ideals.

This guide is about old ideologies and emerging ideologies, including the "end-of-ideology" ideology that pretends to be non-ideological. There is no escape from some system of belief, and the comments herein have attempted to point out some of the assumptions and blind spots that characterize even our most "expert" scholars. The Dolbeares (896) provide a reasonably useful survey of contemporary ideologies, but the "Isms" characterized by Ebenstein (897) are clearly outdated and inadequate. It is quite important to pay attention to emerging ideologies, and to value systems that we ought to have (e.g. Hardin, no. 178; Ferkiss, no. 431) as well as a possible new paradigm for science (e.g. Roszak, no. 303; Maruyama in Spekke, no. 779).

Movements and ideas of the past should serve to inform our present thinking. The survey of American panaceas by the Weinbergs (899) is particularly instructive, and the history of the Technocracy movement of the 1930s (900) bears some resemblances to certain aspects of contemporary "futurism." The history of ideas is a well-established scholarly sub-field, as indicated by the encyclopedic **Dictionary of the History of Ideas** (902). The idea of progress underlies many of the items covered by this guide. Much has been written on the history of this idea, although only two books are mentioned here (903, 904). The extensive taxonomic work on primitivism by Lovejoy et al. (905) suggests a standard for classifying the contemporary thinking documented in the previous chapters.

There are also many volumes that survey utopias of the past, and science fiction images. The two items listed here (906, 907) serve to introduce these two subjects, but are not necessarily the best introductions.

In harsh juxtaposition to the history of ideas, and utopian and science fiction speculation in particular, item 908 on **Implementation** is included at this point as a reminder of the difficulties in realizing well-intended ideas relevant to the good society, and to suggest still another dimension of information that is needed in order to fully consider societal directions and alternatives.

There is much information to consider, and, as pointed out in a 1936 lecture by H.G. Wells, our difficulties will continue until there is some mechanism such as a "world brain" to bring together all of the thinking throughout the world (909). This guide suggests the nature of some of this information, and a possible way to bring it together in some coherent manner. The impetus behind this guide is related to Mead's considerations on stimulating evolutionary thought (911), Stulman's proposals for a global think tank (912), de Jouvenel's argument for ongoing surmising forums (913), and Kochen's effort to promote WISE (World Information Synthesis and Encyclopedia) (915).

The "world brain" of the immediate future will not be (and certainly should not be) a single organization in a single location. Rather, it will be an alliance of information collection efforts, each with a somewhat different swath of information for a different set of concerns and a different set of clients. Documentation of all of the present efforts is too extensive to appear in this guide, and will probably appear in a separate publication from Information for Policy Design. However, two guides are listed (916, 917), one very inexpensive and one very expensive, which might serve as particularly useful companions to **Societal Directions and Alternatives**.

891. SNOW, Sir Charles Percy. **The Two Cultures and the Scientific Revolution.** The Rede Lecture, 1959. NY: Cambridge University Press, 1960. 58 pp. (Also see **The Two Cultures: And a Second Look.** Cambridge University Press, 1965. 107 pp.)   (AB-3)

A widely-discussed lament that "the intellectual life of the whole of Western society is increasingly being split into two polar groups." (p. 3) These two groups are most readily represented by literary intellectuals and physical scientists, and Snow charges that each has a distorted image of the other.

The "Second Look" republishes the original Rede Lecture and adds some valuable commentary. It is felt that the loss of a common culture makes it "difficult or impossible for us to take good action." (p. 60)

"Changes in education will not by themselves solve our problems: but without those changes we shan't even realize what the problems are." (pp. 99-100)

892. KOESTLER, Arthur. **The Call Girls.** NY: Random House, 1973. 167 pp. $5.95 NY: Dell Laurel Editions, 1973. 219 pp. $1.25, paper. (AB-3)

A novel about an international symposium entitled "Approaches to Survival." Held in a Swiss alpine village, the meeting brought together a dozen experts, considered to be the wisest in their fields, in order to work out a plan to save humanity. The participants are experienced at attending similar conferences, and thus the cynical title.

Representatives of "Homo Babel" include a physicist, a neurosurgeon, a behavioral psychologist, a zoologist, an anthropologist, a British Poet, an existentialist, a MIT computer expert, and a Copertinian Brother who studies alpha waves and psi forces. This device allows Koestler to describe the frontier thinking in various specialized fields, and the impossibility of any genuine integration or dialogue.

*** Not much as a novel, but the message of the futile and self-serving meeting of academics is an important one.

893. POLAK, Fred. **The Image of the Future.** Trans. and Abridged by Elise Boulding. San Francisco: Jossey Bass/Elsevier, 1973. 319 pp. $9.50. (First published in The Netherlands in 1955.)   (A-3)

A welcome abridgement of Boulding's previous translation of Polak's lengthy and very weighty work. (NY: Oceana, 1961. Two Volumes, 456 pp.

and 376 pp.) "This book will give an added dimension to our understanding of the historical process by including the interaction between completed and noncompleted time." (p. 1)

Some of the topics from this prophetic approach to history include images of the future from western civilization, dynamics of the image of the future, devastation of the image of the future, and the broken future of western culture.

"The image of the future can act not only as a barometer, but as a regulative mechanism which alternately opens and shuts the dampers on the mighty blast-furnace of culture. It not only indicates alternative choices and possibilities, but actively promotes certain choices and in effect puts them to work in determining the future. A close examination of prevailing images, then, puts us in a position to forecast the probable future." (p. 300)

894. BOULDING, Kenneth E. **The Image: Knowledge in Life and Society.** Ann Arbor: University of Michigan Press, 1956. 175 pp.   (ns)

895. STEBBING, L. Susan **Ideals and Illusions.** London: Watts & Co., 1941. 206 pp.   (AB-3)

An ideal is a state of affairs judged to be good and worthy of attainment. It is an open question as to whether the ideal is realizable or could in fact lead to the good: "to have ideals is not the same as to have impracticable ideals." (p. 5) It is unfair to use "idealist" as a term of condemnation or gentle rebuke: "it is strictly nonsense to assume that to have ideals is equivalent to being a visionary, and that to be a visionary is equivalent to being a utopian." (p. 6)

But Stebbing is also impatient with "vague exhortations to improve our world, platitudinous abstractions masquerading as statements of ideals." (p. ix)

*** Applied philosophy serving to save idealism from those who malign it and abuse it.

896. DOLBEARE, Kenneth M. and Patricia DOLBEARE. **American Ideologies: The Competing Political Beliefs of the 1970s.** Chicago: Markham Publishing Co., 1971.   (B-3)

After the introductory chapter, Ideology: Alive and Well in the United States, individual chapters cover seven positions: Capitalism, Liberalism, Reform Liberalism, Black Liberation, The New Left, American Marxism, and Conservatism.

*** A useful introduction to the conventional positions, but there is no attention to decentralization or the systemic/holistic/ecologic views which could be the most important political beliefs of this decade.

897. EBENSTEIN, William. **Today's Isms: Communism, Fascism, Capitalism, Socialism.** Englewood Cliffs, NJ: Prentice-Hall, 1954; 1967. (B-4)

This well-known political science textbook focuses on the "isms" that shape the world, rather than others that are important, but that have not been decisive. "The major conflict of our age is the struggle between aggressive totalitarianism and the free way of life...This book is a discussion of the main representatives of each side--communism and fascism on the totalitarian side, capitalism and socialism on the democratic." (Preface) The key approach is to use the way of life concept, viewing ways of thought and action that encompass the totality of social life.

The principal characteristics of the Western concept of democracy are rational empiricism, emphasis on the individual, the instrumental nature of the state, voluntarism, the law behind the law, emphasis on means, discussion and consent in human relations, and the basic equality of all human beings. In contrast, fascism distrusts reason, denies equality, is governed by an elite, and is opposed to international law and order.

"...after three decades of the welfare state, the American economy prospers more than ever before, living standards have reached an all-time high, productivity is higher than ever, people live longer and better, and there is more economic equality between the various income groups than in the past." (pp. 207-208)

*** Out-dated and over-simplified, with a severe problem of distinguishing between principles and performance.

---

898. BERGER, Peter L., Brigette BERGER, and Hansfried KELLNER. **The Homeless Mind: Modernization and Consciousness.** NY: Random House, 1973. 258 pp.   (A-4)

An "exploratory argument" by three sociologists who view the problems of modern consciousness from a sociology of knowledge framework. Modernization is the institutional concomitant of technologically induced economic growth. Attention is focused on ideologies that promote and oppose modernization, with a particular focus on the attempt of the counter-culture to de-modernize consciousness.

*** The argument is much narrower than the authors presume.

---

899. WEINBERG, Arthur and Lila (eds.) **Passport to Utopia: Great Panaceas in American History.** Chicago: Quadrangle, 1968. 329 pp. $7.95.
                                            (ABC-3)

Panaceas are defined here as "evangelical responses to crises, answers to disjunctions caused by industrial advances and technological developments, solutions for human frustrations and exasperations." Panaceists are dogmatic individuals, and their grand schemes are well beyond those advanced by mere reformers.

The editors cover the 1825-1935 period, and confine their scope to schemes designed to alleviate political, social, economic, and racial ills. Major political party platforms or third party proposals are not included, with the exceptions of the proposals of W.J. Bryan, Upton Sinclair (see no. 533), and Huey Long's "Share-the-Wealth" program.

The writings of 28 individuals are covered, with an extensive introduction to each. Of particular interest are Robert Owen and the New Harmony community, Henry George and the single tax movement, Edward Bellamy and the Nationalist movement, Margaret Sanger and birth control, Howard Scott and Technocracy (see below), Walter C. Teagle and the "share-the-work" movement, and the above-mentioned political figures. The book is concluded with an unannotated bibliography of about 550 items (pp. 301-329).

*** A fascinating and enjoyable account which could also prove to be very useful for understanding this guidebook to what might be seen as contemporary panaceas.

---

900. ELSNER, Henry, Jr. **The Technocrats: Prophets of Automation.** Syracuse, NY: Syracuse University Press, 1967. 252 pp.   (AB-3)

Societal management ideas originating from the Department of Industrial Engineering at Columbia University attained widespread national recognition in 1932. But attention was already deflated in 1933 when Technocracy, Inc. was formed by Howard Scott, an engineer. The Continental Committee on Technocracy, serving as the educational and coordinating organization, issued its **Plan of Plenty** in 1934. This middle-class movement advocated a bureaucratized society with egalitarian income, universalistic recruitment of elites, and no property rights other than immediate personal possessions. The movement flourished in the 1930's, particularly in the state of Washington (where there were 85 technocracy clubs in 1935). Today, there are still a few thousand members nationwide.

901. PELLS, Richard H. **Radical Visions and American Dreams: Culture and Social Thought in the Depression Years.** NY: Harper & Row, 1973. 424 pp. $12.50.   (ns)

902. PASSMORE, John, "Perfectibility of Man," **Dictionary of the History of Ideas,** Vol. 3, pp. 463-476.   (A-3)

Describes the history of thinking about perfection by means of education, government action, anarchy, genetics, scientific progress, necessary laws, and evolution. Also see Dietrich Gerhard, "Periodization in History," pp. 476-481.
*** The **Dictionary** (Scribners, 1973) is better seen as an encyclopedia, and a fine one at that.

903. BURY, J.B. **The Idea of Progress: An Inquiry Into Its Origin and Growth.** Introduction by Charles A. Beard. NY: Macmillan, 1932. 357 pp. (First published in London in 1920.)   (AB-3)

Progress is a hypothesis which may or may not be true; belief in it is an act of faith. "The idea of human progress...is a theory which involves a synthesis of the past and a prophecy of the future. It is based on an interpretation of history which regards men as slowly advancing...in a definite and desirable direction, and infers that this progress will continue indefinitely." (p. 5)
*** A classic statement that is still quite useful in interpreting the thinking of contemporaries, particularly those holding optimistic views.

904. POLLARD, Sidney, **The Idea of Progress: History and Society.** NY: Basic Books, 1968. 220 pp.   (A-3)

A history of the idea "that things will in some sense get better in the future..." (p. v)--a belief in irreversible change in one general direction only. Particular emphasis is given to the 18th and 19th centuries.

905. LOVEJOY, Arthur O., et. al. **A Documentary History of Primitivism and Related Ideas.** Vol. One. Baltimore: The John Hopkins Press, 1935.   (A-3)

Chapter One, Prolegomena to the History of Primitivism, offers a taxonomy of philosophies of history, among which chronological primitivism (viewing some time in the past as the best state of the world) can be located. Chronological promitivism is distinguished from cultural primitivism, or the discontent of the civilized with civilization, often resulting in primitivistic reformers desiring a return to "nature's simple plan."
The taxonomy is divided into two classes: in which history is assumed to be finite or infinite. Among finitist theories, there are bilateral theories (where history is assumed to have a beginning and an end), and unilateral theories, where there are no assumptions about the end.
Among bilateral finitist theories, there is The Theory of Undulation (ups and downs so that in the long run mankind grows neither better nor worse), Theories of Decline (the general assumption of chronological primitivism, of which there are four variants: fall without subsequent de-

cline, progressive degeneration, decline and future restoration, and the three-phase theory of decline), and Theories of Ascent (of which there are two main forms: continuous progress, and successive progress and decline).

906. ARMYTAGE, W.H.G. **Yesterday's Tomorrows: A Historical Survey of Future Societies.** Toronto: University of Toronto Press, 1968. 288 pp.   (AB-3)

A good survey of Utopian literature in the context of modern forecasting efforts.

907. SARGENT, Lyman, "Utopia and Dystopia in Contemporary Science Fiction," **The Futurist,** VI:3, June 1972, pp. 93-98.   (B-3)

A good overview of the literature, with a listing of 48 recent books, 15 general studies on science fiction and utopias, and a full-page chart that contrasts general characteristics of utopias and dystopias.

908. PRESSMAN, Jeffrey L. and Aaron B. WILDAVSKY. **Implementation** Berkeley: U. of California Press, 1973. 182 pp. $7.50.   (ns)

The lengthy subtitle suggests the sober undertaking of these two political scientists: "How great expectations in Washington are dashed in Oakland; or, why it's amazing that Federal Programs work at all, this being a saga of the Economic Development Administration as told by two sympathetic observers who seek to build morals on a foundation of ruined hopes."
The authors describe how the view from the top is exhilarating, but that leaders have difficulty in imagining the sequence of events that will bring their ideas to fruition.

909. WELLS, H.G. **World Brain.** Freeport, NY: Books for Libraries Press, 1971. 194 pp. (Reprint of 1938 Doubleday, Doran edition)   (AB-3)

A collection of lectures and articles prepared in the 1936-1938 period. In a November 1936 lecture, World Encyclopedia, Wells expressed the need for a new social organ or institution, "the means whereby we can solve the problem of that jig-saw puzzle and bring all of the scattered and ineffective mental wealth of our world into something like a common understanding...a scheme for the reorganization and reorientation of education and information throughout the world." (p. 17) Such an Encyclopedia would be "an undogmatic Bible to a world culture...it would bring together into close juxtaposition and under critical scrutiny many apparently conflicting systems of statement...It is a super university I am thinking of, a world brain, no less." (pp. 21, 22-23, 27)
This lecture is followed by one delivered in America in Fall 1937, The Brain Organization of the Modern World, which castigates our unchanging conceptions of universities and our "preposterous" degrees, in the face of a lag in mental and moral adaptation to our changed conditions. The gist of the problem of world knowledge is that "A great new world is struggling into existence. But its struggle remains catastrophic until it can produce an adequate knowledge organization..." (p. 66) Such an organization would be in direct touch with all of the original thought and research throughout the world.

910. REISER, Oliver, "Building the World Brain," **Free World,** 8:4, Oct. 1944, pp. 363-369.   (AB-3)

"The World Brain is a collective, functional social structure providing an organ of social vision capable of world surveys, planetary planning, and global execution of universal enterprises." (p. 366) It will enable "a super-neural social synthesis" harmonizing the conflicting interests of human groups.

911. MEAD, Margaret. **Continuities in Cultural Evolution.** The Terry Lectures. New Haven: Yale University Press, 1964. 471 pp.   (A-3)

The book is basically concerned with communication and is divided into three parts. Part 1 considers continuities in the light of Mead's field work and describes various kinds of communication. Part 2 describes the evolutionary importance of the cluster--the group of people who stand at the point of divergence in a process of culture change. Part 3 entertains "the question of the conscious creation of conditions within which clusters of evolutionary significance may appear," and how the search for solutions to the crisis of our contemporary world can be undertaken.

"A strategic assay of the world situation, a definition of the state of the period, and a systematic analysis of the potential for evolutionary change... these are the first steps we can take in planning for immediate and responsible participation in cultural evolution." (p. 277)

The problems of a Manhattan Project for the social sciences are acknowledged, but it is still felt that "A first step in activating evolutionary thought is the creation of living intellectual networks which will be conducive to the formation of evolutionary clusters..." (p. 282) Mead warns against groups of cultural innovators who "form a cult and, turning inward, relate more and more to each other and less and less to outsiders." (p. 277)

912. STULMAN, Julius. **Evolving Mankind's Future. The World Institute: A Problem-Solving Methodology.** Philadelphia: J.B. Lippincott Co., 1967. 95 pp. $3.45.   (AB-3)

Stulman is both a businessman and an independent cosmic thinker who first began considering some sort of global think tank in 1941. This brief essay summarizes his thinking to date (see no. 506 for recent publications). All men today are seen as ignorant due to three major failures of perception: the tendency to view change as more of the same, the refusal to recognize both the cataclysmic and beneficent potentials of science, and the failure to organize our intellectual and spiritual resources.

An integrated flow of understanding is needed to lead us to wisdom and to catalyze people to greater growth. Ideological barriers inhibit the free exchange of ideas. "We have come to the point in history when we must set up something we've never really had before: the very best possible interdisciplinary, intercultural, international, nonpolitical intellectual task force--a World Institute--to attack in depth man's interrelated problems. This can be the kind of leadership factor that the whole of mankind and every region and every nation desperately needs." (p. 28)

*** This essay, as well as Stulman's personal encouragement, have been important factors underlying the preparation of **Societal Directions and Alternatives.**

913. de JOUVENEL, Bertrand. **The Art of Conjecture.** Trans. by Nikita Lary. NY: Basic Books, 1967. 307 pp. $7.50. (First published in France in 1964.)   (A-2)

A classic work by a French philosopher and futurist concerned with "the customs of the mind in its commerce with the future."

Of particular concern here is the advocacy of a surmising forum in which forecasts are proposed or debated. A monopoly in the previsions' market would be particularly dangerous." (p. 153) Such a market or exchange should bring together opinions about what may be and what can be done, and this forum must be in continuous operation.

Forecasts are a necessity of modern society; we have no choice in the matter. "We are forever making forecasts--with scanty data, no awareness of method, no criticism, and no cooperation. It is urgent that we make this natural and individual activity into a cooperative and organic endeavor, subject to greater exigencies of intellectual rigor." (p. 277)

914. COUSINS, Norman, "Proposal to a Foundation," **Saturday Review,** April 26, 1969, p. 26.   (B-4)

Editorial advocating a private body, under some name such as the Commission on the World's Future, which would bring together men of stature to consider the whole and prepare an annual State of Mankind report. *** Very limited, in contrast to an ongoing World Institute (no. 912) or surmising forum (no. 913).

915. KOCHEN, Manfred (ed.) **Information for Action: From Knowledge to Wisdom.** NY: Academic Press (Library and Information Science series), 1975. 248 pp. $12.50.   (A-3)

An important collection of essays discussing the "world brain" idea of H.G. Wells and its modern relative: WISE (World Information Synthesis and Encyclopedia), a potential social movement promoted by Kochen (see **J. of Documentation,** 28, 1972, pp. 322-343). In his introduction describing Evolution of Brainlike Social Organs, Kochen argues that a higher priority be given to "systems that help generalists behave more wisely." The WISE orientation would make people more aware of available options, encourage communication across national and disciplinary boundaries, and lead to a reorganization of knowledge.

The 14 papers include the following:
- Edwin B. Parker, "Who Should Control Society's Information Resources?"
- C. West Churchman, "What Is Information for Policy Making?"
- Gerald Feinberg, "How to Know Where We Are Going and Why"
- John Platt, "Information Networks for Human Transformation"
- Karl W. Deutsch, "On the Learning Capacity of Large Political Systems"
- Ronald G. Havelock, "Research on the Utilization of Knowledge"
- Harold D. Lasswell, "Constraints on the Use of Knowledge in Decision Making"
- Alex Inkeles, "Problems in the Utilization of Data for Policy Making"
- Derek de Solla Price, "Some Aspects of 'World Brain' Notions"

916. American Association for the Advancement of Science. **Science for Society: A Bibliography.** (Sixth Edition.) Washington: AAAS, Office of Science Education, 1976. $3.00.   (ns)

The latest edition has not been seen, but previous editions have been noteworthy and are an excellent value. The 105 pp. fifth edition, prepared by Felicia E. West, offers about 2800 briefly annotated items in six broad categories: Reference; Science, Technology, Society; Resources and the Environment; Education; Health; and Conflict and Population. The fourth edition (124 pp.) covers about 3500 items. The third edition (92 pp.) covers about 4200 items. There is little overlap between editions, so one might wish to order the entire set dating back to 1969, if available.

917. Union of International Associations. **Yearbook of World Problems and Human Potential.** Brussels, Belgium: UIA (1 rue aux Laines), 1976. 1136 pp. $65.00.   (ns)

Information on this first edition has just been received, and it would cer-tainly appear to be a potentially valuable reference work with its 12,884 descriptive entries, 58,194 cross-references, and 8 indexes, all comprising "a framework for representation of perceptions of interlinked networks." Sections of the Yearbook are as follows: World Problems (2653 entries), Human Development Concepts (228 entries), Intellectual Disciplines and Sci-ences (1845 entries), International Agencies and Associations (330 entries), Multilateral Treaties and Agreements (931 entries), Integrative, Unitary and Interdisciplinary Concepts (421 entires), Multinational Corporations and Enterprises (606 entries on which firm is in which sector in which country), Human Diseases (77 entries), International Periodicals or Serials (1197 entries), Economic and Industrial Sectors (132 entries), Traded Commodities and Products (241 entries), Occupations, Jobs and Professions (428 entries), and Human Values (704 entries)
*** Much of this information is quite specialized, but some of it is obviously quite germane to considering societal directions and alternatives.

NOTE: Due to last-minute insertions (25a, 25b, 35a, 55a, etc.), the total number of items covered in this guide is 1015.

III. INDEXES

A. Author Index

Note: This listing does not include contributors to anthologies. Reference is to item number rather than page number. Boldface numbers are recommended items selected for "The Civic Curriculum"

B. Organization Index

Note: Date of report is listed for ad hoc bodies. Reference is to item number, rather than page number. Boldface numbers are recommended items selected for "The Civic Curriculum."

C. Chronological Book Title Index

Note: Book and report titles only are listed here. Where information is available, items are listed by their original date of publication, regardless of language. Reference is to item number, and "ns" after a number indicates "not seen"

* All 1976 items not seen (ns) except for Bell, Peter, and Fairlie.

D. Index of Titles for Our Present Society

Where are we? One approach to answering this question is to examine the titles used to describe our present societal condition, found as titles of books, articles, and sections or chapters of books. Some of these titles are well-developed notions, while others are only mentioned in passing. Each title expresses certain assumptions about the present that are an important foundation for thinking about societal directions and alternatives. Unflattering titles usually serve as a preface to some agenda for reform (although Galbraith's "Affluent Society," one of the best-known flattering titles, was originally intended for reform purposes).

The 81 titles are arranged under four broad categories, in the order in which they appear in the guide. These descriptive titles hold some kinship to the 63 stage theories listed in Index E. and should be contrasted with the 206 prescriptive titles for desirable societies that are listed in Index F.

E. Index of Evolutionary Stage Theories

Where are we headed? Descriptions of the future state of society, or the direction of societal evolution, are invariably formulated in a stage theory that locates us in the midst of some transition, with the old society receding and the new society, era, age, or developmental level coming into view.

At present, the most widely used stage theory is that which describes a transition from industrialism to post-industrialism. But this title is so vague as to encompass three broad definitions: a utopian posteconomic vision, a shift in the composition of the labor force, and a turning away from a failed industrialism (see Index of Selected Subjects for references to usage, and introductory comments to Chapter 2.) Those who use the "post-industrial society" concept generally show little or no evidence of having considered any alternatives. There are many alternatives, as this Index indicates, and it would seem to be quite premature to settle on any single notion. Rather, if we are in the midst of a vast societal transformation, every effort should be made to understand every possible dimension, and stage theory analysis-- and synthesis--should be a high priority area for social research.

Although stage theories are expressed in descriptive terms, some are overtly prescriptive, designating a transition to an obviously desirable condition, perhaps in the hope that such prophecy will be self-fulfilling. The most notorious of these is Reich's assertions about "Consciousness III" (no. 150). Other stage theories such as Salk's "Epoch B" (no. 149) and Bates' "Managed Society" (no 34) are more subtle in their mixture of forecast and prescription, suggesting that the next societal stage will come about because it is necessary for our survival. These stage theories therefore overlap with the 206 explicitly normative titles for alternative societies, arrayed in Index F.

The 63 stage theories in this Index are grouped in three broad categories, generally corresponding to chapters 1, 2 and 4. Items are arranged in the order in which they appear in the guide.

Item No.	Present or Receding Stage	Next or Emerging Stage	Author and Date of Publication
General Overviews of Change			
1.	Civilized Society	Post-Civilized Society	Boulding, 1962
2.	Industrial Age	Age of Acceleration	Frankel, 1958
5.	Society as organic entity	Society as organizational entity	Seidenberg, 1950

14.	Liberal Era	Post-Liberal Era	Vickers, 1970
17.	Cofigurative Cultures	Prefigurative Cultures	Mead, 1970
102.	Culture	Post-Culture	Steiner, 1971
105.	Modern Age	New Dark Ages	Lukacs, 1970
167.	Age of Expansion	Age of Equilibrium	Mumford, 1944
170.	Fourth Revolution (Science)	Fifth Revolution (fuel Shortage)	Darwin, 1953

The Technological, Affluent, Service Society

29.	Democracy	Technocracy	Meynaud, 1964
31.	Industrial Society	Technetronic Society	Brzezinski, 1970
34.	Unmanaged Society	Managed Society	Bates, 1974
38.	Democratic Government	Expert Government	Beckwith, 1972
39.	Patrimonial Order	Technocratic Order	Geiger, 1973
40.	Modern Age	Post-Modern World*	Drucker, 1959
43.	Industrial Age	Service Age	Glenday, 1944
44.	Manufacturing Economy	Service Economy	Fuchs, 1965; 1968
46.	Industrialism	Super-Industrialism	Toffler, 1970
48.	Industrial Capitalism	Socialistic Service or Consumer Society	Gartner/Riessman, 1974
53.	Industrial Society	Post-Industrial Society**	Bell, 1966; 1973
60.	Production-centered Industrialism	Neo-Industrialism	Meadows, 1971
62.	Economy of Abundance	Era Four, A Time to Live	Chase, 1960
63.	Era of High Mass Consumption	Beyond Consumption	Rostow, 1960
64.	Politics of National Welfare	Politics of Abundance	Organski, 1965
65.	Mechanization	Socio-Organization	Jaguaribe, 1973
68.	Early Modern Stage	Modern Stage	Peacock/Kirsch1970
669.	Period of Sovereignty	Society of Individual Contracts	MacCallum, 1970
670.	Metropolis, Megalopolis	Ecumenopolis	Doxiadis, 1968
815.	Machine Age	Systems Age	Ackoff, 1974

Cosmic Evolutionary Views

125.	Rational Age	Spiritual Age	Sri Aurobindo, 1949
126.	Noosphere Expansion	Noosphere Compression	Teilhard de Chardin, 1956
131.	Onlooker Age	New Imagination	Davy, 1961
134.	Second Great Awakening	Third Great Awakening	Wolfe, 1973
137.	Second American Frontier (exploiting environment)	Third American Frontier (individual/social change)	Elgin, 1975
139.	Traditional Culture	Somatic Culture	Hanna, 1970
141.	Civilization's End	Dawn of Transformation	Leonard, 1972
142.	Period Ten	Period Eleven	Fuller, 1971
143.	Civilized Survival Society	Civilized Identity Society	Glasser, 1972
144.	Personalistic Existence (F-S Man)	Cognitive Existence (G-T Man)	Graves, 1974
145.	Scientific Exploitative Stage	Communication-Electronic Stage	Calhoun, 1974
146.	Humanic Age	Postindividual/Leptoid Age	Heard, 1964
147.	Childhood of Humanity	Manhood of Humanity	Korzybski, 1921
148.	Relating Stage of Human Development	Postulating Stage of Human Development	Bois, 1972
149.	Epoch A	Epoch B	Salk, 1973
149a	Traditional American Ideology	New American Ideology	Lodge, 1975
150.	Consciousness II	Consciousness III	Reich, 1970
151.	Industrial Civilization	Scientific-Planetary Civilization	Thompson, 1971
152.	Social Organization	Cultural Organization	Jantsch, 1974
153.	Secondary Civilization	A Third Civilization	Rodnick, 1974
155.	Industrial Powers/Socialist States	Universal Civilization	Ribiero, 1968
156.	Machine Age	Power Age	Polakov, 1933
157.	Industrial Society	Power Age	Nearing, 1961
158.	Mechanical Age	Electric Age	McLuhan, 1964

*Etzioni (1968, no. 377) uses "Post-Modern Period," and Ferkiss (1974, no. 431) uses "Post-Modern Era."
**See subject index for other users and uses of "Post-Industrial Society."

F. Index of Titles for Alternative Societies

What kind of society could we have? In addition to societal titles, the following list of prescriptions includes potentially encompassing philosophies, policies, or movements such as ecological humanism, balanced growth, and adhocism. We are not lacking in the quantity of proposals; what we do lack is a mechanism for recognizing and refining them. Many, of course, deserve to be ignored, but there are a sufficient number of deserving notions so as to make these "Banners of Babel" cancel each other out.

Titles are arranged by their order of appearance in the major chapters on alternatives (Chapters 5-13). There is also a category on Improving The Technological, Affluent, Service Society, which borrows several titles from a variety of chapters and a small section devoted to The Christian Future, a vision held by many Americans.

G. Index of Selected Proposals

What are the possible strategies for achieving the desirable society? Many writers focus on specific ideas for new institutions or policies, while a few outline general strategies that are close to characterizing a desirable societal alternative. Some writers make proposals without any suggestion of general future conditions; others make their proposals within the framework of some desirable vision such as those suggested by the titles in Index F.

The following list suggests what a full-fledged "idea bank" might look like. The use of capital or lower-case letters follows that of the author.

H. Index of Selected Criticism

This index includes criticisms of specific individuals, groups of individuals such as "eco-doomsters," philosophies such as liberalism and conservatism, concepts such as "post-industrial society" and "limits to growth," and aspects of society such as science and suburbia. Very general criticisms of conditions such as dehumanization and loss of community are not registered here, because such discontents are the subject of many items in this guide. This index is also not as complete as it could be, in that many annotations were written without thorough attention to every criticism made by every author. However, there is a sufficient quantity of criticism in this guide so as to deserve some separate index that at least might suggest the outlines of a more thorough index.

I. Index of Selected Subjects and Ideas

This is an index to selected descriptive concepts such as "noosphere," "social traps" and "two watersheds" that are readily identified with a particular author (the name appears in parentheses). The index also covers specific subjects such as constitutional reform, goal analysis, and new towns, and makes an attempt to record items that are concerned with general subjects such as leadership, malaise, and planning. Many of the items in this guide deal with these general subjects in various degrees, and many of these subjects are overlapping (e.g., freedom and decentralization) and prone to multiple definitions (e.g., liberalism and post-industrial society). This index is therefore not as extensive as it could be, particularly because the snarls of cross-referencing have been avoided.

Notes

Information for Policy Design welcomes general comments on **Societal Directions and Alternatives.** We also encourage specific suggestions of important items that should be added, and of ways in which the guide might be improved to better serve your information needs.

You may wish to recommend **Societal Directions and Alternatives** to a friend, a colleague, or a library. We will be pleased to send information to anyone whom you suggest.

Information for Policy Design
LaFayette, New York 13084
(315)677-9278